File Organization for
Database Design

McGraw-Hill Computer Science Series

Ahuja: Design and Analysis of Computer Communication Networks
Barbacci and Siewiorek: The Design and Analysis of Instruction Set Processors
Ceri and Pelagatti: Distributed Databases: Principles and Systems
Collins: Intermediate Pascal Programming: A Case Study Approach
Debry: Communicating with Display Terminals
Donovan: Systems Programming
Filman and Friedman: Coordinated Computing: Tools and Techniques for Distributed Software
Givone: Introduction to Switching Circuit Theory
Goodman and Hedetniemi: Introduction to the Design and Analysis of Algorithms
Katzan: Microprogramming Primer
Keller: A First Course in Computer Programming Using Pascal
Kohavi: Switching and Finite Automata Theory
Korth and Silberschatz: Database System Concepts
Liu: Elements of Discrete Mathematics
Liu: Introduction to Combinatorial Mathematics
MacEwen: Introduction to Computer Systems: Using the PDP-11 and Pascal
Madnick and Donovan: Operating Systems
Manna: Mathematical Theory of Computation
Milenkovic: Operating Systems: Concepts and Design
Newman and Sproull: Principles of Interactive Computer Graphics
Payne: Introduction to Simulation: Programming Techniques and Methods of Analysis
Révész: Introduction to Formal Languages
Rice: Matrix Computations and Mathematical Software
Salton and McGill: Introduction to Modern Information Retrieval
Shooman: Software Engineering: Design, Reliability, and Management
Tremblay and Bunt: An Introduction to Computer Science: An Algorithmic Approach
Tremblay and Bunt: An Introduction to Computer Science: An Algorithmic Approach, Short Edition
Tremblay and Manohar: Discrete Mathematical Structures with Applications to Computer Science
Tremblay and Sorenson: An Introduction to Data Structures with Applications
Tremblay and Sorenson: The Theory and Practice of Compiler Writing
Tucker: Programming Languages
Wiederhold: Database Design
Wiederhold: File Organization for Database Design
Wulf, Levin, and Harbison: Hydra/C.mmp: An Experimental Computer System

McGraw-Hill Series in Computer Organization and Architecture

Bell and Newell: Computer Structures: Readings and Examples
Cavanagh: Digital Computer Arithmetic: Design and Implementation
Gear: Computer Organization and Programming: With an Emphasis on Personal Computers
Hamacher, Vranesic, and Zaky: Computer Organization
Hayes: Computer Architecture and Organization
Hayes: Digital System Design and Microprocessors
Hwang and Briggs: Computer Architecture and Parallel Processing
Lawrence and Mauch: Real-Time Microcomputer System Design
Siewiorek, Bell, and Newell: Computer Structures: Principles and Examples
Stone: Introduction to Computer Organization and Data Structures
Stone and Siewiorek: Introduction to Computer Organization and Data Structures: PDP-11 Edition

McGraw-Hill Series in Supercomputing and Artificial Intelligence

Consulting Editor
Kai Hwang, University of Southern California

Hwang and Briggs: Computer Architecture and Parallel Processing
Quinn: Designing Efficient Algorithms for Parallel Computers

McGraw-Hill Series in Artificial Intelligence

Allen: Anatomy of LISP
Davis and Lenat: Knowledge-Based Systems in Artificial Intelligence
Nilsson: Problem-Solving Methods in Artificial Intelligence
Rich: Artificial Intelligence

File Organization for Database Design

Gio Wiederhold

Associate Professor (Research)
Medicine, Computer Science,
and Electrical Engineering
Stanford University

McGraw-Hill Book Company

New York   St. Louis   San Francisco   Auckland   Bogotá   Hamburg
London   Madrid   Mexico   Milan   Montreal   New Delhi
Panama   Paris   São Paulo   Singapore   Sydney   Tokyo   Toronto

To My Family,
Voy, John, Randy

File Organization for Database Design

2 3 4 5 6 7 8 9 0   HALHAL   8 9 4 3 2 1 0 9 8 7

ISBN 0-07-070133-4

This book was set in Times Roman. The editors were Kaye Pace and Joseph F. Murphy; the designer was Joan E. O'Connor; the production supervisor was Denise L. Puryear. New drawings were done by J & R Services, Inc.
Arcata Graphics/Halliday was printer and binder.

Library of Congress Cataloging-in-Publication Data

Wiederhold, Gio.
  File organization for database design.

  (McGraw-Hill computer science series) (McGraw-Hill series in computer organization and architecture) (McGraw-Hill series in supercomputing and artificial intelligence) (McGraw-Hill series in artificial intelligence)
  Bibliography: p.
  Includes index.
  1. File organization (Computer science) 2. Data base management. 3. System design.
I. Title. II. Series. III. Series: McGraw-Hill series in computer organization and architecture. IV. Series: Supercomputing & artificial intelligence. V. Series: McGraw-Hill series in artificial intelligence.
QA76.9.F5W53 1987   005.74   87-2675
ISBN 0-07-070133-4

Contents

Preface   xi

Chapter 1   **Introduction and Definitions**   1
1-1   Definitions   4
1-2   The Role of Files in Data Processing   9
1-3   Performance of Files   14
1-4   Applications   15
1-5   Review   16
     Background and References   18
     Exercises   20

Chapter 2   **Transactions on Files**   21
2-1   Programming for Files   22
2-2   Transactions   28
2-3   Operating Systems   37
2-4   Review   50
     Background and References   51
     Exercises   52

Chapter 3   **Hardware and Its Parameters**   53
3-1   Hardware Choices   54
3-2   Hardware Parameters   65
3-3   Blocks and Buffers   81
3-4   Summary of File Hardware   92
     Background and References   94
     Exercises   96

Chapter 4   **Basic Files**   97
4-1   General Concepts of File Organization   99
4-2   The Pile File   106
4-3   Performance of Piles   109
4-4   The Sequential File   118
4-5   Performance of Sequential Files   121
4-6   Review   127
        Background and References   128
        Exercises   129

Chapter 5   **Indexed Files**   131
5-1   The Indexed-Sequential File   135
5-2   Performance of Indexed-Sequential Files   143
5-3   The Indexed File   152
5-4   Performance of Indexed Files   158
5-5   Partial-Match Retrieval   164
5-6   Review of Indexed Methods   169
        Background and References   170
        Exercises   171

Chapter 6   **Hashed Files and Ring Files**   173
6-1   Description and Use of the Hashed File   174
6-2   Performance of Hashed Files   192
6-3   The Multiring File   202
6-4   Performance of Multiring Files   212
6-5   Review of Hashed and Ring Files   220
        Background and References   221
        Exercises   221

Chapter 7   **Combining File Methods**   223
7-1   Summary of Fundamental Files   224
7-2   Combinations with Sequential Files   225
7-3   Combinations With Hashed Access   232
7-4   Combinations with Ring Access   245
7-5   Review   254
        Background and References   255
        Exercises   256

Chapter 8   **Index Implementation**   259
8-1   Improving the Performance of Indexes   260
8-2   Key Abbreviation   264
8-3   Processing Index Blocks   270
8-4   Serial Processing and Indexes   274
8-5   An Implementation of an Indexed-Sequential File   278
8-6   Summary   289
        Background and References   291
        Exercises   292

Chapter 9 **Alternate File Organizations** 293
9-1 Transposed Files 294
9-2 Tree-structured Files 298
9-3 Hierarchically Structured Data 307
9-4 Files Using Virtual Memory 319
9-5 Summary 323
 Background and References 323
 Exercises 324

Chapter 10 **Storage Organization** 327
10-1 Multifile Architecture 328
10-2 Storage Hardware Selection 332
10-3 Transaction Performance 336
10-4 Free Storage Management 340
10-5 Allocation for Sequential Processing 347
10-6 Database Machines 350
10-7 Review 359
 Background and References 359
 Exercises 360

Chapter 11 **Distributed Files** 363
11-1 Motivation and Organization 364
11-2 Clustered Systems 370
11-3 Remotely Distributed Systems 377
11-4 Federated Systems 382
11-5 Review of File Distribution 385
 Background and References 386
 Exercises 388

Chapter 12 **Analysis Techniques** 389
12-1 Statistical Methods 390
12-2 Simulation 411
12-3 Queues and Scheduling Techniques 414
12-4 Operations Research in Database Design 425
 Background and References 436
 Exercises 438

Chapter 13 **Data Representation** 441
13-1 Machine Representation 443
13-2 Redundancy and Error Correction 449
13-3 Compression of Data 455
13-4 Cryptography 466
 Background and References 475
 Exercises 475

Chapter 14   **File-System Evaluation**   477
   14-1   Benefits of File Services   480
   14-2   Estimation of Transaction Usage   487
   14-3   Matching Load and Capability of a File System   490
   14-4   Sharing of Facilities   507
   14-5   Cost-Benefit Comparison   509
   14-6   Review of File Design   515
            Background and References   517
            Exercises   518

Chapter 15   **File Security**   519
   15-1   Reliability   520
   15-2   Protection of Privacy   527
   15-3   Maintenance of Integrity   539
   15-4   Operating Systems Support   542
   15-5   Review   545
            Background and References   547
            Exercises   548

Chapter 16   **Future Directions**   549
   16-1   Tools for System Design   551
   16-2   Moving to Database Management   557
   16-3   The Future of File Systems   558
   16-4   Epilogue   561
            Background and References   561

Appendix A   **File Systems**   563
Appendix B   **Symbols Used**   568
            Mathematical Symbols   568
            Programming Symbols   569
            Variables used in Performance Formulas   570

            Bibliography   571
            Comprehensive Index   599

Preface

INTRODUCTION   This book presents the issues in the design, implementation, selection, and use of computer files for external storage of data. An analytical approach is followed throughout so that the concepts learned can be applied not only to the examples shown in the book but to any of the wide variety of file structures found in practice, and to those that will appear in the future.

SCOPE   We present the file topics in a setting of transaction processing. Transaction processing introduces modularity into file access programs, and this modularity is beneficial in presentation as well as in actual system design. Performance of entire transactions can be evaluated, both for centralized and distributed systems.

The emphasis throughout is on concepts and evaluation. No actual file systems are described completely, nor are systems surveyed and compared, although specific and realistic examples are used throughout to illustrate points being made.

Because of the wide variety of file design found in the world, we treat in depth six fundamental alternatives, which represent prototypes for all principal file organization seen in use. Subsequently combinations of the fundamental methods are explored and used to illustrate the benefits and liabilities of file design alternatives.

An engineering attitude is stressed in the analyses. Dominant factors are identified and simplifications are made whenever appropriate. This approach provides immediate applicabilty of the concepts learned to the design of file-based systems. Formulas are used to quantify the alternative organizations. The student should try to understand the formulas and may use them for reference purposes, but should not attempt to remember them, nor apply them blindly.

Much of what is learned when following this material is not restricted to files. The quantitative design approach followed throughout is appropriate for any major software project. This material also supports a continuity with the topic of databases, since many of the issues of file access studied here are abstracted into high-level database concepts. With the background obtained here database design decisions can be explained and evaluated in terms of their performance.

ORGANIZATION   We follow a bottom-up approach in presentation, so that each level of abstraction is thoroughly grounded in earlier material. The layout of this book is presented graphically in Chap. 1, as Fig. 1-6, after the introductory definitions have been completed. Foundation material on software and hardware is presented in Chaps. 2 and 3. In Chaps. 4, 5, and 6 the fundamental file structures are presented and analyzed, which are then combined and expanded in Chaps. 7, 8, and 9. Performance of entire transactions is the topic of Chap. 10, and the alternative approaches for distributed files are found in Chap. 11. The remaining chapters present complementary material: Chap. 12 details techniques appropriate for advanced performance analysis and Chap. 13 considers data representation. The analysis of entire file systems in Chap. 14 integrates the prior material, and security issues are considered in Chap. 15. The closing chapter also provides a link to database technology.

CURRICULA   Modern curricula give increased emphasis to files and databases. This book presents all the material recommended for the CS-5 (Introduction to File Processing) as specified in the ACM Curriculum on Computer Science. The quantitative approach taken in this book causes algorithmic and analytic material assigned to courses CS-6 and CS-7 to be included as well, albeit limited by relevance to files. Courses oriented towards data-processing require treatment of files as well, although performance issues may not be emphasized. The importance of competence in performance evaluation and prediction was stressed by Ferrari[86] *.

The teaching of file topics has considerably improved in recent years. It is clear that a graduate with a Computer Science or Computer Engineering degree should be competent to deal with the concepts and techniques of files. Most available books on files describe current file implementation in great detail but do not provide material for conceptualization and analysis. They do provide excellent references and examples for case studies.

An inadequate background in the area of files can make many database courses unsatisfying for student and teacher. The abstractions used when discussing databases imply an understanding of the tradeoffs made in the design and implementation of storage system software.

ORIGIN   Some of the material in this book derives from an earlier book on *Database Design*, and classes based on this book and earlier notes have been given at Stanford University as "File and Database Structures" since 1971. During this period the field has matured, and we can now count on some stability of file concepts, even while advances in many specific areas continue to be made.

A successor book, *Database Design and Implementation*, will stress semantic models and guide rational decisions for implementing database applications. Here too an engineering attitude towards system building is being followed.

---

*   Superior number next to reference indicates the year of publication.

AUDIENCE   The audience for this book ranges from students of computing who have finished a reasonably complete course in programming to applications and systems programmers who wish to synthesize their experiences into a more formal structure. The material covered should be known by systems designers or systems analysts faced with file implementation choices. It probably presents too much detail to be of interest to management outside the systems and database management area itself.

EXAMPLES AND EXERCISES   The program examples throughout the text use a simple subset of PL/1. The programs are designed to be obvious to readers familiar with any procedure-oriented programming language. The introductory examples are annotated to help the reader.

Many of the examples illustrate features of actual systems and applications, but are of necessity incomplete. An effort has been made to note simplifying assumptions. The same should be done in students' design assignments, so that awareness of real-world complexities is fostered without overwhelming the design with trivia.

The exercises listed in each chapter have been kept relatively simple. Some of them were inspired by an ACM *Self-assessment Procedure* (Solomon[86]). It is suggested that an analysis of your local file system be made part of some of the assignments, as indicated in several of the problem statements. The analysis or comparison of actual systems may seem to be an excessively complex task, but has been shown to be manageable by students when the material of this book has been assimilated. Appendix A provides references to a number of file systems.

The primary exercise when this course is being taught at Stanford is a design project. Early in the course students prepare an objective statement for a database application of interest to them. Some individual research may be needed to obtain estimates of expected data quantities and transaction load frequencies. Exercises related to this project appear throughout the text and are labeled with a ^{P}.

REFERENCES   Source material for this book came from many places and experiences. References are not cited throughout the text since the intent is to produce primarily a book which integrates the concepts and ideas.

A background section at the end of every chapter cites the major sources used and indicates further study material. The references provide a generous foothold for students intending to pursue a specific topic in depth. The references can also direct research effort toward the many yet unsolved problems in the area. The bibliography has been selected to include some important material for each of the subject areas introduced.

Trade publications, research reports, theses, and computer manuals are referenced only when used directly, although much relevant information can be found there. Up-to-date information on computer and software systems is best obtained from manufacturers.

I apologize to the authors of work I failed to reference, either due to application of these rules, or because of lack of awareness on my part. A large annotated bibliography is being maintained by me and has been made available. I look forward to distribution of the bibliography in computer-readable form since it is too large to be effectively scanned without computer assistance.

ACKNOWLEDGMENTS   I have to refer to the acknowledgments in the predecessor volume (*Database Design*) for the many collegues and students who have helped with the material as it developed. Significant assistance for this book was provided by Jim Gray and XiaoLei Qian. Material from theses by Dr. Robert Blum, Ramez ElMasri, Sheldon Finkelstein, Arthur M. Keller, Jonathan King, Toshi Minoura, David Shaw, and Kyu-Young Whang has affected the contents of this book. Concepts from papers written with Stefano Ceri, Sham Navathe, and Domenico Saccà have influenced this text as well. Research support for much of this work came from the Defense Advanced Research Projects Agency (contract N-39-84-C-211) for Knowledge Based Management Systems, and applications of these concepts to health care were supported by the National Center for Health Services Research (NCHSR HS-3650 and HS-4389) and the National Library of Medicine (NLM LM-4334). I have also benefited from the computer services at Stanford University, some of which are supported by the NIH Division of Research Resources (RR-785). Systems to support our research have been partially provided by the Intelligent Systems Technology Group (ISTG) of the AI Center of Digital Equipment Corporation in Hudson, MA. The TEX program, developed by Donald Knuth[79], was used to prepare the plates for printing. John Wiederhold helped with the layout and he and Mike Cramer ran the photo-typesetter. The ability to prepare beautiful copy under full control of the author is both an opportunity and a responsibility. I hope to have carried them out adequately. Caroline Barsalou, Mary Drake, and Voy Wiederhold all helped with reading and editing chapter drafts. Any errors in content and format remain my responsibility, and I welcome all kinds of criticism.

Gio Wiederhold

File Organization for
Database Design

Chapter 1

Introduction and Definitions

Consider a future device for individual use, which is a sort of mechanized private file and library. It needs a name, and to coin one at random, "MEMEX" will do. A memex is a device in which an individual stores all his books, records, and communications, and which is mechanized so that it may be consulted with exceeding speed and flexibility. It is an enlarged supplement to his memory.

Vannevar Bush
As We May Think, Atlantic Monthly, *vol. 176, no. 1, January 1945.*

1-0 INTRODUCTION

The objective of this book is to provide the foundations for understanding and developing methods which can manage large quantities of data. Many tasks in an information-oriented society require that people deal with voluminous data. Without use of a computer we would be overwhelmed when attempting to maintain, store, and analyze data. We therefore only consider computer-based management of information, and refer to paper-based methods only occasionally to clarify an issue.

Dealing with large quantities of data is difficult even for computers. Having to handle much data implies that such data will be

- Accessed by multiple people and programs
- Kept on *external storage* devices
- Always reliably available for processing
- Rapidly accessible when information is needed

We will define and deal with all these issues in turn.

We will develop a thorough understanding of how *external storage* for computers is managed. Typical hardware devices for external storage are magnetic disks, ranging from pocket-size *floppy* disks to massive units storing all the information needed for businesses such as banks and airlines. Data is organized for storage into *files*. Processing software for managing the information includes file management and database management programs. Database management makes it possible to deal with multiple files in an integrated manner.

We will also analyze the performance of programs under a variety of realistic conditions. The results will allow us to predict the performance of file systems* for computer applications during their design phase.

CHARACTERISTICS   There are three characteristics of files which distinguish them from other objects that programs deal with:

> **Persistence** Data written into a file persists after the program is finished. The data can be used at a later time by the same or by other programs. Permanence must be further assured by backup facilities.

> **Sharability** Data stored on external storage devices can be shared by multiple programs and by multiple users simultaneously. Conventions and protocols must be established to assure that the integrity of the data can be maintained.

> **Size** Data volumes are typically greater than will fit into the directly addressable memory of the computer. This means that algorithms developed for memory data structures will differ in implementation and performance from those presented here for external storage.

All data management is performed by programs. Such programs may be provided with the computer systems or may be application programs developed by users. The software which handles files and databases has to be well integrated so that one program will not organize the data in a way which would inhibit another program from obtaining the information. An integrated collection of programs becomes a *database system*, as sketched in Fig. 1-1. Files are the primary objects within databases.

THE OBJECTIVE OF KEEPING INFORMATION ON FILES   The objective of computing in general is to provide information so that decisions can be made and actions initiated. What kind of actions are needed depends on the enterprise. For instance, a manufacturing firm needs to order supplies for the products it makes and sells, an airline needs to sell seats, a bank needs to collect interest, and a welfare agency must issue checks. To make the required decisions there must be *data* and *knowledge*. The data needed is stored in files, and the required knowledge for processing the data is encoded in its programs. The programs contain procedures that calculate, say, the amount for the welfare check; the database contains the list

---

* We will use the term *system* throughout this book with care. A system is always an integrated collection of data and programs. The integration means that one component affects all others. Typically, feedback and control are integral to a system, so that the system is stable.

of the recipients. Other programs within the system update the files, for instance, to insert or delete welfare recipient records.

> The collection of data kept on computer files is, from an idealized point of view, a description of the state of the world, reduced in coverage and to a level of detail so that it is relevant to the enterprise.

FILE MANAGEMENT AND DATABASE MANAGEMENT   Files are used to store collections of similar data. A database system includes files and programs to manage the files. A *File Management System* (FMS) manages independent files, helping to enter and retrieve information records. A *DataBase Management System* (DBMS) helps users manage related data kept in multiple files. A DBMS will use file management services to manipulate its many files. It uses additional files to keep directories to the information it manages.

Today most data processing is carried out by programs which use file management services directly, but we see the use of DBMS's increasing. In either case, the performance of applications which manipulate data depends largely on how the files are organized. This book deals with the organization of data files. The Background and References section of this chapter lists some textbooks which complement this book in the database management area.

This book is a text about files. It is not a programming text, although all the work in organizing, maintaining, and retrieving data is performed by programs. We assume that you understand the principles of programming and could write the software needed for the tasks described. Chapter 2 provides some sample programs. In practice, you rarely have to write programs to deal with files directly and you will be able to use existing software. The computational programs needed invoke the file system software to store and retrieve data. Such software is provided with the FMS and DBMS described above.

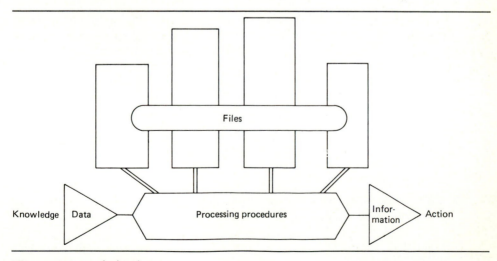

Figure 1-1   A database.

1-1   DEFINITIONS

This section defines data files and their components more precisely, including their relationships to input-output services. Subsequent sections define files in the general setting of information and processing data, and in Sec. 1-3 we introduce a notation for the performance of file algorithms. Section 1-4 of this chapter list some applications where data and files are critical.

Files* are the central objects of our discussion. Procedures in the computers are used to enter data, store data in files, and process the data in response to requests for information. We will first define terms for the objects we deal with and in the next subsection define terms for the operations performed with files. Figure 1-2 sketches a typical file.

1-1-1 Basic Terms

We will now define the terms
- Database
- File
- Record
- Field

which define the hierarchical structure of computer stored data collections. We start from the top down.

DATABASE   A *database* is a collection of related data. The data storage for a database is accomplished by the use of one or more files. A comprehensive database should contain all the information to manage some enterprise, say, a business, a scientific study, or a governmental department. Less comprehensive data collections that support some part of an enterprise are also commonly called databases. A data collection managed by a single-application program is best not considered to be a database.

As indicated earlier, databases can be implemented directly, using file management programs, or a database management system. If a suitable database management system is available, then much work can be saved. All files of one database must be accessible by the computer being used for processing. If the database is distributed over several computers, then its files must be accessible from any of the interconnected computers.

There are applications for which no adequate Database Management Systems are yet available. Such applications are found in situations where there are

1 Heavy computational demands during the processing of data
2 Data distributed over a variety of machines
3 Very strict limits on response times.

We find such instances, respectively, in databases for engineering design, in systems which include previously developed databases, and in real-time systems.

---

* The word "file" will not be used by us to refer to the hardware used to store the data comprising the files.

FILE   A *file* is a collection of similar records kept on computer storage devices. Typical of *external storage* devices are disk drives with magnetic disks, but there are many alternatives.

A file will have a name, known to the operating system, and a structure, or organization, determined by a *file access program*. A file may contain all the records describing employees of an enterprise or a department. It is not a good idea to mix different types of records, say, for employees and for product prices, in one file. On the other hand, having too many files is also awkward, so records for all types of employees for all departments are placed into one file, unless the employees and the computers are widely distributed.

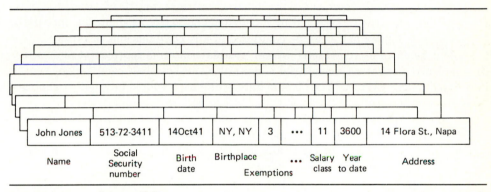

Name	Social Security number	Birth date	Birthplace Exemptions	...	Salary Year class to date	Address
John Jones	513-72-3411	14Oct41	NY, NY 3	...	11 3600	14 Flora St., Napa

Figure 1-2   A payroll file.

RECORDS   A *record* is a collection of related *fields* containing elemental data items. Fields maybe related to each other because they describe some specific instance, say, a person, an object, or an event. A more formal and detailed definition will be developed in Chap. 4. A record of an employee file will contain such information as name, the social security number, date of birth, tax information, current job assignment, and rate of pay for a particular employee. Figure 1-2 shows the first record for our `Payroll` file.

FIELDS   *Fields* contain the basic values which comprise a record. The content of a field is provided to users or their programs on request, say, `14Oct41`, when `John Jones`' birthdate is wanted. Computational processes can manipulate such values. The values are associated with a *type* and a *domain*, as shown in Table 1-1.

Table 1-1   Types and domains for data values.

Type	Domain	Example
Numeric	Salary in dollars	23000
Characterstrings	Person-name	John Jones
Identifiers	Social security number	513-72-3411
Code	Sex{M-F-U}	M
Date	Birthdate	14Oct41
Complex fields	Address(street,town,zip)	14 Wine St., Napa, 94558

The *domain* provides a semantic definition of the value, so that the meaning of the value is understood. For instance, a salary of 23000 is quite different from a weight of 23000. Comparing or adding values from different domains is not meaningful.

The type provides a general specification of the computational constraints for the value. Pairs of values have to be of the same type to permit joint computation such as comparison or addition. An understanding of the domain is needed to decide if such a computation produces a meaningful result. Computations on files are presented in Chap. 2.

For each data type there are alternative representations in computer storage. Numeric data may be represented by floating-point numbers for real-valued data, by integers, or by decimal representations. Characterstrings may be of variable or fixed length. Codes may be represented by mnemonic characters as shown or, internally, by integers. Complex fields can be composed of any combinations of types.

Identifiers can be represented by any adequate internal representation, but are distinguished in that no meaningful computation, other than comparison, can be performed on their values. The domain *date* is best represented internally by integer days after some base date, to permit also *before* and *after* comparison.

Choosing the best type and representation for the information in a database is extremely important. A specific domain is best described by one type and one representation. Inadequate representations can cause irretrievable loss of information. Chapter 13 deals with these issues in depth.

1-1-2 Storage and Input-Output

Computers obtain data from storage and from input devices. Results produced are moved to output devices and placed into storage if needed for further use.

STORAGE   We use the term *external storage* to describe any extension beyond the primary addressable memory of a computer. External storage is characterized by persistence, sharability, and the capability to hold voluminous information. The specific devices are described in Chap. 2, but we note that, in order to assure persistence, the storage devices are logically separate from the central processing unit of the computer, and attached via a cable or a *bus* to the processor and its memory. In small computers they may be housed in the same box, but they are still distinct.

▦▦▦* **Storage Hierarchies**   Instead of making a binary distinction of storage and memory, one can also classify storage functions and their devices into a hierarchy. At the bottom of the hierarchy are the slowest, but largest devices; at the top is the *cache memory* used by processors for frequent accesses. The cache memory, because of its high cost, tends to be small, perhaps several thousand characters on a medium-sized machine. Actual processing takes place in the registers of the processor, there may be less than a dozen of those. Table 1-2 shows some storage types that could be classified into such a hierarchy. Several devices suitable for these functions will be described in detail in Chap. 3.

---

* Fence (▦▦▦) symbols are used to enclose optional sections, which may be skipped when reading without loss of continuity.

Table 1-2　　A storage hierarchy.

Processor registers for arithmetic
Cache memory for high-rate computation
Main memory for program and data, and IO buffers
Small, rapid disks with multiple heads for working storage
Main data storage, consisting of multiple large moving head disks
On-line archival storage, perhaps using optical discs or tape cassettes
Archival off-line storage, often using reels of tape, kept remotely for protection

We will not emphasize the hierarchy in this next, since most of the critical interface for data processing is at the boundary of memory and storage. Any hierarchical structure of memory is handled largely automatically, or on the level of assembly language. The stored data we are concerned with may be periodically archived, but such archiving does not affect the primary data-processing tasks.

Processing Data Stored on External Storage　Whenever processing of data in external storage must be carried out, the following steps take place:
　1　The location of the data on external storage is determined.
　2　The data is read, that is, moved from external storage to memory.
　3　The copy of the data in memory is manipulated by the processor.

If the persistent data must be updated to reflect the result of the computation, then:
　4　The altered copy of the data in memory is written, that is moved from memory to external storage.

If the data is meant to replace old data, then it is written to the place where it was obtained from, otherwise a new place is selected. When new data enters the file, only steps **1**, **3**, and **4** are needed. The details of these steps depend on the organization of the files.

FILE ORGANIZATION　Here we will describe how the records of a file are placed in relation to each other. Given the position of the file we must be able to locate the records and update their fields. Some additional information maybe inserted in the files to facilitate access. Differences of file organization cause great differences in performance when storing and retrieving records. The evaluation and comparison of file organizations is an important aspect of this book.

　Six fundamental file organizations will be analyzed in Chaps. 4, 5, and 6. Subsequent chapters will show some of the possible combinations and permutations of these fundamental file types. A database often requires more than one type of file organization.

INPUT-OUTPUT　*Input* is data which comes from outside the system and is checked and processed before it can enter the files. *Output* is shipped to users and can be printed or communicated so that users can further manipulate the information. It is possible that some output, say, an inventory list, may become input to the stored files after it is verified and corrected.

We must distinguish the reading and writing of files from general input and output services. When reading or writing files, data is transferred between storage and memory devices belonging to the computer system. When reading input or writing output, data enters or leaves the computer system. Files deal with data which remains within the system.

Computer hardware devices are typically specific either to input, output, or storage functions. Some devices can be used for file storage or for input-output.

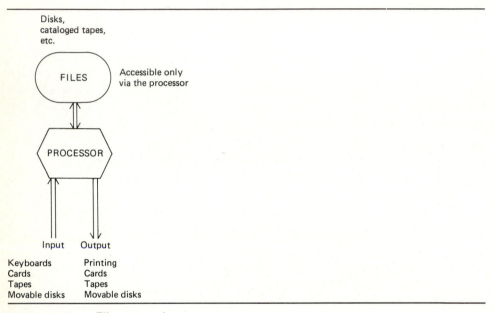

Figure 1-3   Files versus input-output.

Devices used for input and output are visual display terminals (VDTs) and all machines that read or write media in the form of cards or paper tape, printed paper, microfilm, and tapes or disks shipped between computer systems. Reports printed on paper are still the primary form of output.

Examples of devices used for files are nonremovable disks, removable disks that are normally kept mounted, dismountable master tapes or disks kept at the computer site, archival tapes and disks kept in remote vaults for protection, and sometimes card decks containing master lists that are loaded into the system when needed.

Data which is written onto tapes, although the tapes are dismounted, stored, and later mounted and read again, can be part of the storage. Storage has to be secure, so that the contents will not have been altered. Data on tapes or disks which is taken out, made accessible for modification, and then reentered has to be considered new input, since its consistency is not assured.

In some computer systems the distinction of files versus input and output is not clearly delineated. The subject of input and output is at best as complex as file storage and will not be covered in this text. We simply assume, when we talk about database systems, that an *operating system* is available which provides adequate input and output capabilities, including access via on-line terminals where appropriate.

We will not discuss file organizations based on input and output facilities. These approaches tend to regard data as a continuous stream of characters. *Stream files*, as defined by PL/1, UNIX *pipes*, and their equivalents in other systems, are based on the reading and writing of continuous lines of text. Continuous text streams are important for communication but are not suitable for data processing in general.

1-2   THE ROLE OF FILES IN DATA PROCESSING

Databases and their files can be approached from two points of view. There is the comprehensive view, in which the database is seen as a component of an overall information system involving people, organizations, and communication, all of which the database should describe. In contrast, there is a microscopic view, where the database is a collection of the hardware bits and bytes provided by computer technology. This book presents a viewpoint between these two extremes. To provide an understanding of this setting we will in this section present the environment for systems that use files.

1-2-1 Information, Knowledge, and Data

The terms *information*, *knowledge*, and *data* are used liberally when we deal with computers. In this book we will be quite specific when we use these terms, since confusion in this critical area can be costly. We will attach specific meanings to these words that satisfy our objectives. We also try to follow accepted concepts, but cannot satisfy everyone's classifications implied by these words. Consider, for instance, that a classification for flowers used by a botanist is not necessarily useful for a florist, who is concerned with costs and sales, nor for a gardener, who is concerned with planting seasons. Here we are concerned with describing and building systems which provide information, typically information to be used for decision-making in enterprises. Decisions lead to actions, and actions change the state of the world. The database must be changed to reflect the state of the world.

Figure 1-4 indicates two feedback loops: Through one the system obtains new data and through the other knowledge is gained. Feedback is essential to assure long-term stability of information systems. Feedback into the data box occurs through the collection of observations, modeling the *real world*. Feedback into the knowledge box occurs through the development of generalizations and abstractions, perhaps formalized through the scientific loop of hypothesis generation, hypothesis verification, review, publication, and dissemination.

Experts apply knowledge obtained by education and experience to control the flow of data, as illustrated in Fig. 1-4. The first step is selecting which data is relevant to the problem at hand. This selected data provides information. The second step involves reducing this data, again using expert knowledge and knowledge encoded in analysis programs, to produce the answers needed for decisionmaking.

The expert can, by applying knowledge to data selection and processing steps, reduce data to information. We define *information*, following Shannon[48], as data that conveys material that was previously unknown to the receiver. Analysis steps can also be specified, so that decisions can be made without looking through long reports for trends or exceptions. Sometimes even decisionmaking is automated. Supplies may be ordered automatically when their supply is less than the rate used times the time resupply requires. Knowledge is encoded in these programs. Whenever knowledge is used routinely in this fashion it becomes a candidate for encoding in programs or *knowledge-based systems*.

▦▦ **A Test to Distinguish Data and Knowledge** From the definitions given above we can derive a litmus test for distinguishing knowledge from data:

If we can trust an automatic process or clerk to collect the material then we are talking about *data*. The correctness of data with respect to the real world can be objectively verified by comparison with repeated observations of the real world. Eventually the state of the world changes, and we have to trust stored prior observations.

If we look for an expert to provide our material, then we are talking about *knowledge*. Knowledge includes abstractions and generalizations of voluminous material. Such material is typically less precise and cannot be easily objectively verified. Many definitions, necessary to organize systems, are knowledge as well; we look to experts for the definitions which become important building blocks for further abstractions, categorization, and generalization.

These distinctions also cause differences in the storing and processing of data and knowledge.   ▦▦

▦▦ **Storing Data versus Storing Knowledge** Data reflects the current state of the world. It will include much detail, will be voluminous, and will appear in reports used at lower levels of the enterprise for verification. Where circumstances change rapidly much data must be collected over time as well if a complete historical picture is desired.

Knowledge will not change as frequently. Knowledge may be complex but powerful, since it deals with generalizations. It will refer to entire files and their attributes rather than to individual records.

The differences mean that different data structures are appropriate for the representation of data and the representation of knowledge, at least in the preprocessing stages before the decisionmaking process occurs. Structures for data are often simple, to accommodate frequent updates. Files store primarily data.

Today much knowledge is stored within programs, and difficult to change. Knowledge about broader concepts is often uncertain. In *artificial intelligence systems* knowledge is represented and managed formally, and often *uncertainty* is represented explicitly. The representation of knowledge will be more complex, and should permit updating by experts or automated learning strategies.   ▦▦

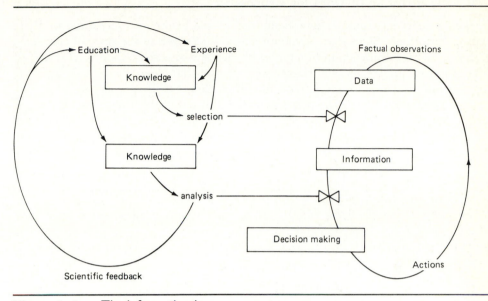

Figure 1-4   The information loops.

▦▦▦ **Knowledge-based Systems** Current research extending files and databases is directed towards the application of rules or other forms of codified knowledge to automate tasks which are now performed by experts. In a traditional environment these experts are using computers only to store and communicate data.

Automation of the decisionmaking processes means that both knowledge and data will be accessed and manipulated. By updating encoded knowledge, rather than programs, maintenance of data-processing functions can also be improved.

We observe that in industry the knowledge source namely the expert, and the information source, the data collector, are most often distinct. It is rare that the expert has time to gather and validate the data as well. Data is collected by participants at lower organizational levels and some of the data acquisition is automated.   ▦▦▦

CONSISTENCY OF DATA AND KNOWLEDGE   Newly acquired data may conflict with existing knowledge. For example, knowledge, encoded in a program, that it takes a week to ship supplies may be proven false in one instance. This information may require that the generalization, made when the program was written, be altered. An immediate increase of the estimate of resupply time may not be wise, however, since then the inventory for *all* items would increase. However, reporting this exception will change the certainty of the expert's knowledge, and lead to eventual changes in analysis programs.

Before revising knowledge, an expert will verify the exceptional data, since in large databases we always find some erroneous observations. Even when the data itself has been verified to be correct, the general base knowledge may be incomplete. New knowledge must now be added which will cover the case in question and similar cases which can be foreseen.

1-2-2 Organization of Data for Processing

Data and knowledge must be physically represented before any operations on them can be performed. Since data is voluminous and changes as the state of the world changes, its representation must support efficiency and ease of update. Our knowledge is more complex and will change more slowly than does the data. Knowledge representations are hence often more complex. This text deals with data.

A database is a structured representation of data which describes a defined and quite limited subset of the real world. The data is represented using files, records, and references between these records. Figure 1-5 presents this structure in the form of a layered pyramid. The breadth of the base symbolizes the volume of data required to obtain information.

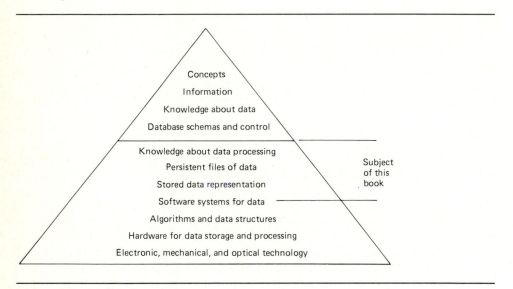

Figure 1-5   Database layers.

By not focusing in this text on the information aspects of files we avoid having to consider the many types of applications and their information needs. The topic of databases and their schemas is covered in other textbooks, including a companion volume, by Wiederhold[87], *Design Concepts and Implementation of Databases*.

The technical aspects of files and stored data are discussed here independently of the meaning of the data value stored. This limitation of focus does not mean that, when we actually implement information processing systems, these considerations can be ignored. Design objectives are derived from particular applications. It is clearly irresponsible if computer professionals ignore the ramifications of the task at hand or their contribution to the social and human environment. The Background and References sections list a number of textbooks which deal with the proper use of information for business and governmental operations and decisionmaking.

We also avoid the engineering side of file technology, namely the design and construction of data storage devices. Although the architecture and performance of computer hardware is central to the evaluation of file systems, very little discussion of hardware-design alternatives is needed to understand the concepts. Of course, an actual system developer must understand the hardware that provides the building blocks of the computer systems. Textbooks are available for the computer engineer at many levels of sophistication (see Chap. 3).

Software support is also required. Although this book is not a programming text some material on programming and programming support will be presented in Chap. 2, since the transaction systems, which now are beginning to provide the major support for file and database operations, are not well covered in existing texts on operating systems.

1-2-3 Layering and Files

By decomposing the problem of data processing into layers we illustrate an important concept in computer science. In each layer a complete set of services is provided for the next higher layer. In turn, each layer depends on services from the layer below it.

The file layer we discuss in this book presents the processes which locate and move data according to demands of database users. Descriptions of data may be manipulated at this layer as well as the data itself.

It is not the content but the *size* and *position* of the data element which is of concern. File systems provide tools to fetch data records containing data according to name or relative position. To execute these services system software is used which provides fixed blocks of unstructured bytes. Efficiency is important, since at this layer data volumes are high. To evaluate design at this layer we can use quantitative tools and provide performance estimates to engineering level accuracy.

Layers are highly dependent on each other. A user can easily specify requirements that the organizational layer cannot reasonably supply using its capabilities and those of lower-level layers. An important measure is the loss of performance introduced in a layer, and one must weigh this loss with the benefits that the transformations provide.

Layering provides isolations from changes occurring in other layers. The applications of a database will reflect the decision maker's concept of the information problems and will vary over time as the needs, analysis tools, and insight of the users of the database mature. Database management systems change as new concepts and data models are being implemented. During this time, the operating systems and computers which support the database evolve and change as well. Survival demands a clean separation or interface between the layers.

To ensure that the separation of layers is kept distinct, systems which attempt to support the concept of distinct layers may hide the structural detail of lower layers from users at the higher layers. This idea of *information hiding* can remain valid only when lower-layer functions are reliable, complete, and reasonably efficient. This independence of the descriptive and organizational layers is also referred to as *data independence*.

1-3   PERFORMANCE OF FILES

Since files can contain large amounts of data they must be handled efficiently. In this book we analyze with care the performance of alternative file management algorithms used in data processing. While it is important to understand the specifics of an algorithm, it is also useful to be able to have a simplified insight into the effectiveness of an algorithm, so that we can avoid wasting time on alternatives which are clearly not effective. Such a simplification is provided by the *big-$\mathcal{O}$ notation*.

1-3-1 The *BIG-$\mathcal{O}$* notation

The *big-$\mathcal{O}$* notation assigns to the symbol $\mathcal{O}$ an expression which omits all constants and factors except the dominating factors. For example, consider some tasks to be performed on an array of $n = 100$ numbers, defined by a program statement as

    `DECLARE numbers[100]`

To go through the array once and pick out the greatest number (the maximum) requires $\mathcal{O} = n$ operations; here `n = 100`. Another task that can be performed on the array is to retrieve a single specific number by its subscript, say `i = 76`. The statement `x=numbers[i]` performs this operation in a time $\mathcal{O} = 1$. This does not mean that finding the maximum takes 100 as long as finding the single element; the computation to locate the array element using the given subscript may take longer than a single element comparison. However the *big-$\mathcal{O}$* notation does tell us that finding the maximum will take proportionally longer for a longer array, but retrieving a specific element will take the same time and does not depend on `n`.

Sorting the array of numbers using a bubble sort requires going through the array n times and comparing and interchanging pairs of numbers. Since each time a smaller part of the array is scanned, the number of operation $\approx \frac{1}{2}n \cdot n$. But in the *big-$\mathcal{O}$* notation we ignore constants and summarize the performance of the bubblesort by saying $\mathcal{O} = n^2$, indicating that the growth of effort with increasing values of n is quadratic, just as $\mathcal{O} = n$ means that growth is linear in n, and $\mathcal{O} = 1$ means that the cost is constant, independent of n.

In data processing many operations are $\mathcal{O} = n \log n$; examples are efficient external sorts, as described in Chap. 4-2-1. Algorithms which require higher polynomials, $\mathcal{O} = n^3$ or $\mathcal{O} = n^4$ are avoided in data processing although they may occur during design evaluation, as shown in Chap. 14-5. Of course, when n is small, algorithms with high order polynomials may still be useful. Throughout this book we avoid algorithms where $\mathcal{O}$ grows exponentially, i.e., where $\mathcal{O} = c^n$. In those cases we search for simplifying *heuristics* which permit computations to be performed in $\mathcal{O} = n^i$ for small i, although the precision or optimality of the result may not be guaranteed.

The *big-$\mathcal{O}$* notation will be used whenever quantitative issues become complex. We will also summarize the basic operations on files in Chap. 7-1-1 using this notation.

1-4 APPLICATIONS

Many applications of computers involve processing of large data volumes kept on files. Commercial data processing is probably the largest segment of computing, and there large files are ubiquitous, but many scientific tasks also require large data collections for analysis and verification of hypotheses. Major groups of applications that depend on large files are:

- Manufacturing, with inventory management, bills-of-material processing, and production equipment scheduling
- Government at all levels, with records on taxpayers and property
- Financial institutions, with lists of individual accounts, assets, and convertibility of funds
- Service industries, with lists of service capabilities and allocation schedules
- Medical services, with patients' records, disease histories, problem classification, and treatment effectiveness data
- Economic planning services, which model production and consumption for resource and effort allocation
- Scientific research, with collections of previously gathered data to be analyzed and used to determine future research directions
- Offices which are automating their document management
- Libraries cataloging abstracts and indexes of their holdings

The Background and References section of this chapter cites some examples from each category. It will help the reader to gain some understanding of the uses to which these systems are put, and to obtain a perspective of the problems discussed.

DEFINING A FILE-ORIENTED APPLICATION In any computer application, the purpose of the effort should be spelled out in detail. Only then can one identify and judge the relevance of the data elements in the files, the processes required to manipulate the data, and the file structures which will enable the processes to be effective. Knowledge of the environment is needed to determine the value of the information produced. We also have to know the response time required by users, since the chosen file organization must ensure timely delivery of the outputs of the system.

A statement of objectives and constraints, specifying the goal and environment of the application, is an essential part of any project carried out in practice. Such a statement should also be presented with any project carried out as an exercise within the scope of this book, as with Exercise 1-1. A frequent error in the formulation of objectives is the inclusion of the method or technology to be used as part of the objective. The proper place for such an account would be the section describing the results of the system analysis.

Objective statements implying that the desire to *computerize* was the reason for development of a database should send a shiver down the spine of any computing professional. If the choice of methods or technology has been intentionally limited, a separate section of the objective statement should clarify such conditions.

1-5   REVIEW

This chapter has provided some definitions for the remainder of this book. It also provides a background for databases and files in general. We have defined a standard terminology which matches much of the literature of this field. Since other terms are used in the literature as well, it will be useful to refer to the index, where many alternative terms are cross referenced to the terms in the text.

We now will review the terms and concepts we have defined in this chapter.

1-5-1 Terms Defined

A file or database system includes persistent data structures and programs which operate on data. The system will include portions which are the users' responsibility, and the basic functions which are supplied with the system.

Database System = Data + User Programs + System Programs

We decompose the data according to a hierarchical* structure:

Database ——→ Files ——→ Records ——→ Fields

Databases and their files provide the persistent storage required for computer applications.

Data for users' applications is managed by a combination of

Database Systems   and   File Management Systems supported by Operating Systems   and   Hardware

and remains under the control of these systems. The systems providing these services should be arranged in layers, to protect them from change and permit independent growth.

The systems we consider provide information according to the rule that

Knowledge   →   Selection   ←   Data ↓ Information

The information obtained may be presented or further processed. Data may be used for multiple applications, which apply different knowledge to the data.

New data enters the system through a separate input mechanism and the results that leave the system are handled by output facilities. Processing and input-output are not topics of this text. Users supply the programs which manage the content of data structures and extract the results required for the enterprise they serve.

---

* We use ——→ to denote a *one:many* relationship, where the *many* depend on the *one*.

1-5-2 Overview of Material to Be Presented

We can group the material in this book into topics as shown in Fig. 1-6.

After the definitions given in this chapter we describe the software and hardware infrastructure. Chapter 2 deals with issues of programming and systems for files. We place program operations into transactions that operate on files. Chapter 3 describes available hardware and reduces its complexities to a small number of quantifiable parameters.

Then we can deal with the topic of files proper. Chapters 4, 5, and 6 present six fundamental types of file organization. In these chapters we also develop evaluation formulas which can be used to predict performance given specifications for the transactions and hardware parameters as defined in Chap. 3.

Chapter 7 compares and combines the fundamental methods to create hybrid file designs. Chapter 8 addresses refinements in indexing methods, and Chap. 9 presents some methods that do not fall into the major classification. The approaches developed in these three chapters can address user requirements that are more complex than those served by the fundamental methods.

The performance of a complete transaction, which can include references to multiple files, is synthesized in Chap. 10. In order to deal with the complexity introduced with multiple files this chapter also covers issues of storage system architecture. Associated topics are free space management and file allocation to storage devices. We also discuss how file services can be provided by specialized database machines.

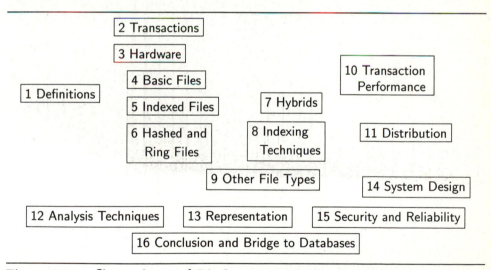

Figure 1-6 Chapter layout of *File Organization for Database Design.*

Chapters 11, 12, 13, and 15 deal with ancilliary topics, and may be skipped or read out of sequence. In Chap. 11 we expand the topic of specialized and multiple file servers by presenting how files may be distributed over multiple, often remote, processors. The analysis techniques presented in Chapter 12 provide a variety of tools to solve hard design and performance problems. We show how concepts from statistics and operation research can be applied to files, and system analysis in general. How data is best represented is considered in Chap. 13; topics include encoding, redundancy, compression, and encryption.

The overall file system design process, beginning with user requirements, is presented in Chap. 14. Criteria are the use and effectiveness of computer-stored files since the best measure of a good design is the overall economic utility of the services provided by the file system. The primary elements of acceptable systems are:

- Reliability
- Speed of access to information
- Ease and speed of update of data
- Economy of storage.

These issues are considered throughout the text. Chapter 15 reviews issues of security and reliability. We end in Chap. 16 discussing future directions, and provide a bridge to database management systems.

BACKGROUND AND REFERENCES

The structure of information systems has emerged slowly. A prophetic paper by Vannevar Bush[45] predicted machines for information retrieval, and in 1948 Shannon[62] published the paper defining the formal concept of information.

Storage devices capable of handling databases became available in the early 1960s, and some early systems such as MEDLARS for medical documentation (Katter[75]), SABRE for airline reservations (Desmonde[64]), and other systems for governmental planning (see Sprague[82]) were initiated. Expectations of use for high-level business management were tempered by disappointments and reassessments (Aron[69], Lucas[75], and in Riley[81]), but Lide[81] stresses that data are critical in the modern world.

At the same time, a scientific approach to problems of data management began to emerge with the concepts of data and data structure (Steel[64], Mealy[67], Bachman[72], Kent[78], Lucas[81], and Tsichritzis[81]). A summary of the history leading to modern databases and a status evaluation is provided in Wiederhold[84a].

Textbooks

As the topics of data management became better understood, textbooks started to appear. This in turn has helped define the field and introduced a consistent vocabulary (Gould[71]). File management issues were addressed by Judd[73], Martin[76], and in Wiederhold[77,83*]. Teorey[82] quantifies many file methods.

For further study many texts are available. An earlier text, which also covers database structures, is Wiederhold[83] *Database Design*. A companion volume to this book also is being prepared (Wiederhold[87]: *Design Concepts and Implementation of Databases*).

Database theory is summarized in Ullman[82] and Maier[83]. Date[85] provides justification for the relational approach to databases. Databases and file management are introduced by Korth[86]. Texts by Kroenke[78], Cardenas[84], McFadden[85], and Salzberg[86] describe a number of database management systems and related topics. A textbook oriented toward data processing is Powers[84].

---

* In the Bibliography the latest editions are cited.

Periodicals

Information about recent work is found in journals and magazines. The high level of activity in the database area has led to publication of several journals devoted to database subjects. Bibliographies and descriptive books become rapidly obsolete.

Major journals in the area are *Transactions on Database Systems* (ACM TODS, since 1975) and *Informations Systems* (Pergamon Press, since 1974). Short notes on research results are found in *Information Processing Letters* (North-Holland Publishing Company, since 1971).

General computer science journals which frequently carry papers on file and database topics include the *Communications of the* CACM (published since 1961) and its *Journal* (since 1968). A substantial number of articles on files and databases appear in the IEEE Computer Society *Transaction on Software Engineering* (since 1975) and the *Computer Journal* of the British Computer Society (published since 1958, with articles on files back to 1970). *Software Practice and Experience* (since 1973) and the *Journal* of the Australian Computer Society carry file and database articles. *BIT (Nordisk Behandlings Informations Tidskrift),* published since 1976 by the Regnecentralen (Copenhagen, Denmark) and *Acta Informatica* (since 1971) often have relevant algorithmic papers. Papers on computational topics are found in the SIAM *Journal on Computing.* There is also the *Journal on Computer and Information Science.*

Computing magazines carrying related articles include *Computer* (since 1970) and *Software* (since 1984) of the IEEE Computer Society. *Datamation* frequently addresses data-processing issues. A recent entry (1984) is Auerbach publishers with *Information Systems Management.*

Newsletters in the area are *Database Engineering Bulletin*, produced since 1977 by the IEEE Computer Society's technical committee of that name, and the ACM-SIGMOD *Record* of the ACM Special Interest Group (SIG) on Management of Data. From 1968 to 1976 the ACM publication was named *FDT*, for File Definition and Translation. Each issue of the IEEE Bulletins is devoted to some topic of current interest. Beginning in 1983 they have been bound annually and republished as *Database Engineering.*

Annual conferences (ACM-SIGFIDET, 1969 to 1974, and ACM-SIGMOD since 1975) sponsored by the ACM interest group present many important papers. A series of conferences on *Very Large Data Bases* (VLDB) cover all database topics. They are held annually. After the first one in 1975 in Massachussetts, they have moved around the world and attracted much international participation. Recent VLDB proceedings are available from Morgan Kaufmann Publishers in Los Altos, CA. Since 1980 the British Computer Society has sponsored conferences on databases, their proceedings are being published by the Cambridge University Press. In 1983 the IEEE Computer Society started sponsoring and publishing the proceedings of the Data Engineering Conferences to cover the engineering issues of databases, knowledge bases, and file systems. Every *Proceedings of the National Computer Conferences*, published by AFIPS, contains several relevant articles.

Many applications areas have journals which emphasize issues of data management. Management-oriented papers are published in the *Harvard Business Review* and *Journal of the Society for Management Information Systems* (Chicago, IL). In medicine we find *Methods of Information in Medicine* (Schattauer Verlag, Stuttgart, FRG) and the *Journal of Medical Systems* (Plenum Publishing). The library field uses the *Annual Review of Information Science and Technology*, published by Knowledge Industry Publications, White Plains, NY, under the sponsorship of the American Society for Information Science. Butterworth, London, since 1982 has published *Information Technology: Research and Development.*

Applications

There is no area of computing where files are not used. General issues of data processing and its relevance are addressed in books by Davis[74], DeGreene[73], Gotlieb[73], and Westin[71]. The design of decisionmaking systems is covered by Sprague[82]. Kroenkhe[83] describes business, and Everest[86] management-oriented applications. An insurance application is described by Allen[68]. The environment for effective systems is discussed in Martin[83]. The demands for engineering design applications are presented by Katz[84]. Lorie[83] contains several papers on that topic. Social science applications are supported by the system described by Ellis[72].

Applications in medicine are detailed in Wiederhold[81] and Javitt[86], the latter includes a chapter on bibliographic files. Traditional bibliographic applications are presented by Dimsdale[73].

EXERCISES

1[P]*   Write a statement of objective for one of the applications mentioned in Sec. 1-3, or for one of your own choosing. Select a subject area with which you are familiar and in which you are interested. Many other exercises in this book can be based on the same application.

2[P]   Provide a list of data elements which you think would be included in the application presented above, and justify their value with a short sentence for each.

3[P]   Identify which elements are likely to change over time as the application or the enterprise grows. State their initial size or number, and the size or number they may attain. Examples are the number of **Employees** and the **Job_lists** in Fig. 2-6.

4   In closing Sect. 1-5-2 a number of points are made. Justify them in single statements. Are there conflicts?

5   ▦▦▦   Look though Fig. 2-4, which shows a program operating on a file, and identify examples of data, knowledge, and information.   ▦▦▦

---

*   Exercises marked with a [P] symbol are steps of a project carried throughout this book and its successor. At the end of a course using this book the project is submitted in the form of a proposal to an enterprise manager. It should be sufficient to define a database and permit the eventual implementation of the required file programs for this application.

Chapter 2

Transactions on Files

To do the act that might the addition earn

William Shakespeare
Othello, Act iv, scene 2, *1604*.

2-0 INTRODUCTION

This chapter provides the background for the manipulation of data on files. This book is not a programming text, although all the work in organizing, maintaining, and retrieving data is performed by programs. We assume that you understand the principles of programming and could write the software needed for the tasks described. In practice you often do not have to write programs to deal with files, but you will be able to use existing software. Such software is provided with the file management systems and database management systems introduced in Chap. 1.

This chapter concentrates on processing issues specifically dealing with data management. The concept of a transaction is becoming increasingly important when dealing with files and provides the focus for this chapter. Programming issues on files differ from programming on memory-based data structures because of three characteristics of files introduced in Chap. 1:

- Persistence
- Sharability
- Size

In Sec. 2-1 we will present the computations which are commonly applied to files. They are implemented using transactions, as presented in Sec. 2-2. Section 2-3 deals with the operating system services which are needed for data files. Included is a classification of various types of operating systems, and their suitability for data processing.

2-1 PROGRAMMING FOR FILES

We assume that readers of this book are familiar with programming in general and so we will only cover programming topics specific to file management. Section 2-1-1 presents operations which apply to files and Section 2-1-2 defines batch and on-line modes of operation. The optional Sec. 2-1-3 introduces concepts of versions of files, tracking files as they are changed. Section 2-1-4 discusses program documentation, and provides the foundation for the material on transaction programs in Section 2-2.

2-1-1 Computations on Files

In the previous section we considered the static structure of data storage, namely the storage of data as files, records, and fields. Now we will look at files from a user's point of view: "What are the operations that are used to process files?"

Operations on files are performed by programs provided with the computer system. These programs often require many thousands of instructions. They are kept in system libraries and invoked automatically by application programs statements as `READ FILE(Payroll) INTO(working_memory)`.

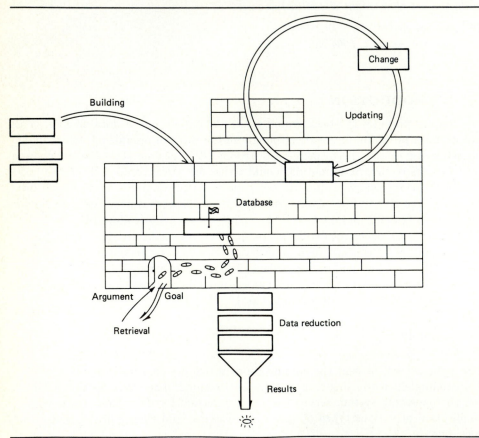

Figure 2-1   Transaction types for a database.

The set of files comprising a database may serve one or more *applications*. Handling a payroll is a typical application. The term *transaction* is used to denote a section of an application which manipulates the database. For instance, giving `managers` a `raise` is performed by a transaction.

Most of the transactions used to manipulate a data collection are conceptually simple. We recognize four kinds of transactions related to files:

1 Building the data collection

2 Updating of data elements in the data collection

3 Retrieval of data from the data collection

4 Reduction of large quantities of data to usable form

An application will use all four kinds of transactions, but certain applications will stress one kind more than others. The kinds are sketched in Fig. 2-1. One may note that the only transaction type which uses the calculating powers of the computer is the reduction of data to yield information.

We now will describe the four kinds of transactions more completely.

BUILDING A DATABASE   To build a database, data must be collected, encoded as the field specifications require, and entered. Input facilities of the computer system are used to enter the data. Programs further check the data and transform their representation before they enter the files. Suspected errors are reported using the computer system's output facilities. This kind of activity is often the most costly part of a database operation.

Building a database can take a long time. A database application will not be able to produce useful information until the files are complete. For instance, to compute a manufacturing schedule, the inventory of parts and the suppliers' delivery capability for all parts not in stock must be known. To predict the outcome of a new medical treatment requires years of testing and recording of results prior to the analysis.

UPDATING   To make the correct decisions data must be up to date. Updating of a database includes inserting new data, changing stored data values as necessary, and deleting invalid or obsolete data.

> The degree of update activity varies much among types of applications. A *static database*, one not receiving updates, may be used in a retrospective study where all the data is collected prior to analysis. A *dynamic* or *volatile database* is encountered in applications reporting current events and situations, such as occurring in ticket reservations systems.

Updating is a continuing activity for most files, so that we can never identify a definite point where all the data have been captured, so that the building phase is complete. One criterion is that the files are sufficient for retrieval of information, updates after that point will cause retrieval to show changes in the data.

RETRIEVAL   Retrieval of data provides the information benefits which justifies
having a database. Retrieved data is considered *information* when it is both previously unknown and useful. A fact stored in a file can be unknown to the receiver,
and hence be potentially information, when it has been forgotten or was entered
by someone else. Often data is entered into files from remote locations. In that
situation a file functions as a communication medium, spanning time and place.

Data retrieval can mean fetching a specific field value to obtain a stored value
or fact, or collecting several related values. Information is often obtained by joining
data to ascertain some relationship among events. To fetch a specific data record,
the file will be accessed using a *search argument*, which will be matched with the
keys in the records. The argument of a search is called the *search key*. In general,
the context clarifies the distinction between the key in the record and the key of
the query.

> In computing, the meaning of the word *key* is unfortunately the opposite of the
> concept associated with a key in common household usage: a person who desires
> something from a house uses a key which will unlock the lock of the proper
> house. With files, a person wishing to retrieve data uses the argument to match
> the key of the proper record.

DATA REDUCTION   Information in the files has much potential beyond simply
presenting collected facts. For instance, out of inventory records and sales of goods
one can compute when to order new supplies. A data-processing system is not
helpful when it simply disgorges masses of facts to users.

Data reduction complements retrieval in the generation of information. It can
also produce information from facts that were known locally, but never brought together for analysis. Data reduction is essential when the data obtained in response
a query is so voluminous that it has to be summarized to make it comprehensible to
the user. Statistical summaries, annual business operating statements, and graphical data presentations are examples of frequently used data reduction techniques.

When the information being obtained is diffused throughout the files, much
of the database will have to be scanned to summarize or abstract data. Even a
query which simply asks for an `AVERAGE salary`* requires reading of every record
of the employee file. Data reduction is very demanding of file performance since the
pace of the user of the information is not slowed down by having to look through
voluminous output.

2-1-2 Modes of File Operation

We distinguish two modes of program operation. The differences are crucial for
programs operationg on files.
1 *Batch operation* means that requests to modify the files or to obtain information
   from a file are collected into a batch, and then processed together at some
   suitable time. Batch processing can use files very efficiently, since the individual
   requests can be rearranged in an optimal sequence. However, users wanting
   information must suffer long delays.

---

*   We use UPPERCASE for programming language functions and lowercase for program variables.

2 *On-line operation* means that each request is processed as it enters the system. An on-line operation requires the use of terminals so that the request and its result can be immediatly displayed. Any errors made in the requests are obvious and an erroneous request can be edited and resubmitted. If updates are also made on-line the results can always reflect current data values.

A request for on-line usage is executed by a *transaction program* and Sec. 2-2 will elaborate on such programs. The distinction also requires very different services from operating systems, and these are defined in Sec. 2-3. We focus throughout on file transaction being executed in on-line mode.

▦ 2-1-3 Versions

When a file is being updated it may be necessary to retain the previous version of the file. Past versions are required for

History maintenance For many analyses it is not only necessary to know the current state of the world but also the events in the time sequence which led to this state.

Backup If the current update is in error, it may be necessary to return to the prior state of the files.

Synchronization It may be necessary to perform a computation using multiple files, where not all files are updated simultaneously. Then matching versions must be selected.

The last case might occur when budgets are updated monthly but payrolls are updated weekly.

Backup provisions are essential where files are used to support *planning* or *design*. Here the files do not represent observation of past events, which can no longer be changed. For instance, in an *Engineering Information System* the files may represent a proposed design for a product, which a subsequent analysis finds not acceptable. The action of *going back to the drawing board* requires going back to an earlier version of the files. The situation gets yet more complex when multiple future plans or designs are investigated and must be maintained in parallel (Katz[84]).
▦

2-1-4 Description and Documentation

To permit implementation and use of files by many people, some documentation must exist to describe both the static aspects, the *file organization*, and the procedural aspects, the *transactions*, which carry out the data transformations.

> We strongly advocate that data and program specifications be documented prior to beginning any programming. The documentation will then reflect the desired behavior of the system. The programmer will then try to write the program so that it satisfies the documentation, and hence the program is likely to have the desired behavior.

On completion, the documentation may have to be updated.

If, on the other hand, the documentation is written after the program is done, it will have to reflect any idiosyncracies introduced while coding. The awkwardness of describing undesirable and inconsistent program behavior may be the major reasons why documentation is often not completed, even for programs that are put into regular use.

For file-oriented programs, because collecting and loading the data to files may take a year or so, full use and testing is often not possible, even when the program is completed. To assure conformance of the program with expectations, early documentation is even more essential, since the programmers will have gone.

DECLARATIVE DESCRIPTION   A picture of the data in terms of files, records, fields, and the relation between items of data contained in these elements defines the relatively static structure of the data portion of an application.

Since many programs can operate on a collection of files, the *declarative* description of the data elements and their assignments typically comprises the primary documention. A *file dictionary* is a carefully formatted description of the files. It is best maintained using on-line computer files for easy sharing and reference. The file dictionary is the document used by those who program file operations and by users who must locate data when directly querying the files.

More information about the use of the data can be placed into such a dictionary, leading to a *data dictionary* as described in Chap. 16-1-1. In a database management system (DBMS), information from the file dictionary is placed into the *schema*. In the schema the structure definitions are kept as computer-readable codes. These are interpreted by the DBMS to automate data management.

PROCEDURAL DESCRIPTIONS   The procedures which operate on files may be given as a formula, a description of program sections to be executed, or a flowchart. In many commercial programming groups much effort is put into *systems analysis* which prepares process descriptions in minute detail for subsequent implementation by coders. It is easy for errors to develop because of communication problems between systems analysts and coders. The analyst may assume that coders are aware of conditions which are actually beyond their knowledge. Coders, on the other hand, may program for cases which cannot occur. The determination of critical sections is often a source of difficulty. No formal methods are yet adequate to fully verify correctness for interacting processes. We therefore prefer detailed declarative data descriptions for the development of files and databases.

DECLARATIVE VERSUS PROCEDURAL DESCRIPTIONS   The declarations and procedural definitions may both be used to describe files. For many simple data-processing problems, however, no process descriptions are needed. A data retrieval has only to indicate which of the elements in the file dictionary are being obtained.

1. A simple update transaction can be described by providing two *declarative* diagrams of a file, specifying the form and contents before and after the transaction. The programmer uses the before-and-after diagrams to write the code.
2. When processing is complex, the user may find that the data organization is implicitly defined by a listing of the steps of the *procedure* which puts the data into the files.

The two documentation alternatives are implied in the two phrases that describe storage structures: *file organization* and *access methods*.

Dispensing with coding entirely is the intent of *report generators*, which accept the file dictionary and the format of the desired output report. Options such as sorting of output or grouping of subtotals are given as format declarations. The sequence of processing steps is implied and the program needed is created by the report generator system.

In high-level query systems an information-retrieval request is stated as a formula and its resolution is the task of a retrieval system. Here the layout may be automatically determined, avoiding the pain and flexibility of specifying the format.

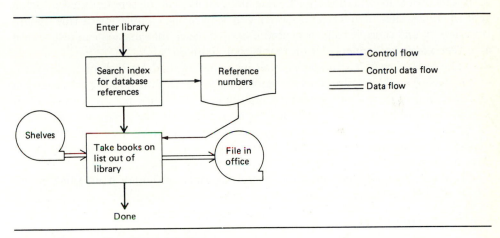

Figure 2-2   Flowchart notation.

FLOWCHARTS In order to describe complex processes and data flow, we sometimes have to resort to a graphic description of the dynamics of an algorithm, a —*flowchart* — as shown in Fig. 2-2. In flowcharts we can distinguish three types of activity:

1 *Control flow*, the sequence of instruction executed by the processing unit under various conditions. This sequence is described when flowcharts are used to document a programming algorithm.
2 *Control-data flow*, the flow of data elements which in turn affect the control flow of the transactions. Typical examples are counts, references, or control switches that indicate whether an operation is permitted, whether an area is full or empty, and so forth. These may be set by one program and used by another program.
3 *Data flow* or the flow of the bulk of the coded data as it is moved, merged, and processed to generate information for the benefit of the users of the system. This flow is typically between files, memory, and input or output devices.

The last two activities are sometimes difficult to distinguish, since often some control data is extracted during data processing. However, the distinction is helpful since the dataflow will grow in proportion of the sizes of the file n, i.e., be $\mathcal{O}(n)$, while the control data flow is only affected by the number of transactions L, and hence will be $\mathcal{O}(L)$. Figure 2-2 shows the three types of flow in the process of using a library.

With modern programming techniques, including the use of higher-level languages, well-defined modules, well-structured processes, and documented standard algorithms, the need for description of the program flow has lessened. Detailed descriptions of file and program state are much preferable unless process interactions are unusually complex. ▦

▦ **CONTROL OF PROCESSING** In general, we assume that processing starts when a transaction or program is invoked by a user. Processing may also be triggered by changes in control variables of the database. A data element kept with a file can state whether a particular file has been completely updated by some type of transaction. A query transaction can require the completion of this update transaction, and cause it to be executed if needed. Such information can also assure a correct execution sequence of programs that share data.

The reason that a transaction was incomplete could be lack of input data. A pay record could require a recent entry of the number of hours worked by the employee. Some transactions could be programmed to decide not to proceed at all in that case; other processes would not be impeded unless they required one of the records which had not yet been brought up to date. We refer to data which is not input but which describes the state of the data for the control of transactions as *control data*.

In practice, much data assumes control functions, although it may not be declared explicitly as such. ▦

2-2   TRANSACTIONS

To produce information by retrieval, perform data reduction, or to update files, programs must define the file operations and the computations on the data obtained from the files. A characteristic of transaction programs used in an on-line mode is that they are typically small, but also that there will be many of them, all dealing with some part of the data collected in the files. These characteristics derive from the characteristics of databases stated in the introduction:

Persistence of data removes the constraint that a single large program must perform all the computations necessary for a result.

Sharability permits computations to be controlled and scheduled by individual users as needed.

Size encourages the splitting up of processing into small chunks, so that interference and delays do not become excessive.

We call programs which have the features of limited size and scope, and which are configured to access shared data, *transactions*. The use of transactions implies that the files are transformed by small, incremental steps. We will in this section introduce transactions from the point of view of users. In Sec. 2-3 we present the operating system services required to deal with transactions. Transaction concepts also have a place in concurrency and reliability control of databases, as indicated in Sec. 2-2-3, but the technical issues of concurrency control are covered elsewhere, such as in Wiederhold[87].

2-2-1 Transaction Programs

A *transaction* is a program dealing with the files for a database. Many transactions are needed to provide all the services that a datab-processing system will provide. A measure of complexity of a transaction is the number of files accessed by a transaction. Up to Chap. 10 we will deal with transactions which access only one file at a time.

> A transaction is a program which, in response to a user request, performs one or more operations on the files of a database.

In Sec. 2-2-2 we develop a sample transaction and show how it may be written. We state in Sec. 2-2-3 the requirements which transactions place on operating systems, and in Sec. 2-2-4 we consider the modularity of programming which transactions bring about.

PROGRAMS AS PERSISTENT OBJECTS The user also expects programs to be always available. This means that files are used for program storage as well. Programs can have more than one representation on files. *Source programs* are files of text lines, mainly created by programmers using word-processing programs. These are transformed by compilers into binary representation, often stored in libraries until needed. Linkers and loaders will bind the individual programs together, and place them on files for use by the operating system.

When the user requests a program from the operating system, the latest bound representation is brought in from the files. If no up-to-date bound version exists, its components may be compiled, if necessary, linked with other programs from the users' or the system library, and loaded into the processor's memory for execution.

╫╫╫╫╫ **Program Files** The organization of files containing programs is determined by the word processors, the compilers, and the operating system, and not specifically discussed in this book. Use of data-processing style files to manage source files and program libraries is an option, but not yet generally used. The capability to manage *versions* of programs, and the ability to compose programming systems using a variety of matching versions of programs is important for program files (Atkinson[85]).

The structure of programs requires capabilities which differ from those required for record-oriented data files. There is little need for decomposition of files into records; however, access into certain points within program files is necessary to link external variables and procedures.   ╫╫╫╫╫

DESCRIBING TRANSACTION PROGRAMS A conceptual descriptions of a transaction for a particular problem can frequently be written in a few lines; the procedures to implement the program may be diagrammed on a one-page flowchart and programmed in a short time. Yet the effort required to bring an application using files into operation frequently involves expenditure of large amounts of time and money.

All transactions have to cooperate with each other while remaining independent. A transaction be executed on request, and hence transaction can occur in

an unpredictable order. To avoid problems they must all have a common understanding of the form, content, and meaning of the data. Some of the stored data
will have control functions, to permit correct interaction. The small size of most
transactions makes it possible to review the program steps and locate for potential
critical interactions. Documentation of such interactions can also be provided in a
declarative form.

We will now examine some typical transaction programs for files. Our example
will use a `Payroll`* file, as illustrated in Fig. 1-2.

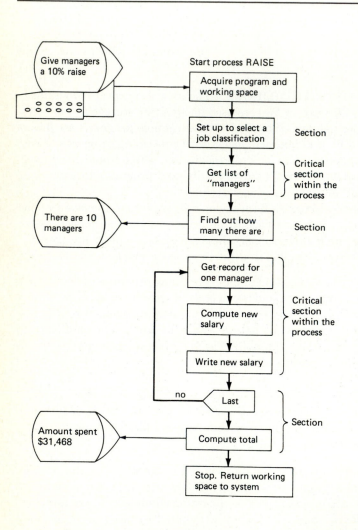

Figure 2-3   Sections of a transaction.

*   We use `Capitalized` names for files.

2-2-2 Programming File Transactions

Up to this point we have dealt with files and programming at an abstract level. Some examples, presented as Figs. 2-4 to 2-6, will help relate programming practice to the concepts which have been presented. To illustrate the use of a file, we will develop a simple program to carry out the actions for a transaction which updates the `salary` field of a record from the `Payroll` file. A successive version will permit multiple records to be updated during the transaction. The third version will use a second file to identify those who should receive the raise (Fig. 2-4). A sketch of the final transaction flow was presented in Fig. 2-3. The programs are not intended to be especially good or bad, but rather typical.

We first program a transaction to give an employee, say `John Jones`, a raise. We cannot know that he is the first employee in the `Payroll` file, so that we have to use a search key. The search key will be found in an input message such as:

"Grant␣'John␣Jones␣␣␣␣␣␣␣␣␣␣␣␣'␣a␣raise␣of␣'10'%"

The *transaction command* name `Grant` will cause the `raise1` transaction to be executed. In this message we have indicated all blanks explicitly, and placed the parameters in quotes. In practice, such a message is formatted on a terminal display.

```
/* Transaction program to grant a raise to an employee */
raise1: PROCEDURE(message);
        DECLARE message CHAR(200);
    s2: DECLARE 1 payroll_ws
                    2 name CHAR(20),
                    2 ssn  CHAR(11),
                    2 dob  CHAR(7),
                    2 pob  CHAR(40),
                    2 exm  INT(5),
                    2 ...  ...,
                    2 s_c  INT(3),
                    2 sal  INT(8),
                    2 addr 3 str CHAR(20),
                           3 cit CHAR(20),
                           3 zip DEC(5);
        DECLARE s_name CHAR(20), pct INT;
 /* parse message */
    s4: s_name = SUBSTR(message,8,20); pct = SUBSTR(message,41,2);
 /* prepare to give raises */
    s5: OPEN FILE(Payroll) DIRECT UPDATE;
        ON KEY(Payroll) GO TO error;
    s6: READ FILE(Payroll) KEY(s_name) INTO(payroll_ws);
 /*   increase salary field of record */
    s7: increase = payroll_ws.sal * pct / 100;
    s8:  payroll_ws.sal = payroll_ws.sal + increase;
        REWRITE FILE(Payroll) FROM(payroll_ws);
 /* report cost of raise */
        PUT SKIP EDIT(increase) ('Amount spent $', F(8,2));
       END raise1;
```

Figure 2-4   A transaction program to grant an employee a raise.

The DECLARE statement labeled s2 defines a working area in memory for a copy of the payroll records. A READ request brings in all of the record. All programs must use the same record definition to avoid errors, for if one program were to declare the size of name to be CHAR(25) all subsequent values will be incorrectly registered. Use of the file dictionary can help avoid such inconsistencies.

The OPEN statement at s5 names the file and specifies its usage. When an OPEN is executed the name of the requested file is found by the operating system (OS) in a directory of file names. Now this file is under exclusive control of this program, at least until the file is released by a CLOSE statement. The execution of the OPEN statements can involve other file operations within the OS, and may take a relatively long time. The ON KEY statement which follows prepares the file system for the possibility of an erroneous key value. We do not show in the example the program statements at the label error, which would be executed in that case.

The READ statement s6 names a particular record of the file identified with a KEY, and — if there is one — moves a copy of this record into the payroll_ws area. The file system will look up and compute the proper record address within the Payroll file. It will then operate the devices to transfer the data to program memory. The address in memory for the payroll_ws area is determined during program compilation and loading.

The program now can extract information, such as salary, by addressing fields in the copy of the record. The copy of the record is modified to reflect the employee's raise. The final REWRITE performs the update of the record in the file. It depends on the record address that was determined by the file system during the execution of the READ statement. The file system saves this record address, for files OPENed with an UPDATE specification, from the time of the READ, for use in the REWRITE.

Some remarks about this program are in order. Since people's names are not neccessarily unique it is likely that in the message and the search key s_name would be replaced by a unique identifier, such as the social security number (ssn). Many file organizations used in data processing require keys to be unique for the records of one file.

NAMING VERSUS ADDRESSING   In this example, the records on the file have been specified using a symbolic identifier or *name*, namely, the s_name. It could also have been the social_security_number. The file system performs some procedure to determine an actual address for the corresponding record and then fetches the record. It remembers this address for any file which is to be updated later to perform a later REWRITE properly. Within the record fetched, the program located data by providing *addresses*; for instance, the sal field was addressed as defined in payroll_ws.

When an address is used, the programmer controls position and size of the data unit. When a name is used, the system performs a search to associate the name with an actual address.

We will now adjust the program of Fig. 2-4 to give raises to all managers, as shown in Fig. 2-5. Let us assume that the salary class s_c for managers is 32. This field is not a likely candidate to be a key for this file, since there will be many Payroll records for each value of a class designator s_c.

The transaction message will now be

"Award'␣32'␣a␣raise␣of␣'10'%"

We change the name of the command invoking the transaction to Award so that the transaction processor can route this message to the proper transaction (raise2). We only discuss now the changes made relative to Fig. 2-4.

```
/* Transaction program to award raises to a class of employees */
 raise2: PROCEDURE(message);
         DECLARE message CHAR(200);
     s2: DECLARE 1 payroll_ws
                   2 name CHAR(20),
                   2 ssn  CHAR(11),
                   2 ...  ...,
                   2 s_c  INT(3),
                   2 sal  INT(8),
                   2 ...  ..., ...;
         DECLARE class, pct INT;
/* parse message
         class = SUBSTR(message,8,3); pct = SUBSTR(message,24,2);
/* prepare to give raises */
     s5: OPEN FILE(Payroll) SEQUENTIAL UPDATE;
         ON ENDFILE(Payroll) GO TO s9;
         total_increase = 0;
     s6: READ FILE(Payroll) INTO(payroll_ws);
         IF payroll_ws.s_c = class THEN
/*       increase salary field of record with matching class code */
           BEGIN
               increase = payroll_ws.sal * pct / 100;
               total_increase = total_increase + increase;
               payroll_ws.sal = payroll_ws.sal + increase;
           REWRITE FILE(Payroll) FROM(payroll_ws);
           END;
         GO TO s6;    /* repeat until end of file is reached */
/* finally report total cost of all raises awarded */
     s9: PUT SKIP EDIT(total_increase) ('Amount spent $', F(8,2));
     END raise2;
```

Figure 2-5   A transaction program to award a class of employees a raise.

We now do not have a KEY, and OPEN the file at s5 for SEQUENTIAL reading. We assume that the Payroll file can be read either way, this assumption depends actually on the file organization. The ON condition now is an essential part of the program. The program keeps reading the file until an ENDFILE condition occurs, then it is done and can produce the final report line.

The READ statement s6 fetches all the records of the file. Only the records which match the class specified in the message will be changed and REWRITtEn.

This transaction will take much more time to execute; if the Payroll file covers many employees the delay for this transaction will be unbearable to the user at the terminal. Note also that during its execution no other program should be able to access the Payroll file.

    To avoid having to search through the entire file of employees we now adapt
this program to give raises to listed groups. The lists defining the groups are kept
on another file, Job_lists, containing the social security numbers of each employee
by title. In this (unrealistic) example we place a fixed limit (250) on the number
of employees for any title, otherwise the program would get more complex and
less clear.

    We also change the record layout of the employee file a bit, and hence give this
file another name: Pay_ssn. The key field for this version of a payroll file is the
social security number, as obtained from the lists of groups.

    "Give␣'managers'␣a␣raise␣of␣'10'%"

```
/* Transaction program to give a raise to a list of employees */
  raise: PROCEDURE(message);
         DECLARE message CHAR(200);
     s1: DECLARE 1 emp_list
                 2 titles CHAR(8)
                 2 id(250) CHAR(11) INITIAL((250)'nobody');
     s2: DECLARE 1 payroll_ss
                 2 ssn  CHAR(11),
                 2 name CHAR(20),
                 2 ...  ...,
                 2 s_c  INT(3),
                 2 sal  INT(8),
                 2 ...  ...,
         DECLARE title CHAR(8), pct INT;
         title = SUBSTR(message,8,8); pct = SUBSTR(message,29,2);
 /* get record listing employees of this group */
     s3: OPEN FILE(Job_lists) DIRECT;
         ON KEY(Job_lists)  GO TO error;
     s4: READ FILE(Job_lists) KEY(title) INTO(emp_list);
         CLOSE FILE(Job_lists);
 /* count how many employees are eligible for the raise */
         DO i = 1 TO 250 WHILE id(i) ¬= 'nobody';  END;
         no_employees = i - 1;
         PUT SKIP EDIT(no_employees, title) ('There are ', I5 /A8);
 /* prepare to give raises */
     s5: OPEN FILE(Pay_ssn) DIRECT UPDATE;
         total_increase = 0;
         DO j = 1 TO no_employees;
     s6:    READ FILE(Pay_ssn) KEY(id(j)) INTO(payroll_ss);
 /*      increase salary field of record */
            increase = payroll_ss.sal * pct / 100;
            total_increase = total_increase + increase;
            payroll_ss.sal = payroll_ss.sal + increase;
            REWRITE FILE(Pay_ssn) FROM(payroll_ss);
         END;
 /* report total cost of all raises */
         PUT SKIP EDIT(total_increase) ('Amount spent $', F(8,2));
     END raise;
```

Figure 2-6   A transaction program to give a list of employees a raise.

The new DECLARE statement s1 defines a working area for the list of employees having a specified title. Statements s3 and s5 OPEN the files for DIRECT access. We have omitted the ON KEY protection for the Pay_ss file, assuming optimistically that there will be no wrong ids in the emp_list obtained from the Job_lists file. Both files are OPENed as late as possible and CLOSEd as soon as possible, so that other users may access them with the least interference. The READ statement s4 fetches the particular list record named by the title 'Managers', as specified by the input message of Fig. 2-3. The transaction then counts and reports the number of employees found in this list.

After OPENing the Pay_ssn file, a loop is set up for these employees. The READ statement s6 uses as KEY name the employee's identifier as obtained from the list. Only records that require updating are READ and REWRITtEn.

This program can still take a fairly long time to execute if there are many employees in a group with a given title, but we cannot expect much less time to be used, since, except for the Job_lists, only records to be changed are handled.

These sample programs were not very elegant. Many improvements should be made in them to make them more foolproof and adaptable to change. For instance, having a limit of the number of employees with a certain title is unacceptable in general. The examples are not intended as an indictment or blessing of PL/1 as a programming language. Few computer languages are both powerful in data access and convenient for general computation. There are many languages which make dealing with files truly difficult.

2-2-3 Types of Transactions

As you have seen, we have developed one type of transaction program, with three examples. For each instance we also considered how many accesses to the files the transaction is likely to make. Many accesses will of course take more time. During its execution time a transaction will require access to the files. The files may be shared with others, they are a common *resource* of the enterprise which established the database.

While one transaction updates data, another transaction should not access the same data. Such interference can lead to inconsistent results. Examples of other transactions which could interact badly with our raise transaction are transactions which demote some employees to nonmanagers or give others a determined, say, $1000, raise. A transaction which updates files should *lock* its data during its execution. Locking prevents simultaneous access to these resources by other transactions.

A transaction is typically restricted in the amount of time it is permitted to run, so that it does not inhibit other transactions excessively. If a transaction cannot complete satisfactorily, it must *abort*, that is, either restore the original state of the files itself, or signal the operating system or the database management system so they can restore the original state. A transaction which completes correctly is said to have been *committed*, and its result will be available to all subsequent transactions.

A transaction which only reads data, a *Read-only Transaction*, cannot disrupt the contents of the files. However, to ensure that results are not based on data that are being changed, a `read` transaction must also lock the records it needs. For instance, a transaction calculating a funds request for the payroll should not be executed while the `raise` transaction is giving raises to people one by one. A similar calculation, but without the consistency constraint, for example,to get a quick look at the budget, may not require locking.

An *Append-Only* transaction can also operate freely, as long as all transactions which require consistent data read only prior versions of the data from the files. This still requires locking of the data being appended until consistency is achieved. For instance, it may be necessary to append simultaneously the list of items in the inventory and the list of suppliers for those items.

TRANSACTIONS AS UNITS OF CONSISTENCY   A transaction is also defined as a unit which preserves the integrity of the files and the database. To assure correct operation transactions requires certain services from an operating system or database management system. This concept of a transaction is critical to reliable and high-performance database systems.

We now introduce a secondary definition:

> A transaction is a computation which, given a database which is consistent, upon completion leaves the database again in a consistent state.

In other words, a transaction leaves the database not in a worse state than before. However, during the execution of the transaction the database may be inconsistent. A failure during the execution of a transaction requires that the database be restored to its original state. If only well-behaved transactions operate on a database, the integrity of the database will always be maintained. For example, if a transaction is to update a `salary` and increment the `budget` amount in a database, it will do either both or neither, so that the sum of the `salary` amounts will always match the `budget`.

2-2-4 Modularity and Transactions

The limited size of transactions has an important effect on the approach taken to programming. In software engineering terms a transaction is a *module*. Modules distinguish themselves by being of manageable size, and having few, well-defined interfaces to other components of a system. The user programs which comprise a database application are *transaction* modules. They interact with each other only through the files, and if executed at the same time, through the operating system.

The `raise` program, for example, is a module which implements one transaction type of a larger payroll system and is called upon when the `message` entered says `raise`. A typical commercial system will have a few dozen modules. A few of these will be used much more frequently than others. The module which records `hours_worked` is the busiest module in a payroll system, while changes of tax-withholding tables, applicable to all employees, occur at most once per year.

A high degree of modularity is needed in data processing because:

1 Projects are undertaken that are of a size where many people have to work together, and individuals take on more specialized functions.
2 Many projects may share a set of files, and the specification of the database becomes the sum of many requirements.
3 The information in the files has a value that makes unlimited access by everyone involved unreasonable. To protect access to private data, access processes are controlled by the operating system.

The users' transaction modules are specified and written by someone familiar with the application. The control-language statements may be generated with the assistance of a specialist. The file system itself (invoked by the file access statements OPEN, READ, and REWRITE) was written by someone unfamiliar with the application, at an earlier time and at a different place. The operating system was designed in concert with the computer hardware.

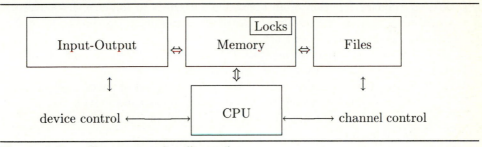

Figure 2-7   Resources to be allocated.

2-3   OPERATING SYSTEMS

We have referred frequently to the services provided by the *Operating System* (OS) of the computer. The primary function of an operating system is to make the capabilities of the hardware available to programs and their users. The motivation for including this material is to introduce a type of operating system relevant to file processing: *Transaction Processing Systems*. Transaction processing systems are used mainly with databases and rarely mentioned in operating system textbooks. Since most operating systems deal with general computations, rather than primarily with database transactions, we will use the term *computation* where we address general use of the computer.

We will first deal with several general operating system issues and in Sec. 2-3-3 consider transaction support systems specifically. In Sec. 2-3-1 we define the resources to be allocated, and discuss scheduling objectives. We also discuss the decomposition of computations into sections, which are the primitive computational units to be scheduled. In Sec. 2-3-2, operating systems are classified according to their methods of allocation of processor and memory resources. This introduction will not present novel material, but serves to offset Sec. 2-3-3. Section 2-3-4 presents the commands used to direct the operating system, specifically for file allocation. In

Chap. 4-1 we will describe the directory information used by the operating system to manage files. Techniques for file allocation are addressed in Chap. 10-4. Section 2-3-5 of this chapter introduces issues of distribution of computation and files over multiple computers.

This book is concerned with internal organization and access to files, but not with specific operating system aspects. This section is needed to establish the environment and vocabulary used throughout this book. The intent of this material is only to provide the background for the presentation of file systems; it will not replace a course on operating systems. We concentrate on issues poorly covered in common textbooks.

2-3-1 Resources to be Allocated

The resources of the computer system include hardware, software, and people. The software cannot run without hardware, and people cannot use the computer without software. A primary function of an operating system is to manage the hardware, which enables the remaining resources. Hardware components, as shown in Fig. 2-7, that have to be allocated to users are:

The Processor. Here we measure the resource in terms of seconds of CPU time allocated to some computation.

The Memory. Here we measure the resource in terms of pages, typically units of several thousand bytes, allocated to the computation.

Storage. Here we measure the resource in terms of pages or blocks allocated to some file.

Input-Output Devices. Here we assign the entire device for some period of time to some computation.

An operating system must also provide **locks**. A computation can set a lock on resources which it has obtained to prevent access by other computations. Locks may be used to disable any access, or permit READ, but not WRITE, access by other computations. Locks are often kept in memory, but may be kept on files if they are to be persistent, that is survive computer failures which damage memory.

To manage these resources operating systems maintain tables of allocated and free resource units. *File directories* describe the storage allocation. Locks are used by the operating system to protect the directories, and other locks will assure that files allocated to some computation will not be accessed by others without authorization.

An operating system measures the use or consumption of the resources, so that it can interrupt computations which use too many resources and so it can bill users when they are done. Finally, an operating system includes a *scheduler*, which selects which computation to start after an interruption.

SCHEDULING FOR MULTIPLE COMPUTATIONS   Scheduling is the operating system process which allocates available resources to the computations needing them. Computations are submitted by users at their convenience. They can be big or small in terms of resource usage and long or short in terms of execution time. They can be broken down into *sections*, as decribed below, and the scheduler may reallocate resources for each section. Some incremental allocation, typically of memory, can be made within the sections, as the computation demands.

The method of scheduling defines the type of operating system. Small and simple machines will have simple schedulers, and hence will utilize the resources less effectively, while large, multiuser systems will have complex schedulers. In systems performing a diversity of tasks multiple schedulers may exist; for instance, some DBMS have their own schedulers which reallocate resources provided by the OS scheduler. Such an arrangement is rarely optimal. Furthermore, the schedulers consume computing resources themselves in direct proportion to their complexity.

Figure 2-8 provides diagrams of the primary scheduling methods. The sketches present the allocation of one resource, namely the memory, over time. Actually, all the resources mentioned above participate in the execution of a computation. When use of one resource reaches its limit, the other resources can no longer be fully used by the ongoing computation. However, having program and data in memory is a prerequisite for using the CPU and controlling files and devices. On computers with a single CPU there will be only one computation *claiming the CPU* at any one time, but claims can be switched rapidly.

A computation will not require resources at a steady rate. Unequal utilization occurs, for instance, when reading data for later processing. The reading process is limited by the maximum speed of the input device, and during that time the CPU uses only a small fraction of its capacity. Subsequently, a large summary calculation using the data just read takes place, and now the reading device waits until it gets new instructions from the CPU.

▥ **BENEFITS AND COSTS OF SHARING**   Any form of resource sharing is associated with a considerable overhead for operation and management. If there is no significant benefit to the use of shared resources, a dedicated system which is of just adequate size is preferable. Such a system will, of course, not be able to cope well with irregular high-intensity demands. Mixed systems, having local and distributed capability as well as access to central shared resources, are of great interest to system designers.   ▥

COMPUTATIONS, PROCESSES, AND SECTIONS   A large computation may be split into independent subtasks. For instance, when data are available in memory, one subtask may format a table for presentation, while another subtask at the same time analyzes data for exceptions, to be reported later.

A computation which is not split further into parallel subtasks is called a *process* in operating systems terminology. A process has a begin, an end, an owner, and a resource allocation. Its resources may be inherited from the computation which owns it and it may obtain additional resources during its life. It is the primary unit for claiming use of the CPU. A process is, of course, associated with a program, and the CPU program counter indicates where the process is active. When it is done it interrupts the CPU so that another process may be started.

A process itself can be decomposed or broken down into a number of successive *sections*. A section is a sequence of program steps during which the operating system does not have to worry about the process. When a process stops, requests data from a file, or requires a new allocation of storage space, a section ends and the operating system has to intervene. When, for instance, a record from a file is requested, the operating system has to check if a lock was set by another process. A section of a process which presents such interaction potential is known as a *critical section*.

Figure 2-3 sketched the flow of a transaction which gives raises to managers. This computation has only one process, nothing occurs in parallel. The transaction process is broken into several sections, as defined by the `OPEN` and `CLOSE` statements which set and release locks. The two sections where the files are open are critical because of their file access. All sections assume that the memory allocated to their program and working data will not be disturbed.

The design and performance of transactions is the subject of most of this book. In Chaps. 3 to 6 we assume that the sections are not affected by activities going on simultaneously in the same or adjacent files. Interference between process sections will be evaluated in Chap. 14-3-4. In databases with many users sharing many files, problems of interference become important.

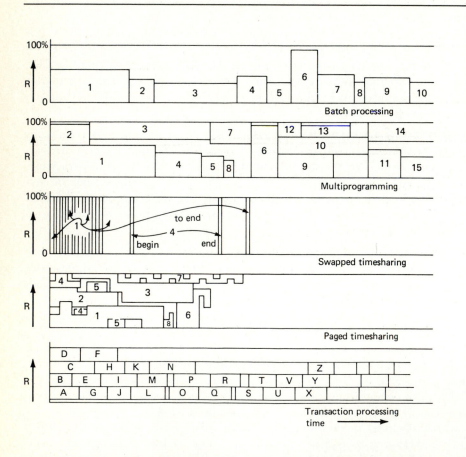

Figure 2-8   Resource allocation for five classes of system operation.

2-3-2 A Classification of Operating Systems

Databases can be established using any of the large variety of operating systems that are available, but their effectiveness will differ. We show now how five different classes of operating systems allocate the memory and the CPU. The classification is based first of all on the allocation strategy used for memory. Figure 2-5 sketches the memory allocation for the five classes. The first two classes are not suitable for an on-line mode operation, as defined in Sec. 2-1-2. The scheduler of the operating system then can schedule a computation which has memory assigned to it.

BATCH PROCESSING   An operating system which only supports *batch processing* schedules all requested computations sequentially. It assigns all available resources of the computer to the one single process claiming the CPU. It is rare that a single computation will be able to use all the available resources. There will nearly always be unused memory, and both the processor and memory will be idle while a computation waits for input or data from files. Batch processing is commonly used on personal computers.

Spooling Batch processing is sometimes combined with a parallel printing service. This service is performed by a simple secondary or background computation, called a *spooling* process, which uses a limited amount of processor time and memory. The spooler runs output tasks initiated by other computations. To execute a unit of spooler activity, the operating system interrupts the primary process after every line printed. For terminal output the interrupt signal may occur after every character. Only a few microseconds are taken from the primary process to place more output into the printing buffer.

MULTIPROGRAMMING   A generalization of the concept of spooling is to permit simultaneous operation of multiple general programs. Multiprogramming exploits system resources more effectively by allocating resources to several computations according to their current requirements. If a computation cannot use the CPU, typically because of insufficient memory or because it must wait for file or input operations to complete, it will give up its claim. The process which has been discontinued will be placed in a *not-ready queue*. When its requests for memory or file or input have been fulfilled it will be reassigned to a *ready queue* for the scheduler. The scheduler, when initiated, will select some process from the ready queue to claim the CPU, frequently the one which has been waiting the longest time.

With multiprogramming individual computations will take longer, but if the resources can be distributed well among the computations, the total productivity of the computer system will be higher. A computation may claim the CPU as long as it can use it, although file-intensive computations are rarely able to run long between requests. Some CPU capacity will be taken from the total available to switch between the computations. Multiprogramming can make it hard to predict when a computation will be finished. For on-line databases predictable performance is desired, otherwise we are wasting the users' time.

TIMESHARING   Timesharing slices computations into fixed, small sections by limiting the length of processing time. Such limitations assure response to users who are waiting at computer terminals. The size of these slices attempts to strike a balance between the productivity of users and the system. Note that the users interacting on-line are also a resource. People, from a computer's point of view, perform very slowly but are quite demanding when they require computation.

Rapid response for on-line users is guaranteed by limiting the competing computational slices to a small fraction of a second by means of a timer-driven interrupt. Computations which are ready are scheduled in round-robin fashion from the *ready queue.* Any new computations that users want to initiate are put in this queue as well, and are executed in turn. The time between successive turns depends on the number of active users, the size of the slices, and the time it takes to switch from one slice to the next.

A critical resource in timesharing systems with many simultaneous users is memory. During inactive periods, users' programs may be "swapped" out of memory and kept on disk or drum storage. Storage space used for swapping of programs is generally not part of the storage space available to data files.

Timeshared use of CPU and core provides effective resource utilization when computations are short. Many database operations deal with users at terminals, and timesharing permits the computation to be inactive while the user responds. Computations which are longer than one slice will take longer to complete than they would have in batch mode, since all other active users will get their slices interposed. Such computations will tie up all system resources for a longer time. A user often has files assigned exclusively to the transaction, and these are now not available to other users. The active user is well served, but the system incurs costs of slicing and swapping, and the periods of file assignment are longer, which may hold up others.

PAGING   An OS with *paging* capability can reduce the amount of memory needed per user, and hence serve more users. Since a single slice of a timeshared computation rarely makes use of all the available core memory, a further division of the memory into *pages* improves sharing of this resource and reduces swapping volume. The total set of pages, in memory or stored on the swapping disks, which are available to the user program is referred to as the *virtual memory.* Pages are generally brought from virtual memory into real memory on demand . The number of *real* pages actually required will vary from slice to slice. Pages for programs used by multiple users, such as file programs, may be shared. Pages which show heavy recent usage are kept in real memory if possible. *Paging capability* can also aid the allocation process when multiprogramming in general.

With paging we have achieved a very responsive and fair allocation of resources. Any user whose computation exceeds a time slice will be placed at the end of the round-robin queue. If intervening users require memory, pages of other users will be removed so that those users lose ready status while waiting. The use of paging for file management is covered in Chap. 9-4.

TRANSACTION PROCESSING SYSTEMS   Operating systems which are dedicated to processing of transactions are quite distinctive. Because of their importance to interactive databases and file systems, we place this approach into a separate section, although it is shown as the final choice in Fig. 2-5.

2-3-3 Transaction Processing

We now present an alternative to the common scheduling strategies presented above, namely *transaction processing*. Now scheduling is oriented toward maximum system productivity, rather than toward fairness to on-line users. Transaction processing is motivated by resource access problems encountered with data-intensive computations. A high resource utilization is obtained by limiting the period that transactions can hold onto resources.

In a system where the resource most in demand is not memory or the processor, but file access, a timeshared paging system will perform poorly. Since an individual computation will be lengthened by intervening demands for the processor and possible loss of ready status, the period that a computation has to hold onto allocated files also increases. While one computation holds onto file resources, others cannot access them.

The concept underlying a *Transaction Processing System* (TPS) is to execute a computation which is holding file resources as fast as possible, so that it will release these resources soon, and permit other transactions to proceed. Many such transactions may be in memory at the same time, but no new transaction is permitted to displace a transaction which is not yet finished. The scheduler hence does not preempt ready transactions, and gives priority to in-memory transactions which are heavy resource users, in the hope of completing them rapidly.

Scheduling On-line Transactions The scheduler for a TPS assumes that the computations are small, in terms of both space and time. A very long transaction could disable all other transactions. Long think times, long loops in programs, and exhaustive searches through files cannot be handled by the TPS. Such computations are decomposed into smaller transactions before being submitted. In a TPS the users' transactions consist mainly of calls to the file systems for reading and writing, a limited amount of numeric and logical computing, and final reporting to the users' terminals. Figure 2-6 showed an example of a typical transaction program.

The scheduler starts transactions as soon as possible after the user requests them and permits them to run as long as necessary to fulfill their computational requirements. Some incoming transactions may have to be queued untill resources are available. When the transaction is started it will have enough memory and access to files, but eventually it may need more information. When a transaction comes to a point where it has to wait for a response from terminals or for data from files, it may yield to the system to enable another transaction process to be started or resumed. At times a transaction may avoid yielding to prevent release of a file which is not in a well-defined state.

A transaction still ties up resources, like files, that have been exclusively assigned to it, but its total computation time will not have been lengthened by slicing and swapping. When a transaction is finished, it will inform the system, which can then free all allocated resources.

Characteristics of a Transaction Processing System are:
- The transaction claiming the CPU keeps the highest priority.
- Transactions which are ready keep all allocated resources.
- New transactions are only started when memory is available.
- If many transactions are queued further requests may be rejected.
- A transaction which exceeds limits of resource usage is aborted.

A transaction processing system will control transactions closely to prevent one computation from locking up the entire system. A transaction which exceeds reasonable limits of resource consumption is abruptly terminated. Limits may be applied to program size, execution time, CPU time, number of subprocesses which can be spawned, number of file accesses, number of messages sent, and locking actions for exclusive use of files. These limits are already applied when the transaction is specified or programmed.

At execution time little checking is performed to protect others from excessive demands by one transaction. Relieved of much of its monitoring responsibilities the operating system can be considerably less complex and more responsive. An example of transaction design constraints are 25 calls to the database system, 2 seconds total execution time, and 25 pages of memory (Inmon[79]). More modern systems have much more liberal limits. Many database actions can be handled very effectively in a transaction processing environment.

Note that a TPS scheduler is not fair to users in the traditional computer service sense. An executing transaction can hold on to all resources within the system limits. A small transaction does not get done until an earlier, perhaps larger transaction releases its claims. A new user is kept queued until resources, sufficient for transaction completion, are free. It is possible to keep new requests entirely outside the system. But, in a TPS the use of system resources is high, and that can benefit everybody. The simplicity of a TPS also reduces the computational high overhead associated with sharing computer systems. There may be higher administrative personnel cost: to assure that the TPS scheduler has to deal only with transaction it can manage, some personnel resources are needed to instruct and check the programmers.

Transaction Protection   We have already introduced the all-or-nothing concept associated with a transaction: either a transaction committs with all its work completed or it aborts without leaving any effect on the files. The TPS has to assure that transactions that do not complete are properly aborted. A variety of mechanisms are available, they all involve *logging* duplicate information. We can distinguish two styles:

1. Optimistic techniques save the previous contents of the file, permitting a restoration of the file when a transaction aborts or fails to finish.
2. Pessimistic techniques may collect all changes on *shadow pages*, and link those shadow pages into the file when the transaction committs.

Although the pessimistic method is simpler, the optimistic method is preferable because success should be much more frequent than failure. More details on this methods are found in database textbooks, since committ protocols become more critical when multiple files have to be dealt with.

The presence of logging files can also help to recover from disasters as file failures. Remote users of on-line transactions expect that once a transaction is accepted that nothing will destroy their work. A TPS has to satisfy that expectation.

▦▦▦ **Batch transactions** In order to increase system utilization many TPS also serve second-class *batch transactions*. These transaction can be interrupted, and perhaps swapped out of memory. At the same time they are not subject to the same time and space constraints of regular, on-line transactions.

A problem occurs if batch transactions set locks. Such locks can cause serious interference. A solution is to set up the batch transaction as a sequence of small independent transactions. For instance, a batch transaction to produce a `sales` report will not lock up the entire `Sales_by_store` file, but extract data incrementally. The result will not be strictly consistent, since some store manager could add recent information entered while the batch was being processed, and its inclusion cannot be guaranteed. Serious errors could occur if an on-line transaction, running at the same time, would reallocate sales amounts from one store to another.

To avoid inconsistencies the "`sales`" batch transaction might use an older version of the `Sales_by_store` file, one which is longer subject to update. Then the results will not completely up to date. With that solution the TPS then has not to concern itself with the execution of batch transactions, except to preempt them as resources are needed.   ▦▦▦

▦▦▦ **A TRANSACTION PROCESSING SYSTEM** To illustrate the concepts of transaction processing we will describe TPF, a system provided by IBM to be used for tasks such as airline reservations and banking. While also advertised as a high-performance database management system, it does not provide the database services that one expects from a general DBMS, such as features dealing with file integrity and backup.

The most severe constraint placed on the transactions is that they may only accept one input message and one output message. To help overcome that limitation a user has a small memory area assigned that can hold data between transactions. Using data from earlier transactions for later ones does not guarantee consistency however, so that any critical file updates must be be made in the initial transaction of a sequence.

Also only the messages are logged, so that crashes can cause loss of old information. The messages can be inspected to restore critical files. All updates to files are written in parallel to two files, so that serious crashes are rare. Having two files available for reading increases at the same time the retrieval performance.

A specific application limits each transaction to 4.7 ms of CPU time, and 4.3 ms is average. Other limits pertain to record sizes. All file records must be either 381 characters or 1055 characters long, so that all programs deal with fixed data units.

TPF maintains three request queues. They are, in order of priority:

1 The ready queue, which contains transactions that had to yield their claims to the CPU because of a file request.

2 The input queue, which contains requests for new transactions initiated by incomming messages.

3 The deferred queue, which contains requests in hold state, either because they will be triggered by a timer, say to print a boarding list for an airline ticket counter an 30 min. before flight time, or because they are batch transactions.

All these constraints help obtain high performance. The average response time for a transaction is 1.5 s., and 90% of the transactions are completed in less than 3 s. Typical TPF systems have thousands of terminals, and each terminal may send up to 1 message per minute.

The parameters are such that computers can be specified to carry the workload once the transaction load is known. Of course, these machines have to be able to handle the load during the expected peak times. Terminals on a network which is widely distributed will present their peak loads at different times.   ▦

2-3-4 Operating System Control

We will now describe the features and language needed by the user or programmer to control an operating system. The operating system controls the allocation of files to storage. Letting the operating system handle addressing of storage provides independence of the program compared to the specification of the storage hardware. The writer of the transaction program expects that there exists somewhere an expert who controls the actual placement of the records of the file in storage. The expert directs the file system, which is generally part of a computer operating system. The expert is restricted to selecting among facilities provided within the computer system by the vendor.

CONTROL LANGUAGE   Statements outside the programming language are used to provide information to the operating system regarding the program. These statements form the *control language* for the operating system. The control languages are not as well formalized as programming languages, although standardization efforts are under way. A lack of communication between the programming language and the control language is often a barrier to effective utilization of computer systems.

A control language statement for the **raise** transaction shown in Fig. 2-6 may read as shown in Fig. 2-9. The transaction expected the requested file to already exist in storage. An earlier transaction will have created the file initially and other transactions will have inserted and deleted employees as needed.

```
FILE(data): NAME('Payroll'), DEVICE(diskdrive), LOCATION(disk5),
ORGANIZATION(fixed records(80 bytes), indexed, sequential)
BUFFERS(2), SIZE(60 tracks),   etc.
```

Figure 2-9   Control language for the **raise** transaction.

The statement in Fig. 2-9 has been made prettier than most control languages permit to aid comprehension. Once this statement is processed, the payroll file is available to the program throughout the entire transaction.

╫╫╫╫ **SPECIALIZATION**   The knowledge required for applications programming may be separate from the knowledge to write control language statements; but in order to write effective database systems, both aspects have to be understood. In order to design the entire database application, considerably broader knowledge is required. The analysis of retrieved data requires a different type of expertise than that required for the design, organization, or collection and updating of data. In order to manage an entire database, a specialist in database administration may be needed.   ╫╫╫╫

FILE CREATION   In the beginning files must be created. We see two methods in practice, some operating systems support both:

1 The file is created by control language statements as given above, perhaps with a modifier `NEW`.
2 The file is created when an `OPEN` statement is executed, which refers to the control language statement above. The `OPEN` statement may have a modifier `NEW` or be a variant such as `CREATE`.

Most systems will ignore a file creation command if the file exists already, others will consider it an error, and some will create a new *version* of the file. The file, once created, will persist after the transaction is completed. The file of the example will be available to subsequent executions of any payroll transactions. It will continue to occupy storage until explicitly deleted. Deletion will be performed through another control language or program statement combination.

DURATION OF FILE ASSIGNMENT   The control language statement is available during the entire program or transaction execution. Does that mean that the payroll file belongs to the program during the entire transaction? Less file resource consumption would occur if the file is only assigned during the period between `OPEN` and `CLOSE` statements, or better yet, only during the interval between `READ` and `REWRITE` statements.

The answer depends on the operating system in use. The question of assignment and exclusive ownership is a concern when multiple programs share access to data. For instance, another transaction, one which `SUM`s all the salaries to prepare a budget, should wait until the entire `raise` transaction is completed to avoid inconsistent results. For this reason most files remain assigned to the transaction until the transaction is completed, although their initial assignment may be deferred to the `OPEN` or `READ` statement.

RESOURCE DIRECTORIES   The operating system keeps track of all system resources, and their allocation to computations and processes. Which process claims the CPU, and allocation of memory and input-output devices is transient information, and kept mainly in memory tables. Persistent information, such as the allocation of files to storage devices, is kept in file *directories*.

Note that the control language does not permit specification of the begin-point for the file shown in Table 4-1. The begin-point is determined by the operating system. Resource directory tables keep track of allocated and free storage space. File directories are described in Chap. 4-1; Chap. 10-4 provides details of storage management.

⧉⧉⧉ 2-3-5 Distribution of Files

The files needed for some computations may not always be located on a single computer. An operating system which supports distribution will permit a computation to access files which are located at remote *sites*.

A distributed file system will have data and processing tasks of local importance executed at a local computer. Tasks that require data or processing that cannot be carried out locally will generate requests to remote computers. Sometimes the 'remote' computer may actually be another local computer or a specialized device attached to the principal local computer.

Distribution causes the file access program to be split over the sites which request data and the sites which store the data. At the requesting site the transaction request will be interpreted. Any subtasks which must be executed remotely will be formulated and shipped to the remote site, where a process is started to execute that portion of the transaction. Results are normally shipped to the requesting site. When multiple sites are involved it may be more efficient to ship partial results to other sites.

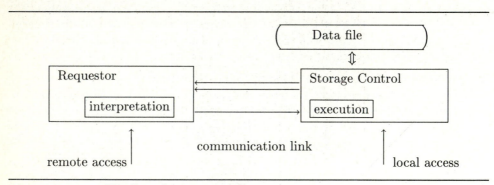

Figure 2-10   Distributed access to a file.

We assume that the storage site is chosen so that the ratio of local accesses to number of remote file access is as high as possible, since shipping of data over a communicating link always adds a delay. The storage site is often the site of the owner of the file, and hence the site where all or most updates originate.

Moving large quantities of data across a long communication line is much slower (2 to 1000 times) than the movement of file data to memory. If data reduction can be performed at the storage site, then the total time for the transaction can be reduced. In some cases sufficient parallelism may be introduced to actually reduce the total transaction time.

In Fig. 2-11 we sketch the best flow for our `raise` transaction from Fig. 2-6, given an assignment of requestor, `Job_lists` file, and `Pay_ss` file to three distinct processing sites.

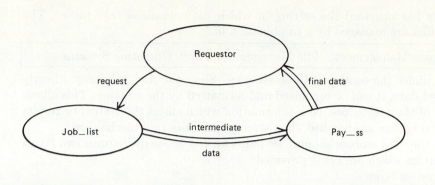

Figure 2-11   Distributing a transaction.

In a *clustered system*, where multiple data-processing systems are located close to each other, communication delays should be less. Furthermore, in such systems the transaction origin can be chosen according to the most suitable processor in terms of file access. The transaction command is used to direct the request to that processor.

Distribution of information is becoming a common feature of modern data-processing systems. Three concepts arise in distributed systems (d) which are also used at times within a single computer system (s), and we list an example of each.

1 Fragmentation: Splitting files into smaller files, appropriate for allocation to remote nodes.
   d The `Pay_ss` file may be fragmented and allocated by company location: New York and London.
   s The `Pay_ss` file may be fragmented and allocated into a current and historical part, putting the infrequently used historical fragment on a slower and cheaper device.
2 Replication: Keeping copies of files or fragments at nodes, to enhance local access.
   d The `Job_lists` file may be replicated to speed employee assignment.
   s Employee `telephone_numbers` are used so frequently by a computerized switchboard that they are replicated on a specialized file to avoid interference.
3 Data derivation: Keeping partial results on files, also to improve access and reduce computation cost.
   d The total `pay_received` by an employee may be kept at the site where taxes are computed.
   s The total `budget_summary` is kept in derived form to permit rapid perusal during sessions where next year's expected income is being allocated.

We see from the examples that these concepts have greater importance in distributed systems, so we will not discuss them until Chap. 11, where distributed systems are covered extensively.   ┼┼┼┼┼┼

2-4   REVIEW

This chapter has provided the setting in which file operations take place. The contents of files are managed by a combination of

Database Management,   File Management,   and Operating Systems

and remain under the control of these systems. Since the user will never directly see the stored data, it can be organized and formatted by the systems. This allows optimal use of their resources. New information which enters the system or results that leave the system are handled via a separate input-output mechanism.

Within the data storage support systems, we can hence distinguish two layers for the functions which are being provided:

1 A file system layer
2 A database system layer

The file system operates without knowledge of the contents of the data, whereas the database system will select data on the basis of the expected contents. A database management system will use a file system for manipulating storage.

Users supply the programs which manage the content of data structures and extract the information required for the enterprise they serve. The data may be used for multiple applications.

User programs—∗ Applications—∗ Transactions —∗ Processes—∗ Sections

These programs use system programs to carry out the actual operations on the files.

Build   and   Update   and   Retrieve   and   Data Reduction

The system services are provided via operating systems which manage the resources.

Operating Systems := Batch or Multiprogramming or Timesharing or Paging   or   Transaction-Processing Systems

Features of these systems are often combined, and, if the systems are distributed over multiple sites, they may differ as to various computers included in the system.

Each of these terms in the boxes conveys broad and complex concepts. Many of these will be covered in more detail later in this book. Concepts specific to database management or operating systems are covered in successor texts. Here, we concentrate on files.

BACKGROUND AND REFERENCES

Every programming language includes some functions which permit manipulation of files, but their integration differs greatly. System-oriented languages, as for instance the C-language, only define a number of subroutines which are included in the library for the compiler. Languages oriented toward data-processing will have built-in statements to READ, WRITE, and parhaps REWRITE records on files. We have chosen such a language, PL/1 for our examples.

Compilers, when translating available language statements to manipulate files, will not generate the complete code required to control the devices. The statements will simply be translated into calling sequences for compiler provided library routines. Even when writing in assembly language it is rare for an application programmer to use files directly. An assembly language may have predefined macros to help in programming, we list some of those in Chap. 8-5-5.

Because of this indirection few texts exists which help with programming for files. Programming for IBM files is presented by Flores[70], Grosshans[86] presents all the operations, both at basic levels and for IBM file access methods, while Claybrook[83] includes some information on CDC systems.

Yourdon[72] considers file management in a system context. The development of file programs, starting from output requirements, is the approach pesented by Warnier[79]. The design of software, using data-oriented techniques, is presented by Orr[84] and Gilb[87]. Making procedures and their versions persistent is considered by Atkinson[85] as an extension for a programming language.

Basic algorithms, such as sorting, table look-ups, and manipulation of data structures such as lists and trees in core memory will have been encountered by most readers. An introductory reference is Stone[72] and a thorough analysis of most techniques is found in Knuth[73F,S]. The ACM Computing Surveys are a useful resource here.

OPERATING SYSTEMS　　Many of the system problems faced in the database area were first encountered in the design of operating systems. Textbooks in this area are Brinch Hansen[73A], Tsichritzis[74], and Peterson[85]. An approach to the design of an operating system, including interrupt processing and device drivers for files, is presented by Comer[84]. Also, here the ACM Computing Surveys is an excellent source for analytic material and further references.

Most texts on flowcarting are naive, but Clark[66] describes data management in IBM-OS, using a large variety of arrows to distinguish control, the various types of control data, and data flow. In Davis[74] some complex dataflows are charted and Davies[82] draws an analogy.

The prime reference for the demands databases make on operating systems is Gray[78]; he describes the role of transactions in in Gray[81] and their control in distributed systems in Gray[86]. Stonebraker[81] addresses specific issues.

A popular transaction processing system on IBM computers is CICS InmonBird[86]. It also manages its own locks, since the underlying OS (IBM MVS a.o.) do not provide adequate locking services. Much higher performance (up to 1000 transactions per second (tps) versus 20 tps) is achieved by TPF, an extension of the airlines reservation system PARS (Siwiec[77])and its TPS ACP Gifford[84]. A number of companies are building systems dedicated to transaction processing Borr[81], Helland[86]. A file system integrated with UNIX facilities is described by Rochkind[82].

Transaction-processing systems have not received in-depth attention: References appear in Martin[67], Yourdon[72], Davis[74], and Holt[75]. Transactions are typically discussed in a database context (Inmon[82]), although some modern operating systems also include that concept. Stonebraker[85] includes the problems to be solved. Inmon[86] provides data on TPS performance. How transactions should deal with integrity constraints has been presented by Abiteboul[85] and concurrency is addressed by Franaszek[85]. *Read-only transactions* and the effectiveness of their various subtypes are presented in Garcia[82]. Programming within a TPS is presented by Lim[86].

Distributed systems are covered by Tanenbaum[81] and Lampson[81]. Jessop[82] describes a distributed file system. Access by remote workstations is evaluated by Cheriton[83].

EXERCISES

1   Rewrite the transaction from Fig. 2-4 to use the social security number. Describe how the file should be organized then.

2   Write a transaction in the style of Fig. 2-4 to insert an employee. The form of the PL/1 statement is WRITE(Payroll) KEY(newkey) FROM(payroll_ws);. Make sure that the employee is not already in the file.

3   Inspect a file-oriented program that you have access to and select statements which typify some of the classifications given in Table 1-2.

4   Rewrite the control-language statement presented in Fig. 2-9 in the language of the computer system you have available.

5   Classify the operating system you have available according to the categories of Sec. 2-3-2. List aspects of your system which you consider especially good or poor for files supporting large databases.

6   Identify the statements equivalent to READ FILE, WRITE FILE, and REWRITE FILE, as used in the transactions of Figs. 2-4, -5, -6. in the programming language you are commonly using. If no equivalents exist, code some subprocedures that can perform the same function.

7[p]   Write the transaction program for three important transactions of the application you defined in Exercise 1 of Chap. 1. You can use any programming language you are familiar with. You may want to use the procedures coded in Exercise 6 above.

Chapter 3

Hardware and Its Parameters

On a clean disk you can seek forever

Thomas B. Steel, Jr.; making a reference to the Broadway musical theme *On a clear day you can see forever*.
at SHARE DBMS *Conference, July 1973*

3-0 INTRODUCTION

This chapter summarizes the hardware used to store data files: mainly tapes and disks. These descriptions will provide background for the understanding of their operation and performance; in other words, the concern here is what the devices do rather than how they do it. After this chapter, all analysis referring to hardware will be made using a limited number of parameters and concepts. Six parameters are adequate to describe the performance of all types of current hardware with sufficient precision.

This chapter contains two major interrelated sections: The first reviews the types of hardware available, and the second discusses the parameters used to describe hardware. Along with basic performance data, cost estimates are provided since the benefits of good performance cannot be separated from the expenses associated with powerful devices. Section 3-3 presents hardware-related programming concepts, and the chapter concludes with a summary of the parameters for recall and reference.

Chapter 10 provides some further discussion of storage system architecture. The remainder of the book needs to make very few direct references to hardware, due to the parameterization. New or improved storage devices are continually being developed, and any description reflects the situation at the time of writing. The reduction of hardware descriptions to the small set of parameters also makes it possible to use the analysis and design procedures in the remainder of the book for devices which are not described or not even invented yet.

Typical values of parameters for the types of hardware discussed are given in Table 3-1 (Sec. 3-2). The use of recent devices will make the problems in subsequent exercises more interesting. The abbreviations used in formulas can be found on the inside covers and in Appendix B.

3-1   HARDWARE CHOICES

Since this section surveys the varieties of hardware available for files, and Sec. 3-2 defines the parameters needed to describe their performance, some cross referencing may be necessary when encountering new terms in the following section.

3-1-1 Mechanical Storage

Some use is still made of mechanical storage for data, using storage media which were developed before the turn of the century.

One such medium is the Hollerith or IBM *card*. Cards store data by having holes punched to encode a character per column. Cards with 80 columns of 12-bit positions each are the most common; other cards exist with 90×6 positions, and special cards are in use for attaching to inventory items.

Paper tape is still used at times to record raw data from measuring instruments. Holes, punched into eight *tracks* across according to the ASCII code (see Fig. 13-1), record data and a *check* bit.

Paper media can be used only once for the recording of data. The punching and reading devices, being mechanical, are slow.

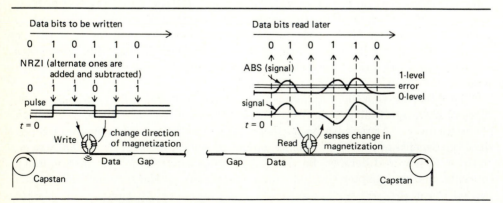

Figure 3-1   Digital-tape recording.

3-1-2 Magnetic Tape Storage

In traditional data-processing operations magnetic tape was predominant. Two categories, typified by cassettes and reels of tape, offer distinguishable capabilities. Tapes and all other magnetic surface devices have identical performance characteristics when reading or writing. Figure 3-1 illustrates the principle of magnetic digital recording.

Limited amounts of data can be stored by the use of *cassette* or *cartridge tape*. The magnetic tape in these packages is 0.150 inch (3.8 mm) or 0.250 inch (6.4 mm) wide and typically 300 ft (100 m) long. A single track of data bits is recorded along the tape, and a parallel track may be used for timing or addressing information. The low cost of purchase and storage of tapes makes their use attractive for storage requirements on workstations. Attempts to standardize these types of tapes have resulted in a plethora of incompatible "standards," so that data interchange to workstations of different types is commonly performed over communication lines, creating distributed systems.

Standards have been developed for large, high-capacity tapes. The physical format has remained stable since before 1960, but the recording density has changed in 5 steps by a factor of 30. Such *industry-compatible magnetic tape* is $\frac{1}{2}$ inch (12.7 mm) wide, comes mainly in lengths of 2400 ft (732 m) on large ($10\frac{1}{2}$-inch, 267-mm) reels, and contains seven or nine tracks across its width.

The linear density of bits in each track is measured in *bits-per-inch* or *bpi*. Some values are given in Table 3-2 (Sec. 3-2-3). A character is recorded by placing a bit in each track. The tape carries that many characters per inch of its length. On 9-track tape, a character is encoded into 8 bits, providing for $2^8 = 256$ distinct symbols. The 8-bit unit, whether used to represent characters or a binary number, is usually called a *byte*. The ninth track is used for error-checking information.

Table 3-1 assumes 9-track tape on 2400-ft reels, having a density of 800 bpi (31.5 bits-per-mm), which uses *non-return-to-zero* encoding, as illustrated in Fig. 3-1. A *phase-encoding* method permits 1600 bpi (63 bits-per-mm). A gap of 0.6 inch (15 mm) separates blocks of data to permit starting and stopping of the tape between READ or WRITE operations. The tape units move the tape at 75 in/s (1.9 m/s) to 225 in/s (5.7 m/s) past their READ-WRITE heads.

Tape units which record and read at densities of 6250 bpi (246 bits-per-mm) have a smaller gap and provide the highest performance currently commercially available. The tape format which supports 6250 bpi uses a group code transformation, using five recorded bits for four data bits and an error-correcting byte in every eighth position, so that the actual recording density is about 9000 bpi (355 bits-per-mm). Error-checking and -correcting techniques are decscribed in Chap. 13-2.

Tape units have very poor random-access qualities. The time to read through an entire tape is on the order of 4 min for reels containing 30M* characters. Many tape units allow tapes to be read in both forward and reverse direction.

---

* We use the letter M to stand for *Mega* or one million (10^6), K for *Kilo* or one thousand (10^3), and G to denote *Giga* or 10^9.

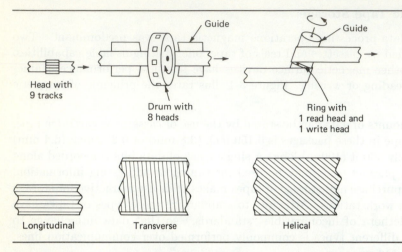

Figure 3-2   Tape-recording methods.

Techniques from video recording are influencing the design of high-capacity tapes for specialized hardware. The high storage capacity is achieved by writing data tracks *transversely* across the tape. The distance between tracks is now determined by the relationship of the head assembly speed across the tape and the forward speed of the tape itself, rather than by the spacing of the parallel heads, as shown in Fig. 3-2. Searching can be performed using the audio and synchronization tracks along the tape edges. Search speeds of 1000 inches per second (in/s) (25.4 m/s) are being used.

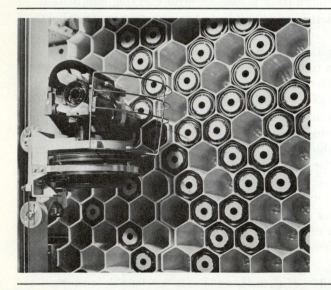

Figure 3-3   Picker mechanism of an IBM 3850 tape-cartridge system.

Helical scanning, as used in home TV recorders, is employed by the tape library shown in Fig. 3-3. The tape cartridges are used to provide backup for disk storage. Each cartridge contains 700 ft of 2.7-inch-wide tape. Data are recorded in helical format (see Fig. 3-2) with each diagonal track containing 4096 bytes across the tape. The tape is moved in steps from track to track.

Such *automated-tape libraries* provide large, but slow to access on-line storage capacity. These are available both for conventional $\frac{1}{2}$-inch-tape reels and for the extra-wide-tape strip cartridges shown above. A mechanical picker mechanism selects the tape, carries it to the tape unit, and puts the reel on the tape unit so that it can be read conventionally.

3-1-3 Rotating Magnetic Storage

The primary type of storage devices which provide large quantities of easily accessible storage for a computer system is the *magnetic disk*. We have the choice of removable media (floppy disks and disk packs) and nonremovable media. The disks may be read and written either by movable access mechanisms or, less commonly, by magnetic heads in fixed positions.

The units with the drive and access mechanisms for these disks go by the generic name of *direct-access storage drives* or DASD, but the term *disk drive* seems more convenient and adequate. Many varieties of the basic design of a disk drive exist. Some of the alternatives give either higher performance or lower cost. In order to increase performance, there are disk units that have multiple moving heads and disks that have both fixed and moving heads.

In many modern devices, known as Winchester drives, the head and disk assembly is enclosed in an airtight and dust-free capsule. The clean environment permits closer tolerances and higher recording densities. Disk drives are available which can store 2500M characters per pack, while in 1970 28M was the highest capacity available in a disk unit of the same physical size and design.

Magnetic disk drives dominate file database storage. Alternative technologies have not been able to keep up with the steady advances made in disk technology, although optical storage appears to be gaining in some applications. Currently *perpendicular recording technology* is providing further increases in storage density. For on-line transaction processing the disks containing an active database are never removed, even though the disk packs and disks may be removable. Removing disks may be wise when hardware maintenance is performed.

Floppy Disks Most popular of all rotating storage devices are the *floppy disks*. They are written and read by one (single-sided) or two heads (double-sided). The larger of these flexible disks are circles of 7.8-inch (19.8-cm) diameter, cut out of coated Mylar material, and kept within an 8.0-inch-square (20.8-cm) envelope. The 5.25-inch (13.3-cm) size is used on personal computers, but is not as well standardized. Disk capacities of 360K and 1 200K are common, but perpendicular recording permits storing 10 900tbf K bytes on a disk. Floppy disks having smaller dimensions exist as well, and are common in portable computers.

Holes in the envelope permit access for spinning, writing and reading, and sensing the position of the disk. After the disk is inserted into the drive unit it is spun by a pressure clutch. The disk is spun only while in use. The reading head touches the flexible disk during access, which permits a relatively high recording density but increases wear.

Diskpack Drives In a *diskpack drive* a set of disks, numbering from 1 to 11, is packaged together in a stack. Multiple disks are separated by spacers from other disks in the stack. The disks are covered with a ferromagnetic oxide, similar to that deposited on tape, and these surfaces are hardened to withstand accidents and the heavy duty expected. The pack of disks can be placed on a spindle and each surface can be read by a recording head mounted on one of a set of arms that moves in or out, relative to the center of the disks, to find a specific track. The heads fly above the surface. The disks rotate continuously once started, and the heads can be switched to read or write information on the disk surfaces. Figure 3-4 presents a sketch of one platter mechanism of a two-platter disk drive, and is similar to smaller units now commonly used in micro-computers as shown in Table 3-1. The entire unit has four heads, one for the top and one for the bottom surface of each disk. The larger drive listed in Table 3-1, a DEC RM-05 type unit, has a stack of 11 disks rotating together. The top and bottom surfaces of the stack are not used and one of the recording surfaces is used to provide timing or position information, so that 19 recording surfaces are available for data.

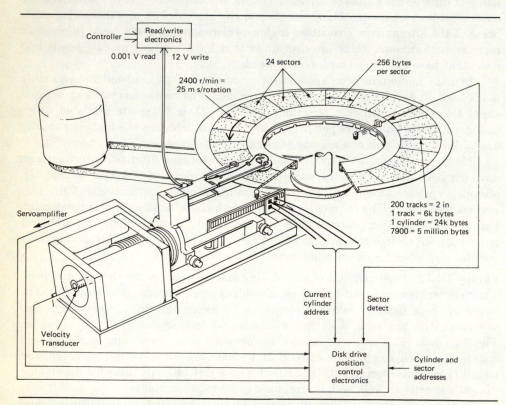

Figure 3-4   Part of a HP-7900 two-platter disk drive. *(Courtesy of Hewlett-Packard Co.)*

CYLINDERS   In a moving head disk all recording heads of the disk drive move in or out together, but only one head will actually transfer data at any one time. No further physical movement of the arm is required to reach any one of the sets of tracks (4 in the HP-7900) that are radially equidistant from the center but on different surfaces. For these tracks the time required to switch from track to track is only due to electronic switching delays and is negligible. This set of tracks forms a hypothetical cylindrical surface at right angles to the physical access directions. Since we often use such a set of tracks together, we will use the term *cylinder* to describe the tracks which we can use without motion of the access mechanism. A disk unit will have as many cylinders as one of its disk surfaces has tracks. Data written sequentially will fill all the tracks of one cylinder before the mechanism will be stepped to the next cylinder.

Nonremovable Disks   We use the term "nonremovable disk" when the disk cannot be removed from the disk unit, other than for repair. The IBM 3380 in Table 3-1 provides an example. These units have moving arms and heads, just as removable disks.

Head-per-Track Devices   Nonremovable disks can also have fixed heads. Such units will need have one head per track on each surface. Now there is no access arm to be moved and hence no delay to locate a specific cylinder position. The heads will be staggered over the surface, since disk tracks are closer to each other than the minimum separation of the read-write magnetic heads. In Table 3-1 we show data for the fixed portion of a disk unit which has both fixed and moving heads.

Geometrically differently arranged, but logically identical to head-per-track fixed disks, are *magnetic drums* where the heads are mounted facing a cylindrical magnetic surface which is rotated past them. This head arrangement is sketched in Fig. 3-5.

Head-per-track devices have very good access-time characteristics but provide relatively little storage capacity since moving-head devices will typically access more tracks. We will use the term *magnetic drum* to refer to any head-per-track storage units, disregarding whether they have a disk or drum-shaped recording surface.

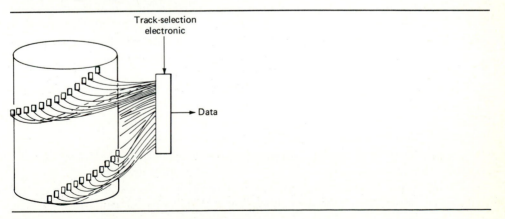

Figure 3-5   Diagram of a magnetic drum.

3-1-4 Large-Capacity Storage Devices

To provide mass storage at low cost, two approaches are followed:

1 Increased storage capacity per unit to reduce storage cost per character
2 Reduction of dependence on manual operation and mechanical parts to achieve more reliability and compactness

Magnetic disks are nearing their limits of storage capacity because of limits in the size of the magnetizable area, which is determined by the surface coating and by the physical dimensions of the READ-WRITE heads. Mechanical limitations are due to the positioning of head assemblies over tracks, even when feedback controls are used which align heads dynamically over the track being read. At the same time the great manufacturing experience with these disks makes their production costs low, and hard to match by other devices.

Increased storage capacity can be achieved by increasing the size of the units, but this adds mechanical delays to the storage systems. To increase data-storage capabilities without also increasing bulk, the space required to store each single bit of data has to be reduced.

OPTICAL TECHNOLOGY   The use of light rather than magnetism to store data has the advantage that the required area per bit is much smaller than the area per bit required for magnetic recording. The availability of the technology from the entertainment industry is spurring the development of optical disc* storage.

Three types of technology exist for optical discs.

1 The discs used for audio and video entertainment are *read-only*. Such discs, also called *CD-ROMs*, are very suitable to distribute large volume data which changes only periodically, say a directory or a catalog of items for sale. For data processing we wish to be able to write data as well. Both *write-once* and *write-multiple-times* discs are under development, and write-once discs are entering the office-system market. The high capacity of optical discs means that write-once disks are often adequate.

2 Write-once, read-multiple (*WORM*) discs are suitable for a large range of data-processing applications. All new data is appended to the end of the previously written portion WORMS have the potential advantage that all past *versions* of the data remain available, providing an excellent historical audit trail. The file organizations available from magnetic disks are not directly applicable to WORM discs; and this is slowing their acceptance.

3 Write-multiple-times discs are still under development. Given the same technology as WORMs they likely to have a lower density, and hence less capacity. Research is directed also to assuring permanency of storage and permitting frequent rewriting, since the surfaces are more volatile.

The applications will eventually determine the trade-off to be made between capacity and retention of versions versus ease of reuse of storage area.

The capacity of announced optical write-once discs varies from 2M bytes to 100G bytes, with 100M bytes becoming a reasonable value for small units. Their

---

* Current engineering convention is to spell optical discs with a "c" access times are less than those of magnetic disks, and, because of their greater capacity, an exhaustive search over their content becomes even less feasible.

Storage capacity will also be affected by the desire to have a single standard for all three types of discs, so that they may be freely interchanged in reading mechanisms. A desire to exploit existing entertainment CDROM technology also affects the performance to be obtained. It is such a proposed standard which is listed in Table 3-1 for optical discs. Having standards will greatly increase their acceptability, and much performance may be traded off. A draft standard was being considered in 1986.

╫╫╫╫ **Recording on Optical Discs** A bit is recorded on optical media by the heat of a laser changing a miniscule spot in the coating of the disc. To read the data, a beam of light at a lower level of energy is guided to the bit position. Changes in reflection will be recognized if a "one bit" has been recorded. Semiconductor lasers of adequately high power make economical optical discs feasible.   ╫╫╫╫

╫╫╫╫ **Other Optical Devices** Other optical recording devices have been manufactured using photosensitive material which is written on directly by intense light. The chemical changes are then read using either transmission or reflection of light. Holographic techniques have been tried as well. The information is then distributed in an interference pattern over a large area. This approach seems attractive because of its ability to ignore local surface irregularities.

Some large storage devices which use photographic media and are based on microfiche technology have been used for some time. Their initial cost and the maintenance required for the automated developing process discourage widespread use.   ╫╫╫╫

3-1-5 Semiconductor Technology

The rapid development of integrated circuitry has made semiconductor technology attractive. We see applications that were based on secondary storage now handled completely in primary memory, thus leaving the realm of databases. At the same time, new applications for secondary storage devices become feasible as their capacity increases.

SEMICONDUCTOR STORAGE Semiconductors can be organized in ways that differ from random-access memory in order to serve specific database storage requirements economically. Very large arrays of storage cells may, for instance, be accessed only from the edges. Data will be shifted to the edges where amplifiers and connectors extract it. Another alternative considered is to have data processed within the arrays so that only results will have to be transferred out of the semiconductor chips. Economies can accrue because the space required for access paths to the data and for control of individual bits of storage can be minimized. One specific architecture of this type, *associative memory*, is presented in Chap. 10-6.

Semiconductor technology proposed for secondary storage includes common MOS (Metal-Oxide) memory, charge-coupled devices, and shift registers. All forms of electronic storage have the advantage that data transmission can be stopped and reinitiated without loss of data or time, whereas rotating devices incur delays when interrupted due to mechanical inertia.

▦▦▦▦ **Bubble Memories** A development which originated at Bell Telephone Laboratories is based on electrical control of small magnetic charge domains on ferrite surfaces. Under the influence of a magnetic field, the surface charges, which are otherwise randomly distributed, will form electromagnetic *bubbles* a few thousandths of an inch in size. These can be rapidly moved along pathways by pulsed electric currents in conductors which have been deposited on these surfaces. These bubbles can be generated and detected by semiconductors. There are some operational similarities with disk drives, but the surfaces and the reading and writing mechanisms stay fixed while strings of data-carrying bubbles are moved along the surfaces between the sensing and the generating mechanisms.   ▦▦▦▦

MEMORY-BASED FILES The reduction in cost of memory has made it possible to keep substantial files in memory for processing. Read access is no longer subject to mechanical delays. To achieve persistence of data a permanent copy is still kept on disk, and any updates are reflected on disk as well as in memory. For modest memory sizes reliability of persistence can be improved by battery power backup.

Searching through large data quantities in memory still requires time, but many more choices exist for effective memory-based file organizations. We will not address these in this book.

3-1-6 Memory

Memory is essential for processing. It contains the active, manipulable data structures used for computing. As shown in Fig. 1-3, all data moves through memory between persistent storage and users with their programs. Memory also contains the instructions of the programs while they are being used.

Memory is randomly addressable at a level of one or a few characters at a time. These units, *words*, are of limited size to allow the processor to manipulate all bits simultaneously through the use of parallel circuits. This type of memory also is relatively fast, so that it can serve to tie other devices, which operate at different rates, together into one data-processing system. Data-storage units which depend on mechanical motion have considerable inertia so that they are not started, stopped, accelerated, or decelerated to suit processing needs. They operate asynchronously, and when they have completed a data transfer to memory, other devices and processes can use the results. Data obtained from storage devices are kept temporarily in buffer areas allocated in core memory. We will discuss buffering in Sec. 3-3-4.

Memory is assumed to be volatile; i.e., deliberate or accidental removal of power will destroy memory contents. Some memories can actually retain data and instructions, but most operating systems do not dare to count on retention of critical information.

VIRTUAL MEMORY On many large computer systems the range of addresses available to refer to memory is adequate for many file requirements. Typical addressing limits in large computers range from $5 \cdot 2^{18} = 1.280M$ to $2^{32} = 4096M$

characters. Only part of the memory space is real; the remainder is virtual and brought in by paging from backup storage when referenced, as reviewed in Chap. 2-3-2. The use of *virtual memory* to support files is analyzed in Chap. 9-4.

Virtual memory, although to the user indistinguishable in function from real memory, cannot be treated from a performance point of view as if it were real. We find that the fundamental performance analyses developed here for general file organizations continue to hold, although the programmer will have little control over the actions of a file system based on virtual memory facilities.

3-1-7 The Cost of Storage

The performance of a system cannot be considered independently of its cost. In Chap. 10-1 we introduce the other hardware components required for using storage devices, namely the channels and controllers which connect the disks, etc., to the processors. In Chap. 10-2-3 storage costs are assessed. Chapter 14-5 reviews the cost-benefit tradeoff over the entire storage architecture.

When the volume of data is large, infrequently used data may be kept *off-line*, on tapes or disks that are mounted by operating personnel when needed. In all other cases we will want to have the data available without manual intervention, i.e., *on-line*.

The cost of keeping data on-line shown in Table 3-1 consists of the cost of the storage medium, the cost of the device that can read and write the data, and the estimated cost of its connection to the computer's processing unit. The cost of keeping data off-line includes the cost of the materials themselves as well as the costs for properly conditioned space for 1 year. The values in the table combine all costs and are reduced to a cost per year using normal lease and maintenance rates. It is obvious that these values are only estimates.

In recent years hardware costs of storage devices and media have fallen by about 20% per year. The purchase cost for disk storage has decreased from $65/M byte in 1981 to $17 in 1985, and it may be $5 in 1989. At the same time personnel and maintenance costs continue to rise. A design for a new system should include a formal projection of all these costs for its lifetime.

Memory costs are substantially higher. To help in making design decisions we note that in 1986 typical prices for add-on memory ranged from $500 to $3000 per Mbyte. The price differential is related to the required interface performance, the low numbers are for micro-computers, and the high numbers for typical data-processing machines. The cost of memory for high-performance computers is much higher. The price of add-on memory does not include the interfaces to the CPU. The price of additional interface capability, if no more memory slots are available, is often equal to the memory price.

Table 3-1   Performance and cost parameters of some storage devices.

Device:	Mag.tape	Disk devices						Units
		Floppy	Micro	Pack	Giant	Fixed	CDROM	
Manufacturer	IBM	Shugart	Seagate	DEC	IBM	IBM	DEC	
Model[a]	9 track	851 8"	XT 5"	RM05[b]	3380	3380-F	RRD50	
Type	1600 bpi	Double	Stack	Stack	Module	option[c]	120mm	
Year[d]	1954	1970	1983	1962	1980	1981	1986	
Physical configuration:								
	Reels	Mylar	Winch.	11 plates	Winch.	head/track	disc	
	of tape	$k=2$	2·2	19	2·15	2·15	1	Surfaces
	2400 ft	$j=77$	306	823	2·885	2		Tracks
Cost per year:								$/M char
Off-line	1.2	17	–	20	–	–	0.05	
On-line	150	200	43	120	20	400	5	
Capacity:								Char
per track[e]	3K	8192	8704	16384	47476	47476		
Min block	6	256	512	512	32	32	512	
Max block	45M	1024	512	512	50K	50K	–	
per device	5.3M	1.2M	10.16M	256M	2520M	5.6M	2M	
Gap size	600	60	130	200	524	524	–	Char
Block access time:								ms
Seek (s)	90K	141[f]	306	31.3	16	0.2[g]	1500	
Latency (r)	250	83.3	8.3	8.3	8.3	8.3	60	
Transfer rate(t):								Char/ms
Write	240	62	655	983	3000	3000	–	
Read	240	62	655	983	3000	3000	150	
Block transfer time (btt)[h]:								ms
(for B char.:	2400	1024	512	512	2400	2400	512)	
Read or Write	10	16.5	0.78	0.52	0.82	0.82	3.4	
Rewrite(T_{RW})[i]	–	167	16.6	16.6	16.6	16.6	–	

[a]   Model refers to the actual device described.

[b]   A later model of the same type unit as the IBM 3330.

[c]   Two fixed heads may be added to each surface of the disk, replacing tracks accessible otherwise by the moving heads.

[d]   Year refers to the first year of use for the general type of device

[e]   Data on track size and transfer rate assume 8-bit characters (char.), also called *bytes*.

[f]   Includes 50 ms to load the heads after having been idle.

[g]   Electronic switching time.

[h]   These values are based on the given block size B, and can be modified significantly by software sytem choices. They are included to simplify comparison of processing times.

[i]   The rewrite delay estimates are based on assumptions stated in Sec. 3-3-6.

3-2 HARDWARE PARAMETERS

We now develop quantitative measures for the hardware used for file storage. This will provide parameters to use when evaluating alternate file organizations. The parameters used in this book are oriented mainly toward disk-type devices, but equivalent parameters can be obtained for other types of storage hardware. We will capture the salient features of a wide variety of hardware and hardware-oriented system choices with half a dozen parameters, summarized in Table 3-5. Some assumptions about the operation and use of the devices are made to simplify those parameters. These have to be verified before building actual systems. Different types of storage hardware need different assumptions.

RANDOM-ACCESS TIME   To access some item of data, located at some known storage position, requires operations which cause an access delay. This delay is called the *random-access time*. It is based on the assumptions that the position of the data to be accessed and the initial position of the access mechanism are randomly distributed over the disk. The assumption of randomness permits the estimation of the average time to reach a specific known position. The random-access time is the most critical parameter of storage device performance. The term is not particularly felicitous, since the access to data is certainly not random. The apparent randomness occurs because data is retrieved or stored in a sequence which is not determined by the device.

The random-access time is broken down into two constituents, *seek time* and *latency*. The former refers to the positioning delay — for instance, the movement of the head mechanism of a disk — and latency is the rotational delay incurred until the data can be read. The time required for the subsequent reading or writing depends on the size of the *block* of data being transferred and on the data-transfer rate of the hardware. So, before proceeding with an analysis of the time needed to get the data, we will present how the hardware organizes the data into blocks.

BLOCKS AND SECTORS   As can be seen in Table 3-1, the capacity of a track can be quite large. Copying such a large quantity of data into memory can take a long time and much memory space. It is hence common to divide a track into a number of *blocks*. A block becomes the unit of data being transferred. The division of a track into blocks may be implemented completely by hardware; such hardware units are termed *sectors*. There will be a fixed number of sectors, typically 10 or 16 per track, each capable of holding a fixed number of characters. In other disk units a track can be divided into sectors by software. Formatting software, provided with an operating system, writes markers onto the disk to define the block boundaries. These markers are recognized by the hardware during normal READ or WRITE operations.

This division of a track into fixed blocks by formatting is sometimes called *soft sectoring*, and the alternative devices are said to use *hard sectoring*. If the size of a hard sector is inconveniently small, it is best to routinely use a number of sectors together as one block. If soft sectoring is not supported by hardware, system software may yet divide data received from a track into smaller units, so that a reasonable block size is obtained. In any case, the block, be it composed of a sector, a number of sectors, a formatted (or *soft*) sector, a track, or a software-defined portion of a track, will be a convenient fixed-size unit for data transfer.

A block then is a collection of coded characters or values, of a fixed size within a computer system or part of a system, which is moved as a unit between the storage devices and the memory for processing. Once the right block is found, it will be read completely in order to obtain the error checking-and-correction information for the block. A block is the prime hardware data unit considered throughout this book. The data units that programs manipulate, and submit to the file system for reading or writing, are called *records*. Section 3-2-4 will discuss the transformation of blocks to records.

BLOCK SIZE   Most files and many databases use one single, predefined block size. Use of the same block size on different devices with differing track sizes can cause loss of storage space, but a careful selection of a block size which fits well into all devices can minimize this loss. Typical block sizes range from a few hundred to ten thousand bytes. The fixed block size reduces complexity in the device-oriented programs. The user programs will still have to deal with a variety of fixed and variable records.

The selection of the optimal size of a block depends on many factors, and in turn the size affects file system performance in a critical fashion. This chapter will discuss the factors which directly relate hardware performance to block size, but throughout the first half of the book the block-size parameter B will appear.

Records, the data units required for processing, vary in size from a few to thousands of characters. A large block size causes more irrelevant data to be moved around when a record is needed and requires more memory. A small block size means that more separate block-access requests have to be made to collect the data required for a task. The trade-off of these inefficiencies depends on the needs of the application and the design of the transaction programs. Chapter 8-4-3 presents an optimization analysis for the block size for indexes.

We can now discuss hardware performance in terms of accessing blocks within tracks. Tracks and cylinders are partitions of storage determined only by the design of disk unit hardware.

3-2-1 Seek Time

The *seek time* , s, is the time required to position the access mechanism over the proper track. Figure 3-6 shows the seek times required to move over various track distances for a moving-head disk, here an old model of the IBM 2314. For this device the relationship of distance traveled and time taken for this travel is not at all linear.

On many modern disks the seek times can be approximated by a linear relationship of the form $s_c + \delta i$, where s_c is an initial startup time, δ is the time to move between adjacent tracks, and i is the distance traveled in terms of intertrack spaces traversed. Most disk units are designed so that the time to move to the nearest track, $s_1 = s_c + \delta$, is less than the time for one revolution. This minimizes the delay for reading cylinders sequentially.

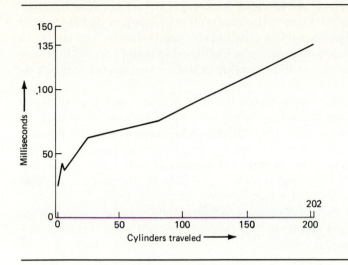

Figure 3-6   Seek times for an IBM 2314 model 1.

To avoid the pain of actually evaluating travel distances for individual disk accesses we will use an average seek time, s, whenever a seek is encountered. Often, an average value for the seek time is provided by the manufacturer. It should be based on a uniform access distribution over all tracks. A lower average seek time can be obtained if important and highly active files are placed on a few adjoining cylinders. In such cases it can be useful to calculate the corresponding expected average seek time.

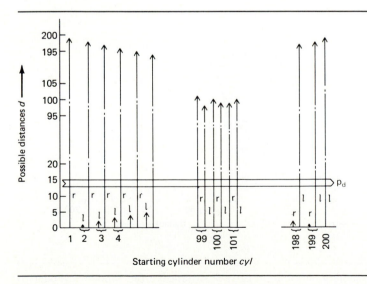

Figure 3-7   Travel possibilities for disk heads.

⧈⧈⧈⧈⧈ **DERIVATION OF AN AVERAGE SEEK TIME**   To demonstrate the computation of the average seek time, the assumption of random distribution of track access will be used here, but other distributions can be handled similarly. In the case of a uniform random distribution, the likelihood of travel is equal from any cylinder to any cylinder. The distribution of distances to be traveled will not be equally likely.

Starting from the extreme cylinders, the heads may have to traverse all of the disk, whereas from the center track they never have to travel more than half the distance. Figure 3-7 illustrates this effect. It shows for some of the 200 possible starting cylinders, cyl, the distances that the reading head may travel to the left (**1**) or to the right (**r**). A seek to the left of distance i, $i = 1 \ldots 199$, is possible from initial positions $cyl \geq i + 1$; and a seek to the right of distance i is possible from $cyl \leq 200 - i$.

For a disk with j cylinders, a distance i, left and right, can be traveled from positions cyl if $cyl \geq i+1$ and also if $cyl \leq j - i$. No travel will occur if the starting point is equal to the destination cylinder.

We will compute the probability of each distance to be traveled by counting the event, left and right, for each cylinder position. There are a total of $j(j-1)$ actual travel combinations between the j cylinders, and we are assuming that they are all equally likely. We note that the probability of no travel is $pd_0 = 1/j$. For a distance i, $i = 1 \ldots j - 1$, the probability of travel of this distance pd_i is

$$pd_i = \sum_{cyl=i+1}^{j} \frac{1^\dagger}{j(j-1)} + \sum_{cyl=1}^{j-i} \frac{1^\dagger}{j(j-1)} \quad = \quad 2\frac{j-i}{j(j-1)} \qquad i = 1 \ldots j-1 \qquad 3\text{-}1$$

This probability distribution is shown in Fig. 3-8a.

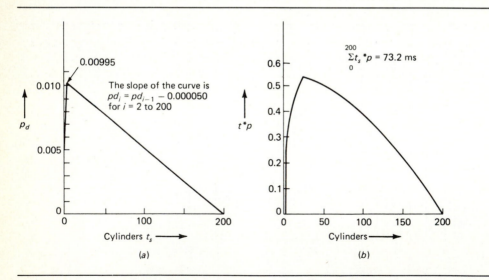

(a)   (b)

Figure 3-8   (a) Probability distribution of seek distances from random cylinder to random cylinder.   (b) Probability distribution of random seek times.

The product of these seek distance probabilities and the time required to travel any of these distances gives the expected seek time distribution. The expected average seek time, s, for this device, with the assumption of random access, is

$$s = \sum_{i=1}^{j-1} s_i\, pd_i \qquad\qquad 3\text{-}2$$

where s_i is the seek time for distance i. A result is shown in Fig. 3-8b for the disk head travel times s_i presented in Fig. 3-6.

Devices with arbitrary seek delays can be evaluated using Eq. 3-2. The case of only using fewer adjoining cylinders can be computed by limiting the range of i to the number of cylinders in use. A nonuniform travel distribution is handled by replacing the numerators(†) in Eq. 3-1 with functions of cyl and i which define the usage pattern for a particular situation.   ⫟⫟⫟⫟

⫟⫟⫟⫟   **Controlling Seek Times**   The value of s for a file may be effectively reduced by certain allocation techniques. We indicated already that when a file occupies a limited number of consecutive cylinders the average movement will be less as long as there is no other file activity on the same unit. Since now only a portion of this diskunit is used by the active file, there is storage available for non-conflicting tasks. Such storage capacity may be used for archive and backup copies of data, and for the programs which are loaded prior to data processing.

For a large file the benefit of having to seek no or only a few cylinders can be obtained by fragmenting the file over multiple disk units. Such a *fragmentation* provides then the use of multiple access mechanisms for one file. Having multiple access mechanisms also provides access overlap, more than one seek can take place simultaneously. The effect of such parallel access is evaluated in Chap. 10-1-2, techniques for fragmentation are discussed with clustered systems in Chap. 11-2-2. Clustered systems provide yet another level of overlap, by using multiple processors.

Other usage patterns can increase the effective seek time. An alternating use of two files on the same disk will result in average seek times that are a function of the distance in terms of cylinders between these files. If the cylinders for the files are far apart we get substantially larger average seek times. In multiprogrammed and timeshared computer systems the probability of multiple use of a disk unit at any time appears large, especially when there are many users relative to the number of available disk drives. Transaction systems attempt to minimize this effect.

Whenever voluminous data can be accessed without interruption and in the same sequence that they are stored on the tracks, a seek needs to occur only once per cylinder. This seek will also require only minimal motion. The cost of seeks per disk access will then be a fraction of the average seek time. We will quantify that effect in Sec. 3-2-5 as a factor in the *bulk transfer rate*.

After the desired track has been located by the seek, it is still necessary to determine where the head is relative to the actual block on the track, since that is the unit we wish to transfer. The begin point for the tracks or of the actual blocks on the disk will be sensed by the access mechanism. There will be a rotational delay before the data can be read or written.   ⫟⫟⫟⫟

3-2-2 Rotational Latency

After the reading and writing mechanism of a disk drive or similar mechanism is positioned at the correct track, a further delay is incurred to reach the desired block on the track. The various delays between the completion of the seek and the actual transfer of data are referred to as the *rotational latency*, r, of storage units.

One type of delay occurs because reading of the recorded data cannot commence at an arbitrary point. This is because we cannot synchronize the single stream of bits coming from the disk with any desired point in memory, until some identification marker is found. Sometimes a track begin point must be reached first, and then it still is necessary to proceed to the desired block. In most devices with fixed sectors a sector count is maintained so that the next complete sector can be transferred, if it is the desired one. If the sector was just missed, most of a revolution will pass before data transfer will take place. In software-controlled formats a block-identifying area or count area is read to determine which of the blocks that pass by is the desired one. A track-begin identifying area (*home address*) is used only by formatting programs when a disk is changed to have new block sizes.

We will first consider the case where a block can be recognized at its own begin point, so that as soon as the desired block is below the reading heads, the data transfer can commence. Then the average value of the rotational latency r is one-half the time required for one rotation of the disk, or

$$r = \frac{1}{2} \frac{60 \cdot 1000}{\text{rpm}} \qquad\qquad 3\text{-}3$$

where rpm is the number of disk revolutions per minute, and the latency, r, is specified in milliseconds. Typical rotational speeds are 2400 and 3600 rpm, leading to values of r of 12.5 and 8.33 ms.

▦▦▦ **Latency with Reading of Track Identifiers** Some disks have at the beginning of each track a field which permits verification that the positioning mechanism is at the desired track or cylinder. Then the above estimate has to be modified to account for the additional delay before data blocks can be transferred. The expected distance between the track-begin point and the data depends on the number of blocks per track. The average time required to reach the track identifier is r, and the average distance from the track begin to the beginning of the blocks, given b blocks per track, is $\frac{1}{2}(b-1)/b$ of the track length. In terms of the previous value of r we find a new total latency:

$$r' = r + \frac{1}{2} \frac{b-1}{b} 2r = r \left(2 - \frac{1}{b} \right) \qquad\qquad 3\text{-}4$$

If there is only one block per track, the block is found at the beginning of the track and the latency remains r. For many and small blocks the latency when having to read track identifiers becomes nearly double the standard latency. This value of the latency is always applicable when writing into unpreformatted areas, since then no block recognition is possible.   ▦▦▦

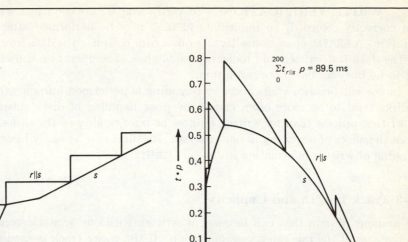

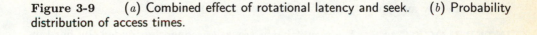

Figure 3-9   (*a*) Combined effect of rotational latency and seek.   (*b*) Probability distribution of access times.

   Seek and Latency Combined   Sometimes the values provided by computer manufacturers have rotational delays factored into the seek times given. Such data, while being essentially honest, tend to blur the correct evaluation of specific system performance. Figure 3-9*a* portrays the combined effect of the two components, seek and rotational latency, for the IBM 2314 of Fig. 3-6, with a one-block-per-track allocation. We expect a delay of *r* to find a block on the current cylinder and, since in this case a new record coincides with the beginning of a track, additional delays of entire revolutions due to seeks from other cylinders. The expected combined seek and rotational latency time provides only a few discrete choices, here *r* (no seek), 3*r*, 5*r*, 7*r*, 9*r*, or 11*r*. By combining this fact again with the previous probability distribution for seek distances, we can obtain for a total expected access time an aggregate as shown in Fig. 3-9*b*.

Certain disk units allow the seek process to continue automatically until a specified sector on the desired cylinder, included as part of the seek destination address, is found. The published seek time then may include the average rotational latency. Such *sector addressing* can reduce significantly the load on the channel which connects the disk unit and the main processor. In this chapter we ignore this type of design. In Chap. 14-3-2, where the total load of an application on a computer system is discussed, we will encounter such disk control mechanisms as class 5 devices.   ▦

⨌⨌ **WRITE VERIFICATION**   To verify that information just written has been correctly recorded, an immediate REREAD may be performed after a WRITE operation. A REREAD operation will carry out a comparison of the data from memory and the data just written and indicate mismatches. The operation causes the disk unit to be busy for one more revolution.

In current practice verification by rereading is performed infrequently. Errors on disks tend to be more often caused by poor handling of disks subsequent to the writing process than by writing failures or poor quality of the disks. We will ignore the effect of rereading in our analyses. Its effect can be easily inserted when rereading of written information is done.   ⨌⨌

3-2-3 Track Length and Capacity

The amount of data that can be read or written with one access determines the effectiveness of the random-access operation. If the entire track is used to hold a single block, then the *track length* is equal to the largest possible block. Otherwise, the track length is equal to the product of the number and the size of the blocks provided per track. The length of a track may be given in terms of bits, characters, or words. The entries in Table 3-1 are standardized by using characters, generally of 7 or 8 bits in length. On many disk units with hard sectors multiple sectors may be read as one block. Blocks will always have to fit within a single track, so that the track length places an upper limit on the block size. If yet larger units of data are required by an application, multiple blocks have to be used.

INTERBLOCK GAPS   We recall that a track is frequently divided, by hard or soft formatting, into a number of blocks of length B each. At every break between two blocks there is a *gap* to permit the head mechanism to prepare for the next operation. The space required for this interblock gap, G, reduces the actual storage capacity, as shown in Table 3-2.

Table 3-2   Storage capacity of tapes and disks for some formatted block sizes.

Capacity for	Characters per block B				
Device	1*	80	200	1000	3000
Tape 800/6	0.038M	2.67M	7.58M	14.2 M	18.9 M
Tape 1600/8	0.047M	3.25M	10.1 M	22.3 M	33.7 M
Tape 6250/8	0.094M	6.75M	22.1 M	60.5 M	107.0 M
Floppy disk (8 in.)	0.045M	1.06M	1.29M	1.386M	1.386M
Disk 11(2314)	0.228M	12.8 M	20.0 M	24.0 M	24.0 M
Disk 11(3330)	0.730M	37.1 M	68.4 M	83.6 M	91.2 M
Disk giant(3380)	79.6 M	2 119.75M	2 272.68M	2 442.6 M	2 389.5 M

* Blocks of one character length are hypothetical for many devices. A minimum number of characters is often required to generate proper redundancy check information. The USASI standard for tape specifies a minimum block size of 18 characters for information interchange.

With high recording densities the gaps displace hundreds of characters. The two Disk 11 devices show how large block sizes have a greater effect on high density than on moderate density disks.

Small block sizes increase the number of gaps, causing significant amounts of wasted disk or tape storage. Large block sizes do make heavy demands on memory capacity and on transmission capability while transferring unused, but adjacent, data. In transaction systems which can have many users, and hence many files simultaneously in use, much memory will be used if block sizes are large: 100 users, each using 3 files with two working buffers each for blocks of 3000 characters will use 1.8M bytes of memory.

▦▦▦ **Gap Size** The size of gaps between blocks of tape or disk depend on the devices used. The older six-data-track tape units had a gap of 0.75 inch (19 mm) and, at their highest recording density, 800 bpi, had a value of G of 600 characters. Eight-track tapes require 0.6 inch (15 mm), or 960 characters at 1600 bpi; and the 6250 bpi tapes have a gap of only 0.3 inch (7.6 mm), but this leads to a gap G of 1875 characters.

Disk units can have complex gaps. The gap on an IBM 3330-type disk consists of the equivalent of

1 Space equivalent to about 135 characters
2 A variable-length block identification field, which may be considered useful space
3 A space between this identification field and the actual block of about 58 characters in length. This space allows for switching from reading — for the identification — to writing of data.

The total gap size G is hence about 200 characters for this device; more values appear in Table 3-1. The block-identification field is used by software to keep a name for the block. The name field can be used to *verify* that the system has located the desired block before a write command destroys its prior contents with new data. ▦▦▦

BLOCK SIZE AND TRACK CAPACITY The reduction in storage capacity shown in Table 3-2 is caused mainly by the gaps between the blocks, and to some extent by the loss when fitting these blocks into the track dimensions of the disks. In order to reduce the loss associated with a poor fit of blocks into the track size -- as seen in the last column for disks — block sizes which make optimal use of the track capacity for the device may be used. An unusual block size will, however, create problems when different devices are used within one system and whenever storage units are replaced by newer types. The desire to use identical block sizes on different devices will cause a compromise to be made. Optimizing space utilization for a variety of storage devices leads to small block sizes. Systems with a single block size for all devices may use blocks of only 128 or 256 characters. Such block sizes will reduce tape and disk capacity greatly.

BLOCK POINTERS In order to refer to a block, we have to construct an address identifying the device and the position of the block on the device. Such a reference address is known as a *block pointer*. A block pointer provides a unique name for every block in a system.

We will use block pointers in the remainder of this section but will discuss the implementation of block pointers in Sec. 3-3-3. The block identification field seen on soft-sectored disks is used by file-system software to keep a name for the block, and hence is a form of block pointer. The size of block pointers will be denoted by the symbol P. In Chap. 5-0 we will encounter pointers to specific records, or *TIDs*.

3-2-4 Records and Blocking

Records are the actual units for data storage on the logical or file level. The fitting of records into blocks is referred to as *blocking*. Records may be of a fixed size, or may be variable in length, as required by the application. We denote the size of a record by R.

Since an evaluation of files for an application has to be concerned with performance in terms of records rather than in terms of blocks, we will now analyze blocking and derive some parameters which relate hardware and block-based parameters to records. The major parameter is the *blocking factor*, denoted by *Bfr*, which gives the number of records expected within a block. Three important methods of blocking are discussed next. When the methods require that all records fit within blocks, we call them *unspanned*. Unspanned blocking applies to fixed- and to variable-length records.

Fixed Blocking   An integer number of fixed-length records is placed within a block as shown in Fig. 3-10. We observe that for unspanned fixed blocking the blocking factor *Bfr* is an integer constant. Any unusable space in a block is wasted.

$$Bfr = \lfloor B/R \rfloor \hspace{3cm} \langle \text{fixed}^* \rangle \text{ 3-5}$$

Fixed blocking is the dominant mode for files written via programming languages, since their record structures are mapped into fixed-length memory spaces.

Variable-Length Spanned Blocking   Records are packed into sequential blocks, and are broken at block boundaries. The continuation is indicated by a pointer to the successor block. *Spanning* is difficult to implement. Records that actually span two blocks are expensive to search and the resultant files are difficult to update.

Variable-length spanning provides application flexibility for the user, but also removes the worry about fitting data into records limited to fixed block sizes. Having to deal with the small blocks found in some systems can be a major burden.

Variable-Length Unspanned Blocking   Only entire records are placed within a block. There is wasted space in most blocks because of the inability to use the remainder of a block if the next record is larger than the remaining unused space. The number of records per block varies if the records are of varying lengths.

Here the records cannot be longer than the block size.

The value of *Bfr* for both types of variable-length blocking will be also affected by the marking scheme used to separate records, as discussed below.

---

* We use ⟨condition⟩ to distinguish cases where a variable is derived in more than one equation.

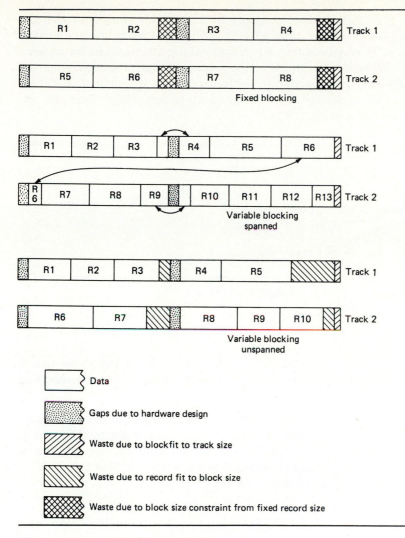

Figure 3-10   Blocking methods.

RECORD MARKS   When manipulating records, it is necessary to know where records begin and end within blocks. For fixed blocking, only the (constant) record length, R, has to be known to locate records within a block. When records of variable-length are packed into blocks, data for marking the record boundaries within the block has to be added to separate the records. When spanned records bridge block boundaries, some reference to the successor block is also needed.

The external specification of the file format, obtained at the time of execution of an OPEN statement, will give the blocking type and marking convention in use. For fixed blocking only the record length R is given. For variable length records three techniques, (shown in Fig. 3-11), are available to mark the records.

Block Marking The blocking descriptor may be a *separator marker* between the records, which can be recognized when searching through a block. Such a marker has to be unique so that data within the record cannot be mistaken for an end-of-record marker. When data is stored in the form of character strings, standard end-of-record characters are available to delineate records within blocks. These character codes are often derived from communication technology; examples are CR, GS, RS, and US (shown in Fig. 13-1).

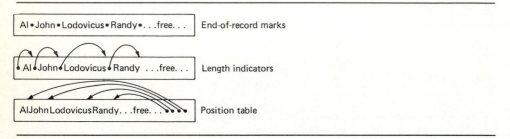

Figure 3-11   Marking of variable-length records.

Another method used to mark record positions within blocks is the use of a *length indicator* preceding every record. The beginning point of the next record can be reached by skipping over the body of the current record.

The third method uses a *position table* within each block giving all the record positions in a block. Each method has its benefits and liabilities. We will often find references to these three choices.

We can now compute the blocking factor, *Bfr*, for variable-length blocking. Each record requires one marker entry, and we assume that the size of one marker entry is about equal to the size of a block pointer, P. For spanned blocking a block pointer of size P to its successor block may be included in each block, so that the pieces of a spanned record can be easily retrieved. Then

$$Bfr = \frac{B - P}{R + P} \qquad \langle \text{var-spanned} \rangle \; 3\text{-}6$$

With unspanned variable-length blocking an average of $\frac{1}{2}R$ will be wasted because of the fitting problem, but no successor pointer is required. Here,

$$Bfr = \frac{B - \frac{1}{2}R}{R + P} \qquad \langle \text{var-unspanned} \rangle \; 3\text{-}7$$

WASTE   Because of the gaps between the blocks, unused space within blocks, and various markers, not all the storage space provided by the devices can be used. Since the effect is often significant, we calculate now the *waste per record* , W, due to these factors. The waste due to gaps W_G will equal the gap size G per block divided by the number of records per block, or *blocking factor Bfr*.

$$W_G = G/Bfr \qquad\qquad 3\text{-}8$$

There is also waste due to unused space from blocking in each block. This is also allocated to each record as W_R. With fixed blocking the record sizes are generally set to minimize the amount of waste, and the wasted space per block is certainly less than one record R. The bounds on W_R are hence $0 \leq W_R < R/Bfr$. We find fixed blocking frequently when records are small, and we recall from Sec. 3-2-3 that gaps are often large. For fixed blocking the waste per record is then

$$W = W_G + W_R \qquad \text{often} \qquad W \approx W_G = G/Bfr \qquad \langle\text{fixed}\rangle \ 3\text{-}9$$

We will now consider the cases of variable length record blocking. The waste due to record fitting and marking has already been discussed in the evaluation of the blocking factor, Bfr. For spanned blocking all the space in a block is usable and the total waste per record is

$$W = P + (P + G)/Bfr \qquad \langle\text{var-spanned}\rangle \ 3\text{-}10$$

and for unspanned blocking we expected a half-record loss per block, so that

$$W = P + \frac{\frac{1}{2}R + G}{Bfr} \qquad \langle\text{var-unspanned}\rangle \ 3\text{-}11$$

Since Bfr is also a function of R, we note that in this last blocking method the waste increases quadratically or $O(R^2)$ with the record size. With a small value for P, and with Eq. 3-7 substituted, $W \approx \frac{1}{2}R^2/B + RG/B$. The waste due to fitting is now quite significant when records are relatively long relative to the block size. This factor has to be taken into account when estimating total storage capacity and effectiveness of data transfer. In order to arrive at an accurate estimate in critical situations, the actual distribution of record sizes should be considered. A discussion of tools to perform such analyses is presented in Chap. 10.

We recall that the size of a record, when spanning is not supported, is restricted to the block size. If this size is not adequate for an application, the problem of proper blocking is passed on to the next higher level of the system. Such inadequacies of the lower-level file systems make other parts of the system more complex and violate the layering concepts discussed in Chap. 1-2-1.

3-2-5 Transfer Rate

We have up to this point discussed the two constituents of the random-access time, the seek time and the rotational latency. When the proper track and rotational position is reached, the actual data block still has to be read or written from or to the disk. This third constituent of a data-transfer operation depends on the speed of actual data transfer. The rate or speed with which data can be transferred is known as the *transfer rate*, t. It is measured throughout this book in terms of characters per millisecond or, equivalently, Kcharacters/s or also Kbytes/s.

The basic transfer rate is dependent on the design of the device used. On most devices the READ and WRITE rates are identical, although exceptions exist for mechanical and some optical recording schemes. On disks the transfer rate is a function of rotational speed and recording density. Manufacturers often provide a raw transfer rate in terms of bits/second, which then has to be adjusted for the number of bits required to encode and check a block of 1000 characters.

The time to read a record of R characters is

$$T_R = R/t \qquad \text{ms} \tag{3-12}$$

and the time required to transfer an entire block is equal to B/t. Since the transfer of a block is such a frequent operation, we will write for the *block transfer time*

$$btt = B/t \tag{3-13}$$

Whereas the transfer rate is determined by the device, the block transfer time is also determined by the block size B. Since blocks can never be larger than tracks, we note that $btt \leq 2r$. Table 3-1 provides some typical values of btt.

BULK TRANSFER RATE   The transfer rate, t, given in the literature provided by a manufacturer is the instantaneous rate during the actual transfer. When transferring large quantities of data sequentially, there are intervals when gaps and other nondata areas are being passed. At the end of each cylinder a seek will occur and during the seek time no data is transferred. In the case of continuous sequential reading or writing, the use of a *bulk transfer rate* simplifies performance analyses. We will now quantify the two factors which affect bulk transfer, and then combine them into a new parameter, the bulk transfer rate, t'.

▦▦▦ **Effect of Gaps and Blocking on the Transfer Rate** The effect of unused space due to gaps and due to blocking of records into blocks was expressed in Eqs. 3-9 to 3-11 as wasted space. We now perform a similar estimation for the transfer time. We ignore any additional gaps that some devices have at the beginning of a track and include only the gaps between blocks, as in computing W. The effect of waste on the bulk transfer rate can be evaluated by considering an entire cylinder, with k tracks and $n't$ records per track. Reading of an entire cylinder takes a period of $k\,n't(R+W)/t$ ms, and during that time $k\,n't\,R$ data characters are transferred. The actual transfer rate for an entire cylinder of data is now computable in terms of W as

$$t_{cyl} = \frac{k\,n't\,R}{k\,n't(R+W)/t} = \frac{R}{(R+W)/t} = t\,\frac{R}{R+W} \qquad \text{characters/ms} \tag{3-14}$$

The value of W for various types of blocking is provided by Eqs. 3-9 to 3-11.

Effect of Seeks on the Transfer Rate In reading even larger quantities of data sequentially, we will have to cross over cylinder boundaries. One minimal seek is required once per cylinder. Even though seeks may be infrequent, the required correction may still be far from negligible because of the relatively long seek times on many units. On disks with few surfaces, seeks will be needed frequently.

In order to account for the effect of seeks, we will consider the seek frequency and seek time, and use the combination to predict an effective seek time per record, s'. The assessment requires some understanding of the operating environment. In a multiprogrammed environment, competition may exist for the seek mechanism, so that a full seek-time delay, s, may be incurred frequently, up to once per block. The effective delay per record is then $s' = s/Bfr$. But when interference is modest or can be controlled during a transaction, the expected delay between blocks is much less. When there is no interference at all, the seek delay will occur only at the end of a cylinder. We use the number of surfaces, k, to determine the size of a cylinder in terms of tracks and then apply the seek delay, s_1. To evaluate seeks per record, the number of records per track, rrt, is also needed; the entire cylinder contains $k\,\mathit{rrt}$ records.

In general, a seek to the next track (s_1) requires less than the time of one revolution ($2r$). The desire to keep $s_1 < 2r$ caused in fact the mechanical complexity which led to the complex seek-time curve shown in Fig. 3-6. Since we continue the reading of records at the beginning of the next track of the new cylinder, we have, if $s_1 < 2r$, a seek delay per cylinder of $2r$. One revolution can again be expressed in terms of the time to transfer all records from a track, so that $2r = \mathit{rrt}(R+W)/t$. Combining these terms we find the minimal effect, from a track-switch delay occurring only at cylinder boundaries, to be $s' = s_1/(k\,\mathit{rrt}) \leq 2r/(k\,\mathit{rrt}) = ((R+W)/t)/k$ per record.

The seek overhead per record for continuous reading s' is now bound by

$$\frac{1}{k}\frac{R+W}{t} \leq s' \leq \frac{s}{Bfr} \qquad \text{(bounds) 3-15}$$

The range of these bounds is great, easily a factor of 100. As a practical estimate the seek time overhead per record, while reading sequentially, may be taken to be equal to the minimum value ($2r = \mathit{rrt}(R+W)/t$), but occurring at every track boundary, so that

$$s' \approx \frac{2r}{\mathit{rrt}} = \frac{(R+W)}{t} \qquad \text{(estimate) 3-16}$$

Measurements indicate that this estimate is still conservative and that in most computing systems interference is modest. If this factor is of great importance to the eventual success of the system, measurements of sequential READ performance should be made on the system to be used, to assure that the estimate is met.

Any assumptions of this type, as having expectations of less than average seek times and seek frequencies less than once per block, should be well documented in any evaluation, so that effects of changes in the operating environment will not lead to unexpected and disastrous performance degradations. ▦

Calculation of the Bulk Transfer Rate The bulk transfer rate includes the effects of waste, W, and seeks, s'. We obtained in Eq. 3-14 above the bulk transfer rate due to waste within one cylinder. For multiple cylinders we add the seek delay per record s' to the transfer time per record and its waste $(R+W)/t$, and obtain the bulk transfer rate

$$t' = \frac{R}{(R+W)/t + s'} \qquad \text{characters/ms} \qquad 3\text{-}17$$

where s' is chosen to reflect the operating environment as detailed in the reasoning leading to Eqs. 3-15 and 3-16.

To combine the two factors for the case of no interference, we consider the time to read an entire cylinder with k tracks and nrt records per track. During this time $k\,\mathit{nrt}\,R$ characters are transferred, and during this time the access mechanism passes each of the k tracks. The lower bound in Eq. 3-15 is based on the loss of an additional revolution once per cylinder for a seek and causes an effect per record of $s' = ((R+W)/t)/k$ or per cylinder of $\mathit{nrt}(R+W)/t$. The time per cylinder is the sum $T_{cyl} = k\,\mathit{nrt}(R+W)/t + \mathit{nrt}(R+W)/t = (k+1)\mathit{nrt}(R+W)/t$. The bulk transfer rate for the entire cylinder is hence

$$t' = \frac{k\,\mathit{nrt}\,R}{T_{cyl}} = t\,\frac{k}{k+1}\frac{R}{R+W} \qquad \text{⟨no interference⟩ 3-18}$$

A similar reasoning can provide the bulk transfer rate for the estimated value of the seek effect given in Eq. 3-16. Now $T_{cyl} = k\,\mathit{nrt}(R+W)/t + k\,\mathit{nrt}(R+W)/t = 2k\,\mathit{nrt}(R+W)/t$ and

$$t' = \frac{k\,\mathit{nrt}\,R}{T_{cyl}} = \frac{t}{2}\frac{R}{R+W} \qquad \text{⟨estimate⟩ 3-19}$$

We can compare this estimate with the value of t_{cyl} given in Eq. 3-14 and note that this level of seek interference halves the estimate of the bulk transfer rate within a cylinder, and doubles the time for sequential data-transfer operations. Factors in this estimate involved the interference per block and the seek distances expected. Note that a change in block size does not affect the estimate directly, although effects of waste W will be less.

Transfer of data at the bulk transfer rate, as computed above, is obtained only if we do not have to delay the reading to perform major computational tasks. We will describe in Sec. 3-3-4 the conditions for computational interference required to make this transfer rate valid. In this section we considered the access interference by other, concurrent tasks. In either case a system environment which creates significant interference will cause delays in the transfer operations, and such delays will in turn increase the opportunity for interference. The effect of interference on the bulk transfer rate quantifies one of the reasons for operating in a TPS, as described in Chap. 2-3-3.

Use of the Bulk Transfer Rate The bulk transfer rate accounts for all additional factors when reading through sequences of records. It has been obtained for the actual data record size, R, so that it can be applied to the units of concern to the user programs. When we apply the bulk transfer rate to entire blocks, only the actual size of the data in a block, $Bfr \times R$, has to be taken into account, since the waste due to gaps and record fitting has been accounted for in the formula for t'. Whenever the instantaneous transfer rate, t, is used, gaps have to be accounted for when reading from block to block.

If a single record is to be read from a random file position, an entire block of size B has to be transferred from the file. The single block is read, following a seek and latency to arrive at the block, with a transfer rate, t. Gaps between blocks can be ignored. In summary:

> **Sequential accessing of records** Use the bulk transfer rate, t', applied to the record size, R.
>
> **Sequential accessing of blocks** Use the bulk transfer rate, t', and the actual data quantity per block, $Bfr \times R$, or, if neccessary, the transfer rate, t, and all of $B + G$ to compute the processing time per block.
>
> **Random accessing of records or blocks** Since an entire block has to be read use the transfer rate, t, and the block size, B, with the random access time, $s + r$, to compute the retrieval time, giving $s + r + B/t = s + r + btt$.

▦▦ **Ignoring Waste** When blocking, the fitting of records into blocks, generates little waste, we can ignore the difference between the net ($Bfr \times R$) and actual (B) block sizes. The use of B where $Bfr \times R$ would be more appropriate will lead to more conservative values when estimating performance. There is little waste with spanned blocking or when fixed records fit precisely into the blocks. In those cases, the number of records per block, the blocking factor Bfr, can always be taken to be equal to the block size divided by the record size (B/R).   ▦▦

3-3   BLOCKS AND BUFFERS

We already have developed the concept of a block in the preceding section and will only review the definitions before proceeding with a number of subjects related to the management of blocks.

3-3-1 Blocks

A *block* is the unit of information actually transferred between the external storage devices and a working area, the *buffer*, in the memory of the computer. The requirements imposed on buffer management to achieve good file performance will be one of the subjects to be discussed.

We presented in Fig. 3-10 three basic methods of placing records in a block:

    1 Fixed blocking

    2 Variable-spanned blocking

    3 Variable-unspanned blocking

The blocking method used affects mainly the quantity W, the wasted space per record. If, in subsequent chapters, the blocking method is not noted, use of the variable-unspanned method can be assumed for dealing with variable-length records, and fixed blocking would be used where we are limited to fixed-length records.

⧻⧻⧻   MIXED BLOCKING TECHNIQUES   Sometimes blocking methods are not consistent throughout a file. An example of such an inconsistency exists in some file systems in regard to updating. To avoid complex update programs, new records are written unspanned into a file which is otherwise spanned, or blocking may be avoided altogether when updating. A traditional file access method, IBM-ISAM, uses this technique. The analysis of such files becomes more complex than the methods shown in the examples in the next chapters.

A mixed blocking strategy also can be employed for other reasons. In an operating system that provides a paged, virtual memory environment, it can be desirable to use pages as the basic unit of data transfer. Since the size of records, when using unspanned blocking, is limited to the size of a block, multiple pages may actually be combined to create larger blocks for file purposes. This approach is used by IBM-VSAM, where a *train* of pages is the basic working unit (see Fig. 3-12). Within the train, records may span pages, but between trains no spanning takes place. Since the entire train is read or written together the entire train acts like a single block. The increased transfer time can cause more interference, even when the pages are maintained in sequence. Multiple gaps appear now within such a block, so that the effective waste will be greater than for a block composed of a single unit. Using B now to denote the size of a train having nPt of pages leads to a blocking factor and wasted space per record

$$Bfr = \frac{B - nPt\,P - \frac{1}{2}R}{R + P} \qquad\qquad \langle\text{VSAM train}\rangle\ 3\text{-}20$$

$$W = \frac{nPt(G + P) + \frac{1}{2}R}{Bfr} + P \qquad\qquad \langle\text{VSAM train}\rangle\ 3\text{-}21$$

Other aspects of this file-access method will be discussed in a detailed example in Chap. 8-5 (also see Fig. 8-15).   ⧻⧻⧻

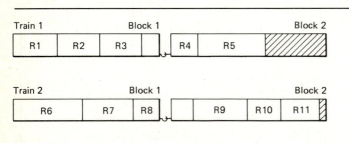

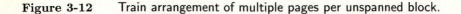

Note that a train is not necessarily equal to a track.

Figure 3-12   Train arrangement of multiple pages per unspanned block.

3-3-2 Density and Locality

Other considerations which can affect blocking decisions are related to the growth of a file. Updating of information in a file may require that new records have to be inserted into the file or that longer records replace earlier, shorter records. The various types of file organizations discussed in Chaps. 4 to 9 all have their own method of handling insertions. Some methods expand files by linking new blocks to full ones via block pointers. Since the successor blocks are assigned at later times, they will not be accessible by sequential reading and are likely to require access to another part of the disk, adding seek and rotational latency costs.

Loading Density If we expect many update operations, we may actually leave some free space distributed within the file for future needs. Each block that is assigned when a file is created or enlarged will initially have some unused space. The fraction of space initially utilized is called the *loading density*. If sufficient free space is available within a block, data can be added without an interspersed random access. When all the free space has been used, a new block has to be fetched and linked into the file, but this block will also have space for several more updates. A disadvantage of a low loading density is, of course, that more blocks have to be read to get the same amount of data when the file is not yet full.

Equilibrium Density A system where the records themselves grow and shrink is forced to move and reallocate records within the blocks. Depending on the design of the file structure, some or much of the space for the file may become fragmented and unusable. Space no longer used can be allocated for reuse to retain the benefits of a low loading ratio. The density expected after a long period of operation is the *equilibrium density*.

LOCALITY A record will be obtained with least delay if it is placed close to its predecessor. When a series of records has to be fetched, the clustering of the series is the most important factor in performance. A similar consideration is encountered in paging systems where it is desirable that all memory references be located within a small number of pages. If this is achieved, there is strong *locality*. If serial references are far apart so that it is costly to get the next record, the locality is weak. Locality as applicable to records in a file is categorized in Table 3-3.

Table 3-3   Locality.

Strong	Record is in the same block and the block is available in memory.
	Record is in the next available block on the same cylinder.
	Record is on the same cylinder.
	Record is on a current cylinder of another device.
	Record is on adjoining cylinders.
	Record is on a known cylinder.
	Record position is unknown, computed using data in memory.
	Record position is unknown, found by reading an auxiliary file.
	Record is on a remote computer in a distributed network.
Weak	Record is on a device not currently on-line.

If the data to be used during some transaction exhibit strong locality, we say that we are dealing with a clustered data structure. *Clustering* applies to data in one or more files, and we will encounter this term mainly in the design of databases which include many files.

In a system where there is a variety of devices, the considerations which determine strength of locality will become more complex. We will not attempt to define the strength of locality as a single quantitative term, but we do use locality as a useful concept in file design.

3-3-3 Block Pointers

The *block pointers* that have been used to link blocks to each other require some more elaboration. Block pointers may address a specific data field in storage.

PHYSICAL DISK ADDRESSES   To refer to a unit of data on a disk, a *physical disk address* will have to specify up to six segments:
1 The number of the physical device
2 The number of the cylinder
3 The number of the surface
4 The sector or block number
5 The record number within the block
6 The field or character number within a record

The complete physical address is composed of a sequence of such segments. Use of such an address as a block pointer is both unwieldy and inadequate. Integer arithmetic applied to a segmented address will lead to erroneous values.

Another problem with a segmented address occurs because different types of physical units in a computer system will have a different number of cylinders, surfaces, and blocks. This means that multiple address formats have to be manipulated within one system.

A third problem occurs when diskpacks are exchanged on a physical device. In that case a physical address does not correspond to a specific item of data.

A final problem is that record sizes and field sizes are application- dependent, so that the maximum number of these components in terms of the next higher component is not fixed. In most systems a *block* is the smallest fixed unit under control of the operating system.

RELATIVE ADDRESSES   An alternative to physical addressing is the use of a *relative address* over the entire file domain. Relative block, record, and character addresses are all used in practice. A relative address is an integer ranging in value from zero (or one) to the maximum number of blocks within the domain of the system which controls the storage of data. Using a relative address to locate an element in storage is similar to the computation needed to find an array element of know size in memory. The diversity in storage systems (Fig. 3-13) makes the computation more complex, as shown in Table 3-4. There will be a unique translation of a relative address to a physical address and vice versa, which allows access to the physical devices to be carried out by operating system routines when a relative address is given.

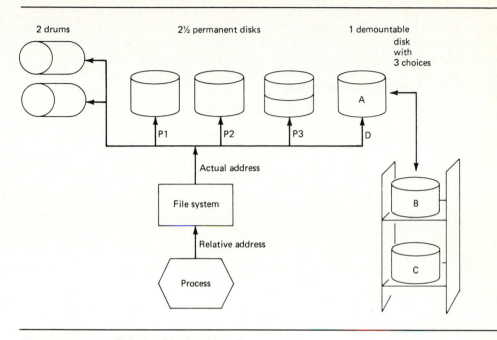

Figure 3-13   Relative block addressing.

SYMBOLIC ADDRESSES   It is also possible to assign a *symbolic address* or *block identifier* to every block or record. There is now no computable relationship between a symbolic address and its value. An address table will provide the physical or relative address for every block in use, and a look-up procedure is executed to obtain the block address whenever a block is requested.

The block identifiers can be integers which select the table entry, or they can use key-to-address transformation techniques as *hashing*. Such methods are commonly used for the linkage of records in the ring-file structures presented in Chap. 6-3.

The use of an address table provides a flexible assignment of blocks to storage. Blocks or records can be moved, and the address table changed appropriately, so that references to the data which use the symbolic identifier remain valid. The address table requires memory and additional accesses to storage when it gets larger than its memory allocation.

USE OF POINTERS   We described three techniques suitable to refer to blocks or records of files. We will use the term *pointer* for any value used to reference a block or record. Any one of the three pointer types described above, (1) the physical hardware address, (2) the relative block or record address, or (3) the symbolic block or record identifier, is adequate to identify a block or a record uniquely. Whenever a specific record is wanted, a pointer is provided to the file programs which fetch the data from storage. The alternative is to retrieve data in physical sequence. Then a pointer may be provided as an additional output to identify the record which was retrieved. When data is stored, a pointer is also provided for subsequent retrieval.

Programs which are at a level closer to the hardware tend to use addresses more; higher-level software will use symbolic references more. A single level of software should, for consistency, use only one pointer type throughout. In the illustrations we show mainly relative addresses.

Table 3-4   Relative block addressing.

Equipment in the domain of the file system

Number	Type	Cylinders per unit	Tracks per cylinder	Blocks per track	*Total*
2	Head per track disks	1	128	16	4 096
2.5	Permanent disks	400	20	8	160 000
1	Disk drive with choice of 3 packs	200	20	4	48 000
					212 096

Relative Block Address ($RBA = 0$ to $212\,095$) allocated to the devices as follows:

Allocated *RBA* Range		Device	Hardware address computation
RBAbeg	*RBAend*	type no.	
0 to	2 047	Head per track disk 1	track=$\lfloor RBA/16 \rfloor$, block=$RBA \bmod 16$
2 048 to	4 095	Head per track disk 2	track=$\lfloor (RBA - RBAbeg)/16 \rfloor$, block=$(RBA - RBAbeg) \bmod 16$
4 096 to	68 095	Disk P1	cylinder=$\lfloor (RBA - RBAbeg)/(20 \cdot 8) \rfloor$, track=$\lfloor ((RBA - RBAbeg) \bmod (20 \cdot 8))/8) \rfloor$, block=$(RBA - RBAbeg) \bmod 8$
68 096 to	132 095	Disk P2	etc.
132 096 to	164 095	Disk P3	
164 096 to	180 095	Disk D, pack A	cylinder=$\lfloor (RBA - RBAbeg)/(20 \cdot 4) \rfloor$, track=$\lfloor ((RBA - RBAbeg) \bmod (20 \cdot 4))/4 \rfloor$, block=$(RBA - RBAbeg) \bmod 4$
180 096 to	196 095	Disk D, pack B	etc.
196 096 to	212 095	Disk D, pack C	etc.

To refer from one record to another record, a field of the referencing record will be used to hold a pointer. The field size for a pointer, P, has to be large enough to hold a value adequate to address all possible records or blocks; in the example of Table 3-4 this requires six digits. A pointer field which is empty is denoted by Λ.

When pointers associated with addressing techniques are used within a file to represent cross references, the resulting structure becomes complex and has to be managed with care. If blocks or records are not moved freely, relative addresses allow efficient use of pointer fields and accessing of data without requiring the look-up of a symbolic identifier. We can consider that the files have been bound with differing intensity or strength, depending on which pointer type is used.

3-3-4 Buffers

The area into which a block from the file is read is termed a *buffer*. The management of buffers has the objective of maximizing the performance or the utilization of the secondary storage systems, while at the same time keeping the demand on CPU resources tolerably low. The use of two or more buffers for a file allows the transfer of data to be overlapped with the processing of data.

BUFFER REQUIREMENTS   Buffers can occupy a large fraction of the memory resources of a system. Let us look at a simple medium-sized computer system where 30 users on terminals can manipulate files. A typical data-processing operation may involve three files. For each file one may use one or two buffers. Then 90 or 180 blocks will be occupying memory buffers. If each block has a length of 1000 characters, 180 000 characters of the memory are used for buffers, while the total memory size may be 250K to 1M characters. Even in systems where memory is backed up by paging storage on disk or drums, those pages which are involved in data transfer of files have to be kept resident in memory. The demand made by a file system on memory for buffers is hence an important part of the resource usage of a file system. The high cost of memory relative to disk storage, as shown in Table 3-1, makes good buffer management very important.

BUFFER MANAGEMENT   To optimize the use of memory assigned to buffers, a buffer-scheduling algorithm allocates buffer spaces to users as needed. As shown in Fig. 3-14, blocks requested more than once will use the same buffer. Any memory not currently in use by other processes may be made available for the buffer manager; but when the requests exceed the available space, the buffer-scheduling process may have to delay a user process or deallocate buffer space of a lower priority process. Deallocation may also be done on the basis of low usage.

If buffer management is to be performed in a paged multiprogramming environment for the entire system, a separate buffer-managing program can be omitted. The paging program will have to take account of the need to keep active buffers resident. In either case, separate management or paged management, it will be useful to match the sizes and boundaries of the buffers, used by the file system, and the pages, used by the operating system, to minimize fragmentation of memory.

```
Q: Check if the block is already in memory using a table look-up.
   If yes, then give the process a memory pointer to the
             buffer which contains the block.
   If no,  then allocate a buffer,
             initiate reading of the block into the buffer, and delay
             the process by putting it into an operating system queue.
             The process is restarted at a suitable time,
             beginning at point Q.
```

Figure 3-14   Block request processing by a buffer management program.

If only one record out of a block is needed, the remainder of the buffer space could be immediately released for other uses. Frequently it is beneficial to keep the contents of the entire block available. This will allow updating of the record and subsequent rewriting of the block with the surrounding records. If the remainder of the block has not been kept available, the block has to be read again before rewriting can take place. Also, if the process at the next request wishes to read a successor record, retention of the block can avoid the rereading from file which improves file-system performance.

Throughout the following evaluations we keep at least two buffers available in memory, as well as directory and other critical information from other blocks which have been read previously. If the algorithms require more buffer space, the descriptions will state this fact explicitly. Two buffers, when used correctly, provide high performance in a file system when reading sequentially.

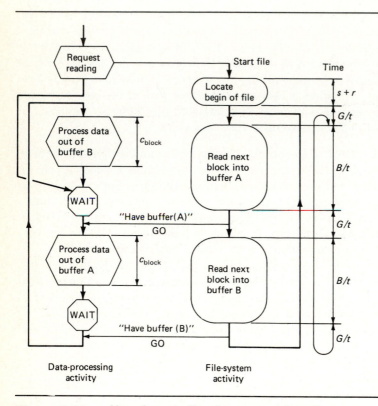

Figure 3-15   Use of two buffers for sequential reading.

DOUBLE BUFFERING   The availability of two buffers permits reading into one buffer while processing the previous buffer contents. This is a prerequisite for the use of the bulk transfer rate, t', for sequential reading; Fig. 3-15 illustrates the algorithm in detail. It is clear that the computational time required for processing one buffer must be less than the time used by the disk units to fill the other one. This algorithm is hence valid as long as the computational time required to process the records of one block, $c_{block} = c \times Bfr$, is relatively small in comparision with the block transfer time.

$$c\,Bfr < btt \qquad \text{or} \qquad c\,Bfr < \frac{B+G}{t} \qquad \text{or} \qquad c < \frac{R+W}{t} \qquad \text{3-22}$$

The gaps between the blocks provide some leeway (G/t), but it should be realized that the sending of the process wake-up message and buffer switching also requires time. This time is the *overhead* caused by buffering. Therefore, we prefer the safer condition, $c\,Bfr < btt$.

The areas indicated as "WAIT" are the periods, $btt - c\,Bfr$, that the CPU is idle relative to this computation. Operating systems which provide multiprogramming will attempt to allocate this time to other processes. To terminate the entire process, a file system will have the capability to pass the message "No more blocks on the file." to the transaction requesting sequential data.

If the condition of continuous sequential processing is violated, the previous buffer is not free to be refilled and we will lose one revolution or $2r$ prior to reading the next block. hence This loss is very significant, and will affect an application greatly if it happens regularly. With two buffers, and $r > c_{block} > btt$, this loss is incurred for every two buffers, and the effective bulk transfer rate is reduced to

$$t' = \frac{2B}{2r + 2btt} = \frac{B}{r + btt} \qquad \text{if} \qquad r > c\,Bfr > btt \qquad \text{3-23}$$

In most cases this causes a reduction of processing speed by several factors.

If $c_{block} > r$, it becomes reasonable to assume a random delay based on search and latency with an average value $c + r$ for every block, so that

$$t' = \frac{B}{c + r} \qquad \text{if} \qquad c\,Bfr > r \qquad \text{3-24}$$

The use of more buffers to hold more blocks in memory will, within the limits imposed by the computation time, c, allow for short time bulk-transfer rates higher than shown in Eq. 3-24. Eventually all buffers will be filled and file reading will have to stop. As long as sufficient buffers are available, the rate of sequential reading or writing is then constrained by two factors, computation and device speed (see Eq. 3-14),

$$t' = \min\left(\frac{R}{c}, \; t\,\frac{R}{R+W}\right) \qquad \langle \text{limit} \rangle \; \text{3-25}$$

The purpose of buffering is to achieve this minimum. The assumption of unlimited buffers is rarely true but having more than two buffers will even out the effects of computation times that vary, but that on the average are $c \approx (R+W)/t$ or smaller. Irregular computation can be caused in multiprogrammed systems by competing computations.

The requirement for two buffers becomes essential when blocks containing spanned records are to be processed, as discussed in Sec. 3-2-4. We assume that blocks involved in spanning are always sequentially allocated.

Double buffering is also beneficial when records are read serially that are not sequential. The reading time for a record will now be longer, $s + r + btt$, and the permissible computation time, c, will be greater. It is then easier to completely hide the cost of computation in the disk access and transfer time.

| Condition for continuous random processing |

$$c < s + r + btt \qquad\qquad\qquad 3\text{-}26$$

3-3-5 Updating Blocks

Updating data within a block requires more time than either the READ or WRITE operation alone, since at least one READ and one WRITE is required. To append a record to the file, it has to be inserted into an existing block containing predecessor records unless that last block happens to be full. This last block may still be read to find out that it is full, unless counters, kept in the file directory in memory, keep track of the status of the last block written. Change of an existing record will always require the block to be read so that all other records, and other fields of the changed record, are available.

After the reading of a block, the new record is inserted into the memory buffer containing the block and the block is rewritten. In most instances it is necessary to rewrite the block into its original position so that the file structure remains unchanged. If the insertion of the record in the memory buffer for the block is fast, it will be possible to rewrite the block during the next disk revolution. Such a REWRITE operation will take one revolution or approximately

$$T_{RW} = 2r \qquad \text{if} \qquad c_{update} \ll 2r \qquad\qquad 3\text{-}27$$

This assumption is made throughout the text, unless explicitly stated otherwise. This condition is not as restrictive as the one required to continuously read sequential data (Eq. 3-22), since $2r = nbt\, btt \gg btt$ for multiple blocks per track ($nbt > 1$), and $c_{update} < c\, Bfr$ for one record being changed at a time.

For devices other than disks the rewrite time has to be specifically analyzed. For magnetic-tape units with the capability to *backspace* a block, the value $2r$ can be replaced by two block transfer times and two delays to account for the gaps, or $T_{RW} \approx 2(B + G)/t \approx 2B/t'$. Some typical values of T_{RW} are given in Table 3-1.

▦▦▦ **CONDITIONS FOR REWRITING IN ONE REVOLUTION** A more rigorous limit on the allowable value of c for disk rewrites can be deduced by inspecting Fig. 3-16. The assumption that $T_{RW} = 2r$, for the rewriting of a single block i, is valid when the time required for computation and update c is such that the following relation will be true:

$$T_{RW} = 2r \quad \text{if} \quad c < 2r\,\frac{(nbt - 1)(B + G) + G}{nbt\,(B + G)} \quad \text{or if} \quad c < 2r\,\frac{nbt - 1}{nbt} \qquad 3\text{-}28$$

If there is more than one block per track ($nbt > 1$) and the system is designed so that the update has sufficient priority, this condition will generally be true.

If a REWRITE is not accomplished in time, a second revolution is lost, so that $T_{RW} = 4r$. When there is a fluctuation of the computational time, sometimes one, at other times two or more, revolutions will be lost. The use of the average value of c in the analysis will give erroneous results, since the relationship between c and T_{RW} is not linear. Chapter 12 will present methods to evaluate such cases. If there is other use of the disk unit, a new search is required when the computation is completed and

$$T_{RW} = c + T_F \qquad \text{if} \qquad c \gg 2r \qquad\qquad 3\text{-}29$$

where T_F is the time needed to fetch a record without any benefit of prior conditions.

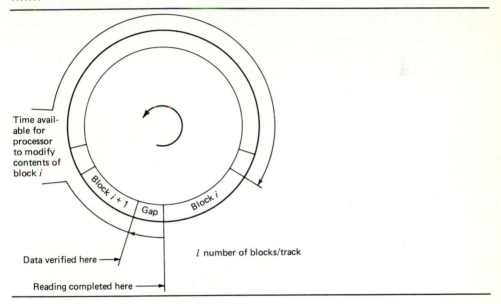

Figure 3-16   Rewrite-time considerations.

3-4   SUMMARY OF FILE HARDWARE

We have, in the preceding sections, taken a variety of hardware types and a number of basic, low-level, file-software implementation choices and distilled their effect into a small number of parameters: seek times, s; rotational latency, r; and transfer rates, t and t'. We use these parameters in the next chapters to produce measures of file-system performance. In Chap. 10 advanced concepts in hardware architecture will be surveyed, and in Chap. 14 we consider the effect of parallel operations of devices on these parameters.

3-4-1 Summary of Hardware Parameters

We summarize these parameters now in the context for which they were derived, namely, the evaluation of the performance of files and databases which use the prevalent disk devices. We will then discuss the applicability of these parameters for alternate storage devices.

Table 3-5   Primary performance parameters for disks.

Parameter	Unit	Code	Function	Condition
Seek time	ms	s	Mechanical delay	Device requires positioning
Latency	ms	r	Rotational delay	Block access or 1/2 reaccess
Transfer rate	char./ms	t	Block transfer	Hardware speed
Bulk transfer rate	char./ms	t'	Sequential transfer	Requires buffering
Block size	char.	B	Fixed transfer unit	Hardware or system specified
Blocking factor		Bfr	Records per block	Blocking method and fit

Estimation of the bulk transfer rate, t', requires determination of the waste, W, due to blocking and gaps, G, and consideration of a minimal seek, s_1, or a latency loss, $2r$, whenever a cylinder break occurs. Bulk transfer implies continuous operation which requires buffering and assuring that $c\,Bfr < btt$.

These and other assumptions made require periodic verification during the design of a database system and evaluation of its performance. The sections where the parameters are derived may have to be reread to assure that the formulas remain applicable in specific situations. We do not include a table of formulas here, since that could encourage their erroneous application. The index of the book can be used to locate the page where the derivation of the parameter begins.

From these primary parameters we derive some useful secondary parameters. The time to transfer a block having B characters, after positioning and latency delays, is $btt = B/t$ ms. The random-access time to a block is then $s + r + btt$, but a block being read sequentially is transferred in a time B/t' ms. A shorthand notation for the time to reaccess a block, typically done in order to rewrite it with changed data, is $T_{RW} = 2r$.

It is clear that this simple parameterization leaves some holes uncovered in the system-design process. In the remainder of this chapter we will raise some warning signs, so that we can avoid distracting the reader from the principal subjects in the chapters ahead. Whenever the simple hardware model used previously does not hold, a system-design process has to reevaluate the results obtained in this and the following chapters. The general methodology employed, however, should remain valid.

3-4-2 Differences among Storage Devices

The relative importance of the hardware parameters differs among the various types of hardware. We emphasize disk-drive units in the next chapters, without ruling out other devices. This means that we stress the effect of the seek time. Files kept on tapes are mainly for periodic processing, so that most access is sequential. They are used also as backup and logging devices.

DISK VERSUS DRUM   Drums and head-per-track disks, as well as most semi-conductor memories, do not require a seek. When the seek time, s, is zero, the effect of rotational latency and transfer rate becomes more important than the discussions imply. All the formulas developed will still hold when $s = 0$. The benefits of double buffering is relatively greater, since it applies to the latency.

DISK VERSUS TAPE   The methods discussed also apply to the use of tape for files. The block size, B, for tape is specified by the system used, and can be used also where the track size is required. Most tape units can read tapes in both the forward and reverse direction and this provides the effective random seek time. Writing may only be possible in the forward direction. The expected random seek time for reading s can be estimated based on forward or backward searching through a third of the length of tape in use. Even when using the ability to read in either direction, this operation will take more than 1 min.

For writing, or if reverse reading is not possible, other values for the seek times will have to be determined, depending on the method used to find a record. A simple approach is to always rewind the tape and then search forward. Better strategies can be used if the current position of the tape is remembered and used. This permits tape to be spaced forward or backward prior to forward search to achieve minimal seek delays.

The latency, r, is due to the time taken to accelerate the tape to full speed. The gap, G, provides the space for getting up to speed and slowing down. The extremely high value of the expected random seek times effectively removes tape as a candidate for the file organizations presented in Chaps. 5 and 6.

Some operations can be faster on tape than on disk. To find a predecessor block on a disk unit takes most of a revolution. On a tape unit with reverse reading such a block can be read immediately in reverse mode. Even without reverse reading it is possible on tape to backspace over the block and then read or write it forward. This assumption was made for the rewrite time in Sec. 3-3-5.

We can incorporate the effect of rewrites for tape to the formulas of Chaps. 4 to 9 by setting the value of the latency, r, to the block transfer time for tape. Similarly, the single cylinder seek, s_1, can be kept as $\approx 2r$. These simplifications introduce errors in the value of s for the seek times, but the effect is negligible because of the long seek times for tape under random-access conditions.

More complex file architectures, as introduced in Chap. 10, require further analysis. The principles underlying the parameter derivations in this chapter can be applied also in those cases. On unusual devices it will be wise to run some tests, comparing measurements with analysis results. Avoiding analyses and only relying on measurements does not help in understanding, and can easily fail to reveal what happens in extreme or boundary conditions.

3-4-3 Directions

New approaches to data storage will continue to be developed. Many of these will be driven by innovation in hardware, and will not have been included in these discussions. The ongoing reduction in the cost of primary memory will permit some applications to avoid secondary storage entirely, or to use secondary storage only for backup purposes, but larger and growing collections of data will continue to strain current and future systems.

Since few truly novel systems have yet attained operational status, little experience is available to judge system-design alternatives. Alternate system organization strategies are often tried by industry while academic institutions provide analysis and evaluation. A detailed analytic evaluation of new and complex systems is often beyond the current state of the art, although many of the engineering-level techniques for performance analysis presented here, combined with simulation and fundamental experiments, can direct further work and avoid expenditure of effort in fruitless directions.

BACKGROUND AND REFERENCES

Storage technology had its beginnings in card and paper-tape filing systems. The original Hollerith card was dimensioned on the basis of the dollar bill in 1890, as documented by Billings[1892]. The dollar and its value have shrunk since then, but storage costs have decreased even faster. Half-inch digital tapes were first used in 1953. Later in the fifties, UNIVAC computers employed coated steel tapes and strong operating personnel. The recording density has increased by a factor of 100 since that time.

The first disk units were used in 1956 on RAMAC (Random Access Memory Accounting Computers), machines which required users to insert wires to specify the logic of their programs. Two read-write heads on one access arm were moved up or down, and inserted between a stack of 20 fixed disks. Seek times were often many seconds. Removable diskpacks appeared in 1962, and in 1973 Winchester diskpacks with integral head assemblies became available. The capacity increase from RAMAC disks with 5M bytes to 1 200M bytes for 3380-type units exceeds the advances seen in tape technology.

Recording technology is described in White[80]. Bell[83] presents current issues in magnetic and optical recording. Developments in magnetic technology are covered in the IEEE *Transactions on Magnetics*; Pugh[71] provides an early overview of storage devices and their use, and Michaels[75] describes a bubble mass memory. Bobeck[75] tells all about bubbles; Doty[80] assesses them for databases. The *Bell System Technical Journal* has many original papers in this area beginning with Thiele[69].

General textbooks for computer hardware and its architecture are Mano[82] and Hill[73], Meyers[81] presents novel storage architectures. More than 30 different types of disk units are now on the market. Surveys of available devices appear regularly in the trade literature and are also obtainable from companies specializing in market surveys. A general reference model was proposed by Miller[85]. Specific information regarding computer hardware is best obtained from manufacturers; frequently their promotional literature omits some of the parameters needed for a proper performance evaluation. A regular feature of computer publications is a projection of future hardware availability and costs; an example is Chi[82]. Prices of computing equipment can be obtained from the price schedules prepared for the General Services Administration (GSA[57,⋯]). Sharpe[69] provides an analysis of storage-device economics. Often, obsolete equipment is used beyond its economic lifetime; GAO[80] cites examples.

An overview of storage technology (semiconductor, tape, disk, bubble, optical devices, automated libraries) is found in Hoagland[84] and projected in Hoagland[85]. Instructive descriptions of hardware-design considerations appear regularly in the IBM *Journal for Research and Development*; see, for instance, Mulvany[74] on the design of a diskpack system with an integral access mechanism. Design decisions leading to the IBM 3330 sector-addressing scheme are considered in Brown[72]. Floppy disk performance is analyzed in Pechura[83] and Dunnigan[84] reviews the small Winchester disks used in personal computers. Smith[85] provides an analysis and measurements of the effectiveness of disk caches as available with csc ibm-3380 disks.

Papers describing new systems and technology appear regularly in the proceedings of the AFIPS conferences and IEEE COMPUTER; Johnson[75] describes the automatic-tape library which provides backup to disks, and Michael[80] and Savage[85] give general specifications. Devices for archival storage are presented by Terdiman[70] and Gentile[71] describes tape files based on video techniques.

Kuehler[66] presents the IBM photodigital mass storage unit. Economical optical discs are announced in Fujitani[84] and a multiplatter optical disc unit, developed for NASA, is described by Ammon[85], while Langworthy[86] describes optical technology as available from DEC. IEEE Symposia on Mass Storage Systems report on new developments, see for instance Bell[84]. An issue of IEEE COMPUTER is devoted to optical storage; In it Copeland[82] argues that its availability will change many habits of data storage. Access software will have to undergo changes, as described by Rathmann[84], Vitter[85], and Copeland[86].

Programming for OS-360 files is taught by Chapin[68]. The relatively low-level programming and performance analysis methods presented have seen little formal publication; some are documented in IBM GC20-1649. Mass storage software is considered by OLear[82].

Most performance issues have been analyzed piecemeal. Knuth[73S] reviews general aspects of disk-performance analysis. Wong[80] minimizes access movement and Gaynor[74] calculates seek times. Anzelmo[71] and Inglis[73] discuss record blocking, while Leung[82] presents the pros and cons of fixed-length records. March[83] considers record fragmentation and placement, and Hakola[80] looks at waste.

The low rate of interference seen in multiprogramming is documented by Rodriguez-Rosell[76]. Effelsberg[84] analyzes buffering and Sacco[82] and Teng[84] consider buffer usage and management. Metrics for buffer performance are considered by Hagman[86].

Salasin[73] evaluates record fetch costs; Waters[72,75] discusses file placement to optimize access. Baber[63] evaluates record access on tape and Ghosh[76] concentrates on optimal sequential placement. Measurement and tuning of systems is covered by Ferrari[83]. Locality of transaction accesses has been reviewed by Kearns[83].

Many techniques used to manage storage are part of programming lore, noted at best as a paragraph in some system description. Often they are specific to certain hardware combinations. On large machines users have little control of the storage system, but on smaller personal or network computers there are many opportunities to improve storage-system performance.

EXERCISES

1   Derive the result stated in Sec. 3-1-2 for the average distance to be traveled when accessing tape randomly (one-third of the length of tape is used).

2   Why is the available surface area a concern when building a magnetic storage device?

3   What is the advantage of many reading heads for a storage device?

4   Read a manufacturer's description of a disk file or other storage device not now included and determine the parameters for Table 3-1.

5   What is the seek time for tape using the simple approach of Sec. 3-4-1? Assume that rewinding over b blocks requires $btt(5 + b/10)$.

6   Design a better method to seek tape blocks when a backspace operation, but no read backward operation, is available. Backspacing over a block takes as long as reading a block btt.

7   Compute the bulk transfer rate for a DEC RM-05 transferring blocks of 300 chars.

8   Determine the net transfer rate seen by the user for the RM-05 if for each block 1.0 ms of computation is required and three buffers are available.

9   Solve the same problem (by simulation?) if the computation time is evenly distributed between 0 and 3 ms.

10   Estimate the performance for someone wanting to convert a compact audio disc player for databases on a microcomputer. The disc revolves at 500 rpm. One disc can contain 60 min worth of music. Transfer rate to the microcomputer CPU is limited by the CPU at 100 chars/ms. The reading head travels at linear rate over the surface and takes 3 s between extremes. The directories of the disc have entries for up to 99 pieces of music (files). Each disc player unit costs $400 and it costs about the same to interface one to the microcomputer.

Estimate all the parameters as a column of Table 3-1. Write down all assumptions made.

11   Your computation takes $c_{block} = 7$ ms per block while the file is being read sequentially and double-buffered. The values of btt and r are respectively 10 and 20 ms. A new computing application on the system runs with high priority and uses 50% of the CPU. How much is your program slowed down?

12[P]   Consider your initial application, as defined in Exercise 1 of Chap. 1. Select some hardware which seems suitable, as small or large disks, tapes, or optical storage of some type. Justify your choice informally in terms of requirements for capacity, access speed, and cost.

Basic Files

All our knowledge may be said to rest upon observed facts.

Charles Sanders Peirce
from "Abduction and Induction" in Justus Buchler: "Philosophical Writings of Peirce"

4-0 INTRODUCTION

The primary features needed in systems that store large amounts of data are fast access for retrieval, convenient update, and economy of storage. Important secondary criteria are the capability to represent real world information structures, reliability, protection of privacy, and the maintenance of integrity. All these criteria tend to conflict with each other. The choice of the file organization method determines the relative suitability of a system according to all these criteria. We will initially evaluate files according to the basic criteria. A good match of the capabilities provided by the file system to priorities assigned to the criteria, as determined by the objectives for the database, is vital to the success of the resulting system.

The number of possible alternatives for the organization of files is nearly unlimited. To make the selection process manageable, we will describe and evaluate in Chaps. 4 to 6 six fundamental file-design alternatives. Most structures used in practice either fall into one of these categories or can be reduced to combinations of these methods. These fundamental types are closely related to systems in actual use. The collection of these six does not represent a mathematically minimal set of independent file organization methods. The selected methods are also reasonable in terms of the secondary criteria, i.e., they are fairly reliable and easy to analyze and implement.

The six fundamental types of files are covered in the chapters as follows:

Chapter 4: Two basic types, that is, files without ancillary access structures:

     4-2 The pile   4-4 The sequential file

Chapter 5: Two types using indexes to aid access

     5-1 The indexed-sequential file 5-3 The multiply indexed file

Chapter 6: Two further types using computer-specific methods

     6-1 The direct file   6-3 The multiring file.

The chapters follow a consistent organization: After a general introduction, one section describes the organization and use of the first method and the next section evaluates its performance. Then a second method and its use is described, followed by a section evaluating its performance. A final section in each chapter reviews the concepts encountered. Chapter begins with a section on general performance parameters.

The design of databases requires analysis for the prediction of performance. After each description a performance evaluation is given. The formulas developed use engineering-style approximations: They concentrate on first-order effects. The formulas are best viewed as concise descriptions of the behavior of the files under normal conditions. The notion used in the formulas is consistent throughout the text; the inside covers or Appendix B can be used to find the significance of the abbreviations employed.

▦ THE METHOD OF ANALYSIS

For the performance analyses a variety of approaches will be used. The general approach is to consider the required hardware functions step by step, consider the values of the computing times, c; any seeks, s; rotational latencies, r; and the transfer rates, t or t', applied to the blocks. Often functions must be executed repetitively. The sum of the values, T, provides the estimate for the cost in terms of time required for a file operation.

When alternative functions are required within an operation, typically dependent on the locality of the data, we have to resort to case analysis. For each choice the probability of using one function on the other is estimated. The expected value is found by taking the sum of the probabilities times the cost of each of the k cases, i.e., $T_e = \sum p_i T_i \mid i = 1 \ldots k$.

To simplify the analysis some assumptions are made. We assume often typical usage ratios of reading versus writing, balanced speed ratios of system components, and commonly seen user behavior. Because of variance in these factors the results will be of typical engineering accuracy, say $\pm 20\%$. This precision is more than adequate for predicting software performance; today, performance is frequently only guessed at and results often differ by orders of magnitude from the expected value. As always, any assumptions should be noted during a design process and later verified, so that unpleasant surprises are avoided.

The consistency of the formulas permits the comparison of expected performance for the fundamental file organizations presented here. A final comparative rating of performance characteristics for the six types of files is given in the introduction to Chap. 7.   ▦

4-1   GENERAL CONCEPTS OF FILE ORGANIZATION

In this section we introduce general concepts of file organizations and their performance. These concepts will apply throughout, but will be specifically stressed in Chaps. 4 to 6.

A file will have some directory information associated with it, but the bulk of the file contains data records. The analyses consider only the data portion of the files. The data portion will follow certain design rules, as defined by the file organization chosen. The previous definition of a file can now be expanded to state

> A file consists of similar records and has a consistent organization.

4-1-1 File Directories

Associated with a file is a directory. The directory contains information describing the owner, the position, and the format of the records comprising the file. Different types of file organization put different requirements on the contents of the file directory. Much of the information kept in the directory is associated with storage allocation and is managed by the operating system.

The directory information also is kept in a file, since it must be persistent as well. The owner of this file is the operating system itself, although it may permit read-access by others, for instance by the file management programs. If multiple computers are used, the directory may be partially replicated in all computers so that the right computer can be selected if a particular file is needed.

Table 4-1   Elements of a file directory.

Directory field	Example
File name	payroll
Owner	Joe Paymaster
Access group	Payroll_dep
Create-date	25DEC85
Device-type	diskdrive
Device-name	disk5
Begin-point	T12B3.000
Organization	ISAM
Max.size	60
Size allocated	40
Size used	35.3
End-of-file pointer	T23B2.234
Last-used date	1JAN86
. . .	. . .

CONTENT OF THE DIRECTORY   We show directory information, as typically kept for each file, in Table 4-1. The names of the owners and authorized users for the file are coded to match the access authorization mechanism for the computer system. More on users and their access rights is presented in Chap. 15-2. The allocation information specifies where and how much storage is allocated to a file. The precise content and organization of a file directory varies greatly among operating systems. Some of the information may be kept in a header record associated with the file rather than in the directory itself. The important elements for access to a file are the name, the begin point, its size or end point, and its organization or structure.

The operating system mainly provides a space with a name attached. Within this named space individual pages or blocks can be addressed, read, and stored. Most operating systems permit files to grow, so that the size can vary over time. Methods used by the operating system to keep track of the storage allocated to a file are presented in Chap. 10-4.

ACCESSING THE DIRECTORY   A practical procedure to deal with directory records is to read these records once, when a computation begins using the file, and retain the information in memory for further reference. Acquisition of directory information is performed during *opening* of a file. When *closing* the file, the file directory will be updated if changes in the file have occurred that should be reflected in the directory. System "crashes" can damage files by failing to update directory records. Data recently stored may then not be accessible. Directory records are not further discussed as part of the subsequent file analyses.

4-1-2 File Description and Use

For each fundamental file organization we provide a description and the type of application it is suitable for. In these descriptions definitions will be encountered that are relevant for the subsequent file organization methods.

Some general criteria for organizing data are
1 Little redundancy
2 Rapid access
3 Ease of update
4 Simple maintenance
5 High reliability

These criteria may conflict, and different file organizations will have a different balance of satisfying these criteria. Reliability is the most complex of these issues and is treated separately in Chap. 15-1.

For economy of storage, we will wish to store data with a minimum of *redundancy*. Redundancy exists when data fields are duplicated in multiple records. Redundancy of data elements also increases the effort required when values of data elements have to be changed, since we expect all copies of a data element to present a consistent description of the world. Redundancy can be useful to provide rapid access to data; it is in fact the primary tool used to increase performance. For instance, in Chap. 5 we will use indexes, which repeat terms used in the file, to rapidly access records containing these terms, just as the index to this book is meant to be used.

Figure 4-1 shows a dense file, a sparse file, and a redundant file. Each of these files presents information in a form useful for a particular purpose.

	Student No.	Class	Credits	Incom- pletes	Current work	Age	Grade type
1	721	Soph	43	5	12	20	PF
2	843	Soph	51	0	15	21	Reg
3	1019	Fresh	25	2	12	19	Reg
4	1021	Fresh	26	0	12	19	Reg
5	1027	Fresh	28	0	13	18	Reg
6	1028	Fresh	24	3	12	19	PF
7	1029	Fresh	25	0	15	19	Reg
8	1031	Fresh	15	8	12	20	Aud
9	1033	Empl	23	0	14	19	PF
10	1034	Fresh	20	3	10	19	Reg

(a) A dense file: Database course attendees

	Student No.	CS101	Courses taken CS102	Bus3	EE5	IE101	Exp. years
1	721	F72	F73		W73		
2	843	F72	W73				
3	1019		S72	S73			1
4	1021		S72			F73	
5	1027	F73		S73			
6	1028				W73		1
7	1029	F73	W73				
8	1031	F73					
9	1033						3
10	1034					F73	

(b) A sparse file: Database course attendees

	Pre- requisite	Student No.	When taken	Years exp.	Acc. credits	. . .	Grade type
1	CS102	721	F73		43	. . .	PF
2	CS102	843	W73		51	. . .	Reg
3	CS102	1019	S72		25	. . .	Reg
4	CS102	1021	S72		26	. . .	Reg
5	CS102	1029	W73		25	. . .	Reg
6	Bus3	1019	S73		25^3	. . .	Reg
7	Bus3	1027	S73		28	. . .	Reg
8	EE5	721	W73		43^1	. . .	PF
9	EE5	1027	W73		28^7	. . .	Reg
10	IE103	1021	F72		26^4	. . .	Reg
11	IE103	1034	F73		20	. . .	Reg
12	Exp.	1019		3	25^3	. . .	Reg
13	Exp.	1028		1	24	. . .	PF
14	Exp.	1033		1	23	. . .	PF
15	none	1031			20	. . .	Aud

Note: the superscripts indicate records where this redundant data element already appeared.

(c) A redundant file: Database course attendees

Figure 4-1   A dense, a sparse, and a redundant file.

4-1-3 File Performance Parameters

Quantitative measures are necessary to evaluate file-system performance. The four types of computations introduced in Chap. 2-1-1 were build, update, retrieve, and data reduction. The balance of these computations differs among applications. If we produce information, rather than operate an archive, the READ frequencies should exceed the number of updates of files and records by a considerable ratio, perhaps 10:1 or more. Hence we are often willing to use data organizations which provide fast retrieval, even when this makes building and update operations more complex.

We now define six basic file operations which are needed to implement these computations, and for each operation measures of performance will be provided. Storage requirements are measured in terms of bytes, while the cost of the file operations is measured in terms of time they require for execution. In Chap. 14-5 storage and time requirements are reconciled by using financial measures.

Seven measures will be provided for each of the six fundamental file organization methods. These are:

R : The amount of storage required for a record
T_F : The time needed to fetch an arbitrary record from the file
T_N : The time needed to get the next record within the file
T_I : The time required to update the file by inserting a record
T_U : The time required to update the file by changing a record
T_X : The time needed for exhaustive reading of the entire file
T_X : The time needed for reorganization of the file

To simplify cross referencing, we use corresponding subsection numbers in this introduction and in the six sections which deal with performance evaluation.

The six operations on files are executed by combining seeks, reads, and writes of blocks, so that the measures to be derived are based on the hardware parameters obtained in the preceding chapter. The use of these parameters provides independence from the physical specifics of the hardware, so that the analysis of file methods can proceed without considering details of the possible hardware implementation.

Decisions to be made in the evaluation of file performance for specific cases are characterized by four questions:

1 Is a seek required, or are we positioned appropriately; i.e., is s to be used?
2 How is the record located; i.e., is the latency 0, r, or $2r$?
3 Are we transferring only data blocks, or are we spacing through a file; i.e., do we use t or t' for the transfer rate?
4 Are we measuring the net quantity of data or the space required; i.e., do we use R or $(R + W)$ as a measure?

For each file organization we have to consider the sum of all these operations.

Parameter 1: Record Size The record stores primarily the data, but may also be used to store descriptive and access information. The files shown in Fig. 4-1 are structured, and the descriptions of the data fields appear only once, in the heading of the files. When data to be stored is more diverse, trying to define all possible fields in the heading will cause many fields to be empty and will lead to large, sparsely filled records. Section 4-2 presents a self-describing organization for records, which is advantageous for heterogeneous data, while Sect. 4-5 will deal with structured files.

Parameter 2: Fetch a Record　To be able to use data from a file, a record containing the data has to be read into the memory of a processor. Fetching a record consists of two steps: locating the position of the record and then the actual reading. We use the term *fetch* when the retrieval of the record is *out of the blue*, that is, no operations to prepare for a simpler locate and read sequence have preceded this fetch. To fetch data efficiently, we have to locate the element to be read fast. A simple address computation, similar to the determination of the position of an array element in memory, seems most desirable but leads to inflexibility when the data is not tabular in nature or the entries in the file are sparse. In general, the records of a file cannot be directly located on the basis of a subscript value or record number.

The use of look-up files or indexes helps in fetching data when the position cannot be directly computed, but having such files increases redundancy. Any changes in the main files will require corresponding updates in any indexes. A look-up file, helpful in obtaining access to the previous files, is shown in Fig. 4-2.

Name	Student No.	Prerequisite entries (variable in number)			
Allmeyer, John	1031	15			
Bushman, Wilde	1028	13			
Conte, Mary	843	2			
Erickson, Sylvia	1034	11			
Gee, Otto	1021	4	10		
Heston, Charles	721	1	8		
Hotten, Donna	1029	5			
Jason, Pete	1027	7	9		
Makale, Verna	1019	3	6	12	
Punouth, Remington	1033	14			

Figure 4-2　　A look-up file.

Parameter 3: Get the Next Record　Isolated data rarely provides information. Information is mainly generated by relating one fact with another; this implies getting the next record according to some criterion. While `Fetch` can be characterized as an *associative* retrieval of a data element based on a key value, `Get-Next` can be characterized as retrieval using a *structural* dependency. A successor record can be obtained most rapidly when related data is kept together; that is, when the *locality* of these data is strong. Records having locality according to some key are considered to be *clustered*. The records in Fig. 4-1a are clustered by `Student No.`

There may be multiple relationships among data, but their representation is difficult. Only one sequential access sequence or *physical clustering* can be directly accomodated on the physical storage devices in which the data resides. To represent further relationships either redundant storage of data or pointers which link successive records can be employed. The reading or writing of records in an order according to any relationship is called *serial reading*. If one serial access path is simplified by physical ordering of the records, we can read the records following that relationship *sequentially*. Figure 4-1c shows the alternate use of redundancy to simplify grouping of records that identify the prerequisite courses.

Parameter 4: Insert a Record Most applications require regular insertion of new data records into their files to remain up to date. Writing into a file is more costly than reading the file. In addition to locating and reading the file, the changed block also has to be rewritten. Adding records is easiest if they can be appended to the end of a file, just extending the file. When a record has to be put in a specific place within the file to permit future clustered access, other records may have to be shifted or modified to accommodate the insertion.

When data is stored redundantly, multiple WRITE operations will have to be carried out to perform a complete file update operation. If the number of Credits of student 1019 has to be changed in the file shown in Fig. 4-1a, only one record is changed; but in the file of Fig. 4-1c three operations are required.

Each WRITE into a blocked file will require the reading of a block to merge the data from the surrounding records before rewriting the entire block.

⫴⫴ **Appending Records** Insertions to the end of the file, APPEND operations, are frequent. To make them more efficient they are handled differently from other insert operations in some systems. If the address of the last block of the file is known the performance of APPEND operations can be improved, since then the locate step is not needed. This address can be kept as a pointer in the directory.

Furthermore, a sequence of APPEND operations may be performed without successive READ and REWRITE operations, since a block needs to be written only when full or when a batch of appends is completed. New blocks, allocated to extend the file, do not have to be read. The relative frequency of encountering a block boundary, which determines the frequency of block writes remaining when appending, is $1/Bfr$. When a single transaction performs only one append, no benefits are derived from batching. Other considerations argue also against batching of appends.

When batching append operations an intervening failure of the computer system will cause multiple appends to be lost. If these APPEND operations are part of distinct transactions, batching of appends violates the integrity constraints of a transactions if the computer fails. The all-or-nothing consistency condition given for transactions hence requires a REWRITE of the block when the transaction is to be committed.

In the analyses that follow we ignore the difference of appends and general insertions and assume that a READ and a REWRITE of a block is done for every type of insert. For applications which append frequently separate evaluations which consider the benefits of not requiring to locate the record, and perhaps on batching as well, could be made.   ⫴⫴

Deleting Records Deleting records is the inverse of insertion. After locating the record, the space that it occupied should be freed for reuse. Maintenance of clustering may require again that other records be shifted.

Often deletion is not performed immediately, but instead the record to be deleted is marked with an indicator that this record is now invalid. The delete is now converted to an update. A marker may be set in a special field containing {valid, invalid}, or the old record space may be filled with NULL characters, or a message such as "* Deleted . . .*;" is placed in the record. We will refer to such a marker as a *tombstone*. We make sure that the tombstone will fit even within the smallest record permissible in the file, so that rewriting of the old record is easy.

We do not cover the performance of deletion operations explicitly, and treat record deletion either with insertion or with update of records, as appropriate.

Parameter 5: Update a Record All changes of data do not require insertion of a new record. When data within a stored record must be changed, the new, updated record is created using the remaining data from the previous record. The old data and the changes are merged to create a new record, the new record is inserted into the position of the old record within the block, and the block is rewritten into the file.

If the record has grown in size, it may not be possible to use the old position. The old record will then have to be deleted, perhaps with a tombstone, and a new record inserted in an alternate appropriate place. Records in the look-up file shown in Fig. 4-2 will grow in size if a prerequisite is added. For a variable spanned organization two blocks will have to be read, updated, and rewritten whenever the record spans blocks. Again, the frequency of that event is again $1/Bfr$.

Parameter 6: Read the Entire File Some application functions require the reading of the entire file. Here again we prefer a dense, nonredundant file to avoid excessive time and errors due to the multiple occurrence of the same data item. If this cannot be achieved, the process of exhaustive reading has to maintain additional information either within the file or in separate tables. There is, for instance, no simple way to use the file shown in Fig. 4-1c to count the number of students or to compute the average credits accumulated by them.

Parameter 7: Reorganize the File Finally, it may be necessary to clean up files periodically. Reorganization removes deleted and invalidated records, reclaims the space for new data, and restores clustering. Reorganization is especially important for file organizations which create tombstones for deletion and updates.

The frequency of this operation is not only dependent on the type of file organization used but varies greatly with the application. Reorganization is initiated when a file has had many records inserted and deleted. If records are mainly appended, reorganization is not needed as often. Reorganization has many similarities with the process of "garbage collection" encountered in some computer-language systems which provide dynamic storage allocation.

Summary of the Parameters We have now defined the operations to be considered when evaluating file performance. We will also use the term *retrieve* for both fetch and get-next, and use the term *access* to denote any reference to a file. The word *search* is used at times to describe the activity of locating a record prior to the actual read or write of a block.

4-1-4 File and Record Structure

Each of the six file organization methods in Chaps. 4 to 6 is described and analyzed in conjunction with one specific record organization. While the combination presented is common in practice, it should be realized that many other combinations are valid. Such alternative combinations will produce different formulas for the performance parameters. The derivations are sufficiently simple to allow readers to evaluate other alternatives on their own.

We now look at two basic file types: the pile and the sequential file. Neither type uses ancilliary structures as pointers or look-up tables. They do differ greatly in file and record organization.

4-2   THE PILE FILE

The initial method presented is a minimal method. This method, the *pile*, is rarely practical but forms a basis for evaluation of more structured methods. Data in a pile is collected in the order that it arrives. It is not analyzed, categorized, or forced to fit field definitions or field sizes. At best, the order of the records may be chronological. Records may be of variable length and need not have similar sets of data elements.

We are all familiar with piles on our desks. They are an easy-to-use form of storage; any information which arrives can be put onto a pile without any processing. They are quickly created, but costly to search.

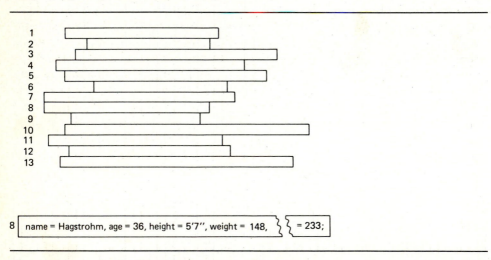

Figure 4-3   A pile file with a representative record.

4-2-1 Structure and Manipulation

Some restrictions, though, will have to be observed to allow for correctness of processing of data. The pile has to be such that we can extract information. A record must be relatable to some object or event in the world. A record should consist of related data elements, and each data element needs to have an identification of its meaning. This identification may be an explicit name, such as `height` in Fig. 4-3, or a code, or a position which indicates its *attribute* type as the records of Fig. 4-1. We use here *self-describing fields*, as shown in Fig. 4-4. If multiple identical domains exist in a record, the attribute type also specifies the relationship to the object or event described by the record: `height of doorway`, `height of tower`. We will use in pile files an explicit name for the attribute description, since this matches best the unstructured form of the file.

> `height = 95`

The value of the data element is `95` and the descriptive name is `height`.

Figure 4-4   Self-describing data element.

The set of two entries in Fig. 4-4 is referred to as an *attribute name-value pair*.

Just one such pair does not make a significant record. We need a number of such pairs to adequately define an object, and then, if we want to associate factual data regarding this object, we will want to attach to the record additional attribute pairs that contain further data.

`name=Hoover,type=Tower,locale=Serra␣Street␣(Stanford),height=95;`

Figure 4-5   Self-describing data record.

When information is to be retrieved we select records by specifying some attributes in a *search argument* and retrieve other attributes as the *goal data*. The attributes of a record to be matched to the search argument of the fetch request are the key attributes. The terms *key* and *goal* define two parts of the record for a query. Different requests may specify various combinations of attributes, so that we do not wish to preassign attributes to the role of key or goal data. The key identifies the record wanted in the file, and the goal is defined to be the remainder of the record.

Extent of Goal Data   If there are no attribute pairs left in our record beyond those required for the search, the only information retrievable is the fact that this object exists in our files. Finding a match is frequently an adequate goal. With the assumptions used in the example worked out in Fig. 4-7, the `height` of the tower still is available as a goal-data element.

▦▦▦ **Complex attributes**   An attribute value may in itself be divided into a number of attribute name-value pairs to permit a hierarchical structure within the record, as shown in Fig. 4-7. Such a *complex attribute* is difficult to manage for a file system. The handling of the contents of a complex attribute is typically the users' responsibility.

```
...,addr.=(place=Serra␣Street,town=Stanford␣U.,
            county=Santa␣Clara,state=California),...
```

Figure 4-6   Complex attribute.   ▦▦▦

Selectivity   The number of attributes required for a search is a function of the *selectivity* of the key attributes. Selectivity is the measure of how many records will be retrieved for a given value of an attribute. When we select a subset of the file according to the value of an attribute, we have partitioned the file into a potential goal set, and a set to be rejected. *Partitioning* can take place repeatedly using other attributes, until only the desired goal set is left.

The selectivity can be given as an absolute count or as a ratio. After the first partitioning, we can imagine that we have a file with a smaller number of records. It is important to isolate this subset of records in such a way that it will not be necessary to search all the original data for a match according to the second attribute specified. The second search should be measured in terms of a selectivity ratio, which is applied to the partition of records produced by the previous search.

Partition sizes are computable by computing the product of the file size, n, and the selectivity ratios. If multiple ratios are used we typically assume that the selectivity of the first search specification is independent of the second search specification. Successive application of all other search specifications narrows down the possibilities until the desired record, or set of records, is obtained. Examples of selectivities are given in Table 5-2.

Let us estimate the selectivity given the record of Fig. 4-5. The specification Tower applied to a file containing all buildings in this world, or at least all towers, would restrict our search to the 10^7 towers in this world (assumption: one tower per 300 people and $3 \cdot 10^9$ people in this world). The name Hoover may have a selectivity ratio of $2.5 \cdot 10^{-6}$ (fraction of Hoovers in the world, based on 40 entries in the San Francisco telephone book: $40/8 \times 10^5$, the fraction of the English-speaking population: $1/10$, and the assumption that half the towers are named after people), so that the second search attribute would yield 4 possible records. (Assumption: As many towers are named after Hoovers as after other family names.) A third specification (the street name) should be sufficient to identify a single specific tower, or establish the nonexistence of a tower satisfying the request.

Figure 4-7   Estimation of selectivity.

Counting the Attributes   Throughout the remainder of this book, we will use the symbol a to denote the total number of attribute types in the file under consideration, and the symbol a' to denote the average number of attributes occurring in a record. If the record in Fig. 4-5 is representative for the file, then a' for that file would be 4. We typically disregard subsidiary attributes as shown in Fig. 4-6 since they cannot be searched independently. We do not need to know the value of the total attribute count, a, of an entire file in the pile organization.

4-2-2 Use of Piles

Pile files are found where data is collected prior to processing, where data is not easy to organize, and in some research on file structures. They also provide a basis for performance comparison within this text.

Data banks that have been established for broad intelligence gathering sometimes have this form, since the potential usage of a record is difficult to assess. In
this type of application many attribute types which defy a priori compartmental-
ization may exist. Many manual data collections, such as medical records, also have
the form of a pile. In pile files, data analysis can become very costly because of the
time required for retrieval of a statistically adequate number of sample records.

Since much of the data collected in real-world situations is in the form of piles
we can consider this file organization as the base for other evaluations. If we consider
piles to be essentially free, we can estimate processing efforts needed to create more
efficient file organizations for retrieval by analysis of the transformation from a pile.

4-3 PERFORMANCE OF PILES

We now estimate the seven performance parameter values for a pile organization
as described in Sec. 4-2. We have already some intuition which parameters will be
small and which will be large.

4-3-1 Record Size in a Pile

File density in a pile is affected by two factors: negatively, by the need to store
the attribute names with the data, and positively, by the fact that nonexistent
data need not be considered at all. The effect is a relatively high density when the
material collected is heterogeneous or sparse, and a relatively low density when the
data is dense and the same attribute names occur redundantly in successive records.

We will denote the average length of the description of an attribute as A, and
the average length of the value portion as V. For Figs. 4-5 and 4-6 the values of
A are 5 and of V are 9 bytes. Since name and data are of variable length, two
separator characters (= and , or ; in the examples above) are stored to mark each
data element. We have an average of a' fields.

Using these definitions the expected average record length will be

$$R = a'(A + V + 2) \qquad \text{4-1}$$

Appropriate values for a', A, and V will have to be based on an adequately sized
sample. Techniques to reduce the values of A and V by encoding are discussed in
Chap. 13-3.

4-3-2 Fetch Record in a Pile

The time required to locate a record in a pile is long, since all the records may have
to be searched to locate a data item that has a single instance in the file. If it has
an equal probability of appearance anywhere in the file, we consider that at least
one, and maybe all (b) blocks will have to be read. Using the big-$\mathcal{O}$ notation we
can state that the T_F operation on a pile-file is $\mathcal{O}(b) = \mathcal{O}(n)$.

More precisely, we can compute the expected average time for a record fetch by taking the sum of all the times to reach and read any of the blocks, divided by the number of choices, or

$$\text{Average blocks read} = \sum_{i=1}^{b} \frac{i}{b} = \frac{1}{2}(1+b) \quad \approx \frac{1}{2}b \quad \text{if} \quad b \gg 1 \qquad \text{4-2}$$

The time to read this number of blocks sequentially is then, using the notion of bulk transfer developed with Eqs. 3-17 and 3-19,

$$T_F = \frac{1}{2} b \frac{B}{t'} \qquad \text{4-3}$$

Figure 4-8 illustrates the process. We now restate the sequential fetch time per record, using the fact that the file size can be expressed as either bB or nR:

$$T_F = \frac{1}{2} n \frac{R}{t'} \qquad \text{4-4}$$

The use of the bulk transfer rate, t', is appropriate here, since we read the file sequentially from its begin point, passing over gaps and cylinder boundaries, until we find the block containing the desired record.

Batching of Requests It may be effective to collect search requests into batches and avoid the high processing cost of a single fetch. A batch of many requests can be processed in one pass through the entire file. The expected length of search through the file will increase from the factor 1/2 in Eq. 4-4 to 2/3 or 3/4 for two or three requests. Eventually this factor approaches 1, so that we simply state for a batch of L fetch requests

$$T_F(L) = 2T_F \qquad \text{for} \qquad L \gg 1 \qquad\qquad \langle \text{batch} \rangle \text{ 4-5}$$

While this lowers the cost per item searched to $(2/L)\,T_F$, the time to respond to an individual request is now twice the original value of T_F. In addition, there is a delay due to the amount of time required to collect an adequate batch (L) of requests. Such batch operations are typically done on a daily cycle to make them profitable. In that case the search costs are reduced as indicated above, and the expected delay is one day for any request. If many requests are processed in one batch, an efficient processing algorithm for scanning the content of the records is required to ensure that the condition of Eq. 3-22 or $c < R/t$ still holds. Batching of requests applies also to other file organizations.

4-3-3 Get-Next Record of a Pile

Since no ordering of records is provided in a pile, the potential successor record may be anywhere in the file. Since the position is not known, the time required to find an arbitrary successor record is also

$$T_N = T_F \qquad \text{4-6}$$

We assume that information from the previous record is required to specify the search for the successor record. If the specification of required attributes for the successor record were known initially, the search for this record could be made during the one combined fetch using the method of batching requests described above.

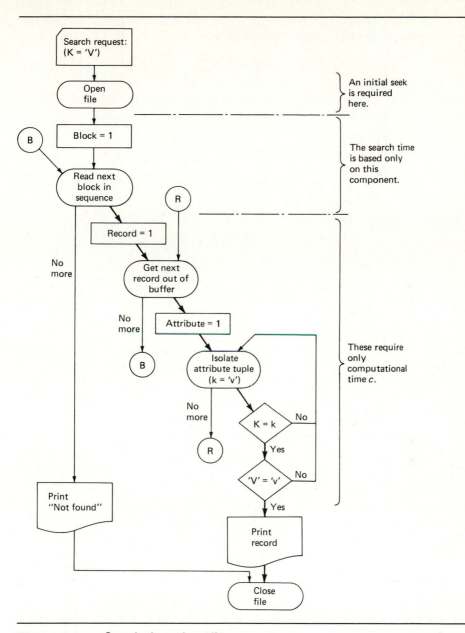

Figure 4-8   Search through a pile.

4-3-4 Insert into a Pile

An insertion of a new record into a pile file will be fast because of its lack of structure. We assume that the address of the end of the file is known, a new record is simply appended, and the end-of-file pointer is updated. To obtain dense packing of records, the last block is read into memory, the new record is appended, and the block is rewritten. The time required then will be

$$T_I = s + r + btt + T_{RW} \qquad\qquad 4\text{-}7$$

When disregarding costs incurred at block boundaries and possible benefits of batching of appends, as argued in Sec. 4-1-3(4), and using Eq. 3-27, we can simplify:

$$T_I = s + 3r + btt \qquad\qquad 4\text{-}8$$

We confirm, as guessed from personal experience, that a pile is very easy to update.

4-3-5 Update Record in a Pile

Updating a record consists of locating and invalidating the old record, and writing a new, probably larger, record at the end of the file, so that

$$T_U = T_F + T_{RW} + T_I \qquad\qquad 4\text{-}9$$

If only a deletion is to be made, the T_I term drops out. Deletion is actually effected by rewriting the old record space with a *tombstone*.

4-3-6 Read Entire Pile

Exhaustive processing of data in this file organization requires reading the file to the end. It is hence only twice as costly as a single fetch, at least if the order in which the records are read does not matter:

$$T_X = 2T_F = n\,\frac{R}{t'} \qquad\qquad \langle \text{sequential} \rangle\ 4\text{-}10$$

If, however, we wish to read this file serially according to some attribute, the repetitive use of n individual get-next operations would cost $T_X = n\,T_N = n\,T_F$.

This cost would hence be $\mathcal{O} = n^2$. We avoid this cost by sorting the records the file, according to the attribute of the search argument prior to processing. Sorting is illustrated in a special box in this section. Using the value for T_{sort}, as given in Eq. 4-12 we reduce the cost to $\mathcal{O} = n \log n$.

Records without a matching attribute may be deleted prior to the sort. The sorted file will provide sequentiality of the attribute values. The resulting sorted file is no longer a simple pile.

Read Entire Pile Serially Using a sort to put the file into serial order prior to processing leads to an exhaustive read time of

$$T_X = T_{sort}(n) + T_X(sequential) \qquad\qquad \langle \text{serial} \rangle\ 4\text{-}11$$

which will be considerably less than $n\,T_F$ for any nontrivial file.

Analysis of External Sorting The box on the next page describes an external merge-sort. The first phase of such a sort requires reading and writing of the entire file content, at a cost of $2T_X$. Since the files are processed sequentially $2T_X = 2b\,btt$ for b blocks of the source file. Parallel operations can reduce that cost, although then the cost of internal sorting must then be considered more closely.

Each merge pass also requires reading and writing of the entire file contents, at a cost $2T_X$. The selection and copy operations during the merge are simpler than internal sorting, and are easily overlapped with buffered input and output.

The number of passes required in the merge phase depends on the size of the initial sort blocks and the power m of the merge. For n records of size R we create $b_s = n/Bfr_s$ sort blocks. To merge b_s blocks requires $\lceil \log_m b_s \rceil$ passes.

An estimate of the total cost for a merge sort with $m = 2$ is hence

$$T_{sort}(n) = 2b\,btt + 2b\lceil \log_2 b_s \rceil btt = 2n \left[1 + \log_2 \left(\frac{n}{Bfr_s} \right) \right] \frac{R}{t'} \qquad 4\text{-}12$$

This estimate will be adequate for most cases. Since many systems have very specialized and efficient programs for sorting, it can be useful to determine the value of T_{sort} in a particular system from documentation or by experimentation.

More details can be found in Knuth[73S], which presents the algorithms and analyzes the performance of a number of external sorts. All have a performance which is $\mathcal{O} = n \log n$, and do not differ significantly from the simple two-way merge-sort described in the box on **sorting** on the following pages.

4-3-7 Reorganization of a Pile

If the pile file is updated with tombstones to mark deleted records, as described above, then periodically a removal of the invalidated records is desirable. The file will shrink, and all retrieval operations will be faster.

Reorganization is accomplished by copying the file, excluding records marked with tombstones, and reblocking the remaining records. If the number of records added during a period is o and the number flagged for deletion is d, the file will have grown from n to $n + o - d$, so that the time to copy the file will be

$$T_Y = (n + o)\frac{R}{t'} + (n + o - d)\frac{R}{t'} \qquad 4\text{-}13$$

Here $\qquad\qquad\qquad\qquad o = n_{insert} + v$

The number of records d to be removed during reorganization is

$$d = n_{delete} + v$$

where n_{insert} is the number of records inserted, $n_{isdelete}$ the number deleted from the pile, and v is the number of records that were updated by creating delete and append entries. The values of o and d are dependent on the file organization, so that this and later formulas using these parameters cannot be directly compared.

4-3-8 SORTING Arranging records in order is the most frequent and time-consuming activity in data processing. It has been estimated that 25% of all computer time is devoted to sorting. Although new approaches to data-processing reduce this fraction, sorting remains an important activity.

Many algorithms for sorting have been developed. When files do not fit into memory we require *external sorting*. Only the class of *merging algorithms* is effective for external sorting. In this box we present the principal algorithm used to reorder the records of large files.

Motivation There are several reasons for sorting data:

1 Presentation: when voluminous results are presented to the users, they should be presented in an easy-to-use form. For instance, a summary of company sales is best shown by product name to help checking if problems with a product have affected sales.

2 Merging of files: often information on files created at different times or at different sites has to be combined. If the files are sorted differently, then looking for related records requires scanning all of one file once for each record in the other file. With files of size n the cost is $\mathcal{O}(n^2)$. If the files are sorted the same way, then scanning the files forward together reduces the effort to $\mathcal{O}(n)$. Sorting is then profitable if it costs sufficiently less than $\mathcal{O}(n^2)$.

3 Creating an index: indexes permit quick retrieval to records, as shown in Chap. 5. An index, even for a large file, can be created rapidly from a sorted file.

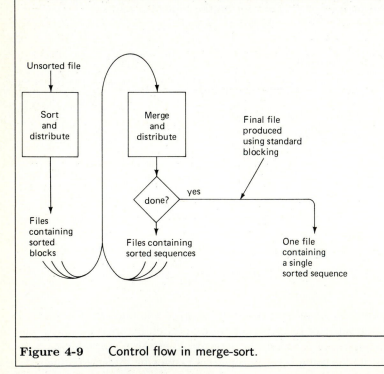

Figure 4-9   Control flow in merge-sort.

A Sorting Method We describe a typical external sorting method, the *merge-sort*. It sorts n records in $\mathcal{O}(n \log n)$ operations. It consists of two phases, sort and merge. The merge phase consists of multiple merge passes, as shown in Fig. 4-9.

The merge-sort operates on sets of records placed into large working buffers in memory, which we call sort buffers. The sort buffers will be written and read onto working files, each buffer will correspond to a *sort block* on file. Sort blocks will be much larger than input or output file blocks. As seen below, the performance of a merge-sort improves when the sort blocks are large.

The constraint on the size of sort blocks B_s is the available real memory. A two-way merge-sort algorithm requires four such blocks, so that the sort blocks may be made as large as a quarter of available memory (as shown in Fig. 4-10), once all systems software, sorting programs, and other buffers have been accounted for.

The Sort Phase We begin by reading in data records from file blocks of the source file, filling a sort-block buffer. A buffer will contain $Bfr_s = B_s/R$ records. Once a buffer has been filled with records, it is sorted in memory, using any reasonable internal sort algorithm which is *stable*. (A stable algorithm keeps records with equal keys in the same order that there were submitted [Knuth73s].)

If we have a fast internal sort algorithm, the time to sort the record can be overlapped with the time needed to fill a second sort buffer from the source file. This requirement is not easily met, but since the sort phase of the merge-sort is not the dominant cost we will assume this condition to be true.

When the first sort block has been sorted, and the second sort block has been filled, we start three processes in parallel:

1 The first sort buffer is written onto merge file i, initially $i = 1$.
2 The second sort buffer is internally sorted. An extra buffer is available if needed.
3 A third sort buffer is filled from the source file.

The processing of the source records is repeated for $i = 2, \ldots, i = m$, where m is the number of merge files to be created. Then i is reset to 1, and the processing continues until the source file is empty and each of the m merge files contain about n/m records. More precisely the merge files will contain up to $\lceil n/m/Bfr_s \rceil$ sort blocks; files labeled $i > 1$ may contain only $\lfloor n/m/Bfr_s \rfloor$ sort blocks.

The number of merge files m may vary from 2 to about 10. Having many merge files permits multiple files to be read or written in parallel. The amount of parallelism available depends on the hardware architecture, as detailed in Chap. 14-3-2. Having more merge files increases the number of sort buffers needed in memory, reducing their size and reducing the effectiveness of the initial sort phase. Since even a two-way merge ($m = 2$) can keep 4 files operating in parallel, we will orient the discussion on $m = 2$, and also assume we have 4 sort-blocks in memory. This means that the merge file address parameter i, used above, alternates between $i = 1$ and $i = 2$.

The Merge Phase We are now ready to merge the merge files. The initial sort blocks from of each of the m merge files are brought into memory input buffers, and their records are compared, starting from the lowest ones.

A Merge Pass The record with the smallest key is placed in a merge output buffer $j = 1$, and omitted from the merge input. This process of selecting the smallest record continues, interrupted only by two conditions:

C1 When a merge output buffer is filled, it is written to a merge output file j.

C2 If a merge input buffer has been processed completely, that merge input block can be ignored during selection. When only one merge input buffer contains records, those records are directly copied to the merge output buffer, and the buffer is written out.

We have now written to the merge output file $j = 1$ a sequence of sorted records that is m sort blocks long. In the case of $m = 2$ we have merged two input blocks, each from one of the from two source files to create a sorted sequence of two output blocks on one merge output file.

We now switch to a new merge output file by incrementing j. For a two-way merge j alternates between $j = 1$ and $j = 2$. Now a new set of m merge input blocks can be read and processed.

The merge processing continues for all input sort blocks. At the end of the merge input we may not have input blocks for all the buffers, but this case is treated as if the input buffers had no records left.

This merge pass is now complete. The input files can be discarded or reused to hold the output of the successor pass.

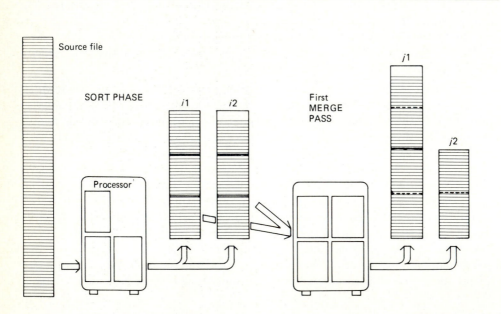

Figure 4-10a   Data flow in merge-sort.

Successive Merge Passes   The files which were the output of the completed merge pass are reset to become the new input files. They now contain sorted sequences of length m sort blocks, and the successor pass has to take this into account. For the condition that an input has been completed, C2 in the description of the initial merge pass, the action is now generalized to become:

C2′ If a merge input buffer has been processed, that buffer is refilled using the next block from the same merge input file until the entire sorted sequence has been read. If the sorted sequence is processed completely, the merge input buffer can be ignored during selection. When only one merge input sorted sequence remains, the remaining records are directly copied to the merge output files and a new set of sorted sequences can be read.

The merging of sorted sequences continues to the end of the merge input files.

The next merge pass processes the output sequences from the prior merge pass. With each merge pass the length of the sorted sequences increases by a factor m. For a two-way merge the sequences double, redouble, etc.

Merge Termination   Eventually the sorted sequence is as large as the source file was. This means that we are done. Only one merge output file is written, and that file contains the desired output. Since we can predict when the final file is being written we can direct the output to a final destination. An output file can be blocked again to standard form or the results can be used immediately, say, to create an index.

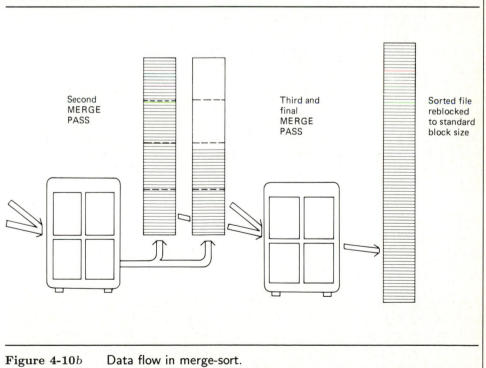

Second
MERGE
PASS

Third and
final
MERGE
PASS

Sorted file
reblocked
to standard
block size

Figure 4-10*b*   Data flow in merge-sort.

It is assumed for the pile file reorganization, as well as in other evaluations of the term T_Y, that the reading and writing activities during the reorganization do not cause additional seeks by interfering with each other. This means specifically that, if moving head disks are used, separate disk units must be used for the old and the new file. It also requires that sufficiently many buffers be available to fully utilize the disks. Overlap of disk operations is further considered in Chap. 10-1. Since reorganization is mostly scheduled to be done at times of low utilization, these conditions can frequently be met.

4-4   THE SEQUENTIAL FILE

This method provides two distinct structural changes relative to the pile organization. The first improvement is that the data records are ordered into a specific sequence, and the second improvement is that the data attributes are categorized so that the individual records contain all the data-attribute values in the same order and possibly in the same position. The data-attribute names then need to appear only once in the description of the file. Instead of storing attribute name-value pairs, an entire set of values, a column, is associated with each name. Methods to manage the attribute names will be encountered in Chap. 16 where the concept of a schema is introduced. This organization looks similar to the familiar tabular format that is generally associated with computer data, and shown in Fig. 4-1.

4-4-1 Structure and Manipulation of Sequential Files

To provide a sequence for the records, we define a key for every record. One or more attributes will become the key attribute(s) for the records in the file. The set of values for the key attributes typically identifies the object described by the record, i.e., the `license number` of a `car` or the `name` of a person. In Fig. 4-11 the `Name` is the key for our `Payroll` file. We expect to be able to identify records uniquely on the basis of their keys. The records in the file are then maintained in order according to the key attributes. One key attribute will provide the primary, high-order sort key, and if this attribute does not uniquely identify the object, then secondary and further key attributes can be specified until the order is completely determined.

Serial reading of the file in the order of the key can be performed sequentially. In Figs. 4-1a and b the `student number` provides such a key attribute, but in Fig. 4-1c there is no single field usable as a key. Two attributes, `prerequisite` and `student number`, can be combined to form a key.

░▒▓ **Artificial Keys** Sometimes artificial fields containing sequence or identification numbers are added to the records to obtain unique key attributes. These artificial keys will have perfect selectivity: The identification number is chosen to be unique for all the records and hence partitions the file into n individual records. Unfortunately, a separate computation may be needed to determine the identification number pertaining to the desired data.   ░▒▓

	Name	Age	Height	IQ
1	Antwerp	55	5'8"	95
2	Berringer	39	5'6"	75
3	Bigley	36	5'7"	70
4	Breslow	25	5'6"	49
5	Calhoun	27	5'11"	80
6	Finnerty	42	5'9"	178
7	Garson	61	5'6"	169
8	Hagstrohm	36	5'7"	83
9	Halgard	31	5'6"	95
10	Kroner	59	5'5"	145
11	McCloud	26	5'8"	47
12	Miasma	27	5'2"	75
13	Mirro	38	5'8"	52
14	Moskowitz	23	5'7"	50
15	Pop	38	5'3"	53
16	Proteus	41	5'8"	152
17	Purdy	37	5'9"	48
18	Roseberry	38	5'7"	70
19	Wheeler	23	5'8"	67
20	Young	18	5'8"	89

Figure 4-11   A sequential file.

Disadvantages With the structural constraints of sequentiality and fixed records, efficiency is gained but a great deal of flexibility is lost. Updates to a sequential file are not easily accommodated. The fact that only the key attribute determines the sequence of the records introduces an asymmetry among the fields which makes sequential files unsuitable for general information retrieval. The common procedure to handle insertions to a sequential file is to collect them in a separate pile, the *transaction log file*, until the pile becomes too big, and then to perform a *batch update*. The batch update is done by reorganizing the file. At that time the transaction log file is sorted according to the same keys used for the main file, and the changes are merged into a new copy of the sequential file.

A sequential file is restricted to a limited and predetermined set of attributes. A single description applies to all records, and all records are structurally identical. If a new attribute has to be added to a record, the entire file has to be reorganized. Every record of the file will be rewritten to provide space for the new data item. To avoid this problem, one finds that sequential files are sometimes initially allocated with space to spare; a few columns of fields are left empty.

The record layout which will appear on the file is a direct representation of the
DECLARE statement in the program, as shown in Fig. 4-12. Such declarations also
imply fixed element and record lengths.

Program declaration	Sample content
DECLARE	
1 payroll_record,	ERHagstrohm . . .10Mar50 1J...
2 name,	ERHagstrohm . . .|
3 initials CHAR(2),	ER|
3 last_name CHAR(28),	Hagstrohm . . .|
2 date_born CHAR(7),	10Mar50|
2 date_hired CHAR(7),	1Jan78|
2 salary FIXED BINARY,	21 000|
2 exemptions FIXED BINARY,	2|
2 sex CHAR(1),	M|
2 military_rank FIXED BINARY,	0|
etc.	etc.|
2 total_wages FIXED BINARY;	23 754|
. . .	

```
WRITE FILE (payroll_file) FROM (payroll_record);
```

Figure 4-12   Record declaration.

The fixed record layout is easy to construct by processing programs. Since similar information is found in identical positions of successive records, data-analysis
programs are easy to write. The record written to the file is often simply a copy
of the data in processor storage. Sometimes data is transformed by the processing
languages so that files are written using a single data type, perhaps ASCII characters, but kept in binary form in memory to simplify computation. Strong support is
given to such record-oriented data through PICTURE specifications in COBOL, FORMAT
statements in FORTRAN and PL/1, and RECORD declarations in PASCAL.

4-4-2 Use of Sequential Files

Sequential files are the most frequently used type of file in commercial batch-oriented
data processing. The concept of a *master file,* to which *detail* records are added
periodically, as sketched in Fig. 4-13, has been basic to data processing since its
inception. This concept transfers easily from manual processing to computers, and
from one computer to another one. Where data is processed cyclically, as in monthly
billing or payroll applications, the effectiveness of this approach is hard to achieve
by other methods. Data kept in sequential files is, however, difficult to combine
with other data to provide ad hoc information, and access to the file has to be
scheduled if the requested information has to be up to date.

    In order to combine data from multiple sequential files, sorts are performed to
make the records of the files *cosequential.* Then all required data can be found by
spacing forward only over the files involved. A sequential file can be in sequence
only according to one key so that frequently the file has to be sorted again according
to another criterion or key to match other sets of files.

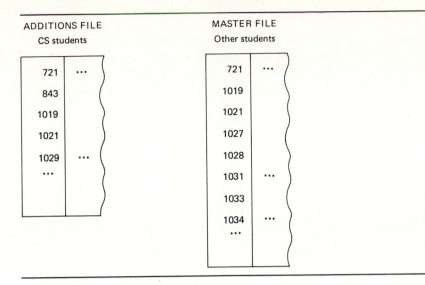

Figure 4-13   Cosequential files.

4-5   PERFORMANCE OF SEQUENTIAL FILES

The performance of sequential files ranges from excellent to nearly impossible depending on the operations desired.

4-5-1 Record Size in a Sequential File

The file storage requirement for sequential files, using a fixed record format, depends on the number of all the possible attributes a. The description of the attributes appears only once per file, and thus the space required for the attribute names can be neglected. The names may appear outside the file itself, perhaps only in program documentation. However, space will be used for values even when attributes have an undefined value or are unimportant in combination with other attributes. The last two entries shown in Fig. 4-12 illustrate such an attribute dependency where for the category sex = F the next attribute value, military_rank, will probably be NULL. The fixed record size is the product of the number of fields and their average size.

$$R = aV \qquad\qquad\qquad 4\text{-}14$$

If many values are undefined, the file density will be low. If the value a' is close to the value for a, the file density will be high. Some methods to reduce storage costs for sparse data $(a' \ll a)$ will be discussed in Chap. 13-3. If insertions are expected, space for the transaction log to hold up to o new records of length R must also be allocated in an associated area.

4-5-2 Fetch Record in a Sequential File

The common approach to fetch a record from a sequential file consists of a serial search through the file. The time required to fetch an arbitrary record can be significantly reduced if we have a direct-access device and use a direct-access technique. In a sequential file direct access can be applied only to the attribute according to which the file has been put in sequence. We describe two direct methods for access to a sequential file organization, binary search and probing, after Eq. 4-17.

SEQUENTIAL SEARCH When the search argument is not the key attribute used to sequence the file, the search is always sequential. The process is similar to the search through a pile file. Since the total size of the file will be different from the size of a pile file due to the difference in record organization, the relative performance will depend on the attribute density a'/a as well as on the relative length of attribute descriptors A and data values V. Half the file will be searched on the average to fetch a record, so that

$$T_F = \frac{1}{2}n\frac{R}{t'} \qquad \langle \text{main file} \rangle \text{ 4-15}$$

For small files this time may be better than the direct methods presented below.

If the file has received o' new records into a transaction log or overflow file, this file should be searched also. The entire overflow file has to be processed to assure that any record found in the main part or earlier part of the overflow file has not been updated or deleted. This file will be in chronological order and processed sequentially. With the assumption that the overflow is on the average half-full ($o' = \frac{1}{2}o$), we obtain

$$T_{Fo} = o'\frac{R}{t'} = \frac{1}{2}o\frac{R}{t'} \qquad \langle \text{overflow} \rangle \text{ 4-16}$$

as the term needed to process changes made to the main file.

We cannot expect that the simple systems which use sequential files will search through both the main file and the log file in parallel. The total fetch time, if both parts of the file are searched sequentially, is the sum

$$T_F = \frac{1}{2}(n+o)\frac{R}{t'} \qquad \text{4-17}$$

where o is the capacity of the transaction log file.

BINARY SEARCH A well-known search technique for memory can be adapted to provide an alternate access method for sequential files. The binary search begins, as shown in Fig. 4-14, with a direct access to the middle of the file, and partitions the file iteratively according to a comparision of the key value found and the search argument. Whenever a block is fetched, the first and last records in this block will be inspected to determine if the goal record is within this block. The number of fetches does not depend on the number of records, n, but rather on the number of blocks, $b = n/Bfr$.

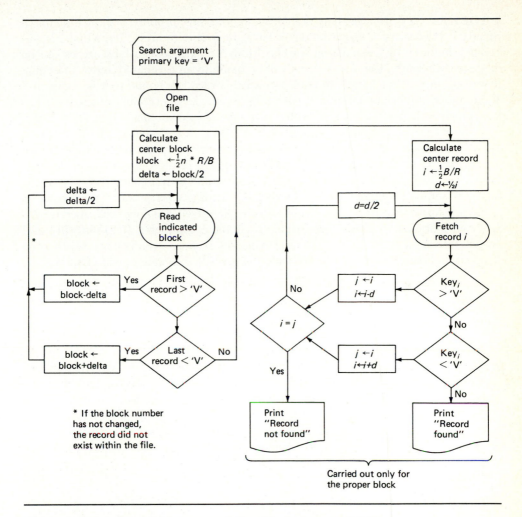

Figure 4-14   Nested binary search in a blocked sequential file.

We find, using the expected number of block access for the binary search $log_2(b)$ (Knuth[73S]), that

$$T_F = log_2 \left(\frac{n}{Bfr} \right) (s + r + btt + c) + T_{Fo} \qquad \langle \text{binary} \rangle \text{ 4-18}$$

The term for processing time, c, is included here, since until the record range in a block has been checked, it is not known which block is to be read next. The efficiencies obtained when reading the file sequentially using alternate buffers have been lost in this case. The value of c may well be negligible compared with the other times involved, but the bulk transfer rate, t', is always inappropriate. The overflow term remains unchanged.

PROBING   A third access method for sequential files, *probing*, is more difficult to quantify. It consists of an initial direct fetch, or probe, to an estimated position in the file, followed by a sequential search. If only forward sequential searches can be executed efficiently, the initial probe will be made to an estimated lowest matching key position, so that having to read backward is rare. Only one seek is made, and the number of blocks read sequentially is based on the uncertainty of the probe.

Likely values for an initial probe have been based on the leading digits of a social security number, if its value is used as a key, or on a percentile expectation for leading characters of names, if names are the key. Names beginning with the letters "E", for instance, may be found after $0.2446n$ records in a file sequenced by name (see Table 13-4). The corresponding block would be numbered $\lfloor 0.2446n/Bfr \rfloor$. There is some uncertainty in the distribution leading to a probe. Since on most devices a forward search is best, one can decide, given a 3% or 0.03 uncertainty, that the probe may actually best begin at the block numbered $\lfloor 0.2146n/Bfr \rfloor$ and search forward. Alternate techniques to access records rapidly are used by the indexed and direct file organization methods described in subsequent chapters.

Summary of Access Methods   We can summarize the three choices of access methods as follows
>   1 Sequential search: $\mathcal{O}(n)$
>   2 Binary search: $\mathcal{O}(\log n)$
>   3 Probing: $\mathcal{O}(1)$

While the *big-O* notation clearly distinguishes the difference in growth patterns for these three alternatives, it ignores the complexity of the programs and the important factors of block access and key distribution. For many modestly-sized files the simple sequential search may remain preferable. Only when the files are quite large are the more complex access methods warranted. The simpler methods are also more susceptible to hardware improvements, as described in the section on database machines, Chap. 10-6-5.

4-5-3 Get-Next Record of a Sequential File

In a sequential file, a successor record is immediately accessible and may well be in the same block. If there is a frequent need for successor records, the file system should be programmed so that it does not discard the remaining records in the block but keeps the buffer with the contents of the current block available. The probability of finding a successor record in the same block is determined by the number of records per block Bfr : in $1/Bfr$ of the cases the next block is required. If the processing speed satisfies the condition of Eq. 3-22, the expected time to get the next record is only

$$T_N = \frac{btt}{Bfr} \approx \frac{R}{t'} \qquad\qquad 4\text{-}19$$

The buffering associated with the bulk transfer rate also evens out any variations in response time, so that performance is not directly affected by the periodic need to read a new block.

4-5-4 Insert into a Sequential File

Insertion of a record into the main file requires insertion into the proper place according to the key. The sequence would not be maintained if new records were to be added to the end. For very small files, records beyond the point of insertion can be moved up to make space for putting the new record in place. This effort involves locating the insertion point by a fetch, and subsequently reading and rewriting the remainder of the file. Each phase involves again half of the blocks of the file on the average, so

$$T_I = T_F + \frac{1}{2}\frac{n}{Bfr}\,(btt + T_{RW}) = n\,\frac{R}{t'} + n\,\frac{r}{Bfr} \qquad \text{(in place)} \ \text{4-20}$$

The assumptions leading to Eqs. 4-15 and 3-27 are employed. This method is feasible for data files only if insertion occurs rarely, for instance, for a list of departments of a company. Several insertions can be batched and handled at the same cost.

   The usual method for inserting data into sequential files is to collect new records into the transaction log file and, at a later time, execute a batch update. We will use o to indicate the number of records collected for deferred insertion. The actual cost of insertions in the file is hence the immediate cost to append the records to the transaction log file and the deferred cost of the reorganization run. Append costs were given for the pile; we use the conservative method (Eq. 4-8) and write each record immediately into the log. The cost of the T_Y is allocated below to the o records that are collected into the transaction log file between reorganization periods. The reorganization time T_Y and the overflow count o are defined below.

$$T_I = s + 3r + btt \quad + \quad \frac{T_Y}{o} \qquad \text{(via log)} \ \text{4-21}$$

The response sensed by the user when inserting a record includes only the initial append terms.

   Our definition of sequential files does not allow insertion of larger records than the original record stored. Problems caused by variable-length records and spanning in insertion and update are hence avoided. The transaction log file can also serve other functions, as described in the chapter on reliability, Chap. 15-2.

4-5-5 Update Record in a Sequential File

A new record is created from retrieved data and new attribute values. If the key value does not change, the record could be rewritten into the main file. If the key value changes, the update is similar to the process of inserting a record but also involves the deletion of a record at another position in the main sequential file.

   Since the main file is not otherwise touched in this method, it is best to use the transaction log file also for record update. The updated record and a flag record indicating deletion are appended to the transaction log file and used for subsequent fetches and in the reorganization process. The flag record will include the key and a tombstone. Note that the tombstone is not placed into the main file either. Both the flag and update records should be added to the transaction log at the same time; the cost of adding two records at a time to a block is not much more than adding a single one, and consistency is enhanced. The cost of an update, which reads the main file and appends to the log file is

$$T_U \approx T_F(\text{main file}) + T_I(\text{log file}) \qquad \text{4-22}$$

Deletion of a record generates only one entry in the transaction log. No tombstone appears in the main file.

After d record deletions and v record updates, $d + 2v$ records will have been added into the count, o, the size of the transaction log file. Multiple updates to the same record will create multiple entries in the log file. Since complex updating is rarely done using this file organization, we will skip further evaluation of updating performance.

4-5-6 Read Entire Sequential File

Exhaustive processing of the file requires reading of the main and the transaction log files in the same order. We assume that data will be processed serially, according to the key used to establish the physical sequence of the main file. The o records placed into the transaction log file must first be sorted to establish this sequence. Then both files can be read sequentially. The total cost is

$$T_X = T_{sort}(o) + (n + o)\frac{R}{t'} \qquad \text{4-23}$$

given that all conditions for the use of t' hold. We find from the comments in the preceding paragraphs that, denoting the number of insertions as n_{insert} and the size of the prior main file as n_{old},

$$o = n_{insert} + 2v + d \quad ; \qquad n_{new} = n_{old} + n_{insert} - d$$

The value of the transaction count, o, includes here insertions, two entries for records being changed, and the number of records to be deleted. The transaction sort has to be stable, as defined in Sec. 4-3-8, so that multiple changes to the same record will be handled in the original chronological order.

If the transaction log file is relatively large ($o \lll n$), it may be best to reorganize the file as well. The records can be analyzed during the merge of reorganization, so that $T_X = T_Y$, as analyzed below.

4-5-7 Reorganization of a Sequential File

Reorganization consists of taking the old file and the transaction log file and merging them into a new file. In order to carry out the merge effectively, the transaction log file will first be sorted according to the same key field used for the old file. During the merge the sorted data from the transaction log file and the records from the old sequential file are copied into the new file, omitting any records which are marked for deletion in the transaction log file. The time required for the reorganization run consists of the sort time for the transaction log file plus the merge time. Merging requires the sum of the times to read both files and write a new sequential file

$$T_Y = T_{sort}(o) + n_{old}\frac{R}{t'} + o\frac{R}{t'} + n_{new}\frac{R}{t'} \qquad \text{4-24}$$

or if the number of records being deleted, $d + v$, can be neglected:

$$T_Y = T_{sort}(o) + 2(n + o)\frac{R}{t'} \qquad \text{4-25}$$

The time required to sort a file of size o as $T_{sort}(o)$ can be estimated using Eq. 4-12, provided in Sec. 4-3-6.

4-6   REVIEW

In this chapter we have introduced a large number of performance oriented concepts, and applied them to two basic file organizations.

Useful concepts encountered are partitioning and selectivity. These concepts will be applied later when selecting indexes and will become critical for database query optimization.

> Attributes of a file have selectivity, ranging from perfect for unique attributes, to small for, say, binary attributes. To find an entry in a file the file is partitioned using selection on the attributes.

Useful techniques are self-describing fields having attribute names as well as values, the use of tombstones to indicate deletion, and use of probing to search a large file space. The use of a transaction file will also be seen to have broader applicability. If the transaction file is retained we have a log of all the changes applied to the file. Such a log can also be used to recover from disasters. Transaction logs provide an audit trail, useful when problems with files or their use or misuse have to be investigated.

The two initial file organizations seen, while both simple, are structured quite differently. The pile file organization is flexible, and costly for information retrieval. The sequential file is rigid, and fast for some simple uses.

> There is a trade-off between flexibility and efficiency. If constraints are applied early in the process of design, flexibility will be reduced, but efficiency will be gained. The difference in efficiency can is typically so great that constraints must be applied to make a design practical. It is important to choose the least onerous constraint.

The distinction can be summarized as follows:

$$
\begin{aligned}
T_U(pile) &= \mathcal{O}(1)   & T_U(seq) &= \mathcal{O}(n) \\
T_N(pile) &= \mathcal{O}(n^2) & T_N(seq) &= \mathcal{O}(1) & \text{4-26} \\
T_F(pile) &= \mathcal{O}(n)   & T_F(seq) &= \mathcal{O}(n), \mathcal{O}(\log n), \text{ or } \mathcal{O}(1)
\end{aligned}
$$

However, to obtain the better performance in sequential fetching requires elaborate programs. To better exploit the potential of sequential files we must add access structures, and that is the topic of the next chapter.

Alternative record structures demonstrated here are applicable to other file organizations, as well. At times, mixed record structures are seen, where stable information is placed into a fixed part which uses unnamed fields, while the remainder of the information uses named fields.

The method used to derive performance formulas should now be clear. The formulas are simply derived from the description of the operation being performed. In essence we obtain factors f which represent the frequency of the primitive computer and disk operations: compute, seek, latency, and block transfer.

$$T_{any} = f_c^* \, c + f_s^* \, s + f_r^* \, r + f_{btt}^* \, B/t$$

The f^* indicates the repetitive nature of the operations being performed.

As the three approaches to fetching data from a sequential file show, it is feasible to have more than one access method for one single file organization. One file organization has to serve all applications, but for a given access application program or transaction the best access method should be chosen.

BACKGROUND AND REFERENCES

The basic file designs presented here can easily be traced to early developments in data processing. A pile is, of course, the most obvious data collection. Most of the pieces of paper that cross our desks are self-describing documents, which can be processed without reference to an external structure description. Citations on selectivity are given with Chap. 5.

Ledgers and card files are the basis for sequential files; they are often divided into pages or folders with headings. There exist corresponding algorithms and structures applicable to memory. But when access is into a homogeneous space the access techniques differ, so that the evaluation of the algorithms and their options leads to misleading results when files are being dealt with.

The benefit of sequential processing is assessed by Charles[73]. Lomet[75] describes the use of tombstones and Leung[86] quantifies their effect in dynamic files. Rodriguez-Rosell[76] shows that sequential processing remains effective even on multi-programmed computers and Slonim[82] evaluates sequential versus parallel access.

File organizations have been analyzed at several levels of abstraction. A pile file is described by Glantz[70] and partitioning is exploited by Yue[78]. A language with a persistent pile file has been implemented by Gray[85]. Gildersleeve[71] and Grosshans[86] address programming for sequential files. Severance[72] evaluates sequential files and buckets, and the difference between fetch and get-next operations. Shneiderman[76] and Palvia[85] analyze batch fetching in sequential files. Willard[86] presents algorithms for direct update of sequential files and Nevaleinen[77] has rules for their blocking.

A detailed analysis of external sort algorithms is provided by Knuth[73S]. All the important algorithms have an $\mathcal{O}(n \log n)$ behavior, and differ by less than 28% between the best and the worst case shown. Many further references are given as well. Advances in hardware have changed the relative importance of the parameters used; for instance, tapes are rarely used today for sorting, so that rewinding and backward reading of tapes are no longer issues.

The problem of merging cosequential files has often been analyzed, a recent example is Levy[82]. In Shneiderman[78] a form of binary search is developed, Li[87] extends it to batched operations. Ghosh[69] proposes to use probing instead of lower-level indexes. Concurrent access of direct primary and overflow areas is proposed by Groner[74].

File systems which implement various methods are described by Judd[73]. Martin[75] describes many file operations in detail and provides design guidance.

References where these files are compared with other techniques are found with Chap. 7. Specific information on file access methods is best obtained from software suppliers, we do not cite their manuals.

EXERCISES

1 Obtain the operating system manual for a personal computer (PC) and locate the table which describes the file directory of the system and compare it with information cited in Table 4-1. Note the differences. For each directory element missing in the PC state what the effects of the lack of information are.

2 Suggest ways to reduce the redundancy in the redundant file of Figure 4-1c.

3 What is the difference between writing a block and inserting a record? What is the difference between reading a block and fetching a record?

4 For the list of applications which follows, choose either a pile file organization, a sequential file organization, or reject both, if neither can perform even minimally. State your reason succinctly.
   a A payroll which is processed once a week
   b A file to collect accident data in a factory
   c An airline reservation system
   d A savings account file in a bank
   e A file listing your record, cassette, and CD collection
   f The files of the social security administration. (They are processed periodically.)
   g The catalog of an automobile factory
   h The catalog of a department store

5 Program the algorithm for a continuous search described as the topic of *Batching of Requests* in Sec. 4-3-2. Test it using a fetch-request arrival rate that is derived from a random-number generator which interrupts a pass through the file 10 times on the average. The file can be simulated by an array in memory. Report the result. Refer to Chap 12-4 for a description of a simulation process.

6 Give the expected insertion time per record inserted into a pile file where $R = 0.7B$ and spanned records are used (Sec. 4-3-4).

7   Determine the time for a batch insertion into a pile (see Sec. 4-3-4). What conditions are required for your result to be valid?

8   To speed retrieval of name records from a sequential file, you want to use probing. Where would you look for data to build the required table? How big a table would you use?

9   Write in a high-level language the procedure to actually insert a record into an unspanned and into a spanned blocked sequential file. Discuss the buffer requirements for both cases.

10   Discuss the differences in updating records for a pile file and a sequential file.

11   When reorganizing a sequential file as described in Sec. 4-5-7, it is possible that a newly inserted record on the transaction file is to be deleted by a later transaction entered in the log file. What does this require when sorting the transactions and merging the files? Draw the flowchart for the merge process.

12^P Consider again your initial file application from Exercise 1 of Chap. 1. List the attributes you will need, and assign them to files. Identify which attributes will require variable length fields.

13^P Discuss if use of pile files or sequential files would be reasonable for some of the files you expect in your application. List any objections the users would have if either method were chosen.

14^P Would periodic reorganization be acceptable for your application? What would be a natural reorganization period? Who would be responsible for assuring that reorganizations were done on a timely basis?

Chapter 5

Indexed Files

Index-learning turns no student pale,
Yet holds the eel of science by the tail.

Alexander Pope,
The Dunciad, I, *1720.*

5-0 INTRODUCTION

In this chapter we describe and introduce files which use indexes. The concept of an index is a familiar one from books: The dense, ordered index entries at the end of a book help to rapidly locate references to desired information in the text. One or several references may be obtained for an index entry. In this chapter we present the principles of indexes as used for computer files. In Chap. 8 we augment this material with features used in implementation.

FILE INDEXES   An index consists of a collection of entries, one for each data record, containing the value of a key attribute for that record, and reference pointer which allows immediate access to that record. For large records, the index entry will be considerably smaller than the data record itself. The entire index will be correspondingly smaller than the file itself, so that a smaller space will have to be searched. The index is always kept in sorted order according to its key attribute so that it can be searched rapidly.

Indexes become effective when files are quite large, so that the index requires many fewer blocks. The search process within a large index itself is aided by again indexing subsets of the index, in Fig. 5-1 we illustrate that concept by grouping social security numbers with the same initial digit.

We have an employee file sequenced by social security number:

TID	Social Sec#	Name	Birthdate	Sex	Occupation	...
1	013-47-1234	John	1/1/43	Male	Welder	...
2	028-18-2341	Pete	11/5/45	Male	Creep	...
3	061-15-3412	Mary	6/31/39	Female	Engineer	...
	...-..-....	....	....	.....	....	...

To find employees we establish an index file as follows:

Index block id	key value	TID
a	013-47-1234	1
	028-18-2314	2
	061-15-3412	3
	...-..-....	.

To find, in turn, the index blocks rapidly we establish a second index level as follows:

Index block id	key value	index block id
m	013-47-1234	a
	102-81-2314	b
	201-51-3412	c
	...-..-....	.

Figure 5-1   Illustration of principles for indexing.

Successively higher levels of the index become smaller and smaller until there remains only a small, highest level index. A pointer to the level can be kept in the file directory, and accessed from memory. There is rarely a need for many levels of indexing.

The recursive nature of a computer index distinguishes it from an index in a book. With every increase in level the search gets longer, but at every level only a block's worth of index entries has to be looked at.

In Fig. 5-1 the top-level index will have 10 entries, and for 500 employees the first level index blocks will have an average of 50 entries. In practice, we want index blocks to be filled to capacity, so that the index divisions are determined by the size of blocks available to the file system, as shown in Fig. 5-5.

The Shape of Indexes

As seen in Fig. 5-1 the entries for an index are quite small, containing only one value and a TID*. Hence, many index entries will fit into one block. The number of entries obtained for each retrieval of an index block is called the *fanout*. A fanout of 100 is not unusual. With two levels we can access them up to 10 000 records and with three levels up to 1 000 000. The index trees are very broad, rather than high.

---

* The abbreviation TID derives from the term *tuple identifier*, used when modeling databases where *tuples* are used to represent records. We use it here to denote any kind of record pointer.

The term used to measure the breadth of a tree is the *fanout ratio y*. Broad trees have few levels and provide rapid fetch access.

In Fig. 5-2 we illustrate symbolically a small and a large fanout ratio. The trees are not presented in traditional computer science upside-down fashion, so that the process to fetch a leaf on the tree starts in the figure from the bottom, at the root. The fanout ratio is a very important parameter in the analysis of indexed file organizations and will be encountered frequently. Similar data structures used in memory, as *m-way trees*, are often quite narrow, most frequently binary ($m = 2$).

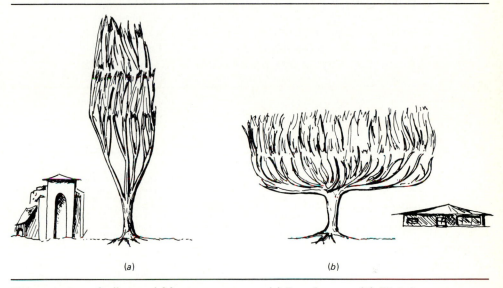

(a)   (b)

Figure 5-2   Italian and Monterey cypress. (a) Low fanout. (b) High fanout.

Static versus Dynamic Trees

The two indexed file organizations presented in this chapter differ greatly in index management. The index of an indexed-sequential file is created at the time of reorganization, and does not change due to updates. New records are placed into an overflow file and linked to their predecessors.

The multiple-indexed file places updates into the main-file. These records must be locatable via the indexes, so that here the indexes are dynamic. We use a *B-tree index*, which trades space for the ability to remain up to date.

INVERTED FILES   A file for which indexes have been created is sometimes referred to as an *inverted file*. This term has its origin in bibliographic indexing and will be used rarely and carefully in this book. Sometimes a copy of a sequential file, when sorted according to another key attribute, has been called an inverted file. The term *fully inverted* generally implies a file where all attributes have indexes, as described in Sec. 5-3.

The terms *inverted index, inverted list, inverted file,* and *partially inverted file* are used inconsistently in the literature, and frequently imply indexing as described in this chapter. We simply avoid using *inverted* in this book.

⧘⧘⧘⧘   **A Concordance**   One older use of inversion is the creation of a single index to all the words in a body of writing. The index has as entries all the unique words (types) in the file, and is essentially a vocabulary. With each entry there will be pointers to all the instances (tokens) in the text where the words appear. If the pointers are augmented by a sample of the text, the result assumes the form of a *concordance*. The language used for the text is, of course, not restricted to English. An excerpt from a concordance is shown in Fig. 5-3.

Following our concepts a text file has only one type of attribute, *words*, and the index has multiple entries per record, one for each word. Partial inversions may exclude high-frequency words or other words not of interest, such as initials of authors. The term *indexing* in a bibliographic context is the selection or creation of significant attribute values for subsequent retrieval. These may be placed with the text sections so that there is now a second attribute type.   ⧘⧘⧘⧘

Sample of text

Key-attribute value	Pointer

```
  quant vit pasmer  Rollant, / dunc out tel doel unkes mais n'out si grant. / Tendit sa mai 2223
 la sele en remeint quaste. / Mult ad grant doel Carlemagnes li reis, / quant  Naimun veit 3451
c. / Co dist li reis: "Seignurs, vengez voz doels, / si esclargiez voz talenz e voz coers, 3627
chevaler." / Respont li quens: " Deus le me doinst venger!" / Sun cheval brochet des esperu 1548
ad mort  France ad mis en exill. / Si grant dol ai que ne voldreie vivre, / de ma maisnee,  2936
d sanc. / Franceis murrunt,  Carles en ert dolent.   Tere  Majur vos metrus an present.    951
ent, / e cil d' Espaigne s'en cleiment tuit dolent. / Dient  Franceis: "Ben fiert nostre gu 1651
alchet ireement, / e li  Franceis curucus e dolent; / n'i ad celoi n'i plurt e se dement,   1825
 ma gent." / E cil respunt "Tant sy jo plus dolent. / Ne pois a vos tenir lung parlement:   2835
 sil duluset; / jamais en tere n'orrez plus dolent hume! / Or veit  Rollant gue mort est su 2023
 devers les porz d' Espaigne: / veeir poez, dolente est la rereguarde; / ki ceste fait, jan 1104
e vient curant cuntre lui; / si li ad dit: "Dolente, si mare fui! / A itel hunte, sire, son 2823
pereres cevalchet par irur / e li  Franceis dolenz e curucus: / n'i ad celoi ki durement ne 1813
aienur, / plurent e crient, demeinent grant dolor, / ploignent lur deus.  Tervagan e Mahum  2695
perere,' co dist  Gefrei D' Anjou, / "ceste dolor ne demenez tant fort! / Par tut le camp f 2946
ance ad en baillie, / que me remembre de la dolur e l'ire, / co est de  Basan e de sun frer  489
amimunde, / pluret e criet, mult forment se douset; / ensembl'od li plus de xx. mil humes,  2577
out mais en avant. / Par tuz les prez or se dorment li  Franc. / N'i ad cheval ki puisset e 2521
ad apris ki bien conuist ahan. / Karles se dort cum huse traveillet.  Seint  Gabriel li a  2525
poeent plus faire. / Ki mult est las, il se dort cuntre tere. / Icele noit n'unt unkes esca 2494
it le jur, la noit est aserie. / Carles se dort, li empereres riches. / Sunjat qu'il eret  718
ent liquels d'els la veintrat. / Carles se dort, mie ne s'esveillat. AOI. / Tresvait la no  736
le cel en volent les escicles. / Carles se dort, qu'il ne s'esveillet mie. / Apres iceste,  724
s  Deu co ad mustret al barun. / Carles se dort tresqu'al demain, al cler jur. / Li reis   2569
et les os, / tute l'eschine li desevret del dos, / od sun espiet l'anse li getet fors,     1201
gemmet ad or, / e al cheval parfundement el dos; / ambure ocit, ki quel blasme ne quil lot. 1588
eruns a or, / fiert  Oliver derere en mi le dos. / Le blanc osberc li ad descust el cors,   1945
ros; / sur les eschines qu'il unt en mi les dos / cil sunt seiet ensement cume porc. AOI.   3222
re joe en ad tute sanglente; / l'osberc del dos josque par sum le ventre. / Deus le guarit  3922
ele les dous alves d'argent / e al ceval le dos parfundement; / ambure ocist seinz nul reco 1649
t li ber. / De cels d' Espaigne unt lur les dos turnez, / tenent l'enchalz, tuit en sunt cu 2445
a fuls: / de cent millers n'en poent quarir dous. / Rollant dist: "Nostre ume sunt mult p  1440
s e l'osberc jazerenc, / de l'oree sele les dous alves d'argent / e al ceval le dos parfund 1648
tet en ad, ne poet muer n'en plurt. / Desuz dous arbres parvenuz est . . . li reis. / Les c 2874
 Dedesuz  Ais est la pree sult large: / des dous baruns justee est la bataille. / Cil sunt  3874
agne, ki est canuz e vielz! / Men escientre dous cenz anz ad e mielz. / Par tantes teres ad  539
t vielz, si ad sun tens uset; / men escient dous cenz anz ad passet. / Par tantes teres at   524
```

Figure 5-3   Sample of a concordance of the *Chanson de Roland*.

5-1   THE INDEXED-SEQUENTIAL FILE

The indexed-sequential file design attempts to overcome the access problem inherent in the sequential file organization without losing all the benefits and tradition associated with sequential files. Two features are added to the organization of the sequential file to arrive at this third file organization type. One additional feature is an index to the file to provide better random access; the other is an overflow area to provide a means to handle additions to the file. Figure 5-4 shows a particular example of an indexed-sequential file. We find in this figure the three important components: the sequential file, the index, and the overflow area. The sketch also has a number of details which will appear in later discussions.

5-1-1 Structure and Manipulation of Indexed-Sequential Files

The indexed-sequential file organization allows, when reading data serially, sequential access to the main record areas of the file, shown in Fig. 5-4. Only some pointer fields, used to handle insertions, must be skipped.

Records which have been inserted are found in a separate file area, called the *overflow area*. An overflow area is similar to the transaction log file used previously, but integrated when we have an indexed-sequential organization. The records in this area are located by following a pointer from their predecessor record. Serial reading of the combined file proceeds sequentially until a pointer to the overflow file is found, then continues in the overflow file until a NULL pointer is encountered; then reading of the main file is resumed.

To fetch a specific record, the index is used.

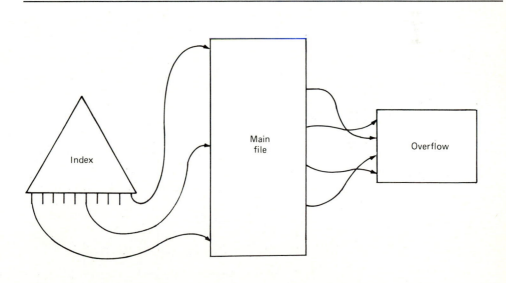

Figure 5-4   Components of an indexed sequential file.

AN INDEX FOR AN INDEXED-SEQUENTIAL FILE   Indexes have been implemented in a variety of ways. We will consider here a static, multilevel index, using *block anchors*. An alternative, dynamic, index method, called a *B-tree*, will be presented with the indexed files of Sec. 5-3. We discuss here the most prevalent version of the indexed-sequential file. Improvements to this scheme are covered in Chap. 8-1.

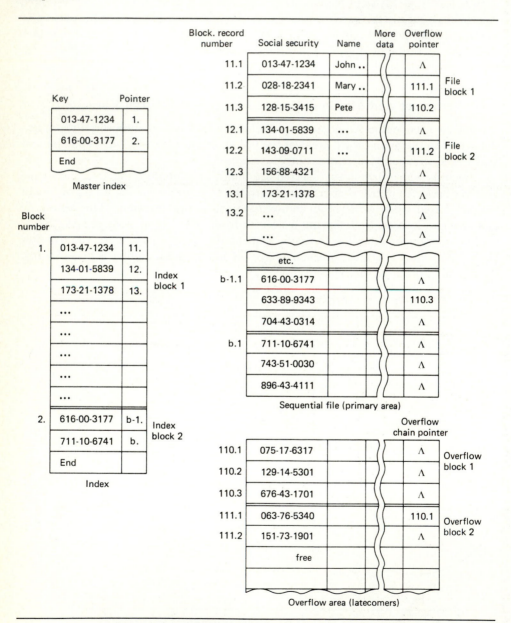

Figure 5-5   Fields of an indexed-sequential file.

Selecting the Key The index for an indexed-sequential file is based on the same key attribute used to determine the sequence of the file itself. For such a *primary index* a number of refinements can be applied. One of these is indexing only the first record in every block — using *block anchors* — and the other is keeping most of the index on the same cylinder as the data records, *cylinder indexes*. The effect of having cylinder indexes will be considered in Chap. 8-1-1.

▦ **Block Anchors** The benefit of the index is to rapidly access a block of the file. Individual records in a block can be found by a search within the block, so that it is not necessary to keep in the index a TID for every record, but only a reference to one record per block. The referenced record is called an *anchor point*, and only the anchor's key value and the block pointer are kept in the index. Natural anchor points are based on blocks, tracks, or cylinders. In Fig. 5-5 the choice of anchor point is the first record of a block.

The cost of searching within a file block for a record is small, since the entire block is brought into memory whenever required and can be kept available in a buffer. A block will contain a number of records equal to Bfr. The number of entries in a block-anchored index is, hence, n/Bfr, and the size of an index entry is $V + P$.

When only block anchors are kept in the index, it is not possible to determine by checking the index alone if there exists a record corresponding to a specific argument. The appropriate data block has to be read also. To determine if the value of a search argument is beyond the last entry in the file, the last data block will have to be fetched, since the anchor point refers to the first record in this block.

If records are often appended to the end of the file, it can be more convenient to keep the key value of the last record in each block in the index entries instead of the key for the first record. The appropriate block for a given search argument is then found in the index through a less-than-or-equal match.   ▦

QUANTIFYING THE SHAPE OF AN INDEX   The shape of an index tree is characterized by two related parameters: *fanout* and *height*. We will discuss these two concepts in turn,

The Fanout Ratio of an Index As stated in the introduction, an important parameter of an index is the referencing capability of a block of index entries, the *fanout*. The fanout, y, is the quotient of the block size, B, and the space required for each entry, $V + P$,

$$y = \left\lfloor \frac{B}{V + P} \right\rfloor \qquad\qquad 5\text{-}1$$

To evaluate the number of levels of indexing that might be required, we will take an example of a fairly large file (one million records) and a block-anchored index. In order to estimate the access time to fetch a record, we need to know how many levels of index are needed for a file of this size. The example of Fig. 5-6 shows this procedure for a general block-anchored index. In Chap. 8-1-1, Fig. 8-1, the same file is evaluated for the case of a block-anchored index kept on the same cylinder as the referenced data.

Estimating the Height of an Index   The height of an index tree is the number of indexing levels, x, required to access all records of the file. To estimate the height we consider the exponential growth of each level, so that

$$x = \lceil \log_y \lceil n/Bfr \rceil \rceil \qquad \text{easily computable as} \qquad \lceil \ln \lceil n/Bfr \rceil / \ln y \rceil \qquad \text{5-2}$$

The estimate should be verified for a specific design, since its value is so critical to performance. Values of x found in practice range typically from 1 to 3. Larger values occur only when the size of the file is very large while the key attribute V is unusually great; in Chap. 8-3 we describe techniques to keep the effective V small.

Given is a block size B of 2000 bytes, a value size V of 14 bytes, a TID pointer size P of 6 bytes, and data records having a total length R of 200 bytes. With this blocking factor Bfr of 10, the 10^6 records require 10^5 data blocks and hence as many TIDs. The size of the index entry is here $14 + 6 = 20$ bytes, and the block size B is still 2000.

Now Eq. 5-1 gives a $y = 100$, so that the 10^5 lowest-index-level entries occupy 10^3 blocks which can be pointed at by 10^3 second-level index entries. This second-level index will occupy a total of $20 \times 1000 = 20\,000$ bytes. The latter number is still excessive for storage in memory, so that a third index level to the second index level will be created. Only $20\,000/2000 = 10$ entries occupying 200 bytes are required at the top level. The term *root* refers to this topmost level. The index levels are numbered from 1, for the level closest to the data, to x (here 3) for the root level.

A record-anchored index for the same file would have been Bfr or 10 times as large but will use the same number of levels, as can be seen by recomputing this example for 10^6 index entries. Its root level (x) will have more entries, of course.

Figure 5-6   Hardware-independent index design.

THE OVERFLOW   In order to insert records into the file, some free space has to be available. Let us consider three choices for placing the records to be inserted
   1 Use a separate file, as in the sequential file organization
   2 Reserve space on every cylinder used by the file
   3 Reserve space in every block for insertions

Let us look at the extreme cases first. A separate insertion file requires a separate access with seek and latency overhead at any point where an insertion had been made. We want to do better now. Allocating space in every block is feasible only if blocks are large and insertions are well distributed; otherwise, it is too easy to run out of space in some blocks. To make such an approach successful requires dynamic space allocation, as used by multiply indexed files described in Sec. 5-3.

Keeping spare space in every cylinder provides a practical compromise. This is the method chosen in the typical indexed-sequential file organization. Locating an overflow record will require rotational latency but not a seek. To insert a record the cylinder address is obtained from the index by matching the attribute key value of the new record to the entry for the nearest predecessor. The new record is placed in the next sequential free position in the cylinder overflow area.

Linkage to Overflow Records   The records in the overflow areas should be found both by `Fetch` and `Get_Next` operations. In both cases the search process begins from the predecessor record and then follows pointers.

Overflow pointers are placed following the predecessor records in the primary data blocks (see Fig. 5-5). The key of the inserted record is not kept there. A search for any intervening record is directed to the overflow area. Modification of the index to reflect the insertion is avoided, but one more block access is needed on every fetch of an overflow record. A request for a nonexistent record will also require going to the overflow file if an overflow pointer is set with the predecessor record.

Chaining of Overflow Records   To locate multiple overflows a *linked list* is created. Linkage pointers are placed in the records in the overflow areas as well, so that all overflow records starting from one source are linked into a *chain*. A new record is linked into the chain according to its key value, so that sequential order is maintained. The chain can go through many blocks of the overflow area.

When the fetch has to proceed via many overflow records in a large number of blocks, following the chain to a specific record may actually be less efficient than simply searching the overflow area exhaustively. On the other hand, serial processing is greatly simplified when we can follow the chain. In order not to lose the records from the sequential file buffer when processing, a separate overflow buffer should be available.

Push-through   Instead of having one overflow pointer per record in the data file it is common to use only one pointer per block. With this method the key sequence in the blocks of the primary file is maintained:

1 New records are inserted after their proper predecessor
2 Successor records are pushed toward the end of the block.
3 Records from the end of the primary block are pushed out into the overflow area.

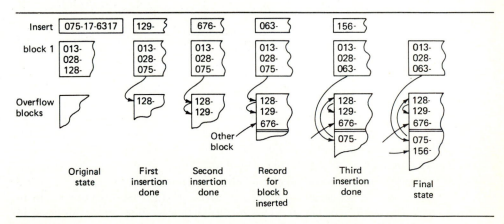

Figure 5-7   Inserting records into a block of an indexed-sequential file.

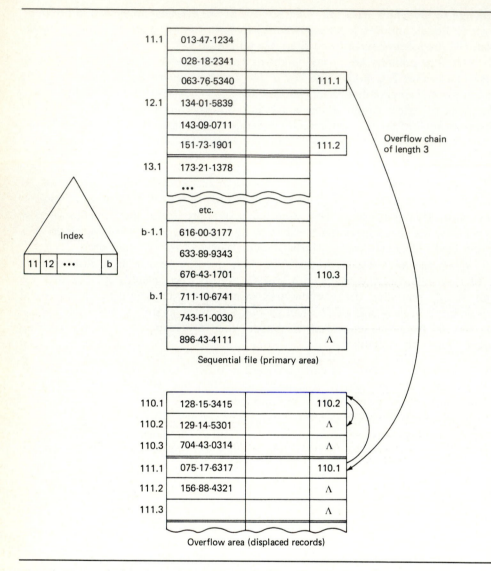

Figure 5-8   Indexed-sequential file overflow with push-through of records.

Figure 5-7 illustrates the *push-through* process using the same insertion sequence which led to Fig. 5-5. The final state of the file is shown in Fig. 5-8. The index is identical, since block positions do not change. Pointers are depicted in the form `block.record` number. Now only one overflow pointer is required per primary block and only one jump is made to the overflow file per block.

The chains will be longer than if each record had its own successor chain in the overflow area, by a factor of *Bfr*. This means that a fetch of a record placed in the overflow area will take longer. The average fetch and serial access will be better since there will be less switching between the sequential file area and the overflow file area, especially when the two areas are not on the same cylinder.

As the number of overflow records increases and with fairly many records per block, under conditions of uniform distribution the probability of having an overflow chain for every block rapidly approaches certainty.

▦ **Processing Overflow Chains** Overflow chains are costly to process. The serial processing required for overflow chains requires fetching a new block for each record. We will consider three issues here.

1 *Searching for nonexisting records.* Half the chain will have to be searched to find a record, but the entire chain must be searched to determine that a requested record does not exist. Maintaining chains sorted by key reduces the search for nonexisting records to about half the chain length as well.

2 *Fetching frequently needed records.* An alternative, keeping records in the chains by order of frequency of use can help find existing records faster. Since recent updates are more likely to be needed it can be beneficial to insert new updates into the front of the chain. This strategy reduces update cost as well.

3 *Considering the distribution of chain lengths.* In practice, overflow chains have quite unequal lengths; for instance, append operations create long chains connected to the last block, unless special mechanisms are used for appends. For an inventory file, activity may be high in a particular item, while other items are unused. In Chap. 12-1-5, Fig. 12-9, we develop estimates of the chain length, Lc, for random insertions, leading to Poisson distributions.

Statistical analysis becomes important if push-through is not used, since then many small chains must be considered.   ▦

Size of Overflow Areas Cylinder overflow areas have to be carefully dimensioned. If insertions cluster in certain areas, the corresponding cylinders will need large overflow areas. If the system provides a space allocation so that all cylinder overflow areas are of equal size, as most do, then much space can be wasted in cylinders that are not receiving many insertions. An escape hatch can be the provision of a secondary overflow area that is used when any cylinder overflow area itself overflows. Now the objective of avoiding seek time is lost for the records placed in the secondary overflow area; specifically, serial access will be quite slow.

Some methods to estimate the size of overflow areas required, given a specific distribution of record insertions, can be found in Chap. 12-1, and an assessment of insert versus inquiry frequencies is presented in Chap. 14-2.

REORGANIZATION At or before the point when the overflow areas themselves overflow, a file reorganization is required. Reorganization can also be needed when, because of the creation of long chains, the fetch or serial processing times become excessive. Such a reorganization consists of the steps shown in Table 5-1. During this process, the reorganization programs will create a completely new index based on new anchor point values for the blocks of the data file. The previous index is simply discarded.

The need for regular reorganization is a major drawback of indexed-sequential files, since it involves monitoring of the files and periodic special processing.

Table 5-1   Reorganization steps for an indexed-sequential file.

---

1 Read the file in the manner that would be used when doing serial processing, using both the sequential and the overflow areas.
2 Leave out all records that are marked deleted.
3 Write all new and old remaining records sequentially into the sequential areas of the new file.
4 Create and insert into a memory buffer an index entry with every block placed into the sequential area.
5 Write the index blocks out when they get full.
6 Create and insert a higher level index entry for every index block written.
7 When all data blocks have been written the remaining index buffers are written out.
8 Free the areas used by the old index.

The frequency of reorganization is dependent on the insertion activity within the file. In practice, one finds time intervals ranging from a day to a year between reorganization runs. Since a reorganization run can take a long time, the reorganization is generally performed before the file is actually full to avoid unpleasant surprises at busy times. It may simply be scheduled at periodic intervals or be done at a convenient instance after the entries in the overflow area exceed a preset limit. In Chap. 14-5 an algorithm for determining reorganization intervals will be presented.

5-1-2 Use of Indexed-Sequential Files

Indexed-sequential files of the basic type discussed above are in common use in modern commercial processing. They are used especially where there is a need to keep files up to date within time frames that are less than the processing intervals which are possible with cyclical reorganization of sequential files. Since individual records can be inserted and retrieved through the index, so that a limited number of block accesses are required, this type of file is suitable for *on-line* or terminal-oriented access. On-line use is not feasible with the pile and sequential file types unless the files are quite small.

At the same time sequential access is relatively simple and efficient. Without overflows, after a reorganization, sequential access is practically as fast as for the sequential file. An indexed-sequential file can, for instance, be used to produce an inventory listing on a daily basis and be reorganized on a weekly basis in concert with a process which issues notices to reorder goods for which the stock is low.

Indexed-sequential files are also in common use to handle inquiries, with the restriction that the query must specify the key attribute. Typical of these are billing inquiries based on account numbers. Sometimes copies of the same data are found sequenced according to different keys in separate indexed-sequential files to overcome this restriction. Updating cost and space requirements are multiplied in that case.

The effects of the specific design implemented for an indexed-sequential file are frequently not understood by the users, so that many applications which use indexed-sequential files take longer to process data than seems warranted. In situations where files receive updates in clusters, the generated chains can be costly to follow. Often, clustered updates are actually additions to the end of a file. By treating these separately, or by preallocating space and index values in the indexed-sequential file during the prior reorganization, the liabilities of appended records can be reduced. Within one indexed-sequential file method the options are often limited, but a number of alternative indexed-sequential file implementation are available from computer manufacturers and independent software producers.

The restriction that only one attribute key determines the major order of the file, so that all other attribute values are not suitable as search arguments, is common to all sequential files. Indexing with multiple keys is presented in Sec. 5-3. There a different scheme of index management is used and the sequentiality of the file is abandoned.

5-2   PERFORMANCE OF INDEXED-SEQUENTIAL FILES

Performance evaluation of indexed-sequential files is more complex than evaluation of the two preceding file organization methods because of the many options possible in the detailed design. We will base evaluation on a simple form similar to the most common commercial designs.

> The index is on the same key attribute used to sequence the data file itself. The first-level index is anchored to blocks of data, and a second-level index has one entry per first-level index block. Push-through is used when records are inserted into a block. Records in an overflow area of size o are linked in key order to provide good serial access.
>
> Records to be deleted are not actually removed, but only marked invalid with a tombstone. An additional field in each record of the main file is used for the tombstone. A field for a pointer for chaining is maintained within the overflow area. For both functions the same field position, of size P, is allocated in the records. We permit records of variable length in our analysis, although only few systems support such records.
>
> After a reorganization the main data areas and index areas are full and the overflow areas are empty. No change of the index takes place between reorganizations, simplifying the insertion of records. All areas are blocked to an equal size B. The total file may occupy multiple cylinders.

5-2-1 Record Size of an Indexed-Sequential File

In the sequential part of the file, a record requires space for a data values of size V and for a possible tombstone of size P.

$$R = aV + P \hspace{3cm} \langle \text{net} \rangle \text{ 5-3}$$

In the main file are n_m records and in the overflow file are o' records. Ignoring deleted records, $n = n_m + o'$. Initially or after reorganization, $n = n_m$. Space is allocated for up to o overflow records.

In addition, there exists an index with entries to locate the file blocks. The first-level index contains one entry per data block, so that, for level 1,

$$i_1 = \frac{n_m}{Bfr} \qquad\qquad 5\text{-}4$$

entries are required. The sizes of higher index levels are determined by the fanout, y, which in turn is determined by the block size, B, and the size of each index entry, $V + P$, as shown in Eq. 5-1. On each successive level will be one entry per lower-level index block, so that

$$i_{level} = \left\lceil \frac{i_{level-1}}{y} \right\rceil \qquad\qquad 5\text{-}5$$

until one block can contain all the pointers to the lower-level index. The number of blocks, bi, required for any index level is

$$bi_{level} = \left\lceil \frac{i_{level}}{y} \right\rceil = i_{level+1} \qquad\qquad 5\text{-}6$$

The total size of the index, SI, is then obtained by summing these until the single block at the root level, $bi_x = 1$, is reached. Using Eq. 5-6 we can simplify

$$SI = (bi_1 + bi_2 + \ldots + 1)B = (i_2 + i_3 + \ldots + 1)B \qquad\qquad 5\text{-}7$$

The total space per record, including space allocated to overflows, is then

$$R_{total} = \frac{n_m R + oR + SI}{n} \qquad\qquad \langle\text{gross}\rangle\; 5\text{-}8$$

The space used for the file remains constant during insertions, until a reorganization frees any deleted records and moves the overflow records into the main file. The new main file then has n records; the overflow file is empty but has space for o insertions, and the index size is probably pretty much the same.

5-2-2 Fetch Record in an Indexed-Sequential File

To locate a specific record, the index is used. The primary fetch procedure consists of an access to each level of the index, and a READ of the data block (Fig. 5-9).

$$T_{Fmain} = x(s + r + btt) + s + r + btt = (x + 1)(s + r + btt) \qquad \langle\text{primary}\rangle\; 5\text{-}9$$

In Chap. 8-1-1 we will present approaches to reduce this cost.

If insertions have occurred, the procedure is to also search for records that have been pushed into the overflow file area. A first-order estimate is that when o' overflows have occurred, the fetch time, T_F, increases proportionally, so that for a file that has n records,

$$T_F = (x + 1 + o'/n)(s + r + btt) \qquad\qquad \langle\text{simple}\rangle\; 5\text{-}10$$

This result is valid while the number of inserted records is modest, say, $o' < 0.2n$. In the next section we investigate the effect of overflow in more detail and derive a more precise value for T_F. However, since many assumptions must be made about uniformity of overflows the derivation shown is mainly to illustrate a method, rather than to provide better estiamtes for typical data retrievals.

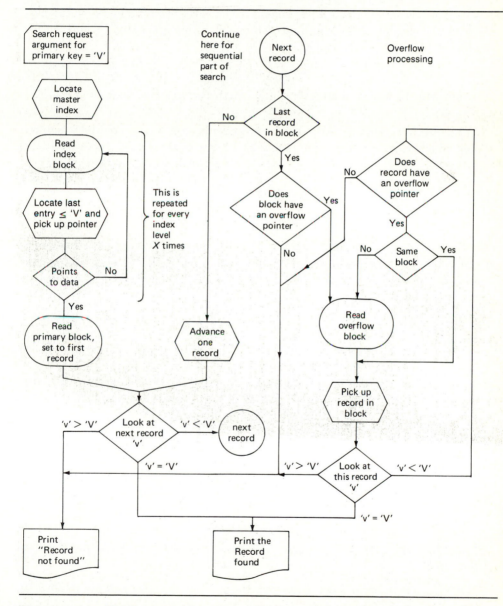

Figure 5-9   Fetch a record in an indexed-sequential file with push-through overflow.

▦▦▦▦ **Estimating Overflow Costs** The probability, Pov, that the desired record is in the overflow area depends on the number of insertions, o', that the file has received since it was reorganized. There are now n records and $n_m = n - o'$ are in the main file. The probability that a record which has been pushed into the overflow area is being fetched is

$$Pov = o'/n_m \qquad\qquad 5\text{-}11$$

The overflow records are attached in a chain to the block retrieved by the initial part of the fetch operation. The length of each chain can be estimated by considering the number of overflow records per main file block

$$Lc = o'\, Bfr/n_m \qquad\qquad 5\text{-}12$$

The number of blocks to be accessed in a search through the chain is $(Lc + 1)/2$ (see Eq. 4-2).

If the area for overflows is on another cylinder, a seek, $s^{\dagger}$, is required whenever the first overflow record of a chain is accessed. Any of the $Lc - 1$ further records from the chain are probably on different blocks, although on the same cylinder, and obtained at a cost of $r + btt$. The expected cost of getting to the overflow area and fetching a record is

$$T_{Foverflow} = Pov\left(s^{\dagger} + \frac{Lc + 1}{2}(r + btt)\right) \qquad\qquad 5\text{-}13$$

Both Pov and Lc are dependent on the amount of overflow, o'. If overflow areas are placed on the same cylinder the $s^{\dagger}$ term drops out. We can express the cost in terms of the overflows using Eqs. 5-10 and 5-11 and assume that the number of insertions was modest, so that $n_m \approx n$. Now

$$T_{Foverflow} = \frac{o'}{n}\left(s^{\dagger} + \frac{1}{2}(r + btt)\right) + \frac{1}{2}\frac{o'^2}{n}\, Bfr(r + btt) \qquad\qquad 5\text{-}14$$

The second term, although squared in o/n, may remain significant since values of Bfr may be such that $(o/n)^2 \times Bfr \approx o/n$.

An adequate estimate for record fetch in common indexed-sequential file configurations and usage is obtained by combining Eqs. 5-9 and 5-14 to give

$$T_F = T_{Fmain} + T_{Foverflow} \qquad\qquad 5\text{-}15$$

$$= x\,s + x\,r + x\,btt + s + r + btt + \frac{o'}{n}s^{\dagger} + \frac{o'}{2n}(r + btt) + \frac{1}{2}\frac{o'^2}{n}\, Bfr(r + btt)$$

$$= \left(x + 1 + \frac{o'^{\dagger}}{n}\right) s + \left(x + 1 + \frac{1}{2}\left(1 + \frac{o'}{n}Bfr\right)\frac{o'}{n}\right)(r + btt)$$

Now, if $o'/n \times Bfr \approx 1$ we can combine the terms due to Eq. 5-11 and Eq. 4-2. We are left with

$$T_F = (x + 1 + o'/n)(s + r + btt) \qquad\qquad \langle\text{shown above as}\rangle\ 5\text{-}10$$

Figure 5-10 provides sample calculations illustrating the precision under the various assumptions. ▦▦▦▦

To estimate the fetch time with overflows we use the same file size presented in the example of Fig. 5-6, so that x is 3. If reorganizations are made when the overflow area is 80% full, the average value of o' will be $0.4o$. If we consider a case where an overflow area equal to 20% of the prime file has been allocated, then $o' = 0.20 \times 0.4\,n = 0.08\,n$. Using the relations above, and a Bfr of 10,

$$Pov = 0.08/1.08 = 0.0741 \qquad \text{and} \qquad Lc = 10 \times 0.0741 = 0.741$$

With these assumptions we arrive at an average fetch time using Eq. 5-15 versus the simplification of Eq. 5-10

$$T_F = 4.072(s + r + btt) \qquad \text{versus} \qquad T_F\langle simple \rangle = 4.080(s + r + btt)$$

If we use $n_m = n - o'$ instead of n we would obtain
$$T_F = 4.0645(s + r + btt)$$

Figure 5-10   Estimation of fetch time.

5-2-3 Get-Next Record of an Indexed-Sequential File

In order to locate a successor record, we start from the last data record and ignore the index. We have to determine whether serial reading can be done sequentially or whether we have to go to another area. We can expect to have to go to the overflow area in proportion to the ratio of records to be found there, o'/n_m, but in the main file we only have to read a new block $1/Bfr$ times. An estimate is then

$$T_N = \frac{1}{Bfr}(s + r + btt) + \frac{o'}{n_m}(r + btt) \qquad \langle \text{estimate} \rangle \ 5\text{-}16$$

A more precise case analysis has to consider all the possibilities which exist and consider the locations of the predecessor and of the successor record. The six cases we can distinguish are illustrated using the record numbers of Fig. 5-8. The process is flowcharted in Fig. 5-11. The result, after simplification, becomes Eq. 5-18.

▦▦ **Path Choices for Next Record**   We consider again block-anchored overflow records, and begin with the most likely case:

a   The current record is in a main data file block and the successor record is in the same block, and hence already available in a memory buffer (e.g., the current record is 11.1, 11.2, 12.1, ...).

b   The current record is the last one in the block, there were no insertions, and the successor record is in a following block on the same cylinder.

c   The current record is the last one in the block, and there have been no insertions, but the record is in a new block on another cylinder. Given that there are β blocks per cylinder, and the file begins at a new cylinder, this would happen between records $\beta.3$ and $(\beta + 1).1$, $2\beta.3$ and $(2\beta + 1).1$, once for each cylinder occupied by the file.

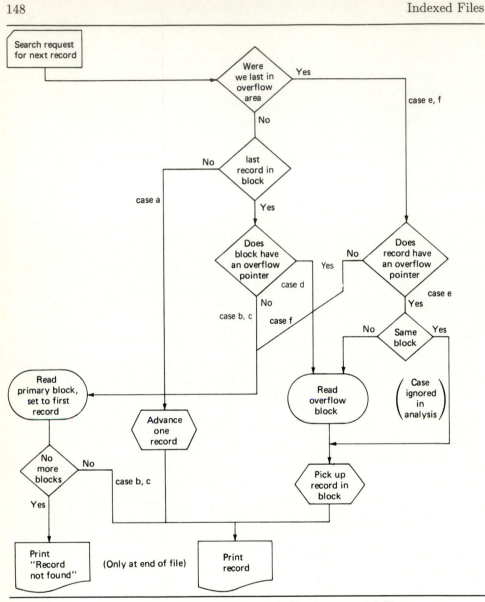

Figure 5-11   Get the successor record in an indexed-sequential file.
                       Note that the flow in this figure overlaps Fig. 5-9 to a great extent.

    d   The current record is the last one in the block, but there has been an insertion, and the successor record will be in an overflow block (the current record is 11.3 or 12.3).

    e   The current record is an inserted record, and the successor is found following the chain to another overflow block on the same cylinder (current record is 110.1 or 111.1).

    f   The current record is an inserted record, and to get to the successor record a new data block has to be read (current record is 110.2, 110.3, or 111.2).

We will evaluate each of these cases using probabilities of the events which lead to their occurrence. The following notation is chosen to define the more likely condition of each event:

Pd: The current record is in a primary data block $= 1 - Pov$.
Pb: The successor record is in the same block $= 1 - 1/Bfr$.
Pm: There has been no insertion into the block $= 1 - Bfr\,Pov$.
Pc: The next block is in the same cylinder $= 1 - 1/\beta$.
Pl: The current overflow record is not the last of the chain. $= 1 - 1/Lc$

These values can now be used for the cases shown in Fig. 5-12.

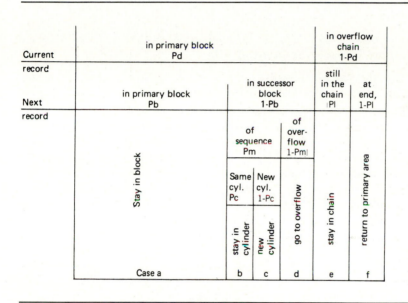

Figure 5-12   Conditions in the search for a successor record.

Figure 5-12 indicates the conditions based on Fig. 5-11. By applying the appropriate combinations of probabilities to their costs, we obtain for the cases considered

$$
\begin{aligned}
T_N = \quad & (Pd)(Pb)(c)+ && /* \, case \, a \, */ \\
& (Pd)(1-Pb)(Pm)(Pc)(r+btt)+ && /* \, case \, b \, */ \\
& (Pd)(1-Pb)(Pm)(1-Pc)(s+r+btt)+ && /* \, case \, c \, */ \\
& (Pd)(1-Pb)(1-Pm)(s^{\dagger}+r+btt)+ && /* \, case \, d \, */ \\
& (1-Pd)(Pl)(r+btt)+ && /* \, case \, e \, */ \\
& (1-Pd)(1-Pl)(s^{\dagger}+\dot{r}+btt) && /* \, case \, f \, */
\end{aligned}
$$

5-17

The seek terms in cases d and f, marked with a †, disappear when the overflow areas are kept on the same cylinders as the corresponding data blocks. The probabilities Pm and Pl can be rewritten in terms of n and o' using Eqs. 5-11 and 5-12.

Simplification of Get-Next Estimate Equation 5-17 was obtained by a detailed case analysis, but as is typical, the result can be made practical by consideration of the relative importance of the terms. If we neglect the memory search time, c, for records within the block, if cylinder seeks can be ignored (i.e., β is large, so that the value of $Pc \approx 1$), and if the overflow areas are on the same cylinders as the data blocks ($s^\dagger = 0$, so that cases b and d, as well as e and f combine), then

$$T_N \approx \left(\frac{1 - Pov}{Bfr} + Pov \right)(r + btt) = \frac{n + o'\,Bfr}{(n + o')Bfr}(r + btt) \qquad \text{5-18}$$

We note that the chain length Lc does not affect this approximation for T_N, but overflows still increase the estimate.   ▥

5-2-4 Insert into an Indexed-Sequential File

Adding a record to the file will always cause an addition to the overflow chain, either because of push-through or because the new record follows serially a record already in the overflow chain. Each insertion requires the reading and rewriting of a predecessor data or overflow block, since a pointer will have to be inserted or changed and also a READ and REWRITE of the overflow block for the pushed or inserted record. The probability of using the same overflow block for both is small if records are randomly inserted into a large data file. We avoid a detailed case analysis now by using the previous result for T_F and making some further assumptions. The fetch time for the predecessor is equal to T_F, the overflow block is on the same cylinder and requires $r + btt$ to be reached, and each REWRITE will take one revolution $T_{RW} = 2r$ (given the conditions of Eq. 3-22), so that

$$T_I = T_F + T_{RW} + r + btt + T_{RW} = T_F + 5r + btt \qquad \text{5-19}$$

The effect of the length of the overflow is incorporated into T_F.

Note that the index is not affected when a record is inserted. The cost of insertion is only due to appending the record to the chain and linking it to the predecessor record. Alternative issues of chain management, discussed earlier, may be considered.

5-2-5 Update Record in an Indexed-Sequential File

An updated record of equal size and identical key can be placed into the place of the previous version of the record, so that the process can be evaluated as a fetch followed by a REWRITE with a cost of T_{RW}:

$$T_U = T_F + T_{RW} = T_F + 2r \qquad \langle\text{in place}\rangle \text{ 5-20}$$

Deletion of a record, done by setting a tombstone into the record, is also done using this process. Equation 5-20 is always appropriate for systems which disallow both the updating of key fields and variable-length records.

In the general case, the previous version of the record has to be deleted and the new record inserted appropriately. The old record is rewritten with the tombstone; the key and pointer fields are kept intact so that the structure of the file is not violated. Then

$$T_U = T_F + T_{RW} + T_I = 2T_F + 7r + btt \qquad \text{(in general)} \ \ 5\text{-}21$$

If the cases which permit in-place updates are recognized by the file system, then T_U is to be computed based on the mix of in-place and general updates.

5-2-6 Read Entire Indexed-Sequential File

An exhaustive search of the file has to be made when the search argument is not the indexed attribute. The file may be read serially by following the overflow chains for every block, or if seriality is not required, the entire data area on a cylinder can be read sequentially, followed by sequential reading of the entire overflow area. In either case, the index can be ignored unless it contains space-allocation information.

Most systems provide only the ability to read serially, so that

$$T_X = T_F + (n + o' - 1)T_N \approx (n + o')T_N = \frac{n + o'\,Bfr}{Bfr}(r + btt) \qquad \text{(serial)} \ \ 5\text{-}22$$

The assumptions leading to Eq. 5-18 are valid here.

In the alternative case the evaluation would consider the effective transfer rate, neglecting the delay when skipping from data blocks to overflow blocks. Unused overflow blocks will not be read, so that o' can be used to estimate the size of the overflow areas read. Now

$$T_X \approx (n + o')\frac{R}{t'} \qquad \text{(sequential)} \ \ 5\text{-}23$$

5-2-7 Reorganization of an Indexed-Sequential File

To reorganize the old file, the entire file is read serially and rewritten without the use of overflow areas. As a by-product a new index is constructed. The prior index can be ignored, since the file is read serially. Additional buffers in memory are needed to collect the new data and index information. For the index it is desirable to have at least one buffer for every level. The new mainfile should be at least double-buffered. All outputs can be written sequentially. Then

$$T_Y = \frac{n + o'\,Bfr}{Bfr}(r + btt) + (n + o' - d)\frac{R}{t'} + \frac{SI}{t'} \qquad 5\text{-}24$$

We assume that o' new records are in the overflow areas; however, the value of o' will be larger at reorganization time than in the cases considered in Eqs. 5-9 to 5-22. The value of o' will still be less than o, the number of records for which overflow space has been allocated.

Following the discussion of reorganization in Chap. 4-1-3(7), we assume that $o' = 0.8\,o$. Such a value is justified if the reorganization policy were as follows:

> *Reorganization of a file is to be done the first night the overflow area exceeds 75% utilization, given that the average daily increase of the overflow area is 10%.*

A simpler assumption that $o' = o$ will provide a conservative approximation for the number of overflow records to be processed.

5-3   THE INDEXED FILE

Indexed-sequential files only provide one index, but searching for information may have to be done on other attributes than a primary key attribute. In a generalized indexed file we permit multiple indexes. There may be indexes on any attribute, and perhaps on all attributes. A number of changes to the file organization follow from that extension.

- All indexes are treated equally:
    1 All indexes are record-anchored.
    2 The concept of a primary attribute is not retained.
    3 No sequentiality according to a primary index is maintained.
- No overflow chains can be maintained:
    1 Any insertions are placed into the main data file.
    2 The main file format should make insertion convenient.
    3 All indexes must be updated to reflect insertions.

We expand on the trade-offs implied above in more detail throughout this section.

By going up the requirement for sequentiality to provide efficient serial access, much flexibility is gained. In the generalized indexed file the records are accessed only through their indexes. There is now no restriction on the placement of a data record, as long as a TID exists in some index that allows the record to be fetched when the goal data from the record is wanted. Each index is associated with some attribute.

The gain in flexibility obtained makes this file organization preferable to the indexed-sequential file organization in many applications. The actual physical placement and format of records in generalized indexed files can be determined by secondary considerations, as ease of management or reliability. Having indexes on more than one attribute greatly increases the availability of the data in information retrieval and advanced processing systems. Variable-length records are common in these applications.

The flexibility of generalized indexed files has created a great variety of actual designs. The variety of designs has unfortunately also created a diversity of terminology, often quite inconsistent, so that anyone intending to evaluate a specific approach to indexed files will have to translate terms used in describing such systems into standard concepts. We will evaluate again a specific approach which is becoming increasingly common, based on the use of *B-trees* for the indexes.

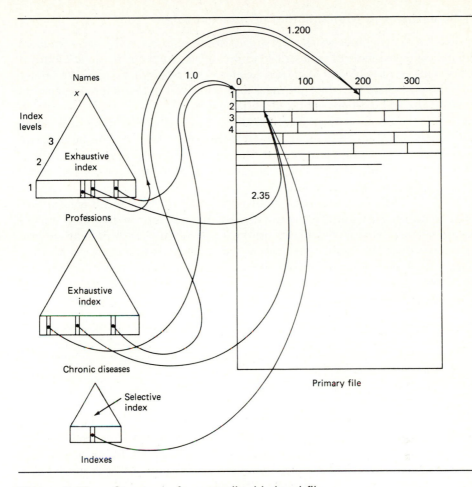

Figure 5-13 Structure of a generalized indexed file.

Figure 5-13 shows schematically three indexes into a `Personnel` file, for the attributes `Names`, `Professions`, and `Chronic_diseases`. Each of the variable-length spanned records of the file can be located by giving a name or profession value. The third record, in block 2 at position 35, has a field with the attribute name `Chronic_diseases` and can also be located via that index.

Directories Since an indexed file with multiple indexes consists of several distinct component files we must be able to determine what indexes exist, how they are organized, and where they are located. An extension of the notion of the file directory, introduced in Chap. 4-1-1, can satisfy that role. Programs which retrieve data or update the file must consult that directory to carry out their function. In database management systems *schemas* take on that role, as indicated in Chap. 16-2. For our evaluations we assume that such a directory is read into a memory buffer when the file is opened, and can be rapidly searched.

5-3-1 Structure and Manipulation of Indexed Files

There may be as many indexes as there are attribute columns in the file; even more if we build combined indexes as described in Sec. 5-5-3. An index for an attribute of an indexed file consists of a set of entries, one for every record in the file. We cannot use block-anchors here to reduce the index size, as we did in the indexed-sequential file, since index and data are not cosequential.

The entries are ordered as determined by the attribute values. Each entry consists of the attribute value and a TID. In indexed files successor records are reached using the next index entry rather than by sequentiality or via pointers from the predecessor record. Each index may again require multiple levels, just as we have seen in an indexed-sequential file.

The data record format may be similar to any of the previous organizations. Records containing attribute name-value pairs, as seen in the pile file, are the choice permitting greatest flexibility; otherwise, structured records may be employed. Since the TIDs in the index specify the block address and record position for every record, there is essentially no restriction on record size or on the placement of records within a specific block. Records can be inserted wherever the file system finds sufficient free space.

Maintenance of Indexes The major problem when using indexed files is that all the indexes to a record must be updated whenever a record has been added or deleted or is moved. A single index has to be changed when a single data field value of an indexed attribute is updated.

In indexed-sequential files dynamic updating of the index was avoided through the use of pointer chains to insertions. With indexing for multiple attributes such overflow chaining is not feasible; each record would need many overflow pointers. The pointers would have to link a new record to many predecessor records. The alternative is to update the actual indexes as the file changes, but a dense index structure as used with indexed-sequential files would require for each insertion or deletion of an index entry the rewriting of the entire index.

⧚⧚⧚ **Exhaustive and Partial Indexes** Indexes may be *exhaustive*, that is, have TIDs to every record in the file; or *partial*, that is, have only TIDs to records where the attribute value is significant. Significance can mean simply that a value exists (is not undefined or zero) or that the value has a good selectivity.

A partial index could occur in a personnel file which includes health data. Only indexes to current employee health problems are maintained, although complete historical data is kept in the records for review purposes. This was shown symbolically in Fig. 5-13 as a `Chronic_diseases` index; here `NULL` or `Healthy` data values do not lead to entries. Another partial index could identify all individuals that smoke, to help in risk assessments.

If there is not even one exhaustive index, there is no easy way to list each record once. Now a space allocation table is required to allow the file to be properly maintained. Such a table gives an accounting of all the space allocated to the file. If the file is read serially according to this table, a record ordering similar to the pile file may be perceived.   ⧚⧚⧚

AN INDEX STRUCTURE FOR DYNAMIC UPDATING — B-TREES   In indexed files every change of an indexed attribute will require the insertion, deletion, or both, of an index entry into the appropriate index block. To make such changes feasible, we reduce the density of the index. Extra space is left initially empty in each index block, and now one insertion will affect only that index block. The blocks can accommodate a number of insertions, and only when the block is filled is another block obtained. Half the entries from the full block are distributed to the new block. There has been a trade-off made here: space has been given up to have reasonable maintenance of the index.

A method based on this solution is the *B-tree*, and we will describe a specific version of this algorithm useful for index trees. A B-tree has index blocks which are kept at least half full; the effective fanout y_{eff} is hence between y and $y/2$ as shown in Fig. 5-14.

B-trees and Index B-trees   The original B-tree was defined with space in each block for y pointers and $y-1$ values. In a block of an index B-tree, however, up to y values are kept, and the value (v_1) appears redundantly, as shown in Fig. 5-14. The value in the first entry (v_1) is the same as the value (v_n) in the entry referring to this block in the next-higher-level index block. This redundancy is avoided in pure B-trees. The index B-tree approach makes the entries consistent in format, permits index blocks to be accessed independently of their ancestor blocks, and has little effect on the analyses when y is reasonably large.

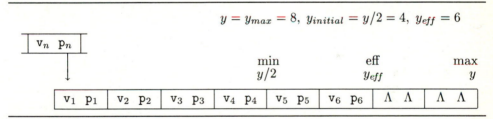

$$y = y_{max} = 8, \ y_{initial} = y/2 = 4, \ y_{eff} = 6$$

Figure 5-14   Block of a B-tree index after two insertions.

INDEX B-TREE ALGORITHMS   The insertion and deletion algorithms for B-trees must maintain the condition that index blocks are at least half full.

Insertion   New entries are inserted into the first-level index blocks until the limit y is reached. The next entry to be inserted will require the allocation of a new, empty index block, which is then initialized with half the entries taken from the block which was full: The block has been *split*. The entry which forced the split can now be inserted into the appropriate level one index block. At the same time a new entry has to be created for the new index block at the next higher level, containing a pair $\{v_{n+1}, p_{n+1}\}$. The value v_{n+1} is the former $v_{y/2+1}$ taken from the split block, which is now v_1 in the new block.

The next-level block may in turn be already full and also require such a split. If the top or root block is full, a new root block is created and initially filled with two entries, one for the previous root block and one for its new partner. The tree has now grown by one level. We note that the root block only may have fewer than

$y/2$ entries; y_{eff} may be anywhere from 2 to y but we ignore the effect due to the root block in our analyses.

This insertion algorithm maintains the value of y_{eff} in the desired range; the deletion algorithm below does the same. For a file receiving only insertions the average y_{eff} for the entire index will become $0.75\,y$, but we will henceforth use a result of Yao[78], which specifies that under conditions of random insertions and deletions the B-tree eventually achieves a density of $y_{eff}/y \to \ln 2 = 0.69$. Then

$$y/2 \leq y_{eff} \leq y \qquad \text{or} \qquad y_{eff} \to \ln 2 \times y = 0.69\,y \qquad\qquad \text{5-25}$$

where y is again defined as in Eq. 5-1 as $\lfloor B/(V + P) \rfloor$. In order to simplify the analysis, we also assume an initial loading density of 0.69.

Deletion in a B-tree When an entry is deleted, an index block may be left with fewer than $y/2$ entries. Its partner should now be inspected. If the total number of entries in both is less than y, they should be combined. An entry in the higher-level index block is now also deleted, and this deletion may propagate and even lead to the deletion of an entry in the root block. If the root block has only one entry left, it can be deleted so that the height of the tree is reduced by one.

In practice, deletion in B-trees is often modified. For instance, if the total of two blocks is exactly y, then it is best not to combine the blocks to avoid excessive costs if deletions and insertions alternate. Furthermore, since the cost of inspecting the partner index blocks for its occupancy is so high, testing for block merging is often deferred. This topic is considered in Chap. 8-1-3.

The Height of B-trees The number of levels of indexing required is a function of the number of index entries, y_{eff}, that appear in one index block. In order to evaluate the height of the B-trees we will assume here that stability has been achieved and that all index levels partition their data evenly. Given that one index will refer to n' records, where n' is determined by the expected number of records having indexable attribute values, we find, similarly to Eq. 5-2,

$$x = \left\lceil \log_{y_{eff}} n' \right\rceil \qquad\qquad \text{5-26}$$

We note that because of the reduced density and fanout the height of the index B-trees is greater than the height of a dense index. The height, x, will be one level greater in many practical cases. A greater increase occurs only in large files with small fanouts, say, $n' > 10^6$ and $y < 12$. With large fanouts there will be wide ranges of n' where the index height is the same for a dense index and a corresponding B-tree.

The height of a B-tree controls the time needed to retrieve records. The search process is flowcharted in Fig. 5-15.

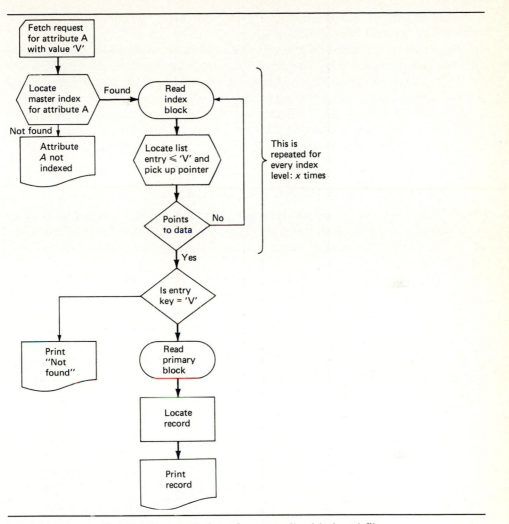

Figure 5-15   Fetch using one index of a generalized indexed file.

5-3-2 Use of Indexed Files

Indexed files are used mainly in areas where timeliness of information is critical. Examples are found in airline reservation systems, job banks, military data systems, and other inventory type applications. Here data is rarely processed serially, other than for occasional, maybe only yearly, stocktaking.

When an item of information is obtained, e.g., an available seat on a certain flight, the data should be correct at that point in time, and if the item is updated, i.e., a seat is sold on that flight, that fact should be immediately known throughout the system.

Having multiple indexes to such information makes it possible that one can find the same data by flight number, by passenger name, by interline transfer record, and so forth, without file reorganization or data redundancy. There is now, of course, redundancy between the contents of the index and the data.

Other instances where indexed files are desirable occur when data is highly variable and dynamic. The flexibility of the record format and record placement available with generalized indexed files does not exist in other file systems. Chapter 8 is devoted to specific alternatives and examples of indexed and related files.

The use of indexed files is increasing, specifically on modern systems, where new software is being developed. There is also more literature in this area than about any other file organization.

5-4   PERFORMANCE OF INDEXED FILES

Indexed files are easier to evaluate than indexed-sequential files. B-trees have a very predictable behavior since all search operations require an effort based on the height of the index tree. The critical design decision is the selection of the attributes that are to be indexed.

The space required for exhaustive indexes for all attributes will easily exceed the size of the original file. In practice, there are always some attributes for which indexing is not justified. Attributes that have low selectivity, as defined in Chap. 4-2-1, are poor candidates for indexing. Not having indexes for these attributes, or the use of partial indexes, will reduce the size of the index space and accelerate updating. Any searches must avoid the use of omitted indexes.

The evaluation which follows considers a completely indexed file, so that all existing attributes of every record are indexed. There will hence be a indexes with up to n, say n', entries. Each index is a B-tree, and the main data file has the form of a pile file. The records may be of variable length and have a variable number of attribute name-value pairs. Insertions are placed into the pile file itself and cause updating of all indexes.

We also assume that steady state has been achieved, so that the density of the index is assumed to be stable at $dens = y_{eff}/y = 0.69$. This means that deletion is done so that partners have never jointly fewer than y entries. The actual space requirement for the index entries is now $1/0.69 = 1.44$ of the net requirement. Note also that the height of the index tree may be greater than the height of a denser index.

5-4-1 Record Size in an Indexed File

The space required for the data portion of such a file is identical to the space required for a pile file, as derived for Eq. 4-1. In addition, there will be a indexes to provide an index for every attribute. Since the data attributes are sparse, there are only a' attribute entries per record; the average index contains

$$n' = n\frac{a'}{a}$$

5-27

index entries referring to data records.

Each index entry is of size $V_{index} + P$ and the size of one index is estimated as

$$SI(one)_1 = n' \frac{(V_{index} + P)}{dens} = 1.44 \frac{n\,a'}{a}(V_{index} + P) \qquad \langle \text{one index} \rangle \text{ 5-28}$$

Higher-level index blocks require little additional space; for instance, the second level adds only $SI_2 \approx SI_1/y_{eff}$ bytes. To account for these higher index levels, we can add 5% to SI, changing the factor 1.44 to 1.5. The total index space becomes

$$SI_{total} = a \sum_{i=1}^{x} SI_i \approx 1.5\,n\,a'(V_{index} + P) \qquad\qquad \text{5-29}$$

The space requirement per record is equal to the sum of data and index space. No overflow area exists.

Since all attribute values which exist in a given record are indexed, the space allocated to a record is

$$\begin{aligned} R_{total} &= R_{main} + a'\,R_{index} \\ &= a'(A + V + 2) + 1.5\,a'(V_{index} + P) \end{aligned} \qquad\qquad \text{5-30}$$

for index and data. If V_{index} is taken to be equal to V, then

$$R = a'(A + 2.5V + 1.5p + 2) \qquad\qquad \langle V_{index} = V \rangle \text{ 5-31}$$

based on Eqs. 5-25 and 5-30. An evaluation is shown in Fig. 5-16.

Consider a Personnel file of $n = 20\,000$ employees, containing an inventory of their skills. Each employee has an average of 2.5 skills so that for this particular index a'/a is actually greater than 1. The skills are given a code of 6 characters. To find an employee record, an 8-digit TID is used which occupies 4 character positions, giving $V + P = 10$ bytes per index entry.

The blocks in the file system are $B = 1000$ characters long, so that $y = 100$ index elements can appear per block.

$$\begin{aligned} n' &= n\,a'/a = 20\,000 \times 2.5 = 50\,000 \\ b_1 &= n'/(0.69y) = 50\,000/69 = 725 \\ b_2 &= b_1/(0.69y) = 725/69 = 11 \\ b_3 &= b_x = b_2/(0.69y) = 11/69 = 1 \end{aligned}$$

Estimating x directly, we obtain the same result:

$$x = \lceil \log_{69}(20\,000 \times 2.5) \rceil = 3$$

An estimate for the space is based on Eq. 5-28, as modified for all levels:
$SI(\text{skill}) = 1.5n\,a'/a(V + P) = 750\,000$ bytes, and used to derive Eq. 5-30.
The space requirement for this index is actually
$SI_{skill} = \sum b_i B = 737\,000$ bytes, because of the high fanout.

Figure 5-16   Calculation of levels for an indexed file.

▦▦▦▦ **Attribute Sizes in Indexes** The value field in an index, V_{index}, is often not the same size as in the data, so that it should be estimated separately. The value field in an index may, for instance, be required to be of fixed length to allow fast searches through the index, so that V_{index} will be larger than the average value field, V, in a data record. On the other hand, if there are frequently multiple records related to a certain attribute value. For example, if the attribute category is `profession`, there will be several entries in this index for an attribute value like `'welder'`); and one value entry may serve many TIDs.

Techniques discussed in Chap. 8-2-2 reduce key value sizes of indexes further, so that often $V_{index} < V$.   ▦▦▦▦

5-4-2 Fetch Record in an Indexed File

The expected fetch time for an indexed file is similar to the time used for an indexed-sequential file. However, no overflow areas exist, and hence the term that accounts for the chasing after overflow records is eliminated. The indexes will be of the larger record-anchored variety and also will contain space for insertions, so that their height, x, will be greater. We add the accesses for index and data and find

$$T_F = x(s + r + btt) + s + r + btt = (x + 1)(s + r + btt) \qquad 5\text{-}32$$

where x is given by Eq. 5-26.

If each index can be kept compactly on a single cylinder, then some seeks can be avoided, so that

$$T_F = 2s + (x + 1)(r + btt) \qquad \langle\text{compact index}\rangle \; 5\text{-}33$$

5-4-3 Get-Next Record of an Indexed File

The search for a successor record is based on the assumption that the last index block is kept available in a buffer, so that only a new data record has to be fetched.

$$T_N = s + r + btt \qquad 5\text{-}34$$

This holds as long as the effective fanout ratio $y_{eff} \gg 1$, since the probability that the current index block contains also the TID of the next record is $Pd = (y_{eff} - 1)/y_{eff}$.

If indeed a successor index block is needed, the second-level index block has to be accessed to locate the successor. If the second-level block is not kept in a memory buffer as well, two block accesses are needed with a frequency of $1 - Pd$. The frequency of having to access a third- or higher-level index block is generally negligible.

5-4-4 Insert into an Indexed File

To add a record to an indexed file, the record is placed in any free area, and then all a' indexes referring to existing attributes for this record have to be updated.

The insertion process will have to find for each index the affected index block by searching from the root block of each index, and rewrite an updated index block at level 1; we will call this time T_{index}. With a probability of $Ps = 1/(y/2) = 2/y$ there will be a block split. A block split requires the fetch of a new partner block, some computation to distribute the entries, and the rewriting of the new block and the ancestor block with a new entry, all this in addition to the rewrite of the old block; the incremental time is T_{split}.

Summing the times for data block fetch and rewrite, for following a' indexes down x levels, for first-level index rewrites, and for the possible split, we find

$$T_I = T_{data} + a'(T_{index} + Ps\, T_{split})\qquad\qquad\text{5-35}$$

$$= s + r + btt + T_{RW} + a'\left(x(s + r + btt) + T_{RW} + \tfrac{2}{y}(c + s + r + btt + 2T_{RW})\right)$$

$$= \tfrac{2}{y}c + \left(1 + a'\left(x + \tfrac{2}{y}\right)\right)(s + r + btt) + \left(1 + a'\left(1 + 2\tfrac{2}{y}\right)\right)T_{RW}$$

Keeping indexes within a cylinder can reduce the time by requiring only one seek per index. Although Eq. 5-35 looks forbidding, it actually shows that cost of insertion is mainly dependent on the number of indexes, or $\mathcal{O}(a'(1 + \log_y n + 1/y))$. If all indexes are small so that $x = 2$, further ignoring the cost of splitting ($y \gg 1$) and using $T_{RW} = 2r$ gives an estimate which is $\mathcal{O}(a')$:

$$T_I = (1 + a')s + (3 + 4a')r + (1 + 2a')btt\qquad\qquad\text{⟨simple⟩ 5-36}$$

In the absolutely worst case the insertion could cause all index blocks to overflow so that they all have to be split. The delay of even several splits could be quite disconcerting to a user entering data on a terminal. A technique, *presplitting*, which reduces the likelihood of multiple splits in one index, is described in Chap. 8-1-2. With deferred updating only one index access and the actual record rewriting is noted by the user.

5-4-5 Update Record in an Indexed File

An update of a record in an indexed file consists of a search for the record, the update of the data record, followed by a change of those indexes for which the new record contains changed values. An update changes one data record and a_{update} indexes. The new field values may be far removed from the old ones, so that the new index entries are in blocks other than the old ones. Now each index update requires the search for and rewriting of two index blocks, the old one and the new one, doubling the term $T_{index} + Ps\, T_{split}$ found in Eq. 5-35. The new index block may require a split because of the insertion, and the block used previously may have to be combined because of the deletion of an entry. We assumed that deletion is as costly as insertion and use below T_{split} for either operation.

The pile organization of the data file leads us to expect that the old data record will be invalidated and a new copy will be inserted ($T_{newcopy}$). The TID value for all indexes will then have to be updated so that the remaining $a' - a_{update}$ indexes also have to be fixed. Fixing the TID requires finding the blocks and rewriting them; no splits will occur here; this term is T_{fixTID}.

We collect all the costs.

$$
\begin{aligned}
T_U &= T_F + T_{RW} + T_{newcopy} \qquad\qquad\qquad\qquad\qquad\qquad \text{5-37} \\
&\quad + 2\,a_{update}(T_{index} + P_s\,T_{split}) + (a' - a_{update})(T_{fixTID}) \\
&= (x+1)(s+r+btt) + T_{RW} + s + r + btt + T_{RW} \\
&\quad + 2\,a_{update}\left(x(s+r+btt) + T_{RW} + \tfrac{2}{y}(c+s+r+btt+T_{RW})\right) \\
&\quad + (a' - a_{update})\,(x(s+r+btt) + T_{RW}) \\
&= (x+2)(s+r+btt) + 2\,T_{RW} \\
&\quad + a_{update}\left(x(s+r+btt) + T_{RW} + \tfrac{4}{y}(c+s+r+btt+T_{RW})\right) \\
&\quad + a'\,(x(s+r+btt) + T_{RW})
\end{aligned}
$$

Making the same simplifications used to obtain Eq. 5-36, we find that a simple update for a modest file will take approximately

$$
T_U = (4 + 2\,a_{update} + 2\,a')(s + 2r + btt) \qquad\qquad \langle\text{simple}\rangle\ \text{5-38}
$$

If the updated record does not have to be moved, the $a' - a_{update}$ indexes do not have to be changed, and now the same simplification gives

$$
T_U = (4 + 4\,a_{update})(s + 2r + btt) \qquad\qquad \langle\text{in place}\rangle\ \text{5-39}
$$

We observe that updating is, in most cases, costlier than insertion and that techniques for deferring part of the update process may be quite beneficial to gain response time for the user. This topic is expanded in Chap. 8-1-3.

▦▦▦ **Small Value Changes** When an update changes an attribute value by a small amount, then it is likely that both old and new index values fall into the same index block. In that case one search and rewrite may be saved. The ratio between out-of-index block and within-index block changes depends on the application. In some cases the behavior of the attribute value changes is predictable. For instance, if the attribute type is a person's `weight`, we can expect the within-index block case to be predominant. If the update changes a value from undefined to a defined value, only a new index entry has to be created. If we define P_i to be the probability of out-of-index block updates, we find for a single update, given all the conditions leading to Eq. 5-39,

$$
T_U = 2(3 + P_i)(s + 2r + btt) \qquad\qquad \langle\text{single change, in place}\rangle\ \text{5-40}
$$

In the general case we have to assume the index changes will be randomly distributed among the blocks of an index. Given the expected loading density of 69%, there will be

$$
b_1 = 1.44\,\frac{n}{y}\,\frac{a'}{a} \qquad\qquad\qquad\qquad\qquad\qquad \text{5-41}
$$

first level index blocks for one attribute; then the probability, given random data changes, of requiring another index block is high: $Pi = (b_1 - 1)/b_1$. For large files Pi will be close to 1, so that Eqs. 5-37 to 5-39 remain appropriate.

However, Eq. 5-40 is of interest whenever it can be shown that Pi will be low because of the behavior of data value changes for updated attributes. Important cases exist in *real-time systems*, where the database receives values from devices that monitor changes in the operation of some ongoing physical process. Changes in `pressure`, `temperature`, or `flow` occur mainly gradually, making Pi small. In such systems the data is often acquired at high rates, so that the improved file performance could be critical.   ▦

▦   **Non-Uniform Update Distribution**   The uniform behavior assumed for insertion and update patterns represents the best behavior that can be expected. Unfortunately the growth of an index is rarely evenly distributed over the range of attribute values. Updating tends to be periodically heavy in one area, and then concentrate again on other attributes. Consider for instance a stock-market file, over some hours there is much activity in a stock which is in the news, and later there will be little activity there. These irregularities affect system behavior. An analysis of these conditions requires statistics about application update behavior which we do not have available here. We will not evaluate their effect here, but note that if there exists a good understanding of the frequency of attribute changes and of the value-change ranges, a more precise estimate of update cost can be made, by refining the concepts presented above.   ▦

5-4-6 Read Entire Indexed File

The basic fully indexed organization is poorly suited for exhaustive searches. When necessary, such searches may be accomplished by using the space-allocation information, or by serial reading of the file using some exhaustive index. An exhaustive index is created when the referred data element is required to exist in every record. A brute force approach using such an index will cost

$$T_X = T_F + (n - 1) T_N \qquad \langle \text{serially} \rangle \text{ 5-42}$$

If one can follow the space-allocation pointers, seeks need to be done only once per block, so that here the read time for a consecutively allocated file would be similar to the time needed to read a sequential file. The records appear to the user in a random order.

$$T_X = nR/t \qquad \langle \text{random seq.} \rangle \text{ 5-43}$$

If the blocks are distributed randomly or found from the space allocation in a random fashion, then, neglecting the time needed to read the space-allocation directory,

$$T_X = \frac{n}{Bfr}(s + r + \frac{B}{t'}) \qquad \langle \text{random} \rangle \text{ 5-44}$$

In this approach the records appear in a logically unpredictable order. A reduction in actual search efficiency may be due to the processing of empty spaces created by previous deletions.

5-4-7 Reorganization of an Indexed File

Indexed files are not as dependent on periodic reorganization as are the previous file organizations. Some implementations of indexed files in fact never need to reorganize the files. Reorganization of the data file may recover unusable fragments of space left over from deletions. A specific index may require reorganization to recover from updating failures or from having poorly distributed index entries due to clustered insertions or deletions. Index reorganization can be done incrementally, one index at a time.

In order to reconstruct one index, the data file is read. A reorganization of an index separately would propagate any existing errors in the index. It is best to use the space-allocation directory, not only for speed but also to assure that every record is read. Since the records will not appear from the data file in the proper logical sequence for the index attribute, it is best to collect them in a dense temporary file having n' small $(V + P)$ records, then sort this file, and then generate the index blocks sequentially. Index generation can be combined with the final sort-merge pass, as indicated in Chap. 4-3-8.

$$T_Y(\text{one}) = T_X + T_{sort}(n') \qquad \langle \text{one index} \rangle \text{ 5-45}$$

Estimates for these terms were given as Eqs. 5-43, 4-12, and 5-27. The sort will be rapid if the space required for sorting $n'(V + P) = 0.69\,SI_1$ is small relative to memory capacity.

If the data file is reorganized, all the index TIDs become invalid. An effective way to reorganize data and the indexes is to read the old data file and write the file anew and reconstruct all the indexes. The time requirement then is

$$T_Y = 2T_X + a\,T_Y(\text{one}) \qquad \langle \text{data and indexes} \rangle \text{ 5-46}$$

We cannot expect to have sufficient memory to process all indexes, so that here a total of a sort files will be generated during the processing of the data file. We do assume that sufficient buffer space exists for all a indexes. Since reading and writing of the main file will frequently be interrupted, Eq. 5-44 is appropriate for T_X in this case.

5-5   PARTIAL-MATCH RETRIEVAL

Having multiple indexes allows access using more than one attribute at a time. Using multiple attributes is beneficial where a single attribute has a poor selectivity, so that too much data would be retrieved by using a single search key. We consider now retrievals where conditions on several attributes are combined in one retrieval request. Such a query is termed a *partial-match query*, since several of many attributes of the record are to be matched. An important use of having multiple indexes is a reduction of search effort for partial-match queries.

Use of multiple indexes for partial-match queries is the topic of Sec. 5-5-1. Selection of indexes to optimize partial-match queries is considered in Sec. 5-5-2. The creation of specialized multiattribute indexes to improve the performance of partial-match queries is the topic of Sec. 5-5-3.

5-5-1 Using Indexes for Partial-Match Queries

A partial-match query with conditions on four attributes is shown in Fig. 5-17. We use an indexed file. For each attribute in the query {style, price, bedrooms, location, ...} an index is available; each key value found will point to many records.

```
LIST houses WITH style      = 'Colonial',
             AND   price      = 31 000 → 33 000,
             AND   bedrooms   = 3,
             AND   location   = 'Wuthering Heights';
```

Figure 5-17   Partial-match query.

USE OF MULTIPLE INDEXES   To restrict the retrieval to one or a few goal records, all arguments in the query are first processed against their indexes. Each index produces a list of TIDs for the candidate records. These lists are then merged according to the expression given by the query, using boolean functions to select the TIDs for those goal records which satisfy all query arguments. Fig. 5-18 sketches how four houses are found for the query shown in Fig. 5-17.

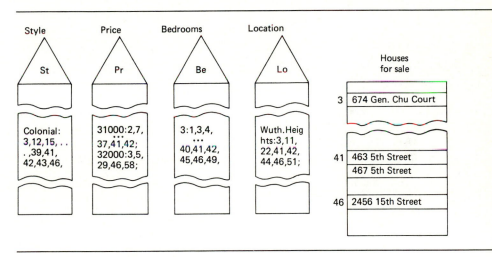

Figure 5-18   Multiattribute indexing for partial-match queries.

Only the goal records needed for the response are eventually retrieved. The cost of processing a partial-match query can be estimated by expanding Eq. 5-32. We use a_Q indexes, merge the lists, and retrieve n_G goal records.

$$T_F(a_Q \cdot n_G) = a_Q x(s + r + btt) + c + n_G(s + r + btt) \qquad 5\text{-}47$$

Estimating the result size n_G accurately is difficult. Using an *independence of attributes* assumption, n_G is the result of the product of n and all the selectivities of the a_Q attributes. Independence is rarely true, but better estimates require knowledge about how attributes are related that is difficult to obtain and manage.

In Eq. 5-47 we made the assumption that each subset of TIDs of the a_Q selected subsets was fetched from one block. If more index blocks are required some additional serial access costs are incurred; the linkage scheme for index blocks presented in Sec. 8-4-1 will minimize incremental costs.

The merging of TIDs is aided by sorting the TIDs initially, so that the retrieval of the blocks containing goal records is conveniently carried out in TID order. The value of n_G is an upper bound, since several records may be found in one block. No block should be accessed more than once. A good estimate of the required number of blocks b_G as a function of n_G, n, and Bfr is given in Chap. 8-4-2 as Eq. 8-6.

5-5-2 Index Selection

Many file and database systems do not have the capability to manipulate TIDs. In that case it becomes very important to select the most selective index for a query. Even when we can combine indexes as shown above, it may not be worthwhile to merge indexes with a relatively low selectivity. The attribute **bedrooms** in the example above is of dubious value. We discussed earlier that attributes with absolute poor selectivity should not even be indexed.

Estimation of selectivity of an attribute is often difficult. Most systems make the assumption of a uniform distribution. Unfortunately, uniform distributions are rare in practice unless the partitioning of the attribute values has been planned that way. Most common in practice are *Zipfian distributions*, as presented in Chap. 13-3-2. Other distributions, as *normal* and *Erlang*, are covered in Chap. 12. All these are distinguished by having frequent occurrences of some values, and fewer occurrences of other values.

Table 5-2 shows some attributes and their likely distribution of values. Then we show for each attribute a sample value expression for a query, and the estimated percentage of the file retrieved using the assumption of a uniform distribution, followed by the actual value, obtained from an experiment using real data.

Table 5-2   Selectivity of some attributes.

Attribute	Range or cardinality	Type of distribution	Query	Estimate of Result	Actual Result
Style	$n = 20$	Zipf	=Colonial	5%	13%
Price	$12K - 262K$	normal	>212K	20%	3%
Bedrooms	$n = 8$	Erlang(2)	=3	12.5%	42%
Location	$n = 20$	uniform	=Wuth.Heights	5%	4.5%

The estimate can be improved if for each attribute additional information is kept. For small value sets the actual counts may be kept. Counts would provide exact values for the **Style**, **Bedrooms**, and **Location** attributes. Keeping, instead of the range, ten decile boundaries of the value distribution permits a more precise estimation of continuous values, as **Price** above. A better scheme is to maintain *distribution steps*, where the partitions have equal sizes (Piatetsky[84]).

Distribution information tends to be associated with indexes, and is best updated as the indexes are. When only a few parameters are kept to describe the distribution, we can expect to find the information in the root block and rapidly retrieved. The values in the root block provide already an initial estimation of the distribution steps, since in the sizes of the subtrees for each entry will be similar. For instance, given that the root block of the `Price` index has 100 entries we would find that the value $= 212K$ will appear in entry 97 or 98, giving a much more accurate estimate of the selectivity than that provided by the assumption of uniform distribution.

All these techniques still ignore the correlation of values. In `Wuth.Heights` the dominant `Style` may be Greek Revival and the `Prices` always above \$150 000. The storage and update demands for such second-order information make its retention impractical.

▦ 5-5-3 Multiattribute Indexes for Partial-Match Queries

We now show techniques for improving the performance of partial-match access, that is, dealing with queries which specify more than one attribute. Having to access many indexes for one partial-match retrieval is costly. We can reduce the number of indexes needed by by creating additional indexes, which combine multiple attributes. The effect is to reduce factor a_Q of Eq. 5-47. Partial-match retrieval using other schemes is shown in Chap. 7-3-5 and 7-4-5.

PARTIAL-MATCH INDEXES   An index is not necessarily based on a single attribute, but can be based on entries that contain the catenation of several attribute values of a record. If we expect two or more attributes to occur together we can construct a single index for those specific attributes.

The number and size of the keys and hence the size of a combined index will be larger, so that the fanout may be less than the size of a single attribute index; but with effective index-abbreviation schemes, the increase will be moderate. Referring to Fig. 5-18, it may be wise to combine `Style` and `Bedrooms`, since `Bedrooms` has a very low selectivity. This combination is denoted in Fig. 5-19 as St∥Be.

St	St∥Be	St∥Be∥Pr	St∥Be∥Pr∥Lo	St →	St∥Be → St∥Be∥Pr → St∥Be∥Pr∥Lo
Be	St∥Pr	St∥Be∥Lo		Be →	Be∥Lo → Be∥Lo∥St
Pr	St∥Lo	St∥Pr∥Lo		Pr →	Pr∥St → Pr∥St∥Lo
Lo	Be∥Pr	Be∥Pr∥Lo		Lo →	Lo∥Pr → Lo∥Pr∥Be
	Be∥Lo				St∥Lo
	Pr∥Lo				Be∥Pr

Null

(1) 4   6   4   1   0   2   3   1

           15 combinations   6 indexes

               (a)   (b)

Figure 5-19   Partial-match indexes. *(a)* Combinations of indexes for four attributes {St,Be,Pr,Lo}. *(b)* A minimal set of indexes for the four combinations.

But the St‖Be index satisfies directly only one attribute combination. If it is desirable to have access capability via one index for *all* queries which specify the logical intersection of attributes, then, for the same example, another eleven combinations are required in addition to the four single attribute indexes (Fig. 5-19a). The number of combinations for a indexes ($\#i$) will be

$$\#i = 2^a - 1 \tag{5-48}$$

This number of indexes soon becomes prohibitive.

Minimization of Combined Indexes The number of indexes needed for full coverage can be reduced, however, since an index ordered on a catenation of multiple attribute values $v_1, \ldots, v_a$ is also ordered for attributes $v_1, \ldots, v_{a-1}$. An index for a attributes can hence also serve to answer queries for one of the combinations of $a-1$ attributes, one of the combinations of $a-2$ attributes, etc. An index for another combination of $a-1$ attributes can similarly serve simpler queries. An assignment of a minimal set of indexes is shown in Fig. 5-19b.

In the minimal set the first index serves four combinations; three indexes serve three combinations each, and two combinations of two attributes remain. Only six indexes are required now. In general,

$$\#ic(a) = \binom{a}{\lceil \frac{1}{2}a \rceil} = \frac{a!}{\lceil \frac{1}{2}a \rceil! \lfloor \frac{1}{2}a \rfloor!} \tag{5-49}$$

indexes will be required. This number is still quite large even for a modest set of attributes a, e.g., $\#ic(9) = 126$. It is possible to reduce the number of indexes further if some merge operations among indexes are acceptable.

The algorithm shown in Table 5-3, provided by Beverly Jamison, generates all combinations.

Table 5-3   Generation of a minimal set of combined indexes.

1	Denote the attributes to be indexed as 1, 2, ... , N.
2	Compute the number of combined indexes needed as NIC $= \binom{N}{N/2}$.
3	Dimension a string array A(NIC) and initialize A(1)="1".
4	FOR K = 2 TO N:
4.1	FOR each string in the last iteration:
4.1.1	If the length is $\geq \lfloor$(N+1)/2$\rfloor$, add a new string to the next available slot. Form the string by deleting the rightmost digit from the current string and inserting the digit K at the beginning.
4.1.2	Append a K to the end of the current string.
5	End

Pragmatic Reduction of Combined Indexes   Fewer combinations of attributes need be stored if for some queries a merge of two or more distinct TID lists is permissible. Then the a attributes will be partitioned into d sets with a_i attributes so that $\sum_{i=1}^{d} a_i = a$. The attributes will be partitioned so that frequent queries require only one set. The number of needed combinations reduces drastically. For $d = 2, a = 9, a_1 = 5, a_2 = 4$ the number of indexes becomes $\#ic(5) + \#ic(4) = 16$; for the simple case $d = 3,\ a = 9,\ a_1 = a_2 = a_3 = 3$ the number of indexes is $3\,\#ic(3) = 9 = \#i$, the original number, although each index will carry more attributes. The increased cost of updates still discourages extensive use of combinatorial approaches for partial-match queries.   ▦▦▦

5-6   REVIEW OF INDEXED METHODS

Indexes are the dominant means to improve access to files. They add a small amount of redundancy and provide rapid access to individual records for fetch and update. Since the performance of indexed files is dominated by the number of index levels accessed, we can summarize the result and state that

$$T_F = \mathcal{O}_{indexes}(x) = \mathcal{O}(\log_y n)$$

Within this growth factor are hidden many parameters, especially the fanout y, which can cause great differences in observed performance.

> Fanout determines the performance of an index.
>   A large fanout reduces the number of index levels.
>   Fanout is increased by having large blocks and small entries.

Abbreviation of entries to increase fanout will be presented in Chap. 8-2.

We showed the alternative of static and dynamic index updating. Static indexes were adequate for indexed-sequential files. Dynamic indexes require much effort when inserting records, but reduce reorganization requirements. In situations where there is little data-processing staff they are preferable. Programs for static indexes are simpler, but create chains. We assumed uniform distributions when following index chains. Nonuniform insertion distributions can increase T_F considerably. The problem gets worse if recently inserted records are referenced more frequently. Push-through reduces that effect. A comparison of retrieval performance is given in Sec. 9-2-4.

Having multiple indexes which produce TIDs permits partial match retrieval without having to retrieve other than the goal records from the data file.

Other decisions which are important when designing indexes are

> •Selection of attributes for indexing
> •Use of record versus block anchors
> •Immediate versus tombstone record deletion techniques

Other design issues are covered in the chapter on index implementation, Chap. 8.

REVIEW OF TERMS   In this chapter we frequently referred to the *search argument* and to the *key* and *goal* portion of the record. These terms are used particularly when files are used for data retrieval. The term *search argument* denotes the attribute type and value known when a record is to be retrieved. The *key portion of the record* is the field to be matched to the search argument. The fields of the record to be retrieved by the fetch process are the *goal*. For example, the search argument may be "`social security number=134-51-4717`"; the key in the specified attribute field of the record contains the matching value "`134-51-4717`", and the goal portion of that record contains the `name` and `salary` for the employee. Search arguments can address other attributes; for instance, "`jobtitle ='welder'`". Now multiple records may be retrieved, each with different keys.

The key is generally intended to identify one record uniquely, so that there is a simple functional dependence from key to record. A key may comprise multiple attribute fields of the record in order to achieve a unique identification. An example of the need for multiple fields might be the title of a book, which often does not identify a book uniquely without specification of author or publisher and date of publication.

It should be understood that another instance of a retrieval request can have a different composition. Then the search argument may comprise a different set of attributes; these may have been previously part of the goal, and the goal can include the former key values.

BACKGROUND AND REFERENCES

In offices, large sequential files in drawers are partitioned using folders. Labels on the drawers provide a second level of partitioning of these files to accelerate access. Multiple indexes, based on title, authors, and subject, can be found in any library.

Chapin[68] includes the programming issues of indexed-sequential files. Further information is available in the literature of software suppliers (see Appendix B). Seaman[66] and Lum[73] treat indexed-sequential files analytically. Allen[68] describes an application using large indexed-sequential files. Indexed-sequential files were considered in Brown[72] to comprise such a significant fraction of disk usage that the IBM 3330 disk system design was greatly influenced by their behavior.

The construction of index trees in memory has been frequently discussed in the computer science literature. It is important to realize when using these references that the index trees found in storage files have very high fanout ratios and do not contain the data within themselves. Trees containing data are discussed in Chap. 9-2. Landauer[63] considers dense, dynamically changing indexes. Bose[69], Welch[75], and Larson[81] evaluate access to indexed files using formal and mathematical models. Maio[84] evaluates block anchors versus record anchors.

The B-tree algorithm was presented and evaluated by Bayer[72O,S]. It is further analyzed by Horowitz[78]; Comer[79] provides an excellent summary, and Knuth[73S] includes some file-oriented considerations. Ghosh[69] combines B-trees with probing. A review by March[83] considers partial indexes.

Yao[78] analyzed the density of B-trees under random insertions and deletions. Held[78] and Aho[79U] evalute B-trees in relational databases. Indexes are used for bibliographic retrieval in Dimsdale[73]. Guttman[84] extends B-trees for spatial data.

An early system using multiple indexes, TDMS, is described by Bleier[68]; Bobrow in Rustin[72] develops this approach. Multiattribute access via indexes is evaluated by Lum[70], Mullin[71], and Schkolnick in Kerr[75]. O'Connell[71] describes use of multiple indexes.

Selection, and its optimization, among multiple indexes is considered by many authors, among them Lum[71L], Stonebraker[72], Shneiderman[74,77], Schkolnick[75] Hammer[76], Yao[77], Anderson[77], Comer[78], Hammer[79], Yamamoto[79], Rosenberg[81], Saxton[82], as well as Whang[85]. The work is limited by assumptions on the distribution of the index value distributions for the queries. Piatetsky[84] suggests modeling the distribution by a stepwise function.

Indexes are used for partial matching by Lum[70]. Strategies of combinatorial index organization were developed by Ray-Chaudhuri[68], Bose[69], Shneiderman[77], and Chang[81]. Procedures for estimating selectivity in a file are surveyed by Christodoulakis[83], Flajolet[85] and Astrahan[87] do it in $\mathcal{O}(n)$, Chu[82] uses statistical models.

Ghosh[76] includes construction of optimal record sequences for known queries.

EXERCISES

1 Compute the average fetch time for an indexed-sequential file where the overflow areas are placed on the same cylinder. Assume overflow area is equal to 25% of the prime file and reorganizations when overflow area is 80% full. Assume $B = 2000$, $R = 100$.

2 Programming lore advises that input should be sorted in descending order when doing batch updates of files which keep overflows in ascending ordered chains. Why? Quantify the effect.

3 Equation 5-30 contains a simplification that upper level indexes add 5% to the index storage space. What does this say about the effective fanout y_{eff}?

4 Compare Eq. 5-16 and Eq. 5-18 for T_N. Why are they different? Evaluate both equations for

    a $n = 100\,000$ and $o' = 1000$ and for
    b $n = 100\,000$ and $o' = 50\,000$.

5 What type of indexed-sequential overflow processing would you chose (assuming you could) for the applications listed in Exercise 4-4.

6 Choose three out of the attributes shown for indexing a personnel file: `name`, `age`, `sex`, `job`, `number_dependents`, `salary_of_dependents`, `salary` ; and explain why you chose them.

7 Estimate the number of goal records obtained for a partial-match query on `sex` and `job` for 500 employees. There are 20 job classifications. Give a specific example of values for these attributes where you expect many more goal records than the average expected, and one where you expect fewer.

8   Prepare a flowchart for and compare the performance of a binary search through an index with the multilevel approach for indexed files.

9   Find a file system where you study or work or in the literature and determine the seven measures of performance $(R, T_F, T_I,$ etc.) for its organization.

10   What is the difference in an index reorganization performance if $2x$ buffers can be allocated rather than just x?

11^P For the project started in Chap. 1, select which files should be piles, sequential, indexed-sequential, or multiply indexed. Evaluate the 7 performance parameters for each of those files, using values of the size parameters n, a, a', A_i, V_i appropriate for your application, and values of s, r, t for a reasonable storage device for that application.

12^P For the project started in Chap. 1, assume you are using fully indexed files. Estimate the selectivity for all attributes, consider their usefulness, and decide which ones should be indexed.

13   You are designing an indexed file system for use on a personal computer. A requirement is that, for 90% of the cases, the insertion of a record should be completed in 1 s. To assure meeting this constraint you will limit the number of indexed attributes permitted on a file. What will this number be? State all assumptions.

14   Design a file and evaluate it for questions as are posed in the epigraph from Vonnegut, on the title page of Chap. 9.

Chapter 6

Hashed Files and
Ring Files

One Ring to rule them all, One Ring to find them,
One Ring to bring them all and in the darkness bind them.

J. R. R. Tolkien
Verse of the Rings, from *"The Fellowship of the Ring"*

6-0 INTRODUCTION

The two final file organization types to be presented in this chapter are the *hashed file* organization and the *ring file* organization. The two methods are quite different, actually so different that they complement each other, so that we will see them used together in Chap. 7. Hashed access uses a computation to determine the file address for a specific record. The ring organization uses pointers to locate successor records.

However, these two file organizations are both distinguished from the file organizations covered in Chaps. 4 and 5 in that they do not derive from any of the previous methods, and also that they have no counterparts in common manual usage. Access methods used with these files are such that a computer is required to manage their complexity. Otherwise the two methods are quite distinct, and not structurally related, so that either section can be read without cross reference to the other section.

6-1   DESCRIPTION AND USE OF THE HASHED FILE

The hashed file exploits the capability, provided by disk units and similar devices, to access directly any block of a known address. To achieve direct addressing, the key of the record is used to locate the record in the file. Hashed access is diagrammed in Fig. 6-1.

There are two components to a hashed file:

1 The file space, organized into m slots. Each slot has the capacity to hold one of the n records of the file.

2 The computation τ which provides a slot address for a record given its key.

We will present the basic organization of hashed files in Sec. 6-1-1. After the general description we will deal in depth with two specific issues: In Sec. 6-1-2 we consider how to compute a suitable address for the record from a key, and in Sec. 6-1-3 we consider what to do when the computation leads to a conflict, or *collision*. In Sec. 6-1-4 we show methods that accommodate growth of a hashed file. In Sec. 6-1-5 alternate algorithms for the key-to-address computation are surveyed and a method for evaluating their effectiveness is provided. Sec. 6-1-6 shows applications which can use a hashed file organization profitably. Section 6-2 then evaluates the performance parameters; for this section the material introduced in Sec. 6-1-1 is adequate.

The earliest direct-access disk files were used by electromechanical accounting machines which would use a key number punched on a card to determine where the remainder of the card contents was to be filed. That number provided the address for *direct* access to the file. Direct access is fast but inflexible. Hashing transforms the key with a computational algorithm before it is used as an address. Hashed access is still fast, since it avoids intermediate file operations. A disadvantage is that the method forces the data to be located according to a single key attribute.

A COMPARISON   We can compare hashed access with an indexed-sequential file in that access is provided according to a single attribute; however, records of a hashed file are not related to their predecessor or successor records. The hashed file methods use a computation to provide the record address for a key, whereas indexed file organizations search indexes to determine the record corresponding to a given key. Index B-trees use extra space to reduce the effort of insertion and avoid reorganization. The hashed file uses extra space in the main file to simplify insertion of records into the file and avoid reorganization.

6-1-1 An Overview of Hashed Files

Hashed files are based on direct access to a file, using a relative address as described in Chap. 3-3-3. In immediate implementations of direct access, identification numbers that provide a relative address into the file are assigned to the data records.

Thus, employee `Joe` is designated as `257`, and that tells us directly that his payroll record is to be found as record 257. We will list a number of problems with the use of direct access to locate data records, and then present the common methods used currently.

Problems with Use of Direct File Addresses

- Identification numbers for a person or item may be needed in more than one file. This requires that one object carry a variety of numbers.
- To reuse space, the identification number has to be reassigned when a record has been deleted. This causes confusion when processing past and present data together.
- Natural keys are names, social security numbers, or inventory numbers where groups of successive digits have meaning. Such keys are long; much longer than is needed to give a unique address to each record. In general, the number of people or items which may be referred to by *natural* keys is much larger than the number of records to be kept on the file. In other words, the key address space is much larger than the file space, and direct use of such a key would fill the file very sparsely.

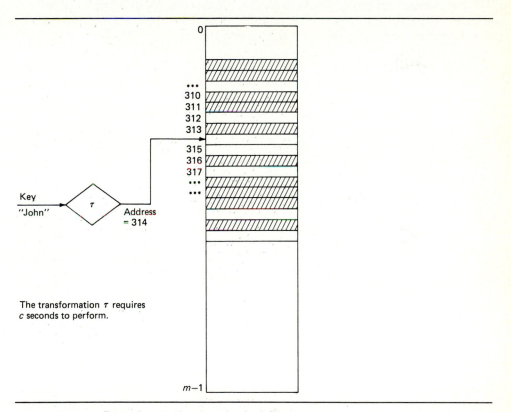

Figure 6-1   Record accessing in a hashed file.

DEFINITIONS FOR HASHED FILES   We define now the concept of a *key-to-address transformation* or KAT, also denoted by the function τ. The objective of the computation τ is to give each arriving record its own slot, based on the key provided. This is achieved if we can distribute the n records uniformly over the m slots. The argument for τ is the key field from the record. When a record is to be stored, the key is given with the record and τ computes the slot address for the insertion function of the hashed access method. The common algorithms for τ perform this task by a *randomizing hashing function* on the argument.

When a record is to be retrieved a search key must be provided. It will be transformed by the same function τ into a slot address, and the retrieval function of the method will fetch the record from the slot.

The file space is partitioned into m *slots*: each slot can hold one record. The result of τ is a *relative slot address*, ranging from 0 to $m - 1$. We need at least one slot per record expected, so that $m \geq n$. In practice the *density* of a hashed file $n/m \approx 0.6$ to 0.95. The higher densities are only feasible for small records, as shown in Sec. 6-1-3.

A subsequent procedure, as outlined in Chap. 3-3-3, translates the relative slot address to an actual storage address. Then the block for this slot can be brought in from storage. An actual access to the file obtains a block or a *bucket* of slots at a time. The size of a bucket, y, is typically determined by the block size so that $y = B/R$. We can expect to find $y_{effective} = \frac{n}{m}y$ records in a bucket.

KEY-TO-ADDRESS TRANSFORMATIONS   The problems identified with the immediate use of keys such as file addresses are solved by interposing a computational procedure. Such a *key-to-address transformation* (KAT) translates the key attribute values into relative addresses within the file space.

The incoming keys may be strings of characters or numbers, defined as the key for the data file. Each relative address to be produced identifies a *slot* into which a record may be placed and ranges from 0 to $m - 1$.

Figure 6-1 shows the access to a hashed file for a new record with key "John". The KAT algorithm τ applied to the string "John" has generated the relative record address "314". The same KAT is applied to a search key when a record is to be fetched.

Most files will have their own key type and slot range. Even with the same key the procedure may differ. The KAT τ to compute the relative addresses from social-security-number key of a person in the 1000 slot Employees file differs from the KAT for the same key in the 150 slot Sales_personnel file.

Requirements for KATs   An ideal key-to-address translation should satisfy two requirements, we mark the second one for further discussion:

1   The source key must be reduced in size to match the slot range.

$2^?$ The slot addresses generated should be unique.

These two objectives conflict. Although the source keys are presumably unique, it is impossible to compute smaller numbers which are unique for arbitrary source keys. Hence, we settle for a lesser criterion

$2^!$ The slot addresses generated should be as unique as possible.

The degree of uniqueness of slot addresses is high if the addresses are uniformly distributed. A uniform distribution of addresses will locate an equal fraction of the keys to each and every slot. Techniques to generate uniformly distributed random numbers form the basis for such transformations.

There is a wide variety of choices for key-to-address transformations. In this section we will use the *remainder-of-division* algorithm throughout.

> We obtain relative addresses using a randomizing KAT
> by computing the remainder-of-division of the given key.

In Sec. 6-1-5 this method is defined in more detail, and other methods, often more suitable, are considered and evaluated as well. All the required principles for hashing can be developed using a single type of KAT. Figure 6-2 shows a small file where records are placed into slots using as KAT the remainder-of-division by 500.

A randomizing transformation for a personnel file uses the social security number as the key. We assume that the value of the low-order digits of these numbers is evenly distributed and hence there is a high probability of deriving out of these digits a unique number for every employee. If one wants to allow space for up to $n = 500$ employees, the value of the key may be divided by 500, leaving a remainder with values between 0 and 499.

Record for	SSN	$\rightarrow \tau \rightarrow$	Slot address
Al	322-45-6178		178
Joe	123-45-6284		284
Mary	036-23-0373		373
Pete	901-23-4784		284

Even though it was unlikely, given 4 out of 500 employees, by chance two identical slot addresses were generated: Joe and Pete both received slot number 284; the records for Joe and Pete will collide if both are placed directly into a file.

Figure 6-2   Key-to-address transformation, with a collision.

The problem with randomizing transformations is that they will generate some identical addresses from different source keys, so that more than one record may be directed to the same place in storage. Such an occurrence is called a *collision*.

Consider using the KAT from Fig. 6-2. The algorithm computed for Pete, with social security number = 901-23-4784, generated a slot number of 284, but this did not provide a free space for Pete's record, since Joe was assigned to that slot earlier.

INSERTION PROCEDURE   As demonstrated in Fig. 6-2, before storing a new record into a slot of a hashed file the content of the slot itself has to be tested. The slot can be

1 empty
2 it can contain an older record for the same key
3 it can contain a colliding record for another key
4 if deletions dont rearrange records it can contain a tombstone

The insertion procedure has to consider these three or four cases. To determine on insertion whether a collision is occurring we check if the slot at the computed address is empty. Insertion into an empty slot is straightforward. If the slot is full, there is a collision. Now we compare the key value of the record found in the slot with the key value of the new record. If key fields match, then earlier a record with the same key was inserted into the file. Perhaps the record found should be replaced by the new one; the implied operation is an **update** of all attributes but the key.

If the new and old key fields do not match, it is a true collision. Then the rules for collision resolution, as set for the particular file organization, must be followed. The most common choice is *open addressing*, where we search through successor slots until an empty slot is found. The colliding record is inserted into that slot.

Fetch Procedure When a record is to be fetched a similar process is followed. An empty slot indicates that there is no record matching the search key. If there is a record, then the search key is compared with the key of the record in the slot. If they match, the record is retrieved from the slot.

If the new and old key fields do not match, then there had been a true collision earlier and we search further to try to locate a matching record. The retrieval process depends on the collision resolution method in use. For open addressing the scheme we will check the successor slots. If the slot is empty we give up, if it is not empty, the key is checked and a matching record will be fetched. If the record still does not match the search is continued through all slots.

Deletion of records from a hashed file using open addressing must be handled with care, since just setting slots "empty" can confuse the retrieval process. This problem is further addressed in Sec. 6-1-3.

Termination Both insert and retrieval procedures are sure to terminate as long as the number of slots m is greater than the number of records n. If m is sufficiently greater than n the probability of finding an empty slot is good, and it will only be rarely neccessary to go to slots in a successor block. These concepts will be expanded on in the performance evaluation of Sec. 6-2.

We summarize both the insert and retrieval algorithm as a decision rule in Table 6-1 below, but first will consider what happens if source keys are not unique.

Nonunique Record Keys Typically, records of hashed files are defined to be *unique*. If in this file application multiple records have the same key, the records to be inserted can still be stored according to the collision resolution scheme used.

If nonunique records, i.e., records with duplicate keys, are to be retrieved, a search up to an empty is needed to find all matches to the search argument. For deletion, either all records with that key must be deleted, or other fields of the record must be inspected.

We will not consider duplicate source keys further in this chapter.

The Decision Rule The corresponding outcomes are now summarized in Table 6-1:

Table 6-1   Decision rules for collisions.

Condition	Insert	Fetch
Slot_key = Λ	Ok to insert	No record found
Keys match	Replace record if permitted	Record found
Keys don't match	Locate free successor slot	Check successor slot

The precise handling of collisions is elaborated in Sec. 6-1-3.

Initialization When a hashed file is created it must be initialized to "empty". This means that for all slots the field to be used for the key is set to some tombstone. In our examples we use Λ to indicate an empty slot.

6-1-2 Randomizing Key-to-Address Transformations

The KATs we consider using use a randomizing transformation when translating the key value into relative file addresses.

Key and File Address Space A key value may range over a large number of possible values, limited only by the maximum size of the key field, V. The number of legal keys is up to 10^V for a numeric key, 26^V for a simple alphabetic key. For a social security number the key space size is 10^9, for a 20-character name field it is nearly $2 \cdot 10^{28}$

The number of records, n, to be kept, and the record space of the file, will be much less for all users, even for the Social Security Administration itself. The available file address space is defined in terms of the record capacity or number of slots, m, of the file. Recall that the number of actual records, n, put in the file cannot exceed the number of available slots, m; hence, if the key uses *base* distinct symbols,

$$base^V \gg m \geq n \qquad\qquad 6\text{-}1$$

Using Alphabetic Identifiers Since many of the key-to-address algorithms depend on a numeric key value, it may be desirable to convert alphabetic keys into integers. If a value from 0 to 25 (`lettervalue`) is assigned to each of the 26 letters used, a dense numeric representation can be obtained using a polynomial conversion, as shown in Table 6-2. Numbers and blanks occurring in keys require an appropriate expansion of the `lettervalue` table which controls the results of this routine. For large keys numeric overflow has to be considered.

Table 6-2   Character string key to numeric key conversion.

```
/* Letters to Integers; applied to the key given in array 'string'*/
   numeric_value = 0;
   DO i = 1 TO length_of_key_string;
      numeric_value = numeric_value * 26 + lettervalue(string(i));
   END;
```

Computing the Relative Address Given a numeric key, we apply τ to yield a relative address. For the remainder-of-division algorithm we must choose a divisor, m. Since the desired density, $\frac{n}{m}$, is an approximate goal, we have some flexibility in choosing m.

A value of $\frac{n}{m}$ of 1 would nearly guarantee a collision for the final, n^{th} record to be inserted, since only one slot will then be unoccupied. A very low density of, say, $\frac{n}{m} = 0.10$, would yield only a 10% probability of a collision for the last record, but the file space utilization would be very poor. We will work below with values of $\frac{n}{m} \approx 0.6$.

The actual value of the divisor, m, is also a concern. Values including factors of 2, 10, 26, etc., may lead to results which are not fully random, since some bias from the key argument may be retained. Good candidates are prime numbers, or at least numbers of the form $2^k - 1$. The latter are often prime as well, and waste only one slot if the storage allocation is in powers of 2, giving 2^k slots. Figure 6-3 provides an example of the reasoning to be followed and Table 6-3 shows the resulting program fragment.

We need to select a divisor for a file of up to $n = 500$ employees. For a desired density $\frac{n}{m} = 0.64$ we find $m_{c1} = n/0.64 = 780$. This number turns out to have factors 10 and 26, so we'd better change it. Given a Bfr of 7 we would be using $b = \lceil 780/7 \rceil = 112$ blocks. Since 112 blocks can hold $7 \times 112 = 784$ slots, we have another candidate $m_{c2} = 784$, still with an undesirable factor 2. The next lower divisor $m = 783$ turns out to be prime. Our function τ becomes then as shown in Table 6-3.

Figure 6-3   Derivation of a KAT divisor.

The file system uses relative addressing, as detailed in Chap. 3-3-3, to translate sequential slot numbers, computed as `rel_address`, from their range of 0 to $m - 1$ into the physical addresses used by the storage devices. If these devices are disk units we can seek directly to the right track and access the block containing the data.

It is actually desirable to just compute block addresses instead of addresses of specific record slots. Records with the same block address will be placed sequentially into the block. The Bfr slots available in such a block comprise a *bucket*. The cost of locating the record in the bucket is negligible. The effect of using buckets is considered below when collisions are discussed.

Table 6-3   Key-to-address transformation using remainder-of-division.

```
/* Slot number for the key; uses remainder-of-division by a prime */
    rel_address = MOD(numeric_value, 783);
```

6-1-3 Collision Management

When we obtain the slot at the address computed above we may find it occupied. The probability of finding every slot in a bucket occupied is much lower. We will first consider slots by themselves, or buckets having only one slot.

When a key-to-address transformation produces identical addresses for distinct records, we have a collision. There is no way that a randomizing procedure can avoid collisions completely, and nonrandomizing KAT procedures (discussed in Sec. 6-1-5) are not practical for large or changing files. We hence have to learn to deal with collisions. Figure 6-20 shows a key-to-address transformation and a collision. In Fig. 6-20 a new entry, `Shostakovich`, collides with an earlier entry, `John`.

The more slots a file has relative to the number of records to be stored, the lower the probability of collisions will be. While we will evaluate such probabilities in detail subsequently, we note that at typical B-tree density ($n/m = 0.69$), we incur a rate of collisions that is quite bearable; even with one slot per bucket, we expect collisions less than 35% of the times we access the file.

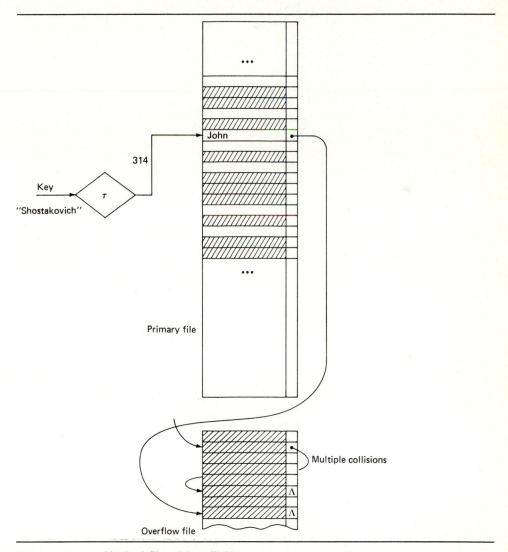

Figure 6-4   Hashed file with collision.

COLLISION RESOLUTION   The resolution of collisions will occupy us in this section. Three strategies are used to resolve collisions, sometimes in combination. Two methods, *linear search* and *rerandomization*, which use the main file for storage of records which have collided, are referred to as *open addressing* techniques. Figure

6-4 shows the third alternative, the use of a separate *overflow* area for such records. The performance of all three methods is significantly improved if first a search through the current block or *bucket* is made.

Search in the Bucket the cost of overflows from collisions can be greatly reduced by grouping of the slots into buckets. A typical bucket is equal to one block, as shown in Fig. 6-5. A search through all the slots in the bucket is used to locate space for the new record. Only computational time is required to access the records within a bucket. Only when the bucket itself is filled will a disk access be needed. The cost of the disk access depends on which of the three alternative overflow methods, shown next, is in use. If the bucket contains y slots there will be space for *ovpb* collisions within the block, where

$$ovpb = \left(1 - \frac{n}{m}\right) y \qquad\qquad 6\text{-}2$$

namely, the fraction of free space times the number of slots. We can use the blocking factor *Bfr* for y if we are careful to remember that we are talking here about slots, and not records. The cost of most collisions is now drastically reduced. An analysis of the effect of the use of buckets is unfortunately quite complex. Figure 6-10 gives results for the use of buckets with a linear search in the file. We find for the earlier example ($n/m = 0.69$) and $Bfr = 8$ a reduction in collision cost from 35% to 5%, as marked in the figure.

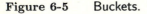 **Bucket Addresses** When buckets are used, the entire block is made available when a record is required. Now a shorter address can be used. If there are y slots in a bucket, the address space reduces from m to m/y and the size of an address pointer will be $\log_2 y$ bits less.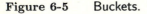

We now consider methods to resolve collisions.

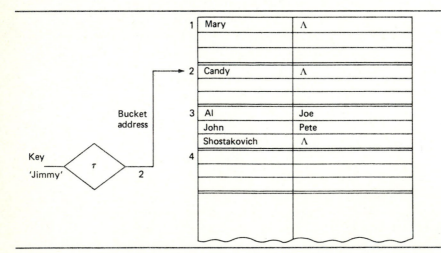

Figure 6-5   Buckets.

Linear Search in the File When an overflow out of the bucket does occur, the search can continue to the next sequential block. This avoids the costs of seek times to new areas but tends to *cluster* overflows together. The linear search method for overflow slots is predominant for hashed files, since it is simple and, one hopes, infrequently invoked. As long as the number of entries is less than the number of slots available $(n < m)$, a record space will eventually be found. Since the availability of a free slot can be determined a priori, no alternate termination method is required.

The problem of clustering is that, when an area of the storage space is densely used, fetches need many search steps. Additional insertions tend to increase the size of the dense area disproportionally. Clustering has been shown to be quite detrimental even for moderately loaded hashed files; an example of how clusters develop is shown in Fig. 6-6.

Rerandomization in the File To avoid the clusters one may assign the bucket for the overflow at a random position in the file. A new randomizing key-to-address computation computes a new slot address in the same file space. Rerandomization, when applied to storage devices, causes a high overhead, since generally a new seek is required. Further collisions can occur, and the procedure may have to be repeated. A randomizing procedure cannot easily guarantee that it will ever locate an empty space. Rerandomization techniques commonly are used when hashing in primary memory, but for files they appear less beneficial. They probably should also be evaluated carefully when it appears that memory is used, but the operating system uses paging for virtual memory management.

Use of an Overflow Area The third method of handling collisions is to put all records which cause a bucket overflow into a separate file with a linkage from the primary record, similar to the overflow chains used in indexed-sequential files. If such a separate overflow area is established, no clustering will take place. An overflow still causes a new seek but avoids the repeated block fetches which can occur with the previous two methods. A difficulty here lies in the allocation of sufficient overflow space, since the number of collisions is not absolutely predictable. The overflow area may fill while the main area has much free space.

▥▥ **Cylinder overflow areas** The cost of overflows out of the main file can be lowered again by allocating overflow areas on each cylinder. This requires modification of the key-to-address transformation to account for the gaps in the primary addressing space. If buckets are already used, it may be better to use this space to reduce the density per bucket.   ▥▥

▥▥ **Linkage to Colliding Records** Once the block for an overflow is located, the record is yet to be found. Overflow records in successor blocks can be found either by simply matching all successive records in the block to the search argument, or by maintaining a chain to link the overflow records together.

Without a chain the search for a record or for a free slot for an insertion terminates when an empty slot is reached. This approach constrains the deletion of records, as discussed below. In a densely loaded file it may take many accesses to find an empty slot, because many intervening slots may be filled by records belonging to the set associated with a different primary bucket address. To identify an arbitrary stored record as a member of the set of colliding records for a specific prime bucket, the key of the stored record accessed has to be transformed to the corresponding address, which is then matched to the initial bucket address. If the addresses are equal, this record belongs to this *collision set*.

The use of a pointer chain avoids accessing records which do not have the same computed bucket address. Now fetches can be limited to the set of colliding records. The use of the chain also improves fetches where the record is not in the file, since the search terminates when the chain pointer is Λ, rather than going on to a free slot.

For insertions it is best to use any free slot in the nearest bucket. If chains are used, the inserted record must be linked into the chain. The linkage of records into the chain at the current block improves locality. This is probably more effective than trying to keep records in sequential order by key or by access frequency.　▦

▦ **DELETION FROM HASHED FILES**　Deletion of a record involves some additional considerations. We have to assure that the freed slot does not hinder subsequent fetch usage, and we also would like to have the slot available for reuse to avoid excessive reorganizations.

We will first consider the cases where a chain is used to link the records of a collision set. The use of a chain requires that deletions mark the slot `Empty` and also that the chain is reset so that any successor records can still be retrieved. If there is more than one record in the collision set, the predecessor record has to be rewritten with the pointer value from the deleted record. Subsequent insertions should use free slots close to the primary bucket, so that the search path does not become longer and longer.

Open addressing methods can be used without a chain. In that case a search for a record to be fetched or for a free slot for an insertion terminates when an empty slot is reached. This means that deleted records cannot just have their slot set to `Empty`, but we have to adjust the file to avoid breaking a subsequent search.

Either a tombstone has to be set, which indicates that this record, although deleted, is still on the path to successor overflow records, or the last record of the collision set has to be moved to fill this freed slot. In this latter case the slot can still not be marked `Empty`, because it may be traversed by some other collision set. Its tombstone, however, can indicate `Deleted`, and show that the slot is available for reuse.　▦

▦ **Dealing with Clusters**　Figure 6-6 illustrates what can happen in these clusters of collision sets when we use open addressing, no chains, and sequential search for slots for overflows. Some deleted record spaces can be reused, but the path length for fetches and inserts includes all spaces not explicitly marked empty. After many deletions and insertions there will be many slots which hold markers and no data. This increases the number of slots to be scanned when searching. The effective density of the file is hence greater than n/m, and this can considerably reduce the performance of a hashed file.

Slot numbers	Time →				

Sequence of additions (+) and deletions (−) to a cluster of a direct file:

Slot numbers		Entry →	Address	Action
40	empty·			
41	empty	+ JOE	42	No collision, insert
42	JOE #	+ PETE	44	No collision, insert
43	MARY	+ KAREN	47	No collision, insert
44	PETE # EZRA	+ MARY	42	Collision, overflow to 43
45	JOSEF	+ JOSEF	43	Collision with overflow,
46	JODY #			second collision, gets 45
47	KAREN empty JERRY	− KAREN	47	Simple delete, empty slot
48	empty	− PETE	44	Cannot mark slot empty to avoid break in search process from 43 or 42 to 45 etc. Mark deleted (#)
		+ EZRA	42	Can reuse slot 44
		+ JODY	44	Gets slot 46
		− JOE	42	Mark deleted to avoid losing overflows from this slot (MARY)
		+ JERRY	45	Overflows to 47
		− JODY	44	Mark 46 deleted for JERRY's sake

A search in this cluster, as it appears now, will require an average of

$$\frac{2(MARY) + 3(EZRA) + 3(JOSEF) + 3(JERRY)}{4(number\ of\ entries)} = 2.75\ comparisions.$$

An optimal distribution, as sketched below, for these entries would require:

41	empty
42	MARY
43	EZRA
44	JOSEF
45	JERRY
46	empty

$$\frac{1 + 2 + 2 + 1}{4} = 1.5\ comparisions\ on\ the\ average$$

Rearrangement of members of chains when deleting can improve the search time experienced in the cluster above.

Figure 6-6   Operations on a file without chaining and with open addressing.

The performance can be recovered during reorganization. Breaking clusters can be performed incrementally, on a block by block basis. During such a reorganization it is possible to collect sufficient information about the collisions to either or both

1 reset deleted slots which are not within any collision set to **Empty** to break clusters no longer needed
2 rearrange the records in any clusters to optimize access

A complete reorganization would rehash all the keys in the block and place the records in order by computed address.

6-1-4 Accommodating Growth of Hashed Files

The familiar notion that a file grows by appending records does not apply to the hashed file. The space to accomodate n records is initially allocated and performance diminishes as n approaches the number of slots m allocated. An increased density, $dens = n/m$, leads to higher rates of collisions, as quantified by Eqs. 6-2, 6-6, etc. Reorganization is a common alternative. For a hashed file reorganization involves determining a new value for m, allocating the space, finding a new KAT, and rehashing all records into the new area.

Such a reorganization, performed by an exhaustive read and a reload of the entire file, is often unacceptable:

1. It causes a long service interruption.
2. Programmer intervention is required to select the new allocation and key-to-address transformation.

Several methods have been proposed to avoid the loss of performance or the need for a complete reorganization.

Extensible hashing techniques add index tables into the file access paths where bucket overflow occurs. The tables will direct retrievals to overflow blocks when warranted, avoiding chains and open addressing. If those tables are kept in memory, all accesses can be kept within a single block access.

Initial allocation was $m = 8$ blocks with $y = 3$, the desired density is $\frac{n}{m} = 0.66$. We insert records with addresses a, d, i, m, j, n, c, x, h, l, z, o, g, b, q, s.

	g							

abc	d	hij	lm	noq	s		xz	
0		2					$m_0 = m_1$	

After 16 insertions the desired density is reached. One bucket (2) overflowed already.

	g			p					

ab	d	hij	lm	noq	s		xz	c
0							m_0	m_1

New insert (of p) causes the first split, on bucket $m_1 - m_0 = 0$, to be performed. Then m_1 is incremented.

	g			p						

ab	d	hij	klm	noq	s	w	xz	c	
0	1						m_0		m_1

After two more inserts (k, w) the next block (1) is split, the new block gets no entries.

		p								

ab	d	gh	klm	noq	st	w	xz	c	f	ij
0		2					m_0			m_1

After the next two inserts (f, t) another split is made; it removes an overflow block.

Figure 6-7   Actions during linear hashing.

Linear Hashing More interesting, and consistent with the general concept of hashed access, is a technique termed *linear hashing*, which is described in the this section and illustrated in Fig. 6-7. The principle of linear hashing is incremental reorganization. In linear hashing (Litwin[80]) the file size grows linearly, block by block, keeping the density approximately constant. A constant density leads then to a constant fraction of overflows.

The file space grows by appending blocks linearly to the end of the hash space. For collisions which still occur overflow blocks are used. We will use m_0 to indicate the initial basic allocation, and let m_0 be a power of 2. The current allocation, m_1, begins with m_0 slots. The procedure operates unchanged until the file reaches a size of $2m_0$ slots. At that point the key-to-address transformation is adjusted as well. No wholesale reorganization of space is required at any time.

The actual space allocation in a file is again by buckets which each have y slots. The file actually grows from $m_1 \Rightarrow m_1 + y$ slots every $\frac{n}{m}y$ insertions. Figure 6-7 illustrates three splits.

Whenever a new block is assigned it is populated by splitting an existing block $m_1 - m_0$. Note that the block to be split is assigned differently from a split seen in B-trees: The block to be split is **not** the block where the collision occurred, but in linear hashing the block to be split is the *lowest numbered* block in the range 0 to m_0 not yet split. This scheme avoids auxiliary tables to indicate which blocks have been split; only the current limit m_1 has to be known.

The method for addressing and the method for splitting cooperate. The KAT produces a `rel_address` for $m = 2m_0$ slots, so that an extra high-order bit is available. The generated address is reduced to the current range $0, \ldots, m_1$ by an additional statement as shown in Table 6-4. This statement corrects the addresses of all blocks not yet split: $(m_1 - m_0), \ldots, m_0$.

Table 6-4   Address adjustment for linear hashing.

```
/* Diminish address if file is still growing */
IF rel_address > m1 THEN rel_address = rel_address - m0
```

When the file grows a new block is appended and the current m1 is incremented. Some of the content of the block at $m_1 - m_0$ is now distributed to the new block. The `rel_address`es of the records in that block and in any overflow blocks attached to that block are recomputed using the KAT and the adjustment with the incremented m_1. All those records will either have the original address (the high-order bit was zero and their `rel_address` = m1-m0) or will have the new address m1, referring to the new block. The records which now belong in the new block are moved and both the split block and the new block are rewritten.

When the file has grown to twice its size ($m_1 = m$) the KAT is revised to produce by another bit: m and m_0 are doubled, and the process can continue with $m_1 = m_0$. No reorganization is required if the new KAT generates the same low-order bits. Methods to actually allocate these blocks are presented in Chap. 10-4.

6-1-5 A Survey of Key-to-Address Transformation Methods

Of the many techniques which have been proposed and evaluated, only some are used for files. We consider here also transformations which do not randomize or hash. Two categories of these computations may be distinguished, *deterministic procedures* which translate identification fields into unique addresses, and *randomizing techniques* which translate the keys into addresses which are as unique as possible but do not guarantee uniqueness.

A *deterministic procedure* takes the set of all key values and computes a unique corresponding relative address. Algorithms for such transformations become difficult to construct if the number of file entries is larger than a few dozen. Adding a new entry would require a new algorithm, since the algorithm is dependent on the distribution of the source keys; hence only static files can be handled. The replacement of a computational algorithm with a table makes the problem of transformation more tractable: We have invented again the indexed file! We will not discuss deterministic hashed access further.

The alternative, randomizing, procedures can cause collisions. A small class of transformations is *sequence-maintaining*; the other algorithms are referred to as *hashing techniques*. The first class tries to preserve the order of the records while computing addresses, but this leads to complexity and inflexibility. The goal of the common hashing transformations is to maximize the uniqueness of the resulting addresses. A family tree of key-to-address transformations is displayed in Fig. 6-8.

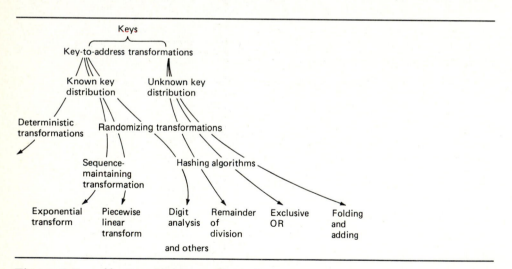

Figure 6-8   Key-to-address transformation types.

DISTRIBUTION-DEPENDENT METHODS   These methods depend on some knowledge of the distribution of keys for the expected records. If we have, for instance, assigned random numbers to identify 1000 samples of some experiment being recorded, we can expect that any three digit positions of the sample identification will be randomly distributed, and suitable as direct-access keys.

The liabilities of distribution-dependent transformations are major, since a change in key distribution can cause these methods to generate many more collisions than previously. A benefit of some distribution-dependent key-to-address transformations is that they allow maintenance of sequentiality. Two distribution-dependent methods are *digit analysis* and *sequence-maintaining transformations*.

▦▦▦▦ **Digit Analysis** attempts to capitalize on the existing distributions of key digits. A tabulation is made for each of the individual digit positions of the keys using a sample of the records to be stored. The tabulation lists the frequency of distribution of zeros, ones, twos, and so on. The digit positions that show a reasonably uniform, even distribution are candidates for use in the slot address. A sufficient number of such digit positions has to be found to make up the full address; otherwise, combinations of other digit positions can be tested. In Fig. 6-2 the three low-order digits of a social security number were considered to be uniformly distributed. Similar use can be made of character-string keys. Here the set of 26 possible letters may be divided into 10 groups to yield digits, or into groups of different sizes to yield factors other than 10 which can be used to produce an access record number.   ▦▦▦▦

▦▦▦▦ **Sequence-maintaining Methods** for key-to-address transformation generate addresses that increase with increasing keys. Serial access is made possible, whereas generally hashed files do not have capability for serial access.

A sequence-maintaining transformation can be obtained by taking an inverse of the distribution of keys found.

This inverse function is applied to the keys. The addresses generated will maintain sequentiality with respect to the source key.

In a *piecewise-linear-transformation* the observed distribution is approximated by simple line segments.

This approximation then is used to distribute the addresses in a complementary manner. An *exponential transformation* is presented in Fig. 12-6 as an illustration of the evaluation of the uniformity of obtained addresses. These approaches are valid only if the source key distribution is stable. It may be difficult to find a simple inverse function.   ▦▦▦▦

HASHING METHODS   The three hashing methods presented here (*remainder-of-division*, *exclusive*-OR, *folding-and-adding*) randomize the source key to obtain a uniform address distribution. Operations such as arithmetic multiplication and addition, which tend to produce normally distributed random values (see Chap. 12-1), are undesirable when hashing.

Remainder-of-Division of the key by a divisor equal to the number of record slots allocated m was used throughout this chapter. The remainder does not preserve sequentiality. The remainder-of-division is in some sense similar to taking the low-order digits, but when the divisor is *not* a multiple of the base (10 in Fig. 6-2 above) of the number system used to represent the key, information from the high-order portions of the key will be included. This additional information scrambles the result further and increases the uniformity of the generated address.

Large prime numbers are generally used as divisors since their quotients exhibit a well-distributed behavior, even when parts of the key do not. In general, divisors that do not contain small primes (≤ 19) are adequate. If the address space m_0 is a power of two then $m = m_0 - 1$ is often suitable. Tests (Lum[71]) have shown that division tends to preserve, better than other methods, preexisting uniform distributions, especially uniformity due to sequences of low-order digits in assigned identification numbers, and performs quite well.

The need to use a division operation often causes programming problems. The key field to be transformed may be larger than the largest dividend the divide operation can accept, and some computers do not have divide instructions which provide a remainder. The remainder then has to be computed using the expression

Table 6-5   Using division to produce the remainder.

```
rel_address = key - FLOOR(key/m) * m
```

The explicit `FLOOR` operation is included to prevent a smart program optimizer from rearranging terms and generating `address=0` for every `key` which would lead to all records colliding. Costly divisions can be avoided by replacing them by multiplication of the reciprocal of m, but the behavior of the result may differ.

Exclusive-OR (X-OR)   is an operation which provides a very satisfactory randomization and can be used when key lengths are great or division is otherwise awkward. The bits of two arguments are matched agains each other. It yields a 1-bit where the argument bits differ and a 0-bit otherwise. The `x-or` operation is available on most computers or can be obtained by a procedure as defined in Table 6-6.

Table 6-6   Key-to-address transformation using X-OR.

```
DECLARE (rel_address,keypart1,keypart2) BIT(19);
    x_or: PROCEDURE(arg1,arg2); DECLARE(arg1,arg2) BIT(*);
          RETURN( (arg1 ∨ arg2) ∧ ( ¬(arg1 ∧ arg2)) );
          END x_or;
    ...
rel_address = x_or(keypart1,keypart2);
```

As Table 6-6 shows, the key is segmented into parts (here 2) which match the required address size. The `x-or` operation produces equally random patterns for random binary inputs. If the segments contain characters, their boundaries should be avoided. For instance, `x_or('MA','RA')` will be equal to `x_or('RA','MA')`, so that "MARA" will collide with "RAMA". Care has to be taken also where the binary representation of decimal digits or characters is such that certain bit positions always will be zero or one. Both problems can be controlled by making the segment sizes such that they have no common divisor relative to character or word sizes. The `x-or` operation is generally the fastest computational alternatives for hashing.

‖‖‖‖ **Folding and Adding** of the key digit string to give a hash address has been used where the x-or has not been available. Alternate segments are bit-reversed to destroy patterns which arithmetic addition might preserve. A carry from a numeric overflow may be added into the low-order position. This method is available in the hardware of some large Honeywell computers. ‖‖‖‖

‖‖‖‖ **PROBABILITY OF SUCCESSFUL RANDOMIZATION** We assess now the performance risks in randomization. A graphic or quantitative under-standing of the processes of transformation can aid in developing a feeling for the effects of various methods to achieve random distributions (Peterson[57]). The num-ber of ways to transform n keys into m addresses is huge; there are in fact m^n possible functions. Even for the most trivial case, say, $n = 4$ records and $m = 5$ slots, 625 transforms exist. Of these $m!/(m - n)! = 125$ would avoid any collisions while loading the file. It would obviously be most desirable to find one of these. On the other hand, we have only $m = 5$ possibilities for a total collision; all records wind up in the same slot, and in those instances, the expected number of accesses for a fetch, using a chain, would be $(n + 1)/2 = 2.5$; the remaining 495 transforms cause one or two collisions.

Since the randomization method is chosen without any prior knowledge of the keys, the selection of any reasonable method out of the m^n choices gives a probability of that method causing no collisions ($o_0 = 0$) of only $p_0 = (m!/(m - n)!)/m^n = 0.2$. On the other hand, the probability of selecting one of the five worst methods for this case, which would lead to $c = n - 1 = 3$ collisions and $o_{max} = 1 + 2 + 3$ extra accesses, is only $p_{max} = m/m^n = 0.008$. The remaining three cases of one collision, two collisions in two slots, and two collisions in the same slot can be analyzed similarly and are shown in Fig. 6-9. Given the assumption that we have just an average randomization, we find that we may expect an average of $p = \sum_c p_c o_c = 0.30$ additional accesses per record loaded.

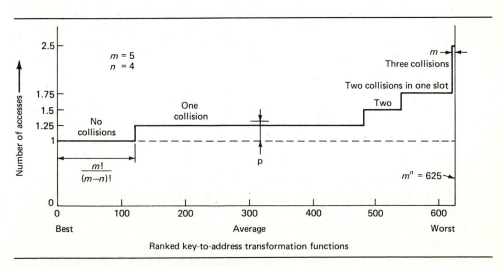

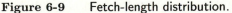

Figure 6-9   Fetch-length distribution.

We expect at the final point that $o = \sum_c p_c c = 1.05$ records collided and were not loaded within the main file; they will have been placed somewhere else. The main file now contains $n - o = 4 - 1.05 = 2.95$ records. The collision probability for the next insertion is $2.95/5 = 0.59$.

The distribution will have a similar shape for other values of m and n. The number of steps rapidly increases with n and m so that the distribution function becomes smooth. Estimates for the number of collisions in the general case are derived in Chap. 12-1, but the intent of this discussion is to show the relative unimportance of the specific choice of randomization method, as long as it is chosen to be outside the obviously worst areas. It might be mentioned here that a change of keys, that is, a new set of data to be randomized, will completely reorder the position of the m^n functions in the figure, but the form of the distribution remains the same.   ▦▦

SUMMARY OF KEY-TO-ADDRESS TRANSFORMATIONS   It is obvious from the above that many choices exist for transforming keys of records to record addresses. We find also that the average performance of reasonable transformations is such that perfectly good results are obtained with less than perfect methods. On the other hand, cute methods, such as deterministic and sequence-maintaining schemes, carry a high risk of failure when conditions change.

6-1-6 Use of Hashed Files

Hashed random access is an invention specific to computers and has been used to access data on the earliest disk files. Hashed files find frequent use for directories, pricing tables, schedules, name lists, and so forth. In such applications where the record sizes are small and fixed, where fast access is essential, and where the data is always simply accessed, the hashed file organization is uniquely suitable. Simple access here means use of a single key for retrieval, and no serial access.

Hashing is not appropriate for attributes which have a poor selectivity. The clusters in the source key are reserved when hashing, and may coalesce with other clusters. Managing deletion in clusters is costly as well.

Hashed files also play an important role as a component of more complex file organizations. It provides rapid access by identifier, as SSN or `inventory_code`, which are already designed to be unique, while other techniques are used for secondary attributes. We will find many uses of hashed access in Chap. 7.

6-2   PERFORMANCE OF HASHED FILES

The performance of hashed files has been more thoroughly analyzed than the performance of any of the preceding methods. The initial parameter in these evaluations is the number of record spaces or slots, m, available for the storage of the n records. The number of records that still cause collisions is denoted here as o.

We will first analyze a simple hashed-access structure with the main file having buckets that hold only a single record and with a separate overflow area to contain up to o records that caused collisions. The records are of fixed length, and contain a single pointer field to allow access to any successor records due to overflows. With the fixed record format the attribute names are not kept within the records, so that space is only needed for the a data values of size V.

Access to the single overflow area will require a seek. There are no identical keys, i.e., all stored records are unique, so that all collisions are due to the randomization. The number of records stored, n, is still smaller than the number of slots, m, so that a perfect distribution would not lead to any overflows and hence keep $o = 0$.

We let overflow records be found via a chain of pointers starting from the primary area. The overflow chain is maintained so that blocks containing overflow records are accessed in sequence. This avoids accessing the same block more than once in a chain.

We will, when appropriate, also make comments which pertain to hashed files using open addressing, and to the use of multirecord buckets, since these methods are used frequently.

6-2-1 Record Size in a Hashed File

The space required for an individual record is the same as for the indexed-sequential file: $R_{actual} = aV + P$, and for an entire file, S_F, as described previously, is

$$S_F = m\,(aV + P) + o\,(aV + P) \qquad\qquad 6\text{-}3$$

or, per record,

$$R_{effective} = \frac{m + o}{n}(aV + P) = \frac{m + o}{n}R_{actual} \qquad\qquad 6\text{-}4$$

The required overflow space is based on the fraction of collisions, p, as discussed below, but one should also consider the expected variability of that estimate, so that this area will, in practice, never overflow between reorganizations. For a file with many records the expected variability is small, and o can be safely dimensioned to be 25 to 100% greater than pn. The estimation of the needed overflow size o is elaborated in Chap. 12-1-5.

6-2-2 Fetch Record in a Hashed File

In order to predict an average for time to locate a record in a hashed file, we must determine the probability of collision, p, since the predicted fetch time is simply the time required for randomization, the time for the single hashed access, plus the average cost of the case of a collision:

$$T_F = c + s + r + btt + p\,(s + r + btt) \qquad\qquad \langle\text{basic case}\rangle\ 6\text{-}5$$

An analysis which estimates the collision cost, p, for this design is given in Chap. 12-1-5, leading to Eq. 12-15. The result of the analysis shows that the expected value of p is

$$p = \frac{1}{2}\frac{n}{m} \qquad\qquad \langle\text{with overflow area}\rangle\ 6\text{-}6$$

for the case of hashing to single-slot buckets and using separate overflow areas for collisions.

EFFECT OF OPEN ADDRESSING   In open addressing with a linear search clusters of collisions can occur. The detrimental effect of clusters increases rapidly with the file density, n/m, as seen in Fig. 6-10 for the bucket size $y=1$. Knuth[73S] has derived, using the arguments of an "average" randomly selected randomization discussed in Sec. 6-1-5, that the number of additional accesses becomes

$$p = \frac{1}{2}\frac{n}{m-n}$$ ⟨with open addressing⟩ 6-7

The result for bucket sizes $y > 1$, as derived by Knuth[73S], is complex and hence is presented in graphical form as Fig. 6-10. The overflow cost is based on the initial probability of an overflow plus all further overflows to be accessed, so that under poor conditions $p > 1$.

It is important to note three aspects of open addressing multi-record bucket hashing:

1 the overflow probability and cost can be kept very small with good combinations of bucket capacity y and file density n/m

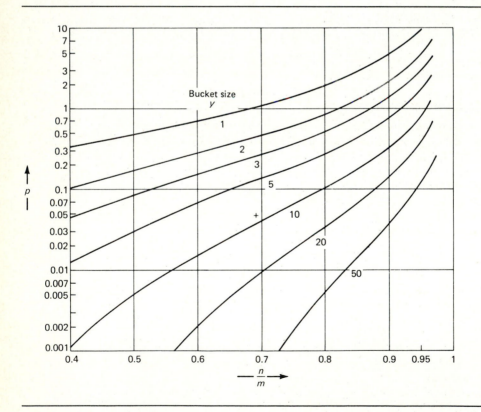

Figure 6-10   Overflow cost for multirecord buckets, open addressing, and linear search.

2 no overflow area is required when open addressing is used, so that for the same total amount of storage the value of m may be appropriately larger. Increasing m to $m + o$ will not compensate fully for the increased number of collisions, as demonstrated in the worked-out example in Fig. 6-11.

3 the deterioration of performance with increasing density is very rapid as shown in Fig. 6-10.

Validation Measurements of hashed files have produced results which are in close agreement with Eqs. 6-5 and 6-6 (Lum[71]). The values shown in Fig. 6-10 have been experimentally verified by Deutscher[75] using the remainder-of-division algorithm to compute the addresses. Even for poorly distributed keys the results became valid when bucket sizes $y \geq 5$.

We can now evaluate the effect of collisions. We will provide 50% more primary space than the amount required for the expected records themselves, i.e., $m = 1.5\,n$. For the basic hashed file — only one record space per bucket and a separate overflow area — we obtain a collision cost of

$$p = \frac{1}{2}\frac{n}{1.5\,n} = 0.3333 \qquad \text{or about 33\% extra accesses}$$

due to collisions when the file is fully loaded. A reasonable overflow area in this case may be based on $1.5\,p$, giving $o = 0.5\,n$.

With open addressing, using the same primary space, m, and still bucket sizes equal to R, the value of p becomes

$$p = \frac{1}{2}\frac{1}{1.5 - 1} = 1.0 \qquad \text{or 100\% extra accesses}$$

Adding the space no longer required for the overflow area, o, to the space for the main file, m, reduces this estimate to

$$p = \frac{1}{2}\frac{1}{1.5 + 0.5 - 1} = 0.5 \qquad \text{or 50\% extra accesses}$$

The use of multirecord buckets has a greater effect. If the record size $R = 200$ and the block size $B = 2000$, the bucket size, y, can be made equal to $Bfr = 10$; this change increases only the computational overhead for a block retrieved into memory. We will *not* add the overflow space to the main file, so that $m = 1.5\,n$. We obtain from Fig. 6-10

$$p = 0.03 \ \text{ for } \ \frac{n}{m} = 0.66, \ y = 10 \qquad \text{or about 3\% extra accesses}$$

Since now only 3% of the fetches will have to access another block, a linear, sequential scan for overflows is reasonable.

Figure 6-11   Collision cost assessment.

LOCATING THE SUCCESSOR BLOCK   In open addressing with linear search-ing, if the decision to read the next block can be made immediately, no revolution needs to be wasted. In general, however, one revolution is required to read the next block if the read decision is based on the contents of the predecessor block, so that the access time for an overflow is $T_{RW} + btt$ or $2r + btt$. Alternate-block accessing, as shown in Fig. 6-12, can reduce this delay to $2\,btt$, leaving a time $c < btt$ for the comparisons within a bucket. The decision of where to place overflows is specific to the procedure for hashed-file access.

We find overflow records in successor blocks by use of a chain. The search for a nonexistent record can be terminated at an end-of-chain flag. Multiple records may be found within the same block. In linear search we can expect, without clustering, $(m - n)/m\,y$ free slots in a block, and these are available for insertion. A failure to find the record in a successor block, p_2, is then

$$p_2 \approx p^{\frac{m-n}{n}\,y} \hspace{3cm} \langle\text{linear search}\rangle\ 6\text{-}8$$

which makes the event quite rare. When needed, successive blocks are accessed using the chain of records extending from the primary bucket.

When a separate overflow area is used, the probability of not finding the suc-cessor block in the same bucket is higher and can be evaluated based on the number of blocks used for the overflow area. This value is

$$p_2 \approx o'/y \hspace{3cm} \langle\text{separate overflow area}\rangle\ 6\text{-}9$$

We will ignore p_2 in the fetch evaluation below, since we will always choose methods with a low primary collision cost, p.

In summary, the fetch time for the various cases becomes

$$T_F = c + s + r + btt + p\,t_{overflow} \hspace{2cm} \langle\text{all cases}\rangle\ 6\text{-}10$$

where the choices for p are given above and the values for the overflow cost are

$$t_{overflow} = s + r + btt \hspace{0.7cm} \text{for a separate overflow area}$$
$$t_{overflow} = r + btt \hspace{0.7cm} \text{for separate overflow areas on the same cylinder}$$
$$t_{overflow} = 2r + btt \hspace{0.7cm} \text{for linear searching, sequential blocks}$$
$$t_{overflow} = 2\,btt \hspace{0.7cm} \text{for linear searching, alternate blocks}$$

and c depends on the complexity of the hashing algorithm and the bucket size.

⊞⊞⊞   **Fetch for a Record Not in the File**   In a fetch for a nonexistent record, we will be forced to follow the chain search until we find a Λ pointer. This time is greater than the time required for fetching an existing record, since we expect to find records on the average halfway into the chain. This condition occurs also when insertions are considered (T_{Iov}), since all the records of an overflow chain have to be tested to locate an empty slot for insertion.

The effect can be estimated by setting the term $p\,t_{overflow} \approx 2\,p\,t_{overflow}$ for the fraction of records(not_in_file) in Eq. 6-10 above.   ⊞⊞⊞

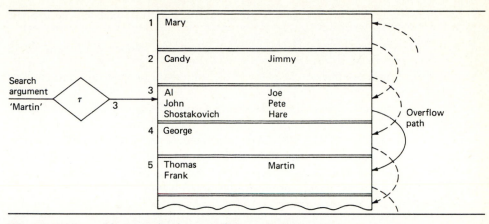

Figure 6-12   Alternate bucket overflow accessing.

6-2-3 Get-Next Record of a Hashed File

No concept of serial access exists with the hashed file. If the key for the next record is known, a successor record can be found using the same fetch procedure used to find any record.

$$T_N = T_F \qquad\qquad \text{⟨known next key⟩ 6-11}$$

If the key for the next record is not known, no practical method exists to retrieve that record.

This represents the major liability for hashing, so that for special cases KATs have been built which overcome that problem.

▦▦▦ **Using a Sequence-maintaining KAT** For hashed files using a sequence-maintaining key-to-address transformation, a successor record can be found. The next record is located by sequential search, skipping over any unused slots. The probability of finding the record in the next slot can be estimated using the density of the main file n/m. A low density reduces performance here. Separate overflow areas must be used to maintain serial linkage of overflows, increasing the cost of fetch and next access to overflowed records. To evaluate the cost a case-analysis approach, as used for indexed-sequential files (Eq. 5-17), is neccessary.   ▦▦▦

6-2-4 Insert into a Hashed File

To insert a record into the file, an empty slot has to be found which can be reached according to the key. The key-to-address transformation generates a prime bucket address. The bucket must be fetched and checked to determine whether there is a free slot for the record. We will consider now again buckets of only one slot and the use of a chain of records which collided. The probability of the initial slot being filled, p_{1u}, has been derived also in Chap. 12-1-5, Eq. 12-18 for the case of a separate overflow area:

$$\bar{p}_{1u} = 1 - e^{n/m} \qquad\qquad \text{⟨overflow area⟩ 6-12}$$

If open addressing is used all records are in the file and we can simply use the density:

$$p_{1u} = \frac{n}{m} \qquad\qquad \langle \text{open addressing} \,\rangle\ 6\text{-}13$$

For multiple records per bucket the value of p_{1u} can again be best determined from Fig. 6-10.

The insertion cost can be computed as the sum of the expected cost for the case where the primary slot is empty, which has the probability of $(1 - p_{1u})$, and the cost for the case where the primary slot is filled, a probability of p_{1u}. In both cases the primary block is fetched first. If the slot is found empty, the record is placed into the empty slot, and the block rewritten; otherwise the existing record is kept and one of the overflow procedures discussed has to be followed.

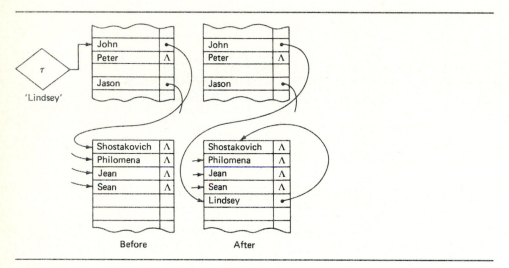

Before   After

Figure 6-13   Overflow record linked as second chain member.

Insert Using a Separate Overflow Area   When a *separate overflow* area is used, the procedure is to link the new record as the second member of the chain, as illustrated in Fig. 6-13. The block with the primary record is still rewritten, now with the existing record and the latest address in the overflow area in its pointer field. The new record is placed into the overflow area at position `last` with the pointer value obtained from the primary record. The two rewrites require

$$
\begin{aligned}
T_I &= c + (1 - p_{1u})(s + r + btt + T_{RW}) \\
&\quad + p_{1u}(s + r + btt + c + s + r + btt + T_{RW} + T_{RW}) \qquad \langle \text{simple} \rangle\ 6\text{-}14 \\
&= c + (1 + p_{1u})(s + r + btt + T_{RW})
\end{aligned}
$$

But placing the insertion immediately does not assure that there are no duplicated records with the same key.

If duplicate records with the same key are not permitted, *all* records in the bucket and in any overflow have to be checked prior to insertion of the new record.

If records are chained the entire chain must be followed. The considerations made when evaluating the fetch of a nonexisting record apply here as well, $p(not\_in\_file)$, and the search time for checking involves the terms used in Eq. 6-10. When the end of the chain is reached (pointer is Λ), a block with the selected prior record and the new inserted record is rewritten. If the block where the search terminated is full, an additional block fetch and rewrite sequence is required. The probability of this event is only $1/y$. The primary block is not rewritten unless it was the terminal block of the chain.

$$T_I = c + s + r + btt + 2\,p_{1u}\,t_{overflow} + T_{RW}$$
$$+ \frac{1}{y}(s + r + btt + T_{RW}) \qquad \text{⟨with checking⟩ 6-15}$$

The cost of following the chain is similar for overflow areas and for open addressing, the parameters used are given with Eq. 6-10.

Equation 6-15 applies also if we wish to optimize the record placement into blocks of the overflow area. Here the simple procedure of Fig. 6-13 is not adequate and the chain will have to be followed until a suitable block is encountered.

When the combination of open addressing, single-slot buckets, and no chaining is used, the entire set of colliding and all the associated clusters (see Fig. 6-6) has to be passed to find a free space. No satisfactory formulation for the linear searching required in this case is known to the author. A low density n/m is important to keep p_{1u} reasonable. Knuth[73S] suggests that

$$T_I \approx \frac{m}{m - n}(s + r + btt) \qquad \text{⟨open addressing, one slot buckets⟩ 6-16}$$

when rerandomization instead of sequential search is used. A special technique for inserting a batch of insertions is given in the discussion leading to Eq. 6-22.

If buckets with many slots per bucket are used, the probability of overflow out of block (p as given in Fig. 6-10) reduces rapidly and any chains will be short. Now we can consider simply that insertion requires just one fetch and rewrite sequence. In open addressing the inserted record is likely to fit into the block found. This is expressed by the factor $\frac{m}{m-n}$ in the final term of Eq. 6-17; use of a separate overflow area would remove that factor, as seen in Eq. 6-15.

$$T_I = c + s + r + btt + p_{1u}\,t_{overflow} + T_{RW}$$
$$+ \frac{1}{y}\frac{m}{m - n}(s + r + btt + T_{RW}) \qquad \text{⟨large buckets⟩ 6-17}$$

The use of large buckets and chaining does affect the value of c.

These evaluations assumed that the number of records n was as expected. When a hashed file is not yet filled there will be fewer, n', records, leading to better performance. This factor is considered in Sec. 6-2-7.

6-2-5 Update Record in a Hashed File

The process of updating the record consists of finding the record and rewriting it into the original slot, so that

$$T_U = T_F + T_{RW} \qquad 6\text{-}18$$

When the key changes, a deletion and a new write operation has to be performed.

Deletion requires the same effort when records are not chained. Depending on the method used for linkage, a tombstone may have to be set. If chaining is used, and it is desirable to set the slot to Empty to make it available for another collision set, then the preceding record has to be rewritten with the linkage pointer obtained from the deleted record.

6-2-6 Read Entire Hashed File

An exhaustive search for a file using a randomizing key-to-address translation can be done only by searching through the entire space allocated to the file, since the discrete transformations from a sparse set of key values do not allow serial reading. The reading is costlier, since the file space also contains empty and deleted slots. The area used by the overflows will also have to be checked. A separate overflow area will be dense, except for deletions, but

$$T_X \approx (m + o)\frac{R + W}{t'} \qquad\qquad 6\text{-}19$$

In practice, hashed files are rarely used when reading of the entire file is an expected operation.

6-2-7 Reorganization of a Hashed File

Reorganizations are mainly required if the total number of records to be kept has grown and no provisions were made for extension of file space; linear hashing was presented in Sec. 6-1-4 as a method to accommodate growth incrementally. Growth causes the density, n/m, to exceed the design goals. Before n, approaches m reorganization is needed. Reorganization allocates a larger space to the primary area for the file; the randomizing procedure has to be rewritten or adjusted. The file is exhaustively read from the old space and reloaded into the new space. The performance of the terms T_X and T_{Load} defined in Eq. 6-20 should be estimated using the old value of m for T_X and the new value of m for T_{Load}.

A simple reloading procedure is to perform n insertions, each taking T_I. Two other alternatives are presented here as well.

Reorganization is also beneficial when many deletions have occurred. Deletions in clusters cause the search paths to be tangled and long. Large clusters in open addressing, the effect of the tombstones left to assure search paths can reduce performance greatly.

If the file cannot be removed from service for a long time, i.e., a high *availability* is desired, an incremental reorganization can reorganize a single cluster (defined as the space between two empty slots) at a time. Otherwise a reorganization will read and reload the entire file

$$T_Y = T_X + T_{Load} \qquad\qquad 6\text{-}20$$

where T_{Load} is the loading time discussed below.

▦ LOADING A HASHED FILE We present three methods for loading a hashed file:

1. Successive insertion
2. A two-pass procedure designed to avoid clusters
3. A procedure where the input is sorted to speed up loading.

Successive Insertion The most obvious way to load or reload a hashed file is to rewrite the records one by one into the new space; then

$$T_{Load} = n\,T_I(n', m) \qquad\qquad 6\text{-}21$$

with a continuously changing value of $T_I(n', m)$ as n'/m increases. Initially there should be scarcely any collisions. The evaluation with Fig. 6-9 was based on loading the file. A first-order estimate to compute the average T_I can be based on a density of $\frac{3}{4}n/m$. Loading still requires much effort; every record will require at least one random block access, and if open addressing is used, the new file will develop clusters as it fills.

Two-pass Insertion A two-pass procedure can be used to reduce the effect of clusters. In the first pass records are stored only if they have primary slots; any colliding records are placed into the remaining empty slots of the file during a second pass. The technique is mainly used for files that are frequently read and rarely updated. The second pass may try to optimize record placement.

Sorting and Block Writing A major reduction in loading cost can be accomplished by sorting the file to be loaded into the hashed file sequence, i.e., by computed address. To do this, the key-to-address transformation is applied to all the record keys of the records to be loaded into the file, and the address obtained is attached to the records. The records are then sorted based on the attached address. Equation 4-12 gave the speed of a sort operation. The sorted file is then copied (without the addresses) into the space for the hashed file; slots which do not have a matching address are skipped, and colliding records are placed into successor slots. This writing time is equal to the sequential exhaustive read time, so that

$$T_{Load} = c + T_{sort} + T_X \qquad\qquad 6\text{-}22$$

The advantage of a substantially reduced loading time is that reorganization can become a valid alternative to more complex schemes used to combat clustering and to manage deletions in a dynamic environment.

Using the technique of sorting by address, leading to Eq. 6-22, to reload the hashed file space permits the entire reorganization to be performed at a cost of

$$T_Y = c + 2\,T_X + T_{sort} \qquad\qquad 6\text{-}23$$

If the last sort pass can be combined with filling the hashed file, then one term T_X drops out. ▦

▦ BATCH INSERTION The reloading method can also be used to add a batch of insertions into the file. The batch would have to be quite large, since a complete sequential pass is needed. If we use n_I to denote the size of the batch, this insertion method would be profitable only if $n_I > (T_Y/T_I)$. ▦

6-3   THE MULTIRING FILE

The three previous file organization methods dealt with the problem of finding individual records fast. This last of the six fundamental methods, the *multiring* file, is oriented toward efficient processing of subsets of records. Such a subset is defined as some group of records which contain a common attribute value, for instance, all `employees` who speak `French`. The multiring approach is used with many database systems; we consider only the file structure of this approach.

Subsets of records are explicitly chained together through the use of pointers. The chain defines an order for the members of the subset. One record can be a member of several such subsets. Each subset has a header record which is the origin for the chain. A header record contains information which pertains to all its subordinate member records. The header records for sets of subsets can also be linked into a chain.

The particular type of chain which will be used to illustrate this approach is the *ring*, a chain where the last member's pointer field is used to point to the header record of the chain. Similar file structures are called *threaded lists* or *multilists* in the literature, and can be implemented either with rings or with simple chains.

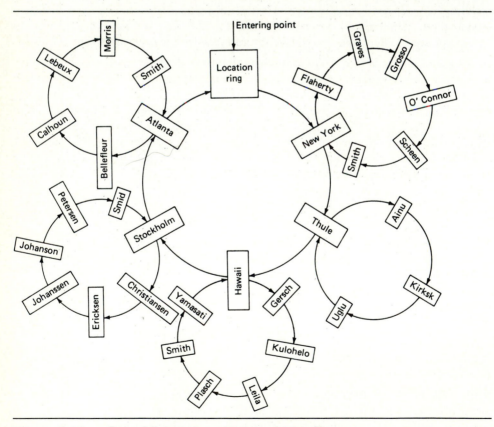

Figure 6-14   Record linkage in a simple multiring file.

Rings can be nested to many levels of depth. In that case member records of a level i ring become the header records of subsidiary rings at level $i-1$. The bottom level rings, with the final data, are considerd to be on level 1.

Figure 6-14 shows a simple hierarchically linked ring structure. The individual records in this example are formatted as shown in Fig. 6-15.

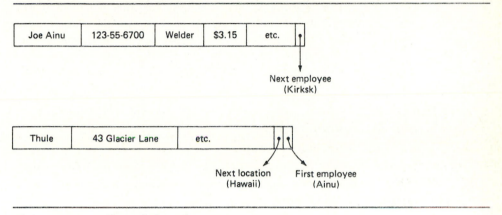

Figure 6-15   Records in a ring structure.

An example of the type of query for which this organization is well suited is

"List all employees in Thule"

A search in a multiring file follows a chain for an attribute type until a match is found for the search attribute value. Then a new chain is entered to find the subordinate attribute records. This process is repeated if neccessary until the desired record or set of records is found. For the example the location ring is read until the record for Thule is found; then the three employees living there could be listed.

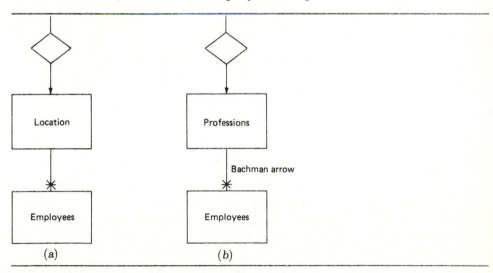

Figure 6-16 a and b   Two employee files.

6-3-1 Depiction of Multiring Files

To simplify the presentation of these rings, we use boxes and a special arrow to indicate rings and their relationship. The concept of the arrow to depict $1 \rightarrow m$ relationship of the one master record to many subsidiary member records is due to Bachman[66]. The shape of the arrow we use ($\rightarrow\!\!*$) is chosen to denote that many records will exist at the terminal point, although only one box is shown in the diagrams. A simple arrow is used to indicate an *entry point*, a ring whose header record is immediately accessible. All rings will be listed in the file directory, and their entry points will provide an initial access for processing queries. Figure 6-16a depicted the structure of the sample shown as Fig. 6-14 with an entry point using hashed access.

INTERLINKED RINGS   Another query of possible interest, which should be answerable from this file, might be

> "List all welders in our company"

Using the structure shown in Fig. 6-14, this would require an exhaustive search, traversing the **department** ring and each **employee** subsidiary ring in turn. Figure 6-16b shows a ring structure which allows answering this second query.

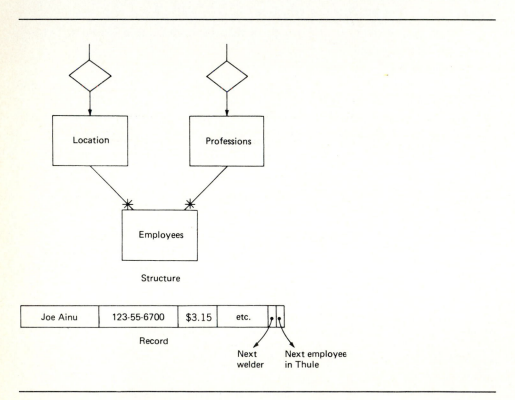

Structure

Record

Next welder   Next employee in Thule

Figure 6-17   Interlinked rings

We now have two redundant `employee` files. They should be combined by linking both by `profession` and `location`, as shown in Fig. 6-17. The actual ring structure with these two relationships becomes quite complex. Real world applications include many more rings.

If we expand the example of Fig. 6-17 by segregating the `employees` in the various `locations` into specific `departments`, allow access also in order of `seniority`, add a `warehouse` at each `location`, and keep `stock` information available, then the structure diagram will be as shown in Fig. 6-18. If the actual connecting pointers had to be drawn, the picture would look like a bowl of spaghetti.

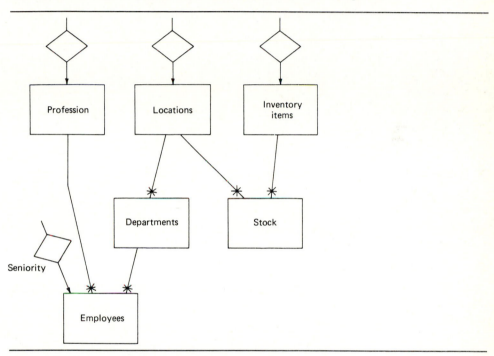

Figure 6-18   Complex hierarchical structure.

Relationships between rings are not necessarily hierarchical. Linkages may be implemented that relate members of the same ring (Fig. 6-19), that provide multiple pathways between records, or that relate lower rings back to higher-order rings. Two examples of multiple pathways occur in Fig. 6-20, which may be helpful to readers who understand football.

Not all constructs are allowed or implementable in practice. The ease with which the membership arrows can be drawn hides the complexity of underlying structure very effectively. Loops and other nonhierarchical relationships between records may require a variable number of pointer fields in the records and are hence undesirable. In Fig. 6-19 an implementation may limit the `spouses` relationship to one entry. The `visit_history` relationship may be best implemented using a search argument from `children` to an index for `clinics`. Network database management systems support such alternatives.

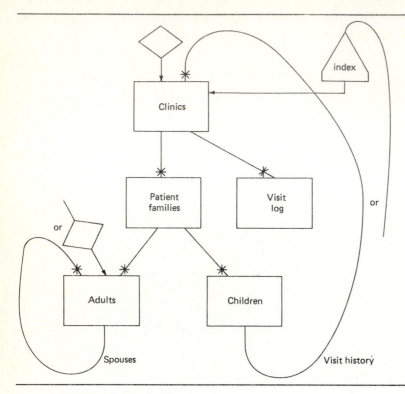

Figure 6-19   Loops in ring structures.

As the structures become more complex, the query processor may have to choose among alternate access paths to retrieve a record or a subset, and the choices may have quite different costs. A query applied to the structure shown in Fig. 6-18 as

> "Find an employee in Thule who can weld"

can be processed beginning at the `location` or at the `profession` ring. The appropriate records will be found at the intersection of any `department` at that `location` and the `welder` ring. The effectiveness of a process in locating a record depends strongly on a good match of the attribute pairs forming the query argument with the structure of the file. If the file is not organized appropriately, the process cannot proceed efficiently, and user intervention may be needed. For instance, if there is no `profession` ring, the path for the query above would have to begin at the entry point for `location`. Since the `location` record does not give a clue about the `profession`, an exhaustive search would be necessary through all `department` rings at this `location`. In an interactive environment, the system might have asked at this point,

> "Which department do you suggest?".

The process of finding the best path for a query to such a database has been termed *navigation* by the principal developer of this file-design concept (Bachman[73]).

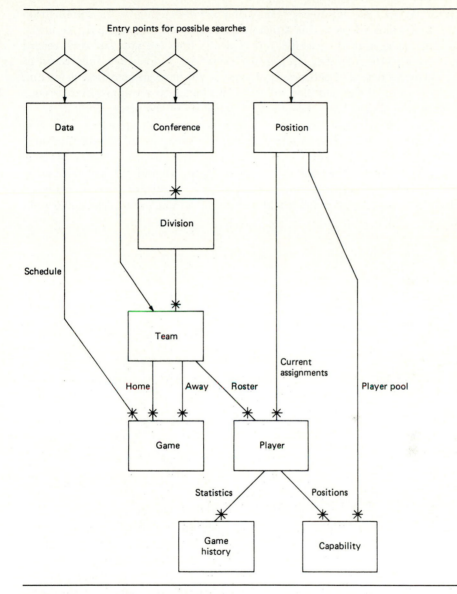

Figure 6-20   NFL football database.

6-3-2 Structure of Multiring Files

In a multiring file all records will have similar structures, but their contents and size will be a function of the rings to which they belong. A multiring file may have a considerable number of distinct record categories. We note here a violation of the earlier definition of a file: The records now are not identical in format, and ring membership as well as file membership has to be known before processing.

RECORD FORMATS The precise format of a record depends on the combination of ring types of which the record is a member. The attribute-value pairs could be self-identifying, as seen in the pile file; but typically they are not, and each record will have a record-type identifier. In Fig. 6-21 the field, t, identifies this record as being an employee record. Each record of type t will have similar data fields and seven pointer fields. This identifier will allow reference to an appropriate record format description, stored with the general description of the file.

To link the records into their rings, many pointers will appear in a typical record. A record can belong to as many rings as it has pointers. A given pointer position in the record format is, in general, assigned to a specific category of rings. In the example above, profession may be such a category and welder one specific ring of that category. If an instance of a record is not a member of a certain category ring, there will be an unused pointer field containing a NULL entry (Λ), as shown in Fig. 6-21.

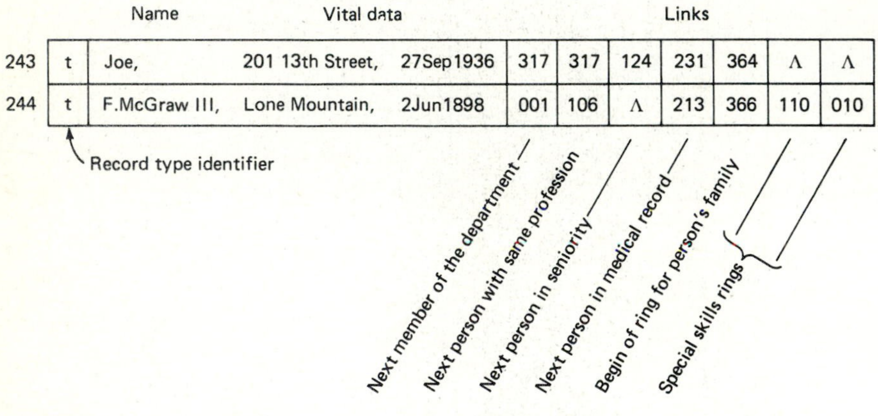

		Name	Vital data				Links				
243	t	Joe,	201 13th Street,	27Sep1936	317	317	124	231	364	Λ	Λ
244	t	F.McGraw III,	Lone Mountain,	2Jun1898	001	106	Λ	213	366	110	010

Record type identifier

Next member of the department

Next person with same profession

Next person in seniority

Next person in medical record

Begin of ring for person's family

Special skills rings

Figure 6-21   Record field assignments for a ring file.

There can also be NULL data fields, but since there are many types of records for specific purposes the overall file will be relatively dense. If all data fields are filled, and no redundant data is kept, the number of fields used is commensurate with the parameter a' which was used to enumerate the number of valid attributes for a record. The use of header records in fact reduces the redundancy of attributes found in files without the structure provided in the multiring file.

HEADER RECORDS Each ring will have a header. This header is either an entry point, a member of another ring, or both. The header for the ring of department employees will be the list of departments; the header for the ring of welders will be a member of the ring of professions; and the employee's record may be the header for a ring listing family members. When a ring is entered during a search, the point of entry is noted so that when this point is reached again, the search can be terminated.

6-3-3 Manipulation of Rings

As shown in the examples above, the typical multiring file organization avoids redundancy of data by placing data common to all members of a ring into the header record of the ring. For example, the name and other data about the `department` of an `employee` appears only in the header record. A negative effect is that, in the basic ring design, whenever a record is to be fetched based on a combination of search arguments, the match of all search arguments with data values applicable to the record cannot always be performed using only the attributes kept in the member or the header records accessed during the search along one path. Two alternatives can be used:

1 A *parallel search* through all rings identified in the search argument can be made, terminating at the records at the intersection of these rings.

2 An *initial search* can be made according to the attribute with the best partitioning effectiveness. The records collected are then checked for appropriateness by locating the header records for the other attribute types needed and rejecting records with inappropriate data values.

This latter process applied to the simple structure of Fig. 6-14 yields the steps shown in Fig. 6-22.

Query:
Find an Employee with Location ='Thule' and Profession='Welder'.
    Enter Location chain;
    For each member record determine if key = Thule;
    When found follow Employee chain;
        For every Employee record the profession must be determined
        Follow the profession chain;
        When its header record is reached,
            then inspect profession header for key = Welder
        If the field matches the search key
            then Employee member record becomes output;
      Continue with the next Employee record;
    When its header record, the Location = Thule is reached,
    then the result is complete.

Figure 6-22   Searching through a nonredundant multiring file.

The importance of the final pointer to the header which transforms a chain into a ring is clear here, but the cost of obtaining data from the header can still be great. Hence it may be desirable to still keep important descriptive data redundantly in the record, or to expand the structure to allow easy access to header records. Auxiliary constructs for that purpose are presented in Chap. 7-4-2.

6-3-4 Design Decisions for Rings

Selecting the attributes for which rings should be established uses similar criteria used for the decisions to determine the attributes to be indexed in an indexed file. The cost of following the chains increases linearly with chain sizes. The sizes of individual chains can be reduced by increasing the number of chains and the number of levels in the structure of the file.

Increasing the number of levels (x) reduces the expected chain lengths (y), since the number of partitions for the lowest-level (1) records increases. If all chain lengths in the file are equal, the expected chain length according to one hierarchy, say `locations, departments, employees` in Fig. 6-18, is

$$y = \sqrt[x]{n} \qquad\qquad \text{⟨equal chain lengths⟩ 6-24}$$

since the product of all the chains (`#locations` * `#departments_per_location` * `#employees_per_department`) is $y^3 = n$. This effect is shown graphically in Fig. 6-27. Numerically Eq. 6-24 is equivalent to stating that $x = \log_y n$, similar to the number of levels found for indexes (i.e., Eq. 5-25). However, in this file organization the partitioning of the file by attributes and hence the number of levels determines the chain sizes; whereas the computed fanout determines the number of levels in an index.

We consider now the case where the desired record can be recognized without having to trace back to alternate headers. The search time for a lowest-level record decreases then proportionally to the xth root of the record count, n, and increases proportionally to the number of levels, x.

Query:
  Find the welder with social security number = '123-45-6789'.
  Given the multiring file of Fig. 6-18 with the following record counts:
      10 000 employees with 10 000 social security numbers,
      and 50 professions (of equal size, 200 members each);
      also 20 locations with 10 departments of 50 employees each.
  The first search alternative is to enter the employee ring at the
      entry provided for ordering by seniority and search for the
      employee by social security number,
          takes 5 000 block accesses.
  The second search alternative - by profession and then
          within a profession -
          takes $25 + 100 = 125$ expected block accesses.
      The optimum for two levels is $2\frac{1}{2}\sqrt{10\,000} = 100$

  A third alternative - by location, department, and then employee -
          takes $10 + 5 + 25 = 40$ block accesses
      but is only possible if location and department are known.
  The optimum for three levels is $3\frac{1}{2}\sqrt[3]{10\,000} = 33$

Figure 6-23   Alternative costs of searching through a multiring file.

The block fetch counts seen here are much greater than the expected number when indexes are used; the retrieval of successor records, however, is more economical in this structure than it is when using indexed files. Locating an entire subset is quite fast, as shown in Fig. 6-24.

An attribute which does not partition the file into multiple levels, such as a social security number which has a perfect partitioning effectiveness, is not very useful as a ring element in a `personnel` file, since to find someone in this manner would require $n/2$ fetches. Finding a specific `welder`, however, is done fairly efficiently by searching down the `profession` chain and then through the `welder` chain. The file designer hopes that these two chains will partition the search space effectively; the optimum is attained when both chains are equal in length, namely, $\sqrt{n}$. In practice this is of course never quite true.

To summarize data for all the `welders`, we expect $25 + 200 = 225$ accesses. This number of records probably cannot be obtained more efficiently by any of the preceding methods. In order to gain a complementary benefit in access time, locality of rings has also to be considered in the file design.

Figure 6-24   Effectiveness of a multiring file.

▓▓▓▓▓ **Clustering of Rings** Records which are frequently accessed together are obviously best stored with a high degree of locality. One single ring can, in general, be placed entirely within one cylinder so that all seeks are avoided when following this particular *clustered* ring.

When frequent reference to the header record of the ring is needed, that header record may also participate in the cluster. Now the ring at the next-higher level will be difficult to cluster, unless the total space needed by all member records and their ancestors is sufficiently small to be kept on one or a few cylinders. With success traversal according to a clustered hierarchy will take very few seeks. In substantial files a given record type at a lower level will require many cylinders, and traversals of rings other than the clustered ring will require seeks.

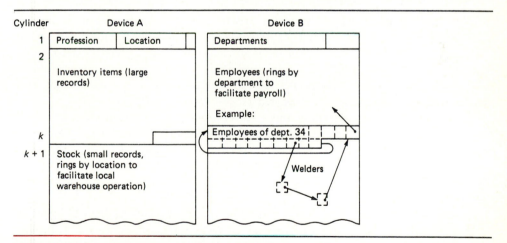

Figure 6-25   Assignment of rings to storage.

A possible assignment for the data of Fig. 6-18 is sketched in Fig. 6-25. Locating an `employee` via `department` will require only a few seeks within the `department` ring, to find the `employee` ring for the `department`. If there are many `employees` in some `department`, there may be some cylinder breaks in the ring. Finding an `employee` by `profession` may require seeks between nearly every `employee` record.

Stock in a warehouse is found with few seeks for a given `location`; these rings are apt to be long, and will require some seeks at cylinder break points. To relate `stock` to the `inventory` data will take seeks between records, but these rings may be short if there are few `locations`.

In a dynamically changing database, optimal clustering is difficult to maintain and its benefits should be partially discounted. A reorganization may be needed to restore clusters.   ▦▦

▦▦ **Categorizing Real Attributes** Some attributes, such as `profession`, can be naturally enumerated as a number of discrete categories, e.g., `welders`, `book-keepers`. Such a categorization will have a powerful partitioning effect, and the file will match well the natural structure of the data. Attributes that represent real or continuous data, e.g., `weight` or `height`, although they may have a high selectivity, do not provide effective partitioning unless they are artificially categorized. A statement to define discrete categories for a continuous variable is shown in Fig. 6-25.

```
DECLARE height
    ONE OF { <150cm, 150-154cm, 155-159cm, 160-164cm, ..., >189cm }.
```

Figure 6-25   Discretization of continuous data.

If continuous variables are used at low levels, so that these rings area reasonably small, then the rings need not be broken. A simple ordering within the ring will aid access. Ordering of members of a ring is frequently used.   ▦▦

6-3-5 Use of Multiring Files

The concept of related master and detail records can be traced to traditional data-processing procedures. Multiring structures are the basis for some of the largest databases currently in use. Management information systems where much of the system operation involves tabulating, summarizing, and exception reporting have been implemented using these multilinked lists. Examples of such operations were shown in the introduction to this section.

Some problems in geographic and architectural space representation also have been approached with a multiring approach. Current developments in integrated multifile systems depend greatly on the capabilities provided by ring structures. A problem with the multiring structure is that a careful design based on prior knowledge of the data and usage pattern is required before a multiring file can be implemented.

Ring structures have been implemented in practice with a number of important additional features. We will mention several of these in Chap. 7-4; they all will make the analysis of file performance more complex.

6-4   PERFORMANCE OF MULTIRING FILES

The performance of a multiring system depends greatly on the suitability of the attribute assignments to particular rings. In the evaluation below, we will assume that the file structure is optimally matched to the usage requirements.

We will analyze the performance for access to lowest level records in a hierarchy of rings. Each record can be adequately identified when accessed, so that no tracing from a candidate goal record to its header records is required. The record formats are fixed within a record type. In each record, there will be a fixed number of data and linkage fields, denoted as a'_{data} and a'_{link}, respectively.

We also assume an ideal partitioning of the file by the attributes, so that the rings on the various levels are of equal size. We neglect benefits to be gained by locality management of the rings, or clustering. The effects of these two factors may balance each other.

6-4-1 Record Size in a Multiring File

Since many distinct record types will exist in a multiring file, an accurate estimate is obtained only by listing all types, with their respective frequency and size.

In a file designed for minimal redundancy we expect that in the most frequent lower-level records

$$a'_{data} + a'_{link} \leq a' \qquad \text{⟨nonredundant⟩ 6-25}$$

since each data element is either explicitly represented or found by reference to some header record; one linkage pointer can replace a number of attributes.

If there is complete duplication of information in attribute fields and linkage fields to permit rapid selection of individual records, but still no empty fields, then

$$a'_{link} \leq a'_{data} = a' \qquad \text{⟨redundant⟩ 6-26}$$

Linkages to the same header record are not included.

In practice we find values in between these ranges, and relatively few linkage fields. Some important data fields will be kept redundantly to avoid excessive header referencing. A reasonable first order estimate is to let

$$a'_{data} + a'_{link} = a' \qquad \text{⟨estimate⟩ 6-27}$$

if the files have been carefully designed to satisfy a known query pattern.

The size of a data field is again averaged at V, and a linkage field contains pointer values of size P. One field of size P is prefixed to each record to allow identification of the record category. Then, for an average record,

$$R = P + a'_{data}V + a'_{link}P \qquad \text{6-28}$$

If the records are members of relatively few rings, the size difference of data values and pointers will not matter, so that with the estimate of Eq. 6-27

$$R \approx a'V \qquad \text{⟨estimate⟩ 6-29}$$

Again, individual record categories will vary about this estimate, and where R is used to estimate y and block retrievals the specific values are needed.

6-4-2 Fetch Record in a Multiring File

The time to fetch a record is a function of the number of chains searched and the length of the chains. We assume that the record contains enough data so that when it is found according to one particular accessing sequence, it can be properly identified. The record hence is found by searching down a hierarchy of x levels. We thus have to consider here only one ring membership per record type.

The length of a ring (y) depends on the size of the file, the number of levels, and how well the file is partitioned into the rings, as shown in Fig. 6-27. An estimate for the ideal case was given in Eq. 6-24. The lowest level (1) contains a total of n records in all its rings together, discounting other record types at higher levels or other hierarchies in the file.

If a single record is to be fetched, the number of hierarchical levels should be matched by the number of search arguments, a_F, in the search key. Example 6-12 illustrated this interdependence.

	#(rings)	#(records)
Level x	1	$y_x \approx y$
Level 3	y_x	$y_3 y_x \approx y^2$
Level 2	$y_3 y_x$	$y_2 y_3 y_x \approx y^3$
Level 1	$y_2 y_3 y_x$	$y_1 y_2 y_3 y_x \approx y^4$

Figure 6-27   File size at four hierarchical levels.

If there are fewer search arguments in the key, an entire ring, i.e., a subset of the records of the file, will be retrieved; if there are more arguments, there is redundancy, and attributes unproductive in terms of an optimum search strategy can be ignored. For a standard fetch the condition $a_F = x$ holds, and with Eq. 6-24

$$a_F = x = \log_y n \qquad \qquad 6\text{-}30$$

In order to traverse one level, we expect to access $\lceil y/2 \rceil$ records, using the same reasoning which led to Eq. 4-2. In order to locate a record at the lowest level, the most likely goal, we will traverse x rings so that $\frac{1}{2}xy$ records will be accessed. Assuming random placement of the blocks which contain these records,

$$T_F = \frac{x\,y}{2}(s + r + btt) \qquad \qquad 6\text{-}31$$

Using the expected number of levels, a_F for the hierarchy used by the query, and the corresponding value for y,

$$T_F = \frac{a_F \sqrt[a_F]{n}}{2}(s + r + btt) = fna(s + r + btt) \qquad \text{(in query terms) } 6\text{-}32$$

where *fna* represents the terms based on the values of a_F and n. We see that this relation is critically dependent on the optimum structure of the data, since the query format matches the relationships inherent in the file structure. Auxiliary rings or linkages will have to be employed if the search length for some foreseen and important search attribute combinations becomes excessive. Unplanned queries are difficult to satisfy with this structure.

Table 6-7 lists values for *fna* given some typical values for n and a_F.

Table 6-7   Values for the file-access factor *fna*.

	fna				
a_F	$n =$ 10 000	$n =$ 100 000	$n =$ 1 000 000	*fna* =	file-access factor
				a_F =	number of levels of rings in the search hierarchy
1	5 000	50 000	500 000	n =	number of records
2	100	318	1 000		on the level to be accessed
3	33	72	150		
4	20	36	72		
5	20	25	32		
6	18	24	30		

The search time may be reduced when important rings are placed so that they tend to cluster on a single cylinder. Large databases of this form have also been implemented on fixed-head disk hardware where no seeks are required, so that the term $s = 0$.

6-4-3 Get-Next Record of a Multiring File

The next record for any of the linked sequences can be found simply by following that chain

$$T_N = s + r + btt \qquad\qquad 6\text{-}33$$

Note that in this file organization we ahve serial ordering by multiple attributes. The "next" record can be selected according to one of several (a_{link}) attribute types. The only other fundamental file organization that provides multiattribute serial access is the indexed file.

If serial access via one particular ring is frequent, the records for one ring can be clustered within one cylinder, as discussed in Sec. 6-3-4. Then $s = 0$ when accessing members of that ring. Getting a next record tends to be an important operation in data processing using this file structure, so that multiring files will often use clustering. It is wise, however, to evaluate the effect conservatively.

6-4-4 Insert into a Multiring File

Adding a record to a multiring file is done by determining a suitable free space for the record, locating all predecessors for the new record, taking the value of the appropriate links from the predecessors, setting it into the new record, and placing the value of the position of the new record into the predecessor link areas.

The total effort, except for placing the record itself, is hence proportional to a'_{link}. Some effort can be saved at the bottom levels when the chains are not ordered. The sum of the fetches in all hierarchies into which the record is linked, the predecessor rewrites, and the placing of the final record is basically

$$T_I = a'_{link}(T_F + T_{RW}) + s + r + btt + T_{RW} \qquad\qquad 6\text{-}34$$

The cost of inserting a new record is obviously quite high, especially if the record is a member of many rings. In Chap. 7-4 structures that allow faster location of the predecessor records are shown.

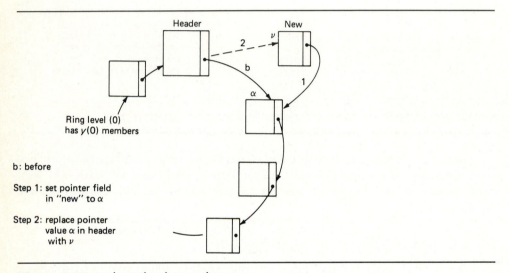

Figure 6-28   Insertion into a ring.

▦ **Unordered Attributes** If the records are ordered by attribute value, the chain has to be searched for the correct insertion point. If the chain connects identical attribute values, such as all `welders`, then only the header record has to be read, modified, and rewritten. For rings where the order does not matter, new records can also be inserted in the initial position. This will result in an inverse chronological sequence. Such a sequence is also desirable for fetching single records, since recent data is found rapidly. The process is illustrated in Fig. 6-28.

This linking has to be carried out for all a'_{link} rings of which the new record is a member. For each ring which is maintained in unordered form, $y/2 - 1$ block accesses can be saved in insertion or update. We will not account for this saving in the evaluations, but the term can be subtracted if appropriate from Eqs. 6-34, 6-36, and 6-34.   ▦

6-4-5 Update Record in a Multiring File

If only data fields are to be changed, the update requires only finding the record and rewriting it. We can assume that updated records do not change type and keep the same length. Then

$$T_U = T_F + T_{RW} \qquad \qquad \text{(unlinked attributes)} \; 6\text{-}35$$

for data field changes. If the record to be updated is initially located via a `Get-Next` operation, as is frequent in this type of file, the initial T_F can be replaced here, and in Eqs. 6-36 and 6-37, by T_N.

Updating of records can also require changes to the linkage. Only linkages whose values have changed need to be altered, since the updated record and its predecessors can be rewritten into the original position. Two cases exist here, since a new predecessor can be either in the same ring or in another ring, although at the same level, as the current predecessor.

If the changed value for one linkage is still within the type of the search attribute used to locate the record, then the point where the new record is to be inserted will be in the same ring and will require only $\frac{1}{2}y$ expected accesses of records in the ring. If, for instance, `stock items` of a given type are kept sorted within their ring by `weight`, a change due to a new design can require an item to shift position within the ring. To achieve such a shuffle, the new and the old predecessors have to be located for every link that is to be changed. We assume conservatively that a circuit of length y around each ring is needed to find both.

To relink the updated record into a new place within the ring, the pointers of the three records are interchanged as shown in Table 6-8:

Table 6-8   Procedure for update in a ring.

The new predecessor is set to point to the updated record.
The old predecessor is set to point to the former successor record
            of the updated record.
The new record is rewritten after all the new predecessor records
            have been read, since its successor links are
            copied from the new predecessors.

For this final rewrite no reading is required, but the position has to be recovered, requiring $s + r$ before the updated block can be written (*btt*).

The total for this case includes the initial fetch, the search for the predecessors of a_U links, the rewrite of these new and old predecessor records, and the final repositioning and rewrite of the new record. All this requires

$$T_U = T_F + a_U \left(y(s + r + btt) + 2\,T_{RW} \right) + s + r + btt \qquad \text{(links in ring)} \; 6\text{-}36$$

If, during the search for the old position of the record, a note is made of each predecessor and also if the new position is passed, the accesses to locate one of the predecessors and sometimes the accesses required to find the new predecessor record can be eliminated. The term, y, can then be reduced to $\frac{1}{2}y$ or even to 1 for one of the links. Since a_U is often 1 or small, the difference can be significant.

If updates cause ring membership changes within the same ring type, the new insertion positions have to be located. An example of this case is an `employee` who changes `departments`. This could be done by searching from the top, as was necessary in the case of record insertion. It may be faster to go to the header records using the ring, and then search through those header records for the desired place (`'Hawaii'`). The predecessor in the old ring (`'Calhoun'`) has also to be located and rewritten with a pointer to the previous successor (`'Morris'`). This process is illustrated in Fig. 6-29. The insertion place (`'Kulahelo'`) still has to be found.

We denote the number of links requiring access outside the current ring by a_W. The first choice, searching for the header records of a_W links from the top of the hierarchy, again requires a_W fetches of time, T_F. For updates less than three levels from the top (level numbers x, $x-1$, and $x-3$), it is advantageous to locate the insertion point from the top. The general approach is to navigate via the headers.

Using the header requires, for each changed outside link, finding the current header, finding the new header, and finding the new insertion point. A fourth scan of a ring is required to find the old predecessor, needed to achieve unlinking. The expected accesses in each ring are again $y/2$. The entire process requires for all fields together $a_W\,4\,y/2$ accesses. The entire process now takes

$$T_U = T_F + a_W\,(2\,y(s + r + btt) + 2\,T_{RW}) + s + r + btt \quad \langle\text{links outside of ring}\rangle\,6\text{-}37$$

In practice there may be both a_U links that can be updated within the ring and a_W links that require the complexity of ring changes. In that case both terms apply with their factors.

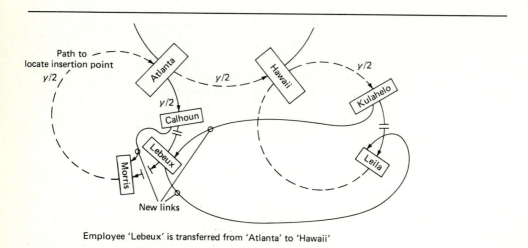

Employee 'Lebeux' is transferred from 'Atlanta' to 'Hawaii'

Figure 6-29   Finding a new linkage point.

6-4-6 Read Entire Multiring File

Exhaustive searches may be carried out by serially following any of a variety of possible linkages. A proper understanding of the file design is required to assure that no records will be read more than once. The cost will be relatively high, since the process will have to follow the linkages given in the records. The alternative, searching sequentially through the space, may not be easy, since the records have a variety of formats, and the description of a record type is necessary to make sense of the fields obtained.

Reading according to the chains requires, in addition, that a header record is accessed for each subsidiary ring. Both the old and new header record is needed to move between two rings, but it should be possible to keep a stack of x old header records in primary memory. Then

$$T_X = n \left(1 + \tfrac{1}{y}\right)(s + r + btt) \qquad\qquad 6\text{-}38$$

6-4-7 Reorganization of a Multiring File

Reorganization is not required as part of normal operating procedures. This is made obvious by the fact that a database system based on multiring files, IDS, available since about 1966, did not have an associated reorganization program available until 1975. Only when reformatting of record types is required will such records have to be rewritten. This may require only a partial reorganization of the file, since the changes are limited to rings of the levels using those records types. If one ring can be processed in memory at a time the costly rewriting of pointers found in updating can be avoided. The entire ring of y records is read, rearranged, and then rewritten at a cost of $y(s + r + btt) + c + y(s + r + btt)$. To fetch the rings to be reorganized we access the headers with one fetch and subsequent get-next operations.

A reorganization of n' records of one level, according to this incremental approach, is then

$$T_Y(n') = c + T_F + \frac{n'}{y}T_N + 2\,n'(s + r + btt) \qquad\qquad 6\text{-}39$$

where, if the reorganization takes place at level λ from the top (level $= x - \lambda + 1$), an estimate for $n' \approx y^\lambda$.

6-5 REVIEW OF HASHED AND RING FILES

In this chapter we covered two very distinct methods. Some of the differences are

	Hashed files	Ring files
Access by	One attribute	Many attributes
Oriented towards	Fetch	Get-next
Record placement	Rigid	Flexible
File growth	Complex	Easy

In practice this causes these two methods to be often combined. Especially, entry points into ring structures are found by hashing.

HASHING   The outstanding feature of hashed files is that the records can be accessed in constant time, $\mathcal{O}(1)$, so that growth of the file has no effect on performance, as long as the density can be maintained. If the density varies, then, for open adressing, $\mathcal{O}(\frac{n}{m-n}) \approx \mathcal{O}(C^{2n/m})$ in common ranges of m/n.

Hashing trades flexibility to gain both constant and high performance. Since record placement is determined by a computation, only one attribute of the record can be used for retrieval. Another inherent restriction due to the computation is that data records are expected to be of fixed length.

Records of randomized hashed files can be accessed only via one precise attribute value and not by range, and not serially. To locate the next record in key sequence requires knowing or guessing the value of the key, and this violates our definitions for Get-Next operations. Guessing a successor key would, in the great majority of fetches, result in a *record-not-found* condition. In practice this choice is excluded from consideration.

Some solutions to the problems listed here are shown in Chap. 7-3; they all carry additional access costs.

RING STRUCTURES   The performance of ring structures is greatly affected by growth. The depth of a search, x, is constant once the design is established, so that the performance then grows as the fanouts, y, grow on each level, so that performance is $\mathcal{O}(n)$.

In this structure speed and complexity was traded to gain generality. In practice they lose some of the generality, because it is rare that all conceptually possible access paths will be implemented in an application. The user has then to know what paths will lead to the data.

Knowing which paths are most important causes the designer to select those that become rings. No changes can be accommodated later when the users and their programs are set, even though that actual usage differs from initial assumptions. It is even difficult to determine that the design was wrong. Measurements only show the implemented paths, and provide no direct information on other candidate paths. The user of ring structures then has to be careful and use foresight during the design phase.

BACKGROUND AND REFERENCES

Hashing   Finding data by transforming keys was first used for data in memory, for instance to refer to symbol tables of assemblers and compilers. Peterson[57] and Heising publicized randomized hashed access for early disk files. Hashed access with chaining and open addressing was analyzed by Schay[62, 63], Buchholz[63], Hanan[63], and Heising[63]. Larson[83] analyzes uniform hashing and Yao[85] proves its optimality. Amble[74] discusses optimal chain arrangements for hashed files. Open addressing with linear probing has been further analyzed by Morris[68], Kral[71], Knuth[73S], and Bradley[85]. VanDerPool[73] analyzes for the steady state the optimal file design for various storage cost to processor cost ratios, both for a file using a separate overflow area and for the case of open addressing.

Many papers concentrate on the choice of hashing algorithms and the expected fetch chain length. Summaries of hashing techniques are given by Maurer[75] and Knott[75]. Gurski[73] considers digit selection by bit, a manual (IBM J20-0235) describes digit selection, Kronwal[65] presents the piecewise-linear-distribution algorithm, and Sorensen in King[75] presents an evaluation of distribution-dependent hashing methods, and Garg[86] describes some applications and algorithms. Kriegel[87] evaluates a variant. Waters[75] defends and analyzes linear transformations.

Bays[73] presents rules for reallocating entries to new, larger hashed access file areas, Fagin[78] uses tables to locate extensions and avoid multiple seeks for collisions. Litwin[80] developed linear hashing and Scholl[81], Burkhard[83], Larson[85], Veklerov[85], and Ruchte[87] present variants. Robinson[86] even maintains sequentiality.

Batch updating of a hashed file is suggested by Nijssen in Codd[71]. Concurrent access of hashed primary and overflow areas is proposed by Groner[74] and Ellis[85] analyzes concurrency with linear hashing.

Ring Files   Prywes[59] first proposed multiple chains for files, and Bachman[64] describes the multiring approach; and Dodd[66] implemented file access based on this concept. These ideas influenced the CODASYL standards, which encouraged numerous applications of this structure. Lang[68] presents another ring implementation and many illustrations are found in Kaiman[73]. Whang[82] provides a design algorithm for ring-structure selection.

Validation of ring pointers is considered by Thomas[77]. Further aspects of ring structures can be found in descriptions of database systems, and more references to specific file methods will be found with Chap. 8.

EXERCISES

1   In Fig. 6-2 division by 500 caused a collision. A nearby recommended value would be $2^9 - 1 = 511$ would not do so. Is that because 500 was a poor choice?

2   Write a program to perform a key-to-address transformation from a 20 character string using the 94 printable ASCII characters as shown in Table 13-1 and generating addresses for 800 entries with a density of n/m of about 0.6 .

3   Insert records labelled r, e, y, ç, u, ê, ä, ö, ü, è, é, v into the file of Fig. 6-7 and diagram the growth of the file.

4   Discuss the collision probabilities when linear hashing is used.

5   Discuss the benefits and liabilities of combining a sequence-maintaining KAT and linear hashing.

6   You have a large hashed file using separate overflow chains. You are aware that 10% of your records are used 50% of the time, and the other 90% of your records are used the remaining 50% of the time. You assume that within both groups the access distribution is uniform (equally probable).

Describe the processes required to keep the average access to records as fast as possible by ordering overflow records. Calculate the gain or loss in total efficiency versus the unordered organization for a file of 10 000 records with a primary allocation of 12 000 slots.

7   Compute the cost of retrieving all 17 welders from files that have as primary attribute the Employees' SSN. Parameters are $B = 2000, R = 125, A = 7, P = 3, s = 50, r = 20, btt = 10$. Make any further assumptions you need explicitly. Do this for an indexed file, a hashed file, and a ring file.

8   What is the performance for T_Y using the two-pass insertion procedure for a hashed file described in Sec. 6-2-7?

9   Sketch the actual ring structure for Fig. 6-17.

10   Evaluate the average access time for a hashed file using buckets of three records, linear search for free record space, and 20% excess capacity.

11^P Are there files in your application which are suitable for hashing? List all files you have defined and give the arguments for and against, and your decision.

12^P Are there natural hierarchies among the files in your application? Sketch a diagram using Bachman arrows among your files, use plain arrows for other relationships. Make a table which lists all relationships, hierarchical or not, and give a name to each, like Author's publications. List for each the destination and the source files, as Author and Books For each file name the attributes which are matched along the relationship, as Author.name and Publication.first_author. Also state the type of relationship (hier or not) and the expected cardinality (0–99 books per author).

Chapter 7

Combining File Methods

When bad men combine, the good must associate.

Edmund Burke
Thoughts on the Cause of the Present Discontents, 1770

7-0   INTRODUCTION

This chapter begins with a summary of the fundamental file organizations covered in Chaps. 4, 5, and 6. Then we present some of the file designs that can be obtained by combining these fundamental methods. The hybrid file organizations produced by such combinations can satisfy requirements that are not fulfilled by any of the fundamental methods.

We recall the general criteria for organizing data stated in Chap. 4-0:
1   Little redundancy: To reduce update and storage cost
2   Rapid access: To have effective information retrieval
3   Ease of update: To aid in having up-to-date information
4   Simple maintenance: To reduce cost and confusion
5   High reliability: To assure good availabilty of information

These criteria conflict. The combinations can achieve a different balance than provided by the fundamental methods.

In Sec. 7-2 some simple structures are described which enhance sequential files. Sections 7-3 and 7-4 discuss combination-based or hashed access and ring structures. A final review in Sec. 7-5 closes this chapter.

7-1   SUMMARY OF FUNDAMENTAL FILES

We review briefly the six fundamental file designs which were discussed in detail in the preceding chapters.

1 The *pile file* provides a fully adequate and flexible, although basic and unstructured organization. The pile file uses space well when the stored data vary in size and structure, is amenable to exhaustive searches, and is easy to update. However, the pile file is quite awkward for fetching specific records.

2 The *sequential file*, containing a collection of ordered fixed records, is, on the other hand, inflexible and difficult to update. It is still awkward for finding single records. But the structure is simple and efficient for the storage of well-structured data and very suitable for efficient, exhaustive processing. Sequential files match well the record facilities available in programming languages.

3 The *indexed-sequential file* adds a single index to the sequential organization. The result is a file which can be efficiently searched and updated according to one attribute, but is otherwise still fairly inflexible. The file is reasonably efficient for the storage of well-structured data and suitable for exhaustive processing.

4 The generalized *indexed file* removes the constraint on sequentiality and allows multiple keys. It can be searched using several search attributes. It is quite flexible, reasonably efficient for data storage, permits very complex updates at some cost, allows convenient access to specific records, but is awkward for exhaustive processes. Much storage may be occupied by the indexes.

5 The *hashed file* provides rapid record retrieval according to a single dimension. Record formats are fixed because of the mapping requirements. Hashing also permits rapid updates, trading speed against storage overhead. Serial and exhaustive searches are, in general, impossible.

6 The *multiring file* provides for a number of record types with many interconnections. Redundant and empty fields are reduced, but some space is required for the linkage pointers. Updates may be performed at a moderate cost. The ring organization provides flexible, but not always fast, access to single records and allows great flexibility for exhaustive or subset searches.

Only the general indexed file and the multiring files provide the capability for access to data according to more than one dimension. These two methods provide the basic building blocks for file designs providing multiattribute access whenever there are many records. Table 7-1 lists these conclusions in a summary form.

REASONS FOR COMBINING FUNDAMENTAL METHODS   There are frequently requirements that are not well supported by any of the file organization types described up to this point. Typical requirements may include the need to collect variable-length records while preserving sequentiality, or the desire to take advantage of the speed of hashed access while requiring retrieval according to more than one attribute.

Not all possible solutions will or can be listed. Many of the methods described here have been used in practice; others are shown in order to provide a logical continuity or to suggest alternate approaches.

Table 7-1   Grades of performance for the six basic file methods.

File method	Space — Attributes Variable	Space — Attributes Fixed	Update — Record size Equal	Update — Record size Greater	Retrieval — Single record	Retrieval — Subset	Retrieval — Exhaustive
Pile	A	B	A	E	E	D	B
Sequential	F	A	D	F	F	D	A
Indexed-sequential	F	B	B	D	B	D	B
Indexed	B	C	C	C	A	B	D
Hashed	F	B	B	F	B	F	E
Multiring	C	B	D	D	B	A	B

A = Excellent, well suited to this purpose $\approx \mathcal{O}(r)$ where r is the size of the result
B = Good $\approx \mathcal{O}(or)$
C = Adequate $\approx \mathcal{O}(r \log n)$
D = Requires some extra effort $\approx \mathcal{O}(n)$
E = Possible with extreme effort $\approx \mathcal{O}(rn)$
F = Not reasonable for this purpose $\approx \mathcal{O}(n^{>1})$

For the combinations presented in this chapter no full set of comparative formulas will be provided. We hope that the reader, using the approaches of Chaps. 4 to 6, will be able to develop formulas to estimate the performance of any file organization method presented in this chapter or encountered in actual practice.

We have not considered the difficulty of programming for the alternatives, but the six fundamental methods as presented became increasingly complex. Combining them into hybrid designs further increases their complexity, but if the services are needed by the application, it is still best to provide them within the file services layer. Not providing adequate file software pushes these problems into the applications programs. This will cause system maintenance efforts to be performed by programmers whose main concern should be the users' problems.

7-2   COMBINATIONS WITH SEQUENTIAL FILES

Since sequential files are supported in every programming language it is natural to find that improvements to sequential files should be common. The indexed-sequential file is, of course, the major improvement of the sequential file, but we present simpler techniques here. Simple files as described here may be the only file support provided on small and personal computers or on systems which were not designed to serve data processing.

These techniques may also be employed by users limited to systems which only provide sequential files. They will write data management software in their program space, which in turn accesses the simpler software provided with the operating system. The extra software layer will typically diminish performance, but avoids that application programs have to deal with file inadequacies.

In Sec. 7-2-1 we will see a direct-access computation applied to sequential files, in Sec. 7-2-2 a TID list, similar to a single-level index, is added, and in Sec. 7-2-3 buckets are used to deal with variable-length records and text files.

7-2-1 Direct Access to Sequential Files

If the attribute values used for referring to records are restricted to integers, a simple hashing-style scheme can be used. It is the responsibility of the users to keep the reference integers unique, since no collision recognition or resolution is provided.

We mentioned this method in the introduction to hashed files (Chap. 6-1-1). Here we assume that a numeric record key will be given by the user. That number specifies a relative record position. Translation of the record key to a number, consideration of the density of the file, and coping with collisions is left to the user of the file. Index numbers are typically constrained to be integers of a limited range.

The specifications for many FORTRAN implementations of *direct* access input and output limit themselves to this level of service. Table 7-2 shows FORTRAN statements defined for this purpose.

Table 7-2   FORTRAN statements for direct access.

```
DEFINE FILE 17(n,R)
. . .
WRITE (17 'key) data
```

The DEFINE statement accesses the file directory and allocates storage for a new file. The number 17 following the keywords DEFINE FILE is the *name* for the file; FORTRAN restricts even the file names to integers. Any integer predefined in a file directory may be chosen, typical ranges for data files are from 10 to 20, The parameter n specifies the maximum size of the file and R gives the maximum record length.

This file is then manipulated by statements such as the WRITE statement shown. If the size of the data field exceeds R, the record written will be truncated; if it is less, the unused space will be filled with blanks, or its contents left unpredictable.

In IBM FORTRAN systems, two additional parameters are provided:

Table 7-3   Defining a FORTRAN file for direct and sequential access.

```
DEFINE FILE 18(n,R,code,nextkey)
. . .
READ (18) last_order
WRITE (18 'nextkey) new_order
```

Sequential access can by simulated by use of the variable nextkey. The value of nextkey is set by a READ operation to the key value of the next existing record in the file. That value can be used as the key for the next READ operation. The code specifies usage: a U indicates file storage while a code of E indicates input-output.

SPACE ALLOCATION AND KEY-TO-ADDRESS TRANSFORMATION   If the entire space for all the expected records is allocated in advance, as shown in Fig. 7-1, a minimal KAT can be used. The transformation, τ, used by the system to locate a record given a **key**, is shown in Table 7-4.

Table 7-4   KAT for direct access of a sequential file.

---

record_address = filebegin + (key-1) * R

The required system software is simple and reliable. A subsystem developer may not want more than these basic services from the system and will then add the logic described for indexed-sequential, B-trees, or hashed files as necessary. On larger systems direct access may be available as an optional building block for file designers unhappy with standard file organization methods.

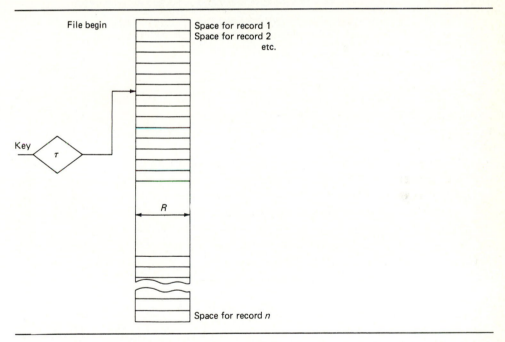

Figure 7-1   File using an integer key with all record spaces allocated.

7-2-2 A TID List for a Sequential File with Direct Access

It is often not convenient to preallocate all the space that might be required for a direct-access file. Augmenting a sequential file with of a list of TIDs for the integer record keys provides some flexibility of space allocation. Now the file can be incrementally or sparsely filled. As shown in Fig. 7-2 the records are assigned to slots as they arrive. The actual data file is now not sequential.

Unused spaces in the TID list can be identified by a marker (Λ). Setting this marker also provides a capability to delete records. Use of these markers also permits a distinction to be made between WRITE and REWRITE operations. Checking the marker can prevent loss of previously stored data due to a WRITE operation with an erroneous key value. A function FREE can allow the user to test the status of a record space.

Table 7-5   Use of statement to identify free slots.

```
        . . .
C       Check if slot is filled
        IF ( FREE(17 'key) )  GO TO 30
C       A record with this key exists in the file
        READ (17 'key) old_data
        IF (old_data.id = new_data.id) GO TO 25
C       Start collision resolution
        . . .

        . . .
C       Tell user that there is a record already.  Ask if
C           an update rather than an insertion is desired.
   25   . . .

        . . .
C       No record with this key exists yet in the file, ok
   30   WRITE (17 'key) new_data
        . . .
        . . .
```

Space for records is taken out of blocks as required. The entire TID list is predefined, and allocated at least to an extent that the highest existing record is included. The actual attribute value or key does not appear in the TID list since the TID slot is found by a computation. The content of the slot provides the reference to the data file, as explicitly shown in the algorithm coded in Table 7-6.

Table 7-6   KAT statements for access via the TID list.

```
        . . .
        TID_address = listbegin + (key-1) * P
        READ (16 'TID_address) reference
        READ (17 'reference) data
        . . .
```

The TID list (file 16) here has a structure identical to the data file shown Fig. 7-1. The storage overhead is reduced for files which are not dense, since we expect that the TID entry, only a pointer of size P, is much smaller than the actual record.

The TID lists are relatively simple to maintain. Data records are easily read and written. Deletion of records should return the free record spaces to the system for reallocation, since just setting the TID entry to Λ would cause loss of space.

Variable-Length records In this organization it is easy to store variable-length records, since the access algorithm shown in Table 7-6 does not depend on a fixed value of R. A record-marking scheme as described in Chap. 3-2-4 will be employed within the blocks. However, if deletion or updating of records of varying size is to be allowed, management of free space becomes more complex.

7-2-3 Buckets

Many systems found in microcomputers and in simple timesharing systems do not provide for variable-length records. Bucket techniques can be used to overcome this limitation.

If data records vary in length and the system only provides fixed-length records, then two approaches are common:

1 The file record size is set to maximum data record size. If the variability is great, much space and transfer time will be wasted.

2 A blocking routine is interposed between the file system and the end users.

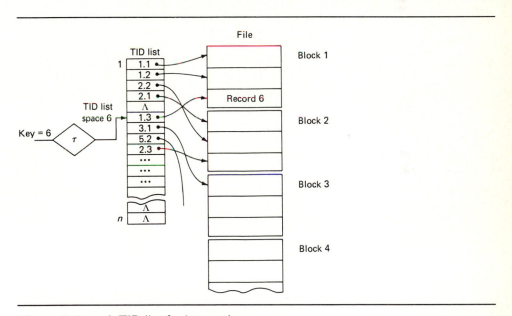

Figure 7-2   A TID list for integer keys.

USER-PROVIDED VARIABLE LENGTH BLOCKING The file system provides the user with buckets, although the simple file system calls it the *records*. Since the file system will read a disk block for every bucket fetch, it is wise to make the size of the bucket equal to or slightly smaller than the system block size.

The number of data records to be assigned to a bucket is such that overflow should be rare. If the density is made too low, then sequential access performance will suffer and space will be wasted.

The user decides on a suitable marker to distinguish the data records, using one of the techniques shown in Chap. 3-2-4, and provides a computation to convert data record numbers to bucket numbers. The computation must take into account the variability of length. If many long records are placed into a bucket, it may overflow. Overflow techniques as presented when hashing (Chap. 5-1) must then be used.

Not all the records in a key range for a bucket need to be present. Records can be packed and searched sequentially in the bucket. For example, records numbered 1 to 60 could be assigned to a bucket using the first entry, 61 to 120 to the second entry, and so on. The buckets accommodate defined partitions of the key range.

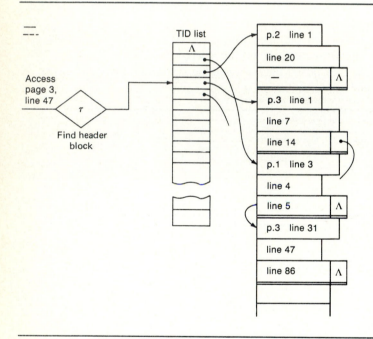

Figure 7-3   Page TID access with linked overflow buckets.

FILES CONTAINING TEXT.   Using bucket's can useful for files consisting of program or data text. The records here are small and of variable length, but the variation between typical pages of text is not very great. Requirements are fast sequential access for processing and searching as well as reasonable access to specific lines to be edited. Keeping the density moderately low provides all these features.

A bucket which contains a page of text may require several blocks. These blocks are assigned as a unit to a TID entry corresponding to a page of text. This file can be read sequentially with a low overhead. Figure 7-3 sketches this organization for a file which uses line numbers of the formsssff, as some BASIC compilers do. For each value of sss only three lines are expected. The text for sss = 3 happens to contain six lines and filled an overflow bucket.

The line numbers are used to compute the block addresses when bucketed files are used to store text data. The bucket number is found by dividing the line number by the estimate of lines that are assigned to a bucket, as shown in Fig. 7-4.

Given $B = 2000$, the desired density (75%), and text lines which average 75 chars. Line numbers are incremented by 100 initially, but we expect one inserted line per original line.

The expected capacity of a bucket is then 1500 bytes. and one bucket should be assigned for each set of 20 lines. We assign lines to buckets by dividing the line number by $20 \times 100/2 = 1000$.

Figure 7-4   Computation of mapping for a direct text file.

7-2-4 Indexed-Sequential with Secondary Indexes

In order to obtain the advantage of sequentiality and yet have more than one index, the two indexing methods of Chap. 5 are often combined. An indexed-sequential file is used to provide a *primary index*, and multiple nonsequential indexes support *secondary* access paths.

The primary index may be dense, as described, or may use a *B-tree* as well, while the *secondary indexes* are typically B-trees. To accommodate insertions into the data file the data records themselves may be organized as B-tree blocks. This adds substantially to the space requirement for the data file, but avoids the loss of sequentiality of records that are placed into the overflow area. This organization is sketched in Fig. 7-5.

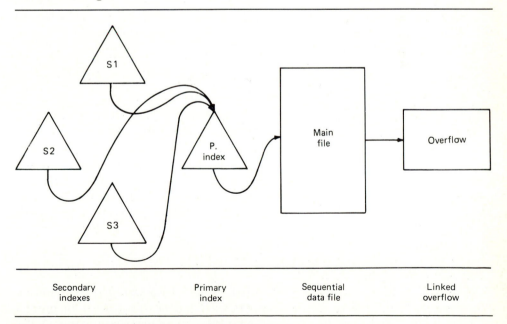

Figure 7-5   Primary and secondary indexes.

The disadvantages of both index organizations are incurred as well. The secondary indexes have to be updated for every new record and for most records being updated. New data blocks assigned to the B-tree will not be sequential and periodically a reorganization is needed to reestablish sequentiality.

The three choices presented in Chap. 3-3-3 for the reference pointers apply also to the references used by the secondary indexes.

1 Block and record addresses refer directly to the records.
2 Relative pointers will refer to entries indirectly, via a list. A suitable list is the lowest level (1) of the primary index. That index must use *record anchors*.
3 Symbolic pointers will refer to the primary key values and be processed through all levels of the primary index.

Push-through , as used in Chap. 5-1-1 ¡verify¿ of records cannot be used in practice with the first choice of secondary index pointers. Moving records from their original location would require changes of all secondary indexes for the records which are being pushed through.

The precise choice of implementing secondary indexes is often pragmatic: A major consideration is how much of any existing indexing programs must be changed. The use of symbolic pointers requires the least change. It is even possible to use multiple-indexed sequential files for these indexes. The performance will be the least desirable: The symbolic references require more space and time for the double index search.

7-3   COMBINATIONS WITH HASHED ACCESS

The hashed-access method presented in Chap. 6 is the fastest means to access records, but three features make the basic method often unsuitable:

1 Its dependence on fixed-length records
2 Fetch access is limited to one key attribute
3 The lack of serial access capability
4 There is no provision for partial-match retrieval

Simple adaptations of hashed access can be used to overcome these three limitations for many applications. A number of these will be illustrated in corresponding sections below. If they are all applied nothing much is left of the simpliscity of the original hashed file organization. Also, since the additions reduce the access speed, hashing rapidly loses its advantage over indexibg.

A fifth section introduces some specialized hashing structures for partial match queries. In the summary of this chapter we will use these examples to illustrate the concept of binding and alternative implementations,

7-3-1 Variable-Length Records

The record length for files accessed by hashing is fixed because of the computation which maps a record key to a slot number in the file area. If a hashed-file organization is desired for its other features, either of two constructs encountered earlier will add variable-length record capability: buckets or indirect accessing.

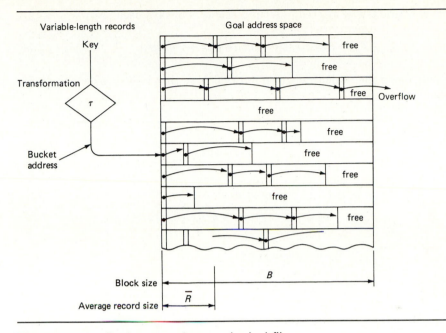

Figure 7-6   Bucket accessing to a hashed file.

BUCKET ACCESSING   Buckets exploit the fetching of blocks to retrieve multiple records at a time. When buckets are used, variable-length records can be accommodated in the buckets. The search within a bucket becomes more complex.

The use of a record mark as shown in Fig. 3-11 enables serial searches through the bucket. Some disk hardware allows the channel or controller to automatically locate markers on a track; this reduces the software effort needed to read through blocks to identify the marks.

If an overflow from the bucket occurs because of the insertion of many records that were longer than the expected average, the existing collision-management mechanism can be invoked. On the other hand, when the records in a block are shorter than average, overflow resulting from collisions due to hashing will be deferred. Deletion of variable-length records is best accompanied by a rearrangement of the records remaining within the block to avoid space fragmentation.

The use of buckets for variable-length records works best if $B \gg R$. The bucket search time, cix, may become a problem, but one of the schemes used to structure index blocks (Chap. 8-3) may help. When pointers are used to mark records, as shown in Fig. 7-6, overflow chains can be maintained using these same pointers. As discussed in Chap. 5-3, overflow chains can reduce the problems due to clusters.

INDIRECT ACCESSING   In this method, a small file containing a list of TIDs is accessed by hashing; the entry fetched provides the location of the actual record, as shown in Fig. 7-7. The organization of the goal data file may be a pile or another organization type chosen according to other requirements placed on the file. The performance is seriously impacted, a second access is always used. Now

$$T_F = c + 2(s + r + btt) + p(s + r + btt) \qquad\qquad 7\text{-}1$$

practically doubling the basic time given in Eq. 6-5, so that indexing becomes quite competitive with hashing.

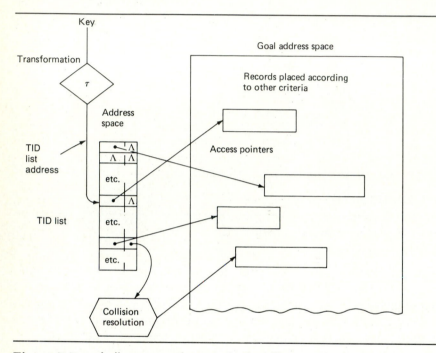

Figure 7-7   Indirect accessing to a hashed file.

The *TID-list* resembles the lowest level of an index, but the position of the entries is determined by the key-to-address transformation algorithm, so that the list is not suitable for serial searching. There will be many entries in a bucket because an entry contains only the key and a reference pointer. Even relatively high densities will give low overflow probabilities, p, as was shown in Fig. 6-10.

Since keys are included in the TID-list entries collision and missing records are recognized without accessing the goal file. The keys of overflow entries due to collisions are also placed in the TID-list, using open-addressing techniques.

Since such a TID-list is kept using bucket techniques, the key is also used to identify the entries. These buckets will have many entries, so that techniques to increase the speed of searching through the bucket are desirable. A binary tree seems ideal for this purpose; The pointers in the nodes can be used for locating lower-level entries or as TIDs to goal records.

The collision rate is determined by the ratio of m/n of the TID address space and the bucket capacity. Only the TID-list has to be given extra space $(m - n)$ and the main file can be kept dense. An adequately high space ratio, m/n, considering the many entries which fit into an index block, *Bfr*, will keep the occurrence of collisions minimal.

   If some part of the goal record is required more frequently than the whole record, a mixed approach is feasible. A fixed-length record segment is constructed containing the most useful portions and placed so that it can be accessed by hashing. The variable segment which remains is retrieved when needed via a TID from the fixed segment. The reduction in the number of entries will increase the collosion rate.

   A third alternative design is to handle collisions *after* accessing the main data records. With this approach no key is placed into the TID-list then required but overflows have to be resolved in the main file. The main file may use linkages to chain colliding records. Having smaller entries in the buckets of the TID-list will reduce the number of collisions. The cost is greater for records not found in the main file.

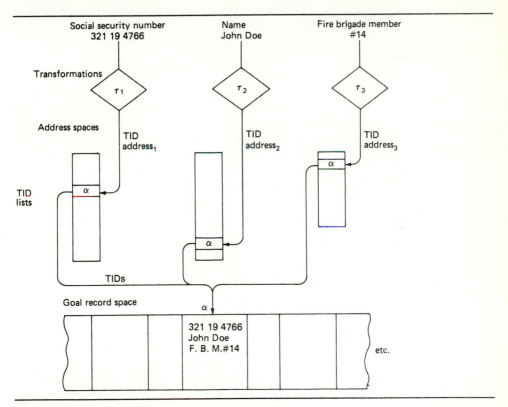

Figure 7-8   Three-way access to a hashed file.

7-3-2 Multiattribute Hashed Access

If the fetch requests are not restricted to one key attribute, the simple hashing access method fails. For each attribute and its value in a goal record, a key-to-address transformation will produce its specific record address. If there is to be only one stored copy of each goal record, indirection via a TID-list provides again a solution.

The TID-list contains only pointers to the actual goal record; the goal is found at the cost of an additional access. Multiple TID-lists will be used, similar to the multiplicity of indexes described for an indexed file. Records can be found according to any attribute for which a transform and a TID-list is provided. The TID-lists are similar to the TID-lists used in Sec. 7-3-1 to deal with variable record lengths. The rate of collisions should again be low.

In this section the earlier definition of a file is violated. It now is difficult to tell whether we are dealing with one, three, four, or even six files. We leave the answer to the taste of the reader.

The records may be located by hashing on the *primary* attribute and resorting to indirection for the *secondary* attributes. However, for symmetry, the system sketched in Fig. 7-8 uses indirection through TID-lists throughout. Not all attributes need to have address spaces of equal length. The goal file itself may have a pile or a sequential organization. An insertion into a file using multiple TID-lists will require changes to all TID-lists in addition to the insertion operation on the main file.

Secondary attributes are rarely unique. For attributes such as `department`, `job_category`, `age`, etc. there will be multiple entries. Attributes which have nonunique entries increase the collision rate. When we dealt with simple hashed files, whose records are stored by key attribute values, we expected uniqueness. The example of Fig. 7-7 is hence atypical; for an extreme case consider the TID-list for `sex = 'male'`. A KAT transforms identical data-attribute values to identical addresses in the TID-list space. The result of the key-to-address transformation will not be uniform. This problem can be dealt with through the collision-handling mechanism, but obviously attributes with poor selectivity can overwhelm the mechanics of many solutions. Overflow buckets rather than open addressing should be used here.

A popular database management system, ADABAS, uses the types of access presented here. The TID-lists may be predefined and maintained, or created dynamically in response to transaction requests.

SHARED TID-LIST   Managing many TID-lists introduces complexity. Especially if the records have an irregular number of attributes, or if the attributes have variable length, the individual TID address spaces must have different sizes. If the content of the file varies, the sizes of the TID-lists may vary dynamically.

In such cases it is also desirable to share a single TID space for several attributes. The space is made appropriately larger and an identifier for the attribute is included in the input to the address transformation function. Figure 7-9 sketches this design using the symbols (I_1, I_2, I_3) for attribute-type identification.

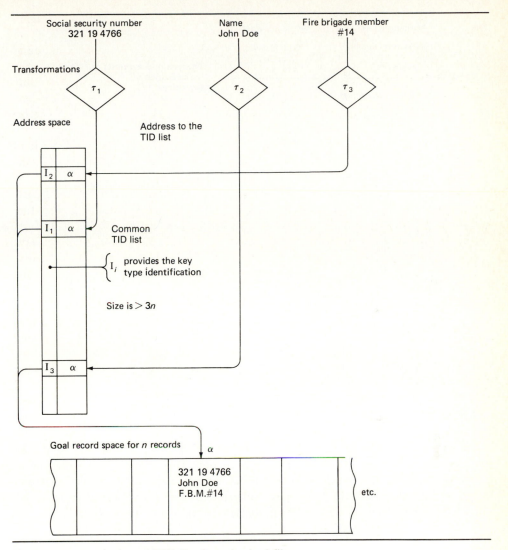

Figure 7-9   A shared TID-list for a hashed file.

▦▦▦▦ **Labeling TIDs** A disadvantage of sharing the TID-list for multiple attributes is that the TID entry has to carry an attribute identifier for verification purposes. The attribute name is best abbreviated. The abbreviation might be a sequence number I, $I = 1 \rightarrow a$ in a file directory dictionary which map to the attributes, and this solution is illustrated. The abbreviation has only to add enough information to the hashing algorithm to compensate for the increase in address space size. The combined input to the hashing algorithm has to be kept to test for collisions.   ▦▦▦▦

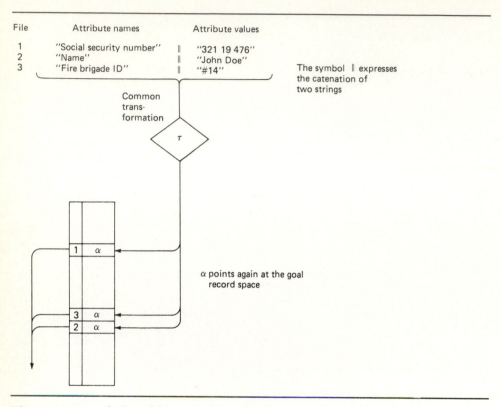

File   Attribute names   Attribute values

1   "Social security number"   ‖   "321 19 476"
2   "Name"   ‖   "John Doe"   The symbol ‖ expresses
3   "Fire brigade ID"   ‖   "#14"   the catenation of
                                                             two strings

Common
trans-
formation

τ

1   α

α points again at the goal
record space

3   α
2   α

Figure 7-10   A shared key transformation for a hashed file.

A SHARED KAT FOR MULTIPLE ATTRIBUTES   A file using many attributes for access may need as many independent key-to-address transformation routines. The definition and use of many distinct routines can be avoided by transforming both the attribute name and value into an address within a single shared TID-list. The sketch in Fig. 7-10 demonstrates the catenation of the name and value strings prior to hashing.

SHARING THE KEY-TO-ADDRESS TRANSFORMATION AND TID-LIST FOR MULTIPLE FILES   We considered in the previous subsections very large goal files, accessed using multiple attributes. As part of most databases many small files have to be maintained as well. Examples of such files are the lexicons which translate from a numeric code to a descriptive character string for output, for instance, a disease_code to a disease_name. In large applications there may be several dozens of such lexicons.

These small files are effectively accessed by hashing, but their individual management is awkward. A technique using a shared access mechanism, as sketched in Fig. 7-11, can be used to provide a single access mechanism for multiple files.

One TID-list is shared among the files, but the goal data are in separate files. The goal files may be maintained simply as sequential files and periodically reorganized. A batch update of the hashed TID file can be combined with a purge of the previous pointers pertaining to a given goal file.

▦▦▦▦▦ **SHARED TID-LISTS TO DISTRIBUTED DATA**　The idea of a shared TID-list can also be used in *distributed files*. A single large file may be partitioned into fragments, so that each fragment will reside on the processor of a site where the data is used the most. An example is the Employees file of a company having multiple locations, as shown in Fig. 7-12

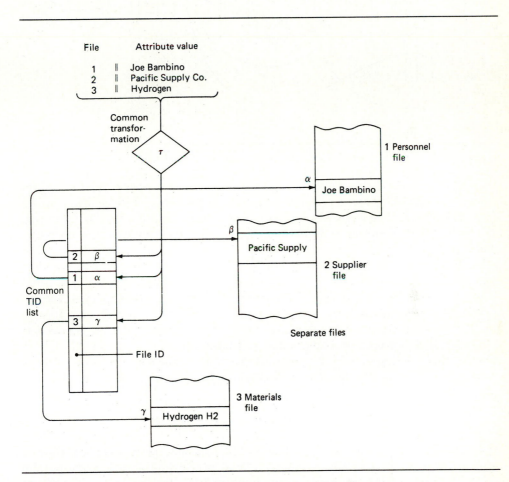

Figure 7-11　　A shared key transformation for multiple files.

Still, the data may be needed at the sites as well. A TID-list to all records in all fragments comprising the entire file can be *replicated* at all sites so that any record can be fetched. The local entries may be distinguished. All TID-lists have to be updated when an employee is added or leaves, but remain unchanged when a pay or work status attribute is updated.　▦▦▦▦▦

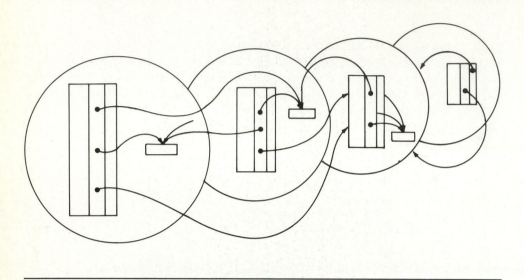

Figure 7-12   A TID-list for a fragmented and distributed file.

Collisions in the TID Space Because of sharing a single TID space for all attributes the amount of unused space is reduced while the probability of exceeding the TID space is kept low. The larger shared space also reduces collisions due to clustering.

To verify that in case of a collision the correct TID is picked, it is necessary that the TID entry can be matched to its attribute name. If this check is not made, problems will arise if two values of different attributes are both identical and produce the same result from their address transformation. An example would be a case where the `health_record_number` for `John` and the `employee_number` assigned to `Peter` are identical and both happen to transform to the same address by different algorithms. The author has come across a system where this case was not considered, but no access failure had ever been reported.

Another solution to the collision problem is to defer the recognition of collisions to the goal records. The implementation will vary depending on the form of the goal records.

7-3-3 Serial Access for Hashed Files

Methods which use indirection by hashing to TID-lists allow placing the data records sequentially according to one attribute. Serial processing of such a file by one attribute is now possible. Insertion into a sequential file, however, remains difficult, so that much of the advantage of a hashed-access file is lost. The use of a B-tree structured data file can keep updates convenient and provide seriality in one dimension.

In order to provide serial access according to multiple dimensions, the goal-record file may be organized as a ring structure. Flexibility of retrieval has been regained at some cost in complexity.

This combination of hashed access and rings is found only in database systems, since procedural management of the complex structure is beyond the ambition of most programmers. The definition of the CODASYL specifications for network databases was predicated on having such a capability. Without TID-lists hashed access is provided for only one attribute, and this is a restriction of many CODASYL systems.

If more general hashed access is provided, the update process has to maintain simultaneously TID-lists and change the ring pointers. The awkwardness of update may make the batch reorganization technique presented in Chap. 6-2-7, leading to Eq. 6-22, appropriate here.

7-3-4 Partial-Match Retrieval with Hashed Access

In basic hashed files, access capability is restricted to one attribute. If intermediate TID-lists are used, as described in Sec. 7-3-2, then access becomes possible by any of a variety of attributes. Partial-match query processing by a combination of these attributes should now be supported.

The buckets storing these TID-lists contain TIDs for specific attribute-name and value combinations. For collisions overflow buckets are employed. Irrelevant entries in the buckets, as determined by their key value, have to be ignored. The sets of TIDs obtained can be merged for partial-match retrieval, so that selection can be accomplished prior to accessing the goal file. The procedure can be visualized using Fig. 7-13 and compared with Fig. 5-18, where indexes were used.

We note that range queries are not supported unless the complications of additional serial access structures (Sec. 7-3-3) are accepted. The attribute values are hence made discrete; the Price, for instance, is given here as two distinct, truncated values $\{31K, 32K\}$ rather than a range of $\{31\,000 \rightarrow 33\,000\}$ when indexing was used. The information loss from truncation increases the number of collisions.

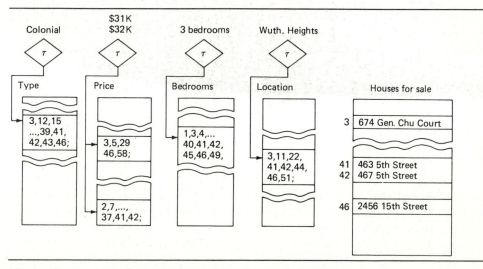

Figure 7-13   Partial-match retrieval using hashed TID-lists.

7-3-5 Hashing Structures for Partial-Match Retrieval

The accessing and merging of many buckets can still be costly. The use of TID-lists and their merging can be avoided by creating hash addresses which support immediate retrieval of records in response to queries which specify multiple attributes in their search argument. A second approach to provide single disk access per record for retrieval in partial-match queries is to develop specialized hash functions. Immediate access by any or all combinations of attributes was already considered for indexes in Chap. 5-5-3.

▦▦▦▦ **Partial-Match by Address Catenation** If we wish to address a hashed file directly for a partial match, using multiple attributes, we have to locate the records to satisfy all the attributes permitted in a query. That solution seems impossible; the number of queries for all possible combinations of attributes is immense. But, recall that hashing converts large keys into smaller addresses. Making the addresses quite small, and catenating the resulting addresses serves the desired purpose. Figure 7-15 shows a TID-list with catenated addresses, and single-record buckets.

As evaluated in Fig. 7-14, the file is constructed by hashing each of 10 attributes down to 2-bit addresses, giving 20 bits, sufficient for nearly a million buckets. For a single attribute the address space is only 2^2, and hence its selectivity will be quite small.

For a file with three million records, a fanout Bfr of 5, a density m/n of 0.6, and $a = 10$ attributes per record

The number of buckets would be $(3 \cdot 10^6)/5/0.6 = 1 \cdot 10^6$.

The address required is $\log_2(10^6) = 20$ bits long.

The KATs should produce $20/a = 20/10 = 2$ bits per attribute.

Figure 7-14   Estimation of catenated hash design.

In the example the number of one-record buckets matches approximately the number of records in the file. This means that not much space is wasted and also that the probability of finding records in a bucket is high. With one-record buckets the collision rate would be high as well, but practical files having buckets with many records would not suffer that fate.

Partial-match queries specify multiple attributes, giving rise to multiple small addresses to be catenated to become candidate addresses to the hash file. The addresses, with missing fields for unspecified attributes, lead to entries in the TID list. Since multiple records may be retrieved for such queries the records to be fetched will be in multiple buckets. Some buckets will have no relevant records, so that the number of accesses needed is more than the number of records being retrieved. If many buckets do not contain a desired record, we lose.

Let us now analyze this design using buckets. The *hash address* is constructed by catenating the hash addresses for all attributes, a. The size of the hash address is based on the number of buckets needed. The number of buckets is chosen to be adequate for the file, with a density so that overflows are rare. If one bucket can hold Bfr records and a density m/n, we want $b = m/Bfr$ buckets. Since $b < a$ the total address space is smaller than assessed in Fig. 7-14.

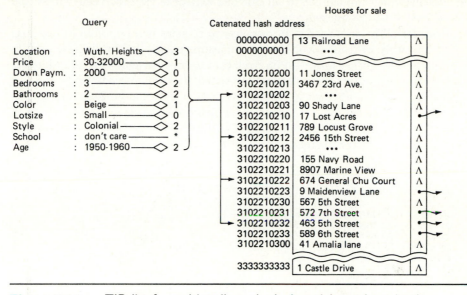

Figure 7-15   TID list for multiattribute, hashed partial-match retrieval.

Using this scheme, the attributes partition the search space only grossly. A retrieval based on only one argument will specify $1/a$ of the file. Here, knowing only 2 bits out of the 20, one could expect that one-fourth of the file will to be retrieved. The situation improves quickly as more attributes are specified in the query. When all attributes are specified, the expected number of relevant and number of retrieved records becomes about one. Figure 7-15 illustrates the case for a nine-out-of-ten attribute query. ▦▦▦▦

▦▦▦▦ **Partial-Match by Precomputing Hash Entries**   The problems of poor discrimination can be avoided by radically increasing the number of entries. The goal record may be replicated for every possible partial match query. For every record with a attributes $2^a - 1$ queries are possible. For our example we would need $2^{10} - = 1023$ entries will be required. The update cost is of course also much greater when so many access paths are maintained. Use of a TID-list with replicated entries can reduce the space explosion, but doubles the access cost on the first retrieval.

In practice this method is applied when we have a small number of attributes, and even then with care. First we will use a TID list. For example, the **houses** in Fig. 7-16 are characterized by $a = 4$ attributes, so that we will place $2^4 - 1 = 15$ TID entries into the TID list for each house. For instance, one of the entries will be for house 41, attributes `type='Colonial'`, `price = $31K`, `bedrooms = 3`, `and location = ANY`. That entry is represented in Fig. 7-16 as the top entry of the third column. A query using these three attributes will retrieve this, and any other houses meeting this partial-match specification, with one access to the TID list and one access per house.

The entries for the four **houses** retrieved for the four-attribute query in the example of Fig. 7-13 are shown in Fig. 7-16. These four **houses** have $4(2^a - 1) = 60$

TIDs. Because they are similar in all but one attribute (`price`) their entries fall into $2^a + 2^{a-1} - 1 = 23$ buckets.

Entries for all records needed in response to a query will be found in one TID bucket; all records with identical key combinations cluster in the bucket, and its overflow area. The bucket may contain irrelevant entries because of the randomization. Since the clustering of popular and few-attribute combinations leads to dense usage of some bucket addresses, a chained overflow to external buckets rather than open addressing is called for. Combinations which do not correspond to records in the file will not generate entries in the TID-lists; there may be, for instance, no "Condominiums" in "Wuth.Heights". ▦▦

Key combinations to be provided for in order to locate houses 3, 41, 42, 46

Col	Col ‖$31	Col ‖$31 ‖3br	Col‖$31‖3br ‖WHs
$31	Col ‖$32	Col ‖$32 ‖3br	Col ‖$32‖3br ‖ WHs
$32	Col ‖3br	Col ‖$31 ‖WHs	
3br	Col ‖Whs	Col ‖$32 ‖WHs	
WHs	$31‖3br	Col ‖3br ‖WHs	
	$32‖3br	$31‖3br ‖WHs	
	$31‖WHs	$32‖3br ‖WHs	
	$32‖WHs		
	3br ‖WHs		

23 buckets

τ

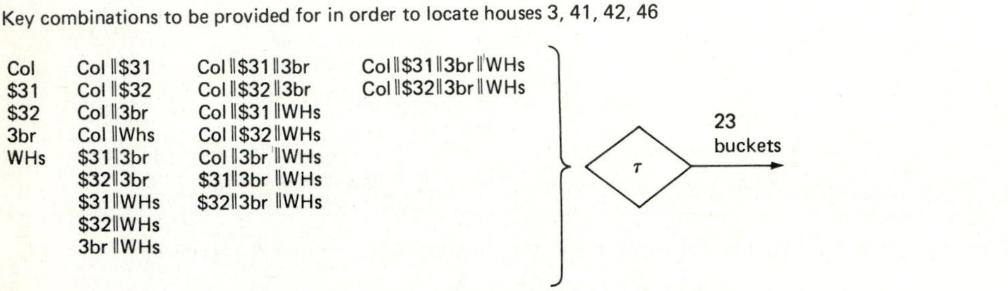

Figure 7-16   Replicated entries for all partial-match queries.

▦▦ **IMPROVING MULTIATTRIBUTE SCHEMES**   The partial-match indexing and hashing schemes presented attempt to always retrieve results using only one TID-list access. But they are not very effective at extreme ranges, when either very many or hardly any results are likely. We can take advantage of their limitations and modify these schemes, so that the update effort is greatly reduced while much of their benefit is retained.

Small Number of Arguments   There seems to be little point in supporting rapid access for queries which lead to retrieval of a large fraction of the file. A valid guideline is:

Search sequentially when looking for more than 20% of the records.

In the case of replicated entries, as shown in Fig. 7-16, update time and storage space can be saved by only entering combinations of several attributes into the access lists, and avoiding single or pairs of attributes which have low selectivity. Queries with few attributes are likely to process much of the file anyhow.

In the case of catenated addresses, illustrated in Fig. 7-15, the retrieval algorithm might as well search sequentially when near-exhaustive requests are made. They can similarly be characterized by having $> 0.3a$ attributes specified in the query. The file storage remains unchanged here. In an interactive environment it is well to have the system respond to a query with poor selectivity with a counter question, such as: "*Do you really want* 13117 *references on the topic:* `system`?".

Large Number of Arguments   The probability that a partial-match query will specify all attributes is slim. It is furthermore expected that, if many search arguments are specified, only a few or no records will respond to a query. Thus, there exists a further opportunity for reduction of file costs. Certain attribute keys can be placed in a *don't care* category, and not entered at all in the lists. When queries are made, the retrieval from the file will fetch some unwanted records. The excess can then be pared down on the basis of the actual key values. In the case of replicated entries (Fig. 7-16), entries for more than, say, $0.8a$ attributes are omitted.

Keeping the Middle   Applying both rules reduces the TID-list of Fig. 7-16 to serving partial-match queries having two or three attributes. Then only 10 entries will be stored per record.

     In the case of catenated addresses, illustrated in Fig. 7-15, the reduction provides an opportunity for better use of the TID-list. Fewer combinations of attributes need be stored if for some queries a merge of two or more distinct TID-lists is permissible. Then the attributes can be partitioned into these sets so that frequent queries require only one set. Some will need two or more, and an odd partial-match query may need one attribute from each set. The number of stored combinations reduced drastically; we considered a similar case using indexes in Chap. 5-5-3.

Superimposition   *Superimposed coding* is a traditional technique used to reduce the number of distinct attribute fields for queries with many attributes. This technique is useful for files where these attributes are sparse. It works best for attributes that have only binary values. With superimposed coding more than one such attribute is assigned to a column. It is also possible to use more complex assignment schemes. For instance, 10 binary attributes can be encoded as the 10 2-out-of-five choices, or in general, $\binom{\#ones}{\#bits} = \#encodings$. We soon run out attributes to encode.

     For *Superimposed coding* to be effective the desired records should be well characterized by the search keys, so that a retrieval will include few unwanted records. A term, *false drops*, for such unwanted records has been retained from manual card processing of references. An attribute can also be assigned redundantly to a combination of several columns to avoid false drops due to a single other attribute. Given adequate information on attribute occurence in the file and in queries, the percentage of false drops can be statistically predicted.   ▦

7-4   COMBINATIONS WITH RING ACCESS

In Chap. 6-3 we presented the basic ring-structure organization. Implementations of file systems based on this structure offer a number of options which allow better performance at some increase in complexity. Such options can be selected to apply only to those rings which play a crucial role in the performance of the file. Language specifications for such options are found in database textbooks which cover the CODASYL database schema language.

     In Secs. 7-4-1 and 7-4-2 we consider augmentation of rings with additional pointers. In Sec. 7-4-3 we consider indexes in rings and in Sec. 7-4-4 hashed access to rings. Partial match access to rings is not presented here, because it involves the addition of index or hashing structures as described earlier. A generalized approach to data management, based on ring structures, is presented in Sec. 7-4-5.

7-4-1 Prior Pointers

The first combination we consider is actually a combination of a ring with a ring. Instead of having pointers connect records in one direction only, going to the next record, pointers may be added that refer to the preceding records. The availability of *prior pointers* simplifies some search and update operations considerably. Prior pointers allow us to space backward through a ring, so that the predecessor record is found using one access rather than using $y - 1$ accesses through the ring.

An example of a query requiring access to predecessor records is a factory database query. Data about machine tools and the tasks assigned to them is kept in files. The machine chains for each type are sorted in order of increasing capability, since one normally wants to assign the least costly machine required. But a query for rescheduling may have as its goal a list of five machines nearly adequate for the task now assigned to machine B. The search finds machine B according to the task chain, and a predecessor search is needed now. Prior pointers make that search reasonable.

Figure 7-17   Use of prior pointers.

Having prior pointers, shown in Fig. 7-19(b), speeds the update process but adds some complexity to all update processes. Use of prior pointers also affects storage requirements.

Update operations need access to predecessor records for all rings to be updated, other than the ring just used for access. This means that update is greatly affected by the existence of prior pointers. Figure 7-19(a) shows a part of a ring structure, and Fig. 7-18 illustrates an update operation on that file.

We have a new piece of improved equipment to insert. Assume that the ("Equipment") ring has been entered from the ring ("Supplier=Earthworm") at record Cat. If the equipment should follow in order then a successor record is to be inserted, and that is relatively easy. To add the successor record Cat2 into the ring, the pointer address to record Dozer from the original record Cat is inserted into Cat2, and subsequently a pointer to Cat2 is inserted into Cat. No other record accesses are required in this case.

If, however, a new Grader2, of lower capacity, is to be inserted in the *preceding* position because (Grader2 is to be put in service before Grader) an update, without prior pointers, becomes costly. All the records of the ring will have to be read, since record Dozer will have to be modified to point to the record being inserted.

Figure 7-18   Updating pointer chains.

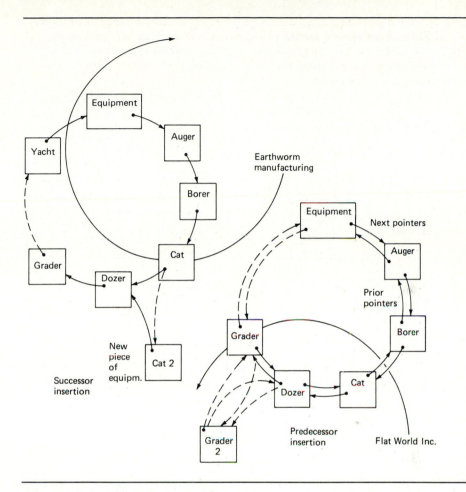

Figure 7-19   Updating a ring file; *(a)* without, *(b)* with prior pointers.

7-4-2 Pointers to the Master Record

Not all the needed data for a query may be found in a goal record. In a ring structure information may be kept in an owner record. A member record can have multiple owner records. To get specific information it may be neccessary to locate the owner record for some specific ring, other than the ring just traversed. A master pointer, from the member to all its owners, can avoid the need of traversing all remaining records of a ring to locate the owner.

     The maintenance of master pointers is relatively easy, since both predecessor and successor records in the ring contain the same information. Some more space is used for the additional pointers. Data which is identical for all members of a ring can be placed into the header records and be easily accessed via the master pointers, saving some space and reducing update costs. New ring types may be defined just to share common information.

An example is a case where a specific personnel record was found during a search for a certain skill. This record can be interpreted by establishing its category, but to determine to which department the employee belongs, the owner record of this department ring must be obtained.

      Ring Using the ring structure the chain has to be followed to its header. The expected cost is $y/2$ accesses.

   Master With a master pointer access is direct, only 1 access is needed.

Figure 7-20   Use of a master pointer.

Typical header record types seen are Department, Supplier, or Equipment. If totals are maintained on a departmental level, relevant changes in a member employee record, such as a salary increase, can be reflected easily in the departmental total payroll field.

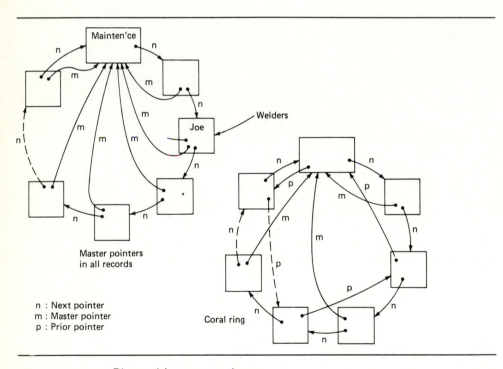

Figure 7-21   Rings with master pointers.

Coral Rings Some implementers let master pointers share space with prior pointers. The result has been called a *coral ring* and is illustrated also in Fig. 7-21. Alternate records have prior and master TIDs. Locating the predecessor record now requires one or two accesses, and locating the header record also requires an average of 1.5 accesses. An indicator is necessary to distinguish the two record subtypes, so that the program knows which way to go.

▦ 7-4-3 Master Records with Indexes

If the need exists to quickly find individual member records in specific rings, indexes may be associated with master records. The resulting substructures have been discussed in the preceding sections. Since records of a ring tend to be similar, and since rings are optimal if they are not very long, simple index structures will suffice. Indexes help especially if individual rings have poor locality. Indexes become more interesting if they are not restricted to the ring hierarchy. In the personnel file example, good use could be made of an index by employee name to permit access to employee records without using department rings.   ▦

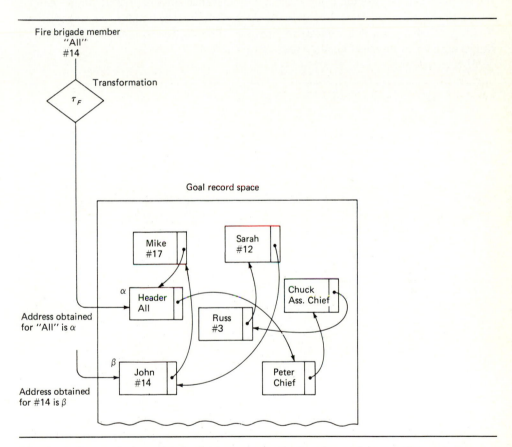

Figure 7-22   A ring with hashed access to the header and to member records.

7-4-4 Rings and Hashed Access

It is possible to combine a hashed-access mechanism with a complex ring structure, since the ring structure makes no demands on the location (value of its own address) of a member record, whereas the hashed-access methods are heavily dependent on them.

The combination can satisfy requests for subsets of data. Hashed access allows rapid fetching of an initial record and following a specific chain provides fast collection of subsequent records.

In order to reach the header record of a ring, a standard identifying term can be used. Figure 7-22 shows such an access. Instead of name of the individual, the standard term "ALL" is given and combined with the class description, "Fire Brigade". The pointer for this combination will lead to the header record for the Fire Brigade, so that the whole ring is available for processing.

Since the transformation controls the placement of the record, only one hashed-access path can be provided per record. For instance, in Fig. 7-22, "John" can be found by hashing as Fire Brigade member #14, but he cannot be accessed by hashing using his social security number. The ability to control placement of ring members to increase locality has also been lost.

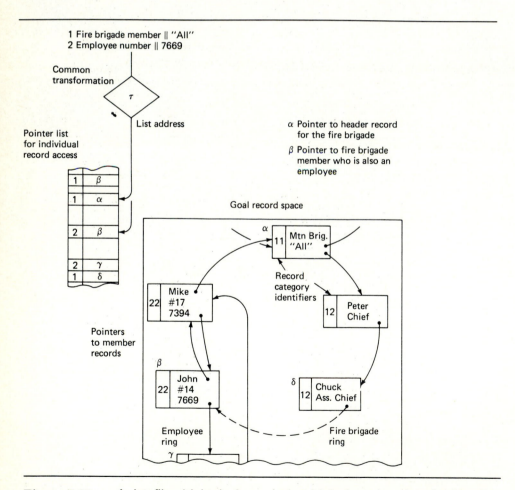

Figure 7-23   A ring file with hashed access to multiple rings via a shared pointer-list.

RINGS WITH A TID-LIST AND HASHED ACCESS   The addition of indirection via TIDs, as introduced in Sec. 7-3-2, can remove the record placement restrictions of simple hashed access to rings. There will be a greater access cost. The use of a TID-list, as sketched in Fig. 7-10, is applied to the previous problem as shown in Fig. 7-23. Now multiple indirect paths to the goal records are possible. There now is also freedom in record placement, which can be exploited to improve the locality of rings, so that retrieval of members will be fast.

The collision-handling mechanism can take several forms. Open addressing was preferred when records were not linked. In the ring structure, additional pointer chains can be considered but may require much maintenance.

A compromise using open addressing is to use the TID-list for file-type verification and the goal record for record category and key identification. No key field is provided in the TID-list, only the record-type or ring identifier is kept in the entry. This becomes feasible when the TID-list is shared by many rings. Most collisions will be recognized in the list, and can be resolved there. A collision which is detected when the goal record is accessed will require a continuation of the open addressing search through the TID-list. The structures defined in such a system lend themselves well to some of the more formal information-retrieval methodologies. We will present a generalized view of such access in the next section.

7-4-5 A Generalization of Multiattribute Ring Access

The combination of hashed access to individual records, and chains to retrieve successor subsets can be effective in dealing with fundamental information structures. We will begin by expanding an example, and then discuss the formal aspects of these structures.

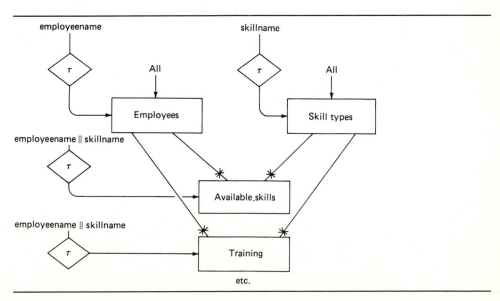

Figure 7-24   Association.

In a ring structure with intersecting rings, as symbolically presented in Fig. 7-24, the subset of records of the ring category "`Available_skills`" represents the *association* of "`Employees`" and "`Skills`". Let the number of `Employees` be ne and the total number of distinct `Skills` be ns. The associative level can be viewed either as ns rings, one for every skill, with ring sizes according to the number of employees who have that skill, $ne(s)$; or as ne rings, one for every employee with ring sizes according to the number of skills which an employee has, $ns(e)$. The number of records in the association `Available_skills` na is then

$$na = \sum_{}^{ns} ns(e) = \sum_{}^{ne} ne(s) \qquad\qquad\text{7-2}$$

If rapid access to the individual members of the association is desired, hashed access can be provided using as the key the catenation of the two parent values.

There can be multiple associations between two parent types; in the figure a second association is called `Training`. In general, there can be any number of associations between two sets of data elements. In order to generalize this aspect, a third parent, say, `Expertise_level`, can be considered to be the header of the set {`Training, Available_skill, Craftsman, Teacher, ...`}, that is, all the associations made between `Employees` and `Skills`. The three-way symmetric concept is indicated in Fig. 7-25. The rings for which this parent provides the header records will link all records for `Training, Available_skill, Craftsman, Teacher`, etc.

IMPLEMENTATION OF A FUNDAMENTAL DATA STRUCTURE   The associative structure of three elements represents the basic unit to carry information. It forms also a minimal record as defined in Chap. 4-2. To identify a record in such an association, three arguments are required; in a programming language implementation of such associations (LEAP-type data structures) these three are called *Object*, *Attribute*, and *Value*, as shown in Table 7-7.

Table 7-7   General associations in LEAP.

Name	or	Sym	Function	Example
Object	or	O	Key	`Employee`
Attribute	or	A	Goal-attribute name	`Skill_type`
Value	or	V	Goal-attribute value	`Expertise_level, Training,` etc.

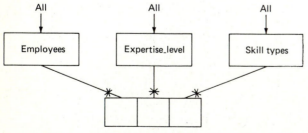

Figure 7-25   Generalized associative structure.

Given this structure, seven types of questions can be asked as in Table 7-8.

Table 7-8   Fundamental queries in data triplets.

#	Format	Example based on Fig. 7-24
1	A(O)=V	Does Jones have Welding as an Available_skill?
2	A(?)=V	Which Employees have Welding as an Available_skill?
3	A(?)=?	Which Employees relate to Welding and how expertly?
4	A(O)=?	Does Jones relate to Welding and how expertly?
5	?(?)=V	What Employees have which Skills Available?
6	?(O)=V	Jones has which Skills Available?
7	?(O)=?	To which Skills is Jones related and how expertly?

The first query can have only the response true or false. Multiple responses will be given, in general, for the other queries; for instance, the last query (**7**) may have as response three triplets:

```
Welding(Jones)    = Available_skill
Machining(Jones)  = Training
Painting(Jones)   = Available_skill
```

Figure 7-26   Response to query about associations of 'O = Jones'.

If semantic considerations are disregarded, it can be seen that any of the three fields can take on any of the three roles.

These structures are used in applications where complex relationships have to be accessed rapidly, for instance, in graphics and in robot operation. When rings have to be followed to retrieve a subset, there is the possibility that the rings will cross many block boundaries, so that the objective of rapid access is not achieved. Good locality can be achieved, as presented in Chap. 6-3-1, for all rings relative to one parent by clustering all member records of a ring within a block. If this is done with respect to "Skill_type", then queries of type **1**, **2**, **3**, and **4** can be answered rapidly. Hashed access can identify the block for a specific argument value of A, and then the position within the block can be obtained by in-memory hashed accessing for O or V to find headers for these subrings, or by hashed in-memory accessing using the catenation of O‖V to locate individual records.

Implementations of LEAP-type structures have used redundancy to provide equivalent access for queries with unknown values of A; a copy of the file is organized based on O or V. The hash for query type **1** does not have to be supported in the second file. These structures have not had goal attributes appended to their records, but this is, of course, possible. The goal parts may be best kept remote, so that the locality of the primary access structure remains high. Collisions also have to be resolved appropriately; this is achieved by use of additional chains from header and member records.

7-5   REVIEW

Techniques described in earlier sections will often be applied again in combination with other file methods. Many techniques improve the data-retrieval capability by adding redundancy, but this increases the amount of space required and makes updates more difficult. The aggregate performance of a system depends on the balance of update and retrieval usage, and will be presented in Chap. 14.

7-5-1 Binding

A concept which can be used to relate many of the alternatives which we have now encountered is *binding*. Binding is the commitment of knowledge and related assumptions, made during the design process, to the choices and decisions necessary to implement a file system.

> During the process of design the designers knowledge is bound into the system being created. If a design decision cannot be made due to lack of knowledge that specific binding must be deferred. Sometimes the decision is made at program excecution time, by checking parameters and input values.
> Late binding increases computation time for retrieval, but can simplify update.

Examples of limited knowledge at design time are the frequencies of the various types of read and update operations, which affect the choice of file organization. Often assumptions have to made earlier than desirable so that systems can be built. Binding time is then the time when decisions are made that determine the processing within the system.

The schemes discussed in Sec. 7-3-5 illustrate concepts of early and late *binding* in information systems. *Early binding* means that the system processes new data asit arrives to make it suitable for retrieval. *Late binding* implies that more processing will be done at retrieval time.

Providing replicated entries to match every feasible query is an early binding decision: Additional work is done when the file is updated so that less work is needed at retrieval time. Also, much storage is needed to keep the result of the early computation.

Late binding is the approach used when we combine the TID-lists when the queries arrive. Less work is done when the file is updated, more work is done at retrieval time. Late binding was of the basis for the pile file design.

Many practical approaches used mixed binding strategies. The handling of false drops is a late-binding procedure; selection of attributes which can be omitted or superimposed is an early-binding process.

Many research results can be categorized according to the criterion of binding. If a new method provides very fast retrieval, then one should look at its update cost. If a new method provides ease of update, then the expectation is that more work will be needed at retrieval time. It is naive to assume that great benefits ensue without costs. With some sophistication one should be able to find the optimum balance for any application.

> By the time a data-oriented information system produces results all information has been bound: The user does not want choices to be presented.

Some *artificial intelligence* approaches do not satisfy this rule. They are designed to be used be experts who can complete the decision-making process before selecting the final action.

BACKGROUND AND REFERENCES

Comparison of the effectiveness of file methods is only possible if consistent measures exist for the files to be compared. This was the objective of the previous chapters. The desire to recognize communalities among several file methods was already expressed by Bachman[66]. Hsiao[70] defined file concepts formally and applied the definitions to retrieval in pile, indexed-sequential, indexed, ring, and redundantly inverted files. Bayer[76] compares B-trees with hashed access.

Stonebraker[80] presents the alternatives used in INGRES. Dodd[69] surveys sequential and various ring and chain techniques. File methods have been compared by many, including Chapin[69] (sequential, indexed-sequential, hashed, and hierarchical), Collmeyer[70] (single and multilevel indexes, and TID-lists accessed by hashing), and Teory[82] (sequential, serial, hashed, indexed-sequential, trees and tries, indexed rings, and hierarchical indexes). Cardenas[77] also considers hierarchical indexes and in Cardenas[73] uses actual data files and considers cost functions for a single-level multiple index, a ring structure, and a single multiple-level index. Lum[70] describes results of parameterization of IBM OS file-access methods to predict file behavior. The model developed by Senko[73] allows description of file-design methods. File systems which implement various methods are described by Judd[73]. Martin[75] describes many file operations in detail and provides design guidance.

Ingenious combinations of fundamental file methods have been part of many challenging file-oriented applications. Descriptions of the techniques used can often be found in user-oriented system descriptions. The lack of a taxonomy of file organization methods has made analysis and comparison of complex approaches difficult. Terminology differs among manufacturers. For instance, in IBM manuals, "direct" refers to both simple direct access and hashed access, and the term "relative" access is used for direct access via TIDs.

Techniques have been used, forgotten, reinvented, and sometimes applied in inappropriate environments, so that it becomes very difficult to trace the history of this subject area. A multi-index file system would be a useful tool for someone attempting such a review.

The simple file systems presented in Sec. 7-1 are commonly provided in systems not oriented toward data processing, such as FORTRAN (Brainerd[78]), minicomputer, and small timeshared systems. Their inflexibility is sometimes hidden in footnotes: "Records are of variable-length, from 1 to 2048 characters (* Users are always charged for 2048 characters per record)". The reason for the surprising charging rate is that the system uses one block per record.

Descriptions of simple systems are not often found in the regular literature, but user manuals often provide enough details so that the structure and hence their performance in various situations becomes obvious. Access to text files is described in Reitman[69], Frey[71], amd Du[87].

New hashing techniques are analyzed by Scholl[81]. Larson[84] uses a single bit hash-table for rapid access and Dimsdale[73] presents details of a system using hashed access to TID lists. Wong[71], Files[69], Burkhard[76,79], Chang[82], and Rivest[76] present partial-match hashing schemes from early to late binding and Nievergelt[84] introduces the *Grid-file*, which uses multiple attributes to hash into TID-lists. SacksDavis[83] applies superimposition to a PROLOG system, and Lee[86] proposes hardware for the task. Before proposed techniques can be adopted, it is necessary to verify that they are applicable to the scale of the intended application. Some interesting techniques require exponentially increasing resources as the file size becomes greater.

Mullin[72] applies hashing to the overflow of an indexed-sequential file. Chains were proposed and analyzed by Johnson[61] to provide multi-attribute access to a hashed file. Systems developed by Bachman[66], Dodd[66], and Kaiman[73] provided hashed access to rings for various applications. Inglis[74] investigates maintenance of indexes using rings. Härder[78] uses both indexes and chains for a DBMS.

EXERCISES

1   Samuel Blockdrawer has been assigned to a group which is designing a regional database application for health records. Some requirements are:
- A large population (3.5 million).
- Records of variable length.
  - Retrieval of patients' records by name as well as by medical registration number. The medical registration number can be assigned at the first patient contact.

Occasionally, the database will be used for research purposes; however, most of its function is the individual health record. A survey establishes some details:

A patient's identification record will occupy at least 150 bytes, at most 280 bytes, with an average of 220 bytes. It contains information such as name, age, patient registration number, and so on. The average person has about three contacts with the health care delivery system per year, distributed as follows:
- Two visits to a pharmacy, for an average of 1.2 drugs; each drug record is 20 bytes.
- 0.72 visits to a physician, with a single complaint; the average visit generates 50 bytes.
- 0.1 hospitalization which generates an average of 500 bytes.
- 0.01 major hospitalization which is summarized to 2000 bytes.

The proposed computer system will use 5-byte pointers, four bytes each for data attribute descriptions and for the data values (names will be compressed to this length). Blocks are 7000 bytes long and the interblock gaps are equivalent to 500 bytes. The average seek time is 30 ms. The rotational latency is 20 ms. The advertised data-transfer rate is 1 million bytes per second. There are six blocks per track and 50 tracks per cylinder.

Sam proposes a design as shown in Fig. 7-27.

Questions:

Provide the appropriate formula and its values at the end of the first year, second year, and fifth year for each of the seven aspects of the file design which are listed below. State any assumption which you have to make in order to obtain the results.

  a The average record size in the system as well as for the total file size.

  b The time required to locate one specific patient's visit by name and date.

  c Time to find the next visit of that patient.

  d The time required to add a visit record.

  e The time to change a data value in a patient's record, if the registration number is given.

  f The time required to collect the patient's entire record.

  g The time required to collect all usage data for one specific drug.

Give three suggestions how this design can be improved and mention for each suggestion both the benefit and the cost considerations. How can we handle people who move out of the region or die?

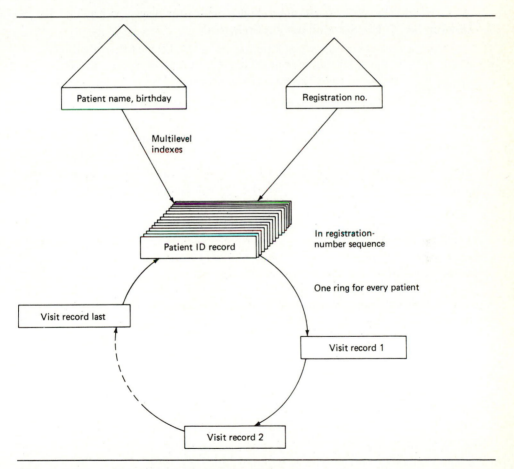

Figure 7-27   Regional health record system.

   2^p For your application, is one of the chosen file structures marked as being poor in Table 7-1 for any aspect? Even though it may not be important to the intended use, propose a hybrid combination to improve the poor aspect.

3   Which file structure provides the best description for the following structures found in our environment? Justify your decision in one or two sentences.

    a Genealogical chart

    b Telephone book, white pages (people)

    c Telephone book, yellow pages (services)

    d Telephone book, green pages (synonyms of service names)

    e Organization chart of a company

    f Manual medical records

    g Railroad classification yard where freight trains are assembled and re-assembled

    h Airline terminal

    i Social security office central files

4   Provide the seven performance parameters for access via a TID list as described in Sec. 7-2-2. State all assumptions made.

5   Compare the performance of fetching using the TID list described in Sec. 7-2-2 with indexed-sequential files and hashing. Why would one chose an alternative having lower performance than the best of the three?

6   Write the programming statements to WRITE into a sequential file accessed via TIDs, corresponding to the READ statement shown in Table 7-6.

7   Derive T_F, W, and the effective R for a text file organization as described in Sec. 7-2-3

8   You want to store pages of text into a file as described in Sec. 7-2-3. Determine the design parameters such as bucket size, number of blocks per bucket, and TID computation for data on your computer system.

9   Determine the optimal bucket size for a text file structured as described in Sec. 7-2-3. The file is to be used for storing text lines of 70 characters and has a block size of 256 characters. No page numbers are available but all lines are numbered. The lines are numbered sequentially, 1, 2, 3, ...

    a In terms of minimal file size.

    b In terms of lowest block-access cost for the sum of 10 exhaustive reads of the file and 1000 random accesses of one line each. Assume a file of 1000 lines. Do not consider more than four blocks per bucket.

10   Review the fundamental methods described in Chaps. 4 to 6 in terms of the binding criterion described in Sec. 7-5-1.

11   Review the hybrid combinations described in Secs. 7-2 and 7-3 in terms of the binding criterion described in Sec. 7-5-1.

12   To reduce the number of entries in a multiattribute, direct-access procedure only queries which catenate at least three of the four key attributes are accepted. How many entries will be required in the TID-list?

13   How many search arguments should you have before using hashed access to the file of Fig. 7-15?

14   How many search arguments should you have before using direct access to the file of Fig. 7-21?

Chapter 8

Index Implementation

The best academy for architects would be the brick-field, for of this they may rest assured, that till they know how to use clay, they will never know how to use marble.

Robin Ruskin,
The House of Venice II, 1853.

8-0   INTRODUCTION

Indexes of various types are the dominant access method for large databases. We introduced the principal concepts of indexing in Chap. 5. In this chapter we present adaptations and approaches which are used in practice for systems with high performance and high functionality. In Sec. 8-1 we will present some techniques which improve the performance of indexes. Section 8-2 deals with abbreviation of index keys, an important technique to assure high index fanout. A high fanout requires more processing once the index block is in memory. Section 8-3 covers techniques to search rapidly through an index block and will deal with alternate index structures which can also ameliorate the problems of long keys. Serial processing by means of an index is considered in Sec. 8-4. There is an interaction of the processing of keys and the optimal block size; the trade-off is evaluated in Sec. 8-4-3. The material leads to an example of a complex indexed-sequential file in Sec. 8-5. Some closing and cross-referencing remarks are provided in Sec. 8-6.

The information presented in this chapter is more technical than that in the previous chapters. Some techniques improve the data-retrieval capability by adding redundancy but this increases the amount of space required and makes updates more difficult. The aggregate performance of a system depends on the balance of update and retrieval usage, and will be analyzed in Chap. 14.

8-1   IMPROVING THE PERFORMANCE OF INDEXES

Since indexes are the primary access structures for files and databases, many specific improvements have been devised. In this section we consider three categories:

1 Reducing the index access costs
2 Reducing interference in B-trees
3 Improving the response time for B-tree updates.

The first category applies mainly to indexed-sequential files, the other two to B-trees.

B-trees provide excellent function for indexing files for general retrieval. The ability to update B-trees immediately, as insertions and updates to the file are made, the avoidance of reorganization, and good retrieval performance are all very desirable. Some problems remain:

1 The update of multiple B-trees takes much effort and the resulting delay in response can hinder on-line update operations. Deferring some of the update effort can help.
2 The possibility that much of a B-tree may be reorganized hinders shared access to the tree, and hence to the data accessed. *Presplitting* provides a solution.

8-1-1   Reducing the Access Costs of Indexes

Two common improvements are made to indexes to increase their performance:

1 Keeping the root of the index tree in memory
2 Locating portions of the index so that seeks are minimized.

We will consider these two adaptations and then evaluate their joint effect.

ROOT BLOCKS IN MEMORY   Since the root level of an index only occupies at most one block it is common to place it in memory, trading some memory for access speed. Keeping the root block (level x) available, once it has been read, avoids repeated disk accesses for that level of an index. The lower levels (levels $x-1, \ldots, 1$) of the index will still be obtained from disk. The root block can be placed into memory when the file is opened. With this scheme we reduce the total number of accesses to disk blocks required to fetch data records from the data file from $x+1$ to x.

CYLINDER INDEXES   Since much of the time cost of fetching a block is due to the seek time required to reach a particular cylinder, access speed can be gained by avoiding seeks during access. The primary index, having a parallel structure to the data file, can be partitioned according to hardware boundaries to yield such benefits.

Specifically, the top of the primary index (level x or levels x and $x-1$) can be used to partition the file into portions that each fit one cylinder. Two such levels are used only if the file is larger than a hardware device, say a disk unit. Then the root level assigns the hardware device and the subsidiary level partitions the storage assigned to one device into cylinder portions. On level 1 is the remainder of the index, its blocks allocated to the cylinders containing the data they reference. Allocating index space within cylinders used for data slightly reduces the capacity for data and increases the bulk data transfer rate, but the access speed gained can be substantial.

To optimize this approach, the size of an index level is best determined by the number of blocks it should reference. Only one low index level (1) needs to be allocated on a cylinder for its records; the number of entries is determined by the data capacity of the remainder of the cylinder. More than one block may be needed for the entries to one cylinder, but since the blocks will be placed adjacent on a track, only additional buffer space and block transfer time (*btt*) is needed.

The next level up, level 2, matches the number of cylinders required. Even if a file uses all of a disk unit, the number of entries will still be only a few hundred. A level $x = 3$ only comes into play when files are greater than one disk unit.

The contents of the entries are also adapted to the hardware. The optional third level uses as pointers references to the operating system directory of disk units. The level two index contains only key attribute values and addresses of cylinder anchors. If the level two entries match sequential cylinders the entries do not even need a pointer field, since entry 1 simply corresponds to block 1, etc. On the initial track of each cylinder there will be the cylinder index. The entries on the cylinder index, level 1, do not need a cylinder address segment; they reference only local tracks, blocks, or records.

We have now a three- or two-level index, with possibly more fanout at lower levels than seen in a block-oriented index design. No seek is incurred between cylinder-index and data records. For files residing on one disk a total of two seeks suffice for data access, one for the root block and one for the cylinder containing index and data. The example shown in Fig. 8-1 evaluates this type of index for a large file and can be compared with Fig. 5-6.

Again given is a block size, B, of 2000 bytes and data records having a total length, R, of 200 bytes. With this blocking factor, *Bfr* of 10, the 10^6 records require 10^5 data blocks. The value size, V, is 14 bytes The TID pointer size, P, of 6 bytes can be abbreviated to 4 bytes with a cylinder.

Using disks with 200 cylinders of 19 tracks, capable of holding 14 000 bytes each and $B = 2000$, we find on each cylinder $19 \cdot 14\,000/2000 = 133$ blocks.

The index to the data on one cylinder, level 1, will require one entry per block, at most $133V = 1862$ bytes, or one block on each cylinder, leaving 132 blocks for data. The portions of the level 2 index to the cylinders are kept on their particular disks. Their entries do not require a pointer field, there is simply one entry per sequential cylinder. On each device we use $200 \cdot 14 = 2800$ bytes or two blocks for the level 2 index. The reduction in disk capacity is negligble. The data file oupies $\lceil 10^5/132 \rceil = 758$ cylinders. This file requires $\lceil 758/200 \rceil = 4$ disk units. We need a third-level index to the cylinder indexes; this root level of the index for the entire file will have one entry per disk, or four entries for this particular file. Only $4 \cdot (14 + 6)$ bytes are needed here.

Figure 8-1   Hardware-oriented index design.

Comparing this example with the original design of Fig. 5-6 we find that the hardware-oriented indexing structure has a higher fanout ($y_1 = 132$, $y_2 = 200$)

than the general, symmetric index structure. A by-product is that the root level is smaller ($y_3 = 4$). For very large files restricting an index to three levels may create larger root blocks. The second-level index is larger and requires additional block reads, costing *btt* for retrieval and additional buffer space.

The actual values for a file depend on the interaction of file, record, and key sizes with hardware boundaries. The hardware-independent index structure is more general and easier to adapt to specific file requirements.

FETCH PERFORMANCE   Using both a root index in memory, and cylinder indexes where the first-level index and the data it references are kept on the same cylinder, we find that

$$T_{Fmain} = (x-1)(s+r+btt) + btt^{\ddagger} + r + btt \qquad \qquad \langle primary \rangle \text{ 8-1}$$

The term marked $\ddagger$ accounts for multiple blocks at level 2.

This formula can be compared with Eq. 5-9 for indexed-sequential files, where $T_{Fmain} = (x+1)(s+r+btt)$). We see that $2s+r$ has been saved. In such designs the corresponding overflow areas will also be kept on the local cylinder, so that no further seeks will be incurred. We obtain a performance that becomes quite competitive with hashing.

For general indexed files with multiple B-trees these improvements are rarely realized.

1 It becomes difficult to keep the root level of many indexes in memory.
2 When there are multiple index subfiles, we can no longer assume that these indexes and the data will both occupy the same cylinder.

8-1-2 Presplitting in B-trees

A problem with B-trees is that they are difficult to share. When a block at the lowest level (1) is split, the resulting insertions at the next higher level may propagate all the way to level x. Another user, wanting to access another portion of the same file, will use the same high-level blocks. If those change while they are being used, the program may not behave correctly.

To prevent errors a B-tree may be locked when in use for update. Then the changes due to the update cannot interfere with other access operations. Now the entire file becomes unavailable to others. In applications where many users may be active, for instance, in a reservation system, such a constraint is unacceptable.

An alternate and improved insertion strategy is *presplitting*. When the search for an index entry is made from the root to the lowest level, each index block read is checked; any index block which is already full ($y_{eff} = y$) is immediately split. This assures that the block at the next level up will never be found full, so that no split has to propagate from the lowest to the higher levels.

This technique becomes more difficult to implement when attribute values, and hence index entries, are of variable length. The definition of *not full* above has to leave enough space for a new entry of any expected size. The pragmatics of deletion operations remain the same.

8-1-3 Updating of Indexes

The maintenance of files which maintain multiple indexes generates many block accesses and rewrites. Every insertion, deletion, and update of a record must be reflected in the indexes. The delay in response to a user caused by updating all indexes can make data entry intolerably slow. It may become impractical to attempt to update all indexes immediately after a record has been changed (see Exercise 13 in Chap. 5).

Deferred Updating of Indexes A solution is to defer the updating of the indexes. The updating of the indexes is then done at a lower priority, when the computer is relatively idle. The data file is kept available. Deferred index updating will be done by separate processes which are active at a modest priority until completed. It is necessary to keep the changed or deleted records in the main file, marked with a tombstone, until all referring indexes have been updated.

A retrieval to such a file may now not include recent changes, and may include records which have actually been deleted. In some applications that may not matter. Many applications can operate with deferred updating. When queries involve management decisions for planning, say, an analysis of a `sales` pattern, use of data which is perhaps a few hours obsolete will not matter. These types of analysis transactions tend to access many records so that a relaxation of their access requirements can be very beneficial to the overall system.

A counterexample is a `sales` transaction which actually commits to deliver specific items from stock. Then an immediate update of the index used for access may have to be forced to assure the stock counts are up to date.

Alternative methods to assure that critical retrievals are up to date when deferred index updating is used are:

1 Assign to the reading process a yet lower priority than the index update process, so that index updating will be completed before any critical retrieval is performed.
2 Mark the indexes which have not yet been updated, and force an index update for attributes used in the retrieval.
3 Search in parallel through the list of records in the process queue for insertion or update to locate any conflicts.

The third method is computationally the costliest, but will not require forced updating of the indexes. In all cases deleted records are recognized by their tombstones.

High-priority fetch requests using the file may be processed before all indexes are brought up to date, with a warning that the response reflects all changes made before a certain time, say $m = 10$ minutes ago. A relatively higher priority may be assigned routinely to a process which updates important attribute indexes than the priority given to other index-update processes. If the priority given is higher than the priority of certain retrievals, these retrievals will always find up-to-date information.

Deferred updating of indexes can also reduce the total effort spent on updating when updates are frequent, or tend to come in batches. The continuous maintenance of indexes is quite time-consuming and a batch of updates may rewrite the same index block again and again.

Thus, we also find systems where indexes are created for a particular analysis but are not kept up to date as the file changes. Without updated indexes recent information will not be accessible. A new index is created when needed, or perhaps periodically. This approach is akin to a periodic file reorganization.

Updating of indexes while the file is otherwise active requires careful sequencing of update operations and the maintenance of status information on incomplete updates. Approaches to monitor concurrent file operations and maintain reliability will be discussed in Chap. 15.

▨▨▨▨ **Deletion Pragmatics in B-trees** Deletion in B-trees, whether done immediatly or deferred, carries with it the high cost of inspecting the partner blocks. In order to find out if the index blocks, where a deletion has occured, can be combined with a partner, the occupancy of its partner has to be such that sum of the entries is y or less.

Many systems use alternate deletion strategies, either to simplify the programs or to reduce effort. Perhaps index blocks will not be checked until one has fewer than $0.69/2y$ entries or will not even be combined at all. In the last case index blocks will be deleted only if they become empty.   ▨▨▨▨

vol I	vol II	vol III	vol IV	vol V	vol VI	vol VII	vol VIII	vol IX	vol X	vol XI	vol XII
A ANA	ANA ATH	ATH BOI	BOK CAN	CAN CLE	CLI DAY	DEA ELD	ELE FAK	FAL FYZ	G GOT	GOU HIP	HIR IND

vol XIII	vol XIV	vol XV	vol XVI	vol XVII	vol XVIII	vol XIX	vol XX	vol XXI	vol XXII	vol XXIII	vol XXIV
INF KAN	KAO LON	LOO MEN	MEN MOS	MOT ORM	ORN PHT	PHY PRO	PRU ROS	ROT SIA	SIB SZO	TAB UPS	URA ZYM

Figure 8-2   Volumes of the 1890 Encyclopaedia Britannica.

8-2   KEY ABBREVIATION

The keys used to identify data records can be very long. Examples of long keys which can be encountered are names of individuals, technical terms, names of diseases, and addresses. Long keys are also often of variable length.

Long keys in an index waste space, but more seriously, reduce the number of entries that can be kept in one index block. The resulting reduction of fanout in turn increases the number of levels of indexing and this increases the processing time significantly. In Fig. 8-2 we show key abbreviation used to locate reference volumes.

Since the low-order parts of the keys do not aid at all in the discrimination process between the books, fixed-length, low-order key abbreviation was used here. On the other hand, when an index refers to many records, there will be long sequences with identical high-order parts of the key field. Then the key field can be shortened by judiciously abbreviating the high order part of the key. In Fig. 8-2 you can tell that Vol. II covers A even if the entry were shown as .NA − .TH.

VARIABLE-LENGTH KEYS   Variable-length keys occur naturally, but are also a result of abbreviation algorithms. Without abbreviation space for the maximum possible size must be allocated to a variable length identifier. Truncation to a fixed length, leaving out the low-oder characters, can cause loss of the uniqueness that computer retrieval depends on.

Figure 8-2 shows a problem due to a fixed-length abbreviation: In which volume would you find "Canoe"? When processing data automatically, it is necessary that only one record be selected in response to a fetch request. To assure uniqueness we would abbreviate this entry less, so that the volume, or the record, can be uniquely identified by that key alone.

Naturally occurring variable-length keys, for instance, people's names, should in any case be allocated to variable-length fields, since a fixed allocation of adequate space for the longest key may be prohibitive. When the length is unknown, because the memory representation uses fixed-length character-string fields, deletion of low-order blanks is common. Once this step is made other abbreviations follow easily. Hence, key abbreviation requires variable-length fields and having variable-length fields encourages further key abbreviation.

Markers are needed to delimit variable-length key and record boundaries; alternatives were shown in Fig. 3-11. In this section we use special characters to indicate the boundaries, the system described in Sec. 8-5 uses length indicators. The markers reduce the benefits of the abbreviation. For short keys a fixed allocation may still be preferable.

LIMITS OF ABBREVIATION   Note that abbreviation is feasible in particular when the keys appear in a sorted sequence. That is true in an index. The portions of the key which do not discriminate between adjoining keys can then be deleted.

Formally, keys can be abbreviated since keys should not need more bits than needed to discriminate among the n items being referenced. A theoretical minimum is a length of $\log_2 n$ bits, and within one index block only $\log_2 y$ bits should be needed for each key.

Abbreviation of long keys may be made *externally* before records are put into a system, or may be performed *internally*, completely within the file system. Some key abbreviation algorithms are designed to be convenient in either case.

8-2-1 External Key Abbreviation

In order to introduce the topic of key abbreviation, we will present a scheme oriented toward manual use. This scheme also randomizes the key values, so that buckets used to store the records are evenly filled. This method has hence also a hashing objective.

In Fig. 8-3 we present a mailing label, with a code which is intended to be understandable by clerks who have to deal with subscription renewals and delivery complaints of newspapers and magazines. The file is accessed based on the coded key in the top line. The zip code and characteristics of the name and the street address are composed to obtain the abbreviated key. This method is similar to a sequence-maintaining hashing technique but can also be carried out manually. The method used does not guarantee uniqueness unless a sequence digit is added.

60282HGS5155POT31

Edgar R. B. Hagstrohm

155 Proteus Park

Chicago, Ill 60282

A mailing label code.
The underlined parts of the address are
included in the code.
Counts are given for the dotted characters.
A sequence digit 1 is appended.

Figure 8-3   Abbreviated address key.

In many European countries identifiers for individuals are constructed using similar techniques. When such an abbreviated key is reconstructed at a later time, the sequence digit is not known, so that no unique transformation can be made. In that case multiple records have to be retrieved and checked using further information, similar to the collisions occurring in a direct file organization. A trade-off is made between the length of the abbreviated key and the number of key collisions.

8-2-2 Internal Key Abbreviation

Figure 8-5 illustrates opportunities for abbreviation of long keys with blocks at two levels. The index shown uses the highest value of the key as the block anchor point. The keys in our examples are numeric and letters indicate block addresses. We will show how to delete redundant high-order and low-order segments of keys.

HIGH-ORDER KEY ABBREVIATION   If all index entries in an index block refer to keys within a certain range, the high-order part of the key will be identical and this *high-order segment* can be deleted. In Fig. 8-5 the two leading digits of entries in block C of the second-level index are redundant, and were deleted from the individual entries. In block D only one digit could be deleted, but in both cases the number of entries per block and the fanout ratio y has increased.

The redundant segment can be marked in the predecessor block, leading to a so-called *prefix B-tree*. In practice, we keep in a header portion of each index block the value of the high-order segment to allow reconstruction of the key from information within the index block.

B : 000+13=a,+29=b,00+407=c,   D : 118+00=p,+10=q,11900=r,1
     +704=d,0+2050=e,10+094=f   2+130=s,1220+1=t,+5=u,+9
     ,+151=g;   =v,12+210=w,+384=x;

The stored segments are separated by markers { + = , ; }. The high-order segment
is repeated in front of the + symbol whenever the truncation changes.

Figure 8-4   High-order key abbreviations.

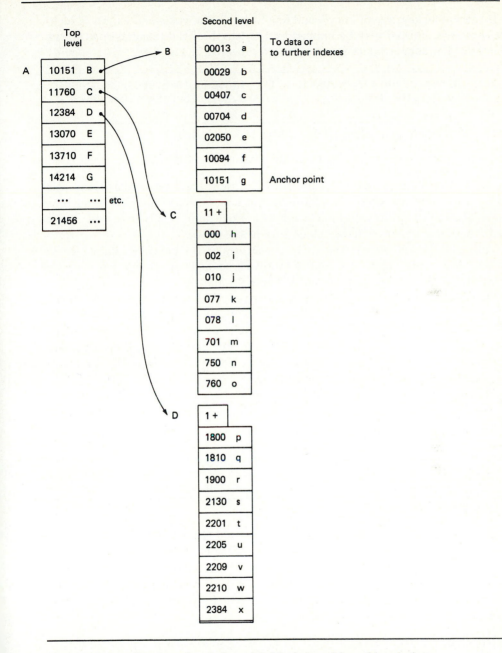

Figure 8-5   Part-number index with block-based key abbreviation.

Key abbreviations may be also applied to individual entries within blocks, as is shown in Fig. 8-4 for blocks **B** and **D**. Now the individual entries are variable within a block. Some analysis is needed to make the truncation optimal for the entire block.

If the source keys are of known and fixed length, the value and length of high-order segments omitted may be implied by the length of the remainder, as shown in Fig. 8-6. The source values for block D are repeated in Fig. 8-8.

B : 00013=a,29=b,407=c,704=d   D : 11800=p,10=q,900=r,2130=
    ,2050=e,10094=f,151=g;   s,201=t,5=u,9=v,10=w,384
                                             =x;

Figure 8-6   High-order abbreviation for keys of known length.

Avoiding markers reduces the entries by 25% versus Fig. 8-4.

LOW-ORDER KEY ABBREVIATION   The right-hand side of keys may also be shortened. Indexes where the attribute is a long string of characters, such as a name, sometimes arbitrarily limit fields to a fixed number of characters. Some records then may no longer have unique keys in the index.

This method was seen in the volume headings of the encyclopedia shown in Fig. 8-2. Three characters here did not provide enough discrimination between Volumes 1 and 2, 2 and 3, 4 and 5, nor between 15 and 16.

For automated processing uniqueness is desired. The contents of an index block can be inspected to determine how many low-order digits can be safely deleted. In the earlier example (Fig. 8-5), two low-order digits of the first index level (block A) can be deleted without loss of discrimination. For insertion, omitted digits are taken to be nines. The third character cannot be deleted because of the density of entries in the range between 13 000 and 14 000.

Abbreviating the individual entries makes the keys yet shorter. Blocks A and, for comparison, block D of Fig. 8-5 are shown in Fig. 8-7 with low-order abbreviation applied to the entries.

A : 10=B,11=C,12=D,130=E,13=   D : 1180=p,118=q,119=r,121=s
    F,14=G,...,21=...   ,11201=t,11205=u,12209=v
                                             ,122=w,123=x;

Figure 8-7   Low-order key abbreviation.

Low-order key abbreviation has the disadvantage that the actual data file has to be accessed to determine whether a record corresponding to the full key exists. Now a search for a nonexistent record, via a record-anchored but abbreviated index, will require one more access. Without abbreviation, the lack of the record is recognized when the lowest-level index entries do not yield a match. When using block anchors, the file has to be accessed in either case.

COMBINED ABBREVIATION   Both types of abbreviation can be applied at the same time. The result is not easy to to decode, but combined abbreviation is effective. When there is likely to be little high-order abbreviation — there are few references relative to the key space — low-order abbreviation is effective, and vice versa.

In Fig. 8-8, again based on block D of Fig. 8-5, both abbreviations are applied to the entries. We show the original entries on the left. In this block, with already short entries, adding low-order abbreviation does not help; Fig. 8-19 shows a successful example.

D : 11800=p,11810=q,11900=r,   D : 11.80=p,-8=q,-9=r,12.1=s
       12130=s,12201=t,12205=u,   ,-20.1=t,-5=u,-9=v,12.2=
       12209=v,12210=w,12384=x;   w,-3=x;

The point '.' symbol defines segments; the dash '-' indicates an omitted segment.

Figure 8-8   Original keys and their combined high- and low-order abbreviation.

8-2-3 Other Opportunities for Abbreviation

Two other opportunities for abbreviation can be exploited: repeating keys and the TIDs.

REPEATING KEYS   In indexes where the keys are not *unique*, so that more than one record for a given key can exist, it can be profitable to avoid restating the key. With the flexible key organization obtained with abbreviated keys, such a facility is easy to implement, as shown in the example of Fig. 8-9.

E : 1241.1=y&z,-2=...

Two records, stored at y *and* z, *both have a key value of* 12411.

Figure 8-9   Abbreviation of repeating keys.

The partial match example, shown in Fig. 5-17, used this technique.

ABBREVIATING TIDS   If the goal records occupy only a part of the file space, then the pointers to the goal records may be similarly abbreviated. The high-order segment of the TID in any block can be significantly shortened, especially in the case where the indexed entries are used to point to a sequential file in index order.

     The number of entries referenced can now differ greatly in the various blocks. The method for index selection of inferring *distribution steps* from the entries in the root block, described in Chap. 5-5-2, now may no longer work.

8-2-4 Use of Abbreviated Index Entries

Abbreviation of keys is effective when keys are relatively long and files are big. Often, one level of index can be saved. In these small examples the effect is less obvious than in practice, where index blocks are long. In practice, fields with length indicators are often, instead of the marker characters shown, as = , .   - ;. An actual implementation is described in Sec. 8-5.

     When there is no need to access data serially, a hashing algorithm can perform the same service without the complexity and computational overhead of variable-length keys. Hashing, however, causes collisions, whereas the abbreviation techniques maintain uniqueness. Since the keys are denser in the record-anchored indexes associated with multi-indexed files, key abbreviations can play an important role there. The abbreviation of TIDs complements abbreviation of the keys and can lead to further savings.

8-3   PROCESSING INDEX BLOCKS

Having a high fanout means that many entries have to be scanned when processing index blocks. Although the high fanout, y, reduces the number of block accesses, the computation can now cause delays exceeding the time needed to fetch blocks from high-speed disks. Since index blocks are not accessed sequentially this does not affect the assumptions made for the bulk transfer rate made in Chap. 3-2-5, but the delays and the demands on CPU resources are significant.

Having abbreviated keys requires even more index processing time than would be required if a simpler index entry format were used. Measurements have allocated 14% of total database CPU usage to abbreviation and expansion of keys. In a multiprogrammed environment the CPU is used at the same time for other processes and is too valuable to spend on excessive index processing.

In this section we consider methods to reduce the processing time, cix, of index blocks that are in memory. Some alternate index block structures change the structure of the index blocks to achieve fast search. We present three structures for index blocks to support fast search. In Sec. 8-3-3, *jump search*, preserves seriality of index entries, an issue discussed in Sec. 8-4. The other two structures, *index trees* in Sec. 8-3-4 and and *tries* in Sec. 8-3-5, have better performance but do not keep index entries in serial order. We first consider the base cost.

8-3-1 Linear Processing

Processing all the y keys in a linear sequence requires comparing about

$$cix = 1/2\,y \qquad\qquad \langle\text{linear search}\rangle\ 8\text{-}2$$

entries with the search argument.

Approaches described in the remainder of this section reduce cix by replacing the linear search of the entries in the current index block. The use of rapid search in an index block regains computational time lost because of abbreviation.

8-3-2 Binary Search in Index Blocks

A binary search can provide rapid access to entries within an index block. Since entries in an index block are always sequential, a binary search seems applicable, but the entries should be of fixed size and not be abbreviated. Then

$$cix = \log_2 y \qquad\qquad \langle\text{binary search}\rangle\ 8\text{-}3$$

We presented the algorithm for binary search within a sequential file in Chap. 4-5-2, Fig. 4-14.

Variable-length entries disable the computation of an entry position in the center of the block. Abbreviation disables the comparison of an entry found. However, the use of a *position table* for marking the variable-length entries (see Chap. 3-2-4) permits a binary search to be used through indirection.

8-3-3 Jump Index Search

A simple scheme groups the y index entries within one block into a number of sections to provide a second level. The number of sections is chosen to be about equal to $\sqrt{y}$. An initial search pass *jumps* from section to section and compares one entry in each section. A subsequent pass searches within the proper section through the $y/\sqrt{y} = \sqrt{y}$ entries found in a section.

The expected number of comparisons of sections and entries is $\frac{1}{2}\sqrt{y}$ each, so that the total number of comparisons cix expected is

$$cix = 2\left(\tfrac{1}{2}\sqrt{y}\right) = \sqrt{y} \qquad\qquad \langle\text{jump search}\rangle\ 8\text{-}4$$

which is the minimum obtainable with two passes and linear searching. The number of comparisons, $\sqrt{y}$, to find an entry is within a factor of 2 of the optimum, a binary search, for typical values of y. This additional pseudolevel does not require redundant entries of the key or pointers, only a means to locate the sections.

If the records are of fixed length the location of the sections in the index block is computable. Otherwise, $\sqrt{y}$ section pointers can be used in each index block to define a two-level tree. These section pointers σ have to be distinguishable so that they will not interfere with sequential processing of index entries. An implementation is shown in Sec. 8-5-3 and Fig. 8-17.

8-3-4 Binary Arranged Index Tree

To achieve binary search performance for entries of arbitrary length we can rearrange the entries. Explicit successor pointers direct the search. The addition of pointers takes some space and reduces the fanout. These entries can also be abbreviated; high-order or prefix abbreviation works best.

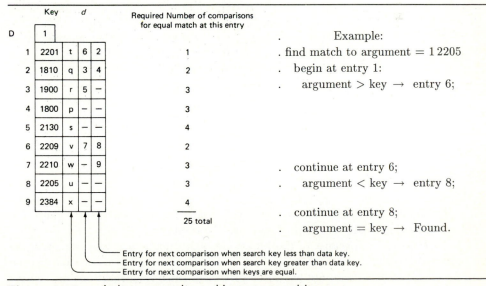

Figure 8-10   Index arranged as a binary tree and its use.

Figure 8-10 shows block D from the earlier example in Fig. 8-5. The search begins at the first entry, containing the center value. Two fields per entry direct the search algorithm to the next index entry to effect a binary partitioning. In this example, the maximum number of comparisons is four, and the expected number is $25/9 = 2.78$. In a sequential search, $(1 + 9)/2 = 5$ comparisons would be expected. In general, the tree search will require on the order of

$$cix = \log_2 y \qquad\qquad \langle\text{binary tree search}\rangle\ 8\text{-}5$$

comparisons. This is significant when there are many entries per index block.

The index shown has grown in size because of the pointers which relate the index entries to the tree structure. Of these pointer fields, $y + 1$ will be empty. In the example the comparison is based on the whole value of the key and some opportunities of high-order key abbreviation are lost.

8-3-5 A Trie

An alternate arrangement to enable rapid search is based on partitioning the search using individual digits of the key. Files based on this idea are named *tries* (pronounced "try-s"). A trie also uses a table to drive a sequence of binary decisions, but instead of comparing the entire value, as done in the binary tree, only a digit of the value is used.

Figure 8-11 shows an index trie for the index block D used earlier. The first column of the trie-table says which digit position is to be used, and the second column gives the comparison value of that digit. A digit value partitions the keys into two subsets. Columns three and four again direct the procedure to successor steps. Note that the full key is not represented here. To locate an entry the digit position for the first comparison is found and the corresponding digit is extracted from the search key. Comparing the search key digit with the stored value directs the search to one of two successor lines, partitioning the search. At those lines some other, or the same search key digit is picked up and compared with the comparison value stored there. The search continues until it is directed to a TID-pointer.

Building a trie means selecting digits from the keys which provide the best partitioning of the search space. For our source keys the value 0 in position 5 splits the keys into a subset of 5 and one of 4 entries, as shown in the decision tree of Fig. 8-11. The first digit (which anyhow could be omitted from the block) was of course never useful for partitioning the key space, but even the second digit was never used.

We expect some more comparisons than for a binary search, since we cannot guarantee that the space will be optimally partitioned. In this example we expect $29/9 = 3.22$ comparisons per key. In large indexes the improvement over sequential searching will be significant. The method produces also an effective abbreviation of the key, since entries are represented by only one digit.

In practice, tries, because of the binary decisions made, are best implemented by basing the comparison on a single bit, rather than on a digit. In this case no column with comparison values has to be provided, since the conditions are always only "=0" or "=1".

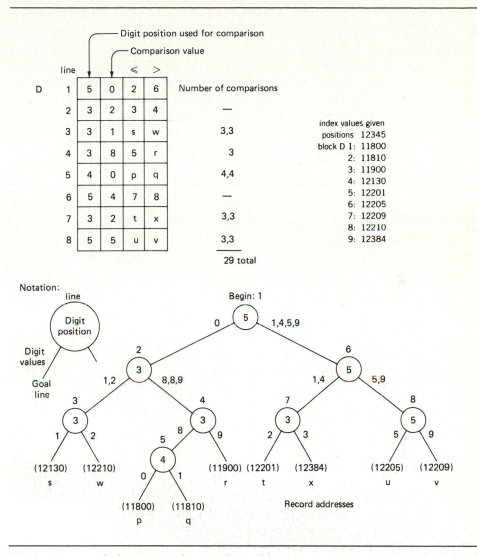

Figure 8-11   Index arranged as a trie, and its use.

The number of entries in a block of a trie leading to y records n_e is determined by the number of decision nodes, $n_d = \lceil y/2 \rceil$, and their ancestors in the tree $n_d - 1$, and hence $n_e \approx y$. The space required for the key segment of a binary trie entry is composed of the bit position of the key and two references. Trie entries are hence smaller than index entries, and there will be an increase in fanout.

A search for a missing record has to be resolved in the data file. Since the trie is built by rearranging data from the source keys indexes based on trie structures as shown are suitable only for record-anchored indexes, with entries pointing to each individual record. Intermediate search arguments will not lead to an anchor point for serial access. These tries are hence not useful at index levels > 1.

8-4   SERIAL PROCESSING AND INDEXES

The need to perform serial searches and retrieve many resulting records has to be considered in the design of indexed files. Serial access is required for `Get_Next` and `Read_Exhaustive` operations. Long sequences of repeated `Get_Next` operations occur when a subset is to be retrieved. A general term for such requests is *range queries*. We consider first how to obtain the TIDs efficiently and then how to use the TIDs to fetch blocks containing goal data. We assume here that the number and size of the TIDs for one query is such that we can collect them in memory, prior to accessing any of the data blocks containing the desired results.

We close this section by evaluating the optimum block size for indexed files, taking many of the factors discussed here into account.

8-4-1 Range Queries

A query may specify a *range* of values, say all

   `Employees having salaries between $20000 and $30000;`

so that records must be serially accessed. Serial access is also needed to access values that do not match exactly, say

   `Find an Employee with a salary > $50000;`

Such requests may be part of *partial-match* queries. We encountered such a query in Chap. 5-5:

   `FIND Houses priced 31000 → 33000`
      `∧ Style = 'Colonial';`

If the attribute that is indexed can have nonunique values, many entries may have to be retrieved for a single search argument, say,

   `FIND Houses with 3 bedrooms;`

These are the types of queries for which serial access capability through an index is essential.

File structures that deal well with **Get-Next** operations, as indexes, potentially process range queries well. An index provides an ordering for the data records, so that it is possible to find TIDs to successive records by scanning through the index blocks at level 1.

We considered serial access within a block in Sec. 8-3, and consider here access between blocks.

SERIAL LINKAGES In the case of the indexed-sequential file, which we examined in Chap. 5-1, serial access according to a single attribute was established through the location of the data records themselves and through a linkage for any overflow records.

Files with multiple indexes establish multiple serial access paths within the indexes themselves. The alternative, multiple direct linkages of data records themselves is used in the design of the multiring file. With indexes, serial access to the data records remains indirect; they are fetched according to the TIDs found in index entries.

Since indexes are small, it is easier to achieve a high degree of locality for indexes than for data records. If few records are to be obtained per serial retrieval, multiple indexes with linkages will perform as well as multiring structures. For further manipulation of subsets obtained, as needed for partial match retrieval, the indirection via an index and use of TIDs is more convenient than following a ring.

SERIAL ACCESS BETWEEN B-TREE INDEX BLOCKS   To process a B-tree type index serially we obtain TIDs from a block on level 1. When the entries in the block have been exhausted, the next index entry has to be found in a successor block. Since the next key value is not known, no fetch using a search argument equal to the next key is possible; the successor has to be found by navigation up and down the index.

Keeping all current ancestor index blocks available helps such navigation. At the end of a level 1 index block, we locate the next entry at level 2. This entry leads us to the successor level 1 index block. Generalizing, at the end of any block we must locate its successor via an entry from the superior level. To perform this process we use a stack of x ancestor blocks and the position of their current index entry.

A linkage of index blocks on level 1 can avoid this pain. The solution is shown in Fig. 8-12. The linkage pointers will have to be maintained with care. For a B-tree this adaptation is called a *B+ tree*. The pointers are reset when a lower level block is split. The linkage pointers also identify the partner block to be checked when deletions make recombining of index blocks desirable.

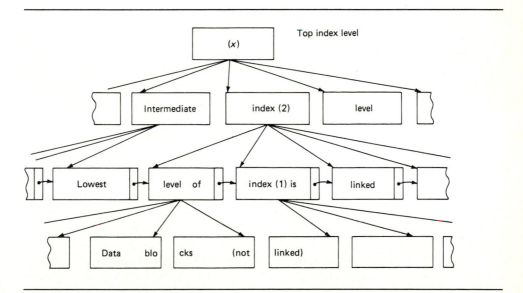

Figure 8-12   Linked lower-level index blocks for a B+ tree.

8-4-2 Accessing Data Blocks

When many records were requested we will expect many block accesses, in the first instance as many as we have TIDs. But some blocks may contain two or more goal records. By putting the TIDs in order by block number we can be assured that each block will be accessed only once; all goal records in one block will be obtained at the same time.

To estimate performance now we need to know the number of block fetches, b_G, required to retrieve n_G goal records in TID order from a large file of n_{file} records with Bfr records per block. The file uses $b_{file} = n_{file}/Bfr$ blocks. We will first consider the extreme cases. For small results ($n_G \ll n_{file}$), the value of $b_G \approx n_G$, since only rarely will one block fetch more than one result record. For large numbers of n_G the value of $b_G \to b_{file}$, if the retrieval is carried out in TID order, since nearly every block will be accessed once.

In the important intermediate region, where a substantial fraction of all records is selected from the goal file, some blocks will yield multiple records and others will not be needed at all. An estimate of the number of block fetches required to retrieve n_G records in TID order from a file of n records with Bfr records per block, for the cases $n_G \leq n_{file} - Bfr$, is computable as (Whang[81])

$$b_G = \frac{n}{Bfr}\left(1 - \left(1 - \frac{Bfr}{n}\right)^{n_G} + \frac{Bfr}{n_G^2}\frac{n_G(n_G-1)}{2}\left(1 - \frac{Bfr}{n}\right)^{n_G-1}\right.$$
$$\left. + \frac{1.5}{n_G^3 Bfr}\frac{n_G(n_G-1)(2n_G-1)}{6}\left(1 - \frac{Bfr}{n}\right)^{n_G-1}\right)$$

8-6

This formula is a good approximation in the range of values seen in databases of the computationally difficult function required to produce an exact result (Yao[77]). To a retrieval time computed on the basis of this technique the computation time, c, required for sorting of the TIDs in memory prior to file access, has to be added.

8-4-3 The Interaction of Block Size and Index Processing

Up to this point we have used the block size as a given parameter in the design of indexes. In many cases this is a valid assumption, but it is instructive to see how changes in block size affect the performance of an index. The size of an index entry will be denoted below as Rix, and the number of index entries by nix. The positive effect of large block sizes is a high fanout ratio ($y = B/Rix$, from Eq. 5-1), which reduces the number of levels required. The number of levels, x, is again determined by $x = \log_y nix$ (Eq. 5-2).

The detrimental effects of large block sizes are the increased block transfer time, $btt = B/t$, the increased computational effort, c, to locate the appropriate index entry in a block, and the cost of memory occupancy. The computation is a function of the number of records which have to be searched in memory, cix, and the time for a unit access and comparison, c_1.

Figure 8-13 shows the combined effect of these factors except the memory occupancy for a fairly large index. The fetch time within the index is computed as

$$T_{Fix} = \lceil \log_y n \rceil (cix\, c_1 + s + r + y \frac{Rix}{t})$$ 8-7

where $cix = \frac{1}{2}y$ ⟨linear search (Eq. 8-2)⟩
and $cix = \log_2 y$ ⟨binary search (Eqs. 8-3, 8-5)⟩
Figure 8-13 does not show $cix = \sqrt{y}$ ⟨jump search (Eq. 8-4)⟩
which is in between, but close to the binary search.

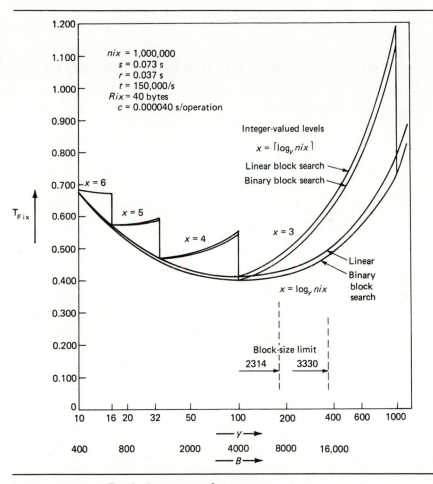

nix = 1,000,000
s = 0.073 s
r = 0.037 s
t = 150,000/s
Rix = 40 bytes
c = 0.000040 s/operation

Integer-valued levels

$x = \lceil \log_y nix \rceil$

Linear block search
Binary block search

x = 6
x = 5
x = 4
x = 3

$x = \log_y nix$

Linear
Binary
block
search

Block-size limit
2314   3330

—y—

400   800   2000   4000   8000   16,000
—B—

Figure 8-13   Fetch time versus fanout.

 **Evaluating Index Block Sizes** The optimum length for index blocks in the case shown, a 2314-type disk, is 4000 bytes. The steps in the function are an effect of the discrete assignment of index levels. The lower, continuous curve represents use of optimal index processing; approaches were described in Sec. 8-3.

An assumption made to generate Fig. 8-13 is that the time needed to inspect one index entry, c_1, is 40 microseconds (μs). The validity of this assumption depends on the index implementation. Abbreviated entries will take longer to process and will raise the left side of the curve, especially if linear searches are made through the index blocks, but their use will also decrease the size of an average index entry, so that the same fanout will correspond to a smaller block size.

The disk parameters are for a relatively slow unit. Devices with a shorter seek time will favor shorter block sizes, while devices with a higher transfer rate will cause minimal values of the fetch time to occur with larger blocks.   ▦

8-5   AN IMPLEMENTATION OF AN INDEXED-SEQUENTIAL FILE

A practical example of a comprehensive indexed-sequential file system is provided by IBM in their Virtual Storage Access Method (VSAM). The term *virtual* refers only to the fact that the programs used to implement VSAM depend on the virtual addressing provided by IBM's 370 type of computers. The approach is a hybrid of techniques presented in Secs. 5-1, 5-3, 8-2, 8-3, and 8-4.

We can describe the file design, using the terminology developed in the previous section, as follows:

VSAM is an indexed-sequential file organization. It permits multiple secondary indexes. The indexes and the data file use a B-tree algorithm. The primary index has a fixed number of levels, thus limiting the file size, albeit to a very large number of records. Anchor points are the keys with the highest value in a train of blocks. Records and keys may be of variable length; their marking is by length indicators (see Chap. 3-2-4). There is high- and low-order abbreviation of keys as well as abbreviation of TIDs. The variable-length elements of the index are also described by length indicators which specify the original key length and the amount of low-order abbreviation. Jump search is used to reduce the CPU cost of index processing. The lowest index level is linked to maintain seriality.

In addition, a number of practical considerations have been given attention in the design, and we will discuss some of these in detail.

It also is possible to use the structure of VSAM files while bypassing the processing procedures to provide record retrieval by *relative byte addressing* as presented in Chap. 3-3-3. The conversion of record keys to relative byte addresses is a user responsibility. Of interest in this section is only the use of VSAM facilities to obtain indexed-sequential access to variable-length records.

When evaluating the performance of a VSAM file, consider that the unit of data moved from disk to memory is an entire train of blocks rather than just one block. First, the cost of moving a train of sequential blocks has to be estimated; then this result can be used with care in the formulas based on variable-length unspanned blocking; Eqs. 3-20 and 3-21 provide the basic parameters.

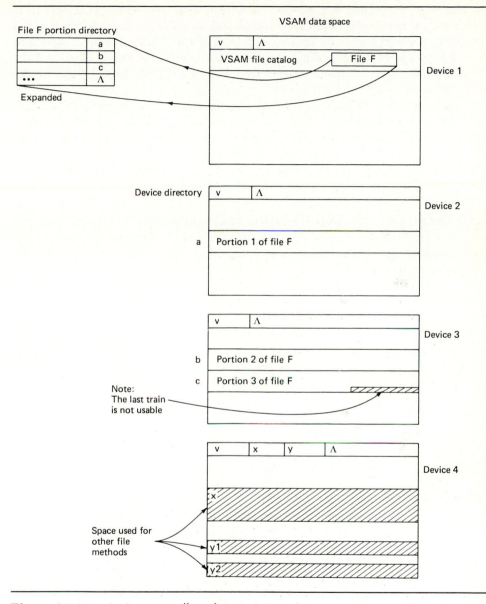

Figure 8-14   VSAM space allocation.

8-5-1 Space Allocation

When a file is established, a large *portion* out of the available disk space is allocated to the file based on estimated future file-space requirements. The intent of such a *bulk allocation* is to keep the records closely together, so that the locality within a portion of a file is high.

When all the trains in a portion have been used, but space for a new train is required. a new portion will be allocated and an entry for this portion inserted at the top level of the VSAM B-tree; this level is called the *directory*. The first (low-order) half of the trains will be copied to the newly allocated portion, and the space freed from the trains moved will be put in a list (see Chap. 10-4-3) of free trains for reuse in the original portion.

The new portion is also obtained by a bulk allocation, but it may be smaller. It will not necessarily be close to the old portion. Benefits of locality are important for sequential processing of the data, and if the number of portions are small, will be obtained. These benefits of locality will of course be lost when other users intersperse file requests on the same device. A disadvantage of bulk allocation is that substantial storage space may be unused if the file size and growth is not well estimated.

ALLOCATION AND RECORD MANAGEMENT

ALLOCATION AND RECORD MANAGEMENT   Allocation of portions is controlled by a directory specific to VSAM. The allocation of trains within the portions is also done using the B-tree algorithm. The blocking and insertion of records into trains exploits markers to reduce indexing effort. The loading density can be negatively affected by the number of B-tree levels. The code complexity is high, so that VSAM requires unusually much CPU effort.

Directory   A directory to the allocated portions is kept as part of an entry for every VSAM file in a VSAM file catalog. The directory is limited to 256 entries. A possible allocation is shown in Fig. 8-14. The size of the allocation to the initial and to any further portions is determined by the expected maximum file size, as estimated from parameters given at the original file definition time. These parameters also are kept in the file catalog entry. The entire catalog contains many file descriptions and is itself a VSAM file.

Blocking   VSAM uses the *train* concept presented in Sec. 3-3-1 to achieve blocking. Each train has a fixed number of blocks, also determined at the time of initial allocation, and is treated as one logical unit. Within a portion there will be space for a number of trains. Some of these may be in use; others may be free. Trains in use contain a variable number of records.

The records may be of variable length and may span blocks within a train. A partially filled train is shown in Fig. 8-15. The actual data records are packed into the forward area of the train; the 3-byte markers giving the length of these records are stored in reverse order in the rear of the train. Adjoining records of equal size are controlled by a single double-sized marker. A control field for the entire train gives the amounts of space used by the markers and left free.

Record Insertion   The free space in a train can be used to insert records and position information without requiring index manipulation. The new record is merged into its proper position. Some shifting within the train will nearly always take place to achieve this. The markers may have to be shifted, too. Since they contain only the length, old markers retain their values.

If there is insufficient space in the train, a free train will be requisitioned. The B-tree algorithm is carried out in three steps, performed in a sequence which reduces vulnerability of the data in case of system malfunction.

1   The records comprising the first half of the full train are copied into
    the new train, and the new train is written out to disk.
2   The index is updated to include the new train at the appropriate point;
    the last record provides the key value for the index entry.
3   The old train is adjusted by shifting the latter half of the records to
    the front, and this train is rewritten.

During this sequence, the record which was to be added is put into the correct
position, and the length markers are set for the old and the new train.

We already have discussed the measures taken when there is no free train in
the portion, so that a new portion has to be allocated. Both overflow handling
algorithms are B-tree based; they differ mainly in terms of the size of the units that
are being manipulated.

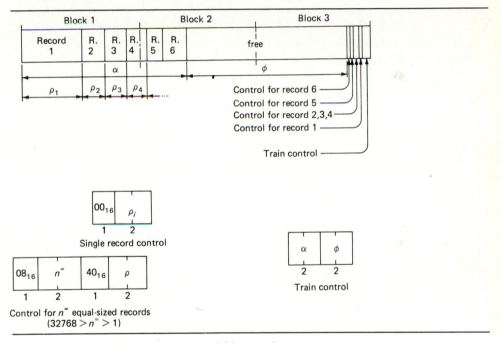

Figure 8-15   Record allocation within a train.

Loading Density To allow updating of the files without immediately forcing the
splitting of trains and portions, the initial file density is specified at < 1. Here
the B-tree algorithm is used for an indexed sequential file, trading space to avoid
deterioration of performance due to insertions. Reorganization is not normally
needed.

A file which undergoes much updating will eventually achieve an equilibrium
similar to the equilibrium conditions described in Eq. 3-47. We used the result that
space utilization will approach 69% so that we expect the trains eventually to be
69% occupied. In addition, there will be some storage loss from unused trains in
portions.

The directory to the trains in one portion provides for the allocation of initial free trains. Trains which are freed are made available for reuse only within the same portion, so that here also a space utilization of 69% is expected when equilibrium conditions are reached. It will take a very long time to achieve this equilibrium, since portions will not be split frequently if the initial loading density and train allocation was generous. However, a specific portion can overflow while there is yet much space in all but one of the trains.

If trains are initially filled to 60% and portions to 90%, the initial storage utilization will be $0.60 \cdot 0.90 = 54\%$. After a number of updates equal to 40% of the initial loading, the storage utilization will be $1.40 \cdot 0.54 = 75\%$. This is the expected density for the trains under random insertions only. For this case we can expect that now many trains are filled, but also that little portion overflow has yet occurred. Beyond this point portions will overflow more frequently, and the portions will also achieve this density. Eventually the total storage density will approach the limit of $0.75 \cdot 0.75 \rightarrow 0.5625$, or 56%. If insertions and deletions both occur at high rates, the eventual equilibrium density may become as low as $0.69 \cdot 0.69 \rightarrow 48\%$.

If better utilization of space in a highly dynamic environment is desired, a reorganization can be used to reload the file to a desired density.   ▦

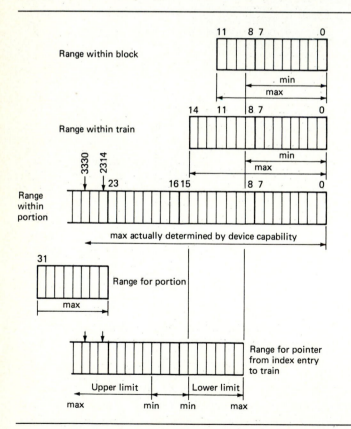

Figure 8-16   The components of the relative byte address.

8-5-2 Addressing

A relative address space is set up for every file. The address begins with the initial portion and continues through all further portions allocated to the file. The components used to construct the address are shown in Fig. 8-16. The size of some of the components is established for the life of the file, using estimates of future file size which are provided by the user or estimated by the system at file-creation time.

If no records are inserted, deleted, or replaced by records of differing size, the relative address of a record will remain the same. Such addresses then can be used to access data records in a VSAM file directly. The addresses are used in an extension of VSAM to provide multiple indexes. A primary file will contain the actual data records, and secondary files have lower-level entries which refer to the records of the primary file.

Relative addresses can be obtained by a program as a by-product of any operation on a record of the file to enable such usage. With relative addressing, sequential access can be carried out more rapidly. Any change of record arrangements due to updates or insertions will, however, invalidate such addresses.

LIMITS   Any implementation of a file has limits. Many limits here are related to the assignment of components of the relative address used for pointing, as shown in Fig. 8-16. The size of the entire address is limited to 32 bits, so that the size of a file is limited to $2^{32} \approx 4.29 \cdot 10^9$ bytes. A portion is limited to one device. Up to 256 portions may be allocated, so that a file has to grow by substantial increments if it is not to run out of portions. Blocks may be {512, 1024, 2048, or 4096} bytes long, and a train is limited to a total of 32 768 bytes. The size of a record is limited to the space available in one train. There are some other implementation limits to allow simple fixed sizes for the marker fields seen in Fig. 8-15.

8-5-3 Index Manipulation

A multilevel index is used to access the data records. The index is considered to be a separate but related file. The index entries at the lowest level point to the beginning of the train, but the value associated with each index entry is the highest or last value in the train. Every train in a portion has an index entry, but entries for free trains do not have a key value and are collected at the end of the index. The assignment of fields within a single index train is given in Fig. 8-17. The index entries in a train are grouped into sections to permit a jump search algorithm to accelerate the search within a block. In order to appreciate the issues addressed in a specific B-tree implementation, we will describe the VSAM index in more detail.

LEVELS   We indicated earlier that the number of index levels, x, is fixed for a VSAM file. Three levels are easily identifiable; the grouping of index entries into sections provides intermediate levels. It is convenient to regard $x = 3$.

If the file uses multiple portions, the level 1 index will be split into corresponding pieces. In the example in Fig. 8-18 these pieces have been located adjacent to the corresponding data portions, which can help to obtain good performance. Locating the pieces of the index on separate devices or on devices with a smaller access time than the data can increase the fetch performance even more. One candidate is the IBM 3880, with its fixed head option, as listed in Table 3-1.

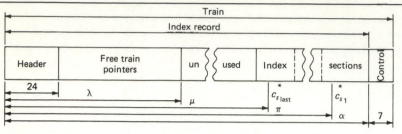

Complete index record

The header describes the remainder of the train format.

Header contents

The base value for data trains δ is 0 in all but the lowest-level index since all other indexes are kept within one portion ϵ is the pointer to the next index train

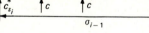

The size of the pointer field γ is always 3 except for the lowest-level index, where
$$\gamma = 1, 2, \text{ or } 3$$
Free train pointer

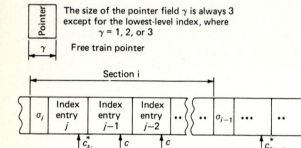

Section of index entries

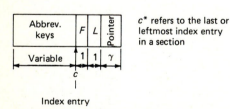

Index entry

c^* refers to the last or leftmost index entry in a section

Figure 8-17   Components of an index record.

The next higher index level (2) provides at the same time information regarding the location of the allocated disk portions and the indexes. It encompasses the portion directory discussed in Sec. 8-5-1.

If a portion is split, a new level 1 index is built for the new portion, the old index is changed to indicate the trains that are now free, and one new entry is made in the second-level index. Since there is a limit of 256 portions, index level 2 is limited to 256 entries, and one third (x) level block provides the root. If the root block is frequently referenced, the paging scheme should keep this block in memory, providing fast access.

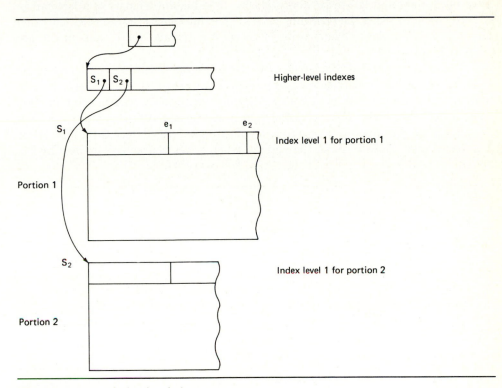

Figure 8-18   Index levels in VSAM.

⌗⌗⌗⌗ **BLOCKING OF THE INDEX**   The index file uses trains of a size appropriate to its own needs. One index record appears to fill one train completely, but within each record there are three types of fields: a header, entries for free trains, and index entries. There may be unused space between the two variable-length areas to allow for changes in the contents of the index record. Figure 8-17 shows the various components of an index record.

The index entries are again stored from right to left within an index record. They are grouped into a number of sections to reduce the index search time. The significance of the various fields is indicated through the matching Greek-letter symbols. In order to read or write programs to interface with the file structure at this level of detail, the reference manuals should be used.   ⌗⌗⌗⌗

KEY ABBREVIATION   Since VSAM deals with general keys, often long names, effective abbreviation of keys is necessary to have a fanout which can address all records in a file using only the fixed three levels. Figure 8-19 shows a set of keys and how they would appear in abbreviated form.

⧼⧼⧼⧼ **Key Abbreviation Algorithm** The key abbreviation of VSAM algorithm uses two length indicators, each of fixed size, to describe the extent of abbreviation. The first field (F) indicates the number of characters omitted from the high-order part of the key, and the second field (L) indicates the number of characters remaining after both high- and low-order abbreviation. The high-order part of a key can be reconstructed by using the preceding entries. The initial entry establishes the range for the first data block. The F value of the first entry and the L value of the last entry will always be zero.

The low-order part is reconstructed with highest possible values in the character collating sequence. For clarity we assume this character to be "Z". All records to be inserted subsequently with keys from the begin value to the reconstructed boundary value for the first train (BEZ... in the figure) will be added to this first train. The boundaries for all subsequent trains are similarly established once the abbreviation has been done. Note that, in the entries, when fewer characters are required to define the next entry, the size of the actual key entry will be zero.

Source Key	Key	F	L	Remarks			
BADE	BA	0	2	Begin value			
BERRINGER	E	1	1	First train:	BAA....	to	BEZ....
BIGLEY	I	1	1	Second train:	BFA....	to	BIZ....
BRESLOW	RES	1	3	Third train:	BJA....	to	BRESZ..
BRETSHNEV	T	3	1	Fourth train:	BRETA..	to	BRETZ..
BRODY	O	2	1	Fifth train:	BREUA..	to	BROZ...
BRUCKNER	none	2	0	Sixth train:	BRPA...	to	BRZ....
BUHLER	U	1	1	Seventh train:	BSA....	to	BUZ....
CALHOUN	CALH	0	4	Eighth train:	BVA....	to	CALHZ..
CALL	none	3	0	Ninth train:	CALIA..	to	CALZ...
CROSS	none	1	0	Tenth train:	CAMA...	to	CAZ....

Figure 8-19   VSAM key abbreviation.

This example shows the abbreviations as if there were only one record per data train. In practice, one extreme record per train is chosen as an anchor. The anchor in VSAM is the immediate successor record, that is, the first record in the next train. Otherwise it could not be determined if a reference to "BIGLOW" would be an existing entry in the third train or a new entry in the second train.

When the index is used, the entries have to be searched serially. The number of matching high-order characters is counted. If the number of characters provided in the index is equal to the number matched, the proper index entry has been found. A proper match occurs also when the search-argument character in the current position is smaller than the matching index-entry key character, or if the index key entry is abbreviated so that no further key character is available.   ⧼⧼⧼⧼

INDEX SEARCH   The number of index entries within a train, y, can be substantial, and the basic procedure to reconstruct the keys for matching is very time-consuming. In order to reduce the search time, a jump search, as described in Sec. 8-3-3, is implemented, leading to $cix = \sqrt{y}$ (Eq. 8-4). The index entries within one train are grouped initially into $\sqrt{y}$ sections. After insertions and deletions the sizes of the sections may differ from this optimum.

The key for the last index entry in each section, the section key $c^*_{s_j}$ of Fig. 8-17, is abbreviated less, to permit reconstruction for jumping from the preceding section key $c^*_{s_{j-1}}$. The first search pass uses this section key and skips from one to the next section using the section length indicator, σ_j, to find the proper section. When the section has been found, a search pass for the appropriate entry is restricted within that section. This additional pseudolevel does not require repeated entries of the key or TIDs, only a reduced key abbreviation for the section keys.

▦▦ **TIDs** The referencing TIDs are also abbreviated. The index pointers on level 1 to the data trains include only the displacement within a portion in terms of trains. For instance, if there are 300 trains in one portion, $\gamma = \lceil 300/2^8 \rceil = 2$ 8-bit bytes suffice for the pointer entry. To calculate the byte address of the train, the contents of the pointer field is multiplied by the train size and the beginning address of the portion δ is added. ▦▦

8-5-4 Sequential Access

In VSAM the index has to be read to process the data trains serially. To obtain high-performance serial access, the use of higher levels of the index is avoided. The linkage pointer (ϵ) is used to locate successive lowest-level index trains, and the data trains are fetched using the TIDs of the index entries.

After many dynamic changes of a VSAM file the trains will no longer be in a physical sequence. Within each train, however, the record sequence has been maintained. For large trains fewer seeks are required, but the train size is limited in practice because of buffer capacity and the relative addressing scheme. A file with portions covering multiple cylinders will have its trains distributed over this space, so that seeks during serial access still can add substantially to the time required to read the file.

▦▦ **Locality Control** There are some optional features to increase search performance through improved locality. One of these features allows replication of the index on a track of a rotating device so that the average rotational latency for reading of the index can be reduced. Other options provide for the close location of index file components and the data file itself to minimize seek times. Index and data can also be placed on separate devices to provide overlap of access. This is especially useful when processing the file serially. ▦▦

8-5-5 Programming

Programmers who use a file-access method can operate on one of three levels:
1. They can write instructions to manipulate the file on the basis of understanding the logical functions to be executed.
2. They can attempt to also understand the underlying physical structure in order to produce programs that are efficient within the perceived system environment.

3 They can use attractive features of the file system and attempt to bypass or disable parts of the file-system support which do not suit them, and replace these parts with programs of their own invention.

Each of these choices has associated costs and benefits, and the decisions should be made based on documented evaluations of the trade-offs which were considered. The cost of the first alternative may be inadequate performance and the cost of the third alternative may be intolerable inflexibility.

A philosophy in structured programming, *information hiding*, advocates the imposition of the first approach by not revealing the underlying structure of system programs. This is sometimes unintentionally aided by the lack of clear system documentation. The author prefers to work with a good knowledge of the available tools and use them to a maximal extent.

When programming tools are inadequate and have to be rejected, good documention of the reasons will help successors maintain the programs and may also give guidance to the developers of newer tools. It is hard to induce from a description of a new system what the problems were that led to rejection of prior systems or other design alternatives.

STATEMENTS   The operations that are basic to the use of VSAM and similar methods include the following statements.

1 An OPEN statement is to be issued before the file can be processed. The OPEN statement is used to specify the file name, the type of operations to be performed, and, optionally, a *password* to be verified. The OPEN statement also specifies the area or areas where the parameters for further processing requests will be found. The catalog, the file listing all files, will be searched to locate the file. The device or devices which contain index and data will be accessed and directory information extracted. A check to ensure the use of the right versions of the index files and the data file is made by matching the contents of a field in each file directory which contains the most recent update times. Buffer storage for file processing also is obtained and initialized.

2 A CLOSE statement is used to indicate that processing of the file is completed. The CLOSE statement empties any outstanding buffers and updates the file directory.

3 A GET statement is used to read data from the file. Before its execution the search argument and other parameters are placed into a parameter area which specifies what is to be read. The parameters to be set for indexed access include the key value and indicate whether an exact or a less-than-or-equal match is desired. The position and length of the area into which the record is to be placed have to be specified. An area for receiving error messages should also be provided. A further parameter states whether the process will wait until the reading is completed. Otherwise the process can continue computation while the system executes the GET process asynchronously. The calling process can check later if the system process is complete. The length and address of the record read will be placed into the parameter list upon completion.

4 The advantage of using a separate fixed area for the parameter list is that only parameters that change have to be respecified when the next GET is issued. To

provide more flexibility of operation, it is possible to generate new or to modify existing request parameter areas during program execution by means of GENCB and MODCB statements.

5 The PUT statement initiates the writing of a record, again using parameters contained in the specified parameter area. When writing, the length of the record has to be set into the parameter list prior to execution of the statement. The parameter area can be separate since its address is specified as part of a GET or PUT operation.

6 The ERASE statement causes deletion of the indicated record.

7 The POINT statement provides a capability to reset the current-record TID for serial GET and PUT statements.

8 The CHECK statement is used to determine whether a previous asynchronous operation has been completed.

9 The ENDREQ statement can be used to terminate an outstanding request. This will cancel an operation which is no longer desirable, perhaps because of a detected error or because a parallel operation has delivered the desired data already.

▦ **ESCAPE PROCEDURES** Optional parameters allow the specification of program segments which are to be executed when the file system performs certain operations or senses certain conditions in the file. One use of these escape procedures is to compress or expand data records to save file space. Others can be used when End-of-file conditions occur. Considerable modification of the basic operations is possible when these escape hatches or exits are used.

These facilities are also exploited to create multi-indexed files within VSAM. Upon insertion of a record into the data or primary file an escape procedure will initiate updating of all secondary indexes.

The programmer who uses escape procedures has access to all the options and the underlying code at the same structural level. Now the distinction between the three levels of programming described above is not very explicit, and good intentions can easily come to naught. Programs which are invoked as escape procedures may introduce errors which are not visible when the program which invokes the file services is checked out. These escape hatches can also easily be misused to violate system security. ▦

8-6 SUMMARY

We have treated index structures in great detail. We find that bringing the conceptually simple index structure into practice requires much knowledge and many trade-offs. If an existing indexed access method is used, much work can be accomplished without understanding the details, but when performance becomes an issue or when the records or access patterns are irregular, an understanding of the underlying structure can make much difference.

In databases alternative index methods may be available. The method detailed in Sec. 8-5 is but one of the file systems used for database support on large IBM systems. This material should help in setting database parameters for efficient operation.

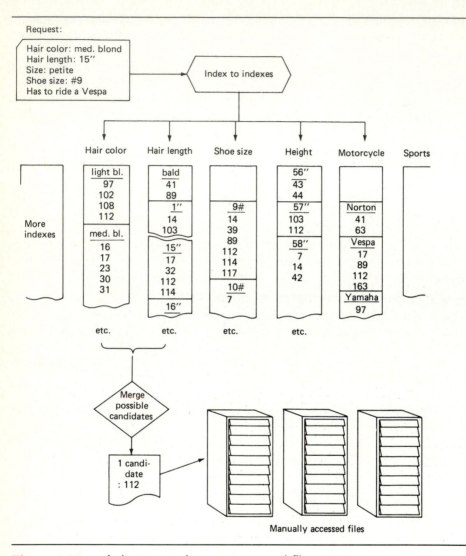

Request:

Hair color: med. blond
Hair length: 15"
Size: petite
Shoe size: #9
Has to ride a Vespa

Index to indexes

Hair color   Hair length   Shoe size   Height   Motorcycle   Sports

light bl.   bald   56"
97   41   43
102   89   44
108   1"   9#   57"   Norton
112   14   14   103   41
More   103   39   112   63
indexes   med. bl.   89   Vespa
16   15"   112   58"   17
17   17   114   7   89
23   32   117   14   112
30   112   10#   42   163
31   114   7   Yamaha
               16"   97

etc.   etc.   etc.   etc.

Merge
possible
candidates

1 candi-
date
: 112

Manually accessed files

Figure 8-20   Indexes to a phantom or manual file.

8-6-1 Phantom Files

To illustrate the power of indexes we present an example where the indexes contain
all the information, and the data file becomes a *phantom*. We noted earlier that
the key information in an index duplicates information in the file records. Having
indexes for all attributes duplicates the entire file.

　　　If this information is not needed as goal data when the record is accessed via
other paths, the indexed attributes do not have to be kept in the goal records
themselves. This data may still be stored on an inactive backup file so that it
remains available for periodic regeneration of the index. If many fields are handled

in this manner, a large portion of the goal file will not exist in active storage. We will refer to data which is used only for accessing, but is not available for result generation, as *phantom* data.

Requests for goal data using multiple attributes can be resolved completely within the indexes by matching addresses of the goal records. Such an application is shown in Fig. 8-20, which is an example taken from a file system designed for a casting agency selecting models for TV advertisements.

If all goal data is kept only in indexed form, the entire file has become a phantom file. Files approaching this design have been called fully inverted files in the literature.

Another case of a phantom file can be found in bibliographic indexing. Searches through indexes are made using logical combinations of request parameters which in the end produce a set of call numbers for books. The call numbers are equivalent to the TIDs of the goal data. The goals are the books on the shelves of the library. A library which would always be accessed in this manner could store its books according to considerations other than the sequentiality of subject codes. If, instead of call numbers, the system would provide the actual shelf number and position, then books could be stored according to size, to minimize space used, or according to frequency of access, to minimize retrieval time. Browsing in such a library would be less productive but more surprising. Currently, such optimizations are, in practice, restricted to computer files.

8-6-2 Further References to Indexes

Subsequent chapters will also consider specialized aspects of indexes. For instance, in Chap. 9-2-3 we will describe R-trees, a version of B-trees adapted to geometric data. Issues of reliability, privacy and integrity protection also affect decision made about index design. These will be touched upon in Chap. 14.

BACKGROUND AND REFERENCES

Many specifics of index implementations are gleaned from manuals or implementors. Lefkovitz[74] presents a variety of index-organization techniques. The technique of pre-splitting is due to Guibas[78]. Deferred updating is analyzed by Sarin[86]. McCreight[77] considers the effect of paging and Huang[85] constrains B-trees further to improve their performance.

Index abbreviation is analyzed by Hu[71] and Wagner[73]. How to deal with range queries is addressed by Willard[85].

Tries were described by Fredkin[60] and analyzed by Knuth[73s]. Rathmann[84] uses them for WORMS. Burkhard in Kerr[75] and Litwin[81t] look at tries and direct access. Comer[81] developed a heuristic for trie minimization.

The number of block accesses to retrieve many records is accurately predicted by Yao[77], and Whang[81] developed a computationally feasible formula which is accurate in the practical ranges. Cheung[82] and Luk[83] present alternatives. A dynamic clustering algorithm to minimize block accesses is given by Yu[85]. Nievergelt[74], and Bayer[76] consider access frequencies. The trade-offs in blocking factors are analyzed by March[77] and Nevaleinen[77].

Detailed specifications for VSAM can be found in various IBM manuals. A description of its design is given by Wagner[73], Keehn[74] explains the effect of its parameters, while Bouros[85] is a reference for the application programmer and Atkinson[83] focuses on converting from ISAM. Its storage allocation is discussed by Chin in Kerr[75] and optimized by Schkolnick[77]. Allgeyer[87] uses an expert system to help in file configuration. Reorganization intervals are estimated by Maruyama[76]. This file system is the basis for much database development where IBM equipment is used.

Wong[71], Files[69], Burkhard[76,79], Chang[82], and Rivest[76] present partial-match hashing schemes from early to late binding. Before proposed techniques can be adopted, it is necessary to verify that they are applicable to the scale of the intended application. Some interesting techniques require exponentially increasing resources as the file size becomes greater.

Bibliographic systems as described by Lancaster[79] have phantom goal data.

EXERCISES

1   Evaluate the three alternatives shown in Sec. 8-1-2 of handling critical retrieval operations in terms of response time and additional CPU time needed. Assume retrieval access interferes with updates in progress for the entire file 50% of the time, with the specific index 10% of the time, and with the specific record 1% of the time. Assume five indexes are actively being updated, each with 20 records. Time to complete an index update is 1 s. and CPU time for one comparison 1 ms.. Ignore all other CPU cost.

2   Apply the four techniques of key abbreviation illustrated in Sec. 8-2-2 on all the blocks of Fig. 8-5.

3   Devise a method for implicit high-order key-segment deletion. Illustrate the effect on the example given in Fig. 8-2.

4   Write a program to produce full keys given the abbreviated text of Fig. 8-5, starting at the beginning of any index block, selecting markers where needed.

5   Write a program to produce full keys that can start at any entry of Fig. 8-6.

6   Estimate the average search time for a record in a multi-indexed file according to one search key using:

   a   Conventional multi-indexed organization

   b   Abbreviated keys

   c   Tree-structured files

Parameters for the evaluation are:

Block size $B = 2000$ characters	Full key size $V = 20$ characters
Record size $R = 200$ "	Pointer size $P = 8$ "
Number of records $n = 100\,000$ characters	Abbreviation factor for keys 50%
Time to seek and read one block $T_B = 50$ ms	

Assume a uniform key distribution. Document all other assumptions.

7   Prove the statement in Sec. 8-3-4, that the number of empty pointer fields in binary index trees is $y + 1$ (Fig. 8-10).

Chapter 9

Alternate File Organizations

Balyard had stopped off at the local personnel office for the name of a representative American in the neighborhood.
The personnel machines had considered the problem and ejected the card of E. R. B. Hagstrohm, who was statistically average in every respect save for the number of his initials: his age (36), his height (5' 7"), his weight (148 lbs.), his years of marriage (11), his I.Q. (83), the number of his children (2: 1 m.9; 1 f.6), his car (3 yr. old Chev. 2 dr. sed.), the number of his bedrooms (2), his education (h.s.grad., 117th in a class of 233...)

Kurt Vonnegut, Jr.
Player Piano.

9-0   INTRODUCTION

In this chapter we show alternative methods of organizing files. These file designs can satisfy requirements that are not fulfilled by the basic methods or their combinations.

Section 9-1 presents transposition, an approach to structure files by attribute, appropriate when files are used for data analysis. In Sec. 9-2 tree-structured files are presented, leading to hierarchical files with an example in Sec. 9-3. The final section discusses files based on virtual storage.

The information presented in this chapter is more diverse than the contents of other chapters. The underlying principles are still the same. Little formal analysis will be applied to these techniques, but Sec. 9-2-4 includes a comparison of the performance of tree-structured files versus indexed-sequential and B-tree indexed files. Many techniques improve the data-retrieval capability by adding redundancy, but this increases the amount of space required and makes updates more difficult. The aggregate performance of a system depends on the balance of update and retrieval usage, and will be presented in Chap. 14.

9-1   TRANSPOSED FILES

In some applications, frequently all values of a given attribute are required. For instance, to compute the `average height` the height field from all employee records must be accessed. To generate this single result requires that, in any of the file organizations presented up to now, all records are accessed. The delay (T_X) will seem excessive to the user of the transaction. Similar operations are needed to find other statistical descriptors as `MAX`, `MIN`, `AVERAGE`, `VARIANCE` of single attributes. The costly operation may not be obvious:

> "Give 'managers' a raise of '10'%,
> but make it at least equal to the MAX of their employees."

The simple change to the transaction shown first in Fig. 2-5, made by adding a constraint to the amount of the raise, means that now exhaustive reading is needed. The transaction cost grows from $\mathcal{O}(r \log n)$ to $\mathcal{O}(n)$. Most statistical queries are characterized as having to access all or many records, but they require only one or a few values from each of the records. Exhaustive reading is slow, so that statistical analyses were only done on-line if the files to be analyzed were quite small. Being forced to batch operations means that fewer alternatives will be explored.

A *transposed file*, as shown in Fig. 9-1, which stores data stored by attribute, provides a solution to the problem of retrieval performance. A transposed file contains one record per transposed attribute type from the main file, and each record has a number of data values which is equal to the number of records in the source file. If all attributes are transposed, the transposed file will be equal in size to the source file. Only one record is fetched per attribute from a transposed file, and this record contains the values of this attribute for all entities, e.g., n persons, in the file.

New record number	Field ID	| Original record number										
		1	2	3	4	5	6	7	8	9	10	
1	2	55	39	36	25	27	42	61	36	31	59	Ages
2	3	5'8"	5'6"	5'7"	5'6"	5'11"	5'9"	5'6"	5'7"	5'6"	5'5"	Heights
3	4	95	75	70	49	80	178	169	83	95	145	IQs

Figure 9-1   The personnel file from Fig. 4-11 transposed.

All values in a record of a transposed file are ordered as the source records would have been. The record contents is similar to the lowest level of an exhaustive index, but not reordered. A transposed file stands on its own; it does not contain pointers from the transposed file to any main file.

Use of transposition presents opportunities for the discovery of trends or functional dependencies among attributes which are otherwise not obvious. Many research-oriented data processing tasks will take transposed data and group, select, and correlate the values found.

The processing effort for such long records is significant. The potentially very long records, $R = nV$ for one attribute, require long or multiple buffers. They may exceed the array size limits of conventional analysis programs, although most modern computers have adequate memory space for at least one transposed record. In analyzing large quantities of data the numerical stability or accuracy of the analysis algorithm use must be considered as well. The assumption, made in most other examples, that the computational time can be neglected, is not valid when processing records from transposed files.

Updating of transposed files is difficult. A transposed file is oriented to aid selection or evaluation of data according to a dimension which is orthogonal to the data entry or update dimension. Insertion of the data corresponding to one source record requires accessing all records. Updates are hence always batched, and recent changes are kept on a transaction log file.

If the file is relatively small and storage is affordable, the creation of duplicate data files, one straight and one in transposed form, is the easiest solution to the update problem. Since transposed files are used typically for statistical purposes, the updating or re-creation of the transposed file is then done only periodically. This process is analogous to a file reorganization.

It may be convenient to use a transposed file as input to a program which generates indexes to the source file. To help in creating the TID portion of the entries, the transposed file can contain one record with values of all the source file record positions.

9-1-1 Transposition of a File

The effort needed to transpose a large file with many attributes is great. We assume that neither the source nor the transposed file fits in memory. The most obvious procedure is to construct one transposed record during one exhaustive read of the file. To transpose all of a file in this manner will require a time equal to aT_X, for the a passes over the file. If multiple buffers (*buf*) permit blocks for multiple transposed records to be built up in memory at one time, only $\lceil a/buf \rceil$ passes over the file are required.

More sophisticated algorithms are available. Floyd[74] describes two transposition algorithms which take $\mathcal{O}(\lceil \log_2 w \rceil)$ passes where w is the greater of n or a. The simpler algorithm generates records increasing gradually in size to n; the second algorithm is given as Fig. 9-2 and generates each transposed record as a sequence of pieces of size a and requires only three buffers of that size.

TRANSPOSITION PROGRAM   The program shown as Fig. 9-2 transposes a source file using $\lceil n/a \rceil (2 + \lceil \log_2 a \rceil) a$ fetches and as many insertions. The complexity of this program is hence $\mathcal{O}(n \log_2 a)$. Most of the operations are not sequential and will require a seek. The benefit of this procedure will become substantial when $a/buf \gg 10$.

```
/* Program to transpose a source file of 'n'records of length 'a'.
   The input and output files are sequential.
   The program contains three distinct sections:
       1. Copy groups of 'a'records to a work file, resequencing
   all but the first record of a group in inverse order.
   Values in these records are circularly shifted so that the
   first column elements form a diagonal.
   The last group is padded with zeroes.
       2. Record pairs within groups are selected, and within each
   pair alternate entries are transferred to rotate columns by
   1,2,4,8,.. using powers of two in log2(a) passes per group.
       3. When all groups are rearranged, the work file is copied,
   shifting each record to the final position in the output file.
                                                                  */
file_transpose: PROCEDURE(source,transposed,n,a);
          DECLARE(source,transposed,work) FILE;
          DECLARE(spacein,spaceout,save)(a);
          DEFAULT RANGE(*) FIXED BINARY;   DECLARE(MOD,MIN)BUILTIN;
       /* The transposition proceeds in groups of 'a' records */
          groups = (n-1)/a+1;   amin1 = a-1;   record_in = 0;
       /* Perform sections 1 and 2 for each group and leave re-  */
g_loop: DO group = 1 TO groups;         /* sults on the work file */
       /* Copy and rearrange a group for permutation */
loop_1:   DO out_rec_pos  =  a TO 1 BY -1;
             IF record_in<n  THEN READ FILE(source) INTO(spacein);
                             ELSE spacein = 0;
             record_in = record_in+1;   base_out = a*(group-1)+1;
       /* Shift records to align columns so that transposition
                               can proceed in parallel blocks */
             CALL movearound(out_rec_pos);
             record_out = MOD(out_rec_pos, a) + base_out;
             WRITE FILE(work) KEYFROM(record_out) FROM(spaceout);
             END loop_1;
       /* Set up number of passes to permute one group */
             order = 1;   order2 = 2;
loop_2:   DO WHILE( order<a );
       /* Permute records by order = 1,2,4,8, ... */
             CALL rearrange(base_out);
             order = order2;   order2 = order*2;
             END loop_2;
          END g_loop;
       /* Now copy the result from each transposed group to the */
loop_3: DO shift = 0 TO amin1;                      /* output file */
       /* Each record contains 'groups' segments of length 'a'*/
   a_loop: DO rec = shift+1 BY a TO base_out-1;
             READ FILE(work) KEY(rec) INTO(spacein);
             CALL movearound(shift);
             WRITE FILE(transposed) FROM(spaceout);
             END a_loop;
          END loop_3;
```

Figure 9-2   Floyd's second transposition algorithm.

```
/*    Dick Karpinski helped with checkout and structuring */
  /* Subprocedures */
   /* Procedure to copy records, elements are circularly shifted */
   movearound: PROCEDURE(move);
            DO i = 1 TO a;     /* note that last (a) precedes 1 */
               j = MOD(i-move-1, a)+1;  spaceout(j) = spacein(i);
            END;
        END movearound;
   /* Procedure to pair alternate records */
   rearrange: PROCEDURE(beg_rec);
    /* The record pairs exchanging data will be:
         pass=1: (last,1),(last-1,last),(last-2,last-1),...;
         pass=2: (last,2),(last-2,last),(last-4,last-2),...;
         pass=3: (last,4),(last-4,last),(last-8,last-4),...;etc. */
            rec_in, rec_save = beg_rec + order;
      /* Loop through all 'a' records in the group */
    t_loop: DO transfer_count = 1 TO a;
               IF rec_in=rec_save
                   THEN DO;  rec_out = rec_in-1;
      /* This record is saved to provide data for its partner */
                      READ FILE(work) KEY(rec_out) INTO(spaceout);
                      save = spaceout;  rec_save = rec_out;
                      END;
                ELSE DO;  rec_out = rec_in;
                      spaceout = spacein;
                      END;
               rec_in = MOD(rec_out+amin1-order, a) + beg_rec;
      /* Use saved record when it comes */
            IF rec_in=rec_save THEN spacein = save;
                   ELSE READ FILE(work) KEY(rec_in) INTO(spacein);
      /* Shift data values from 'spacein' to 'spaceout' */
            CALL transfer;
            WRITE FILE(work) KEYFROM(rec_out) FROM(spaceout);
      /* Terminate when all records have been processed */
            END t_loop;
        END rearrange;
  /* Procedure to move alternate elements in records selected   */
  transfer: PROCEDURE;              /*  by the rearrange procedure */
      /* Elements to be moved from 'spacein' to 'spaceout' are for:
         pass=1, order=1: 2,4,6,8,etc.
         pass=2, order=2: (3,4),(7,8),(11,12),etc.
         pass=3, order=4: (5,6,7,8),(13,14,15,16),etc. */
            DO i = order BY order2 TO amin1;
             limit = MIN(i+order, a);
            DO j = i+1 TO limit;  spaceout(j) = spacein(j);
            END;
        END transfer;
  /* This completes the file transposition program */
    END file_transpose;
```

Figure 9-2   Floyd's second transposition algorithm, continued.

9-2 TREE-STRUCTURED FILES

Up to this point we have discussed indexed organizations where the index was *distinct* from the data portion of the file. In this section, we describe file organizations where the goal portions of records are merged with the index structure into a *tree*. Combining both into one structure saves some space and may simplify programs. We will find that the performance is worse for many practical instances. Since the goal records are placed into a single tree, this organization is akin to the indexed-sequential file. Seriality is established according to only one attribute.

Providing for more than one attribute increases complexity, as shown in Sec. 9-2-3. Section 9-2-4 summarizes the material by comparing the performance of such files with indexed-sequential and indexed files. Section 9-2-5 leaves the forest with a sketch of an implementation of a tree-structured file

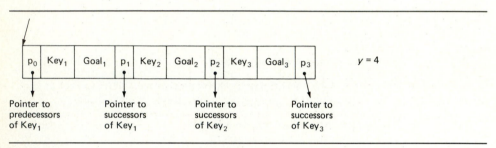

Figure 9-3   A block of a tree-structured file.

9-2-1 Structure of a Tree-Structured File

A block of a tree-structured file is shown in Fig. 9-3 and can be compared with the block of an indexed file shown in Fig. 5-14. The position of the entire record is determined by the position of its key. The tree-structured file organization is seen in Fig. 9-4.

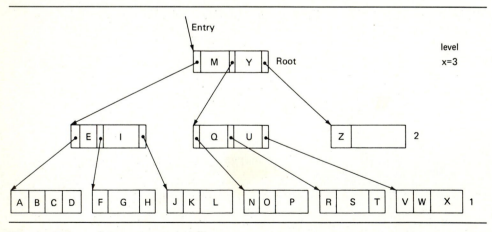

Figure 9-4   A tree-structured file.

Table 9-1   Obtaining records serially from a tree.

```
proceed: go to the left subtree,
              if not terminal block
                   then  →  proceed,
                   else process the records of the terminal block,
              go up to the root for this subtree,
              if there is a record,
                   then do; process the record,
                        go to the next subtree,
                        →  proceed, end;
              else do;
                   if this is the root for the entire file,
                        then  →  done,
                        else  →  proceed, end;
    done:       . . .
```

The process of accessing the records of the file serially is a generalization of *inorder traversal* for binary trees (Knuth[73F]). Table 9-1 sketches the algorithm.

A tree-structured file will be *balanced* if the number of levels is equal or nearly equal for all branches of the tree. Given that record requests are uniformly distributed, a balanced tree will require on the average the least number of block accesses to locate a record.

BALANCING TREES   In order to retain good performance in tree-structured files, it is desirable that the tree be *balanced*. An optimally balanced tree has only path lengths to terminal nodes of size x or of size $x-1$. Inspection of Eq. 9-1, which predicts the search time, will show that any other distribution of the records will lead to higher expected search values.

In tree-structured files the performance of the file can degrade after insertions and deletions are made, since insertions are connected to their ancestors. For instance, insertions of records F1, F2,... in Fig. 9-4 will increase the file height $x \to 4$, and the path length to these records will also be 4.

The strict B-tree algorithm does not need explicit balancing, since here insertions affect eventually the root, and not the terminal leaves. In a B-tree irregularity of insertions and deletions causes a reduction in density and thus longer path lengths, but the effect is bounded by the condition that $y_{eff} \geq y/2$. In tree-structured files balancing has to be done explicitly, either during update operations or by reorganization. Balancing has been extensively analyzed for *binary trees*.

BINARY TREES   A tree where each record contains only one value and two branches ($y = 2$) is of interest for two reasons:
- The structure is appropriate for memory because of its simplicity, and hence is also useful within a block of file storage.
- The behavior of dynamically changing binary trees has been investigated both theoretically and statistically.

A basic record in a tree is called a *node*. Figure 9-5 shows a binary tree equivalent to the file tree of Fig. 9-4.

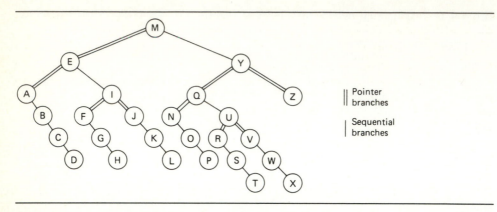

Figure 9-5 Binary tree.

In Fig. 9-5 the file tree has been mapped to a binary tree, while distinguishing sequential branches, implemented by successor nodes in a block, and pointer branches, which connect tree nodes that are not sequential.

Algorithms to keep trees balanced are covered extensively in Knuth[73S], and their performance is presented by Karlton[76]. For certain file trees useful results can be derived from the analyses of binary trees kept in memory, although equal access costs between linked nodes were assumed. When applying these results to file trees, having multiple nodes within one block, one must consider that the access cost along sequential branches in a block is much less than the access cost along pointer branches. Only if the node records are so large that all nodes will reside on distinct blocks will access costs be equal.

MAINTENANCE OF TREES   Tree balancing is done when the file is being updated. Insertion of new records extends the tree, generating new leaf nodes. If space is of concern, then reorganization to reallocate leaf node blocks may be needed. We find that frequent reorganization is needed for tree-structured files.

If a file is reorganized, it can be more efficient to generate a new tree sequentially for each level instead of performing n insertions. The operation on the file is similar to the recreation of the index for an indexed-sequential file, but now the data fields are moved as well. After y_{eff} entries are written into a block for level 1, one entry is taken for level 2, etc. If a certain pattern of growth is expected, the reorganization algorithm can make decisions which will lessen the effect of unbalanced growth. This is easily done when most update activity is expected to occur at the end of the file. On each level some space will be left free for new records.

9-2-2 Evaluation of a Tree-Structured File

The major advantage of this structure is the nonredundancy of storage. The goal record is directly associated with its key. Key fields appear only once, they are not replicated at other levels. An operational benefit of trees is then that keys are stored in only one place, and hence are easier to update.

In the evaluation which follows we assume that the records are densely packed into blocks, although not spanned. Insertion performance would be better if a non-dense B-tree scheme were used, but the reduction in density reduces the effectiveness of the tree structure.

We find goal records at all levels of the tree. The number of block accesses needed to obtain records differs as well. Records residing near the root block are accessed rapidly. This benefit is shown in Fig. 9-4, where some records (7 out of 26) are closer to the root and hence easier to retrieve.

A disadvantage of the tree-structured file is that the fanout can be significantly reduced versus the fanout of an index so that many more seeks may be required to retrieve an average record of a large file. The effect of poor fanout will outweigh the reduction in access path for high-level records unless the goal records are quite small. This happens when a tree file is used itself as an index, but then another access is required to access the data file.

The difference in the expected number of block accesses of tree files versus indexed files depends on the ratio of key sizes to goal record sizes, which controls the change of the fanout. If the goal attributes are as small as the pointers in an indexed file, the fanout ratio is equal and the tree file is faster.

Records of tree files can be of variable length, since the access algorithms do not depend on a specific number of records per block. In order to simplify the analysis, an average value for R will be used below. The results will be close if there are many records per block ($R \ll B$).

By inspection of Fig. 9-3 we find for the fanout ratio of the tree

$$y = \left\lfloor \frac{B-P}{R+P} \right\rfloor + 1 \qquad\qquad 9\text{-}1$$

Even though the lowest level does not require further pointers, space for such pointers is frequently allocated, since this simplifies further growth of the file. Then the fanout ratio y is the same at level 1.

We assume now that the file is filled at the top levels ($x, \ldots, 2$). This minimizes the sum of all the access paths to the data. The number of records at each level is again determined by the number of blocks on a level and by the fanout ratio. Note that here, as with the original B-tree, the number of records in a block is one less than the fanout.

$$n_{level=x} = y-1; \; n_{level} = (y-1)b_{level} = (y-1)y\,b_{level+1} = y\,n_{level+1} = y^{x-level}(y-1)$$

If the tree is balanced, only the bottom level (1) will be partially filled; it will contain the remaining records, computed by subtracting the records on levels $x \rightarrow 2$ from the total file size n

$$n_1 = n - (y-1)\sum_{i=x}^{2} y^{x-i}$$

We assume at least a two-level tree here, i.e., $n > y - 1$. To find the number of levels in the tree, we follow Eq. 5-26. For $y \gg 1$ an estimate for x is

$$x_{est} = \lceil \log_y n \rceil \qquad\qquad 9\text{-}2$$

The exact height of the tree can be obtained by summing the number of records at the successive levels $n_{level=x}, n_{x-1}, \ldots$, and stopping when all records are stored.

The fetch time in a tree structure varies by level, so that the average is not determined by the integer height of the tree, as were the indexes shown earlier. The expected, i.e., average, fetch time can be computed by taking the fetch time for the n_{level} records at each level and allocating the sum to the n records in the file. The access path increases from 1 for $level = x$ to x for the bottom level, and this accounts for the first factor $(1 + x - level)$ in the summation below

$$T_F = \frac{s + r + btt}{n} \left((y - 1) \sum_{level=x}^{2} (1 + x - level)\, y^{x-level} + x\, n_1 \right) \qquad \text{9-3}$$

Also, if the tree itself is used as an index, the pointers in the tree to the remote goal data can exist at various levels. The smooth curve in Fig. 8-13 is hence appropriate to describe the fetch time to fanout relationship seen here.

9-2-3 Multidimensional Trees

The restriction of having only one access path to data has often been attacked and a number of variant tree structures have been developed. Few have seen practical use; it appears difficult to improve on multi-indexed files using B-trees.

MULTIATTRIBUTE INDEX TREES   In order to handle more than one attribute in a tree a variety of structures which discriminate according to a different attribute on successive levels has been proposed. The K-d tree (Chang[81]) is a development for external storage. The tree is expected to be used as an index.

Given K attributes to be used for retrieval, we arrange the root level index block as a binary tree, similar to Fig. 9-5. The first entry (M) discriminates based on the first attribute, the two successor entries (E, Y) each on the second attribute, etc. The entries after K comparisons discriminate on the Kth attribute. After the Kth discriminant the scheme restarts with attribute 1, until all the TIDs are accounted for. This pattern continues over all x levels of the index tree. This internal binary index structure will hence have a height $X = log_2 n$, distributed over x levels of index blocks.

Since K attributes are used for discrimination the selectivity of an individual attribute will be less by a factor K. This technique can be related to the catenated key hashing technique seen in Chap. 7-3-5. The leaf entries partition the records based on all K attributes. If rapid access for range queries is desired, the data blocks may follow that partitioning.

When the file is used for retrieval, search is simple when all K attributes are specified in the search. If some attributes are not known then their internal index level provides no discrimination and both successor entries must be followed. In general, if partial-match queries are incomplete, we must also expect to access multiple data blocks.

Insertions affect the entire subtree, since a new value requires a leaf entry. Keeping blocks partially full, as done with a B-tree, can reduce the number of blocks accessed as the X attributes are added into the x blocks. When an index page overflows it is split. A new discriminating value must be selected at the split level, and two new entries accommodated at the next level. In experiments with uniformly distributed data, the discriminators were chosen to be the median value. For practical files with reasonable fanout, K is expected to be small.

INDEXING FOR GEOMETRIC OBJECTS   Geometric objects are characterized by having multiple dimensions. Solid objects can be characterized in Euclidean geometry by a lower and a higher value in each dimension, bounding the object. *R-trees* (Guttman[84]) are index trees which have in each entry a pair of bounds for each dimension. Entries for proximate objects, that is, objects at minimal distances, are grouped into blocks. At level 2 and above the entries contain the bounds for the collection of objects defined in the lower level blocks being referenced.

The search argument is typically a range interval as well. Since it is possible for adjacent entries to overlap, it can be neccessary, even when searching for a single point, to follow more than one descendant entry to its blocks. If the data are well structured, the number of paths to be followed reduces rapidly. If the objects overlap, or are complex or curved, then it is likely that many objects must be investigated. Access to the actual data is needed, since objects may not fill their rectilinear boundaries.

For insertion a single path has to be chosen: The entry which needs no, or the least, expansion of its bounds to handle the new object. Finding this node is costly, and heuristics are used to find an adequate candidate rapidly. To improve update performance the blocks, as in B-trees, are partially filled. Splitting may be needed, and requires a recomputation to determine the boundary values of the two new entries at the superior level. Deletion requires checking if now the superior bounds can be reduced. Block deletion may also be triggered but blocks to be combined are not restricted to neighbors. The best combination is the one that yields the least increase in superior entry boundaries. Update of the size fields of a record requires deletion and insertion of entries in the R-tree.

9-2-4 A Comparison

We now compare the retrieval performance of tree-structured and similar B- tree indexed and densely indexed files. A dense index is as encountered in an indexed-sequential file. The tree-structured file (alternative **1**) uses blocks densely and will hence be much harder to update than the B-tree file of alternative **2**. The dense index of an indexed-sequential file (alternative **3**) is hence more comparable with the tree structure and may perform better in retrieval than a B-tree.

Since the size of the goal record is an important parameter for trees, we consider for each type of file two cases: (**a**) short, and (**b**) long records. In case **a** we assume that an `employee` record contains only a key, the `social security number` of nine characters (V_K), and a goal field, a `skill code` of six characters (V_G), so that $R = 15$. In case **b** we use a still modest record length of $R = 180$ characters.

For the remaining parameters we will use values as were used in the example of a personnel file given in the example of Fig. 5-16 of Chap. 5-4-1.

We compare accessing three file types according to one key attribute.
The required parameters are $R_a = 15$; $R_b = 180$ characters; for both cases $n = 20\,000$ records, $B = 1\,000$ characters, $P = 4$ characters.

1   Tree-structured file

For the tree-structured file we assume a dense packing of records, and use Eqs. 9-1, 9-2, and 9-3. To verify that x_{est} is indeed equal to x, we also present the contents of each level of the files.

Case a

$$y = \left\lfloor \frac{1000-4}{15+4} \right\rfloor + 1 = 53$$

$$x_{est} = \lceil \log_{53} 20\,000 \rceil = \lceil 2.49 \rceil = 3$$

Case b

$$y = \left\lfloor \frac{1000-4}{180+4} \right\rfloor + 1 = 6$$

$$x_{est} = \lceil \log_6 20\,000 \rceil = \lceil 5.21 \rceil = 6$$

The files are then constructed as follows:

Level	Blocks	Records	Pointers	Blocks	Records	Pointers
6				$= x : 1$	5	6
5				6	30	36
4				36	180	216
3	$= x : 1$	52	53	216	1 080	1 296
2	53	2 756	$\leq 2\,809$	1 296	6 480	$\leq 7\,776$
1	331	17 192		2 445	12 225	
Total	385	20 000		3 964	20 000	

Hence $T_F =$

$$\frac{1 \cdot 52 + 2 \cdot 2756 + 3 \cdot 17192}{20\,000}(s + r + btt)$$
$$= 2.86\,(s + r + btt)$$

$$\frac{1 \cdot 5 + 2 \cdot 30 + \ldots + 5 \cdot 6480 + 6 \cdot 12225}{20\,000}(s + r + btt)$$
$$= 5.53\,(s + r + btt)$$

2   B-tree index to a data file

An alternative to a tree-structured file is a file accessed via a B-tree index. Here we can consider two further subcases, one where the file is record-anchored, as required for multi-indexed files, and one where the file is block-anchored, for a primary access path, which compares best with a tree-structured file. When the file is record-anchored, the record size does not affect the fetch time, but in the block-anchored case the short records of case **a** require only $\lceil n/Bfr \rceil = \lceil 20\,000/\lfloor 1000/15 \rfloor \rceil = 304$ blocks and corresponding pointers, whereas the longer records require $\lceil 20\,000/\lfloor 1000/180 \rfloor \rceil = 4000$ pointers for the data blocks. The fanout in the index is determined by the density and the entry size $V_K + P = 13$. The file remains easy to update.

Record-anchored	Block-anchored	
Cases a and b	Case a	Case b
$y = \left\lfloor \frac{0.69 \cdot 1000}{13} \right\rfloor = 52$	also $y = 52$	$y = 52$
$x = \lceil \log_{52} 20\,000 \rceil = \lceil 2.51 \rceil = 3$	$x = \lceil \log_{52} 304 \rceil = 2$	$x = \lceil \log_{52} 4\,000 \rceil = 3$

Fetching a record requires one more access to the file; hence on all cases $T_F =$

$(x + 1)(s + r + btt) = 4(s + r + btt)$ $3(s + r + btt)$ $4(s + r + btt)$

3   A dense index to a data file

As a third alternative we will evaluate a dense index, one that is as hard to update as a tree-structured index. The same considerations of record anchors versus block anchors apply, but the fanout is greater. With block anchoring this case is the indexed-sequential file design presented in Chap. 5-1.

Record-anchored	Block-anchored	
Cases a and b	Case a	Case b
$y = \left\lfloor \frac{1000}{13} \right\rfloor = 76$	also $y = 76$	$y = 76$
$x = \lceil \log_{76} 20\,000 \rceil = \lceil 2.29 \rceil = 3$	$x = \lceil \log_{76} 304 \rceil = 2$	$x = \lceil \log_{76} 4\,000 \rceil = 2$

Fetching a record requires also here one more access to the file; hence $T_F =$

$$(x+1)(s+r+btt) = 4(s+r+btt) \qquad 3(s+r+btt) \qquad 3(s+r+btt)$$

if no overflows have occurred.

Figure 9-6a   Comparison of performance of tree-structured and indexed files.

SUMMARY   In comparing these three methods applied to this problem, we see that the best performance is obtained for short records with the tree structure, but that this method is the worst for long records. The indexing methods discussed in Chap. 5 are more robust but cannot match the instances where the tree structure is optimal.

To complete the example of Fig. 9-6a, we will list for the six cases the fetch time in terms of block accesses and the file space used.

Record size	Short $R = 15$	Long $R = 180$
Tree-structured file	$T_F = 2.86, b = 385$	$T_F = 5.53, b = 3964$
B-tree index on one attribute	$T_F = 4, b = 698$	$T_F = 4, b = 4269$
Block-anchored	$T_F = 4, b = 311$	$T_F = 3, b = 4080$
Indexed-sequential	$T_F = 4, b = 573$	$T_F = 4, b = 4269$
Block-anchored	$T_F = 3, b = 310$	$T_F = 3, b = 4054$

Figure 9-6b   Comparison of performance of tree-structured and indexed files

Using Trees as Single Indexes   If the records are long, a tree structure still can be employed to store the keys of an index. In this case the nonkey portions of the records, the goal portions, are placed into a separate file. Elements in this file are found by pointers from the tree entries so that some of the considerations developed for overflow of files have to be applied here.

One extra access will be required to fetch the goal record; so that the performance will not differ much from indexed files. Indexed-sequential access would be faster, but then only block anchors are available in the tree. There may be an advantage to such trees when operations that operate solely on the key are frequent. Such is the case when keys are used to produce counts or subset TID pointers.

The next section illustrates a mixed approach.

9-2-5 An Implementation of a Tree-Structured File

As an example, we show a block layout for a tree-structured file system used for information retrieval (Fig. 9-7). This system addresses the problem of poor fanout with large goal records with a compromise. Large records are split into a node segment (located within the tree), and a residual segment, kept in a separate file, to be accessed indirectly.

Fields of the record which remain in the node segment benefit from immediate access. The key, of course, will always be placed within the node segment and will not be replicated in the residual part. The record-marking scheme uses a *position table* as shown in Fig. 3-11. The entries in the position table contain control information, namely the type of record being referenced. The remaining content of the block should be self-explanatory.

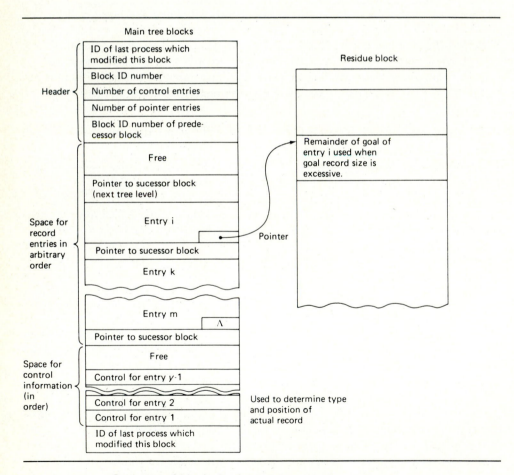

Figure 9-7   Contents of blocks in the SPIRES system.

9-3   HIERARCHICALLY STRUCTURED DATA

In the previous section, we started with trees which were indexed according to one attribute, and then considered some index trees to accommodate multiple attributes. All data records were of the same type. Tree-like structures have found more appropriate use where data has a natural hierarchical organization. Figure 9-8 shows a data structure which is naturally hierarchical in concept.

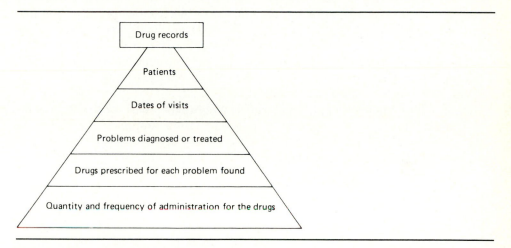

Figure 9-8   A hierarchical data structure.

We have already encountered hierarchical data structures when multiring files were presented in Chap. 5-3. In this section we use trees to manage hierarchical structures.

A classical example of such data is a genealogical tree or an organizational structure. We often need to describe the relationship of records in a hierarchy. A nomenclature which is common and nonsexist is shown with the tree in Fig. 9-9: *parent* and *child*, and with recursion, *ancestors* and *descendants*. The ultimate ancestor is the *root* of the hierarchy; children of the same parent are *siblings*.

A list of assemblies, subassemblies, parts, and material in a manufactured product is an important hierarchical structure found in many database applications. This example, also called a bill-of-materials database, is shown in Fig. 9-9. Use of indexes to refer to such a hierarchy requires a long, composite key and does not provide a convenient model to the user. The key for "dial" is

Products‖washing_machine‖control‖dial.

We restrict hierarchical structures to form proper trees, without cross connections at the lower leaves. Linked structures that form banyan-type trees are called *networks*. The latter type permit a goal record to be accessed via more than one path. In the bill-of-materials example, this condition would occur if a certain type of "Switch" is used in several of the subassemblies and only one record is to contain all the data for this switch. The record "Switch" would then have three parents. In a hierarchical file every record has only one parent.

9-3-1 Criteria for Hierarchical Data Files

In tree-structured files access is optimized by generating a well-balanced tree. Since the records are similar throughout the file, the fanout ratio is made equal at every level. A hierarchical file is structured by the data; the number of levels and the fanout is controlled externally. The fanout at the **Product** level of Fig. 9-9 is three, and will only change if the company changes its products. We must distinguish now the fanout y, which is due to the values occurring in the data, from the number of entries per block, which is based on the mechanical blocking factor, *Bfr*. In order to process hierarchical data structures effectively, certain conditions are to be met.

1. The hierarchy selected must provide a reasonable fanout at each level. The number of ¡children¿ for one record should not be so small that too many levels would be required to find level 1 data. Neither should there be so many children that the search for a specific child will be difficult.

2. An equal level number implies an identical record type. This constraint permits generalized programs to be written. Referring to our example in Fig. 9-9, this means that the hierarchy must not be changed by inserting a level below **Spin Dryers** which distinguishes electric spin dryers from gas spin dryers, if this is not to be done for all products.

Since this type of file structure is so closely related to the data structure for an application, we will present hierarchical files by means of a detailed example of a simple system.

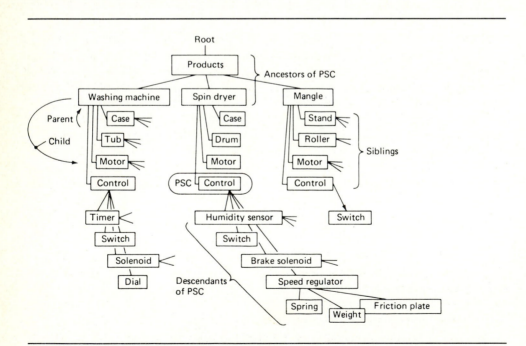

Figure 9-9   Nomenclature in a hierarchy.

9-3-2 MUMPS

As an example of an implementation of a hierarchical file we will describe the file system which supports the requirements of the MUMPS language. This language is oriented toward interactive computing on small systems. It was standardized in 1976 by the ANS institute (O'Neill[76]) and is finding increasing use. The syntax and user interface are close to those found in BASIC language systems. A unique feature is that a hierarchical file-management scheme is embedded in the language, so that it is frequently used for database implementations.

MUMPS operates in an interpretive mode, and hence no declaration of any variables is required. The MUMPS language allows great flexibility in the assignment of values to variable names. All data is represented by strings of up to 255 characters. A class of variables called *globals* are always fetched from and stored onto data files. To distinguish global variables in the language from program local variables, they are prefixed with the symbol "↑" or " ^ ".

The names of MUMPS global variables are stored in a directory level of the user's file space, so that the name of a data file is permanently associated with the name of the global program variable. There is no control language to associate a file name from a system directory to a reference file name used within a program, but the language provides indirection so that any string can be used to address globals.

Each global is a potential hierarchical tree, containing many values. If there is a single value associated with a global, as is the case in this write statement:

```
SET ↑username='Penelope'
```

Figure 9-10   Storing a single-valued global in MUMPS.

The string 'Penelope' will become the value of the global named **username**. Single globals of this type appear in the top level of the hierarchy. They provide a useful means for the communication of status variables, as DONE in Fig. 9-15, between transactions.

At each level integer subscripts are used to provide keys for the globals. There will be one subscript added per level, so that low levels in the hierarchy are addressed with many subscripts, as shown in Fig. 9-13. The subscripts have a permissible range from 0 to 999 999 999. To store one patient's name with a key of **patno** into a **drug** global patients file, a subscript is used, as

```
SET ↑pharmacy(patno)='Manuel Cair'
```

Figure 9-11   Storing a value at a high level into a MUMPS hierarchy.

To read the value of the name of patient identified by **hospno**, one writes

```
SET name=↑pharmacy(hospno)
```

Figure 9-12   Reading a value in MUMPS.

The number of subscripts, ns, used determines the level number in the hierarchy, $level = x - ns$. Note again that the subscripts are not used for address computation, but as search arguments and keys for the hierarchical global files.

The datatype of each value is stored with each value in a *segment*, as shown in Table 9-2. This feature increases the storage flexibility of MUMPS, as seen in Fig. 9-13. Here the field for drug frequency on level 1, item 3, is set to a string data value: `'RPN'`, indicating *as needed*, ratherthan the usual numeric data element specifying a frequency, which appears in corresponding record segments, as seen in Fig. 9-15.

```
    . . .
SET icdno=49390    for Athlete's foot
SET ↑pharmacy(patno,dateno,icdno,1,1)='Desenex'
SET ↑pharmacy(patno,dateno,icdno,1,2)='454'
SET ↑pharmacy(patno,dateno,icdno,1,3)='PRN'
```

Figure 9-13   Setting parameterized globals in MUMPS.

An analysis of MUMPS files also provides an example of the capabilities which can be provided by systems that are considerably less massive than those that support the elaborate indexed-sequential files discussed earlier.

STORAGE STRUCTURE   To begin with an example, we consider the following structure used for records in a clinic pharmacy. The description which follows will assume a B-tree data file approach followed in modern implementations. Since MUMPS does not need statements to define variables and storage, we will use a PL/1 notation to document the intended data.

```
DECLARE
    1 pharmacyrecord,
        2 patients (n1),
            3 patient_number,                      }  2
            3 patient_name,
            3 visit_dates (n2),
                4 treated_problem (n3),
                    5 drugs_prescribed (n4),
                        6 drugname,
                        6 quantity,                }  3
                        6 frequency;
```

Figure 9-14   Declaring a hierarchical data structure.

This structure implies a hierarchy which provides storage for n1 patients with *2* data values {patient_number, patient_name} each and a subtree for n1 · n2 visits, n1 · n2 · n3 problems, and n1·n2·n3·n4 drugs with *3* data elements per drug. Conventional languages and their files will have to allocate excessively large amounts of storage to accommodate the possible maximum array sizes.

▦▦▦   **Hierarchies versus Arrays** If 5 000 patients may be members of the clinic, if some patients might have 100 visits and might have 20 diagnosed problems, and if treating a problem can require up to 10 drugs, then the array space required for the data items on each level is

$$1 + 5000 \cdot 2 + 5000 \cdot 100 + 5000 \cdot 100 \cdot 20 + 5000 \cdot 100 \cdot 20 \cdot 10 \cdot 3 = 310\,510\,001$$

At some point there may actually be 4 500 members, their average number of visits is 8, the average number of problems per visit is 2.3, and the average number of drugs used for a problem is 1.2, so that only

$$1 + 4500 \cdot 2 + 4500 \cdot 8 + 4500 \cdot 8 \cdot 2.3 + 4500 \cdot 8 \cdot 2.3 \cdot 1.2 \cdot 3 = 425\,881$$

data fields would be occupied at that time, and more than 310 000 000 will be empty.

We wish to avoid these null entries because of the storage cost, and even more because of the processing cost incurred when fetching and rejecting empty fields. The hierarchical structure provides a method to achieve compact storage. ▦▦

Segmenting Records Hierarchically A MUMPS data file stores each data value in a distinct *segment*. The relationship of segments will be explained using the nomenclature of Fig. 9-9. A segment is identified through its position in the hierarchy of ancestors and by a key which distinguishes multiple children of one parent. The segments which are logically part of one record are not stored together. Segments of different records that are at the same level are stored together. Those segments on one level that belong to the same parent are arranged to form a continuous *segment sequence*. A logical record can be constructed by assembling from each level the segments that are related by a parent-child binding. Among multiple children the child with the desired identification can be chosen. For example, a record of Fig. 9-9 is made up of keys and data found at each level from `Product` to `Dial`.

A segment forms a triplet or quadruplet {level, key, value, and/or child}. The level is implied. Table 9-2 describes the stored components of a segment.

Table 9-2   Components of a MUMPS data segment.

Function	Code	Typical value
Key (integer)	V_{key}	5 chars.
Type identification for the value field combination	Pid	1 char.
Data string value (if entered)	V_G	15 chars.
Pointer value to children (if entered)	P	2 chars.

Multiple children of the same parent, *siblings*, are appended to their particular segment sequence in order of arrival. Siblings which do not fit into the initial block referenced are put into successor blocks. Blocks are split as required. A linkage between blocks, as presented in Sec. 9-2-3, is maintained to assure rapid access to all segments of a sequence.

The actual implementation of the conceptual hierarchy is shown in Fig. 9-15. The position of the segment sequence with all children is defined by a single pointer from the parent. The key for a data item is part of the segment, so that a search for a sibling is done at the same level used to keep sibling data. The number of pointers in a block is relatively high, since a segment contains only one or zero data elements, and hence is quite short. The actual format of the segments is described later. We will now consider the data found in this file structure.

CONTENTS OF THE FILE   An entire hierarchical structure is known by one global variable name kept at level x, here ↑PHARMACY. The variable names stored are limited in length to 8 characters to provide a high density of segments per block (Bfs_x) at the top level. There are no names associated with the variables at the lower levels, and extrinsic documentation is required to explain the meaning of levels in the hierarchy.

At level $x - 1$, we find the patient number as key and the name as data. At level $x - 2$, the date itself provides the key, and no actual data field is required. To permit use of the date as a key, the value of the date is represented in storage as an integer, say, 31272 for 3DEC72. We prefer an unambiguous representation. Note that patient Cair has had three visits recorded; the other sibling records are for 3Aug73 and 12Oct75.

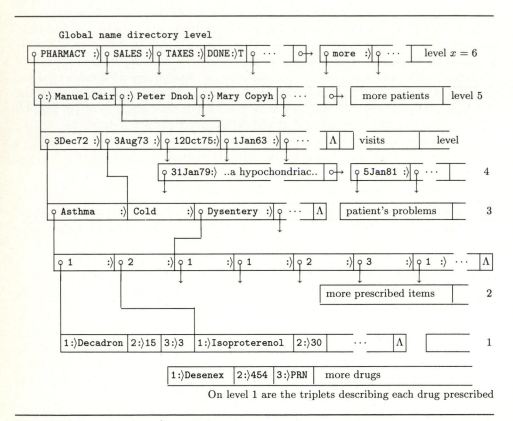

Figure 9-15   MUMPS **data storage.**

The pointer field of the date segment allows retrieval of the problem list on level $x - 3$. A problem name could be kept as data; here the problem is identified through a standard coding method. A suitable key might be the ICDA code (International Classification of Disease) which assigns numbers of the form xxx.xx to diseases. For a value of this code, 493.90, the key would be 49390. We have again a segment without an explicit goal field. Patient `Cair` had only one problem treated at his 3Dec72 visit. On 3Aug73 he had at least three problems.

Level $x - 4$ contains as a key a sequence number of each drug given in the prescription for this problem. For each drug there is a pointer to a segment sequence on level $x - 5 = 1$. `Cair`'s prescription for `Asthma` had two items; on a later visit for his `Cold` nothing was prescribed, but his `Dysentery` was treated.

At this final level we find the actual data segments for a drug name and dosage. In our example this segment sequence has always three segments with keys of `1,2,3` and associated data fields. These segments have no further pointers.

To retrieve `PHARMACY` data, we have available as key the sequence of patient number, visit date, problem number, a drug number and a dosage description element number. The fetch statement to get the name of the drug provides 5 keys:

　　　　`SET drugname=↑pharmacy(patno,dateno,problemno,drugno,1)`

and would require the seven steps shown in Fig. 9-16 for execution. Intermediate level data, such as the patient's name, can be found with fewer accesses.

Access the initial root block containing the global names to find 'pharmacy',
　　if neccessary read through successor blocks until the desired global is found;
Follow the associated pointer to successor level = x-1 block;
Search at that level for patient segment key_1 = `patno`;
　　/ If we have many　patients, many blocks may have to be searched. */*
When found, follow pointer in segment to date level block;
Search for visit date key_2 = `dateno`;
When found, follow pointer in segment to problem level block;
Search for problem number key_3 = `problemno`;
When found, follow pointer in segment to prescription level block;
Search for drug number key_4 = `drugno`;
When found, follow pointer in segment to drug data level block;
Finally search for drug data segment key_5 = `'1'`;
When found, pick up data field (`'Decadron'`) out of segment.

Figure 9-16　　　Navigating down a hierarchy.

In all hierarchical files the natural structure of the data has a great effect on file performance. Within a single level the length of the segment sequence, y, is the critical parameter. This length is determined by the number of siblings on one level and is not controlled by file-system procedures. Let *Bfs* denote the average number of segments in one block; a B-tree implementation will permit

$$Bfs = 0.69\,B/V_{seg} \qquad \text{(MUMPS B-tree) 9-4}$$

where V_{seg} is the segment size. We find the same concerns encountered in the Ring-files of Chap. 6-3: when the natural hierarchy controls the structure, nature sometimes must be adjusted to improve performance. In Sec. 9-3-3 we evaluate and subsequently optimize a MUMPS file structure.

In MUMPS the sibling segments within a segment sequence, i.e., having the same parent, need not be kept in any particular order. To locate a specific sibling requires only sequential access to segments in a block and, if the sequence y extends beyond the block, serial access to the successor blocks on that level. To minimize the cost of accessing long sequences, most MUMPS systems do attempt to maintain locality of blocks when a block split occurs.

9-3-3 Evaluation of a MUMPS File

Following the general description of the MUMPS file structure, we will evaluate a typical organization in greater detail so that some criteria for proper utilization of hierarchical files, as exemplified by MUMPS, become clear.

CHAINS   The number of seeks or block fetches is determined by the number of levels and the length of the chains at each level. Figure 9-15 shows a structure where most segment sequences were short. Exceptions are the list of patients on level $x - 1$ and the sequence of visits of a hypochondriac on level $x - 2$.

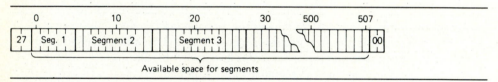

Figure 9-17   A block in MUMPS.

The number of blocks to be accessed on one level depends on the number and size of sibling segments and on the size of the blocks used. In order to use little memory, the implementers of MUMPS choose fairly small block sizes, from 128 to 512 characters in length. Figure 9-17 shows such a block. We will assume for our example a system with 512 bytes per block.

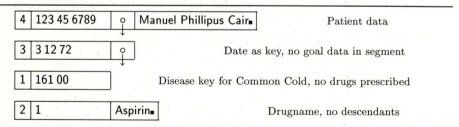

The *type identification* indicates what type of fields this segment contains. Two bits are required to encode the four possibilities:
{ 1: key only; 2: key, data; 3: key, pointer; 4: key, data, pointer; }.

The *key* field extends from the identification field and requires up to 9 digit positions. In binary form the value could be encoded in 33 bits.

A *pointer*, when present, occupies two character positions. Its presence indicates that this segment has a descendant subtree.

Data when present is of variable length, up to 255 characters, and is terminated with a special end-of-string marker.

Figure 9-18   Segments in MUMPS files.

Two fields in each block are used for block management. One indicates the number of characters used in the block, and the other one contains the successor-block pointer. Binary integers are often used as pointers so that fields of 2 bytes in length can contain positive integer values up to 65 535. This value is not adequate for all blocks on a large disk unit, so that this block number is specific to one user. To each user, a number of cylinders are assigned, within which all the global variables are allocated, so that all the files of one user are limited to 65 535 blocks total.

SEGMENT FORMATS   A segment consists of a type identification, the key, and as a goal either or both pointer and data fields. Figure 9-18 shows some possible segments.

EVALUATION OF THE HIERARCHICAL DATA STRUCTURE   We now will evaluate the pharmacy file level by level using the assumptions made earlier. We will assume segment sizes based on the values in Table 9-2. The average length of the data strings (15 characters) includes the end-of-string marker. Computation of the segment size

$$R' = Pid + V_{key} + V_G + P \qquad\qquad 9\text{-}5$$

has to consider if a data or pointer value exists at the level. The example contains data at only two levels $\{1, 5\}$ and pointers are needed on all levels but the bottom one $\{1\}$. Denoting the size of a segment of a record at level i as R'_i, we find that the number of segments per block

$$Bfs_i = dens \left\lfloor \frac{B - 2P}{R'_i} \right\rfloor \qquad \text{(hierarchical file) } 9\text{-}6$$

The density for a B-tree data file implementation can again be estimated with Eq. 3-47 as $dens = 0.69\%$. Large segment sizes can lower the density further if spanning of blocks by single segments is avoided.

Since segment sequences can span blocks, a number of block accesses may be required to find a specific segment at one level. The expected number of blocks comprising an entire segment sequence of fanout y is

$$b_i(y_i) = \lceil \tfrac{1}{2} + y_i / Bfs_i \rceil$$

The extra half-block appears because a segment sequence may start at an arbitrary position in its initial block.

If $b_i \gg 1$, the fanout y_i is too high at level i because the number of block accessed will be large on one level. There will also be fewer segments in the last block of the sequence, so that for arbitrary sequences the number of accesses can be precisely estimated using the procedure leading to Eq. 9-3, assuming an equal frequency of access to all segments of the sequence. The number of expected block accesses is the sum of accesses to the first block, accesses to reach intermediate blocks, if any, and accesses to reach the remaining segments in the final block, all divided by the number of segments in the sequence.

$$b_G = \frac{1}{y_i} \left(\tfrac{1}{2} Bfs_i + \sum_{j=2}^{b_i-1} j\, Bfs_i + b_i \left(y_i - \tfrac{1}{2} Bfs_i - \sum_{j=2}^{b_i-1} Bfs_i \right) \right) \approx \left\lceil \frac{b_i + 1}{2} \right\rceil \qquad 9\text{-}7$$

The approximation applies when $y_i \gg Bfs_i$ so that the lesser number of segments in the first and last blocks does not affect the result greatly.

In MUMPS we find on level x the directory of file names or globals for a user. At this level the name strings are limited to 8 characters and no other key is needed. If the average global-variable name is 5 characters, the segment size $R'_x = 9$ and $y_x = \lfloor (512-4)/9 \rfloor = 56$. When there are many global files, including unsubscripted globals, it is likely that more than one block is required for the directory level of the user.

The initial segment for the `pharmacy` file will be created when the first patient is stored by a statement as

---

```
SET ↑pharmacy(patno)='Manuel P. Cair'
```

Figure 9-19   Starting a MUMPS subtree.

The segment in level x will consist only of the key `pharmacy` and a pointer, and a block on level $x - 1$ will be allocated to store the key value from `patno` and the string with `Cair`'s name and the end-of-string mark. We assume for `patno` a nine digit or five character encoding. The above patient's segment will require $R'_{x-1} = 1 + 5 + 15 = 21$ characters, but as soon as lower-level segments are entered, a pointer field will be inserted, so that the level $x - 1$ segments will actually become 23 characters in length. This will make $Bfs_{x-1} = \lfloor \frac{512-4}{23} \rfloor = 22$ so that there can be this many patient segments in a block. For the 450 patients seen in the clinic, the segment sequence will occupy 21 blocks. These have to be searched sequentially for every reference, requiring an average of 11 block accesses on this level. An approach to avoid this high cost is given at the end of this section.

We will summarize the remaining levels of the example rapidly since we find that all further segment sequences will fit into a block. On level $x - 2$ the `visit dates` are stored as keys. This means that no `SET` statements with only two subscripts will be executed. This level will be filled indirectly when the `dateno` is used as a subscript to lower levels. On level $x - 3$, we find the problem treated during the visit. Again, the problem is encoded as the key, `'Asthma'` $\rightarrow$ `icd=493.9` $\rightarrow$ `icdno = 49390`, and the key is set implicitly. If no drugs are prescribed for the problem the hierarchy terminates here with a segment of type 1.

Level $x - 4$ provides pointers to the drug description. An alternative design could store the drug name as a data field on this level. It again contains segments having only a key and a pointer. Level $x - 5$ contains the actual drug data as a sequence of three segments. This level would be loaded by statements such as

---

```
SET ↑pharmacy(patno,dateno,icdno,dno,1)='Decadron'
SET ↑pharmacy(patno,dateno,icdno,dno,2)=15
SET ↑pharmacy(patno,dateno,icdno,dno,3)=3
```

Figure 9-20   Loading data into leaves of a hierarchical file.

⁐⁐⁐⁐⁐ **NAKED VARIABLES**   To simplify and speed execution of such sequences, an option is available that will allow reuse of a previously reached node, so that redundant searches down the tree can be eliminated. The absence of a variable name implies the reuse of the previous global variable and all but the last one of the subscripts. Further subscripts leading to lower levels can be appended. Using the *naked* variable notation, the last two statements become as shown in Fig. 9-21.

```
SET ↑(2)=15
SET ↑(3)=3
```

Figure 9-21   Shorthand loading of leaves in a hierarchy.

The number of block accesses to reach this level $(x - 5)$, assuming one block access for the directory level, is $T_F \approx (1+11+1+1+1+1)(s+r+btt) = 16(s+r+btt)$. Some seeks may be avoided, especially on level $x - 1$, if locality is maintained. Further naked accesses to the same segment sequence are free if the buffers are retained, at least until the end of a block is encountered.

OPTIMIZATION BY CHANGE OF THE HIERARCHY   Optimal fanout would avoid sibling overflow blocks. When the fanout $y \gg Bfs$, the hierarchy becomes a poor match for the file, as seen on the patient's level $x - 1$. A solution is to change the hierarchy originally envisaged for the file. We will apply this notion to the patient's level of our example.

In order to obtain better performance, this level might be split into two levels, perhaps by using half of the patient's number as the three-character key for each level. The name will appear only on the lower level $(x-2)$. Now $R'_{x-1} = 1+3+2 = 6$, $Bfs_{x-1} = 84$ and $R'_{x-2} = 1 + 3 + 15 + 2 = 21$, $Bfs_{x-2} = 24$ (Eq. 9-5). The original fanout $y = 450$ is distributed over two levels, so that $y_{x-1}, y_{x-2} = \sqrt{y} \approx 22$. Both $y_{x-1} < Bfs_{x-1}$ and $y_{x-2} < Bfs_{x-2}$, so that most segment sequences will fit into one block. The block fetches for the patient's data have been reduced from 11 to slightly over 2. This file will have six levels, and $T_F \approx 6(s + r + btt)$.

If the file would have to hold information for all patients seen during a long period, say a year, then at least two and probably more patients' levels will be needed to provide adequate performance.   ▦

9-3-4 Storage Allocation

Occasionally, long chains of sibling data create long segment sequence, and the optimization process described above on the patient's name. The search for children down the hierarchical tree also follows pointers. Optimization of locality for the serial blocks according to both dimensions is hence important. Most MUMPS implementations, therefore, attempt to allocate the next block in a series within the next accessible sector. A *sector* is defined to consist of all the blocks which can be read on one cylinder at the same rotational position.

Figure 9-22 shows a series chained on an unwrapped cylinder surface. Optimal placement has been achieved for the first four of the five blocks of chain C shown. Accessing blocks of C avoids latency, r, and seek time, s. The example assumes that the next sequential sector can be read. On computer systems where buffering constraints prevent this, alternate block referencing is preferred (see Fig. 10-7).

To locate the best block from the free chain, a table entry for each sector is maintained which points to the first block of a chain of free blocks within the sector.

If there is a free block in the sector, it is assigned to the chain which requested it, and the table is updated with the link value from this newly obtained block. If all of a cylinder is filled, so that the new block has to be placed on another cylinder, no rotational optimization is attempted. In fact, an extra sequence of file accesses may be required to store the old free-space table and fetch one for the new cylinder.

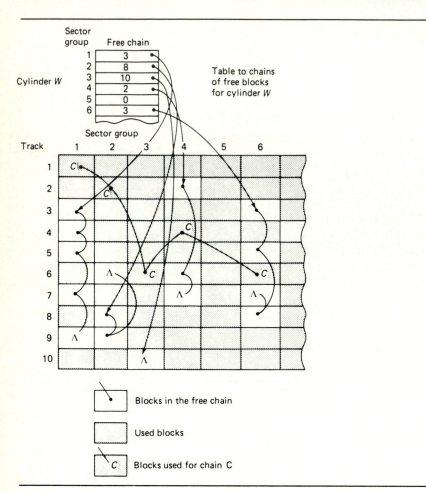

Figure 9-22   Storage for a MUMPS cylinder.

When storage is released by the delete statement KILL, such as

```
KILL ↑pharmacy(patno)
```

Figure 9-23   MUMPS delete statement.

All descendants of the deleted segment are also released. A lower-priority task collects all freed blocks and attaches them to the appropriate free-space chains. These blocks can then be reused. Alternate methods for free-space management are discussed in Chap. 10-4.

9-3-5 Conclusion

The method used by programs to reference data in hierarchical systems such as MUMPS is closely interwoven with the file structure. This interdependence is both an advantage and a liability. When a hierarchical file structure is called for, careful data analysis and data dimensioning have to precede a file design. Intermediate indexes or hash-access lists may be interspersed to provide adequate performance over the expected range of quantities of data on each level. The interdependence of data and file structure could also be perceived earlier, in Chap. 5-3, when discussing ring-structured files, which also implement a hierarchical design.

Hierarchical views of data may also be provided by more general database systems which can provide a data-independent system design. When the range of data and applications cannot be adequately assessed initially, the higher overhead costs of a more general system will be less than the cost of frequent rewriting of the database and database programs to match the data structure.

9-4　FILES USING VIRTUAL MEMORY

Most modern computers permit the use of *virtual addressing*. A virtual address refers to an address space that is much larger than the actual memory available. A mechanism consisting of both hardware and software components translates the virtual memory addresses. The virtual memory address becomes a real memory address for pages available in memory, and brings pages from storage into memory for virtual addresses not now in memory. To make space for pages being brought in from storage, pages currently in real memory have to be invalidated and, if they contain changes, written to storage. A flag bit for each page notes if a page is *dirty*, that is, that some write operation has occurred that could have changed the contents of the page.

This approach is referred to as an operating system using demand paging or a *virtual memory* system. We classified the operating systems choices available in Chap. 2-3-2.

There will be a division of the address space into working units called pages. A *page* is identified by the high-order digits of the address and will be a few thousand characters in length. A hardware table, possibly with a software extension, will record which pages from the entire address space are actually represented in memory at any given moment. A page-not-present interrupt occurs when a referenced address falls into a page not currently in memory. When this happens, a system software mechanism is invoked to find or to create free space in memory, fetch the required page from drum or disk, update the page table, and resume execution of the interrupted task, as shown in Fig. 9-24.

If enough address space exists to handle the size of expected data files, virtual addressing provides a very convenient mechanism for handling files. Systems have been written that perform key-to-address transformations into this data space, and use these system facilities for all further page transfers in and out of memory. A collision-resolution mechanism remains necessary. The page size of a virtual system will, in general, define the effective block size of the file system.

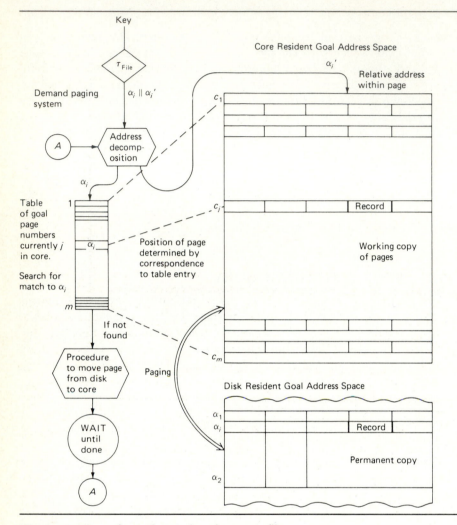

Figure 9-24   Accessing a virtual-storage file.

Two types of virtual systems can be found: those which have a single address space, and those which employ multiple named address spaces, called *segments*. The use of a single address space erases any formal distinction between the area used for programs, the area used for program data, and the area used for files. Boundaries between these areas are set up by convention. Such a convention could be that a file will consist. of the space between two address values of α_1 and α_2. Reliability can be compromised if the conventions are difficult to enforce.

More sophisticated virtual systems will provide the capability for several separately named address spaces, called segments. Figure 9-25 sketches this approach, but details of the paging mechanism are omitted here.

A sequence of high-order bits of the hardware virtual address is used to pick up an entry from a segment table. One or more storage segments can be viewed as files, and the segment entry may have associated with it information regarding protection and sharing of such a file. The allocation of segment pages to disk storage and their movement to memory when needed is again an operating-system function. Such a file still presents only a linear address blocked into pages, and no assistance is provided by the operating system to map records into this space. To better manage the virtual-address system, some operating systems, such as TENEX and TOPS-20 for the DEC-10/20 series of computers, map only those file pages that have been referenced into the address space. Multiple processes can share an available file page. When the process using the files terminates, the file pages will be rewritten, if they were modified, and then released.

The use pattern associated with files may not have been considered by the designers of the virtual-memory system, who were concerned mainly with the manipulation of program sections and data referenced directly by these programs. Paging systems are especially effective if memory references, during time intervals commensurate with the time required to move a page to memory, cluster within a limited number of pages.

To use a virtual-access mechanism effectively, it still is neccessary to be aware of the page size and page boundaries and also to utilize pages densely. For instance, aligning blocks to page boundaries avoids accessing two pages for a single block request. The storage density can be very low if the file is not carefully allocated to the virtual-address space. No matter how little is stored in a page, it will take a page in memory and an entire page block on the disk used for backup storage. Completely empty pages may or may not occupy file space, depending on the sophistication of the support system. The techniques used for blocking remain valid, since the same density considerations apply.

Sequential files, with fixed records, are easily mapped densely to a virtual-address space, since we do not expect dynamic update. The performance of files using explicit block read access and virtual direct access will be similar, except that there will be no buffering to overlap computation with block reading in virtual systems. Paging facilities do provide good buffering when writing blocks, so that rewrite delays can be neglected except in terms of total system load.

Indexing is very desirable when using virtual memories, since it reduces the number of pages that have to be read. The pointer obtained from an index entry is an address in the virtual space. Only the high-order bits are kept and extended for reference by catenating $\log_2 pagesize$ zeros.

The use of direct-file approaches is simplified by the large address space, although effective space utilization has to be considered. The file storage density can be very low if the file is not carefully allocated to the virtual-address space. The performance will be identical for similar values of m and Bfr. Open addressing with linear searching can make good use of pages already in memory.

In systems with a single address space, shared use of the space by multiple files using a common transformation simplifies control of storage allocation. With ring structures locality remains a concern if excessive paging load is to be avoided when rings are being traversed.

Some paging algorithms assign priorities according to the ratio of CPU-time to paging-rate. Whether this will penalize or benefit file-oriented programs depends on the objectives of the system administrators who set the parameters.

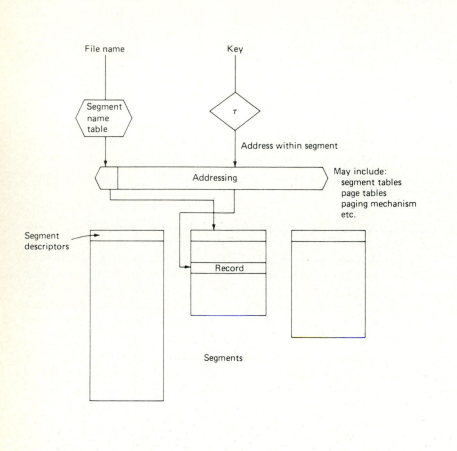

Figure 9-25   Segmented virtual addressing.

We find then that the use of virtual storage does not change the approach to file design greatly, except that it does provide an alternative for the lowest level of file management. A trivial file system, as described in Chap. 7-2-1, is completely replaceable by virtual-storage access. Some database systems have been built directly on top of such virtual-storage systems, but these systems have incorporated within themselves one or more of the file-organization techniques presented to control locality while paging. A number of database systems for demonstration and educational purposes have not considered how to use the paging mechanisms effectively, since the implementers did not expect to operate in a production environment.

An evaluation of the performance of files based on paging can be obtained by combining data on file behavior in terms of block reads and writes with measurements regarding paging-system performance and available workspace size.

9-5   SUMMARY

In this chapter we described a variety of file types which have been developed to cope with special application demands. Before deciding to use a non-standard file structure two questions must be answered:

1 Is the benefit, typically a again in performance, significant and important?

2 Are the liabilities, which always come with such approaches worth it?

If the performance of a special type of file is not better by a significant amount, typically at least a factor of two, then it is probably not worth further consideration. improvements in hardware keep coming along, and a factor of two may well be gained by hardware before novel file software is debugged.

Even if the performance improvement is significant it may not be important. For files that are only used occasionally the simplest implementation is best. It has the greatest chance of still working when it is needed next.

It is easy to forget about liabilities. Many high-performance schemes rely on early binding, as described in Chap. 7-5-1. Implied is then that update is costly and flexibility is limited. We will list some tradeoffs encountered in this chapter.

File Type	Usage	Benefits	Liabilities
Transposed	Statistical	Rapid access to data in columns	Costly update Long records
Trees	Simple lookup	Minimal redundancy, Large body of related theory	Single access path, Balancing needed, Performance gets worse if records get longer
K-d trees	Complex query	Multiple attributes	Poor partitioning, Partial match queries search multiple paths
Hierarchies	Sparse data	Good space utilization	Rigid access paths
Virtual files	Dense data	Little programming	No buffer or locality control

It is of course good to be aware that alternatives exist. There remain situations where standard file methods do not perform to the users' satisfaction. Since performance may be issue any specific proposal should be accompanied by a performance prediction. Although we have not analyzed these methods thoroughly, the comparison in Sec. 9-2-4 shows how easy it is to compare methods using the performance analysis approaches illustrated here.

In the next chapter we will consider the performance of entire transactions, including those which access multiple files.

BACKGROUND AND REFERENCES

Transposed files are used by Easton[69], Selbman[74], Weyl[75], analyzed by Batory[79], and surveyed by Wong[86]. They are used in several large statistical database implementations.

Landauer[63] and Sussengut[63] describe trees for file systems. Binary trees were described by Hibbard[62] and analyzed by Arora[69], and Overholt[73]. Bentley[75] extends a binary tree to deal with multiple attributes. The balancing of binary trees has had much attention. Adel'son-Vel'skiĭ and Landis presented a basic algorithm (AVL-trees) in 1962. An extensive analysis is in Knuth[73S]. Baer[75], Nievergelt[74], and Bayer[76] consider access frequency. The SPIRES system is presented by Schroeder in Kerr[75].

Many concepts for multidimensional trees have been published, for instance Gopalakrishna[80] and Lee[80]. R-trees are described by Guttman[84] and K-d trees, similar to those described by Chang[81] are examined by Flajolet[86] (who compares them with tries).

Hierarchical structures are found in many applications. Examples are found in Connors[66], Benner[67], andDavis[70]. Many more are cited in Senko[77].

Descriptions of MUMPS can be found in Allen[66] and in Greenes[69]. The MUMPS system was developed at Massachusetts General Hospital to support computing applications in medicine. The general system design was based on one of the earliest and best timesharing systems: JOSS. The file system was designed to match specifically the hierarchical organization of data perceived in the area of medical record keeping, as seen by the developers at MGH and General Electric in their FILECOMP system which preceded the MUMPS implementation. Modern implementations use B-trees, but the hierarchical layering remains a concern, as illustrated in Safran[86]. MUMPS implementations following the standard (O'Neill[76]) are now available on many computers.

Daley[65] presents the virtual systems approach to files; its application is described by Rothnie[74]. Denning[71] compares the objectives of storage and memory systems. Hatfield in Freiberger[72] evaluates locality in paged systems.

EXERCISES

1   In Fig. 9-26 elements of a file system are shown: A Device and Unit Table indicates that we have two devices, one of type Unicon, a mass-storage unit, and a moving-head disk of type 2319. On the first track of each device is a pointer to a File Name Table (FNT) which lists the files stored on the device. The files on the disk are Personnel, Equipment, etc. Each file has a directory, which lists a.o. the subfiles. The Equipment file is comprised of a Data subfile, a Schema subfile, which lists the attributes stored in the Data file and indicates if they are indexed, and a number of Index subfiles. As shown in Fig. 9-26 two types of index structures are used: dense indexes with overflows (I) and TID-lists accessed by hashing (τ). Note that Horsepower is not indexed at all. The actual Data file is stored on the mass-storage unit (INFSYS02), at position thr4.

Identify and list the various component tables of Fig. 9-26 and indicate for each whether they belong to the operating system or to the file structure.

2   Initially the operating system obtains the Device and Unit Table in Fig. 9-26. To begin processing, a user transaction issues initial OPEN statements which copy the relevant file directory entries into memory. Make these two steps the beginning of a processing flowchart. Then continue the flowchart, showing the expected file access steps for a transaction program to answer the following questions:

a Find the inventory number of our 'Shovel'.

b Find the inventory number of our 'Hoe'.

c Find the inventory number of equipment purchased '12Jun83'.

d Find the inventory numbers of equipment having > 200 horsepower.

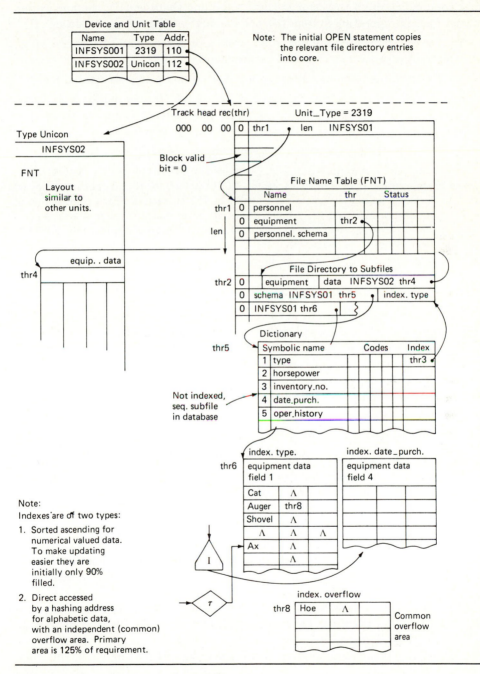

Figure 9-26   Structure of some files.

3   * Mark in the flowchart made in Exercise 2 a dozen possible error conditions. Make a table with entries giving suitable diagnostic messages for each error condition and a code indicating if the error is likely to be due the user (U), the application designer (A), the operating system (S), the file method (F), or the hardware (H).

4   For the transposed file in Fig. 9-1 write a program to find the average man and compute the program's expected performance.

5   Describe the difference between an indexed and a tree-structured file.

6   Design a K-d tree, as described in Sec. 9-2-3, for the multiattribute file shown in Fig. 5-18. Estimate its performance parameters. Compare the performance with the multi-indexed TID merge shown in Chap. 5-5-1.

7   Does MUMPS use an early or late binding approach?

8   A supplier's manual of MUMPS provides the following design example: We wish to store patients' identifications, each of 60 characters, for 10 000 patients numbered from 1 to 10 000. The blocks have a net capacity of 762 characters. Each combination of segment-type identification and key requires three character spaces, a pointer also requires three, and the end-of-string character one space. Due to the design of the machine, segments have to be multiples of three characters.
   a How many segments fit into one block if all segments are on one level?
   b What is the number of blocks used?
   c What is the expected search time exclusive of the directory search?

9   We can get faster access in the above case by using segments consisting of a pointer only on level $x - 1$ and keeping the patient's identification on level $x - 2$.
   a How many segments will be in one block on level 1?
   b How many segments will be in one block on level 2?
   c How many blocks are being used?
   d What is the expected search time?

10   Do you see any problem if the segment length in Exercise 8 would not always be 60 characters, but rather 60 characters on the average?

11   Compare a MUMPS segment with a LEAP record.

12   Discuss the equilibrium density for the two indexed files described in Chap. 5, the hashed file of Chap. 6-1, the tree-structured file of Sec. 9-2-1, and a MUMPS file of Sec. 9-3. State all assumptions made regarding insertion, update, and deletion patterns, and use them consistently.

13   To save programming time you decide to use virtual memory for a dynamic file. You have to provide for 9 000 entries of 410 characters each. Frequently only 1000 entries will be in use. You know that the pagesize for your virtual memory is 4096 characters. Up to a thousand virtual pages can be available.
   a Evaluate hashed access to that file. What is the expected access cost in terms of block fetches when the file is nearly full and when the file is in its average (1000 entries) state.
   b Suggest and evaluate an alternative storage design, still using virtual memory.

---

* More exercises for this problem are found in Chap. 10.

Chapter 10

Storage Organization

This thinker observed that all the books no matter how diverse they might be, are made up out of the same elements: the space, the period, the comma, the twenty-two letters of the alphabet. He also alleged the fact which travellers have confirmed: In the vast Library there are no two identical books. From these two incontrovertible premises he deducted that the Library is total and that its shelves register all the possible combinations of the twenty-odd orthographical symbols (a number which, though extremely vast, is not infinite): in other words, all that is given to express, in all languages. Everything: the minutely detailed history of the future, the archangels' autobiographies, the faithful catalogue of the Library, thousands and thousands of false catalogues, the demonstration of fallacy of the true catalogue, ...

Jorge Luis Borges
from "The Library of Babel", a story in the "Labyrinths"

10-0 INTRODUCTION

In the preceding chapters we dealt with one file at a time, although the example in the introduction (Fig. 1-1) already indicated that typically multiple files are needed for a data-processing task. In this chapter we will consider issues of having multiple files. We start by reviewing the architecture of storage systems. In Sec. 10-2 estimate the storage demands for a file and then describe how the files are allocated to storage. In Sec. 10-3 we evaluate the response time for transactions.

The storage capacity made available by the hardware will not be allocated immediately to the user files. Keeping a pool of free storage permits the sharing of storage resources as some needs increase and other needs diminish. In Sec. 10-4 we consider the management of free storage. In the remainder of the chapter we present some techniques to improve file performance; Sec. 10-5 considers some software methods and Sec. 10-6 hardware methods, especially file servers and database machines. In Sec. 10-7 we also review systems having multiple processors, leading into Chap. 11 on distributed processing.

The material in this chapter provides background for Chap. 14, where we evaluate the performance of entire file systems. For such an analysis we have to be able to take into account the effect of having multiple files, multiple processors, and distributed processing.

10-1   MULTIFILE ARCHITECTURE

We now review the architecture of storage systems, going beyond the coverage of Chap. 3, where only the actual storage devices, typically disks, were considered. When only one file is used then the performance of the disk unit is the primary determinant of system performance. When two or more files operate together, then not only the disk unit, but also their connection to the processor will determine the aggregate performance.

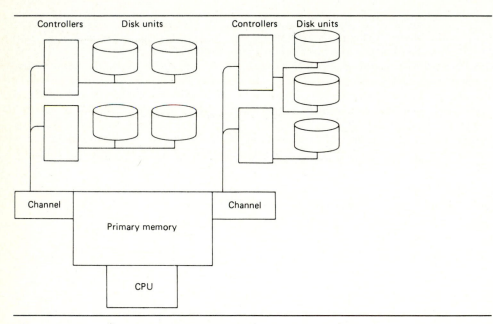

Figure 10-1   Storage-system components.

10-1-1 Storage System Components

The primary hardware components of a system to provide data storage are of course the storage devices themselves. We found disk units easy to characterize. We will now also consider the hardware units required to attach disks to the processors, *controllers* and *channels*. Here the differences among different hardware systems are great. A personal computer will have minimal additional hardware connecting disks to its processor, whereas large data-processing systems often have specialized subsidiary computers to control the storage units. Figure 10-1 shows the organization of hardware components for a major storage system.

The term *channel* designates equipment which provides a path for data to move from the memory of the processor to and from the disk. The term *controller* designates equipment which schedules the seek, block search, and data transfer operations for a disk. The performance and cost of a complete storage system are affected by the performance and costs of channels and controllers as well as the performance and costs of the disks.

MULTIPLE UNITS   Databases using multiple files often require multiple disks and somtimes multiple controllers and channels as well. If the quantity of data to be stored, D, exceeds the capacity of one of the available disk units, multiple units will be employed. Table 3-4, in presenting the computation of relative block addresses, also provided an example of the computation of the available storage capacity of a system:

$$D_{available} = \sum_{dt=devicetype} No_{dt} Cap_{dt} \qquad 10\text{-}1$$

The amount of available storage, $D_{available}$, is determined by integer multiples, No, of the capacity, Cap, of the devices to be used, unless we can convince others sharing the processor to purchase the remnant. In the large configuration shown in Fig 10-1 $No = 7$.

If the entire computer system is being configured for a specific data-processing application there is freedom in equipment selection. In general, it is desirable to select storage devices so that a few disks will satisfy storage needs without the complexity of many units.

When the data-processing applications is incremental to the system, less flexibility is available.

We also need storage for backup and archiving. It is best to assign separate units to these tasks, so that a failure will not destroy the primary data and the backups. Since the requirements for backup and archiving tend to differ from the needs of direct data-processing services, the types of storage devices and their connections tend to differ as well.

To evaluate the effect of multiple devices we will in the next section analyze device operations in more detail.

10-1-2 Controllers

In most computers, disks are not directly coupled to the processors but require a *controller*. A controller executes selected commands, provided by the processor or the channel. The commands are related to the basic operations — seek, latency, and data transfer — presented in Chap. 3. If the controller has the capability to hold and process the argument of the commands, then it can execute commands such as sl, sk, sh, and perhaps sr without continued involvement of the processor or the channel.

A controller may be able to handle 2, 4, 8, or 16 disk units, but perhaps only one at a time. Controllers typically have only one connection path via the channel or the processor to memory. This means they can only handle one of the data transfer commands such as tr, tw, or tv at a time. If a sector is identified by a software determined identifier, then it is likely that an sr command will also require access to memory, so that the block identifier can be compared.

If many disks are to be used, there will be more than one controller. At least the sk commands, which move the head assembly to another cylinder, can be handled in parallel. The effect of that overlap can be significant since seeks take a long time.

Table 10-1   Typical controller commands.

sl	select d: commands following are for disk unit d
sk	seek a: move disk arms to cylinder a
sh	set head s: commands following use surface s
sr	sector rotate b: wait until disk sector b is available
tr	read m: transfer contents of next block into memory starting at m
tw	write n: write next block from contents of memory starting at n
tv	verify n: check that block on disk matches memory starting at n

10-1-3 Channels

On the larger computers, controllers are connected to the processor by *channels*, which provide the data path into the processor memory. A channel may serve a large number of controllers. Multiple *channels* are used to provide multiple simultaneous data access paths, giving a greater bandwidth of data into the computer. Each channel can serve a tr, tw, or tv command, so that as many data transmissions can take place as there are channels.

Each channel is assigned a priority. If multiple channels need access to memory simultaneously, the requests are processed in order of priority. High speed devices are best attached to channels having high priority. The amount of data transferred to memory per request is small, and depends on the *width* of the memory access path, typically 4 to 32 characters for large computers using channels.

A limit on the number of channels permissible on one processor is due to total bandwidth capability of the memory. If channels try to read or write more than the memory can handle, loss of data will occur in lower-priority channels. System software will cause retransmission of data when such failures occur, but the retransmission increases the bandwidth requirement further, so that channel failure rates should be kept low.

10-1-4 Using Multiple Processors

Multiple processors are found in an increasing number of computer systems. The low cost of simple processors makes it attractive to build systems using many simple components. Use of multiple processors does include complexities, which have to be dealt with if performance is to increase as computational tasks are assigned to more processors.

Interconnections are required to make multiple processors function as a system. The network of interconnections is used to communicate requests and data. The processors within a system may be controlled by individual users' processes or may be system-controlled subprocessors. Some subprocessors may carry out highly specialized tasks in response to an overall system scheduler, for instance, maintaining an important file. General subprocessors simply share the general workload.

We distinguish two major types of systems according to the independence of the operation of their component processors:

1 *Multiprocessor computer systems*, where several processors operate as a single system, often sharing memory, storage, and operating systems control. Multiprocessors behave nearly like single processors. They provide increased computational power and can reduce overhead from frequent process switching. Multiprocessors are typically *closely coupled* using direct hardware *busses*.

2 *Distributed systems*, where processors control their own devices and priorities. Distributed systems may be remote from each other. Communication delays prevent direct sharing of hardware and the processors operate more or less autonomously. We classify distributed systems further into three types:

2.1 *Clustered processors* still appear to the user as single systems. They have their own memory and storage. A shared operating system must allocate data-processing tasks so that data storage is accessible to the process which needs it. Clustered systems are typically connected by *local networks*.

2.2 *Remotely distributed systems* do not share operating systems, and a user accesses the system through a local processor. The operating systems communicate with each other through a network, and cooperate to execute users' requests. Network services may be provided by a *computer network* vendor.

2.3 *Federated systems* are under separate management, available to share information over a computer network or by public telephone line access.

Distributed systems may process transactions more rapidly, but that is rarely the primary motivation for their existence. Distributed systems will be presented in much more detail in Chap. 11 on distributed systems. In this chapter we only deal with closely coupled multiprocessors, to gain more performance.

MULTIPROCESSORS   Multiprocessors behave so similarly to single processors that we need not treat them in great detail. To the user of the multiprocessor the system may appear as if it were a high-quality centralized processor.

Some performance differences appear due to specifics in their connections to memory and storage. When the processors fully share memory and storage they can exchange tasks and data rapidly, and only increased CPU capacity results. Because of interference, however, most multiprocessors do not share resources fully.

Often the processors will have local *cache memories*, which provide rapid access to local data and without interference. Use of caches complicates buffer management, since now file buffers are not shared. Buffers may have to be locked to prevent errors when one file can be shared among transactions using different processors.

The storage systems for multiprocessors have two architectural alternatives:

1. Each processor can access all the storage devices. Processors may use distinct channels to access the same storage controller. A *lockout mechanism* prevents conflicts due to simultaneous access. For instance, once a controller has issued `select` commands `sd`, `sk`, `sh`, or `sr`, it should not lose that disk position prior to attempting data `transfers` `tr`, `tw`, or `tv`.

2. Each processor accesses only its owned subset of storage, and any data it needs which resides outside this subset is requested from the owning processor. Such a system is then closer in behavior to a clustered distributed system.

Mixed architectures are also available; for instance, systems where pairs of processors share access to the storage units, and the entire system comprises several such pairs. Data transfer between pairs is by request. Such an architecture is motivated by improved availability in case of failures due to the shared storage; having multiple pairs permits growth and reduces the capacity loss if a processor fails.

The benefits of having multiple processors, from the data-processing point of view, are increased computational capability and backup in case of processor failures. If failure protection is required against storage-device losses, storage must also be replicated.

10-2   STORAGE HARDWARE SELECTION

In selecting a computer system for a data-processing application we first determine the amount of storage required. The reason for making storage requirements the initial criterion is that we want to design a *reasonable* system. In such a system the cost of the storage does not exceed by a large factor the cost of the processor.

The benefits of storing data arise from the use of data. The use of data may be vague and distant, but its probability needs to be evaluated and measured. The availability of stored data is, of course, a prerequisite for use of data processing. If the computer system is used primarily for data-processing applications the processor will also not be much more costly than the storage.

We summarize the initial procedure in Table 10-2.

Table 10-2   Storage hardware selection.

---

1 Estimate the data storage requirement for data files and programs.
2 Estimate total storage capacity needed by adjusting for effective density.
3 Select an adequate disk capability.
4 Find a reasonable computer for the disk.
   Reasonable may mean having a cost in the range of 20 to 200% of the disk cost.

After selecting the storage devices, the controllers, and the channels they need, we must determine if performance of the transaction is adequate. In Sec. 10-3 we consider performance of applications and transactions, in Chap. 14 we analyze the adequacy and cost-benefit relationships for the aggregate systems.

10-2-1 Storage Requirement

For each fundamental file organization we have developed formulas giving the expected record length, R_f, taking into account the attributes being stored. In addition, there will be *wasted space*, W, because of unspanned packing of records into
blocks, which reduces the number of blocks needed for some records. As part of the
load estimation we have estimates of the size for each file, n_f.

We must not forget files used for backup and archiving. Traditionally, tapes
were used for this function, but the high reliabilty of disks and their convenient
access for recovery and audit make backup and archival storage on disk more common. Some additional storage capacity is needed for files used by the operating
systems and to store programs.

The total net storage capacity, D, required for the files, $\mathcal{F}$, making up the
collection of files for the data-processing operation being analyzed is then

$$D = \sum_{\mathcal{F}} n(R + W) \qquad \langle \text{net} \rangle \ 10\text{-}2$$

In practice, often considerably more storage will be needed.
1 There will be temporary files created by applications which copy data from the
base files prior to analysis.
2 There will be working files created by utilities as sorting programs.
3 Past transaction logs may be kept untill the completion of updates has been
assured.
4 Storage for programs in source and executable format requires space. Often
multiple versions are retained.

Also, for many applications the volume of data increases steadily over time.

The estimation of the file size requires knowing both the number of records n
and the record size R. The value of n is directly related to the application. To
estimate R we look towards the application for the total number of attributes a and
the average number of attributes in a record a'. The lengths of the value fields V
and the attribute description fields A are also a factor.

The various file designs will combine these fundamental parameters in different
ways, so that at this point we are actually not prepared to evaluate the file size,
since the design decision is yet to be made. The storage demand presented by a
pile organization (Chap. 4-2), if substituted in Eq. 10-2 above, provides an order of
magnitude estimate which is adequate to select hardware for the proposed file.

10-2-2 Storage Utilization

When files undergo frequent and dynamic changes, not all the available file capacity
can be utilized. Depending on the file organization used, considerably more space
should be available. A density factor, u_D, is used to adjust the expected storage cost
throughout the design process. The author has seen values for u_D ranging from 90%
(stable files in an environment which provided good space-allocation capability) to
25% (dynamic files in a structurally limited environment).

A low value of u_D does not necessarily imply an undesirable file design. In files using direct access, for instance, available space will considerably enhance operational performance. Problems of reorganization are also reduced if the storage capacity is generous.

The total storage capacity required for the files becomes then

$$D = \sum_{\mathcal{F}} n \frac{R + W}{u_D} \qquad \langle\text{total}\rangle \ 10\text{-}3$$

An initial value of the utilization can be obtained by surveying similar systems. A value of 50% is a reasonable starting point. Only if systems are carefully designed to minimize space will the utilization be significantly higher.

The parameters n, R, W, and u_D will be different for each file, but in this presentation we ignore these differences to keep the notation simpler. The value D provides the initial estimate of the total storage needs for a system.

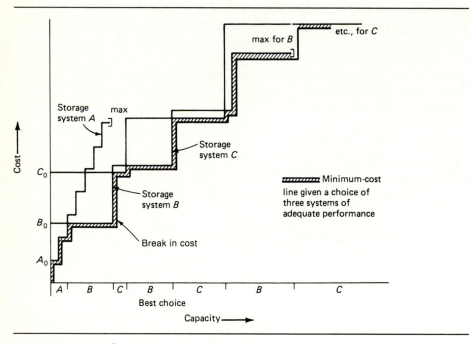

Figure 10-2   Cost versus storage capacity.

10-2-3 Counting the Devices Needed

We can now estimate the types and number of components needed to satisfy the storage requirements for the files. For each proposed hardware configuration we make sure that

$$D_{available} > D \qquad\qquad 10\text{-}4$$

The estimate of D made above has much uncertainty. Since the actual file organizations are not yet known, one can obtain a range of devices needed by establishing a range of the storage capacity needed, estimating the requirements at a low level of waste, free space, and redundancy (say $W = 0, u_D = 80\%) \rightarrow D_{low}$, and at a high level (maybe $W = R, u_D = 25\%) \rightarrow D_{high}$ of these conditions.

THE STORAGE DEVICE TYPES   Once the range of storage requirements is defined, we can limit the evaluation of alternative hardware to an appropriate range. Since a similar range of disk devices is available from many manufacturers, we can concentrate initially on types of storage units, and avoid selection of a specific vendor. We will select from the alternatives a file configuration which promises minimum cost. Figure 10-2 shows cost estimates for three storage hardware combinations (A, B, C,) versus their capacity, $D_{available}$.

Discontinuities exist in these cost functions because of disk type alternatives, controller increments, and choice of reasonable channel assignments. Since an approximate range for the storage requirements has been established, only a segment of the curve is of interest. Three outcomes are possible: *Fixed, Break,* or *Variable.*

F The actual storage cost is fixed because a minimal number of units are adequate for the range of capacities being considered. The high limit should be reasonable and adequate for the foreseeable future. A specific file design can be chosen on the basis of other parameters.

B There is a significant *break* in the cost function within the range of interest. One can attempt to design the file hardware to remain at the low side of the break. Careful evaluation is needed to assure that in the worst case the storage, D_{high}, will never exceed the capacity at the break. The selection of file-design choices will be constrained. The alternative is to play it safe, acquire the higher-capacity device, and use the excess capacity to increase performance. Many file-organization methods, such as B-trees and hashed files, respond well to increased space.

V The cost varies by relatively modest incremental steps as capacity changes. Now the cost can be modeled adequately by a continuous function within the range being considered. This situation is frequently true for a large data-processing system, because we are using many devices so that the cost function has many breaks. This means that file cost is incremental, and that there is only an economic storage constraint in choosing a file method, as discussed in Chap. 14-5.

Costs are also incremental if the data-processing application is added to an existing computer system. The cost per increment of file storage is then known, but not controllable. Now we do not start from point zero, the cost function for our application starts at some point of the curve shown in Fig. 10-2.

THE NUMBERS   Once we have selected a hardware type, A, B, or C, some review is in order. In practice, the method used to select the storage required may not be as mechanical as outlined above. Long-term growth expectations may make the eventual quantity D_{high}, and hence the cost range, impractically large. The rapid development of new hardware may make a design based on current storage device information impractical.

If projections of future hardware capabilities are being used, the delay between the introduction of new technology and its availability with full software support has to be considered; 3 years has been a typical interval. If one of the design objectives is a good understanding of a number of hardware-design alternatives, assuming a fixed storage cost (F or B) is inappropriate.

In most instances, approximate methods provide adequate initial results. A reverification, both of needed capacity and available capability, is always in order before a final commitment is made.

10-3 TRANSACTION PERFORMANCE

In Sec. 10-2 we considered satisfying the storage capacity. Now we check if the hardware satisfies the response-time demands placed on it by the transactions. Here we only consider individual transactions, and the applications that give rise to them. The analysis of aggregate file system performance is covered in Chap. 14-3.

A transaction, or any data-processing application in general, will make multiple references to multiple files. To estimate the time required to execute such a program we must add all the times required for computation and accesses to all files. We continue to use the term *transaction*, even for long-running application programs.

We do not analyze here the time required for the actual user computation. In most data-processing applications this time is small, but many exceptions exist. Analysis of algorithms for computations are found in many textbooks, for instance Knuth[73A&F]. An alternative to analysis is measurement, running the program with dummy data, and perhaps without file accesses, for a number of cases, and extrapolating from these measurements to the expected general behavior. Simulation is appropriate when the program is too complex to be pretested. Chapter 12 includes techniques for these approaches.

10-3-1 Decomposing a Transaction

A transaction, T, may use several files, F. Most data-processing applications will use at least two files, one as a source of information and one to record the computed results. Applications performing updates often use three files, a source and a result file for the data, and an input file containing the update information. When operations are logged for later audit or recovery, an additional file is needed, to which the log records are appended.

Small inquiry transactions may avoid having a result file, since responses are presented directly on the screen and small update transactions may not need a file for update information since they obtain updates directly from the users. However, transactions are typically logged, so that having a log file is common.

Having selected the CPU and storage hardware we have values for the hardware parameters c, s, r, and t. Selection of a suitable block size, B, is also possible now, taking limits of physical sectors into account, and perhaps optimizing the size using the considerations provided in Chap. 8-4-3. Now btt and derived values such as W and t' can be estimated as well.

Computation of the basic performance measures T_h requires selecting the file organizations for each of the files $\mathcal{F}$ as well. A reasonable approach is to use Table 7-1 for an initial selection among fundamental file types. The selection will consider the expected response times.

We have also learned enough about the various file organizations to know that some file types are not suitable for certain on-line operations. In practice, constraints of the actual file support available must be considered as well. If performance problems are found, then alternate file organizations, combination schemes (Chap. 7), refinements in indexing (Chap. 8), or special file organizations (Chap. 9) may provide solutions.

Given storage hardware parameters and an organization of the files we can compute values for the file performance parameters. Each file, $\mathcal{F}$, used by a transaction, τ, may have multiple operations applied to it. For each operation, h, we can estimate the time, T_h, using the six performance parameters defined in Chap. 4-1 and used throughout:

1 The expected fetch time: T_F
2 The expected get_next time: T_n
3 The expected read_exhaustive time: T_X
4 The expected insert time: T_U
5 The expected update time: T_U
6 The time required for reorganization: T_Y

Transactions, τ, are composed of sequences of operations described by the timing measures shown above: search and update. For convenience we treat reorganization as a transaction as well.

Figure 10-3 uses an airline ticket sale transaction to show a decomposition. There are two tasks during such a decomposition of a transaction:

1 Determining which files are accessed by the operation.
2 Determining how often the operations occurs. In simple transactions the frequencies will be low, and perhaps fractional for conditional accesses. In large application programs there may be loops with thousands of accesses.

10-3-2 Transaction Response Time

The time required to perform a transaction, T_T, is obtained in Fig. 10-3 by summing the times, T_h, of all its operations. In general, the total time, T_T, for the transaction is

$$T_T(\tau) = \sum_{f=\mathcal{F}} l_F T_F(f) + l_N T_N(f) + l_I T_I(f) + l_U T_U(f) + l_X T_X(f) + l_Y T_Y(f)$$

10-5

Here l_h denotes the number of operations of type h that a transaction, τ, performs using one of the files f of $\mathcal{F}$. This equation is adequate in the first instance, but we must consider some differences among file organizations that require some mapping between the counts, l_h, and the performance parameters, T_H. For instance, no performance parameters were developed for operations as update_next, used in step 3 of Fig. 10-3, extend record, append, and delete.

The airline has a Seats_counts file with entries for each flight segment between two points.

A Passenger_list is kept as a separate file and refers to the Seats_counts file. We have analyzed the activities at the ticket counter and find

- a The average ticket sold contains 2.7 segments.
- b The average number of people flying together on a ticket is 1.61.
- c Five percent of the time no ticket is sold because of insufficient seat availability.
- d Twenty percent of the tickets sales are actually changes.

We now analyze the primary transaction:

ST Sell Ticket
  1 Fetch seats_free for the first flight segment from Seats_counts file.
  2 Get successive flight segments needed from Seats_counts file and check their seats.
  3 If seats are available, update the Seats_counts file segments.
  4a Insert new passenger information into the Passenger_list.

or

  4b Update the Passenger_list with the flight information.
  5 For ticket changes also change previous Seats_counts.

Now count the FETCH, GET–NEXT, INSERT, and UPDATE accesses for ST.

1 $1 \cdot T_F$ (Seats_counts)
2 $(2.7 - 1) \cdot T_N$ (Seats_counts)
3 $0.95 \cdot 2.7 \cdot T_U$ (Seats_counts)
4a $0.80 \cdot 1.61 \cdot T_I$ (Passenger_list)
4b $0.20 \cdot 1.61 \cdot T_U$ (Passenger_list)
5 $0.20 \cdot 2.7 \cdot T_U$ (Seats_counts)

Multiplying these operation counts by their timings, T_h, then gives an estimate of the total transaction cost, T_T

$$T_T \leftarrow \{1 \cdot T_F + 1.7 \cdot T_N + (0.95 + 0.20) \cdot 2.7 \cdot T_U\}_{\text{(Seats\_counts)}}$$
$$+ \{0.95 \cdot 1.61(0.80 \cdot T_I + 0.20 \cdot T_U)\}_{\text{(Passenger\_list)}}$$

Other transactions operating on these files are
  WL Place passenger on wait list
  CT Cancel ticket
  CS Check schedule
  PT Pay for ticket
  RT Refund ticket
  SP Search passenger list
  PF Prepare flight manifest
  CP Cleanup passenger list
  .. etc.

Figure 10-3   Transaction decomposition.

If we consider only our six fundamental file methods, we find for other operations on files a mapping such as shown in Table 10-3. We note that the operation counts l_i and l_U also do not map directly to the file performance parameters T_I and T_U, since their functions are not directly supported by all file organizations.

Some cells in the table are marked to indicate that the fundamental organization is not suitable or relevant for the operation type. For other file organizations similar mapping rules can be developed, so that a small number of performance parameters can continue to serve our needs. The performance analyses which follow assume that such a mapping is available.

Table 10-3 Parameter mapping for file operations.

Operation:	file	Pile	Seq.	Index Seq.	Index	Hashed	Ring
fetch	l_F	T_F	T_F	T_F	T_F	T_F	T_F
get_next	l_N	T_N	T_N	T_N	T_N	∞	T_N
read_exh.	l_X	T_X	T_X	T_X	T_X	T_X	T_X
update	l_U	T_U	T_I	T_U	T_U	T_U	T_U
update_next	l_V	T_U	T_I	$T_N + T_{RW}$	$T_U - T_F$	∞	$T_N + T_{RW}$
extend	l_E	T_U	$-$	$-$	T_U	$-$	T_U
insert	l_I	T_I	T_I	T_I	T_I	T_I	T_I
insert_next	l_J	$-$	$T_I - T_F$	$T_I - T_F$	T_I	$-$	$T_I - T_F$
append	l_A	T_I	$T_F - Trw$	T_I	T_I	T_I	T_I
delete	l_D	$T_U - T_I$	T_I	T_U	T_I	T_U	T_I

10-3-3 Satisfying Response-time Requirements

Given the values of T_T for all important transactions, T, we can now see if they require the requirements presented by the users of the application. We must add to the values for T_T any significant computational costs incurred within the transactions.

If we find that the response time for some transactions is inadequate we have the choices shown in Table 10-4. The choices are not ordered since the suitability of one versus the other depends on many factors. Each of these topics has been covered in earlier chapters, except for parallel operations.

Table 10-4 Improving transaction response times.

- Select a better file organization from the ones available on the computer system.
- Use more indexes or TID-lists to avoid file search.
- Use combined indexes or TID-lists to reduce number of access structures being used.
- Use a specialized file organization for critical data files.
- Rewrite the transaction programs to reduce accesses or computation times.
- Obtain faster hardware.
- Try to use hardware in parallel for multifile transactions.
- Obtain more hardware and use it in parallel.

We can gain from parallel operation on the storage devices, on the controllers, on the channels, and by having multiple processors. In the ST transaction of Fig. 10-3 we had to access two files, Seats_counts and Passenger_list. If these use different channels and controllers the transaction may be speeded up. An analysis is neccessary to determine the overlap possibilities. In the ST transaction steps 1 and 2 have to be completed to assure seat availability, but steps 3, 4, and 5 may overlap. In this transaction the reduction of T_T may amount to 30%. The benefits of parallel operation are greater among multiple transactions, and that issue is treated in Chap. 14.

10-4   FREE STORAGE MANAGEMENT

When we have obtained storage space for our file application, as presented in Sec. 10-2, we have to consider how to allocate the storage for the various files. This task is a function of an operating system for a computer, as indicated in Chap. 2-3.

We discuss the methods used by an operating system to manage the *free space* here, because there is an interaction between file structure and allocation policy. File organizations which do not use indexes or pointers to locate blocks require contiguous space; other file organizations can receive space incrementally. Two methods to keep track of the *p portions* allocated to files and of the space which remains free have already been encountered in Chap. 8-5 (VSAM) and 9-3 (MUMPS). In this section we will review this subject more completely.

The assignment problem becomes more complex when a computer system has to support a variety of files of different types. We see at times more than one allocation scheme in use. VSAM, for instance, has its own suballocation scheme within the standard IBM operating system.

INITIAL STATE   In the beginning the system establishes the file area required for its operation and then defines the areas available for users. The user's area is without form and void. The first task for the system is the creation of a directory to all available storage units. During operation the system has to identify removable diskpacks, tapes, etc., which are currently mounted. The storage-device directory is re-created whenever the system is initialized, and directory entries are updated upon receipt of a "ready" signal from a device on which a diskpack or such has been mounted.

On many machines new diskpacks or floppy disks have to be formatted before use. Formatting defines the blocks that the system will use, giving each block an identifier for future reference. During formatting a verification may take place. Any blocks found that cannot be successfully written and read may be marked "bad" and omitted from the set of blocks available for allocation.

The initialization process has established the *free space* available in the system.

10-4-1 Assigning Portions

When the free space has been defined, users can come forth and demand their share of the resources. We use the term *portion* to designate a unit being assigned to a user's file. The minimum size of a portion will be one block, but if locality is important then portions may consist of many blocks at a time.

We note that the allocation of space is a function carried out at a level which is more basic than the level on which the file systems operate. When multiple file systems share one computer system, the operating system may have to support more than one space-allocation strategy. Good space management is essential to keep the system's ecology in balance.

Portions, Size versus Number   Space will be allocated to users in response to their requests. The shape, number, and size of the portions of the system storage space given to users is a compromise between the requirements for efficiency by the individual files and overall system efficiency. The items to be considered in the trade-off are:

1 Contiguity of space increases performance, especially for get_next operations, and greatly for transactions running in a transaction-oriented operating system.
2 Having a large number of portions increases the size of tables needed to manage the allocation information.
3 Having fixed-size, simple portions, for instance blocks, simplifies the reallocation of space.
4 Having variable size or small portions minimizes the waste of unused storage space due to overallocation.

These items interact, and there are two major alternatives: variable, large, contiguous portions or blocks. We can summarize the trade-off of the alternatives as follows:

1 Large portions improve performance. They should be variable in size to avoid excessive waste. They can use small allocation tables, but the space is hard to reuse.
2 Small portions improve flexibility. They are typically of fixed size, but may require large tables or complex structures for their allocation. Contiguity has been abandoned, blocks are allocated incrementally as needed.

To achieve high performance it is best to allocate large portions. Some users and some file systems request large amounts of storage prior to need, even if incremental allocation is the provided alternative, and they allocate that space to their files internally. This was the approach used in VSAM, where the user can prespecify eventual file size. With large portions much space may remain unused, but the user will pay for the excess.

If contiguous space is to be allocated, large portions are needed to make the contiguity effective. To prevent waste of storage space for small files, the portions will be of various sizes. Allocations may be restricted to a small number of portions; this number is, for instance, limited to 16 in IBM's OS. The tables used to keep track of allocated storage in OS are relatively small. Some operating systems are able to utilize the extra space given when the user is done.

In systems with a high degree of multiprogramming it is not very beneficial to provide contiguous space for users, so that allocation can be based on blocks (CDC SIS) or trains of blocks (IBM VSAM). The user's request will be rounded to the next larger unit.

Allocation by variable portion leaves more total free space, but in less usable form, than allocation by block or train. The storage efficiency of block allocation improves with smaller block or train sizes. When allocating blocks or small multiples of blocks, the storage allocation tables will be larger.

Figure 10-4 sketches a storage space layout after an identical space request and release sequence for variable and block allocation. We see that after the release of the variable portions used by process C some space could be used by successive requests of processes D and B, but fragments of those spaces remained unused. It is likely that small fragments will never be used. The blocked allocation assigns more space intially, but uses less space in the end.

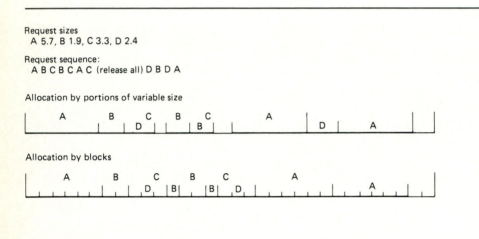

Figure 10-4   Storage allocation alternatives.

A DYNAMIC ALLOCATION POLICY   A scheme to avoid the problem of preallocation versus waste or lack of contiguity is to allocate portions of increasing size as the file grows. If the next portion is always doubled, the size of the portion table for the file is limited to $\log_2(n/Bfr)$ entries. Less than half the allocated file space is unused at any time.

This scheme can be improved by allocating fractional portions, say, four portions of 25% of the previous allocation, before doubling the allocation size. Now the portion table is four times as large, but a file of 10^6 blocks still requires only 80 entries. Less than 25% of the allocated file space is unused at any point.

10-4-2 Management of Allocated Portions

Since external storage is typically allocated over long periods of time, the storage-control tables reside on disk. The record of allocated space has to be updated whenever a portion is allocated to avoid problems when the system fails.

Consider the scenario of Fig. 10-5.

Step 1 A user, Y, stores information on a file in the portion allocated to user Y.

Step 2 The system fails before the allocation information is persistently recorded.

Step 3 The system is restarted.

Step 4 Another user, M, requests storage and is allocated the same portion, or a part of it.

Step 5 User Y accesses the same portion via a reference kept inside the file.

Figure 10-5 Storage allocation disaster.

Some schemes can prevent such disasters.

1 One can delay user access to the portion until the update of the allocation table has been completed.

2 One can check on restart after a failure that all blocks used on disk are in the proper allocation table.

3 One can mediate all accesses to disk and verify that any block accessed is allocated to the user or file giving the access command.

In the latter two schemes additional storage is taken from each block to maintain the identification.

The second scheme has a very high cost when a failure occurs, since all blocks have to be read. The cost can be reduced if it is only performed for files that were in use or open when the disaster occurred. In that case, the timestamp for the last CLOSE of the file precedes the OPEN timestamp. The cost for the second scheme can also be deferred by only checking when a file is OPENed again for use, but at that time more damage may have been done to that file.

The third scheme distributes a small loss in performance over all accesses, independent of the failure rate. When the inherent failure rate is low, as we hope, its cost will be relatively greater.

The first scheme is the only one that actually prevents errors. It has, however, a significant effect on performance when small portions are allocated frequently. The cost of keeping storage secure in this manner can triple the users' cost of writing a new block. To avoid this overhead, a batch of entries denoting free portions can be kept in a working area in core storage. The algorithm in Table 10-5 is intended to keep the *batch storage allocation* secure.

Table 10-5 Batch storage allocation.

1 Obtain batch of free portions from the storage-control table on file for allocation into a work area.

2 Mark these portions in the work area as 'in use'.

3 Rewrite the storage-control information to storage.

4 Allocate portions from the work area to the users as requests are received, and identify the portions allocated.

5 When the batch is used up, rewrite the storage-control table again to incorporate the actual assignment information.

6 Return to step 1.

With a batch storage allocation scheme, there will be entries for portions after a failure marked "`owned by user X`", entries for portions marked "`free`", and entries for portions marked only "`in use`". The latter portions will not be reallocated. If the allocated portions themselves are identified with their owner, date, and time of most recent `WRITE` operation (as required by the other schemes), it is possible to check the portions whose entries are marked "`in use`" when they are again retrieved by the user and correct the storage-control table eventually. Other techniques for cleanup are possible, depending on the file system's protocol.

Cleanup and other housekeeping tasks may be deferred and combined with file-reorganization tasks, since the storage-control table remains usable. It helps to use a verification such as alternative scheme 2 above routinely when reorganizing files. Chapter 16-1-4 discusses some long-term aspects of file maintenance.

Systems which ignore the problem altogether lose robustness, and the user may waste much time picking the pieces up after a failure. Even users who were not aware of the failure can be subject to damage.

ALLOCATION OF FREE STORAGE   The storage-control table also contains, explicitly or implicitly, information about the external storage areas which are not yet allocated and hence free to be given away. To assign storage to a user from the free space, a section of the storage-control table is fetched from the disk and analyzed to determine which space to give to the requesting user. When variable portions are used, decisions have to be made whether to allocate according to *first fit* (done above), *best fit*, or closest to the previous allocation for the file to increase locality. It is not clear which strategy is best.

10-4-3 Storage-Control Tables

The structure of the storage-control table is affected by the allocation procedure it has to support. Three methods are in common use to define the available storage space and its allocation:

1 Table of contents
2 Chaining of portions
3 Bit tables

We will discuss these in turn.

TABLE OF CONTENTS   A file maintained by the system on every unit may be used to describe space allocation, using one or several records per file. A file may have an extensive description. Typically included are such items as the owner's identification, the file name, the date of creation, the date of most recent use, the date of most recent updating, and for every portion the position and size. This technique is typically used for systems which allocate large portions. Such a *table of contents* is kept on every disk in the system and is found from a fixed position on every unit.

Free portions could be located by searching the table and finding unallocated space, but this is apt to be costly. To avoid this cost, a dummy file with owner `SYSTEM` and name `FREE_SPACE` is kept in the table of contents. Since the number of portions of free space can be larger than the limit of portions per single file, the free portions may be chained to each other and found from a single or a few entries.

CHAINING OF PORTIONS   The free portions may be chained together through the free-space portions themselves. This method is also applicable when portions are smaller, for instance, in block-based allocation. It has negligible space overhead since it uses free space for storage of the free storage-control data. Only one, or a few, header entries are kept in a pseudofile entry. When space is needed, the headers from the portions are fetched one by one to determine the next suitable free portion in the chain. Then the portion is removed from the chain and the chain is rewritten, taking care again not to leave the free storage control data vulnerable to system failure.

Multiple chains may be kept to group cylinders or sectors in order to create efficient user files. MUMPS uses free chains in that manner (Fig. 9-22). If variable-length portions are being allocated, there may be multiple chains to implement a best-fit algorithm. Files will obtain portions from the chain appropriate for the size of portions required, and large portions are preserved until needed.

Chained free-storage management does not keep track of data allocated to the user's file. It is desirable for the operating system to be cognizant of all allocations made. When there is no table of contents, this can be achieved by an extension of the chaining method. The allocated portions are chained together for each file using a header similar to the header used for free storage management. The relative space overhead to do this depends on the size of the portions allocated but will be bearable unless portions are of a size much less than a thousand bytes.

BIT TABLES   A third approach to manage free space is to keep a *bit table*. This method uses an array containing one bit per portion in the system. It is used only when all portion sizes are the same, generally equal to one block. Each entry of a "0" indicates a corresponding free portion, and a "1" indicates a portion which is in use. The list of portions allocated to a specific file is kept as part of the file mechanism. A bit table has the advantage that large sections of the table can be kept in core memory and that the allocation and deallocation cost is minimal. This advantage is important in highly dynamic environments. The tables, on the other hand, are quite vulnerable to errors, so that they tend to be practical only where the file system keeps track of its allocation in a manner which can be used by the operating system. It is then possible to reconstruct or verify the bit table by checking through all the individual file tables.

File systems themselves can also use bit tables to locate their member portions. The use of bit tables is especially effective where the portion-allocation data does not have to be kept in serial order. Bit tables for a specific file tend to be very sparse, but their efficiency can be increased by a technique of packing. The packing of a sparse bit table is achieved by indexing groups of the bit array. A group which has only zero entries is indexed by a zero, and not actually represented. The index itself can be recursively grouped and indexed. Figure 10-6 illustrates this technique for File **B**. Bit arrays have also been used where portions, or records, are being shared by multiple files. Since no space is required within the portion, there is no limit to the number of owners that such a portion can have.

We see that there are a number of possibly conflicting objectives in the design of a free-storage management algorithm. The primary conflict is again speed versus space. To increase file performance, it is desirable to provide large portions, and also to locate new portions close to the predecessor portions. To decrease the cost of space management, one may also wish to allocate large portions, which reduces the frequency of allocation as well as the size of the required tables and lists. To use storage space well, it is desirable to allocate variable or small portions.

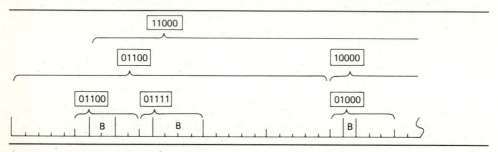

Figure 10-6   A packed bit array.

SUMMARY   Table 10-6 summarizes these three methods to manage free space. The basic methods can, of course, be improved at some cost in complexity, time, and core requirements.

Table 10-6   Evaluation of three free-space management techniques.

Criteria	Methods	1. Contents directory	2. Chained free portions	3. Bit tables
Portion size		Large	Large or small	Small
Portion variability		Variable	Variable or fixed	Fixed
Allocation frequency		Low	Low to high	High
Time to allocate space		Medium	Long	Short
Free space .control		Poor	Medium	High
Basic crash security		Medium	Medium	Low
Core space required		Moderate	Low	Moderate

An operating system which does not provide good management of storage space imposes a greater load on the file system. Some file systems allocate separately for files within a larger space assigned to a user (MUMPS), or allocate from a very large space allocated by the operating system for all files in its purview, as seen in VSAM in Chap. 8-5.

10-4-4 Reliability in Allocation

An important aspect of free-space management is file reliability. The assignment of permanent file resources to a user is even more critical than the assignment of core memory to the user's processes. While there are routine hardware-protection features which require a storage key to be matched for every data reference to core storage, equivalent facilities have to be implemented through software in the file-system area, except in those systems where files are considered extensions of virtual core storage segments. In Chap. 15 we will discuss some file-protection structures. It is the free-space allocation routine and hence the operating system, however, which controls ownership and has to set the privilege codes and keys which enable file protection schemes to perform their work.

Because of the great risk inherent in the reassignment of space, computer systems have been designed which would never have to reuse an address. This is achieved by providing a large virtual address space ($\gg 10^{20}$). The MULTICS system achieves this goal for all data at a given point in time. In more commonly available hardware some of this protection can be achieved by assigning portions for reuse that have been free for the longest period. Then there is increased recovery capability when portions have been released to free space in error, either by the system due to a program error, or by the user due to a mistake. Unfortunately, many systems assign free space on a LIFO basis rather than according to the safer FIFO rule, since the "last in first out" method is much easier to implement when free-space portions are maintained in chains. A ringlike structure could be used to hold free portions of storage for FIFO allocation.

10-5   ALLOCATION FOR SEQUENTIAL PROCESSING

In many data-processing applications entire files have to be read periodically. Typical of such processing are daily account balancing, weekly preparation of payrolls, or extraction of data subsets for further analysis. Buffering provides the most important tool to improve sequential performance. We will present here three techniques that are used to further improve sequential processing. In the previous analyses we did not assume that these techniques were being used, since we concentrated on transactions applied to individual records.

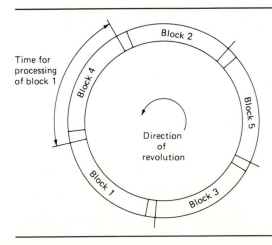

Figure 10-7   Alternate-block arrangement.

10-5-1 Interleaving of Blocks

Sometimes a processor cannot process the blocks in time, violating the constraint of Eq. 3-22 that $c_{block} < (B + G)/t$. This occurs frequently on personal computers, because they cannot overlap computation, c, and disk transfer time, btt. Another cause can be insufficient memory, so that only one buffer is being used.

Where data is often read sequentially, use of *interleaving* avoids paying the full latency cost, $2r$, to read successive blocks. By changing the relative addressing algorithm to arrange serial blocks on a track in an alternating pattern, time for interblock processing can be gained.

Figure 10-7 illustrates the method with an *interleave factor*, if, of two. The number of blocks being skipped is adjusted to provide good sequential performance. The interblock processing time obtained is $(if - 1)(B + G)/t$, so that the time to transfer and process one data block is $btt + (if - 1)(B + G)/t \approx if(B + G)/t$. The bulk transfer rate for this arrangement, using an interleaving factor, if, is then

$$t''_{\text{interleaved}} = \frac{1}{if} \, t'_{\text{full rate}} \qquad\qquad 10\text{-}6$$

Interleaving is commonly used on microcomputers, since these cannot overlap data transfer with processing of incomming data. For instance the `FORMAT(04)` command on an IBM PC permits the specification of an interleave factor of 1 to 16; a value of 3 is common for *hard disks*. Distinct interleave factors can by specified for individual tracks (05) and for bad tracks (06). When alternate disk drives or CPUs are placed in such systems, a change of the interleave factor may be needed for best performance.

10-5-2 Scatter Block Reading

A seek which commences the reading of a train of many sequential blocks can in some systems, avoid the full latency time, r, to begin transferring data from a cylinder. If the file system can read any block of the train as it appears at the reading head, identify it, and deposit it in a buffer for later processing, useful data can be transferred as soon as some block can be read. We expect to have at least enough buffers available for every block on the track, so that any block appearing on the selected track can be read. The average latency delay is now equivalent to $\frac{1}{2}$ block or

$$r'' = \frac{1}{2} \frac{B + G}{t} \qquad\qquad 10\text{-}7$$

This type of operation is called *scatter reading*.

If the identification of the block can be carried out prior to the reading of the block, the block number, i, can be deposited into the buffer numbered i. Otherwise the file system will maintain a table with entries giving the correspondence (`block_no`, `buffer_no`) and will direct record requests to the appropriate buffer.

The computational algorithms will still process the data records in a logically sequential order independently of the order in which the blocks were read. There are also instances where data can be processed in any order. For instance, if the sum

of all values of a certain field within the records is required, the processing sequence
is immaterial. Then scatter reading of blocks can allow significant reductions in
reading time.

The algorithm also can be used for writing of data. *Gather writing* picks buffers
from core memory as the appropriate blocks appear at the heads of the disk unit.

10-5-3 Track Stagger

Staggering the begin point of tracks of successive cylinders provides minimization
of the effect of rotational latency encountered when reading information sequentially. The amount of stagger is determined by the time required to perform a seek
operation to an adjacent cylinder, s_1. The amount of stagger has to be adequate to
account for the mechanical variability in the seek time. Looking at Fig. 10-8, one
can derive that the stagger, ϕ, in degrees should be

$$\phi = \frac{360}{60 \cdot 1000} \text{ rpm max}(s_1) \qquad\qquad 10\text{-}8$$

where rpm is the number of revolutions per minute and the seek time for a one
track distance, s_1, is in milliseconds.

Stagger is especially useful if the seek time to an adjacent cylinder is much
less than the rotational latency. For the examples used earlier the seek time for
one track was just less than $2r$, so that the appropriate amount of stagger was
$\phi \approx 360° = 0°$. Devices with few tracks per cylinder will also benefit more than
disks with many surfaces.

Where no hardware track stagger capability exists, but sector addressing is
available, the effect can be accomplished through sector renumbering by file software. Staggering between cylinders is easiest if done using the relative block-
addressing mechanism, analogous to the method used to provide alternate-block
reading within cylinders.

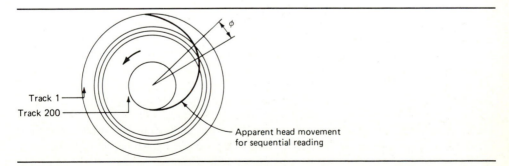

Figure 10-8   Stagger of track-begin points.

10-6 DATABASE MACHINES

Database machines use specialized hardware to improve the performance of operations using external storage. Most efforts concentrate on making file access faster
by placing important operations into hardware, but an important by-product is the
modularity of systems which is needed to achieve such a partitioning.

Opportunities for performance improvement exist at all stages in the flow of
data in a computer system:

1 Faster disk access by parallel access to data on disk
2 Faster data transfer by early selection and projection of relevant data
3 Faster operations by hardware implementation of operations
4 Reduced competition for the processor by performing the data reduction in a
   separate back-end computer
5 Better tracking of modern technology by being able to improve back-end or
   main processors independently, as it becomes advantageous.

Some conditions must be satisfied before the advantages will be realized.
The database machine should perform hardware functions rapidly as a centralized
machine. Two issues must always be considered:

1 The hardware must use algorithms that are as effective as the algorithms available in software.
2 The increased communication overhead due to partitioning of the operations
   must not exceed the benefits gained.

A database machine provides file access and manipulation capability for a computer system. To perform its task a specialized processor is coupled to the computer
which receives the users' data-processing requests. The steps needed to execute a
transaction using a database machine are shown in Table 10-7.

Table 10-7   Steps in using a database machine.

---

1 The main processor receives a transaction request.
2 It analyzes what tasks can be performed by the database machine.
3 It prepares task requests for the database machine.
4 It sends task requests to the database machine.
5 It waits for the results of the requests.
6 It receives the results from the database machine.
7 It processes the task results as needed.
8 It returns the answer to the transaction request to the user.

Steps 3, 4, 5, 6, and 7 may be executed repetitively for a complex transaction.

Performance Gains If the database machine is faster than the main processor,
then step 5 will take less time, and, if steps 3 to 6 do not take much additional time,
the response time to the transaction request will be shorter. Even if the response
time is not better, it may now be possible for the main processor to perform other
useful work during step 5.

10-6-1 Classification of Database Machine Tasks

We can classify database machines according to the tasks they perform, or we can classify them according to how they perform the task. In this section we will consider their capabilities, and in successive sections present various technologies to achieve these capabilities. We will start with the simplest type of task. Many current database machines are simple, since it is risky to build complex hardware.

File Scanning   Files have to be processed in their entirety to fetch sets of data by attributes which are not indexed, hashed, or partitioned via rings. Having a separate machine to carry out this function can provide a great advantage in offloading the main processor.

   If the subset being fetched to the main processor is large, the advantage is less because step 6, receiving the results, will take as much effort as is gained by not reading data from storage.

   Being able to handle variable length data, or data formats such as occur in pile files, can make a file-scanning machine quite useful, since much processor time may be freed. Multiple simple database machines might work in parallel on a large file.

Aggregate Computation   If a database machine can scan rapidly, it might be extended to extract some information during the scan. Such a machine can assist in data reduction and much data transfer to the main processor can be saved. Producing COUNTs, TOTALs, SUMS_OF_PRODUCTs, etc., for sets and subsets of data can support basic statistical data analysis. Searching for MAXima and MINima can help in locating exceptions and special events. Obtaining references to related data and then fetching such data can reduce the need for task interaction and the attendant delays.

Record Selection   Scanning is not an effective approach to replace indexed or hashed access, even if carried out by separate processor. If the database machine can also take on the tasks of retrieval of records by the key, then the services it provides become more complete. The load on the main processor can be greatly reduced. Effective selection may require that the database machine maintain and use indexes internally, otherwise the response time to the user will be worse than local processing with software indexes.

Attribute Selection   The volume of results to be transmitted to the main processor can be greatly reduced if irrelevant attributes can be projected out. A request to generate a telephone listing for the employees will require only two fields out of the dozens of fields in each employee record. Update requests often involve only a few fields and can benefit greatly from not transmitting large records in and out of the main processor.

   The capability to select attribute fields requires that the database machine understand and parse the record formats. Some formal description has to exist to make such communication feasible. Database management systems support schemas to make search communication easy, but some modern file systems have schema capability as well. We will discuss schemas further in Chap. 16-1-2. If records have a fixed format, then the main processor can simply specify beginning- and end-positions, and perhaps the data representations.

COMBINING RESULTS FROM MULTIPLE FILES   If the database processor can combine results from multiple files, and continue computation without interaction with the main processor, then further computational effort, transmission requirements, and interaction costs incurred by the main processor will be reduced. An example of a transaction accessing two files was shown as Fig. 2-6. It is easy to see that not having to ship the intermediate results to the main processor is beneficial.

Now the database machine carries the majority of the *load*, and the response time will be largely determined by the capability of the database machine.

We will now present alternatives for database machines and begin with a solution which has all these capabilities.

10-6-2 A Database Machine Using a Standard Processor

By using a standard processor all needed capabilities can be performed in the separate database machine, and the main processor load can be significantly lightened. If the two processors are equal in performance no gain in response time will be realized.

If the task requests and results are small, and the connection between the processors has a high bandwidth, additional delays will be minimal. If the effort needed to execute the tasks is large, much processing power will be freed in the main processor. Careful balancing of tasks issued and main processor data analysis may, in fact, reduce response time.

An otherwise standard processor may be speeded up by avoiding layers of software needed to provide general user services. There will be no need to process interrupts from user terminals, and possibly no need to page software in and out of memory. More memory can be allocated to file tasks, and buffer management can be simplified if all blocks are the same size.

Having a separate processor also generates a less obvious benefit: Software system maintenance is simplified. Often, problems with data-processing services occur when software in a processor is updated to deal with new terminal devices, new network connections, or processor improvements. In the database processor such changes can be ignored or deferred to a suitable time. On systems serving many diverse demands, the increase in reliability due to the flexibility gained in software maintenance can alone make the use of a distinct database machine worthwhile.

OPTIMIZING PERFORMANCE   Since this type of processor has all the capabilities needed for data processing, it can easily be overloaded as well. In an extreme case, the main processor only provides terminal access and message-switching function. Such a processor is then termed a *front-end processor*, to distinguish it from the database machine, the *back-end processor*.

10-6-3 Servers for Large Files

In many modern systems we find back-end computers that deal with voluminous data, reducing the file costs for the main processor or for a network of processors.

Examples of the first class are *archive data staging systems*, and for the latter, *file servers*. We will discuss both classes in general terms.

DATA STAGING SYSTEMS   Up to this point we have mainly discussed devices where the storage unit feeds data directly into the main memory. When voluminous data must be kept on more economical, slower storage devices it can be effective to use a specialized back-end processor to select data and make it available on higher speed storage as needed. An illustration of a storage unit used with staging is shown in Chap. 3 as Fig. 3-3.

The staging processor is typically not accessible by the user. The user requesting data is delayed until the staging processor has placed the file on the faster storage unit. That faster unit is then jointly accessed by the user's processor and by the staging processor. When a users program is completed, the operating system may signal the staging processor, if the file was changed, that it should be rewritten to slow storage.

The effectiveness of staging is based on the observation that some large data files are used intensively for limited times, and then remain unused for long periods. The concept of staging can be generalized to a complete *hierarchical storage organization*, as sketched in Table 1-2, where each layer automatically moves less frequently used data elements to the next, slower and more economical layer. Multi-layer staging, based on single paradigm, has not been seen in practice; the volume ratios are too large to permit consistency. Disk staging devices are in use to manage archival data. Interactive use tends to be prohibitively slow.

When staging is used, parameters such as the average seek time have to be computed carefully, using the methods shown in Chap. 3-2, and taking into account the pattern of access to the file. The mixture of operations must contain the proper balance of short, direct accesses to the faster unit and long, indirect accesses when data is being staged.

FILE SERVERS   File servers are used in situations where processors have little or no disk storage capability themselves. We see that condition in two situations:

1 In a network of personal workstations, where individual computers are configured to be economical, so that having many small and yet fast disk units would be very costly. These are often high-performance systems, with users who would not be well served by limited solutions such as floppy disks.

2 In large scientific computers, where it is inefficient to use the costly processor to perform file and input or output tasks.

For instance, in the large CDC systems the file devices are controlled by a peripheral processor, which obtains the data blocks to be read, verifies correct transmission, and then retransmits the blocks which have been read to the main processor. Data may be preanalyzed and reduced within the peripheral processors, so that less data has to flow to the central processor. The process is sketched in Fig. 10-9.

In *network file servers* the serving node behaves similarily, but has only access to remote nodes via the network. A network file server is hence more passive, only responding to requests, whereas a directly attached file server can participate in scheduling processes on the machine it serves.

The proper analysis of performance of these systems becomes more complex than the cases of direct data transfer considered up to now. While there are some obvious delays in the system, the ability to reduce data can compensate partially for the delays.

·A file server can also rearrange the data on its storage devices for optimal use, whereas a user will rarely make that effort. Since user transactions do not need to know where data actually resides, the server processor controls the file allocation. Active files or records can be placed on faster devices, or on devices which have less total load and interference.

The discussion of distributed systems in Chap. 11 is also relevant to the analysis of network file servers.

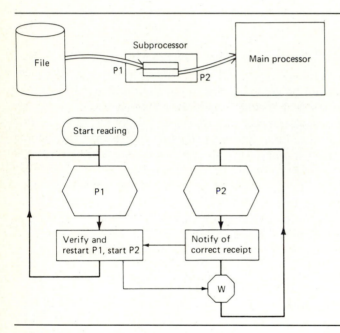

Figure 10-9   File access via a file server.

10-6-4 Machines with Rapid Storage Access

In Chap. 3-3 and Sec. 10-4 we found some schemes to improve the processing of data by careful management of buffers. Specialized hardware, which acquires and checks blocks in local buffers, can reduce delays and increase processing power.

PIPELINING   The underlying concept involves *pipelining*, decomposing the process into separate sections, with each section being managed by specialized hardware. Each section of the pipeline hands its results over to the next section.

Pipelining in data processing is more difficult to achieve than in numeric processing, where the concept had its origin. The individual sections have to handle large data units, so that it is costly to transfer the intermediate results. An architecture where blocks are read into buffers and specialized processors successively operate in them may be more beneficial but has not been tried as far as we know. It is not easy for users to determine how database machines achieve their performance by reading the available marketing literature.

To be effective, such machines require much memory to hold data. In general, it may be desirable to hold an entire cylinder in memory, so that seek time is incurred only once.

PARALLEL STORAGE ACCESS   If we can process many buffers of data rapidly, then the bottleneck of reading data from disk is exacerbated. Reading data in parallel into buffers can accelerate this phase, especially if many blocks are needed.

Conventional disks having multiple surfaces can only read data from one surface at a time. The physical movement of the entire access mechanism is controlled to optimize reading or writing one particular selected surface.

Disks which can read multiple surfaces simultaneously have been built, but are quite costly since additional hardware and higher precision of mechanical components is required. Tracks of drums, bubbles, and charge-coupled devices are easier to use in parallel.

An alternative, to overcome the problems of multiaccess disks, is to use multiple disk units in parallel. Although more hardware is used, the simple replication of standard disks is economical. Systems using this principle are now available.

PARALLEL PROCESSING OF STORAGE FUNCTIONS   The low cost of simple processors makes it feasible to replicate processors once storage access is replicated. Now the operations carried out serially in a pipelined processor can be carried in parallel by such *storage processors*.

A storage processor is attached to every read station, and each processor can test and select data in parallel. For a disk we would expect a processor per track, so that all tracks of an entire cylinder are searched during one rotation. The possible degree of parallelism is hence equal to the number of tracks per cylinder.

It will be necessary to communicate among the parallel processors since partial results in one machine can affect the computation in another machine. There will typically be one more processor to control the operations of the storage processors. This *storage control processor* will also mediate all communication with the main data-processing machine. For instance, several storage processors may have results for the main processor at the same time. Such requests must be handled in some order.

To avoid excess complexity in the main data processor it is desirable that task requests can be issued without considering which of several storage processors will carry them out. Then the number of storage processors, and the assignment of files to them, becomes immaterial. The single storage control processor will then also take on the job of assigning task requests to the individual storage processor. Now the storage control processor is in danger of becoming the bottleneck of the operation.

ASSOCIATIVE STORAGE   Storage processors permit associative searching for a value stored on their storage areas. One pass through storage by all processors replaces a serial search. Associative storage differs from associative memory, presented in the next section, that the storage device itself remains unchanged.

To retrieve data associatively, all storage processors are loaded with a search program and a search argument. When a processor finds matching data, it may set a mark, or it may transfer the record to the central processor for further manipulation. If the central processor is just receiving a record from another track processor, a delay and possibly a second revolution will be needed.

The storage processors can have relatively sophisticated programs, so that multiple and conditional matches can be performed on each record, without involving the central processor. Less data will need to be transferred and interference will be less. The record formats may also be variable, since the track processors can decode the record and field marking schemes that are used. Work in this area is progressing, although the degree of speedup is limited to the parallelism of the device reading mechanisms.

SUMMARY OF STORAGE ACCESS PROCESSORS   We see that systems involving advances in storage access take on the roles of advanced controllers and channels, expanding on the functions presented in Sec. 10-1. Many control units and channel devices on large systems have, in fact, the capabilities required, but can carry out only a small fraction of the possible tasks since they have to be compatible with older architectures.

If we extend these concepts and make the units of the database machine more autonomous, then we move to the realm of multiprocessors and distributed computing, as described in Sec. 10-1-4 and Chap. 11.

In the next section we will present yet more specialized hardware to accelerate the processing of data.

10-6-5 Associative Processing

Associative storage processors distinguish themselves in that, instead of accessing data by using a given address for the data, they find data that satisfies certain given requirements.

Associative addressing locates records by matching one or several *key* fields of the stored records with a search argument. Multiple records may simultaneously satisfy the search request. To state this in a simple form: The search request does not specify *where* but rather *what* it is we are looking for.

ASSOCIATIVE MEMORY   Associative memory uses semiconductor devices that are arranged into arrays with long word lengths — we again will call them blocks — in a manner that permits comparisions to be executed on all or many of these blocks in parallel. The data records are stored one per block within the associative memory. Within the data records are fields which may be selected as retrieval keys. A match register is used to define which parts of a record are to be taken as key fields, as shown in Fig. 10-10. The block size and match register will be fixed by the hardware design, and limits record sizes and field arrangements within the record. Every block may have an active flag to indicate if it is to participate in the next operation.

A search operation presents a search argument, which will select all blocks having active records with a matching key value, setting a marker, X, for these blocks. Subsequent operations will fetch one marked record at a time to the processor, resetting the marker, until all records are processed. Other associative operations may be available which permit such simple operations as incrementing, summing, shifting, or replacement to be applied to defined fields of all marked records in parallel.

COMBINING ASSOCIATIVE MEMORY AND STORAGE   Since associative access to storage can rapidly retrieve all relevant data from multiple files and bring it into memory, and associative processing in memory can rapidly link related information from those files, the combination of the two technologies could provide order of magnitude gains in data processing.

As an example where matching records from multiple files have to be brought together for data analysis, we can consider two files, Sales_by_region and Population_centers_by_region. An associative system permits matching records on the attribute region to be brought together for analysis without expensive intermediate sorting by region. A speedup yielding linear performance, $\mathcal{O}(n)$, versus the best sort performance, $\mathcal{O}(n \log n)$, is conceivable.

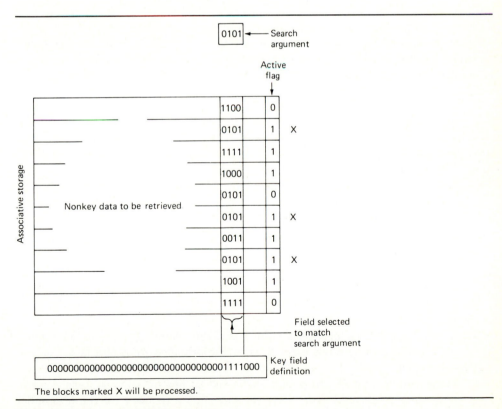

The blocks marked X will be processed.

Figure 10-10   Associative memory.

Associative memories have been built only on a small scale, or used in highly specialized data-processing applications, for instance, for the processing of data obtained from radar observations. The evaluation of their performance is not covered in this book. It appears that, using VLSI (Very Large Semiconductor Integration) technology, such memories could be built at a unit cost less than double the cost of *regular* semiconductor memory.

Analyses of machines combining associative memory and storage have been made, and experiments have been conducted and published. However, the risk and complexity of combining two radical technologies has prevented any commercial demonstrations.

10-6-6 Status of Database Machines

A number of specialized database machines are now available, and they provide some part of the advantages described in Sec. 10-6-1. It remains difficult for hardware solutions to keep up with advanced algorithms rapidly implemented in software, so that it is difficult to beat the performance of well designed software systems. For instance, associative access is also provided, at only somewhat higher cost, by index and hash mechanisms. The software, while complex, tends to deal better with problems of varying fields, variable file sizes, and long records. We hence find associative technology used in only highly specialized systems.

We note also that associative access is logically equivalent to the key-based software methods to access records described throughout this book. The use of specialized hardware typically increases performance but reduces flexibility and capacity.

To obtain high productivity from systems which include database machines, the loads on the various components must be balanced carefully so that no unit is consistently a bottleneck for all others. Different transactions will, of course, have different patterns of component usage, so that excessive optimization is apt to be futile.

We find then in practice:

1 Back-end conventional processors to offload heavily loaded central computers. Some database management systems have the option that all transactions addressing intensively used but limited size files are assigned to a distinct processor which can keep all or most of those files in memory.

2 File servers, composed of conventional processors configured to only provide file services. These are especially common in distributed environments, since they permit users to select any of a number of connected processors for their computation.

3 Back-end specialized processors which perform scanning and simple primary key access to rapidly fetch selected data. Performance gains of a factor of 2 or 3 are typical.

4 Systems using multiple processors dedicated to one or a few storage devices. They may interpret arbitrary retrieval and update requests for the files under their control.

5 Computers using associative memory for rapid analysis of data blocks, used in specialized applications such as image data processing and sensor data reduction.

Up to now specialized database machines have not had the impact expected by their promoters. There seems little doubt, however, that systems with multiple processors, including specialized machines for databases, will become common. It is hard to see that a single architecture will dominate the field.

10-7   REVIEW

We have now introduced the complexity of multiple files, using systems having multiple disks, multiple controllers, multiple channels, and multiple processors. This permitted the prediction of the behavior of complex transactions using multiple files. Data processing applications will be composed of numerous transactions, sometimes many small ones, initiated from on-line terminals, sometimes mainly large programs, executing in batch mode and producing voluminous results. The same considerations apply to the analysis of both types. Large programs, of course, will take longer to analyze, since they execute many more accesses to the storage devices.

We see the use of smaller transactions increasing, because of the flexibility they provide, the ease in changing patterns of use, and the improved maintainability of smaller programs. This trend is made possible by having greater on-line storage capacities, so that costs of keeping information accessible is now quite low.

Satisfying user requirements for transaction response times was a major concern in this chapter. We considered the allocation of storage space, since achieving high locality can improve performance greatly. We then covered some software and hardware techniques which can be used to help improve performance.

We have not yet considered the total effect of executing many transactions many times on the computer system. Evaluation of the aggregate demands of users and the aggregate capabilities of computer systems is the topic of Chap. 14.

Performance can also be improved by having more processors. In the introduction we cited four classes of systems using multiple processors. Section 10-6 discussed the first class, and provided its own summary of five subclasses in Sec. 10-6-6. The important and growing class of distributed systems, where files are controlled by distinct processors, will be analyzed in the next chapter.

BACKGROUND AND REFERENCES

The architecture of storage systems differs by manufacturer and also by computer series within a manufacturer. To determine the commands for channels and controllers the detailed architectural specifications have to be perused.

The concepts of transactions were referenced in Chap. 2. Combinations of operations are estimated by Demolombe[80].

Specific procedures for storage allocation are found in the internal documentation of operating systems. BrinchHansen[73] reviews some of the techniques used. Frey[71] provides an evaluation of a file system with block allocation and many reliability considerations. Knuth[73F] shows that "first-fit" storage allocation performs better than expected.

There are a number of devices which improve performance at various hierarchical levels, some were cited in Chap. 3 as mass storage devices. A database computer using video mass storage is described by Marill[75]. Canaday[74] proposes a back-end computer for file control, and Epstein[80] introduces an implementation. The topic is surveyed by Maryanski[80]. A European product is described by Armisen[81] and Epstein[80] describes the popular BRITTON-LEE system. Network file servers are surveyed by Svobodova[84], Brown[85] describes a server in an ethernet.

Research efforts toward database machines using associative storage, for instance Ozkarahan[77] and Lin[76], are surveyed in a collection edited by Langdon[79]. Their principles are discussed in Su[80] and Hawthorn[82] provides a comparative analysis. King[80] has doubts about their effectiveness. System examples are found in Appendix B. An early associative memory system is described by Rudolph[72]. An economical associative memory is proposed by Doty[80]. Addis[82] describes the language for CAFS, an associative file storage device produced by ICL. Shaw[80] proposes a system combining associative memory and storage which would use new algorithms to carry out database operations. The effectiveness of database machines was questioned by King[80]. An annual workshop on database machines is sponsored by Syracuse University, and proceedings of a series of International Workshops on Database Machines are published by Springer-Verlag in their series, Lecture Notes in Computer Science; the machine described by Salza[83] stores the data in transposed form.

Systems using multiple processors to increase performance are becoming common. They may in turn be combined into distributed clusters. The TANDEM computers led the development of such transaction systems (Borr[81]). A research system sponsored by IBM is described by Andler[82] and Schkolnick[83]. The larger DEC VAX systems rely on having clusters of processors.

New architectures have been presented annually since 1975 in the *Workshops on Computer Architecture for Non-Numeric Processing*, published by the ACM special-interest groups SIGARCH for architecture, SIGMOD for databases, and SIGIR for information retrieval.

EXERCISES

1   Rank the following items in the order that a file designer has the most and the least control over (Solomon[86]):
- transaction time T_T
- storage space S
- CPU time c
- memory space Buf
- ▦ Wait time in queues (see Chap. 12-3) ▦

2   Describe the free-space-allocation procedure of the system you have available. Is it safe? Is it efficient? If you want contiguous space, how do you get it?

3   Do the calculations from Exercises 2-7 to 2-9 in Chap. 2 for transfer via a file server as illustrated in Fig. 10-9.

4   Calculate the total space required for a file as shown in Fig. 10-11, using record-anchored indexes. The calculation will initially evaluate the capacity of one cylinder and then determine the number of cylinders required.

Parameters to be used:
$R = 200$ (including the linkage pointer of 6 bytes length),
$B = 2000, V = 14, P = 6,$
Blocks per track = 7, surfaces per cylinder $k = 19$, Overflow allocation = 20%.

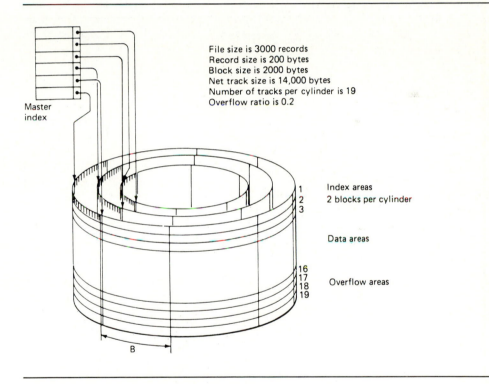

File size is 3000 records
Record size is 200 bytes
Block size is 2000 bytes
Net track size is 14,000 bytes
Number of tracks per cylinder is 19
Overflow ratio is 0.2

Master index

Index areas
2 blocks per cylinder

Data areas

Overflow areas

Figure 10-11   Illustration of indexed sequential file layout.

5   Make a flowchart for a general program which can deal with queries of the type indicated in Exercise 9-2, use again the files sketched in Fig. 9-26:
Given attribute_1 = (or $\geq, >, \neq, <, \leq$) find attribute_2.

6   Generalize the program for Exercise 10-6 for complex questions. Such questions may involve references to multiple files as well as usage of multiple indexes. Since the sketch is not complete, you have some freedom in the implementation of details. As in all other questions list any assumption made in a table to be appended to the answer to this question.

7 Derive a predictive formula which can be used to give an estimate of the length of an inquiry response time from the inquiry parameters and the file dictionary only, using again the above file design.

8 Evaluate the formula derived above for the following query:
"Find an unmarried man between 25 and 30 years old with recent experience operating Caterpillar D-10 equipment."
where the operating history is given in an equipment file and the personnel data are provided in a personnel file. Use values from Table 3-1 for the disk and optical disc estimates for the mass storage device.

9 Calculate the average seek time for a file on a mass storage device having a seek time distribution as shown in Fig. 10-12.

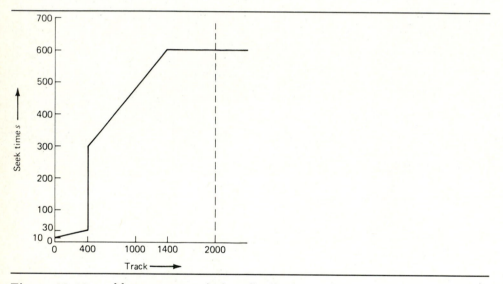

Figure 10-12 Mass storage seek-time distribution.

10^p For the three important transactions of your application, identified in Exercise 2-7:

    a Identify which of your files they will access
    b Estimate with what probability each access will occur
    c Compute the expected total time for each transaction

You will be making assumptions about the use of the transactions. State all assumptions you have made clearly, in a separate table.

Chapter 11

Distributed Files

'Tis distance lends enchantment to the view.

Thomas Campbell
The Pleasures of Hope, vol. I, 1799

11-0 INTRODUCTION

We have concentrated up to this point on files that are stored on hardware connected, directly or indirectly, to one central processor, although in the previous chapter we also considered central computer systems having multiple processors. There are a number of situations where the use of a centralized system is not the best solution. In such cases we distribute both the files and the processing of the files to multiple systems.

Chapter 10-1-4 introduced three types of distributed systems: clustered systems, remotely distributed systems, and federated systems. When distributed systems are mentioned without further qualifications it is likely that a remotely distributed system is implied. However, there are major differences between the three types, and each type has its specific benefits and liabilities. We find that sometimes, in literature about distributed systems, benefits or liabilities associated primarily with one type of system are assigned to other types.

Some of the confusion is due to a mix of motivation for distribution. In Sec. 11-1 we will consider the motivation for distributed processing; subsequent sections will investigate the technology: clustered systems in Sec. 11-2, remotely distributed system in Sec. 11-3, and federated systems in Sec. 11-4.

Some definitions are in order. We refer to the processor or processors which operate as a closely coupled multiprocessor as a *node*. A node is the unit of distribution and includes processing capability, memory, and storage. Nodes are linked by a communication network. Nodes comprising multiple processors will have internal interconnections as well, but we will ignore these in this chapter.

Associated with distribution are three concepts which determine how to allocate the information contained in files onto the nodes of a distributed system. *Allocation* is the primary issue in designing distributed systems.

1 Fragmentation: Splitting files into units suitable for distributed allocation. This topic is addressed already with clustered systems in Sec. 11-2-2, but as relevant to remotely distributed systems.

2 Replication: Allocating more than one copy of the data. This topic is addressed with remotely distributed systems in Sec. 11-3-3.

3 Data derivation: Computing and storing intermediate results for local use. This topic is addressed with federated systems in Sec. 11-4-4.

The association of the three concepts with three types of distributed systems is to simplify exposition of the material. The association does not imply a rigid binding of these concepts with the types of systems being discussed. Similarily to the exposition of file organizations, we associate concepts with primary types of systems, but realize that hybrids are common.

These three concepts can also be used to allocate data on files of a single processor using storage devices of different capability. In that case we allocate files within a *hierarchical storage system*. Layers of hierarchical storage were listed in Table. 1-2. This topic was touched upon in Chap. 10-6-3, a hardware example was cited as Fig. 3-3.

Section 11-5 summarizes and discusses the modeling of these systems. Material for quantitative performance evaluations is also found in Chap. 14.

11-1   MOTIVATION AND ORGANIZATION

Reasons for distributed processing are varied. Important concerns which motivate distribution are:

Functional   A system carries out a number of distinct functions, and it is desirable to develop and manage these functions separately. If the activity within a function is greater than the interaction between functions, a system where functions are distributed to specialized processors will be more manageable.

Geographical   If groups of users are located in distinct sites, it may be efficient if substantial local processing can be carried out on a local processor.

Performance   Retrieving data from local nodes avoids communication delays. Replication reduces retrieval costs but increases update effort. Highly specialized nodes can provide high performance for certain functions, without having to alter other aspects of a data system. *Back-end* database processors or *front-end* communication systems are examples of such specialized nodes.

Autonomy   In an organization, when responsibility over business or scientific areas has been delegated, a corresponding delegation of control over the related information also is implied. Delegation is made explicit by distribution of the data. Access privileges, quality-control responsibilities, reliable communications, and access convenience can then correspond with the pattern of responsibility.

Availability   If parts of a data system can be isolated, much of the system can continue to function when one processor or its storage devices have failed.

Recovery   If parts of a data system are damaged, data replicated on other nodes can be used to restore the damage. If necessary, a new node can be assigned to collect the data and take over the function of the damaged node.

Growth   If demands on a data system grow, adding a new node can provide additional capacity without replacement of the entire system.

While all these motivations lead to distribution, they do lead to conflicts. For instance, autonomy may not help improve performance or recovery.

For a system designer it is important to recognize the driving force in a given case of information distribution. Often, technical reasons of efficiency and reliability are presented, while autonomy is part of a hidden agenda. Autonomy is in fact beneficial, since with distribution of authority comes a distribution of responsibility. Responsibility can lead to a better effort in maintaining quality of data.

11-1-1 Motivation and Architecture

The systems listed as distributed systems in Chap. 10-1-4 show increasing levels of autonomy. The choice of system architecture is strongly related to the motivations for distribution. We now review these relationships for the three distributed architectures.

1. Clustered processors still appear to be single systems. The user does not address a transaction request to a specific processor. The system and the system's administration control all allocations.
2. Remotely distributed systems communicate through messages. A user accesses the system through a local processor. The system may make local and remote access functionally *transparent*. Even if transparency is achieved the user will sense differences in response times for local and remote accesses.
3. Federated systems are explicitly under separate management. Typically, they only respond to read requests. Some coordination is required to make the information obtained sharable among nodes. Any remote updates are reprocessed by their own systems to assure compatibility and integrity.

Indirectly related to autonomy is distance and locality. Central management becomes more difficult when nodes are remote. The rules for resource allocation change drastically with these three types of systems.

In a clustered processor transactions and their data are grouped onto nodes to optimize system use. Distance increases communication delays, so that locality of data becomes a greater issue in remote systems. In remotely distributed systems it is desirable that most transactions be completed locally. Files may be reallocated among nodes to achieve that objective, or data will be replicated so it is available at more than one node. Updates to replicated data have to consider all nodes.

Since in federated systems there is no central management authority, no re-allocation of primary files to improve performance is feasible. But replication is common, although now such replicated data is awkward to keep up-to-date. Some-times only selected data is extracted and kept for local use. The issues covered when talking about federated systems section deal mainly with coordination to achieve data compatibility.

Note that the type of system is not directly related to distance, although there is a strong correlation. We do see at times processors that are physically close and connected only by a telephone link, so that they behave as a distributed or a federated system.

11-1-2 Effects of Communication Networks

For multiple processors to be integrated into one system, a communication network has to exist among nodes. If the processors are clustered, using technology as used for their storage devices, they can communicate at rates t_r similar to the highest disk or drum transfer rates, about 1M char/s. As distances increase to span buildings, the effective rate is reduced by a a factor of 10 or more. Use of telephone lines reduces the bandwidth by a factor of more than 100, and that rate, requiring 56K baud service, is quite costly. Transmission of data over public dial-up lines is at best at a 9600 baud rate, adequate for about 1.2K char/s, but due to cost and reliabilty concerns much transmission occurs at lower rates. Terminal access to information services, sometimes used to download information to local files, is often limited to 1200 baud, yielding at most 150 char/s.

Table 11-1   Performance of communication links.

Network type	Typical maxi-mum distance	Typical bandwidth t_r
Computer bus	20 meters	5 000 000 char/s
Local network (Ethernet)	200 meters	500 000 char/s
(with gateways) or token ring	2 000 meters	100 000 char/s
Leased line to workstations	20 000 meters	6 000 char/s
Remote computer linkages	unlimited	6 000 char/s
Computer network service	unlimited	1 200 char/s
Switched phone line	unlimited	300 char/s
Dial-up information service	unlimited	150 char/s

If we recall the typical times needed to access data on attached disks we note that, especially in remotely distributed systems, the interprocessor transmission delays dominate. It is hence important to distribute processing in such a manner that local processing reduces demands on the communication network.

OPERATION   Let us review the use of distributed files as introduced in Chap. 2-3-5. In general, remote nodes are accessed to obtain data needed for some transaction which is maintained at remote nodes for the convenience of their owners or to increase system performance.

1 Requests originate at a source user node.
2 At the source node the transaction request is analyzed and, if necessary, decomposed into subtransactions for remote execution.
3 The subtransactions are forwarded to other nodes or subnodes.
4 The subtransactions are analyzed and processed at the remote nodes.
    a Further subtransactions may be generated and forwarded to other nodes.
    b The logical capabilities of subnodes are used to eliminate the need to pass data containing no information to the user machine.
5 Relevant data is returned to the requesting source node.
6 The source node processes the data obtained and returns the final result to the user.

Steps 2 to 5 depend on knowledge about the location of the files. Since allocation of files may shift as efficiency concerns or user responsibilities change, all accesses for files in a distributed system should be mediated by system software. We call such interface software a *file access interpreter*.

Directories for Distributed Files   A File Access Interpreter (FAI) will receive each file request and ship it, as needed, to the remote node. When the allocation is changed, only the FAI will have to be changed. Without such an interpreter the users' transaction programs have to be modified for every change of file allocation. The FAI is driven by a *global directory*, similar to a file directory, but having less detail. The global directory will refer to the local directories for specific information on file storage allocation, last-used times, etc.

1 If reallocation is infrequent the FAI tables may be managed by a system adminstrator.
2 If files move around frequently the FAI tables must be updated automatically.

Maintaining a complete global directory at each site having a FAI can be costly. Local nodes may not keep complete global directories; only those files that are referenced at the local node may have *cached entries*.

When a file is not listed in the local *directory cache*, the local FAI must invoke a directory update procedure. Such a procedure may again involve a system administrator or be accomplished by automated requests:

    2a A global table is consulted. It refers to the last known owner site.
    2b A broadcast is sent to the network, requesting the current owning site to respond with information to build a FAI entry.

Because of the possibility that sites may receive requests for files they no longer hold, many protocols require that tombstones be kept in local directories for obsoleted files.

Distribution of Effort   If the intent of distribution is also to reduce the processing effort made by the source node, then specialized nodes, following some of the concepts presented with database machines in Chap. 10-6-3, can help. Frequently, data blocks are fetched from a file only to obtain references to other blocks; and in these cases a capable file server node can carry out a large fraction of the work. Some specialized subnodes may be used to merge and analyze data retrieved from one or more such file server nodes. Yet other nodes in a network will carry out the function, switching user requests and data between the other nodes.

We will consider only generalized nodes in the remainder of this chapter. If we have specialized nodes, certain transactions or data will be assigned to them. Although the physical system will be more complex, the use and tasks of all the nodes are still analyzed as before. Any preassignments to specialized nodes reduce the range of design alternatives and simplify the design process.

11-1-3 Transaction Cost in a Distributed System

To satisfy the response time requirements for transactions in a distributed environment, we have to consider now the additional cost due to remote access. The cost of the actual file access should remain the same, as given in Eq. 10-5, although one will have to account for differences in equipment or interference at other nodes. If a file is remote then the costs shown in Table 11-2 are also incurred.

Table 11-2   Costs in remote operation.

Symbol	Definition	Estimation	Typical range
c_l	Local interpretation		< 1 ms
c_m	Preparing the request message		< 1 ms
mtt_q	Message transmittal	$100/t_r$	Up to 20 ms
c_r	Remote interpretation		< 1 ms
T_{tr}	Remote processing	Eq. 10-5	20 to 500 ms/block
c_r	Preparing the response		< 1 ms
rtt_r	Response transmittal	B_r/t_r	1 to 400 ms/block
c_p	Local processing		< 1 ms

Note that we measure the size of results being returned to the requestor node still in terms of blocks, rather than as actual data quantities. Communication systems also break large data quantities into blocks, and buffering considerations are similar as for files. Since error recovery is typically by block as well, large blocks have great penalties when communication lines generate errors. Small data quantities are rarely efficiently transmitted, so that it is best to allocate an integer block for performance evaluations.

We see that the costly items depend greatly on the bandwidth and will dominate the processing, especially if the bandwidth of the network, t_r, is modest. For that reason we will ignore below the processing costs $c_l + c_m + c_r + c_r + c_p$, although they comprise a major fraction of the total cost in complex systems with fast communication.

TRANSACTION COSTS For any given allocation of files the cost of executing any single transaction can be estimated. The cost of execution of a subtransaction accessing a file at a node is T_T, as developed in Chap. 10-3-2. We must often distinguish the cost local incurred at the local node $T_T(\text{lp})$ and the costs incurred remotely $T_T(\text{rp})$. In addition, we must take the communication cost into account; we will use the estimate 100 from Table 11-2 to account for the size of the queries sent. If we access $\mathcal{F}_r$ remote files, and acquire $B_{\mathcal{F}_r}$ blocks from each of them, an initial estimate of the time required to execute a transaction becomes

$$T_T(\text{d.e.}) = T_T(\text{lp}) + \sum_{f=1}^{\mathcal{F}_r} \left(T_T(\text{rp})_f + \frac{100 + B_{\mathcal{F}_r}}{t_r} \right) \qquad \langle\text{distributed effort}\rangle \; 11\text{-}1$$

This equation measures the total effort expended at all nodes to process the distributed transaction. Since it is likely that some of the operations on distinct files will be overlapped, the response time seen by the user will be less.

The extent of overlap depends on how the transaction was written and how the scheduler handles the subtransactions that address distinct files. With full overlap, possible only if the subtransactions shipped to remote nodes do not depend on each other, the response time could be as low as

$$T_T(\text{d.r.}) = \max \left(T_T(\text{lp}), \max_{f=1}^{\mathcal{F}_r} \left(T_T(\text{rp})_f + \frac{100 + B_{\mathcal{F}_r}}{t_r} \right) \right) \qquad \langle\text{distr. response}\rangle \; 11\text{-}2$$

If we find that an important transaction has a poor response time, it might be allocated specially by binding it to a node with a low utilization. Such a reallocation will not reduce the total effort expended.

SYSTEM COST The same priority exists in distributed design as in general transaction design: (1) we must satisfy the response-time requirements for each of the given transactions, (2) we design best total system. The design methods will differ for the three types of systems we consider, but the cost evaluation is identical.

Equation 11-1 estimated, for a given allocation, the cost of executing a transaction. The cost of executing a set of T transactions can now be estimated, possibly taking the importance of the transaction, I_t, into account. In practice, only a few transactions will be assigned an importance $I_t > 1$. Say that each transaction T is executed L_t times in a given period. Then the global cost of a given allocation is

$$Cost(\text{alloc}) = \sum_{T=1}^{T} L_T I_T T_T(\text{d.e.})_T \qquad 11\text{-}3$$

Design methods for distributed files can propose a number of alternative allocations. Each proposal should now be evaluated according to thwo more criteria:

1 Are any of the individual nodes overloaded, that is, stressed beyond their CPU, disk access, or storage capacity?

2 Are the demands made on the communication network for transmittal of requests and data within its capacity?

If several of the alternative allocation designs are satisfactory, the allocation which has the lowest cost is chosen. In the three sections following we will consider how appropriate allocations, suitable for the three system classes, can be generated.

11-2   CLUSTERED SYSTEMS

The objective of a clustered system is to distribute processing over multiple nodes to increase total capacity and availability, and permit incremental growth of the system. In a clustered distributed system we find a collection of processing nodes which each have their own memory and storage. There may be multiple processors within a node, but this aspect does not concern us here. The nodes in a cluster are connected via a high-capacity network. Typical networks use direct coaxial cabling and *Ethernet* or *token-passing* communication protocols. Aggregate transmission rates of up to 1M char/s are seen.

11-2-1 Transaction Origin Node

In a clustered system the user is not connected to any prespecified node; the initial network node is assigned by a front-end terminal processor. A common choice for the front-end processor is to assign a new user to the least-busy node. This technique is used, for instance, by DEC in VAX clusters. In a *transaction-processing* environment, however, the assignment should be by transaction. The command invoking the transaction is used by the transaction processing system to determine the node to be assigned for execution. In Chap. 2-2-2 we encountered the commands to give raises: `Grant`, `Award`, and `Give`.

Since these three `Raise` transactions use the same `Payroll` data, it is likely that they are best assigned to the same node. Any `Buy` and `Sell` transactions will be allocated to a node managing the `Inventory` data. A transaction `Pricing` goods uses primarily the data on the inventory node and will be assigned there, but may require also access to the `Salary` file on the `Payroll` node.

11-2-2 Fragmentation

For effective use of distributed resources two design tasks are applied to the files: *fragmentation* and *allocation*. Fragmentation creates subfiles for allocation. We consider fragmentation first, although the criterion for an effective fragmentation is that it permits a good allocation of data to nodes. A good allocation is one that minimizes transaction costs, especially costs induced by distribution of data to remote nodes. Fragmentation for clustered systems is conceptually identical to fragmentation for remotely distributed systems, but the allocation criteria are not. There is not a simple one-to-one correspondence between files and transactions.

1 One transaction may require data from multiple files.

2 Data from one file is accessed by multiple transactions.

A transaction will not need all data stored a file.

Data requirements of a transaction depend on its type and the parameters given by the user. We can predict to some extent what data may be needed by considering only the type of the transaction. Data needed by the `Mail` application, as the `electronic_mail_address`, is not needed by the `Payroll` application. Similarly, data records for administrative employees are accessed frequently by transactions scheduling office tasks, while data on factory employees is accessed mainly by transactions scheduling production orders.

Fragmentation partitions the file in units that permit localized allocations of data to the transactions that use the data. For the case of the `Mail` and `Payroll` application we would fragment the file *vertically* by attribute. For the second case of `Scheduling` distinct classes of employees the `Employee` file would be fragmented *horizontally* by record descriptor.

A fragmentation suitable for one transaction may split the file into units that are meaningless to another transaction. Now some of the transactions which access a fragmented file will need to access multiple subfiles. Fragmentation increases the complexity and cost of access for such transactions.

Evaluating Fragmentations
The number of fragments should be limited, both to reduce complexity of allocation and expense of operation. In general, one has to balance potential benefit due to the ability to place each fragment with the transactions which use it heavily versus the liability that now some transactions will need to access two fragments. Cost measures can help make the decisions.

We again first assure that individual transactions, now accessing fragments, do not exceed the limits of response times specified. The transaction response time T_T(d.r.) is computed identically to the times developed in the cost of having unfragmented distributed files, as developed in Eq. 11-2, but now we consider each fragment. This also means that the decomposition, underlying the terms T_T(local) and T_T(remote), must be reevaluated. In general, transactions on fragments should perform better than the same transactions accessing larger, although possibly fewer, files.

We now also consider the aggregate cost of the system using fragments. For any proposed fragmentation into $\mathcal{F}$ fragments many allocations to the $\mathcal{N}$ nodes of the network are possible. The cost of individual transactions and their aggregation is also identical to the cost of having unfragmented distributed files, developed as Eqs. 11-1 and 11-3 in Sec. 11-1-3, but now we consider each fragment.

For any given fragmentation and allocation the cost of executing the set of $\mathcal{T}$ transactions can be estimated, again taking into account the importance of the transaction, I_t, and its frequency, L_t, in a given period. Again, the fragmentation and allocation which have the lowest cost while satisfying response time and capacity constraints, should be chosen. The problem, however, becomes quantitatively much more difficult, because the number of possible alternative designs has grown exponentially.

The possibility of not fragmenting a file at all should be considered. In particular, if the fragmentation does not lead to well-differentiated groupings, the overhead due to fragmentation may not be compensated for by the advantage of local processing. However, if the file use is so intense that any single node will be overloaded, then fragmentation is needed.

Now we will analyze the two types of fragmentation, horizontal and vertical, in more detail.

HORIZONTAL FRAGMENTATION Horizontal fragmentation creates multiple shorter subfiles out of larger files. The fragments created will be fully adequate for some of the transactions. For instance, an `inventory` file may be split into fragments containing data for `vehicles, supplies`, etc., since most transactions only deal with one type of inventory. The total file size should not change.

The rationale of horizontal fragmentation is to produce fragments with the maximum potential locality with respect to transactions. This means that all relevant data from a file for a transaction, and as little as possible irelevant information, should be kept in a fragment. Of course, data irrelevant for this transaction may be relevant for another transaction. A good fragmentation makes allocation of transaction-fragment pairs to the nodes easier.

Different transaction classes may use different attributes for selection. The payroll application may have distinct transactions for three classes of employee: salaried, hourly, or occasional; while the personnel application may have its transactions split by five regions: East, South, West, North, and Central. The horizontal fragmentation of the `Employee` file used by both applications will have $3 \times 5 = 15$ fragments.

▦▦ **Derived Fragmentation** Once a file has been horizontally fragmented there may be other, related files, which require a matching fragmentation. For instance, if the `Employee` file is fragmented, then the file `Skills_of_employees` should be fragmented identically.

If related files are not fragmented or fragmented differently, then the subsequent allocation phase will be greatly compromised. Relationships among files can be obtained from database models, so that a precise treatment of derived fragmentations is beyond the scope of this book. In many practical cases the relationships requiring derived fragmentations will be obvious.   ▦▦

VERTICAL FRAGMENTATION Vertical fragmentation creates several smaller records out of larger ones. Each record of a vertical fragment must still carry a key field for identification, so that, in contrast to horizontal fragmentation, the total file size will grow somewhat.

The rationale of vertical fragmentation is to produce records which are used by different transactions, so that attributes frequently used together are grouped together. An ideal vertical fragmentation exists when transactions use subsets of attributes without any intersection; otherwise, some transactions will be harmed, since they will need to access two fragments, when one access was adequate before.

Finding vertical fragmentations consists of grouping attributes of each file according to their usage. Often a good vertical fragmentation is obvious, then it only has to be evaluated. If the fragmentation is difficult to perceive, formal methods can be considered (Navathe[84]); the procedure is discussed below.

▦▦ **Fragmentation According to Affinity.** A formal approach to vertical partitioning creates an *affinity matrix*, A. The matrix has a rows and a columns for each attribute $1, \ldots, i, \ldots, a$ of the file, and in each cell, $A_{i,j}$, an affinity value is placed. The affinity of attribute i and attribute j is the sum, over all transactions T being considered, of the joint use of those attributes $\{i, j\}$. We set a value $a_{i,j,t} = 1$ if both the attributes are used by the transaction, t, and keep it 0 otherwise. The joint use in turn is weighed by the product of the frequency of use of that transaction, L_t, and the importance of that transaction, I_t. Infrequent and unimportant transaction types can be omitted from this computation. It is typical that 20% of the transaction types account for 80% of the total load on a system (see Zipf's law and Chap. 12-1-6). The values in the affinity matrix are hence

$$A_{i,j} = A_{j,i} = \sum_{t=1}^{T} a_{i,j,t} L_t I_t \qquad \text{11-4}$$

where T is the total number of transactions being considered. If no transactions use both attributes i and j, then the entry in cell $A_{i,j}$ will be zero. High values indicate that the attributes are often used jointly.

The matrix can then be inspected for natural groupings. A more formal procedure is to diagonalize the matrix and use it as input to a partitioning process. Diagonalization places all high values along the diagonal by permuting rows, and because of the symmetry, the corresponding columns (McCormick[72]). To track the result, the names of the attributes on the sides are permuted, too. After diagonalization the attributes appear in a more suitable order along the sides of A. The zero entries $A_{i,j}$ will appear in the upper right and lower left of A, indicating a low affinity of attributes at the top and bottom of the reordered sides.

The partitioning process then splits the matrix A into submatrices, typically 4, then 9, 16, etc., representing 2, 3, 4, etc. fragments. The submatrices on the diagonal, which now have the highest values of A, represent activities within a fragment, and the other submatrices represent activities that go across fragments. To balance the use of the fragments, each submatrix near the diagonal should have a similar total internal affinity load. For one particular file a few partitions suffice, since each partition doubles the number of fragments. For the complete set of files there should be sufficiently many fragments that the total usage can be easily allocated over all the nodes.   ▦▦▦

THE FINAL FRAGMENTATION   Fragmentation design iterates applications of horizontal and vertical fragmentation to files to determine candidate units of allocation for the subsequent allocation phase. The allocation phase will be covered next, in Sec. 11-2-3. After that phase, any fragments of the same source file that wind up on the same node are best recombined. Of course, if no transactions ever need both fragments, then the recombination is only motivated by ease of file management and not by increased efficiency.

Transparency   It is important to make fragmentation *transparent* to the transaction programs. A *file access interpreter* dealing with fragmentation will receive each file request and satisfy it from the file fragments. Without such an interpreter the transaction programs have to specify the location of every fragment. It would become infeasible to change the node allocation of the fragments when growth or changes in usage pattern make a reallocation desirable.

11-2-3 Allocation in Clustered Systems

Since each node has its own storage, the data and transactions that use the data must be allocated so that the total system performs effectively. Having to move data from one node to another always involves a delay.

ALLOCATION CRITERIA   There are three criteria for effectiveness:
1 Any individual transaction must perform satisfactorily.
2 No node should be overloaded.
3 The global system should be as economical as possible.

If important and demanding transactions are also frequent, then all criteria may be satisfied together. Low individual transaction response times are achieved by balancing the loads on the nodes, and the low costs of transactions lead to low global costs.

There are many applications, however, where some infrequent transactions must be processed rapidly. For instance, in systems supplying information to deal with emergencies, the required emergency transactions must be designed first. These transactions will not affect the balance of the load or the minimization of aggregate cost. We dealt with satisfying transaction requirements in Chap. 10-3-3 and Sec. 11-1-3.

THE GLOBAL ALLOCATION PROBLEM   When all transactions which have response time constraints are allocated, at least in a general sense, then the global allocation problem can be addressed. A dual allocation problem arises in clustered systems:
1 Allocate execution of transactions to the node where most of the required data are located.
2 Allocate storage of data to the node where most of the transactions needing those data are executed.

These problems have to be solved in light of constraints of storage and processing capacity of the individual nodes. If there were no such constraints the best allocation would place all data and all transactions on the same node!

Since there will be capacity constraints in the nodes of most clustered systems, the fragments and transactions must be allocated to distinct nodes. The variety of possible allocations is immense. The sum of costs of all individually optimized transactions for one proposed allocation is the measure of the goodness of that allocation. Optimizing global allocation has been shown to be very difficult. Getting a good solution is easier.

Not obtaining a good solution can have a serious consequence if the cluster is heavily loaded. If the resources are not effectively used, the system as allocated may not be able to deal with the total load. This does not mean that the allocation must be optimal for the system to succeed. We will not design a system so heavily loaded that less than optimal use will cause it to fail.. However, a poor allocation can still overload a system that was designed to be moderately loaded. If, for instance, every data request for a transaction had to access another node, and an internode access costs 10 times the effort of a local access we would have a load demand that is 10 times greater than the equivalent single processor would have to support.

To drive a global allocation algorithm we must have a global cost function. A good allocation should achieve a minimal, or at least a reasonable total cost. The cost function may be available if the cluster transaction-management system tries to optimize its processing, since then it will assess the cost of transaction-processing alternatives for a given allocation. If this function is not available then the estimation of transaction-processing cost, as outlined in the prior section, will have to be invoked for each transaction being considered.

An Algorithm for a Nearly Optimal Allocation   The effort required to find an optimal result, if done exhaustively, consists of the following steps:

1 Finding the finest fragmentation of files
2 Generating all possible allocations of the fragments to the files
   a Checking constraint satisfaction
   b Computing the cost for all transactions to be executed during some time period using this allocation
3 Selecting the best allocation

Unfortunately, the exhaustive approach to design will require years of computation, even for a modest system having a hundred fragments and a dozen nodes.

Informal, heuristic rules can reduce the high cost of computation associated with a best algorithm. We outline here a modestly costly algorithm to allocation in a clustered system, which, however, does not guarantee the best solution.

The algorithm is termed *Greedy—First-fit* (GFF) because it combines the *greedy* heuristic of first taking the most promising initial step with the *first-fit* heuristic. The first-fit heuristic states that, if a total allocation evaluation is too costly, then it is better to fit these variably sized objects into existing bins rather than try to optimize bin allocation piece by piece. Both heuristics have been applied separately in number of design problems.

In this case we cannot afford to try out all allocations; instead, we will start with one partial allocation, and, being greedy, select the one which seems to reduce costs the most. Now only one allocation per iteration is evaluated. But, even now we cannot afford to recompute anew the costs for all the allocations that are feasible in the next step. Instead we estimate the new costs from the old ones.

The total cost for executing all desired transactions for the cluster in a certain time period will be called **C**. This cost will include CPU, disk access, and communication components, weighed to reflect their relative costs. We use the cost function giving **C** to direct us from a fictitious initial costly network configuration to a good one.

This fictitious network has one node for each individual fragment and transaction. Each partial allocation combines a transaction and a fragment it uses, or a fragment with a previously allocated transaction-fragment pair. Each partial allocation reduces costs: Communication cost because two objects previously on separate nodes are now together; processing cost, because no messages have to be formulated and parsed; and disk access costs if fragments from the same file are being combined. The steps of the allocation process are as given in Table 11-3.

The algorithm is driven by a benefit matrix, giving information about which objects (transaction and fragments) are good to combine. The computation of these benefits is very costly. The full computation of the benefit matrix is done only once in the method shown in Table 11-3. Subsequent updates to the matrix assume no effects on other objects. This assumption, made in step 9, that benefits are additive, is a gross simplification, but it avoids the high cost of having to recalculate the matrix **M** every iteration through steps 8 to 10.

Table 11-3   Heuristic Greedy—First-Fit algorithm for global allocation.

/* Initialization */
   1. We create a fictitious network of nodes,
        with one node for each of $\mathcal{F}$ fragments and
           for each of $\mathcal{T}$ transactions.
   2. We evaluate the total cost C_{worst} for executing
      the desired transactions on this network.
   3. For all $o = \mathcal{F} + \mathcal{T}$ objects, fragments and transactions,
      we perform steps 4 to 6.
   4. For each of the $\mathcal{F}$ fragments we perform steps 5 and 6.
   5. We combine the object with the fragment onto one node,
      reduce the network size by one, and
      evaluate the cost $C_{i,j}$ of
      executing the transactions in this smaller network.
   6. We record the benefit $C_{i,j} - C_{worst}$
      in a benefit matrix $\mathbf{M}$ of size $o \times f$.
/* Reduction loop to convert the fictitious network to the actual one */
   7. Using this benefit matrix we accept the most beneficial
      combination, say $\mathbf{M}_{k,l}$.
     /* This pair is initially a transaction and a fragment,
       in later stages the pair can include objects created by previous pairings. */
   8. We assign the pair k, l as an object to a single node,
     8.1 normally one of the source nodes, if capacity constraints permit
     8.2 to the next adequate node, if capacity constraints are exceeded
       and so reduce our fictitious network by one node.
   9. We correct the benefit matrix $\mathbf{M}$ by eliminating
      rows k and l and columns k and l and
      inserting a new row and column which reflects the
      node containing the pair.
 10. If the reduced fictitious network is still larger than the number
      of nodes permitted in the cluster, we return to step 7.
/* fini */
 11. We are done, and may recompute the global value $\mathbf{C}$ for
      the reduced, actual network.

In critical cases, however, it can be wise to recompute the benefit matrix, $\mathbf{M}$, as the fictitious network nears its desired size. Four alternative methods for estimating $\mathbf{M}$ is given in Sacca[84].   ▦▦

11-2-4 Summary for Clustered Systems

We have now completed the design allocation process for a clustered distributed system. The major steps were defining the files and their transactions, possibly fragmenting the files to create smaller units for allocation, and allocating them so that a good total cost is achieved, while no node is excessively loaded.

Allocation Tables   Now the transactions and the files or fragments all have assigned nodes. The front-end processor will receive a *transaction allocation table* informing it at which node the incoming transactions are to be processed. The file request interpreters in every node will receive a *file allocation table* informing them where files or fragments are located, so that data requests will be executed correctly.

If the file allocation tables are very large, then each node may only contain a subset of the tables, namely the table of its own files, and those files actively being accessed by its own transactions. A request for a file not in the table is broadcast through the network, and the remote node which owns that file will respond, and permit the local node to augment its file allocation table. Entries for remote files not accessed for a long time may be dropped. Unsuccessful attempts to locate data according to the file allocation table indicate that a reallocation has taken place which has caused the entry to be deleted. Then a broadcast is in order.

11-3 REMOTELY DISTRIBUTED SYSTEMS

A system of remotely distributed nodes is most commonly implied when *distributed systems* are discussed in the literature. The principal conceptual difference of this type with the clustered system is that, due to the distance, a user accesses the system through a known local node. Any accesses to remote files are communicated through a network which typically has much less transmission capability or bandwidth than is available among local computers. The configuration for remote query was shown in Fig. 2-10.

The fragmentation steps presented for design in a clustered system are also valid for remotely distributed systems, but some of the criteria will change. The allocation will differ, since we can no longer place fragments according to global criteria, we have to consider where the major users are located.

11-3-1 Accessing Remote Nodes

When nodes are *remote* from each other, the storage facilities are not shared in the same manner. Access to remote sites is indirect, via communication lines and the remote node. We do not find direct connections to remote storage devices useful, unless the storage device is used for remote input or output, and input and output remain outside our interest.

Distributed operations distinguish local and remote access, and transactions may be decomposed into subtransactions containing requests for distinct sites. A local request is processed as in a centralized system, but a request to access remote data has to be communicated first to a remote node. That node obtains the result and returns it to the originator.

As shown in Table 11-1, the capability of remote lines, t_r, is an order of magnitude less than that of disk devices, t. Now, because $btt_{comm} \gg btt_{disks}$, the balance of a system design changes considerably when it is remotely distributed. To overcome slow access to remote sites, some of the data may be *replicated* into multiple nodes. Replication increases the cost of update but improves retrieval dramatically. Data that is frequently read and infrequently updated is a prime candidate for replication at the sites where queries originate. If replication is used, the storage demands, D, increase, affecting Eq. 10-2.

In any distributed system the partitioning and allocation of data over network nodes is a critical aspect of the design effort. In networks of remote nodes, local processing of transactions dominates. Typical fractions of local processing are above 80% of file accesses. This means that capacity constraints of individual nodes are not likely to control the allocation of files used remotely, as they do in clustered systems.

In allocation of files or fragments first we must consider local demands, to avoid stressing the individual nodes. The totality of shared files should be partitioned so that the system throughput is maximal.

11-3-2 Allocation in Remotely Distributed Systems

Optimal allocation requires some management decisions since priorities have to be set. The condition of local system access and relatively slow access to remote nodes means that it is important to have the greatest portion of the data needed by local transactions on the local node. This constraint actually simplifies the allocation process: Fragments are allocated where they are most frequently accessed.

Again. the first concern is to satisfy response times. Any specific transaction response constraints have to be considered prior to aggregate optimization. Such constraints can be satisfied by assigning fragments to nodes which execute their transactions, prior to application of a global optimization procedure. The inability in remotely distributed architecture to allocate transactions to any node makes it more difficult to satisfy response times than in clustered systems.

Since in a remotely distributed system we cannot cluster the users at the nodes which contain the files or fragments that they need most intensely, a new tactic is needed. Replication of intensely used fragments provides a solution.

11-3-3 Replication

Replication of data permits local access to shared data at multiple nodes. Because of the cost of communication over remote networks, replication of data becomes common in remote distributed systems, more so than in clustered systems. The additional storage required by selected replication will matter less, since remote access is only a fraction of the total load on most nodes of a distributed system. Since files or fragments may be replicated, we will here, for simplicity, refer only to replicated files.

Performance is not the only reason for replication. If data must be locally available because communication may be unreliable in an emergency, then replication provides a solution. Without replication, distribution of data can reduce availability, although availability is one of the original motivations for distribution.

USING REPLICATED DATA   Replicated data can be read locally at any node which keeps copies of the data. Now any updates made at the primary storage site must be shipped to the remote sites, but all requests can be answered locally. To avoid inconsistencies, any updates which originate at remote sites are typically first shipped for execution to the primary storage site. This means they may not be immediately reflected at the local site, and the person updating files remotely has to realize what is happening.

If, on the other hand, updates were to be accepted and processed at any storage site, then conflicting updates. For example, assigning a person to some task, could be entered into files at multiple nodes during the same time, and the eventual content of the files would be hard to predict.

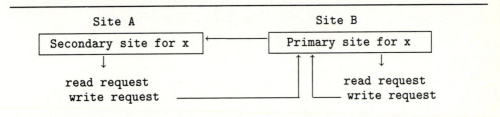

Figure 11-1   Accessing replicated data with primary copies.

Suitability for Replication   Since updating replicated data is costly, files differ in their suitability for replication. Files updated rarely may be replicated at all nodes of a distributed network. Directories, for instance, lists of part_numbers and their names, are referenced by many transactions at all nodes. Since such directories do not change frequently, the cost of update is low and the major cost of replication is storage.

Files updated continuously, for example, real-time measurements obtained from a manufacturing process, are rarely replicated directly. Information may be derived from such data, as described in Sec. 11-4-4, and those results may then be replicated. Fragmentation can reduce costs of updating by isolating information with high update frequencies and avoiding its replication. In an Employee file the current task assignment may not be replicated.

Files which are used only at some nodes need only be replicated there. Selected replication reduces both storage and update costs, although occasional access from a remote site will occur.

If communication costs are the same among all nodes, the least busy site holding a replicated copy will be the best server for remote requests. We can hence use replication also to balance the load among sites.

If communication capability among nodes differs greatly, then transactions will choose the most accessible copy of the replicated file.

UPDATING REPLICATED FILES   The simplest technique to update a replicated file is to ship out a *new copy of the file* whenever a change is made. This technique is feasible only when updates are infrequent, and files are of modest size. This approach to updating replicated files is typically done on a scheduled basis. Even when other techniques are used, updating by copying entire files can be used occasionally to assure that the copies match exactly.

Transactions for Replicated Update   The other alternative is *update by transaction*. Any transaction which updates the file is also transmitted to all nodes that hold copies, and the update is carried out there as well. We consider two approaches here: (1) updating all copies within the transaction versus (2) updating a primary copy, and let secondary updates be disseminated later.

In either case, concurrent or primary copy update, the system must be reliable:
1 No update message should get lost.
2 All remote nodes should be operational, so that transactions can be executed.
3 None of the remote transactions should fail.
4 Acknowledgments should be returned to inform the origin site that the updates are complete, so that incomplete updates can be dealt with.

The total effort is great. The response time at the originating site can become quite poor if one waits until all remote updates are completed. If one does not wait, the the information in the network could be inconsistent.

Concurrent Update of Replicated Data   The most straightforward approach to maintaining consistency among replicated files is to keep all files synchronously identical. This means that any change to a file will be propagated immediately to all copies. Any conflicting access must be locked out. The required steps for concurrent update are shown in Table 11-4 and form the basis for the so-called *two-phase concurrency control protocols*. Many variations have been analyzed, to reduce the high cost of message passing, the effect on response time, and the problems caused if components are unreliable. These protocols are presented in database and distributed database textbooks.

Table 11-4   Concurrent remote file update.

---

1 Inform all nodes that an update to the file is about to occur, so they can lock the files against further access;
2 Wait for acknowledgment from the nodes that the file has been locked and is now available to the update. If all acknowledgments are not received in some time interval, abandon the update for the time being by going to step a-2;
3 Send the update to all nodes, with the warning that this update may have to be undone;
4 Wait for acknowledgment from all nodes that the update has been completed; If the update acknowledgment does not arrive, abandon the update by going to step a-4;
5 Advise all nodes that the update has been completed and that they can release their locks and delete the backing version of the data. This step is called the *commit* phase.

We now present the various termination steps called for on case of an *abort* of the update.
   a-2 Advise all nodes that the locks they acquired can now be released, and advise the submitter of the transaction that the update failed.
   a-3 If a remote node does not receive further requests in time from steps 1 to 3, it may *time-out*, release its locks, and revert to its original state. It must then refuse to act later on the update, if any requests are received after the time-out.
   a-4 Advise all nodes that the update cannot be completed, and that the backup copy of the data should be reinstated and then the locks released. Then the submitter must also be informed.
   a-5 If step 5 is not completed, inquiries may be sent out to find out what happened, but the update has been comitted.

The cost of concurrent update remains quite high. The major problem is the delay induced at the submitting node, and the loss of access to the file during long lockout periods. If replicated copies exist at many nodes, the probability of not being able to complete all remote updates is great. In distributed systems with dozens of nodes, there is nearly always some node which is out of order. In that case, strict currency requirements have to be relaxed and alternative approaches chosen.

Primary Copy Update In systems with many nodes, it becomes rare that all nodes are operational, and then concurrent update techniques cannot be used.

A *primary copy update* method, as shown in Fig. 11-1, is then used. The node holding the primary copy generates secondary transactions to update nodes holding secondary copies. These transactions are managed individually, and if they fail are re-sent. There will be intervals where the replicated copies are not identical so that the files in the network are not consistent. For important queries, accessing only primary copies provides a partial solution, but has to be combined with version access as outlined in Sec. 11-3-4.

It is not necessary that one node always holds the primary copy. A flag or *primary copy token* can be associated with a node, and that token can be moved to another node after establishing that the other node is current. Locks have to be used while the primary copy token is used, but here we only interact among a pair of nodes. During the transfer both nodes hold potential primary copy tokens, but as soon as a node accepts updates the other node becomes the secondary node.

11-3-4 Consistency of Retrieval

Updates to replicated files can be requested while a retrieval is in progress. They also should be delayed to avoid inconsistent results, similarily to the protocol to protect updates shown in Table 11-4. Even when concurrent updating is used, inconsistencies exist during the update. If primary copies are used the inconsistencies last longer.

⧈ **Version Access** If retrievals are frequent or important the cost of delays becomes excessive. To permit continued retrieval access, while providing consistent results of transactions which access multiple files a technique based on retaining past *versions* can be used.

An update sent to a node creates a new version, with a timestamp, but the node also retains previous versions of the file. A read request will also carry a timestamp, and will receive data only from versions not updated after its own timestamp.

Synchronization messages with timestamps can be used to establish that all read requests after a certain time have been completly processed, permitting the release of older versions being held.   ⧈

⧈ **Non-audit Results** The costs of guaranteeing concurrency of results in distributed systems are such that many transactions in systems do not attempt to assure consistency. Only selected transactions, such as funds transfers, invoke the full mechanisms available. Since financial records on files are equivalent to real money, such files are never replicated as multiple equal copies, although secondary copies may be used to make information available. Such copies follow the rules seen in federated systems.   ⧈

11-4   FEDERATED SYSTEMS

The least coordination among nodes of a network is found in so-called *federated systems* or *multidatabases*. Here the nodes are under separate management, although jointly accessible via a network. They are still distinguished from wholly independent computer systems in that data formats and content will be coordinated to some extent, so that transactions using files on federated nodes can produce correct answers. We can refer to the management at each of the remote node as the *owner* of the data. A remote federated node may of course itself contain multiple processors in some configuration.

Table 11-5   Candidate levels of coordination among nodes.

Level	Description
	Example
Entity	Records describing the same entity should use the same key.
	Use same stock_numbering in both nodes.
Entity set	Number of records should be the same.
	All stock_items exist in both nodes.
Entity subset	No distinct entities should have the same record key.
	An employee is only assigned to one node.
Attribute name	Identical attributes should have the same name.
	Do not use salary in one node and pay in the other.
—	Different attributes should have different names.
	Do not let s_c mean salary_class in one node
	and social_class in the other.
Domain	Identical attributes should have the same domain.
	Do not encode colors as R,G,B in one node
	and as V,B,G,Y,O,R in the other.
Representation	Identical values should be represented the same.
	Do not encode the value color = red by 'R'
	in one node and by 1 in the other.

11-4-1 Coordination

Computations using federated nodes need to be concerned about several levels of coordination. Often coordination will not be achieved at all these levels, but it is important to either plan coordination or make users aware that no coordination exists. The results of a transaction using uncoordinated data are likely to be incomplete, and perhaps wrong. Table 11-5 lists levels where coordination should be considered. The issues are presented in terms of having two nodes, but any number can be involved. Coordination is difficult to achieve if the files existed prior to the federation. The owner cannot afford to make changes that would hinder local use of data.

Solutions to the coordination problem involve having intermediate programs translating data between nodes or perhaps translating all communicated information to a higher level. Unfortunately, a common higher level is hard to define. To resolve domain and representation differences it is necessary to choose the most general common denominator. However, such a common denominator is apt to be too general, and much valuable information may be lost in the process.

11-4-2 Accessing Federated Nodes

A file access interpreter will have a harder task in interpreting users' requests in federated systems than in centrally managed systems. A locally maintained table will keep information about data of interest available at remote nodes. Typically, only some of the remote data is made globally accessible.

The table is initialized from information exchanged between the user and the holder of the data. Perhaps an update strategy for the table is also initiated, perhaps by giving access to remote data control tables. The requests to remote nodes will be formulated using the local information. A failure to obtain data indicates that a reallocation has occurred at the remote node. Then the remote table may be reaccessed and interpreted, or the owner of the data may have to be contacted.

If a node changes content information may have to be obtained from another node. If priorities change at a node, data may remain, but may not be kept up to date. It is wise to check the timestamp on files received from federated nodes to assure currency of information.

Techniques of version access, as presented in Sec. 11-3-4, can be employed here as well, if owners are willing to maintain and give access to past versions.

UPDATING FEDERATED FILES   Since the files at remote nodes are under different management, there is typically no direct update capability. If updates are needed, they are sent as messages to the owner of the data at the remote node.

The owner can then process these messages, and, if they are acceptable, submit them to a local update transaction. If updates arrive regularly from other nodes, then the update process may be automated. It becomes the responsibility of the transaction which handles update messages from other sites to accept only those updates which are allowable.

11-4-3 Fragmentation and Replication in Federated Systems

The absence of central management makes formal fragmentation rare in federated systems, although information will be fragmented by interest and responsibility of the management of the node. Now fragmentation will not be *transparent* to the transaction programs.

REPLICATION IN FEDERATED SYSTEMS   To simplify use of information from federated nodes, entire files may be copied to the user node and replicated there. Any conversion or editing required to permit local use of the data is performed while the replicated copy is generated.

However, there is a major distinction in the management of replicated data in federated systems versus the methods that dominate in remotely distributed systems. Data may be replicated, but since the secondary nodes are not under the same management no responsibility exists to keep such data current. In federated systems it is the user at the secondary node who will, periodically, obtain a fresh copy of the replicated data. The formal issues of concurrency control, discussed under replication in Sec. 11-3-3, rarely apply.

Snapshots   The copy obtained in this manner is called a *snapshot*. A snapshot file should be consistent, and hence its generation requires that an *exhaustive-read* be performed without any interference. Snapshots are hence often created at periods of low activity. Transmitting snapshots at such times also reduces transmission costs.

In database systems we must also be concerned about the mutual consistency of diverse files. For instance, a snapshot file, obtained from a remote site, will remain unchanged while the local files continue to be updated. Processing dynamic local files and snapshots together can lead to inconsistent results: inventory moved from the remote site to the local site can appear in both files. If consistency is a concern it may be neccessary to also create local snapshots: a *version* of the local file which receives no further updates. It is discarded when new snapshots from remote sites are received.

11-4-4 Derived Data

Derived data is data obtained from other files, perhaps from other nodes, processed to make it suitable for local use, and stored. Often the data is reduced in the process, so that the volume of derived data is less than that of the source data. Storing reduced data also reduces computational effort at the local node.

Although derived data is not literally replicated, it is redundant vis-a-vis the source data. All the issues of maintaining replicated data, presented in Sec. 11-3-3, apply also to derived data. Validation of correctness of derived data requires recomputation of the values.

A typical derivation is the list of departmental `Budgets`, computed from detailed files of `Expenses` and `Income`, using `ledger_number` to group the data and classify the subtotals. If we have nodes keeping the detailed data and a node which collects data for management planning activities, then the management node will contain derived information from other nodes.

The derived data is less costly to use, both because it is precomputed and because the information (not the data) is locally replicated. Keeping only the derived data locally also reduces the local data storage needed.

The derived data cannot be used to re-create lost or damaged primary data, since in general the derivation cannot be inverted. This means that derived data does not contribute much to the recovery objectives of having distributed systems.

CURRENCY OF DERIVED DATA   Similar issues arise in currency maintenance for derived data that we found earlier in replicated data. Although the quantity of derived data to be transmitted is less than if all the source data were to be replicated, maintaining derived data is still costly. Maintenance of past versions of derived data is less costly, since the data volume will be so much less.

Currency requirements are often relaxed in federated systems. A transaction which can be effective using derived data can probably also stand having the derived data only updated periodically. For some applications periodic updating is in fact desirable: For instance, the `Budget_summary` should only be produced weekly. Using daily source information can be inconsistent, since the data may show daily `income` but only weekly `payroll` costs.

11-5   REVIEW OF FILE DISTRIBUTION

This chapter covers a topic of increasing importance in file system design. It is becoming rare that all the information needed for an application can be found on one computer. Many primitive solutions exist, anywhere from shipping data tapes around by express mail, to reentering data printed out on other computers. The economics of computing are forcing greater automation, with distribution of data via networks.

The concepts described here

Fragmentation, Replication, and Derived Data and the Allocation of the resulting fragments

provide the foundations for responsible and correct automation. These concepts also apply to systems having one processor, but multiple levels of storage with distinct performance and storage capabilities.

Specific issues of processing in a distributed environment may be handled by distributed database management systems, but these all rely on the concepts of file distribution presented here.

We recognize, in Chap. 10 and here, several classes of systems that benefit from having multiple processors:

1 Multiprocessors
    1.1 Systems using multiple identical processors
        1.1.1 With full sharing of memory and storage
        1.1.2 With memory caches and sharing of memory and storage
        1.1.3 With private memory and shared storage
        1.1.4 With private memory and storage
2 Systems using specialized processors
    2.1 Back-end processors
        2.1.1 Back-end processors using standard computers
        2.1.2 File servers for managing voluminous files
        2.1.3 Specialized processors for fast file access
        2.1.4 Specialized processors for fast data processing
    2.2 Front-end processors for managing on-line user access
3 Distributed systems
    3.1 Clustered distributed systems
    3.2 Remotely distributed systems
    3.3 Federated systems

Many systems are hybrids within these classifications. Issues of file processing are raised mainly by the final three classes. Since many files may be involved in data distribution any further analysis becomes a database topic.

11-5-1 Status

No comprehensive and generalized distributed systems for data processing are available today from manufacturers, but all the components are available. Many working systems exist, although they all involved some careful design if high transaction performance and shared access to data were made available.

The handcrafting needed to build effective distributed systems has caused *file access interpreters*, which we consider essential, to be rarely used. Today the users' programs are often aware of the distribution, and will have to be modified if a reallocation is needed. Adaptation of distributed systems to changes of user demands is still a manual process in today's practice.

Specialized front- and back-end processing nodes are common now, as are local networks interconnecting machines. Remote files are mostly explicitly accessed by the transactions that need them. Sometimes file access across the network is made transparent. Scheduling some of the dat-processing to remote nodes is still explicit, except in some research and development systems.

Prognosis   The availability of generalized distributed systems is sure to change rapidly, as the need to manage distributed data increases. Many results are available now which permit the construction of distributed systems that are easily adapted to the users demands, reliable, and sufficiently efficient. File access interpreters are available, althogh not as flexible as they should be to deal with changes in request patterns.

In order to facilitate general solutions, it will be necessary to develop high-level data request and response protocols. We will discuss this issue in Chap. 16. Optimization of distributed systems is difficult, but finding a satisfactory system may not be, since incremental hardware is not costly. To avoid excessive data transfer and to increase reliability in distributed systems, some information will be replicated in multiple nodes.

Replication is in common use, but the design trade-offs are not yet formally well understood. Much work has been done on concurrency control algorithms, so that once replication has been decided upon, a plethora of methods are available. These are well covered in database textbooks. Experience with systems in operation today will be important in developing the concepts and techniques of the future.

BACKGROUND AND REFERENCES

Distributed computing systems are introduced in Tanenbaum[81] and Lampson[81]. A comprehensive survey of networks is presented by Quarterman[86]. Conferences on distributed computing include research papers on distributed files as well. The journal Computer Networks has carried several such papers. A common clusterd architecture is provided by DEC VAX computers. Unfortunately the allocate transactions to the least busy machine, which is probably not the best choice for data-processing.

Wah[81] addresses a variety of distributed data management issues. Tutorials published by the IEEE include Mohan[84] and Larson[85]. A textbook for distributed databases is Ceri[84]. A recent critical summary is by Gray[86].

Madnick[75] and [Gardarin in Lochovsky:80] present proposals for distributed database architecture. Badal in Lochovsky[80] presents a global analysis for these systems. Their reliability is considered in Bhargava[81].

The problem of allocating files in a network of computers has been dealt with in Chu[69], Casey[72], Eswaran[74], and Wah[84]. Morgan[77] considers the constraints due to the dependencies between programs and data. Bernstein[81] and Dutta[82] present methods to minimize processing costs for distributed data. The topics have been surveyed by Epstein[80] and Hevner[82]. Streeter[73] found few economic reasons for distribution.

Proposals for distribution have been made by Stonebraker[79]. Read-only access can use a variety of currency criteria (GarciaMolina[82]).

Data access for federated systems is addressed by Litwin[84], while Popek[82] and Shroeder[84] present implementations. Adiba[81] generalizes snapshots and derived data. Their consistency is considered by Jajodia[87M] and Czejdo[87]; Dittrich[87] reports on cooperation among engineering sites.

Prototypes of distributed systems have been extensively described. At CCA investigations were based on the design of SDD-1 (Rothnie[80] and Chan[83]). The CCA Multibase system is an example of a federated approach, it only provides remote read access (Landers[82]). A nationwide French project is summarized by Bihan[80]. A testbed for development of distributed systems (Honeywell DDTS) is described by Devor[82], experiences of development at DEC are reported in GarciaMolina[84]. Burkhard[87] focuses on replication. Several experimental systems, such as POREL (Neuhold[82] and Studer[80]) and IBM R-* (Williams[82], Wilms[83], and Lindsay[84]) have attracted much attention. A federated system experiment is reported by Demurjian[87].

A commercial file system, which supports horizontal fragmentation, is TANDEM's ENCOMPASS system (Borr[81]). A version of IBM's transaction system CICS/ISC, also permits distributed file access (Acker[82]). Other distributed file access mechanisms are part of distributed extensions of database management systems.

Research on distributed databases typically assumes the relational model of data (Codd[70]) because fragmented relations are still relations. The relational model is also appropriate because links among files are not beneficial when files are at different sites. Chang[80] indicated the way in which a relation can be fragmented and by giving a methodology for relation decomposition into fragments. They used the terms *horizontal* and *vertical* in the opposite way they are used in all the subsequent literature on fragmentation and also in this book.

The theory of horizontal fragmentation was studied by Maier[81], Ceri[82], and Dayal[84]. Dependency-preserving horizontal decompositions are discussed by Grant[84]. The problem of determining an optimal horizontal fragmentation has been investigated by Ceri[83]: The formulation of the allocation problem without replication is given by a linear integer program, and heuristics are presented for decomposing the problem into smaller subproblems and to determine replication starting from the optimal nonreplicated allocation.

The problem of vertically partitioning and clustering of attributes from a single file was addressed by Hoffer[75] and Hammer[79]. An excellent overview is presented in Dowdy[82] and expanded by Kollias[83]. Vertical fragmentation was addressed for centralized databases by Hammer[79];an application of vertical fragmentation to systems with memory hierarchies (i.e., with a "fast" and a "slow" memory) is presented by Eisner[76]. March[84] discussed how vertical fragmentation can be useful for the recovery of databases. Navathe[84] and Cornell[87] studied vertical fragmentation by considering affinities among attributes.

The problem of partitioning files both horizontally and vertically and allocating the fragments obtained to a network of computers has been studied by Ceri[81] and Apers[81]. Sacca[85] describes fragment allocation procedures for a clustered architecture.

Withington[80] presents the motivation for replication. The number of copies to be made is optimized by Coffman[81]. An algorithm for intensly used resources is given by Fischer[81]. ¡Daniell[83] presents a scheme for dynamic replication using primary copy concepts. The cost and time savings of replication are evaluated by Barbara[82] and Yoshida[85].

The literature has not yet dealt well with the issues of distributed update. Cheng[80], Minoura[82] and Chu[85] use different primary copy schemes. Most of the papers cited assume that all replicated copies must become current for transactions to complete. This is clearly impractical for large systems; a model for relaxing this constraint is presented in Wiederhold[87]. Jajodia[87] addresses the issue when the network is broken.

Concurrency is covered by more papers than can be cited, several approaches are analyzed and compared by GarciaMolina[81]; Hac[87] models performance; a thorough summary of methods is by Bernstein[81]. Two-phase protocols to protect databases are presented there and in database and distributed database textbooks as Korth[86] or Ceri[84]. The case for read access is analyzed in GarciaMolina[82]. Skeen[85] has devised a three-phase protocol which deals better with communication problems.

Issues of resiliency have been addressed by Minoura[82] and Apers[85]. The IEEE conferences on Reliability in Distributed Systems and Databases are a source for material on this important topic.

EXERCISES

1   Locate two descriptions of distributed systems and determine the type as clustered, remote, or federated. If it is hybrid assign its features by type.

2   For two distributed systems evaluate the distribution software provided to determine if it matches the hardware type.

3   For two distributed systems describe how information about remote files is kept.

4   How can fragmentation be supported if the distributed system software does not recognize fragmentation?

5   Determine a common denominator for each of the examples of levels to be coordinated shown in Sec. 11-4-1.

6^p Consider if vertical fragmentation is feasible for the files of your application by listing for a variety of transactions the attributes they are using. Suggest some vertical fragmentation and discuss its desirability.

7^p Assume that the users of your system are geographically dispersed. Consider which horizontal fragmentation makes sense. Investigate how the fragmentation is inherited by related files, as defined in Exercise 6-12.

8^p Now that you have fragmented your files, list each fragment and its best site. Estimate local access and remote access ratios or frequencies. Is replication of any of the fragments likely to be helpful? Assign secondary sites to some fragments.

Chapter 12

Analysis Techniques

But then chiefly do they disdain the unhallowed crowd, as often with their triangles, quadrangles, circles, and the like mathematical devices, more confounded than a labyrinth, and letters disposed one against the other, as it were in battle-array, they cast a mist before the eyes of the ignorant. Nor is there wanting of this kind some that pretend to foretell things by the stars, and make promises of miracles beyond all things of soothsaying, and are so fortunate as to meet people that believe them.

Desiderius Erasmus (1509)
  on philosophers, from "The Praise of Folly"

12-0 INTRODUCTION

Throughout this book we have analyzed disks, file organizations, and transaction patterns. So we could proceed rapidly in the prior chapters, details of the methods used for the analyses have been ignored. Some of the techniques will now be covered in this chapter, always in the context of file design.

The analytical techniques applied when designing data-processing systems are derived from applications in areas beyond the subject of this book. Many important tools are available from the field of statistics. Statistics may have been applied first to agriculture, but the techniques can be used in all fields where events are frequent and varied. In order to apply statistical techniques, the distribution patterns of the events which are to be analyzed have to be understood. A typical collection of events are the transactions placed on the file system. The lengths of fields in variable-length records will also show a certain distribution pattern.

Section 12-1 discusses types of distributions which are frequently encountered and applies basic statistical tools to some file problems. Section 12-2 introduces simulation as a means to obtain performance estimates. A high level of demand for service leads to delays and generates waiting lines or queues which are discussed in Sec. 12-3. Some aspects of queuing theory and other disciplines from the area of operations research are touched upon in Sec. 12-4.

The objective of this chapter is to demonstrate the availability of well-developed tools which should be in the satchel of a serious computer system designer. To make the techniques easy to use, many algorithms are presented in programmed form.

The casual reader may skim over the topics in this chapter and proceed to the remainder of this book, which will address general issues of system design and operation.

12-1   STATISTICAL METHODS

Analysis and design often can make use of information collected from the observation of the operation of related systems. Statistics provides a means to summarize and simplify detailed data. The results which are obtained allow transfer of the experience to improved or new systems.

In order to apply statistical techniques to a process, a number of sequential activities must take place:

1 The process being analyzed has to be understood, so that a model can be built.
2 Parameters which affect the operation will be listed.
3 Data about the operation will be
   a Collected
   b Displayed with the relevant parameters to identify patterns
4 The cause of patterns seen in the data values will be explained in terms of the parameters used.
5 Transfer functions will be developed to permit the application of the collected information to new systems.
6 The validity of the transfer will be tested in the new setting.

We will touch upon these points while using examples from file system applications. The actual knowledge of statistics should be obtained from a course or textbooks in this area. The section is kept simple so that a background in statistics is not needed to follow the arguments.

MODELS AND PARAMETERS   In the preceding analyses of file systems a number of basic parameters were used to explain the operation of files. The set of functions or logical rules using these parameters form the *model* for the systems being described. If the system being observed can be described with the parameters used throughout this book, then this description provides an adequate model. A model should be complete, that is, it should include all variables that contribute to the observed results. In practice, completeness is difficult to achieve. We are happy if a model describes the result modestly well; in engineering sciences, obtaining 20% precision is often satisfactory. The remainder is the *unexplained* portion of the result, comprising all effects of variables which were not considered in the model.

An instance of the model is defined by setting parameters for all variables of the model. The basic operational parameters are often difficult to measure, and performance measurements taken often represent the combined effects of many parameters. The power of statistical techniques is that observations of complex and random phenomena can be analyzed if the underlying model is understood. The results obtained can be used for further system development, since arbitrary parameters can be submitted to the model and the expected results computed. Care must be taken that the parameters do not take on values for which the model is not valid.

12-1-1 Typical Demand Distributions

We analyzed many problems using averages. There is an inherent danger in these evaluations, since we must realize that average records and average files are as rare as average people. In most instances where averages were used, the measures we obtained were reasonably robust, that is, not greatly affected by a certain amount of variation from the mean or average value. Unless rigidly constrained, however, the observed values such as record lengths and field lengths, and frequencies of events such as queries will deviate from the mean.

Measurements of varying events are often profitably presented by graphical techniques, and explored in that form. Data presented as a histogram can show the frequencies of occurrence of events, classified by value type. We say that the histogram presents a *distribution* of occurrences. For this short summary all values on the ordinate are considered to be frequencies and values along the abscissa to be categorized values of events. If there is no variation, all events will fall into the same column of the histogram, and we have a *constant* distribution.

A number of possible distributions are shown in Fig. 12-1. We will describe conditions which lead to these distributions and then describe their behavior.

Data from file system operations can be sampled and plotted for data exploration. When frequencies of events are finely categorized, the graph will often have the shape of one of the popular distributions. Rarely will the match be exact, but if events show consistent patterns, the rules associated with the matching distribution type can be used to develop appropriate analysis tactics.

HOW DISTRIBUTIONS HAPPEN   When we understand a process and its events we can often expect a characteristic distribution. Then it is possible to validate our expectations for correctness, and use this knowledge to help build a model. Before analyzing the distribution types individually we will consider the type of events occurring in file systems which lead to certain distributions.

Uniform distributions arise when all events being considered are equally likely to occur. This means they are obtained when simple independent events are categorized. Uniformity may be obtained through truncation of high-order effects.

The latency time when accessing data within a cylinder of a disk, given that the time between accesses, c, is many times greater than the revolution time for the disk, $2r$, is apt to be uniformly distributed.

Uniformity is often a desirable feature of file system processes. Uniformity of record distribution into a direct file minimizes interference and collisions. The truncation of high-order effects is the idea behind the key-to-address transformations discussed in Chap. 6-1, typified by the remainder-of-division method.

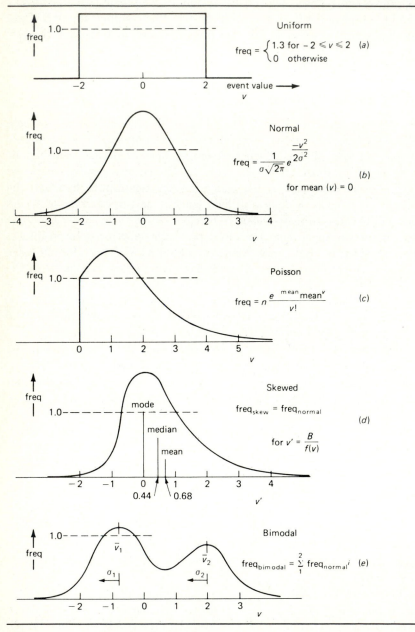

Figure 12-1   Popular distributions.

Normal distributions occur naturally when the events being measured are the sums and products of many independent actions, and the events have a constant probability, p, of occurrence. The normal distribution is, in fact, the limit of the binomial distribution, used to calculate the probabilities of discrete events, which is reached as the number of samples, f, tends to infinity. If the product $fp > 15$, the normal curve becomes an adequate approximation.

Consider placing into buckets the catenation of a fixed number, f, of records of two different sizes which occur with equal probability ($p = 0.5$). If $f > 30$, the expected length of the catenation will be normally distributed. Figure 12-2 shows the distribution developing for three distinct sizes. If the distribution of the record length varies uniformly, the normal distribution is an adequate approximation with even fewer records per block

---

To visualize what happens as a distribution becomes normal, we use a record type which can be 30, 40, or 50 bytes long, with equal probability, and then construct sequences composed of three of these records. The sequence can be from 90 to 150 bytes long, each of the 27 possible record arrangements has been drawn on the left. Each sequence has equal probability. Next to them is the distribution of record lengths ($p = \frac{1}{3}, \frac{1}{3}, \frac{1}{3}$) and of the total lengths ($p = \frac{1}{27}, \frac{3}{27}, \frac{6}{27}, \frac{7}{27}, \frac{6}{27}, \frac{3}{27}, \frac{1}{27}$). Even with this small aggregation of values from a discrete uniform distribution, the total begins to look like a normal distribution. The final shape, for larger sets of values, was shown as Fig. 12-1*b*.

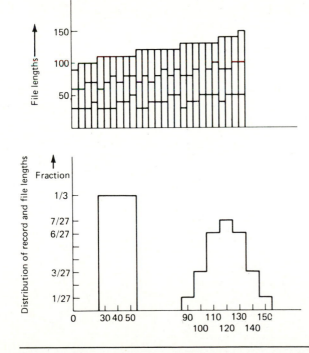

Figure 12-2   How normal distributions come about.

Catenations of records whose lengths are symmetrically distributed according to any patter will rapidly become normally distributed. If the record lengths are already normally distributed, their catenations will be always normally distributed.

Exponential distributions occur when the probability of values of a series of event types increases or decreases rapidly as the event values increase. Increasing exponentials are difficult to manage in models and in reality. An example of such disconcerting behavior in databases is the number of interconnection possibilities among its elements, and hence the time required for thorough checking of a complex database; the time required for sorting also goes up more than linearly with file size.

Negative exponentials decay initially quite rapidly, but then reach their asymptotic value of zero slowly. An example is seen in Fig. 12-3. Distributions of a similar shape arise when measurements of terminal requests and of access frequencies to records of files are made. These are best described by the Erlang and Zipf distributions noted in Sec. 12-1-6.

Our example shows the distribution by date of charges for hospital services which have not yet been settled. Bills older than 18 months (August a year past) are either turned over to a collection agency or written off. A total of 94 048 bills were outstanding. The distribution has the form of a negative exponential, as shown by the curve fitted to the data using visual comparison on a display screen. The long tail of this distribution is handled through the imposition of the arbitrary cutoff date.

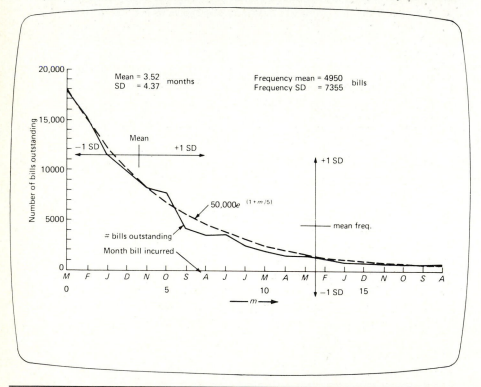

Figure 12-3   Distribution of outstanding bills by date.

A negative exponential distribution is typically generated by a succession of mutually dependent events of the same probability. In Figure 12-3 it appears that the probability of a customer paying an outstanding bill is about 20% every month. Negative exponential distributions are also found when the times between random arrivals of service requests are displayed. Exponential and Erlang distributions are important when queues of service requests are analyzed.

Poisson distributions occur when important contributing events have a small probability p. This distribution is the limit of the binomial distribution for the case where the likelihood of a particular event is small. The Poisson distribution becomes a valid approximation when the number of events $f > 25$ while $fp = mean < 5$. When the mean becomes large ($fp > 30$), the peak is sufficiently away from the left boundary that a normal distribution can be used to approximate the Poisson distribution.

For a moderate sample size, the Poisson distribution diminishes more rapidly than the exponential to the asymptotic value of zero. A Poisson distribution is typically caused by independent events, whereas an exponential distribution occurs more often where successive events are related. Poisson distributions which have a mean value of less than one do not show the initial rise shown in Fig. 12-1 but decline immediately and hence look similar to exponential distributions.

We wish to model overflows due to insertions in an indexed-sequential file organization for a file of 400 blocks. We expected to insert 550 records between rorganizations. The probability of a block being updated is only $1/400$ per insertion, a nd fp is 1.38. With this information we know that a Poisson distribution is likely. This means the distribution curve will be as shown in Fig. 12-1c. The intersection at **freq 1.0** gives the relative count fr_0 of 0 insertions in a block. About the same number will receive two insertions (fr_2), but most blocks ($fr_1 = 1.35 fr_0$) will receive one insertion. Some blocks will receive up to 6 insertions. The specific details are worked out in Fig. 12-10.

Figure 12-4   Using a Poisson distribution.

It can be shown that, for events which have an exponential interarrival-time distribution, the number of expected arrivals in a given time period has a Poisson distribution.

Skewed distributions occur whenever nonlinear transformations affect the outcome of events. A distribution as shown in Fig. 12-1d can represent the number of records, *Bfr*, in a block. Since the operation $Bfr = B/R$ is not linear for R, the normal distribution of record sizes, R, is distorted. Skewed distributions are characterized by the fact that their mean occurs at a different point than their median; the median is the value with an equal number of observations to either side; in Fig. 12-1d the mean is at 0.63, but the median is 0.44. Yet another measure of *central tendency* is the mode, the position of the most frequent value, here at zero. For moderately skewed distributions,

$$(mean - mode) \approx 3(mean - median) \qquad \text{12-1}$$

This relationship can provide a quick estimate of the median from the mode and the mean, which are easier to compute.

Bimodal distributions occur when the events being measured are due to two separate, underlying phenomena. An example is the response time for queries, where some can be answered by using an index and others require an exhaustive reading of the file or a subset of the file.

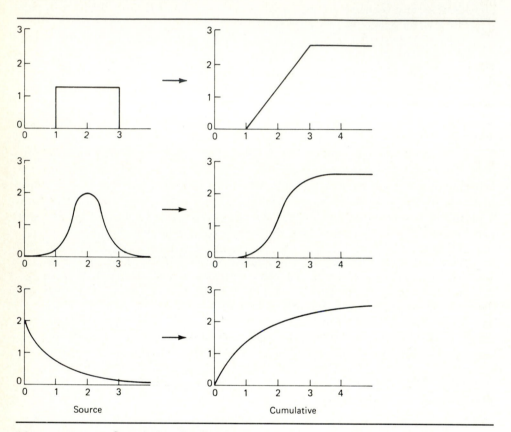

Figure 12-5   Cumulative distributions.

CUMULATIVE DISTRIBUTION FUNCTION   Often a frequency distribution is used to obtain an estimate of the fraction of cases exceeding a certain limit. For each distribution shown a *cumulative distribution function (c.d.f.)* can be obtained by summing or integrating the frequency distribution from left to right over time. The height of the curve is directly proportional to the number of events occurring with values less than the corresponding value. A few c.d.f.s are shown with their source functions in Fig. 12-5. Table 12-7 and Fig. 12-31 use c.d.f.s to predict the fraction of desirable or undesirable events.

These cumulative distributions may also appear in the system measurements, since often only the aggregate effect is observed. Differencing or differentiation of these functions can be used to re-create frequency distributions. Skew, multiple modes, etc., are more difficult to recognize when they occur in c.d.f.s instead of in frequency distributions.

12-1-2 Describing Distributions

When the result of a measurement generates a distribution, a similarity to one of the distribution types shown will provide some clues about the process causing this distribution. As a next step, some quantitative measures can be obtained. Two basic parameters useful with nearly any observed distribution are: the *mean* xbar and the standard deviation *sigma* σ of the observations, given f samples x(1),x(2),...,x(f). In order to have an unbiased estimate, these sample observations should be a random sample of the events. For the standard deviation we will use the symbol σ in equations, but sd in program examples.

For any collection of observed events we can compute the *mean* and σ parameters:

Table 12-1 Mean and Standard Deviation of an array of values.

```
/* Mean (xbar) and Standard Deviation (sd) of array x */    /* 12-1 */
       xsum,xsqsum = 0;
       DO i = 1 TO f;
           xsum = xsum+x(i);
           xsqsum = xsqsum+x(i)**2;
       END;
       xbar = xsum/f;
       sd = SQRT((xsqsum-xsum**2/f)/(f-1));
       ...
```

The number of samples, f, should be large enough so that we can have confidence that the sample set used is representative of the events occurring within the system. Any of the statistics texts referenced can be consulted for tests which provide measures of confidence. A *chi-square test* will be used in an example in Sec. 12-1-5.

12-1-3 Uniform Distribution

If a distribution looks flat or uniform over a range of values, many estimation tasks are simplified. A uniform distribution of events has often been assumed in examples in the earlier chapters, since the uniform distribution often gives a relatively poor, and therefore conservative result. A uniform distribution of addresses of seek requests to a disk will cause a higher average seek time than all but a bimodal distribution. The probability that a next record is not available in the current block is greater for a uniform distribution of requests than for any other. The average cost, however, of following overflow chains is lower when update insertions were distributed uniformly and greater for nonuniform update distributions.

Table 12-2 Parameters of the uniform distribution.

```
/* Parameters of the uniform distribution */                /* 12-2 */
       height = f/number_of_categories;
       range = MAX(x) - MIN(x);
```

A uniform distribution is described by its height, that is, the frequency of occurrence of categorized events, and by its range, which has to be finite for a finite number of events as shown in the program segment in Table 12-2.

To visualize the uniformity of the distribution the size and value for each category icn = 1, ..., number_of_categories is computed in Table 12-3. CEIL and FLOOR functions are used to improve the presentation of the information in a histogram.

Table 12-3   Create histogram categories for the frequency distribution.

```
/* Create histogram categories for frequency distribution     12-3 */
      size_of_category = CEIL(range/(number_of_categories-1));
      base = FLOOR(MIN(x));
      category_low_value = base + (icn-1)*size_of_category;
```

If an investigation is made to determine the amount of cylinder overflow for a direct or indexed-sequential file, then f may be the number of records, and the number_of_categories may be the number of cylinders allocated to the file. The expected mean and standard deviation of samples which present a perfectly uniform distribution are

Table 12-4   Expected mean and sd of a uniform distribution.

```
/* mean and sd of a uniform distribution */                    /* 12-4 */
      xbar_uniform = range/2;
      sd_uniform = SQRT(range**2/12);
```

If the observed xbar and sd from the program segment in Table 12-1 do not match these values well, other distributions should be considered.

Even if the parameters match well, the observed frequencies will vary about the expected height, so that it may be desirable to analyze how good the fit is. In the example, variations can cause the capacity of some cylinders to be exceeded. The frequency distribution can be plotted from an array, fx, filled from the observed values, x, as follows:

Table 12-5   Computation of the frequency histogram of observed values.

```
/* Compute the frequency histogram of observed values */    /* 12-5 */
      DECLARE fx(number_of_categories);
      fx = 0;
      DO i = 1 TO f;
          ifr = CEIL((x(i)-base)/size_of_category);
          fx(ifr) = fx(ifr) + 1;
      END;
```

Computing the standard deviation of the frequencies, sdfreq, and obtaining a value which is small when compared to the height in the graph, the mean frequency, indicate a satisfactory degree of uniformity. We will apply these concepts to a problem posed by the need to combine rapid access with sequential access.

In order to use fast direct access to the billing file of Fig. 12-3 for frequent inquiries, while keeping the file in chronological order, a sequentiality-maintaining,
exponential key-to-address transformation, based on the inverse of the cumulative distribution function, was investigated. The file was to be stored on
100 cylinders, each with a capacity of 1197 records, so that $m = 119\,700$, for
$n = 94\,048$. The key-to-address algorithm computes a cylinder address for a
given date, taking into account the weekends, which have lower billing rates.
The name of the person billed provides the record address within the area allocated to the date. Figure 12-7 shows the distribution of records over cylinders.

The expected frequency is 940.5 per cylinder. The resulting distribution
is quite uniform, with some irregularities due to the fact that the low-order
cylinders are affected by the many recent bills generated on single days and also
by irregular billings from some holidays. Only one cylinder overflow occurs with
this sample. Further analysis is needed to determine the rate of block overflow,
given the distribution of names and buckets of 63 records using blocks of 14 000
bytes. The results are shown in Fig. 12-7.

Figure 12-6   Creating a uniform distribution for direct access.

Hashing provides the solution for rapid access. We create a specialized key-to-
address transformation which is *sequence-maintaining*. For reference the family
tree of hash functions, presented in Fig. 6-8, may be useful.

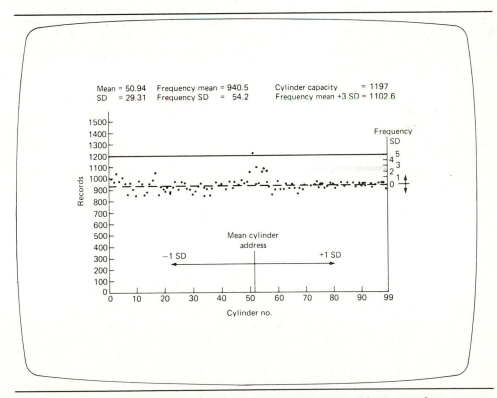

Figure 12-7   Test of uniformity of an algorithmic key-to-address transform.

12-1-4 Normal Distribution

The difference of observed and expected frequencies can often be expected to be a
normally distributed variable, since it is based on many independent samples from
the observed events.

To describe a normal-looking distribution found in array fx, the mean value
of events, xbar, and the standard deviation, sd, as computed in Table 12-1 are
the parameters. Using these two parameters from the observed values, an expected
normal distribution can be generated for comparison purposes. Using the equation
for the normal curve, programmed for f observations, we obtain values in array xnf
which should match the values fx, if the distribution was indeed normal.

Table 12-6   Expected normal frequency distribution function xnf.

```
/* Expected Normal Frequency Distribution Function xnf */  /* 12-6 */
     DECLARE xnf(number_of_categories);
     scalefactor = f/(sd*2.5066283);   /* 2.5066283 = sqrt(2*pi) */
     shapefactor = -0.5/sd**2;
     DO i = 1 TO number_of_categories;
         category_center_value = base + (icn-0.5)*size_of_category;
         xnf(icn) = scalefactor*EXP(shapefactor*
                 (category_center_value-xbar) **2);
     END;
```

The observed frequencies at x(i) can be compared with the values exp(i) generated
by this function.

If a distribution is approximately normal, many useful estimation rules can be
applied. In file design, it is often desirable to estimate how often a certain limit will
be exceeded; for a distribution which is approximately normal, the cumulative area
of the normal curve beyond the limit provides the desired estimate. Table 12-7 lists
some of these values in terms of t, the difference between the mean and the limit
as a ratio of the standard deviation, σ.

Table 12-7   Normal one-tail probabilities.

t	p($value > limit$)	
0	0.500	$limit = mean + t\,\sigma$
0.25	0.401	
0.50	0.309	
0.75	0.227	or
1.00	0.159	
1.25	0.106	t = (limit-mean)/sd
1.50	0.067	
1.75	0.040	
2.00	0.023	
2.25	0.012	
2.50	0.006	
2.75	0.003	
3.00	0.001 3	
4.00	0.000 03	
5.00	0.000 000 7	

Infrequent Events   Table 12-7 shows that events of value greater than the *mean +* 3σ are quite rare.

Applying these values to the example in Fig. 12-6, we first tabulate the frequencies. We obtain a mean of 940.5 records per cylinder with an σ of 54.2. It takes $t = +4.73\sigma$ to exceed the cylinder capacity of 1197. For a normal distribution this is expected to happen less than once in a million cases (Table 12-7), but the distribution of bills per cylinder was not quite normal, due to seasonal variations. In practice one overflow was found in 100 cylinders, as shown earlier in Fig. 12-7.

Even when data is truly normally distributed, rare events can, of course, still happen; in fact, the high activity rates in data-processing systems can cause rare events to occur with annoying regularity.

BLOCK OVERFLOW DUE TO RECORD VARIABILITY   When the normal distribution was introduced, the statement was made that distributions, when summed, become more normal. This phenomenon is known as the *the central limit theorem*. In the example which follows that rule will be applied to the problem of packing records into blocks for the tree-structured file evaluated in Chap. 9-2-4, Fig. 9-6.

In order to pack fixed-length records effectively into one block, the capability of a block in terms of record segments was computed.

$$n_{block} = y - 1 = \left\lfloor \frac{B - P}{R + P} \right\rfloor \qquad \text{12-2}$$

A certain number of characters per block remained unused. We will name this excess G' and find that

$$G' = B - P - n_{block}(R + P) \qquad \text{12-3}$$

These files are designed to always place n_{block} entries into a block, so that $G' < R$. The file-space usage for fixed-length records was most efficient if $G' = 0$.

If the records are actually of variable length, the distribution of R has to be described. A normal distribution may be a reasonable assumption if the average length is sufficiently greater than the standard deviation; otherwise, record-length distributions tend to be of the Poisson type. To make a choice, it is best to look at a histogram. When assuming normality, the distribution is determined by the value of the mean record length, *Rbar*, and the standard deviation, σ.

In Example 9-6 we had fixed length records with the following parameters: $B = 1000, R = 180$, and $P = 4$, so that $n_{block} = 5$ and the excess per record was $G' = 76 \approx R/2$.

Now we take variable length records that are still on the average 180 characters long, and have a small standard deviation σ of 20 characters. We allocate all the space in the block to the five records ($G = 0$), providing $(B-P)/n_{block} - P = 195$ characters of space for each record. The parameter t of Table 12-7 defines the space between mean and limit in terms of the σ: $t = (195 - 180)/20 = 0.75$ From Table 12-7 we find that 22.7% of the records will not fit into their allotted space. In Fig. 12-9 we try to do better by using buckets.

Figure 12-8   Fixed space allocation per record.

SUMS OF NORMALLY DISTRIBUTED VALUES   Often, many variable-length records will be packed together in a bucket within a block, so that space not used by one record will be usable by other records. The relative variability of a sum is less than the variability of individual items, so that we can expect that the numbers of overflows will be reduced. For n_{block} records per bucket, the `mean` and `sd` for the sequence of records in a bucket are

$$mean_{block} = n_{block} \, mean_{record} \qquad\qquad\qquad 12\text{-}4$$

$$\sigma_{block} = \sqrt{n_{block}} \, \sigma_{record} \qquad\qquad\qquad 12\text{-}5$$

and, if the ratio of extra space is the same,

$$t_{block} = \sqrt{n_{block}} \, t_{record} \qquad\qquad\qquad 12\text{-}6$$

and the the overflow probability per bucket is less, as evaluated in Fig. 12-9.

If five records with the same behavior as those of Fig. 12-8 share a bucket, then

$$t_{block} = \sqrt{n_{block}} \, t_{record} = \sqrt{5} \times 0.75 = 1.68$$

From Table 12-7 we find that the overflow probability with bucketing is less than 6.7% (actually 4.7%) versus the 22.7% for single record slots, each with their maximum.

To demonstrate the space versus overflow trade-off more vividly we will use the same standard deviation $\sigma = 20$ used in Fig. 12-8, but applied to smaller records ($Rbar = 66$ vs. 180) so that the effect will be even more pronounced. Given is also $n = 10\,000$ and $B = 762$. Now, with the average $Rbar = 66$, an initial value of $n_{block} = \lfloor 762/66 \rfloor = 11$, and the number of unused characters per block $G' = 762 - 66 \cdot 11 = 36$. The total file will occupy $b = \lceil 10\,000/11 \rceil = 910$ blocks.

With $\sigma_{record} = 20$ the σ_{block} for the sequence of 11 records is $20\sqrt{11} = 66.33$ and the $mean_{block}$ is $11 \cdot 66 = 726$ characters. Table 12-7 indicates for $t = 36/66.33 = 0.54$ a probability of overflow of about 29.5% per block. If we allocate and link an overflow block to each overflowing primary block $910 \cdot 0.295 = 269$ additional blocks will be required. The total used for this file is now 1179 blocks.

If, on the other hand, only $n_{block} = 10$ entries are placed in every block, then 1000 primary blocks are needed instead of 910, but 102 characters are available to cope with the variability of the length of the entries. This makes $t = 1.54$ and reduces the overflow to 6.2% or 62 blocks. This generates a net saving of $1179 - (1000 + 62) = 117$ blocks. There will also be a proportional savings in expected access time.

A further reduction to nine entries reduces the overflow probability to 0.61% but requires a total of 1118 blocks instead of 1062. The expected access time will still be slightly reduced.

Figure 12-9   Allocation of variable-length records to a block.

OPTIMIZATION OF ALLOCATION FOR VARIABLE-LENGTH RECORDS
It is sometimes wise to use a value of n_{block} which is less than the value computed based on the average, to reduce the probability of overflows further. In dense files overflows can be costly and using some additional space can provide a good trade-off. Figure 12-9 shows this effect also, using small variable-length records.

12-1-5 The Poisson Distribution

Poisson distributions occur due to independent events. The shape of the Poisson distribution is fully described by the value of the mean of the observations, since in this distribution the mean and the variance are equal. The variance is the standard deviation squared, σ^2. To avoid introducing another symbol for the variance, we will use σ^2 or sd**2 as appropriate. To compare an observed distribution with the curve describing a Poisson distribution, the corresponding values can again be computed. The program segment in Table 12-8 computes expected values for event counts from 0 to 20 following a Poisson distribution.

Table 12-8   Poisson distribution for 21 categories.

```
/* Poisson Distribution for 21 Categories  */              /* 12-8 */
      DECLARE expfr(0:20);
      expfr(0) = n*EXP(-mean);
      DO ov = 1 BY 1 TO 20;
         expfr(ov) = expfr(ov-1)*mean/ov;
      END;
```

A sample problem is tabulated in Fig. 12-10, which shows the observed distribution of insertions and the equivalent Poisson probability computed in Table 12-8 given above. When the two columns are compared, a Poisson distribution appears likely.

The events which lead to this distribution of Table 12-5 are such that a Poisson curve is indeed likely: The distribution is the sum of many events, each with a low probability, and the probability for events in high-numbered categories tends to zero. Table 12-9 modifies the program of Table 12-8 stopping the generation of categories when less than one entry is expected.

Table 12-9   Poisson distribution with grouping of low frequencies.

```
/* Poisson Distribution with Grouping of Low Frequencies       12-9 */
      DECLARE expfr(0:20);
      expfr(0) = n*EXP(-mean);
      left = n-expfr(0);      /* number of blocks for assignment */
      prod = expfr(0)*mean;
      DO ov = 1 BY 1 WHILE(prod<ov);    /* ok if next expfr > 1 */
         expfr(ov) = prod/ov;
         left = left-expfr(ov);
         prod = expfr(ov)*mean;
      END;
      last_category = ov; /* used in Table 12-10 below */
      expfr(last_category) = left;
```

TESTING FOR GOODNESS OF FIT   A more formal test to determine if a distribution fits the data can be made using the *chi-square* function. The *chi-square*, or χ^2, test compares categories of observations and their expectations, but each category should contain at least one expected sample. To avoid invalid categories, the Poisson values of less than 1 can be grouped with the last good category as shown in the program of Table 12-9.

There were 550 insertions into a dense indexed-sequential file of 400 blocks. These insertions caused $0, 1, 2, \ldots$ overflow records to be written for each of the blocks. The mean number of insertions per block is `mean` $= 550/400 = 1.38$. The expected frequency is computed for `n = 400`.

No. of overflows	Observations		Expectations
	Frequency	Records	Frequency
ov	fr(ov)	ov·fr(ov)	expfr(ov)
0	101		101.4
1	138	138	139.1
2	98	196	95.6
3	45	135	43.8
4	11	44	15.1
5	5	25	4.1
6	2	12	0.9
7	0	0	0.2
...	0	0	...
	400	550	400

Figure 12-10   Poisson distribution of insertions for an indexed-sequential file.

The observed values, listed in Fig. 12-10 are best inspected again visually. A better presentation for that purpose would be a histogram, `fx`, as can be generated by the program segment in Table 12-5. The cells of low expected value are combined into a single, the last category, by accumulating them in a program loop as shown in Table 12-9.

Then the chi-square values are computed, as shown in Table 12-11, to see how well the actual observations fit the assumed Poisson distribution. The final results are seen together in Fig. 12-11.

Table 12-10   Combining tail values of an observed frequency histogram.

```
/* Combine tail values of observed frequency histogram */ /* 12-10 */
      DO i = last_category+1 TO number_of_categories;
         fx(last_category) = fx(last_category) + fx(i);
      END;
```

Table 12-11   Computation of Chi-square value for goodness of fit test.

```
/* Computation of Chi-Square Value for Goodness of Fit */ /* 12-11 */
      chisquare = 0;
      DO ov = 0 TO last_category;
         dif = fx(ov)- expfr(ov);
         chisqterm = dif**2 / expfr(ov);
         chisquare = chisquare + chisqterm;
         PUT DATA( ov, fx(ov), expfr(ov), dif, chisqterm);
      END;
      PUT DATA( SUM(fx), SUM(expfr), chisquare);
```

Values obtained for χ^2 can be compared with standard values, which are based on the assumption that the difference of distributions was caused by random events. These standard values for χ^2 can be computed as needed using approximations of binomial distributions or can be found in statistical tables and graphs.

Figure 12-12 presents the standard χ^2 distribution in graphical form. In order to use the χ^2 distribution, the number of degrees of freedom, df, has to be known. Where we distribute our samples over a specific number of categories, c, df will be equal to $c - 1$.

ov	fx(ov)	expfr	dif	χ^2term
0	101	101.1	0.1	0.001
1	138	139.1	1.1	0.009
2	98	95.6	2.4	0.060
3	45	43.8	1.2	0.033
4	11	15.1	4.1	1.113
last	7	5.3	1.7	0.545
$n =$	400	400		$\chi^2 = 1.761$

Evaluation:
The value for χ^2 is 1.761 at a $df = 5$ for the indexed-sequential file observations shown in Fig. 12-10. The value for this comparison falls within the area of Fig. 12-11 which is appropriate for most cases which match an expected distribution. The point is off-center, close to the "good" side, so that it seems likely that the file updates are not quite random, but somewhat uniform. Perhaps many of the insertions are due to some regular customer activity.

Figure 12-11   Testing a Poisson distribution.

A very high value of χ^2 makes it unlikely that the frequencies are related; a very low value could cause suspicion that the data is arranged to show a beautiful fit. The chi-square test is useful when distributions are being compared. Other tests, such as the t-test and F-test, can be used to compare means and standard deviations obtained from samples with their expected values, if the distribution is known or assumed to be known.

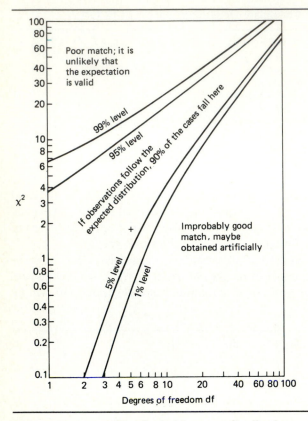

χ^2

100
80
60

Poor match; it is
unlikely that
the expectation
is valid

40
30
20

99% level

10
8
6

95% level

If observations follow the
expected distribution, 90% of the cases fall here

4
3

2

Improbably good
match, maybe
obtained artificially

1
0.8
0.6

5% level

1% level

0.4
0.3

0.2

0.1

1   2   3 4 5 6 8 10   20   40 60 80 100

Degrees of freedom df

Figure 12-12   Standard chi-square distribution.

COLLISION PROBABILITY   To derive Eq. 6-5 in Chap. 6-2-2, use was made of a relationship which gave the probability of occurrence of collisions in direct access slots given n entries into m slots. This result will now be derived using the tools developed.

Each record has a probability of $1/m$ of being assigned to any one slot. The probability for one slot to receive q records is given by the binomial distribution

$$P_b(q) = \frac{n!}{q!(n-q)!} \left(\frac{1}{m}\right)^q \left(1 - \frac{1}{m}\right)^{n-q} \qquad 12\text{-}7$$

For the case that $n \gg 1, m \gg 1, q \ll n$, we can approximate this expression by the Poisson distribution for the mean density n/m:

$$P_b(q) = e^{-(n/m)} \frac{(n/m)^q}{q!} \qquad 12\text{-}8$$

$P_b(0)$ is the probability of the slot remaining empty, and $P_b(n)$ is the (very small) probability of this slot receiving all n records (see again Fig. 5-19). If q records appear in one slot, causing $q - 1$ overflows, then the number of accesses to fetch all these records, which form one sequential chain, will be

$$0 + 1 + 2 + \ldots + q - 1 = \tfrac{1}{2}q(q - 1) \tag{12-9}$$

Taking the sum of all the $P_b(j), j = 1 \ldots n$, multiplied by their cost in terms of disk accesses, gives for any one slot the expected access load AL

$$AL_{slot} = \sum_{j=0}^{n} \frac{j(j-1)}{2} P_b(j) \tag{12-10}$$

The successive terms of the Poisson distribution are related to each other by the iteration

$$P(j) = P(j - 1)\frac{mean}{j} \tag{12-11}$$

The mean is here n/m, so that using the Poisson distribution for P_b

$$AL_{slot} = \frac{1}{2}\frac{n}{m} \sum_{j=0}^{n} (j - 1) P(j - 1) \tag{12-12}$$

Since at $j = 0 :$ $P(j - 1) = 0$ and at $j = 1 :$ $j - 1 = 0$

$$\sum_{j=0}^{n}(j - 1)P(j - 1) = \sum_{j=2}^{n}(j - 1)P(j - 1) = \sum_{k=1}^{n} k\, P_b(k) \tag{12-13}$$

where $k = j - 1$. The expected record load RL per slot is the mean, which in turn is equal to the cumulative frequency distribution, specifically the sum of the products of the number of records per slot i and the probability of the occurrence of the event $P(i)$

$$RL_{slot} = \frac{n}{m} = \sum_{i=1}^{m} i\, P(i) \tag{12-14}$$

and when $m \approx n$ the series terms are equal, so that the expected increase of accesses for overflows due to collisions per record p is

$$p = \frac{AL}{RL} = \frac{1}{2}\frac{n}{m} \tag{12-15}$$

If multiple records $(Bfr = B/R)$ can be kept in a *bucket*, the probability of another record entering a slot can be predicted using $P_b(q)$ as derived above. The number of buckets will be m/Bfr and the number of collisions per bucket will be higher. There will be no overflows, however, until Bfr records have entered the bucket, so that the cost of accessing overflows AL becomes less. For this case Johnson[61] derives similarly,

$$p = \frac{1}{2}\frac{n}{m/Bfr} \sum_{k=Bfr-1}^{n} (k - Bfr)(k - Bfr - 1)\, P(k) \tag{12-16}$$

Of course, the processor's computing effort, cix, to search within one bucket increases now. An evaluation of this effect in indexed files is given in Chap. 8-4-3.

COLLISION EXPECTATIONS FOR DIRECT FILES   The results obtained above can be further developed to give the expected overflow space requirement or the average overflow chain length, Lc, due to collisions. These can then be compared with observations from the operational file.

The probability of a slot being empty was approximated by the zero term of the Poisson distribution so that

$$P_b(0) = e^{-n/m} \qquad\qquad 12\text{-}17$$

The probability of a slot of the primary file being used is then

$$P1u = 1 - e^{-n/m} \qquad\qquad 12\text{-}18$$

and the number of records in the primary file is then $m\,P1u$, and in the overflow file is

$$o' = n - m\,P1u \qquad\qquad 12\text{-}19$$

The overflow area contains the tails of all the Poisson-distributed record sequences. Using Eq. 12-5 for the σ of a sequence and the fact that σ^2 of a Poisson distribution is equal to the mean n/m, we expect a standard deviation of o' of

$$\sigma = \frac{n}{m}\sqrt{m} \qquad\qquad 12\text{-}20$$

and this σ applies of course to the entire file. If an observed standard deviation is less, we can deduce that the keys are more uniform than a Poisson distribution-based model expects and that a smaller prime or overflow area may suffice. If the observations are worse, the key-to-address transformation is not doing its job.

For a file as used in Fig. 6-11 (Chap. 6-2-2) $n = 1000, m = 1500$, we find with Eq. 12-18 $P1u = 0.49$, and expect $o' = 265$ with a σ of 25.8. This value can be compared with observed values from operational measurements.

Figure 12-13   Estimating a collision probability.

When the buckets contain more than one record ($Bfr > 1$), the above computation can be carried out using the cumulative Poisson probability for the records 1 to Bfr being in the buckets and the records from $Bfr + 1$ to n overflowing. Tables of the values of the mean total accesses $1 + Lc_I$ are used in Knuth[73S] (page 535) to compute the length for an unsuccessful fetch leading to an insertion. The value of

$$P1u = n/m - Lc_I \qquad\qquad 12\text{-}21$$

so that the case of Fig. 12-13 corresponds to $Lc_I = 1000/1500 - 0.49 = 0.18$.

12-1-6 Other Distributions

When a distribution does not seem uniform, normal, exponential, or Poisson-like to an acceptable extent, the behavior may follow one of many other functions which are available to describe distributions. An important reciprocal distribution, similar in shape to a negative exponential, is presented by *Zipf's law* (Eq. 13-6). This distribution is used to describe activity ratios of records and type/token ratios of words in text.

Zipf's law can be viewed as a generalization of *Heising's rule*:

> 80 percent of accesses to a file address 20 percent of its records.

An example of its use is given in Chap. 13-3-3.

When requests arrive from users at terminals, queues can form due to conflicting requests of independent users. The requests from each single user are mutually dependent, so that the total set of requests is more complex than a Poisson distribution. This behavior is modeled well by Erlang distributions; they are presented in Sec. 12-4-1.

Some cases where the distributions are not simple can be solved by algebraic transformations of the observations until some fit to a known distribution is obtained. Reciprocal, logarithmic, and hyperbolic functions are used frequently. Observations may also be broken down by differencing or decomposed into sums or products of functions. Differentiation or taking successive differences helps to remove the effect of aggregation if the observations are some form of c.d.f.. A visual display of the transformed data is helpful to rapidly establish the benefit of a transformation.

Any transformations are best based on an understanding of the underlying phenomena, so that we have some model of what is happening. In the examples shown earlier we tried to find a causal mechanism; for instance, utility customers pay in regular cycles and the hospital patients in Fig. 12-3 pay according to individual pressures. If such an empirical model fits the observations well, it can be used with some confidence for extrapolations and the design of databases that work in general and over a long term. The algebraic transformations of the observations based on the simple patient-payment model were adequate to exploit the distribution for effective direct access.

If transformations make observed data tractable, but the underlying model which generates the observations is still not understood, then much care has to be taken in applying the results. The use of many variables or of complex transformations to describe observations is apt to generate very misleading results when the values obtained after the fit for these variables are used to *extrapolate* the behavior of new systems. Empirical functions based on a few reasonable variables can be used for *interpolation*, since this procedure is less risky. Since there is a degree of arbitrariness in assigning a transformation function, subsequent testing for validity should be done with fewer degrees of freedom, *df*.

SKEWED DISTRIBUTION   If a distribution appears lopsided or skewed, it is wise to analyze the relationships being considered for nonlinearities. It may be that the parameter being measured is some function which distorts the behavior of parameters of the model at a more basic level.

The skewed distribution in Fig. 12-1 occurred because the blocking factor, *Bfr*, was described for a fixed number of variable-length records per block. The underlying measure, the distribution of record lengths or the inverse, $1/Bfr$, had a normal distribution.

BIMODAL DISTRIBUTION A bimodal distribution as shown in Fig. 12-1 can best be decomposed by fitting two normal distributions to the data. Four parameters have to be determined: $mean_1$, σ_1, $mean_2$, and σ_2. If the modes are well separated, the means can be estimated at each node and fitting of two normal curves will be simple. It helps if the σ's are equal or have a predetermined relationship. Sometimes the position of the means can be determined by alternative reasoning.

UNRECOGNIZABLE DISTRIBUTIONS Even when the shape of the distribution does not match any known distribution, there is still a conservative statistical tool available, *Chebyshev's inequality theorem*, to describe the behavior of the variables.

Given the mean and the standard deviation, which are always computable for a set of observations, Chebyshev's inequality provides directly the probability of values from the set of observations $x_i, i = 1, \ldots, n$ falling outside a range. The range, rg, is defined in terms of a number, c, of standard deviations, σ, to either side of the mean of x. The mean and standard deviation are computed from the observation without any assumptions regarding the behavior of the distribution. If the sample observations are not biased, then for some k

$$p(x_k \text{ not in } rg) \leq \frac{1}{c^2} \qquad \text{where} \qquad mean - c\sigma < rg < mean + c\sigma \qquad \text{12-22}$$

This relationship can, for instance, be used to state that given any observed distribution, 90% of the values will be within $\sqrt{10}\,\sigma = 3.162\sigma$ to either side of its mean. If the distribution is approximately symmetrical, we can assume that only 5% of the values exceed the $mean + 3.162\sigma$. The worst case is that all 10% of the values exceed the $mean + 3.162\sigma$.

If the distribution has a single mode and is symmetric, then

$$p(x \text{ not in } rg) \leq \frac{2}{3c^2} \qquad \text{12-23}$$

and, correspondingly, the probability that a value, x_k, of the observations exceeds the *mean* by $c\sigma$ is

$$p(x_k > mean + c\sigma) \leq \frac{1}{3c^2} \qquad \text{12-24}$$

For the direct file used to illustrate Eq. 12-20, the Chebyshev inequality can be used to evaluate the chance of exceeding a primary overflow area of a given size. The distribution of overflows is not symmetric, so that the worst case approximation should be used. Given was $o' = 265$, $\sigma = 25.8$, and we wish to guarantee that in all but 1% of the cases the records fit into the primary overflow area. Here

$$c = \sqrt{100} = 10 \qquad \text{and the required space} \qquad o = o' + 10\sigma = 523$$

This value is based on the sample observations. Multiple samples should be used to verify stability of the result.

Figure 12-14   Estmating file overflow with the Chebyshef inequality.

12-1-7 Other Statistics

At times, an observed response is a function of multiple variables. With assumption of independence among these variables we can separate the effects given a sufficiently large number of observations. Two types of analysis methods are in use for this work: *multiple regression* and *analysis of variance*. Regression analysis determines a line describing a linear relationship between the individual variables and the resulting dependent variable. Many relationships in computer systems are not linear. Analysis of variance relates causes and effects by discrete groupings and has been used to analyze the performance of paging operating systems based on the variables: memory size, program size, loading sequence, and paging algorithms. Both regression and analysis of variance assume linear relationships of the combination of independent variables on the dependent variable.

12-1-8 Help with Statistics

It is not necessary to be a statistical expert to use the methods and results that statistical research and development have provided. Many statistical packages exist to help perform these calculations. Graphical output can make the models being used accessible to people who are not comfortable with the numerical aspects of statistics.

You cannot expect that statistical experts will solve systems problems. The understanding and modeling of the system being evaluated remains as important as the application of analytical techniques. This also means that expertise about the computer system being evaluated and its applications must be available as well when an analysis is being made. Especially, the actual design process cannot be delegated to specialists in a single narrow area, and neither programmers nor statisticians can be expected to provide acceptable system evaluations by themselves.

12-2 SIMULATION

When no source of data is available which can be used to predict the behavior of a new system, it may be necessary to build a scale model to generate predictive data. Such a simulation model will be based on the process and hardware to be used in reality and will be fed with a sequence of descriptions of the desired computations. The output of a simulation will not be the results of the computation, but rather measurements of parameters collected in the simulation process.

The principal components of a discrete, event-driven simulation are shown in Fig. 12-7. The input to the simulation itself is an event queue, which contains entries of events that are created external to the system being simulated, for example, a request to retrieve a record; and internal events, for example, a completion of a seek. The output is a log of events with their times, which can be further analyzed.

External event entries may be generated by a program. It will use the expected distribution of external requests to make up request types and their times.

Another source for external events may be a log file from an existing system or a synthetic program which generates event requests during its execution. Logs or programs have the advantage that they provide a standard for system testing.

THE PROCESS OF SIMULATION   A simulation has its own timing mechanism. To determine how long the simulated computation will take in real life, the simulation uses a variable `clock` to keep the simulated time. The `clock` is incremented to the next event to be simulated. An external event may specify:

"At time = 29.1:   `Fetch Record for employee 631 (' Jones' )`"
After setting the clock to 29.1 and logging the receipt of this event, the steps of the process are simulated to the extent required.

If a hashed access to a disk or similar unit is being simulated, the steps shown in Fig. 12-17 are appropriate. We see that, because of the existence of queues, requests may not be processed when they arrive. Queuing is the subject of Sec. 12-3.

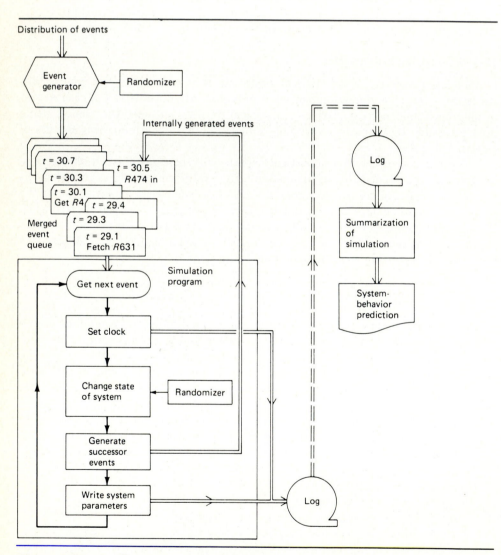

Figure 12-15   Components of a simulation.

A problem with simulations driven by external events lists is that there is no feedback from the system to the generator. This is fine if the process requesting services is indeed independent of the system.

---

1 An independent request function would be the distribution of flight inquiries by phone from potential passengers.

2 If the requests are issued by airline reservation agents, then a poor response rate by the system response will reduce their actual rate of entering inquiries.

Figure 12-16   Independent and non-independent request sources.

Dependent requests are best modeled internally within the simulation. A response function based on data as shown in Fig. 5-3 can be used to describe the effects of the user-machine interaction. When randomly generated events are used, multiple tests or partitioned long tests are needed to verify the stability of the simulation results.

The parameters of interest are either processed incrementally or written on a log file for later summarization. Typical parameters of interest are the total time to process all the events, the time required to process individual events, and the activity ratios of the devices used. The data obtained is again conveniently presented as histograms or described as distributions. Then predictions can be made, such as, "The response time to an inquiry is less than 10 s 90% of the time."

---

1 A status table for the simulated devices, as shown in Fig. 12-18, is checked. If the device being requested is busy skip to step 13.

2 A block address is computed for record with key 631 using the key-to-address transform being considered. A constant value, c, for the KAT is obtained separately.

3 The desired cylinder position is determined.

4 The amount of seek, cyl, from the current position is calculated.

5 The required seek time, s_{cyl}, is found.

6 A random latency, r, is generated.

7 The block transfer time, btt, is calculated from the transfer rate, r, and the block size, B. It will be constant for a given system.

8 A random function based on m/n is used to determine if there is a collision,
   if yes, go to step 3 to compute the incremental times, else

9 The completion time is computed as $29.1 + c + s + r + btt$, say, 29.4.

10 The status of the disk unit used is set to "busy".

11 Now an internal event is generated which states that

"At time 29.4: `Record 631 ('Jones') is in core, and disk D is free`"

---

12 The internal events are merged with the external events, and the simulation continues until the event list is exhausted.

13 When a device is found busy, the requests are put into a device queue.

14 Eventually A "`device is free`" signal from the internal queue resets the status, and directs the simulation to look at the device queue, select a request to be processed, and simulate it, continuing with step 1.

Figure 12-17   Simulation steps.

WRITING A SIMULATION   The use of simulation techniques to investigate file system behavior is simplified by the large gap between processor and file speeds. Adequate results can often be obtained from a simulation which concentrates on file delays and models the computation only in a gross fashion.

In one area, computational delays, other than those affecting bulk transfer, have to be considered. Much of the computational overhead in file operations is due to complexity in operating systems. Frequently, several milliseconds can elapse between the execution of a CALL for service and the emitting of a command to actually move the disk arm. Mean overhead times for these operations can sometimes be obtained from manuals, or are otherwise obtained by executing a large number (n) the disk operation in question. The known disk access times can be subtracted from the elapsed time, or the CPU time measurement may be available from the system. Dividing by n gives the mean CPU time for servicing the operation. If no paging of code occurs, this value should have a very low standard deviation.

A number of simulation languages are available and have been used extensively for system simulation. The author has found that simple simulations can be written rapidly on an interactive system in any higher-level language. The simulation languages now commonly available use batch processing techniques. When a simulation becomes large, the computing time required can become a significant item in the design budget, and the simulations have to be planned carefully so that they will return an adequate benefit for the expended effort.

A simulation model which includes many variables will first be tested by changing the variables one by one to select those which have a major effect on the outcomes. Then these important variables can be evaluated by having the randomizer generate test values throughout their range, while keeping the variables which had less importance constant. When a desirable model has been found, the minor variables will be tested again to verify that the perceived lack of effect is also true at the final setting of the model variables.

Another approach to handle simulations of large systems is to attack the simulation hierarchically. First, the cost of primitive operations is simulated, and the results are fitted to a simple mathematical formulation. These formulations are then used by simulations of more complex tasks. Several simulation levels may be used until the needed results are obtained. At each level a verification is done so that the parameters used do not exceed the range simulated at the lower level, since extrapolations based on fitted functions are risky. This scheme requires some sophistication so that the mathematical abstractions from each level are viable.

12-3   QUEUES AND SCHEDULING TECHNIQUES

When a computation requests service from a device which is busy, the computation will be delayed. Since the computation should not be abandoned, the request will be noted as an entry in a *queue* for the device. A single process of a transaction is delayed when it requests a file operation until it gets permission to use the file. The user's file requests may be issued directly by the user's programs, or indirectly by systems programs. The elements that make up a queue for a device are shown in Fig. 12-18.

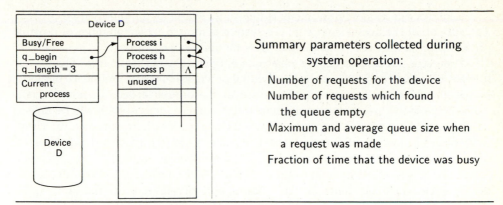

Figure 12-18   Elements of a queue.

The parameters listed are vital when systems are monitored for planned augmentation and improvement. If the queue is being simulated, then not only these variables will be collected, so that the entire usage distribution can be reconstructed.

QUEUES AND PROCESSES   One computation may initiate multiple processes which will independently go to the file system to request services. The entire computation cannot proceed beyond certain joining (P) points until outstanding processes have been completed. Figure 12-19 shows the progress of a small computation, which spawns processes for each file operation. Processes which have to read data frequently require delay of computations. Processes which write data may only prevent the final termination of a computation.

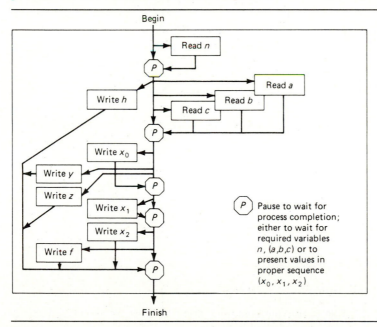

Figure 12-19   A transaction with multiple file processes.

Each service request in a queue is due to a request by one individual process. The sum of all the queue lengths in the system is limited by the number of possible processes in the system. This number may be quite large.

Processes, unless specifically constrained, operate asynchronously. This means it is not wise to generate a bunch of individual processes to write a sequence of blocks into a file: The blocks may not be written in the desired order. If, however, the blocks have individual addresses, a smart queue-management system will be able to write the blocks onto the file in an order which minimizes hardware delays. Every write or read process will be associated with one or more buffers to hold the data. The number of buffer lists possible limits the number of active file processes and hence the degree of parallel operation possible. The number of buffers permitted per file limits the queue lengths. The total number of buffers is limited by memory. This limit in turn keeps the number and sizes of queues manageable.

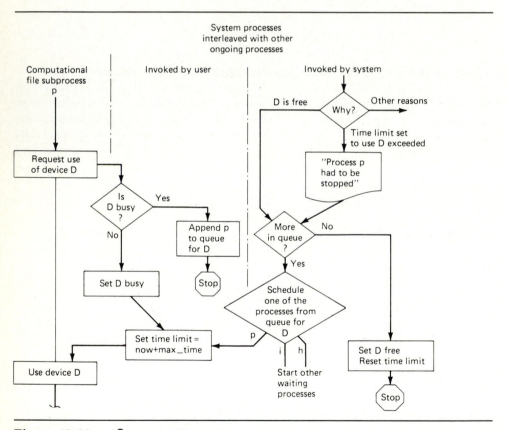

Figure 12-20   Queue management.

12-3-1 Queue Management

The activities which are part of the queue management for files are shown in Fig. 12-20. There will be at least one queue for every file device and there may be also a number of queues for other device types, all scheduled by the same *queue-management program* (QMP). The QMP is invoked either by a user, who wishes access to a device being managed by the QMP, or by the operating system, when it has analyzed that a signal for service involves the QMP.

The typical reason for the operating system to invoke the QMP is that a device has been released by the process that was holding it. Such a release is often initiated by a hardware signal which indicates the completion of the actual data transfer for device D. This will be followed by a verification procedure, after which device D is no longer needed by the process. It can now be assigned to another process.

Occasionally, because of a failure of the hardware or of a program, a process does not release, or maybe does not even begin to use device D. If a time limit or *time-out* is set, the faulty process can be canceled when the allowed time is exceeded, and the device given to another process. In systems where no time limits are set, all computations requesting D will come to a halt, and eventually all activity of a system will cease.

Some simple transaction systems attempt to prevent time-out errors by having all file access processes use code sections which are provided as part of the transaction operating system. This, of course, increases the complexity of the operating system itself. Excessive restrictions imposed by a system on the user for the sake of protection indicate an excessively weak operating system.

In order to provide space for infrequent large queues, a QMP may share the space for all queues active in the system, using linked-list structures. In interacting systems the queues for a few devices are often long, while other queues are empty. The monitoring of queues is important when systems are to be tuned for best performance. Queues may be created dynamically when a new resource is added to the system.

When more than one process is waiting in the queue for the device, one of these processes has to be selected. The selection or *scheduling* of service requests from a queue is the topic of the remainder of this section.

12-3-2 Scheduling from a Queue

The scheduler selects one of multiple candidate processes, which are waiting for service, for execution. The scheduler is the big diamond-shaped box in Fig. 12-20. It is invoked by the queue-management programs but should be a distinct module. Queue management concerns itself with the correct operation of the devices. The scheduler implements management policy, and is frequently subject to change. Many operating systems are built so that correct operation may be compromised when a scheduling policy is changed.

The choice of policy to select request elements from a queue is wide. The intuitively fairest policy is to select the process which has been waiting the longest, that is, use *first in first out* (FIFO) as the scheduling policy. Table 12-12 lists scheduling policies that have been employed, using the abbreviation which is most common in the queuing literature. Most of these policies have also been given computer-oriented names; several of these abbreviations are provided in Appendix A. The reason for alternate scheduling policies is the diversity of objectives to be achieved. Objectives in file and database scheduling are: minimal user delay, minimal variability of user delay, maximum utilization of the processor, maximum utilization of the transfer capability from the device, or maximization of locality for a currently active process so that a single process at a time is flushed through the system as fast as possible. Objectives may also be combined; a typical combination is the maximal utilization of the device, constrained by a requirement to provide an adequate response time for any user.

The scheduling choice is important to system performance only when the queues are filled; when there is no, or only one, process to be served, all algorithms behave equally well.

SCHEDULING POLICIES FOR A CYLINDER   We first consider only one cylinder of a disk. When using a FIFO policy, an average of one rotation will be lost between successive block accesses to a cylinder. Since other blocks may pass under the reading heads during this time, it is desirable to arrange that any requested blocks are read when they appear, rather than read strictly in the order in which they were requested. Such an approach is called *shortest service time first*, or SSTF. Control units for disks are available which allow the maintenance of multiple requests, one per sector, and these requests will be processed in sector sequence. Examples are the UNISYS B6375 and the IBM 2835.

When block lengths are fixed and track-switching time is predictable, an SSTF schedule can be implemented through software arrangement of requests. Sector-specific queues are shown in Fig. 12-21, with an example of the selection path for the next sector of a fixed head disk. The gap between sectors provides the time needed for switching tracks. If all sector queues $Q1, \ldots, Qb_{track}$ are filled, then b_{track} blocks can be accessed during one track revolution, giving the maximal *utilization factor uf*, defined as #(user blocks accessed)/#(disk blocks passed), of one.

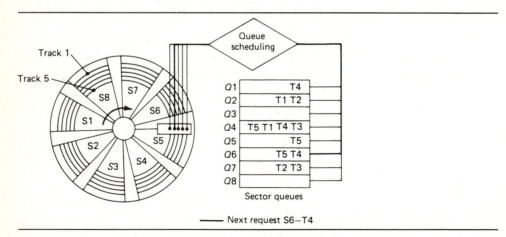

Figure 12-21   Queue optimization for a cylinder surface.

Even if b_{track} or more blocks are waiting to be processed, there will usually be empty queues. In Fig. 12-21 there are 12 requests for the five tracks in the 8 sector queues, but Q8 for sector S8 is still empty, and unless a request arrives for this queue during the next two sector times S6,7 the time for passing sector S8 will be unutilized. The probability of having an empty queue will be less for the sectors about to be accessed (S6, 7, ...) than for the sectors which have just been processed (S5, 4, ...). If the arrival of requests to the cylinder has a certain distribution, the arrival of requests to a sector queue (if they are independent of each other) will have the same distribution.

Long queues increase productivity, so that SSTF scheduling promotes a stable equilibrium as long as

$$uf = \frac{\lambda \, 2r}{b_{track}} < 1 \qquad\qquad 12\text{-}25$$

where $\lambda \, 2r$ is the number of arrivals during one revolution.

A $uf = 0.75$ corresponds, for the cylinder of Fig. 12-21 with $b_{track} = 8$ sectors and a rotation time of $2r = 50$ms, to an arrival rate $\lambda = 0.120$ requests per ms, or 120 requests/s.

Figure 12-22   Computing the arrival rate.

Unfortunately, a high utilization is associated with long queues, and hence long delays to processing requests. The mean delay for waiting in a sector queue, w, which has to be added to $r + btt$, has been derived for a Poisson-type distribution of arrival times by Coffman[69]. For a moderately large number of sectors ($b_{track} > 3$) the effects of the discrete sector boundaries can be disregarded; then

$$w = \frac{uf}{1 - uf} \, r \qquad\qquad \langle\text{Poisson arrivals}\rangle \; 12\text{-}26$$

giving a total average processing time for a request of

$$T_F = w + r + btt \qquad\qquad \langle\text{cylinder queue}\rangle \; 12\text{-}27$$

While a high utilization rate does increase the productivity of a cylinder, the waiting times, and hence the queue lengths, increase rapidly with heavy utilization.

At a utilization $uf = 0.75$ the waiting time, w, becomes $3r$, or the equivalent of one and a half revolutions. Given $r = 25$ms, the delay $w = 75$ms.
At $uf = 0.9$, the delay becomes $w = 9r$; and as $uf \to 1$ the queues get longer and longer, and will never be worked off if the arrivals don't cease.

Figure 12-23   Queue delay due to high utilization

A result of queuing theory, *Little's formula* (Jewell[67]), states that at equilibrium the total number of requests queued, Rq, depends on their delays, w'

$$Rq = \lambda w' \qquad\qquad 12\text{-}28$$

For the case of Fig. 12-23 we include in Rq the requests in the queue due w and r. Let $w' = w + r = 100$ms, then $Rq = (0.120 \text{ requests/ms})100 = 12$ requests.

Figure 12-24   Computation of the queue length.

Denning[72] has analyzed the case of uniform distribution of arrivals in the sector queue, taking into account the changing density before and after access. Uniform arrivals are a reasonable assumption if cylinder requests are due to sequential processing or due to direct-access algorithms. Here, the utilization

$$uf = \frac{1}{\frac{1}{2} b_{track}/Rq + 1} \qquad \langle\text{uniform arrivals}\rangle \; 12\text{-}29$$

Under extreme conditions ($Rq > 10, \lambda 2r > 10$ or $Rq < 1, \lambda 2r < 1$) the models behave similarly under either arrival distribution.

For cylinders the other scheduling algorithms listed in Table 12-12 are of interest only when variable-length blocks are collected. Since such usage is uncommon, we will proceed to consider disk units.

SCHEDULING POLICIES FOR DISKS   For disks with many tracks the intensity of use per sector will tend to be small, so that the expected length of the sector queue often becomes less than one and the cost of scheduling by sector does not provide commensurate benefits.

However, an optimization of seek times can improve performance significantly for disklike devices. This requires again the use of scheduling policies other than common queuing (first-in first-out or FIFO). The minimization of seek time is completely independent of the minimization of rotational latency within a cylinder so that two different schedulers may be operative within one file system at the same time. Each of the policies listed in Table 12-12 will now be considered.

LIFO   Transaction systems can use LIFO to optimize the use of the disk by minimizing disk distances. The idea here is that, by giving the device to the most recent user, no or little arm movement will be required for sequential reading of the file. LIFO can also minimize congestion and queue lengths, since jobs, as long as they can actively use the file system, are processed as fast as possible.

Table 12-12   Scheduling algorithms.

Name	Description	Remarks
Selection according to requestor:		
FIFO	First in first out	Fairest of them all
PRI	Priority by process	Control outside of QMP
LIFO	Last in first out	Maximize locality and resource utilization
RSS	Random scheduling	For analysis and simulation
Selection according to requested item:		
SSTF	Shortest service time first	High utilization, small queues
SCAN	Back and forth over disk	Better service distribution
CSCAN	One way with fast return	Lower service variability
N-step-SCAN	SCAN of N records at a time	Service guarantee
FSCAN	N-step SCAN with N = queue size at begin of SCAN cycle	Load-sensitive

Priority   The use of *PRIority*, frequently given to small computations, also has the effect of flushing selected computations through the system. If the number of computations having equally high priority becomes large, the disk usage efficiencies diminish. Users with large computations and low priorities often wait exceedingly long times. Priority-driven systems will have a high rate of completed computations and small queues. Statistics from these systems are used by computer center directors to demonstrate the effectiveness of their operations, while the users split their computations into small pieces to share in the benefits. This type of operation tends to be poor for databases.

     If the current cylinder position of the disk-access mechanism is known, scheduling can be based on the requested item rather than based on attributes of the queue or the requestor.

Shortest Service Time First   The SSTF algorithm for disks is equivalent to highest locality first. All requests on the current cylinder will be processed, and then requests on the nearest cylinder. A random tie-breaking algorithm may be used to resolve the case of equal distances. Since the center tracks are apt to be favored, an alternate tie-breaking rule is to choose the direction of the nearest extremity. This means that if the current position is 115 out of $j = 200$ tracks and requests are waiting at 110 and 120, then 120 will be chosen.

Guaranteeing Service   Any of the methods shown above, except FIFO, can leave some request unfulfilled until the entire queue is emptied. It is hence necessary to modify these techniques to reintroduce some minimum service level into the system. One augmentation is the addition of a dynamic priority structure which is based on the length of time that a process has been delayed. The rate of priority increase has to be chosen to satisfy response time constraints while not losing advantage of improved locality.

     The SCAN algorithm adds regularity of control to a SSTF method. When all requests on a cylinder have been served, it proceeds to one specific side, and this direction is maintained until the extreme cylinder is reached. The service direction changes whenever the inner or outer cylinder is reached. A modification of SCAN (LOOK) reverses direction as soon as there are no more requests in that direction. A SCAN policy will operate similarly to SSTF unless the request pattern is particularly poor, since the probability of requests in SSTF is biased against the area most recently processed.

     The CSCAN method reduces the maximum delay times of the scan by restricting the SCAN to one direction. If the expected time for a SCAN to go from inner to outer track is $t(SCAN)$, the expected service interval for blocks at the periphery is $2t(SCAN)$ using SCAN and less than $t(SCAN)+s_{max}$ for CSCAN, since in the shorter time interval fewer requests will enter the queue.

     The relative productivity of SCAN and CSCAN depends on the ratio of incremental seek times to cylinder processing times, and on the maximum seek time. For SCAN this ratio varies with cylinder position, since the most recently processed area is processed first.

     Figure 12-25 sketches the queue behavior for the case of perfect processing equilibrium. The arrival rate is uniform (1.5 per unit of time). The top boundary

of the queue area B→C→ ... indicates the aggregate arrivals; during the period
to point F their volume is proportionate to the area A,B,C. The lower boundary
of the queue area D→E→ ... indicates requests that have been served and which
have departed from the queue. The areas (A,B,C)=(D,E,F) and the areas (A',B',C')=
(D',E',F'), since under long-term equilibrium conditions arrivals and departures have
to be equal in each cycle. SCAN encounters increasing numbers of requests per track
as it goes back and forth. CSCAN encounters a steady load but is idle during the
seek to the beginning of the cycle.

The seek time from inner to outer track s_{max} is taken to be one-third of the
sum of single-track seek times $(j\,s_1)$. It can be observed that the average queue
length is slightly greater under CSCAN than under SCAN (about 100 versus 90),
since during the time s_{max} no requests are serviced.

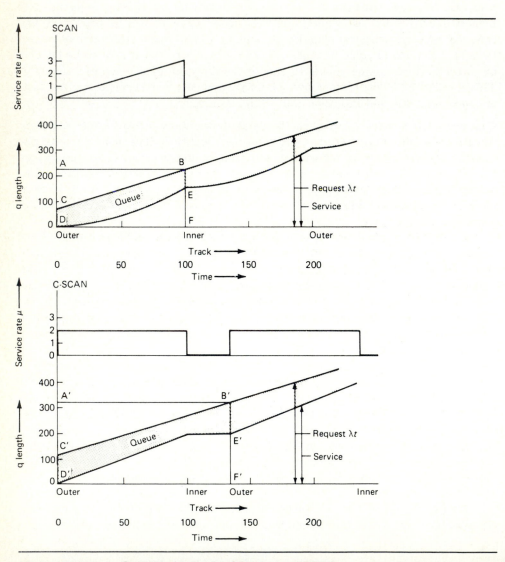

Figure 12-25   Queue behavior for SCAN and CSCAN.

The simplifying assumption made here, that processing time is linearly related to track position and does not depend on the number of requests per cylinder, is valid only when the average number of requests per cylinder during a scan is ≤ 1, or at least much less than the number of blocks or sectors on a track, so that no additional rotational latency accrues.

Making Scanning More Fair   SSTF, SCAN, and CSCAN may still fail to move the access arm for a long time. If, for instance, two processes have high access rates to one cylinder, they can monopolize the entire device by interleaving. High-density multisurface disks are more likely to be affected by this characteristic than disks with a low capacity per cylinder. To avoid forgetting requests for long periods, the request queues may be segmented, and one segment processed completely before any requests from the next segment are taken. This approach is refined in the N-step-SCAN and the FSCAN policies.

The N-step-SCAN places requests into subqueues of length N. Within a subqueue requests are processed using the SCAN policy. If fewer than N requests are ready at the end of a cycle, all of them are processed as a cycle.

With a large value of N, the performance of the N-step-SCAN approaches the performance of SCAN, while with $N = 1$, the service is equal to FIFO.

The scan has only to cover the range required for the N subqueue requests. User response time within a group of N requests might be best if SSTF were used within a cycle. Policies which leave the arm at the end of a cycle in an extreme position will contribute to the performance of the next cycle.

FSCAN is an implementation of an N-step-SCAN which uses as N the total length of the queue when a cycle commences, and defers all arrivals during the cycle to the next cycle. FSCAN shows improved efficiency as the load increases over CSCAN. The maximum queue length, however, increases to the number of arrivals per cycle. For the values used in Fig. 12-25 the average queue length becomes $1.5j/2 = 1.5 \cdot 200/2 = 150$ entries.

An *Eschenbach scan* extends the optimization used for a cylinder of a disk to the entire disk area. This is done by limiting the time to be spent at each cylinder position. A cylinder with a queue may be allotted between $1 \rightarrow k$ rotations, where k is the number of tracks on the cylinder. A parameter, E, is used to indicate the order of the Eschenbach scan. An order $E = k$ scan will obtain all the blocks from a cylinder position and is hence similar to a CSCAN, except that incremental requests requiring more than k revolutions will not be serviced in the current cycle. A small parameter of E $(1, 2, \ldots)$ will obtain blocks while the queue for the cylinder is still relatively long and will hence deal with higher average sector densities.

Fig. 12-26 shows the effect of the Eschenbach scheme applied to the single cylinder shown in Fig. 12-21. The results do not account for the small probability of new arrivals for this cylinder during its processing.

It is obvious that the Eschenbach scheme trades longer queues and greater waiting times for the capability to provide a very high utilization rate. It is clear that a high device-utilization rate will provide, at an equal request rate, better aggregate service to the user. For an Eschenbach scheme to be effective, the request rates will be high. This method has been used more in message switching and in the collection of transactions for subsequent batch processing than in the area of standard file services.

E	Blocks accessed	uf
1	6 out of 8	0.75
2	+4 out of the next 8	0.625
3	+1 out of the next 8	0.457
4	+1 out of the next 8	0.375
5	Skip since track is empty	0.375

Figure 12-26   Utilization factors using Eschenbach scans.

The Eschenbach scheme does not provide a service guarantee, but since the scanning cycle time, t_{cycle}, is guaranteed

$$t_{cycle} \le j(s_1 + 2\,E\,r) + s_j \qquad\qquad 12\text{-}36$$

where j is the number of cylinders allotted to the file, a service guarantee for priority messages can be provided. The required augmentation is the rearrangement of the sector queues to place priority requests at the head of the line. Unless a cylinder has for one sector more than E priority messages, t_{cycle} will be the maximum queue delay.

12-3-3 Use of Scheduling

Other techniques to optimize disk usage include the placement of frequently used blocks in the central cylinders of a disk. A SCAN policy will then access these cylinders most effectively; and even FIFO will show lower average seek times. FIFO and PRIority policies are frequently used because of their simplicity and the fact that the more complex scheduling policies excel at utilization rates not often reached in practice.

Scheduling is needed to overcome for poor performance of systems which collect transactions from many terminals for later batch processing (Winick[69]). If we represent data from a transaction coming from terminal T during the time interval I as (T,I), the file containing data from these transactions will be approximately arranged in the sequence
    { (1,1),(2,1),....,(t,1), (1,2),(2,2),....,(t,2), ..., (1,i),(2,i),....,(t,i)}.
When this file has to be processed, the data from one source terminal repesents a batch, requiring access in the order { (1,1),(1,2),....,(i,1)}, followed by { (2,1),...., } etc. This transposition of access places extremely heavy loads on the file services supporting these systems, loads which can be considerably ameliorated by effective queue scheduling policies.

In many operating systems the scheduler is integrated with other functions, so that implemented scheduling policies are difficult to discern and nearly impossible to change. Since the scheduler, after making the scheduling decision, allocates not only resources but also assigns access privileges to users, as described in Chap. 15, the interaction can be complex. Some concepts, for instance the notion of a *monitor* to protect critical sections of programs (BrinchHansen[73]), encourage such integration. The lack of modularity which exists in those systems can make it difficult to implement effective scheduling techniques.

12-4   OPERATIONS RESEARCH IN DATABASE DESIGN

Operations Research is an area of applied mathematics which addresses problems faced by the management of enterprises in the scheduling, operations, and development of facilities. In this context, Operations Research (OR) is closely identified with *management science*, although it is obvious that there is more to the science of management than the application of OR techniques.

Tools of OR include:
- Queuing theory
- Inventory theory
- Linear and integer programming
- Decision theory

Each of these fields is now a discipline in its own right.

12-4-1 Queuing Distributions and Their Application

Because of the importance of queues in manufacturing and communications, the subject of queues has been intensively studied. The parameters required for the mathematical treatment of queues include:

Description of the source of requests for service
r.1 Number of requests
r.2 Arrival rate distribution
Description of the queue waiting for service
q.1 Queue capacity
q.2 Scheduling policy
Description of the service
s.1 Number of servers
s.2 Service time distribution

The previous section has described queues as they are managed in file systems. A convention used to classify queuing models for analysis, *Kendall's notation*, specifies

arrival process/service process/number of servers,

using standard symbols for the distributions of arrival or service processes:

M	:	Exponential
D	:	Constant or otherwise determined
$E(m)$	:	Erlang
I	:	General and independent
G	:	General

Of interest to problems in file analysis are primarily queuing models of the type $M/G/1$ and $E/G/1$.

Events leading to queuing are described by their average arrival rate (λ). An alternative to the arrival rate is the distribution of interarrival times, t. In Fig. 12-25 the requests arrived uniformly distributed, the arrival rate λ was 1.5 per time unit, and the interarrival time t was a constant 0.66.

We have encountered exponential and constant distributions in Sec. 12-1. We associate exponential rates with independence of successive events and constant rates with complete dependence of the arrival time on the time of the preceding event. The important case where the distribution of arrivals are neither completely random nor constant is described by distributions of the Erlang type.

The servers are characterized by the potential service (μ) rates they represent. The service types in the systems we describe are dominated by seeks and latencies which can be determined using hardware parameters. Requests will depart from the system at a throughput rate, $\rho = uf\,\mu$, As seen earlier a high utilization, uf creates delays.

During equilibrium arrivals λ and departures ρ are equal. The number of departures is limited by the number of arrivals: at any time t_i after initialization $\lambda\,t_i \geq \rho\,t_i$ and any unprocessed arrivals are held in queues.

When a service request addresses a specific file, the applicable number of servers is one; only in communication networks between processors, access to fully redundant files, or when writing without specifying the disk address can the case of multiple servers occur.

ERLANG DISTRIBUTIONS   When the demands for service to file and communications systems are measured, it is often found that the times between services requests are distributed in a pattern which is due neither to completely random nor to constant behavior. The behavior may be explained by the fact that after a service request has been granted, the time for the service and analysis of the obtained data is not at all random, so that one computation will emit service requests in a cyclical pattern. Similar but randomly interleaving patterns are presented by other, independent computations being processed.

To capture the range between random and constant interarrival times a parameterized distribution, Erlang(m), can be used. Figure 12-27 shows some Erlang distributions for an average arrival rate, $\lambda = 1$. Figure 12-27 and the accompanying Eq. 12-32 show that the Erlang distribution for $m = 1$ is equal to the exponential distribution, while as $m \to \infty$ the distribution becomes constant. The parameters for the Erlang distribution are

$$mean(t) = \frac{1}{\lambda} \quad \text{(of course) and} \quad \sigma(t) = \frac{1}{\sqrt{m}\,\lambda} \qquad \qquad \text{12-31}$$

Table 12-13   Computation of Erlang parameter, m.

```
/* Computation of Erlang Parameter */                          /* 12-13 */
      m_erlang = (mean/sd)**2  ;
```

The appropriate Erlang parameter, m, for an observed Erlang-like distribution can hence be found from the computed mean and standard deviation, as shown in the program statement of Table 12-13. High values of `m_erlang` (> 10) indicate little variability in interarrival times.

The frequency distribution for an Erlang distribution is

$$freq(t) = \frac{(\lambda m)^m t^{m-1}}{(m-1)!} e^{-m\lambda t} \quad \text{for } t \geq 0 \qquad \text{12-32}$$

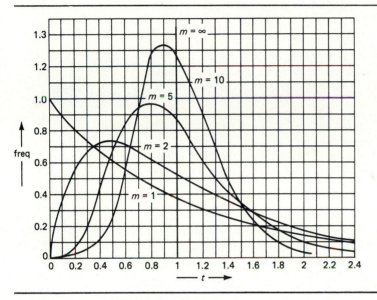

Figure 12-27   Erlang distributions.

The Effect of Variability   That random service times or service requests have a detrimental effect on service performance can be demonstrated with the simple example of Fig. 12-28. The probability to arrive at a *bad* time is 50/fully compensated by *good* times.

There are two disks which provide service at mean intervals of 30 ms. The expected delay for one randomly arriving request arriving in the interval $(0, 120)$ to receive service from disk D1 is 15 ms, but the delay for that request for disk service from D2 is

$$\frac{15}{120}\frac{1}{2}(15) + \frac{15}{120}\frac{1}{2}(15) + \frac{60}{120}\frac{1}{2}(60) + \frac{30}{120}\frac{1}{2}(30) = 20.6\text{ms}$$

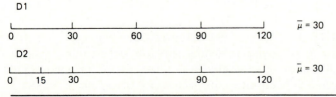

Figure 12-28   Disk service times.

Queue Length and Delays for Erlang Distributions   When the order of the Erlang distribution for requests, and the utilization factor of the service facility are known, the queuing behavior is defined. Formulas and graphs (IBM F20-7[71]) can be used to compute queue length and delay times given m_erlang and uf. The computations required are shown in Table 12-14.

Table 12-14   Computation of expected queue length and waiting time.

```
/* Computation of Expected Queue Length */                  / * 12-14a */
     idlef = 1 - uf;    ufsq = uf**2;
     factor1 = 1 - 1/m_erlang;    factor2 = 1 - uf/2*factor1;
 /* Queue Length */
     queue_bar = uf * factor2/idlef;
     queue_sd = SQRT(uf * (1 - uf/2*(3
                    - (10*uf-ufsq)/6 - (3*idlef + ufsq)/m_erlang
                    - (8*uf-5*ufsq)/(6*m_erlang**2)) ) ) / idlef;
/* Waiting Time before Begin of Service */                  /* 12-14b */
     w_bar = (s+r+btt) * factor2/idlef;
     w_sd = (s+r+btt) *
        SQRT( (1-(4*uf-ufsq)/6*factor1)*(1+1/m_erlang)
                                        - factor2**2) / idlef;
```

The availability of computers is appreciated when Erlang distributions are used.

The factor idlef=1-uf had already been encountered in the analysis of cylinder scheduling. It accounts for the rapid decline of performance when a high utilization is achieved while arrival or service times show random or stochastic variation.

Given that the times needed to fetch a large number of records from a file system have been collected. The mean time was 90 ms, and the standard deviation 40 ms. A histogram of the distribution makes an Erlang distribution likely. The appropriate Erlang parameter, according to the statement in Table 12-13, is
    m_erlang = (90/40)**2 ≈ 5.0
The disk unit was busy during the test 40% of the time, so that uf = 0.4. The queue length expected is computed, using the program in Table 12-14a as
    queue_bar = 0.56
    queue_sd = 0.84
Given that the mean service time s+r+btt is 50 ms we find from the program segment in Table 12-14b the mean delay and its standard deviation
    w_bar = 70.0 ms
    w_sd = 42.8 ms

Figure 12-29   Calculation of a queue length.

USE OF PERCENTILES TO DEFINE PERFORMANCE   The type of distribution with its mean and standard deviation defines the distribution of events in a system precisely. The result has to be translated into terms useful for operational decisions. The use of fractions or percentiles of occurrence of certain events is a well-understood approach. Figure 12-31 provides this information for Erlang and hence exponential distributions.

It provides the values of t where the areas of the Erlang distribution from $0 \to t$ are 90%, 95%, and 99% of the total area. Events that fall into the tail for $t \to \infty$ will have longer delays. The result is that the waiting time is less than $w(p)/\overline{w}$ times the average waiting time $\overline{w}$ in $p\%$ of the cases.

Let us provide the waiting-time limit for 90% of the record fetches in the example above. For **m_erlang = 5** the 90th percentile in Fig. 12-31 gives a ratio of 1.6, or a delay of $1.6 \cdot 70 = 112$ **ms**.

A Chebyshev inequality can only promise for the 90th percentile a delay of less than $70 + \sqrt{10}\, 42.8 = 205$ **ms**, and this is the value to be used if the distribution does not match the Erlang curve for **m_erlang = 5**.

Figure 12-30   Waiting time limit using Erlang and Chebyshev assumptions.

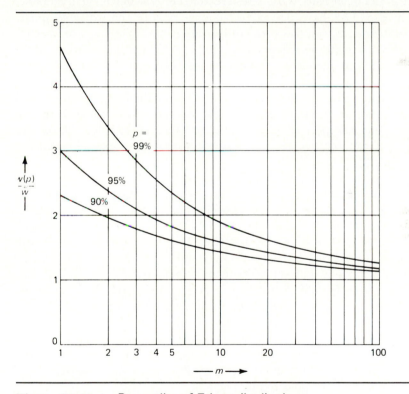

Figure 12-31   Percentiles of Erlang distributions.

MIX OF DISTRIBUTIONS   When the behavior of a mixture of different services is needed, the joint distribution and the mean will be the sum of the scaled distributions. The expected mean and standard deviation in the mix will be

$$mean_{mix} = \sum_{h} pc_h mean_h \qquad\qquad 12\text{-}33$$

$$\sigma_{mix} = \sqrt{\sum_{h} pc_h^2 (\sigma_h^2 + (mean_h - mean_{mix})^2} \qquad\qquad 12\text{-}34$$

where pc_h is the proportion of the computation h in the mix (IBM F20-7[71]).

12-4-2 Transients in Service Demands

Up to this point we have discussed queuing models which are in equilibrium, so that within all intervals considered, the service rate was adequate to provide the requested services. In many systems, however, there will be certain periods where the rate of arrival of requests for service, λ, exceeds the service capacity, μ. Such a period is called a *transient*, since it can only be a temporary situation; a situation where the average rate of arrivals, $\overline{\lambda}$, remains greater than μ is of course intolerable.

Examples in Sec. 12-3 have demonstrated how rapidly the expected queue length and the wait time, w, can rise as the utilization factor, $uf = \overline{\lambda}/\mu$, approaches one. If later $\overline{\lambda} \to \ll \mu$, the queues will empty and $w \to 0$. Unused computing capacity is a very perishable commodity; it cannot be put into a bank to provide later benefits.

Transients are fairly difficult to analyze using the probabilistic techniques used earlier, so that graphic constructions based on flow concepts will be used here. We will consider now only the part of a queue due to overload and not the part of the queue which is generated because of the delays caused by seek and rotational latency.

Figure 12-32 shows the cumulative arrivals as line A and the cumulative service requests which are being processed as line D. Processing of requests (D) is limited both by the slope μ giving the service rate capacity and by the arrival of requests, A. The space between A and D depicts the queue which is generated. The queue begins forming at $t = t_0$ where for the first time the instantaneous arrival rate $\lambda(t) > \mu$. At t_2 the arrival rate has subsided and $\lambda(t) = \mu$, but the queue has yet to be worked off. The queue will not be reduced to zero until time t_3, where D, continued at angle μ from t_0, intersects A. The average rate of arrivals λ during the total transient between t_0 and t_3 is equal to μ, but the overall $\overline{\lambda}$ in the cycle of t_c is less than the available service rate μ. The values are given below.

If the shape of the arrival distribution, A, is known, a graphical construction can provide the desired values of queue lengths. This graph can easily be interpreted, for instance, for a FIFO scheduling discipline the waiting time for an arrival at t_i, when the queue length is q_i, is indicated by line w_i.

In order to treat a transient analytically, an assumption regarding its shape has to be made. The simplest relationship which can describe a cyclic transient of $\lambda(t)$ is a sine curve. In Fig. 12-33 we show this curve with a basic cycle of 100 s. To this curve are applied three arrival and service parameters, as listed.

Figure 12-32 shows the queue beginning to form at t_0, where $\lambda(t) = \mu$. Substitution of this value in the sine-wave equation for $\lambda(t)$ allows computation of this point. The arrival rate is maximal at $t_1 = t_c/4$. Symmetry about t_1 determines t_2.

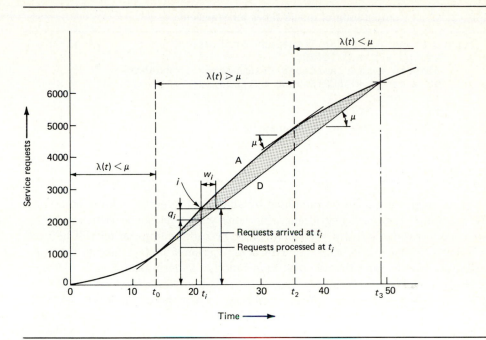

Figure 12-32   Transient arrivals.

$$\lambda(t) = \overline{\lambda} + (\lambda_{max} - \overline{\lambda}) \sin(t \frac{2\pi}{t_c})$$

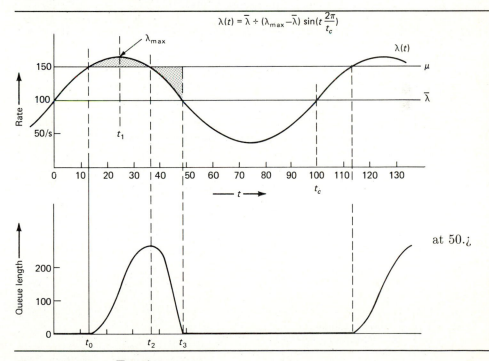

Figure 12-33   Transient queue.

Table 12-15   Computation of queue times for transient.

```
/* Compute Queue Times for Transient Arrivals */            /* 12-15 */
        two_pi = 2 * 3.14159;
        sine_t0 = (mu-lambdabar)/(lambdamax-lambdabar);
        t0 = cycle * ARCSIN(sine_t0)/two_pi;
        t1 = cycle/4;
        t2 = t1 + (t1-t0);
```
Executing this program gives for the example values
```
        t0 = 13.6 s
        t1 = 25.0 s
        t2 = 36.4 s
```

The queue length at t2 can be computed by analytical integration between t0 and t2 or by finite, stepwise integration. The time when the queue vanishes, t3, is tedious to derive analytically, so that a simple stepwise computation will be used which simulates the queue behavior. This computation will step through time and estimate arrivals λ using the assumed *sine* function superimposed on $\bar{\lambda}$. When λ exceeds the possible service rate, μ, the excess arrivals are added to a queue. If there is a queue, it is decreased by any excess $\mu - \lambda$. When the queue length becomes zero, the time t3 is computed and printed. At each second of the cycle the queue length is reported.

Table 12-16   Queue length and total time for transient.

```
/* Queue Length and Total Time for Transient */             /* 12-16 */
      radius = lambdamax - lambdabar;
      queue = 0;
      lastlambda = lambdaba;r
      DO second = 1 TO cycle;    angle = second/cycle*two_pi;
          lambda = radius*SIN(angle) + lambdabar;
          IF lambda>mu THEN
 /* Approximate Arrivals by Average in Interval */
              queue = queue + (lastlambda+lambda)/2 - mu;
          ELSE DO;
              IF queue > 0 THEN DO;
     /* Work off Queue */
                  decrease = mu - (lastlambda+lambda)/2;
                  IF decrease < queue THEN queue = queue - decrease;
                  ELSE DO;
      /* queue is gone, interpolate between seconds */
                      t3 = second - 1 + queue/decrease;
                      queue = 0;
                      PUT DATA(t3,queue);
                  END;
              END;
          END;
          lastlambda=lambda;
          PUT DATA(second, queue);
      END period;
```

Applying the program of Table 12-16 to our example computes a completion time of $t3 = 48.2$ s, so that there are here three similar intervals,

Phase 1:   Increasing rate of queue growth: $t1-t0 = 11.4$ s
Phase 2:   Decreasing rate of queue growth: $t2-t1 = 11.4$ s
Phase 3:   Queue collapse : $t3-t2 = 11.8$ s

Figure 12-34   The three phases of a transient.

⊞⊞⊞⊞ **Behavior of Transients**   The pattern of equal thirds observed in Fig. 12-34 can also be analytically deduced. The time to work off the queue depends on the ratio of $\overline{\lambda}$ to μ. If there is a reasonable margin between $\overline{\lambda}$ and μ, the transient takes less than half of the total cycle, t_c. If now $t_3 \approx \frac{1}{2}t_c$ we find four phases in a cycle as shown in Fig. 12-33: no queue from 0 to t_0 and the three phases of queue growth increase, growth decrease, and collapse to t_3. In the last phase t_2, t_3 the steepness of the arrival rate λ is about twice as great for cyclic or quadratic functions as the steepness of λ during growth in t_0, t_1 and t_1, t_2. Because of this difference the queue will collapse in about half the time it took to grow. The two phases of growth are equal because of the symmetry we assumed for the cycle. The reasoning of double steepness and symmetry continues to hold for transients with $t_3 < \frac{1}{2}t_c$ or transient lengths $t_3 - t_0 < \frac{3}{8}t_c$. This pattern of equal thirds is typical and has also been concluded for other second-order assumptions.

When transients increase in length, the time to work off the queue increases relative to the transient length. At the limit for long-term operation, $\overline{\lambda} = \mu$, $t_2 - t_0 = t_3 - t_2$ and the time for the queue to grow is equal to the time needed for the queue to disappear. This can be easily visualized in Fig. 12-33 by reducing μ to 100; then t_3 occurs at the end of the cycle, namely, at $t_c = 100$ s.

When the transients are not due to cyclic phenomena, the same analysis method can still be used by fitting the sine curve according to observed values of any two of the time points { t0,t1,t2,t3 } in addition to using the service and arrival rates as before.

The expected queue length, as computed here, is entirely due to the transient, and additional queue capacity is required for random variations of arrivals and service, and for hardware-caused delays.   ⊞⊞⊞⊞

12-4-3 An Application of Inventory Theory

In classical inventory theory, there is a collection of goods which are gradually consumed. Before the inventory is exhausted, an order is to be placed, so that the supply is replenished. A cost is associated with placing an order, with storing the inventory, and with having run out of the goods. There are many models available to solve inventory problems.

A file or database tends to become less efficient over time until an order to reorganize is placed, so that its behavior presents a similar cost function as shown in Fig. 12-35. The cost functions depend on the overflow parameter, o, seen in Chap. 3. In direct files the cost is related to the degree of clustering and to the file density.

After reorganization at a cost $C_Y = f(T_Y)$, the file will be more efficient. The original efficiency should be regained unless the file has grown. If statistics about record activity are available, reorganization can be used to improve the file efficiency. While the method and its effect depend on the file organization, usage costs will be lower if records of highest activity are reloaded first. In a direct file, for instance, the frequently accessed records will be found at the initial address.

We will consider only the case of a static file because the principle of the analysis remains the same. The reorganization cost is equivalent to the cost of placing an order, and the time required between the placing of the order and the receipt of the goods can be ignored.

The cost of operating the file system can be split into the component for the static portion, $n\, C_n$, and for the overflow portion, $o\, C_o$, where $C_{n,o}$ are the costs per record of the file fragments. To simplify matters further, a linear growth of overflow, o, over time, t, is assumed, so that $o = c_o t, t = 0 \rightarrow t_Y$. The cost of overflows at a given instant can be written as $t\, c_o C_o = t\, C_o'$. Reorganizations are performed after an interval, t_Y, and the cost of operating the system during such an interval can be estimated from the two areas shown in Fig. 12-33 and the cost of reorganization

$$C_{op}(t_Y) = t_Y n\, C_n + \frac{1}{2} t_Y^2 C_o' + C_Y \qquad\qquad 12\text{-}35$$

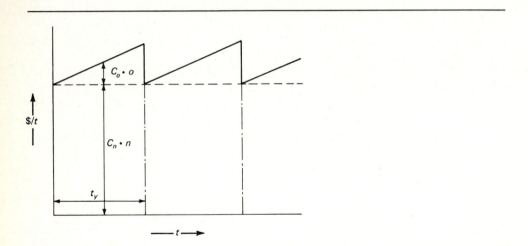

Figure 12-35   Cost function of a file which is being updated.

During a long period, Per, there will be Per/t_Y reorganizations and the cost over Per will be

$$C_{op}(Per) = Per\, n\, C_n + \frac{1}{2} Per\, t_Y C_o' + Per\, \frac{C_Y}{t_Y} \qquad\qquad 12\text{-}36$$

Given are load quantites of

$$L_F = 20\,000/\text{day fetch requests}$$
$$L_I = 300/\text{day new records, causing overflow } o$$

The file has $n = 40000$ records of length $R = 500$ on blocks of size $B = 2000$, the index has a fanout $y = 100$. We derive $Bfr = B/R = 4$, $x = \log_{100}(n/Bfr) = 2$. We assume that the index level, x, is in core, also that level $1(x-1)$ is on the same cylinder as the data and that $n/o \gg Bfr$, so that we can use Eq. 5-14. We simplify the overflow term $o'/(n+o')$ to o/n, since we use o here to denote the current overflow and $o \ll n$.

$$T_F = c + s + 2(r + btt) + \frac{o}{n}(r + btt)$$
$$T_Y = 2n\frac{R}{t'}\frac{SI}{t}$$

The low ratio of insertions to fetch operations $L_I/L_F = 300/20\,000 = 1.5\%$ permits T_I to be ignored.

Continuing the estimation process, it is assumed that the index SI requires 5% space over the rest of the file and hence a proportionate effect to rewrite. Then

$$C_Y = 2.05\,n\,\frac{R}{t'}\,0.5\,cost$$

For a 2314-type disk unit the parameters for this file will be

$r = 0.025$ s
$t' = 120\,000$ bytes/s
$btt = 0.005$ s

and for simplicity, we set the processor cost at

$$cost = \$0.10/\text{s}$$

The actual absolute values of these parameters are not very critical since they tend to cancel each other out. With this *cost*

$$C_Y = \$17.10 \qquad \text{and} \qquad C_o' = \$0.45/day^2$$

so that

$$t_Y(\text{optimum}) = 8.7 \text{ days}$$

Figure 12-36   Calculation of reorganization period.

The lowest cost as a function of the reorganization interval can be found by taking the derivative with respect to t_Y and setting it to zero.

$$\frac{1}{2} Per C'_o - Per \frac{C_Y}{t_Y^2} = 0 \qquad \text{giving} \qquad t_Y(optimal) = \sqrt{2\frac{C_Y}{C'_o}} \qquad \text{12-37}$$

This rule is applied in Fig. 12-36 to the indexed-sequential file presented in Chap. 5-2-2.

For an indexed-sequential file the relationship for $C_o = f(T_F)$ is, given the assumptions in the example, linear in respect to o and T_Y is independent, as required by the assumptions made in the model used to optimize the reorganization time. Then

$$C_o = \frac{r + btt}{n} \qquad \text{12-38}$$

and with one overflow per insertion L_I

$$C'_o = L_F L_I (r + btt) \frac{cost}{n} \qquad \text{12-39}$$

where *cost* is the processing cost per second. The reorganization will be scheduled for lower cost time, so that $0.5\,cost$ was used in Fig. 12-36 to compute C_Y.

BACKGROUND AND REFERENCES

Basic References   Of the many available statistics texts, Dixon[69], Freund[62], and Snedecor[67] provided the required background. Feller[71] presents a comprehensive foundation of probability theory. Moroney[56] is a very readable introduction, and Huff[54] warns of many pitfalls in the use of statistics.

Useful mathematical techniques can be found in Knuth[69,73S] and in Acton[70]. An excellent compendium for statistical and mathematical procedures is Press[86]; programs are available for its procedures.

The application of a variety of techniques to computer-system behavior analysis is demonstrated in Freiberger[72]. An example is given by Hill[87]. There is not much incentive to publish the routine application of statistical techniques to system design, and because of this void, it is difficult to judge how much these techniques are used and how powerful they have shown themselves to be (Ferrari[86]).

Distributions   Agarwala[70] addresses the problems of recognizing distributions, and Bhattacharya[67] separates bimodal mixtures of normal distributions. Statistically based analysis of file systems has concentrated on direct access methods: Peterson[57], Johnson[61], and Buchholz[63]. Christodoulakis[84] is justifies optimism about the assumptions of uniformity made commonly.

Simulation   Simulation as a tool has been used for planning a large variety of technical and social projects and is often associated with database efforts to provide the required input to the simulation model. A journal, *Simulation*, is devoted to this field. An early textbook in this area is Gordon[69], who is the designer of GPSS, a simulation program often used for computer-system modeling. Kiviat[69] describes SIMSCRIPT and some applications. A careful exposition of simulation is given by MacDougall[82]. Maryanski[83] is a general text which covers both discrete (GPSS) and continuous simulation (CSMP).

Simulation has been used in many performance assessments, other chapters cite results by Effelsberg[84], Salza[83], and Whang[84]. Computer systems have been simulated to evaluate interacting processes (Nielsen[67] and Skinner[69] are examples), but the relative importance of file operations has been low in these studies. Seaman[69] includes input-output processes applicable to files. Glinka[67] discusses a simulation of an information-retrieval design. Reiter in Kerr[75] presents the development of a simulator to handle a variety of files. Fishman[67] analyzes the problem of the validity of simulation results generated from random inputs. Özsu[85] simulates control of distributed files.

Measurements   Measurements of access patterns are provided by Lum[71,73], Deutscher[75], and both Ousterhout[85] and Maloney[87] for UNIX. Cheng[69] describes the use of logging files to drive simulations. Buchholz[69] presents a synthetic file-updating program, and Sreenivasan[74] uses this program to derive a workload for testing. Measurement of file operations is described by Krinos[73], Huang[74], Sreenivasan[74], and Heacox in Kerr[75]. Salza[85] describes the workload for testing advanced hardware models.

Queue Scheduling   Any computer managing more than one process at a time will need queue management as part of required operating system services. Methods to obtain effective scheduling of queues were initially tried in the teleprocessing environment, where message queuing was a familiar concept. Seaman[66] mentions scanning to improve disk access, and Weingarten[66] presents the case for sector queuing, the Eschenbach scheme, and in Weingarten[68] extends this method to disk. Denning[67] gives a simple analysis of practical queue scheduling policies. These and other early papers take into account track-switching delays, which are no longer important.

Coffman[69] gives results for queue optimization with SSTF. Burge[71] and Denning[72] resolve the problem of drum performance for random arrivals of requests which access sectors uniformly, using Markov processes. Jenq[87] describes experiments.

Frank[69] analyzed SCAN and N-step-SCAN for uniform requests and complex disk devices using discrete probabilities and simulation. Teorey[72] analyzes and simulates a number of scheduling algorithms, and proposes CSCAN as well as switching of scheduling policies. The assumptions made in these analyses have to be considered very carefully before the results can be used. Coffman[72] analyses FSCAN; it is the technique used in the CII SIRIS operating system which supports the database system SOCRATE. Stone[73] compares SSTF with other scheduling disciplines for drums with variable-length blocks. Wilhelm[76] presents the case where FIFO outperforms SSTF on disk and Goldberg[79] presents a problem in paging. Fuller[75] summarizes queuing policies and their analyses; included are confirmations of results in earlier reports. More recently, Atwood[82] simulated actual hardware with great care and concluded that seek scheduling was ineffective with their assumptions.

Operations Research   OR has emerged as an applied science mainly because of the problems faced by the industrial mobilization of World War II. Much of the mathematical background was already available. Queuing theory had been developed and applied to telephone systems by A. K. Erlang in 1909; a recent example of their use is by Kelton[85].

A basic and easily read textbook describing methods used in OR is Wagner[75]; Hillier[67] or Hertz[69] provide fundamentals. Feller[71] includes some examples of queuing in his treatment of probability theory, and Kleinrock[75] covers the theory and practice of queuing systems.

Queuing analysis   Hellerman[75] and Stone[75] consider queuing problems in computer systems; Graham[78] and Denning[78] provide surveys. Kobayashi[78] approaches performance issues formally. BrinchHansen[73] analyzes queuing in time-shared processing, but many of the assumptions do not hold for file systems. Allen[75] and IBM F20-7[71] summarize queuing theory for message-processing systems, and Martin[72] includes some approximations to queuing results. Newell[71] applies queuing to rush-hour transients, using a parabolic approximation; the sinewave-based approach presented here was original in Wiederhold[77,83] and appears simpler. Many of the analyses of scheduling disciplines in the previous section use results from queuing theory.

Linear Programming   Morgan[74] describes replacement algorithms for files on mountable diskpacks and uses linear programming (LP) for some solutions. Benner[67] uses LP to optimize record allocation in an IMS-like hierarchical structure, and Stanfel[70] uses LP to optimize fetch time in trees. Chu[69] and Severance[72] apply LP to file design. A CODASYL database is optimized by De[78]. Ramamoorthy[79], Chen[80], and Ceri[82] use OR to design distributed databases. Levin[78] uses a branch-and-bound method. Pelegatti in Bernstein[79] and Ceri[82] minimize the communication costs.

Reorganization Analyses   The use of techniques developed for inventory control to determine the time interval for file reorganization is due to Shneiderman[73]. Arora[71], Vold[73], Yao[76], Tuel[78], and Batory[82] address the same problem. Sockut[78] models concurrent reorganization and provides a survey (Sockut[79]). Young[74] and Lohman[77] use a similar technique to obtain the required interval for writing file backup copies.

EXERCISES

1   Redo Exercise 7-8, given that the text lines are of length 70 with a standard deviation of 30 characters.

2   Redo Exercise 2-9, given that the request rate for tracks has a Poisson distribution over the track numbers with a mean of 0.5.

3 a   Sketch a distribution of the access times between blocks on tape.

 b   Calculate the standard deviation.

4   Do Exercise 3 for a disk or other direct-access unit.

5   What queue-scheduling policy is used by the file system that you have been using? Do you find the policy reasonable? Which users are being favored and which are being discriminated against? Prepare an argument to management for changing the policy.

6   In Fig. 12-6, used to demonstrate the normal distribution, space was saved by placing fewer records into a block. When is the technique apt to be effective in an indexed or in a direct file?

7   Reevaluate the same example for the case that the distribution was not normal, but symmetric and unimodal.

8 Section 12-1-6 stresses understanding of the model when applying transformations. What was the model used for the billing data? Does it make sense? Using this model, what is the expectation of outstanding bills if the hospital doubles size and billings? What can cause failure of the model?

9 Specify the simulation steps for
" 29.4: Record 'Jones' is in core and disk D is free."

10 Read a scheduling algorithm other than FIFO used for processor scheduling and apply it to a file system. Compare the effectiveness and the validity of the analysis in the file environment.

11 During lunch hour a large number of orders for stock purchases are placed at a brokerage, creating a queue within the processor which updates the order file. Estimate the earliest time when the entire order file can be tabulated.

12 Write a program to simulate the queue management problem, and apply it to two selection algorithms. Compare the processing of two identical workloads. Explain the differences in behavior.

13 Describe how a random-number-generating routine generates a uniform distribution. Describe how a normal random-distribution routine generates values which are normally distributed, using a uniform-distribution-generating routine. The listings of the programs used can be found in the documentation of your computer service.

14 Using the Poisson distribution of Sec. 12-1-5 as an example, compute the median and the mode, and use Eq. 12-1 to estimate the median from the mean and the mode. Apply these to some moderately skewed distributions.

15 Recalculate the expected update cost for an indexed file (Chap. 5-4-5), given that it has been determined that data changes are distributed normally around the current data value, with a relatively small standard deviation, say 100 for $n = 10\,000$.

16[p] We now will apply some distributions to the files of your application and their use. Consider the length of the records. Let the records be of variable length and assume the standard deviation of the length to be of at least 30% of the average record length R. If you use variable-length and unspanned blocking:

  a How many records fit into a block if consider only the average record length?

  b How many records fit into a block if consider only the record length to be normally distributed, and you want to exceed the block less than 1% of the time $(t = 2.32)$?

  c How many records fit into a block, again with less than 1% overflow, if you cannot predict the distribution, so that you have to use the Chebysheff assumption?

17[p] Write a simulation where variable length records are placed into blocks, up to the estimated *Bfr*. Use the same parameters assigned for Exercise 16.

  a Assume a uniform distribution with the same length and standard deviation parameters.

   b Do the same with a normal distribution. (If you dont have a function to
generate normally distributed random numbers take a sum of say, 16 uniform numbers, from a distribution having a quarter of the desired standard
deviation, as shown in Eqs. 12-4 and -5.

Count the number of overflows. Compare your results with the prediction. Which
distribution is better? Justify the result.

   18^p Assume that your record lengths have an Erlang distribution. Compute
the Erlang m parameter.

   19^p Create a scenario where, for a transient period, more requests are coming
into your system than it can handle during some period (i.e., $L_{period}T_T > t_{period}$).
Assume that the excess load distribution in that period has a sinusoidal shape, as
done in Sec. 12-4-2. Establish a start and and end time for the transient.
   a Sketch the behavior of the transient.
   b Compute the length of the transient.
   c Compute the expected waiting time in the queue which will form during
he transient. For This problem you may want to compute the standard
deviation over the transient, and find a distribution which approximates
the excess.
   d As an alternative or verification of the result of Exercise 19-c determine
the queue length by averaging the queue as computed in steps as shown
in Table 12-6.
   e Discuss if the distribution you selected to solve Exercise 19-c is an optimistic approximation to the shape of the transient.
   f Compute the overall expected waiting time in the queue, considering that
that the transient is only in effect some fraction of the day.

   20^p Compute the optimal reorganization period for your files.
   a Assume that you are using indexed-sequential files.
   a Do the same for the file organization you have actually chosen.

State carefully all your assumptions on file usage. Chap. 14 gives some examples of
usage estimation.

Chapter 13

Data Representation

We do not recommend the use of "Roman Numerals" in Western Electric Information Systems.

M. J. Gilligan
in H. E. McEwen, Management of Data Elements, *1974*

13-0   DATA AND THE WORLD

The collection of data on files is intended to be a representation of the real world. It is desirable to have an accurate and complete representation of our knowledge about reality, so that decisions made on the basis of extracted information are applicable to the real world. It is, however, soon obvious that the model of the real world, as stored on files, is both crude and incomplete.

While searching for a representation there is a reliance on abstraction: One speaks of a specific individual as an employee, a welder, a manager; and then this abstraction is encoded into numbers or characters, which are subsequently transformed into binary computer codes.

In Chap. 1 and Table 1-1 we introduced the concept of a *domain* for an attribute as the range of values it can take, and distinguished it from the *representation* of values, the *bitstrings* we see in the computer.

In this chapter we will be concerned with the encoding process, namely how values, limited by domain definitions, are efficiently represented in a computer. A concept which occurs throughout is that a string of b binary bits can be used to represent 2^b distinct values. If these values are numbers, we can immediately assign meaningful values to the bitstrings. If the domain contains arbitrary symbols, some interpretation will be needed.

Standard codes will be presented in Sec. 13-1. Codes for error correction are presented in Sec. 13-2, followed by a presentation of code-compression techniques. The chapter closes with a presentation of encryption codes and their use.

This material is presented to provide guidance to applications designers when faced with the initial stages of a file design problem. It is not unusual that a programmer is asked to *computerize* an information problem. Since a traditional computer science or engineering education has been concerned only with the processing of data as given, rather than with the transformation of real-world observations to representable data, this facet of the design effort is easily neglected. Decisions about their representation will bind the stored data for many years during their use. Designers of data-processing systems should be aware of alternatives of representation so that the system will support the diversity of information found and only restrict the unreasonable.

Bit positions 4321 → 765

4321 \ 765	000	001	010	011	100	101	110	111
0000	NUL	DLE	blank	0	@	P		p
0001	SOH	DC1	!	1	A	Q	a	q
0010	STX	DC2	"	2	B	R	b	r
0011	ETX	DC3	#	3	C	S	c	s
0100	EOT	DC4	$	4	D	T	d	t
0101	ENQ	NAK	%	5	E	U	e	u
0110	ACK	SYN	&	6	F	V	f	v
0111	BEL	ETB	'	7	G	W	g	w
1000	BS	CAN	(	8	H	X	h	x
1001	HT	EM	)	9	I	Y	i	y
1010	LF	SUB	*	:	J	Z	j	z
1011	VT	ESC	+	;	K	[	k	{
1100	FF	FS	,	<	L	\	l	|
1101	CR	GS	—	=	M	]	m	}
1110	SO	RS	.	>	N	^	n	~
1111	SI	US	/	?	O	_	o	DEL

Bit numbering is right to left within a character.

ACK	Acknowledge	ESC	Escape	NUL	Null
BEL	Audible signal	ETB	End of transmission block	RS	Record separator
BS	Backspace	ETX	End of text	SI	Shift in
CAN	Cancel	FF	Form feed	SO	Shift out
CR	Carriage return	FS	File separator	SOH	Start of heading
DCx	Device control	GS	Group separator	STX	Start of text
DEL	Delete	HT	Horizontal tabulate	SUB	Substitute
DLE	Data-link escape	LF	Line feed	SYN	Synchronous idle
EM	End of medium	NAK	Negative acknowledge	US	Unit separator
ENQ	Enquire			VS	Vertical tabulate
EOT	End of transmission				

American Standard Code for Information Interchange

Figure 13-1 ASCII character coding.

13-1   MACHINE REPRESENTATION

We distinguish three basic types of representation
  1 Numeric — integer or floating-point
  2 Character strings — using some standard code for individual characters
  3 Coded — using arbitrary bit strings with defined meanings

Other data values can be represented by combine of multiple instances of these basic types. A common example is a complex number, represented by a pair of floating-point numbers, or a date, represented by a sequence of digits and letters, such as 9AUG86. We will consider the various basic types in turn.

13-1-1 Numeric Data

The representation of numeric data is generally determined by the computers being used. Numeric values are processed in terms of *words*, often of size $b = 16$ or 32 although sizes of $8, 12, 18, 36, 48, 60, 64$ are found as well. Larger word sizes reduce the effort when numeric values are large, but hardware costs increase more than linearly with word size for the same performance.

INTEGERS   *Positive integers* are obtained from counting, and are easily represented by ascending binary integers, up to $2^b - 1$ for fields of length, b. Zero is represented by b zeroes. *Signed integers* are typically represented in *two's complement* notation, where positive numbers are also represented as positive by binary integers, up to a size of $2^{b-1} - 1$. Negative numbers are obtained by counting down from zero, so that a bitstring of b ones represents -1 and the smallest number representable in b bits is -2^{b-1}.

If small integers make up much of the stored data it can be profitable to store the data on files in small fields and re-create the fields required for computer arithmetic when bringing data into memory. We will talk about compression in general in Sec. 13-3. This technique is also appropriate when files are shared among computers with differing integer word sizes.

REAL-VALUED NUMBERS   Real values, as obtained from measurements, can in general not be represented precisely in computers. Floating-point representations approximate real values by storing the sequence s, e, f of an expression of the form $r = s \cdot f \cdot b^{e-g}$ where s is a sign ($+$ or -), f is a fraction, and e is an exponent. To evaluate the result the exponent is adjusted by subtracting a constant groundvalue, g, and taking the result as the exponent for the known base value, b. In all cases the size of e determines the range of values and the size of f its precision in terms of the base b.

The field sizes and constants differ among computers, but the total will fit into one or more words. The representation used by IBM 360 computers uses one bit $s = 0, 1$ to denote $+, -;$, a base $b = 4$, $f = 24$ or 56, and $e = 7$ with a value of g of 200_8. A comprehensive standard adopted by the microprocessor industry uses s, $b = 2$; 24, 53, or 111 bits for f with field sizes for $e(g)$ of 8(127), 11(1023), or 15(16383) bits in single, double, and quadruple word precision. The leading bit of f may be omitted in the single and double word formats, since with a base $b = 2$

they are always normalized to "1". This permits the representations to fit into
32, 64, or 128 bits. To permit more precision extended fraction formats are also
defined. Two special exponent cases are recognized. If $e = 0$ the value is either ± 0
or $\pm f$ as a pure fraction. If the exponent is all ones $111..111$ the number is used
to represent exceptional cases, namely ∞ if $f = 0$ and other special non-numbers
as: *uninitialized number*, pointer to a number, or results of overflows or invalid
operations $(\sqrt{-1}, (+\infty) - (+\infty), 0 \times \infty, \ldots)$

Conversion problems among dissimilar computers can be severe for floating-
point values, and repeated conversions can reduce the precision of the data. It
is not unusual to store real numbers in a character-string encoded floating-point
format on shared files, and perform conversions as needed for processing.

13-1-2 Character String Data

When data is stored in character string form, the data element is represented by
a sequence of binary coded characters, typically of varying length. Figure 13-1
presents the standard encoding for characters in the interchange of information,
i.e., files and communication lines. Each character is represented by 7 bits; on
machines with 8-bit character spaces, 1 bit will remain unused. Alternate character
encoding methods in use for data storage are listed in Table 13-1.

Table 13-1   Character codes and their sizes.

Common name (organization)	Size	Number of symbols		
		Data	Control	Undefined
Baudot (CCIT)	5 bits+shift	50	5	3+
BCD (CDC)	6 bits	64 or 48	0	0 or 16
Fieldata (US Army)	6 bits	48	16	0
ASCII (ANSI)*	7 bits	95†	33	0
EBCDIC (IBM)	8 bits	133	64	59

*   American National Standards Institute. A similar code has been adopted by ISO,
         the International Standards Organization.
†   For international usage some characters can represent alternate symbols.

Control characters   are used in data communication to designate empty spaces,
to separate data units, and to control output device functions such as `linefeed`,
`carriage return`. In files control characters are useful to delimit variable-length
fields and to represent UNDEFINED. The ASCII symbols `FS`, `GS`, `RS`, `US`, and `DEL`
may be suitable.

Identifiers   Much data in computers, especially key data used to identify objects
and events by name, is neither numeric nor arbitrary text. Arbitrary, unique bitstrings are sufficient to name objects internally. It can be useful to be able to enter
and print identifiers, and they may be compared and sorted. Most other operations
are meaningless. Identifiers can use numeric or string representations.

Table 13-2   A Sampler of standard codes.

Subject area: Entities code name	Organization location	Number of entries or: format of code†
Geography:		

States of the US
   USPS identifier
	National Bureau of Standards
	  FIPS 5-1 Gaithersburg MD
		`56:AA or :NN`

Counties in states	NBS, FIPS 6-2	`var:NNN`
Standard metropolitan statistical areas	NBS, FIPS 8-3	`:NNNN`
Congressional districts	NBS, FIPS 9	`:NN`
Countries	NBS, FIPS 10	

Place names in US and
   a class code for each
	Comp.&Bus.Equip.Manuf.Ass.
	  (CBEMA) Washington DC
		`130000:AANNNNN C`

Mailing addresses, ZIP code
   for block faces, businesses, .. .
	US Postal Service
	  Washington DC
	Canadian and British PO's
		`22 500 000`
		`:NMMNN-MMMM`
		`:ANA-NAN`

Organizations:		

Businesses
   D-U-N-S
	Dun and Bradstreet, Inc.
	  New York, NY
		`>3000000`
		`:NNNNNNNNN`

Employers Identification
   EIN
	Internal Revenue Service
	  Washington, DC
		`:XX-YYYYYYY`

Occupations	Bureau of the Census	`:XXXX`
Supplies:		

Parts
   Federal stock numbers
	Defense Logistics Serv.Ctr.
	  Battle Creek MI.
		`A*,N*,N*,AA,`
		`(* means variable)`

Automobiles	Consumers Union	`cars since 1970`

Commodities (US Transp.)
   STC code
	Assoc. of Am. Railroads&
	  DOT, Washington, DC
		`:NNNMMMMM`

Commodities (Internat. Trade)
   SIT classification
	United Nations
	  New York, NY
		`8 codes·350`
		`categories:NNNNN`

Biologically active agents
   SNOP
	College of Amer. Chemicals:
	  Pathologists. Enzymes:
		`700:NNN`
		`200:NNN`

Electric equipment and parts
   WE standards
	Western Electric, Inc.
	  Newark, NJ
		`various`
		`:hierarchical`

Groceries
   UPC (Bar code)
	Distribution Codes, Inc.
	  Washington DC
		`:NNNNN MMMMM or`
		`XBBBBB BBBBBX`

Publications
   MARC
	Library of Congress
	  Washington DC
		`(3 standards,`
		`100 elements)`

Scientific instruments
   Guide to Sc. Instr.
	Am. Ass. Adv. of Science
	  Washington DC
		`:NNNNN`

Miscellaneous:		

Data-processing outputs
   AMC-DED
	Hdq. US Army Material Command
	  Alexandria VA
		`9000:`

Device failures
   WE Standard No. 10178
	Western Electric, Inc.
	  Newark NJ
		`:NNNMMM`

Human body
   SNOP
   (Systematic Nomenclature)
	College of Amer. Topology:
	Pathologists Morphology:
	Skokie IL Etiology:
	             Function:
		`2000:NNNN`
		`1300:NNNN`
		`1500:NNNN`
		`1200:NNNN`

Motorists (accidents, insur-
   ance, vehicles, highway plan.)
   ANSI-D20
	National Highway
	  Safety Administration
	  Washington DC
		`various`

Work injuries ANSI Z16.2	Am. Nat. Stand. Inst.	`7 categories`

†`A,C` *denotes an alphabetic,* `N,M` *a numeric, and* `X,Y` *a mixed, alphanumeric code.*

13-1-3 Standard Codes

When data has to be shared among many users, a coding convention has to be agreed upon to ensure correspondence, completeness, lack of ambiguity or redundancy, and appropriateness of level of aggregation. Developing such code lexicons is a time-consuming task.

Many organizations have found it necessary to define standard encodings for a large variety of data elements. Activities in the field have been led by industry, as the Bell System, trade organizations as the IEEE and the ASTM, and goverment agencies, as the defense department, federal procurement agencies, and the Bureau of the Census. Some international standards are also developing.

If a standard encoding can be used, a considerable amount of system-design effort can be saved. Integration of the stored data with data provided by others is also simplified. The assignment of observations or concepts to the terms provided in a coding lexicon can still cause some debate when an existing code is brought into a new place and a new environment.

Not only place, but time is also a factor in understanding codes. The meanings of words used in the definitions change over time. An example of a compound problem is the assignment of values to a currency code, as conversion rates vary among countries. This issue gets worse for the many countries which have different conversion regulations for investment and for tourism.

Table 13-2 provides some references to standard code tables. The list is by no means exhaustive. Many of these codes are available on tape to simplify their incorporation into data-processing systems.

13-1-4 Coding of Names of Individuals

The coding of names remains as one of the major problems in data processing. The use of the social security number to identify individuals is restricted to files which relate to activities involving payments of taxes or disbursements from federal insurance or support programs. These are quite pervasive so that the social security number is used in many files, including some where its use is not appropriate. The use of names is hampered by two issues.

CLUSTERING   One problem with the use of names is the fact that some names appear very frequently. The Social Security Administration (SSA[57]) has found about 1 250 000 different last names in its files, but also that 48% of the people share the 1514 most common names. Thirty-nine names occur with a frequency greater than 0.1%. The use of first names can resolve the clusters to some extent, but 768 four-letter combinations comprise the four initial characters of more than 90% of the first names. Endings of first names show frequent changes (i.e., Johnny for John) and hence are not very reliable as identifiers. Duplication of entries for single individuals seems inevitable. When queries to name files are made in an interactive query situation, all collisions of the search key can be presented. A choice based on further data (address, age) can be made if the full name displayed is not yet adequate.

NAME SPELLING VARIATIONS   An even more serious problem is the fact
that the spelling of a name is not necessarily consistent. Whereas clustering leads
to retrieval of too many names, variation of spellings causes failure to retrieve
information. Examples of common variations are listed on the left in Fig. 13-2.
Cross referencing can be used to refer to frequent alternatives, but the synonym list
soon becomes large.

McCloud, MacCloud, McLoud, McLeod, M'Cloud	M243,M243,M243,M243,M243,M243
Ng, Eng, Ing	N2, E52, I52
Rauchers, Rogers, Rodgers, Rutgers	R262,R262, R326,R326
Smith, Schmid, Smid, Smyth, Schmidt	S53,S53,S53,S53,S53
Wiederhold, Weiderhold, Widderholt, Wiederholdt, Wiederhout	
	W364,W364,W364,W364, W363

Figure 13-2   Name variations and SOUNDEX codes

‖‖‖‖   **Soundex Coding**   A technique to bring all similar sounding names together
which has seen intensive use is the SOUNDEX method defined in Table 13-3. It can
be viewed as a type of phonetic hashing.

Table 13-3   SOUNDEX procedure.

```
 1. All nonalphabetic characters (',-,␣, etc.) are eliminated.
 2. All lowercase letters are set to uppercase.
 3. The first letter of the name is used to initialize the result.
 4. The remainder is converted according to steps 5 to 8:
 5. The frequently unvocalized consonants H and W are removed.
 6. The following replacements are made:
```
Labials	: B,F,P,V	→	1
Gutturals, sibilants	: C,G,J,K,Q,S,X,Z	→	2
Dentals	: D,T	→	3
Longliquid	: L	→	4
Nasals	: M,N	→	5
Shortliquid	: R	→	6
```
 7. Two or more adjacent identical digits are combined;
        thus, LL→  4, SC→  2, MN→  5.
 8. The remaining letters (vowels: A,E,I,O,U, and Y) are removed.
 9. The first three digits obtained are catenated to the result.
10. The result is one to four characters long.
```

We show some names liable to inconsistent spelling this procedure will generate
the SOUNDEX codes shown in Fig. 13-2. It can be seen that many variations are
completely merged, although some remain distinct. This scheme appears biased
toward Anglo-Saxon names; other codes have also been constructed.

Use of SOUNDEX codes as a primary key increases the number of collisions.
This code provides at most $26 \cdot 7^3$ or 8 918 choices, and the alternatives are not
uniformly distributed. The first letter alone causes a poor distribution as shown
in Table 13-4 (SSA[57]). For comparison the occurrences of English words in a text

of 4 257 692 words and the distribution of 5 153 unique words in this same text are
also shown (Schwartz[63]).

When the identity of an individual has to be resolved, secondary information
such as address, birthdate, profession, birthplace, parents' names may
still be required. Which parameters are appropriate will differ according to cir-
cumstance. The month of one's birth, for instance, tends to be remembered more
reliably (98%) than the day of birth (96%) or the year of birth (95%).

Table 13-4   Distribution of names, words, and word types by initial letters.

Initial Letter	Names(tokens) %	Rank	Text (tokens) %	Rank	Dictionary(types) %	Rank
A	3.051	15	12.111	2	6.229	4
B	9.357	3	4.129	9	5.550	7
C	7.267	5	3.916	10	9.722	2
D	4.783	10	2.815	13	6.016	5
E	1.883	17	1.838	18	4.386	11
F	3.622	13	3.911	11	5.162	9
G	5.103	8	1.960	16	3.086	16
H	7.440	4	6.937	5	3.842	12
I	0.387	23	8.061	3	3.707	13
J	2.954	16	0.427	23	0.776	21
K	3.938	12	0.576	21	0.602	22
L	4.664	11	2.746	14	3.474	14.5
M	9.448	2	4.429	8	4.560	10
N	1.785	18	2.114	15	1.844	18
O	1.436	19	6.183	7	2.271	17
P	4.887	9	2.897	12	7.801	3
Q	0.175	25	0.199	24	0.427	23
R	5.257	7	1.880	17	5.317	8
S	10.194	1	6.787	6	12.886	1
T	3.450	14	15.208	1	5.608	6
U	0.238	24	1.008	20	1.417	20
V	1.279	20	0.428	22	1.436	19
W	6.287	6	7.643	4	3.474	14.5
X	0.003	26	< 0.001	26	< 0.001	26
Y	0.555	21	1.794	19	0.369	24
Z	0.552	22	0.002	25	0.039	25

The relative freedom with which individuals in the United States can change
their names makes positive identification of an individual difficult. The social benefits of this data-processing difficulty may outweigh the costs. Concerns about
protection of privacy everywhere are discouraging the use of personal identification
numbers. Some European countries are discontinuing their use.

The use of numbers as identifiers will not disappear. Individuals have many
numbers as identifiers: tax accounts, license numbers, bank accounts, employee
numbers, etc.   ▦▦

13-1-5 Conversion

Input data is converted to the binary representations when entered. Most common are computational procedures which take character strings and convert the character representation to the desired values.

Sometimes the input choices are presented on a screen or form to be checked. Then the input consists of x-y coordinates which must be converted to internal symbols, corresponding to the label of the choice presented to the user. Data-entry techniques can influence the choice of data representation. We discuss problems of data entry in Chap. 15-3.

13-2   REDUNDANCY AND ERROR CORRECTION

Data representations for long-term storage and communication also must consider protection against errors. There are two aspects to error control:

1 Errors must be detected.
2 Detected errors must be corrected.

Detection and correction can be separate or combined, but both phases must cooperate. Both phases can be performed manually or automatically.

Obviously, errors that are not detected will never be corrected. This means also that error detection must be automated before correction can be automated. Since we expect to have on the whole few errors compared to the volume of data we will first discuss error detection methods.

Error detection and correction depends on *redundancy*. Information is represented so that there are two copies, and, if the copies conflict, there must be an error. The copies need not be identical, and in manual error detection, not even on the computer. A user easily recognizes when a computer-produced result is completely out of line with the user's information about the real world.

Redundancy in computer-encoded data is obtained when data units (bytes, words, blocks, etc.) are expanded to provide more information than is strictly necessary. The data units then can be checked for internal consistency. If they are found to be in error, they may be corrected.

13-2-1 Natural Redundancy

Even without explicit addition of redundant information, we find that much data coding is highly redundant. A prime example is information coded in English or any other natural language. If the data being processed is English text, a dictionary search can be used to detect errors. Hashed access is commonly used here. *Spelling-checking programs* can suggest corrections based on similarities of the unrecognized words and words in the dictionary file. Suggestions are based on common errors:

1 It is a word listed as commonly misspelled.
2 The error is due to a transposed pair of characters.
3 The error is due to a missing or extra character.
4 The error is due to a wrong single character.

In a sense, such a program mimics, with intelligent processing, human beings when reading text with typographical errors. A large fraction of the suggestions will be accepted by the user for correction.

Frequently the number of choices in coded data is much more limited than the whole of the English language, and simple searches of lexicon files accessed rapidly by hashing can determine whether an entry is valid. Such look-ups are performed routinely to verify items entered, such as employee names, identification codes, and similar data elements in many processing systems.

There frequently is a considerable amount of redundancy within the character encoding itself; and this too can be used for error detection. An 8-bit code, for instance, allows 256 characters, but frequently the data is restricted to uppercase letters (26) or alphanumeric (36) characters, as seen in Sec. 13-1. Filtering to detect erroneous characters can be done at little incremental effort during other text-processing operations. Filtering should also be used during output because serious problems can be caused when wrong characters enter communications channels. A "bad" character may have unexpected control functions such as mode shifts, disconnect, or screen erase on displays.

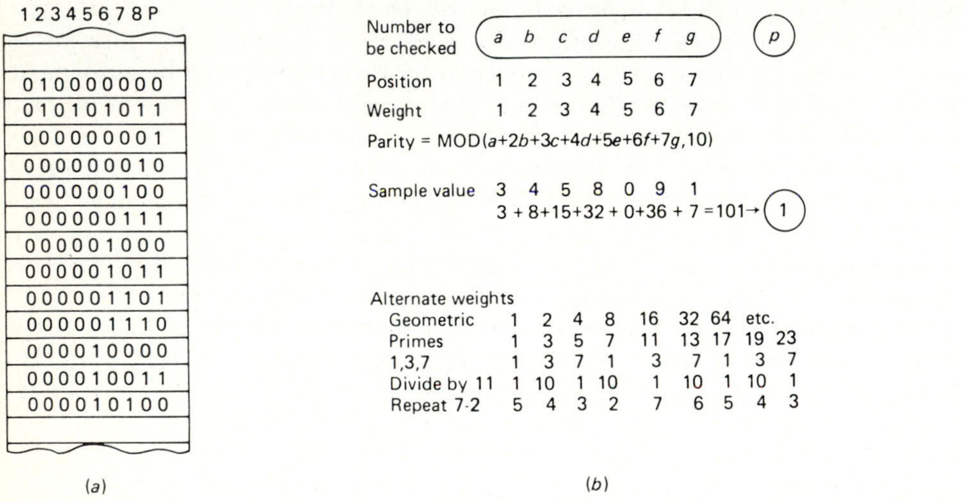

Figure 13-3   Parity. (a) Section of tape with odd parity. (b) Check-digit computation.

13-2-2 Parity

A simple form of redundancy is obtained in computer codes by appending a *parity bit* to elemental data units. Characters on tape or in computer memory frequently have a parity bit added when they are initially generated. The count of the number of bits of value 1 in the character representation is termed the *Hamming weight*. If the character is represented by 8 bits, the parity bit in the ninth position will be set so that the Hamming weight of the combination is odd (odd parity encoding) or even (even parity encoding). Odd parity is the preferred code, since it avoids any occurrences of all zero or all blank sections on the recording medium, which is useful to assure detection of the existence of a character, especially on tapes. Figure 13-3a shows odd-parity encoding for some 8-bit characters on a 9-track tape.

Odd parity produces a code with a minimum Hamming weight of 1. The counting of bits is done easily by computer hardware, and some machines have specific instructions for bit counting. The encoding and checking processes are performed without user intervention until an error occurs.

Parity Coding　The addition of the one parity bit doubles the number of possible symbols that a code can transmit. Half of these codes are not valid characters and should not occur in the received input. Appearance of invalid codes signals an error condition. The number of bits which are different between the intended and actual code received is termed the *Hamming distance* of the two codes. The Hamming distance is hence equal to the difference in the Hamming weights of the two codes. Simple parity coding only detects odd Hamming distances. Howerver, since errors tend to appear in bunches, a bunch has a little chance of being undetected.

Check Digits　Techniques similar to parity encoding are also used for numbers which are transmitted outside of computer systems. Decimal identification numbers may have check digits appended which are verifiable. Since accidental *transposition of digits* is a frequent error, the check digit is best computed not as a simple sum but as a sum of products of value and a weight (assigned to each position) as shown in Fig. 13-3b. Only a one-digit remainder of the sum is retained for checking. An interchange of 3 and 4 in the sample will generate a check digit $p = 0$ instead of $p = 1$. Many systems invert the check digit to simplify verification, so that $p = 1$ becomes 9. Now the check-digit is also added, and a zero result indicates that all is well.

Decimal, or modulo 10 addition, as used in Fig. 13-3b, will not detect certain transposition errors between alternate columns; in the sample a transposition of 5 and 0 will not be detected. Because of the high frequency of transposition errors, use of modulo 9 or 11 ($p = 10 \rightarrow 0$) is preferred, even though it reduces the power of the check digit. Digits in the position equal to the modulus are not checked at all using the simple successive arithmetic weights scheme. Alternate weight assignments which have been used are also shown in Fig. 13-3b; the series $(1, 10, 1, \ldots)$ is obtained in effect by division of the number by 11.

Parity coding and check digits are independent of the content of the data. Only detection is provided, and even the detection capability is limited. However, the schemes are simple and effective. In Sec. 13-2-4 we will discuss error-correction.

▦　13-2-3 Batch Checking

Where data is manually processed before submission to an input transaction or where additional software checking is desired, *checksums* or *batch totals* may be employed. A checksum is the sum of all values in a critical column. Checksums are typically computed before data entry and within the transaction, and these sums are compared. This method is conceptually identical to parity checking, but since the result is a large number rather than a single bit, the error-detection probability is quite high. For a large batch the added data quantity remains relatively low.

The method cannot be used for correction, except for some transpositions. Transposition of adjacent digits is a common error in manual entry and can easily be spotted in checksum comparisons, since transposition causes a checksum with errors in two adjacent digits, with a digit error sum of 9; an example is given in Fig. 13-4.

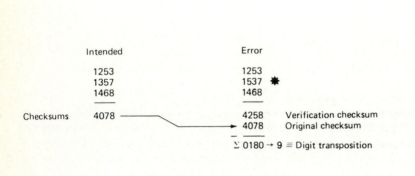

Figure 13-4   Example of checksum.

Transaction Numbering   Another technique to avoid errors in manually prepared data is the use of *transaction sequence numbers*. Each batch of input documents for one transaction is assigned a sequential identifier and this number is also entered. The data-entry program can check that all transactions have been received. If it is important that transactions are processed in the same sequence, the check can simply verify that transaction numbers increase by one. Many such systems check transactions in this manner, but the sequentiality constraint may place unnecessary constraints on operations. If one batch is late, all processing ceases.   ▦

▦   13-2-4 Error-Correcting Codes

Error-correcting codes provide a high degree of the benefits obtained by replication of data without all the costs. Here a certain number of bits are added to each data element. These check bits are produced similarly to the parity bits, but each check bit represents different groupings of the information bits. These groups are organized in such a fashion that when an error occurs an indication of which bit is in error will result. The principle is shown in Fig. 13-5.

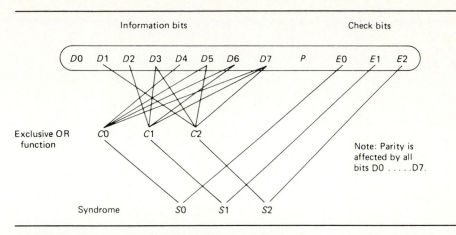

Figure 13-5 The idea behind error correction.

If the parity bit, P, indicates that there is an error, the three error-code bits, C0, C1, and C2 can be generated from the data bits and compared with the check bits E0, E1, and E2 that were carried along. A difference in these bits is obtained in the syndrome, S, and this will indicate (in binary) the number of the bit in error. For example, an error in D5 will cause a *syndrome* of 101, implicating data bit 5. This example is incomplete, since it does not provide error control for the parity and the error-correction bits themselves.

Redundancy versus Correction and Detection The number of check bits, r, required for codes which can correct ec bits and can definitely detect errors of up to ed bits is determined by a minimum Hamming weight of

$$Hw_{min} = 2ec + ed + 1 \qquad\qquad 13\text{-}1$$

for the complete error-correcting data codes.

If a frame of coded information has a total of n bits it can represent 2^n codes. For the byte with 8 data bits in Fig. 13-5 the value of $n = d + r = 12$. We can now consider that out of the 2^n codes received, only 2^d codes are correct. Out of the remainder $(2^n - 2^d)$, those codes which have a low $(ec = 1, 2, \ldots)$ Hamming distance to any of the correct codes are used for correction by being converted to their neighbors. The correct codes have to be seperated by a Hamming distance of at least 2 ec. The remainder of the codes is undecodable, and hence will detect, but not correct an error.

Procedures are available to select a code transform matrix which will generate the least number of check bits, r, from the information bits, d, given ec and ed. From the transformation matrix, a check matrix can be obtained which will generate a zero if the code received was correct (or possibly had more than ed errors) and which generates on error a bitstring which can be used to correct an incorrect code, if there were not more than ec errors. An example for $n = 7$, $d = 4$, $r = 3$, $ed = 3$, and $ec = 1$ is shown in Fig. 13-6.

```
Position           1     2      3      4      5      6      7
Data pos.                       D0            D1     D2     D3
Sample value                    1             1      0      0
Hamming codes
  Pos. 1       H0 = ODD(        D0     +      D1     +      D3) →1
  Pos. 2            H1 = ODD( D0                +    D2  +  D3) →0
  Pos. 3                     H2=ODD(D1  +    D2   +  D3) →0
  Stored         1     0      1      0      1      0      0

  Fault  ──────────────────────────────────────►  •

  Read           1     0      1      0      0      0      0
  Check 1    C0 = ODD(        D0     +      D1     +      D3) · 0, S0 = 1
  Check 2        C1 = ODD( D0                 +   D2  +   D3) · 0, S1 = 0
  Check 3                    C2=ODD(D1  +    D2   +   D3) · 1, S2 = 1
Syndrome is 5
Correct position 5 ──────────────────────►  X
Corrected data          1             1      0      0
```

Figure 13-6   Hamming-code error correction.

Assuring that all errors involving a limited number of bits are checked is appropriate when errors occur independently. For $ec = 1$ and $ed = 2$, it has been shown that the minimum number of check bits required is determined by

$$2^{r-1} \geq r + d > 2^{r-2} \qquad\qquad 13\text{-}2$$

We see that for $d = 8$ this capability is obtained with $r = 5$ check bits.

Increasing the number of check bits increases the number of errors detectable and correctable. There is a trade-off when selecting the transformation matrices between the numbers of errors detected and the number of errors correctable. In either case the number of check bits required is a logarithmic function of the length of the data unit. This means that the cost, in terms of bits, is relatively low when the units are long ($d \gg 8$), although the circuitry becomes more complex.

Some error-correcting codes, such as Bose-Chaudhuri and Fire codes, are more advantageous for variable-length blocks, since they are cyclic and can correct errors occurring in a data stream rather than only by transformation of a complete block. They also can be designed to cope better with burst-type, that is, dependent bit errors. Data blocks must be at least a cycle long.

The error correction process also delays transmission by the length of the error-correcting cycle. However, since a longer cycle uses relatively fewer check bits, the net penalty in the transmission rate will be less. Advertised data-transmission rates generally include only the net information bits, while the actual disk-to-controller bit transfer occurs at a higher rate. The difference between the data and the real transfer rate can be great; the 6250-bpi tapes and mass-storage units described in Chap. 3-1-1 have actual bit densities of approximately 9000 bpi.

Occasional but large bursts of errors found in communication lines make the use of error-correcting codes in data transmission less profitable. Here, detection and retransmit techniques are prevalent. Files, however, are maintained on closely coupled devices with controllers which have the logical capability to generate error codes as well as to check and correct errors. Error correction on files permits a drastic increase in storage density. ▦

13-3   COMPRESSION OF DATA

Data storage remains an important cost factor in many applications. Often, representation of data leads to unused space and redundant representation of data. While some redundancy may be part of schemes to improve reliability, significant opportunities for data compression remain. Compression is possible when any of the following conditions are true:

- High frequency of undefined or zero elements
- High frequency of small integers in fixed-size words
- Low precision requirements for floating-point numbers
- Values which range over a limited domain
- Values which change slowly
- Fixed length spaces for character strings
- Redundancy in character strings
- Character sizes in excess of character set needs

We will consider only schemes which allow complete reconstruction of the data when the compressed data are again expanded. In Chap. 8-2 we encountered *abbreviation* methods for index entries, which did not permit full reconstruction.

There is, of course, a trade-off between the degree of compression and the cost of processing time. Compression will also reduce data-transfer requirements so that file operations may become faster. The total trade-off to be considered is compression CPU time versus file access speed and storage cost.

13-3-1 Compression of Numeric Data Elements

For computational purposes, it is desirable that numeric values occupy full words. Frequently the data forms large, regular matrices to allow rapid computation across rows and columns. In scientific data processing the volume of data can be such that the representation used for computing is too costly for storage.

We present three approaches, which overlap in part:

1 Removing null data elements
2 Shrinking the representation of small values
3 Shrinking the representation of imprecise values

COMPRESSION OF SPARSE DATA   Whenever data represents observations of real-world phenomena, it is not unusual that positions are allocated for values that have not been collected (u) or are of zero value.

By *storing only nonzero data values with their coordinates* the zero elements are compressed out of the file. Table 13-5 below applies this idea to a record having $a = 20$ numeric data spaces, including one undefined value, indicated by u.

Table 13-5   Coordinate coding for sparse data.

Original record:
        0,14,0,0,0,15,0,0,0,3,3,0,0,0,0,0,0,423,0,u;
Coordinate representation:
        2:14,6:15,10:3,11:3,18:423,20:u;

Now the record requires $2a' = 12$ data spaces. This method is reminiscent of the record format shown for the pile-file organization presented in Chap. 4-2.

An alternative is the use of a descriptive *bit vector*. One bit is used per field, a zero indicates the absence of a value. Now the same record is represented as shown in Table 13-6.

Table 13-6   Bit vector coding for sparse data.

Original record:
      0,14,0,0,0,15,0,0,0,3,3,0,0,0,0,0,0,0,423,0,u;

Result: Bit vector and six actual values:
      01000100011000000101_2:   14,15,3,3,423,u;
or, if the bit vector is shown as a single decimal integer
      280068:   14,15,3,3,423,u;

If both zeros and undefined values occur, the bit vector can be used to describe the three choices.

Table 13-7   Coding two special cases.

       0   Zero value
      10   Undefined value
      11   Actual nonzero value to be stored

Original record:
      0,14,0,0,0,15,0,0,0,3,3,0,0,0,0,0,0,0,423,0,u;

Compressed record (bit vector and five values):
      $0110001100011110000011010_2$: 14,15,3,3,423;

In the example shown with Table 13-7 there is no benefit; where **undefined** values are plentiful the effect will be felt. The bit vector of Table 13-7 is more difficult to manage, since its size will change depending on the values in the record. In an application where values repeat frequently, four choices can be coded as shown in Table 13-8.

Table 13-8   Coding three special cases.

      00   Zero value   01   Repeated value
      10   Undefined value   11   Stored value

Original record:
      0,14,0,0,0,15,0,0,0,3,3,0,0,0,0,0,0,0,423,0,u;

Compressed record (bit vector and four values):
      $0011000000110000011010000000000110010_2$: 14,15,3,423;

The encoding for compression shown in Table 13-8 was applied to a file system which supported multiple databases using a total of more than three diskpacks and gave a reduction of 44% when applied to all files and 45% when applied only to records which became smaller. Some large statistical files were reduced by more than 80%.

Figure 13-7   Effect of numeric compression.   ▦

▦ **CODING FOR SMALL DOMAINS**   When the *range of numeric values is small*, the numbers can be placed into a smaller space. It is unfortunately difficult to indicate boundaries within a bit string, so that a variable-space assignment for single numbers is awkward to implement. If numeric data is coded as decimal digits of 4 bits each, one of the $2^4 = 16$ codes can be used to provide a boundary. Such a code can be generated using the four low-order bits of the ASCII character code (Fig. 13-1) for the ten digits, leaving space for six symbols, as: * + - , . and US, since these symbols are useful with digits and have complementary bit patterns.

For binary values the conversion to fixed-size decimal digits does not make sense; it is better to use a fixed size for a record based on the values to be stored. A scan of the record can be used to determine the largest required space, and this size can be kept as another prefix with the record. Using again the same values, we find that the largest data value fits into 9 bits. The records will now consist of a bit vector, a size indicator, and the set of recoded values, as shown in Table 3-9.

Table 13-9   Coding to size.

Original record:
     0,14,0,0,0,15,0,0,0,3,3,0,0,0,0,0,0,423,0,u;

Compressed record (bit vector, size indicator, and four values):
     $0011000000\ldots000110010_2$:   9,014|015|003|423;

                    We use | to indicate the boundaries of the 9-bit units.

In Table 13-9 one word plus 36 bits is required instead of four words. The method is defeated by the presence of any single large value in the record.

An alternate input for compression can be a data dictionary which specifies the range of values. Then the record can be formatted appropriate to the range in any column. If we know that the range of a number, for example, student_age, is limited from 5 to 26, then the age values can be represented in fields of size $\lceil \log_2(26 - 5 + 1) \rceil = 5$ bits each.   ▦

▦ **CODING FOR PRECISION**   Low-order positions of floating-point number fractions can be truncated if the required precision is low. Such a decision would also depend on the specifications provided through the data dictionary. Instrumentation data is often of low precision, and 16-bit floating-point formats with 10-bit or three-digit precision and a range up to $\pm 10^9$ have been devised. If floating-point numbers are used to represent integers or fractions with a known binary point, then a representation using binary integers may save even more space.

If data elements represent attribute values which *change slowly*, it can be attractive to store the differences of successive values, using *delta coding*. A capability to store small numeric values efficiently is required to make this scheme effective, as shown in Table 13-10. Four bits are sufficient in the example to store the successive differences. Unless we are dealing with transposed files, records containing sequential values tend to be rare. The method could be applied to selected columns over many records, but then the record cannot be processed unless it is sequentially accessed.

Table 13-10   Delta coding.

Original sequence in record:
     854,855,857,856,859,860,863;

Compressed record (initial value, size of deltas, and deltas):
     854,4,+1|+2|-1|+3|+1|+3;

A special case of delta coding is *Aztec coding*, where only one bit is used, indicating up or down. A sequence that is not changing is then encoded by alternating up and down bits. This code can be effective when real-time data is being collected. The frequency of observations has to be sufficiently high that one bit can follow a steeply rising or falling phenomenon.   ▦▦▦

13-3-2 Compression of Character Strings

Compression of character strings is more frequent than compression of numeric values. One reason is that there are a number of large systems specifically oriented toward textual data, and a pragmatic reason is that systems which have to support text already have had to support variable-length data elements and records, so that the additional complexity introduced by compression is less.

Most schemes to compress text limit themselves to compression of the text representation. There is also a great deal of semantic redundancy within language sentences. It is estimated that 50% of English text is redundant. The redundant information, however, is not distributed in any regular fashion, so that automatic deletion of this redundancy is difficult.

In Chap. 8-2 techniques for abbreviation of words in indexes were presented. These techniques were effective because the keys appeared in sorted order, so that the redundancies were easily eliminated. The same techniques may at times be of use to compress data portions of files. Low-order abbreviation, however, causes loss of information. Abbreviations are frequently used independently of data processing. They may range from

        M for "Monsieur"

to   ADCOMSUBORDCOMAMPHIBSPAC for "Administrative Command,
          Amphibious Forces, Pacific Fleet, Subordinate Command."

Such abbreviations present a degree of data compression prior to data entry.

Abbreviations can reduce data-entry volume as well as storage costs. When abbreviations are developed specifically to deal with the database, their effect should be carefully considered. Compression of terms within the computer may be more economical than the abbreviations which simplify manual processing, but a reduction of manual data-processing errors is extremely worthwhile.

RECODING   The most frequent technique used to compress textual data is the representation of the data in a character set of smaller size. Data may, for instance, be recoded from an 8-bit set to a 7- or 6-bit set. With 6 bits it is just possible to represent the digits, upper- and lowercase characters, a hyphen, and the blank, since $2^6 = 10 + 2 \cdot 26 + 2$. Most 6-bit codes do not retain the lowercase characters in order to provide a more complete set of special characters.

Recoding from 8 to 6 bits saves 25% of the space. This is often accomplished by deletion of the leading two bits of the ASCII code. Most modern output devices can present both upper- and lowercase characters; for much of the public the rule that *computer output is always uppercase* still holds. It seems unwise to remove the humanizing appearance of upper- and lowercase print to achieve data compression.

Single-case characters alone can be represented by 5 bits. If alphabetic and numeric characters appear mainly in separate sequences, the use of a method similar to Baudot coding, which uses a shift character to switch between sequences, can be used to represent text in an average of slightly more than 5 bits per character.

If the data represents digits, only the four low-order bits of most codes have to be retained. Starting from ASCII a blank (⊔) becomes a '0' but the six characters listed earlier (* + - , . and US) will be kept as distinguishable codes.

Table 13-11   Character group encoding alternatives.

Character set	Set size	Group	Group range	Bits	Limit	Saving, %
Digits	10	3 digits	1 000	10	1 024	16.6
Single-case alphabet	26	4 letters	456 976	19	524 288	5.0
Alphanumerics+28	90	2 characters	8 100	13	8 192	7.1
Alphanumerics+18	80	3 characters	512 000	19	524 288	9.5
Alphanumerics+22	84	5 characters	$4.18 \cdot 10^9$	32	$4.19 \cdot 10^9$	8.57

The savings are computed versus an ungrouped dense encoding. The bit sizes for the groups may not match word boundaries, so that multiword units have to be handled to exploit this type of compression. However, the final grouping of five alphanumeric characters allows a 32-bit word to be used to represent five characters, a saving of 20% over the common 8-bit-per-character encoding.

▦   **Encoding Groups of Characters**   Compression by recoding symbols into a specific number of bits is optimal if the number of symbols to be represented is close to, but less than, a power of two. This is not the case for character sets containing only the 10 digits, or the basic character set needed to represent common text, containing upper- and lowercase characters, digits, and the 16 common special characters from ASCII column 010. These sets of 10, respectively 78 symbols, require

4 or 7 bits per character, adequate for 16 or 128 symbols. Recoding groups of a few characters into a single bit-string can produce a denser compression, as shown in Table 13-11. The limit of symbols for a group is, of course, 2^{bits}.   ⧻⧻⧻

DELETING BLANKS   In formatted data there tend to be long sequences of blanks. A simple technique to compress such sequences is to replace a string of i blanks by a sequence of two characters '⊔i' as shown in Fig. 13-8. The value of i will be limited by the largest integer that can be kept in a character space (63, 127, or 255). In the scheme shown a single blank is actually expanded and requires two spaces. This can be avoided by letting single blanks remain and replacing longer strings of blanks by some otherwise unused character, followed by the count.

Giovannini 123.89		Giovannini 1123.89
Jean 87.50		Jean 887.50
Johann 103.76	→	Johann 5103.76
John 154.66		John 7154.66
Sean 88.34		Sean 888.34

Figure 13-8   Compression of blank sequences.

Table 13-12   Relative frequency of letters in English written text.

E	133	D	43	G	14
T	93	L	38	B	13
O	85	C	31	V	10
A	81	F	29	K	5
N	75	U	28	X	3
I	71	M	27	J	2
R	70	P	22	Q	2
S	65	Y	15	Z	1
H	61	W	15	Total	1032

Table 13-13   Algorithm for constructing a Huffman code.

```
1   A list is initialized with an entry for each symbol,
        its frequency, and a space for its code.
2   Take the two entries of lowest frequency in the list;
        assign them the bits 0 and 1.
3   If an entry is a result of a previous combination,
        then catenate the new bit to the front of each code;
        otherwise initialize the code field with the bit.
4   Remove the two used entries from the list and
        insert a single, combined entry which has as frequency
        the sum of the two entries and attach the two used entries.
5   Repeat steps 2, 3, and 4 with the two entries which now have
        the lowest frequency, until all symbols have been processed.
6   The code values can be obtained from the tree of entries.
```

VARIABLE-LENGTH SYMBOL ENCODING   Characters do not occur with equal frequency in languages. Frequencies for English are given in Table 13-12. A technique, *Huffman coding*, takes advantage of this fact to compress data. The most frequent symbols are assigned to the shortest codes, and all longer codes are constructed so that short codes do not appear as initial bit sequences of the longer codes. No further marking bits are required to designate the separation of one character field and its successor.

Next element	Encoding steps		Next element	New code for previously encoded elements
fr(Z)=1				
fr(Q)=2	Z→ 0	Q→ 1	fr(ZQ)=3	
fr(J)=2	J→ 0	ZQ→ 1	fr(JZQ)=5	Z→ 10 Q→ 11
fr(X)=3	X→ 0	JZQ→ 1	fr(XJZQ)=8	J→ 10 Z→ 110 Q→ 111
fr(K)=5	K→ 0	XJZQ→ 1	fr(KJZQ)=13	X→ 10 J→ 110 ... Q→ 1111
fr(V)=10	V→ 0	KXJZQ→ 1	fr(VKXJZQ)=23	K→ 10 ... Z→ 11110 Q→ 11111
fr(B)=13				
fr(G)=14	B→ 0	G→ 1	fr(BG)=27	
fr(W)=15				
fr(Y)=15	W→ 0	Y→ 1	fr(WY)=30	
fr(P)=22	P→ 0	VKXJZQ→ 1	fr(PVKXJZQ)=45	V→ 10 ... Z→ 111110 Q→ 111111
fr(M)=27	M→ 0	BG→ 1	fr(MBG)=54	B→ 10 G→ 11
etc.				

Figure 13-9   Construction of a Huffman code.

Using the frequency of single characters in English given in Table 13-12, the optimal space Huffman encoding begins as shown in Fig. 13-9 The codes which are generated for this important case are given as Table 13-14. The encoding can also be represented by a tree as shown in Fig. 13-10. This tree construction can, in general, be used to minimize access to items of unequal frequency, as long as the access cost per link is equal.

Table 13-14   Huffman code lexicon for English text.

E	100	D	11011	G	001111
T	000	L	11010	B	001110
O	1111	C	01110	V	001010
A	1110	F	01011	K	0010110
N	1100	U	01010	X	00101110
I	1011	M	00110	J	001011110
R	1010	P	00100	Q	0010111111
S	0110	Y	011111	Z	0010111110
H	0110	W	011110		

We find that for English text, given the frequencies of occurrence $fr(i)$ shown in Table 13-13, the average character length, lc, becomes

$$lc = \frac{\sum fr(i)\, len(i)}{\sum fr(i)} = 4.1754 \qquad \text{bits} \qquad\qquad 13\text{-}3$$

where $len(i)$ is the number of bits of symbol i in the Huffman code. This result can be compared with the $\log_2 26 = 4.70$ bits required for a minimal nonpreferential encoding of 26 symbols and the $19/4 = 4.75$ bits achievable with a grouping of four characters seen in Table 13-12.

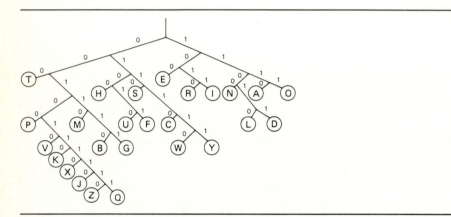

Figure 13-10   Huffman code tree.

VARIABLE-LENGTH STRING HANDLING   An important factor in string compression is the support of variable-length strings. Names of individuals, organizations, titles of books, and references vary greatly in length, and to accommodate the maximum without truncation is rarely feasible using a fixed string length.

A marking scheme, as introduced in Fig. 3-11, is required. Most character codes provide a control character which is appropriate to terminate a character string. In the ASCII code (Fig. 13-1) US is in general appropriate. An alternative is the use of initial count field, although this imposes limits on the maximum string length. A count field of 8 bits limits strings to 255 characters, which is adequate for simple lines of text but is sometimes exceeded when formatting macros are included or when underlining is specified within the line. The use of a count field has computational advantages, since character strings move and catenation operations can be prespecified. When a US character is used, the string has to be scanned during processing.

REPLACEMENT   Although Huffman codes are easily docoded left to right, their use is awkward on most machines. The facilities for handling characters are often much better than bit-oriented operations. Schemes to use *free characters* to replace frequent long strings can be easy and effective. Both unassigned and unused control and data characters can be free. Table 13-1 shows that especially 8-bit codes, representing characters by bytes, have many free spaces. Up to about 150 of these character codes will not occur in normal English in the text.

Table 13-15   Length of names and words in a dictionary.

Length	Names (tokens)		Words (types)	
	%	Cum.%	%	Cum.%
5 or less	29.53	29.53	40.44	40.44
6	24.22	53.75	17.37	57.81
7	21.56	75.31	14.96	72.77
8	12.81	88.12	10.23	83.00
9	6.10	94.22	7.03	90.03
10	2.87	97.09	5.05	95.07
11	1.15	98.24	2.66	97.73
12 or more	1.76	100.00	2.27	100.00

Since blank sequences are frequent, some, for example, four, free characters can be assigned to represent two blanks, three blanks, four blanks, or eight blanks. If other characters are expected to occur in long sequences, this technique can be extended to those characters. If many of the characters are apt to be repeated, the free characters can be used to indicate two, three, four, or eight repetitions of the preceding character.

If certain words appear with great frequency, they can also be replaced by single free characters. Which words occur most frequently in a text depends greatly on the universe of discourse. Words such as

     THE OF A TO AND IN THAT IS IT FOR ON ARE

are universally frequent, and hence are, in general, candidates for replacement by single character codes.

ZIPF'S LAW   In natural text, unfortunately, the shortest words occur already with the greatest frequency. A rule, *Zipf's law* provides an estimate for the relationship between frequency and size in many situations. If n words $w_i, i = 1 \ldots n$ are listed in the order of their size, from smallest to largest, we can expect that their frequency of occurrence $fr(w_i)$ will be

$$fr(w_1) = c/1, \ fr(w_2) = c/2, \ fr(w_3) = c/3, \ \ldots, \ fr(w_n) = c/n \qquad \text{13-4}$$

The constant, c, is adjusted to generate the appropriate total. Words of equal size have to be ordered according to the frequencies observed.

If the frequencies, fr, are expressed as fractions, then $c = H$, the harmonic number for n. Knuth[73S] shows that for $n \gg 100$,

$$H_n \approx \ln n + \gamma \qquad \text{13-5}$$

where γ or Euler's constant is $0.5772\ldots$.

One can consider replacing longer but yet frequent words by shorter multiple letter combinations, in a sense intensifying Zipf's law by inclusion of unpronounceable combinations. In a stored database textbook the replacement of "␣database␣" by "␣db␣" could be profitable. The lexicons required to effect this translation can become quite large. This approach has been used in files of names. Zipf's law can also be applied to estimate the progression of the type-token ratio for words in a text, ranked according to their frequency of occurrence, or individual type-token ratio. Knuth[73S] shows how a better fit to Zipf's law can be obtained by adding a parameter to the divisor in the sequence, so that

$$fr(\text{item}i) = \frac{c}{i^{1-\theta}} \qquad \text{13-6}$$

With $\theta = 0.1386$ the sequence expresses Heising's 80-20 rule stated in Chap. 12-1-6, and with $\theta = 0.0$ the sequence expresses the type-token ratio for the words from the text by Schwartz[63] used for Table 13-5 for the words ranked from 5 to 4000. Extremely high and low frequencies do not quite match.

Since (as discussed in Sec. 13-1-4) a limited number of last names of individuals accounts for many of the names in files (SSA[57]), it is possible to replace these names by shorter representations. These short names can be made up out of the 20 consonants, giving, for instance, 8000 three-consonant combinations for more than half the names in use. Use of two letters and a digit in an arbitrary position of the representation would avoid the rare but possible confusion with an existing name and provide 20 280 combinations, beginning with "1AA" and ending with "ZZ9". The names with extremely high frequency can be represented by combinations of two characters, "1A" to "Z9". Lexicons to control replacement of names or words can be generated by analysis of the file or of a sample of the file.

If a fixed-field encoding is desirable, some of the codes can be used to refer to an overflow file for names which could not be encoded. A format Zaa, for instance, could use the digits aa to point to records containing unencodable names.

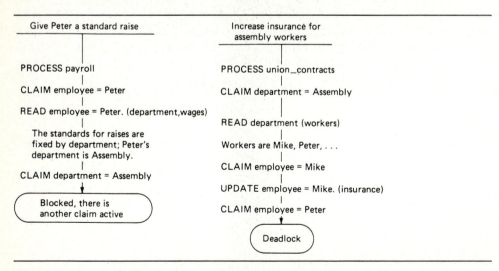

Figure 13-11   Dynamic string replacement.

DYNAMIC REPLACEMENT   If adequate processor time at data-entry time is available, the selection of a lexicon to control replacement can be done dynamically. The lexicon which is specific to a record now has to be carried along with the record. An example from DeMaine[71] is shown in Fig. 13-11.

Compression of 40% to 60% is reported on strings ranging from 400 to 1500 characters using up to 10 patterns in the lexicon. The same technique is possible using arbitrary bit strings. In this case the record can contain numeric or string data, as well as results from previous compression algorithms.

A Huffman code could also be generated dynamically, but here the code tree would have to be appended to the record. The code tree is difficult to represent in a compact form. A general decoding program for variable character codes will also be larger and slower than a program oriented to a particular Huffman encoding.

13-3-3 Implemention of Compression

Compression schemes can be best evaluated by applying them to a representative sample of the data. Several parameters have to be measured. The simplest measurement is the reduction of storage requirements. Changes in data transfer time are another benefit which should be evaluated. The processing cost for compression and expansion can be significant and should not be neglected. Since data retrieval is more frequent than update, complex compression schemes which generate encoding that are simple to expand are preferable. Evaluation requires that the retrieval to update ratio be known.

More than one method can be used in combination with others. In that case, the order in which compression algorithms are applied will make a difference. Replacement should precede Huffman coding, for instance, but if replacement leads to a more uniform use of character codes, subsequent Huffman coding will lose its advantage.

PROCESSING POINT FOR COMPRESSION   Compression or expansion can be performed at various points in the data acquisition, storage, and retrieval process. If compression is done soon after data entry and expansion is done just before information presentation, the volume of data to be handled throughout the system is less. Data elements which only control selection of other data elements will not be expanded at all, so that processing time for expansion will be saved. On the other hand, extensive usage of compressed data will require that all processing routines can manage compressed data. If computational use of the data requires expansion, the data elements fetched may be expanded many times during processing. Statistical-analysis programs especially tend to require data elements that are of consistent size and cannot cope with compressed elements.

The alternative is to assign data compression entirely to the file system. File systems can be equipped with compression algorithms through the use of database procedures or file-system escape procedures, so that compression and expansion become fully transparent to the user. Now the degree of compression performed can be adjusted by a database administrator according to storage versus CPU cost ratios applicable to a particular system or system era.

The automatic management of compression by the system can lessen the involvement of the user with the hardware and reduce binding of programs to system features. A user who is worried about storage costs is apt to adopt the use of representation techniques which are not optimal from the human interface point of view.

Compression of numeric values in storage can be used to let all expanded numbers used in processing be of equal precision and size, without sacrificing storage space. The use of fixed data-element sizes in processing programs can increase the sharing of standard programs.

Hierarchical files, through their multiple record formats and lack of array structure, tend to benefit less from compression than files which are formatted as tables. There are instances, as shown in Chap. 9-3, where the benefits of dense storage are a major factor in the decision to use a hierarchical approach. The availability of compression reduces the importance of this particular factor.

COMPRESSION AND FILE DESIGN   The compression of data has a significant impact on the file design:

> Compression of files generates variable-length records. Updating of records in compressed files can cause these records to change size. Compressed files need a file organization with the capability to store and update variable-length records.

Since many current file systems do not support varying length records fully, the compression of data has been forced from the level of a file-system support option into the database system or into the user level.

The user who is limited to fixed-length records also has to create mechanisms to store the representation economically in addition to being burdened with the problem of finding an effective representation for the real-world data. The combination is frequently a difficult task for the user. There are important applications where the data is broken into many linked fixed-length records since variable-length records were not available.

In the opinion of the author this abdication of responsibility by file-system designers is the major reason why the use of file systems has remained a problem in computer systems. These same systems do provide compilers, editors, and libraries to attract users to their facilities. All these facilities provide a better match to the users processing concepts at the cost of some computing overhead. The provision of equally elegant file-support facilities is the next step.

13-4   CRYPTOGRAPHY

Another objective of changing to the representation of data is to keep information secure, perhaps secret. Encoding in the sense used in cryptography protects data by transforming it into a form that does not provide information when intercepted. Cryptographic methods can provide privacy in otherwise insecure environments and can provide effective secrecy if access to nonencrypted versions of the data is controlled. Encryption can protect data while stored in files and while being transmitted over communication lines. Encrypted data is not suitable for processing without decoding.

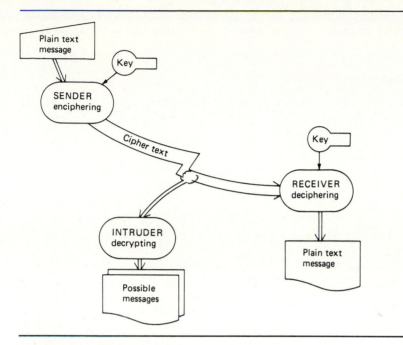

Figure 13-12 Elements of cryptography.

Three basic techniques are available:
1 Encoding of information
2 Transposition of codes representing data
3 Substitution of codes representing data

Encoding of data is a common process even without privacy consideration. Letting the value "1" mean `male` and the value "2" stand for `female` is a form of encoding, which will protect that field to someone who does not have access to a code book or lexicon, as shown in Sec. 13-1-3.

Operations where basic symbols are transposed or substituted to garble the data are referred to as *enciphering*. Such a transformation creates *cipher text* from *plain text*.

In order to understand the message, the recipient will have to *decipher* the cipher text, according to rules and a key used in the enciphering operation. The intruder, who wishes to understand the text, will have to resort to *decrypting* techniques. Figure 13-12 shows the components of cryptography.

We will consider mainly operations on data consisting of alphabetic messages. It should be noted that in fields outside of cryptography, the term "code" is commonly used for processes regarded as a "cipher" within the field. Only in this section will we be careful and make the appropriate distinction.

How well cryptography works depends on the plain text to be enciphered. Natural-language text has very distinctive patterns, and also provides much redundancy which promotes both comprehensibility of garbled text in day-to-day use, and the decrypting of enciphered data by analytical methods. We first will present the two basic enciphering methods and then discuss the security which they provide.

▦ 13-4-1 Ciphering

A *transposition cipher* operates on a group of characters. A key indicates the rearrangement pattern, as shown in Fig. 13-13. If the block length is N there are $N!$ possible rearrangement patterns.

N:	1	2	3	4	5	6	7	8	9	10	11	12	13	14	15	16	17	18	19	20	21	22	23	24	25	26	27	28	29	30	31	32	33	34	35
P:	W	h	o	'	s		g	o	i	n	g		t	o		d	o		t	h	e		j	o	b		o	n		E	P	I	A	C	?
K:	34	6	2	10	23	27	9	29	25	18	32	7	20	24	22	30	11	14	3	13	5	15	28	26	4	1	35	19	18	17	31	12	21	16	33
C:	C		h	n	j	o	i		b		l	g	h	o		E	g	o	o	t	s		n			W	?	t	o	o	P		e	d	A

N: character number, P: plain text, K: transposition key, C: cipher text.

Figure 13-13   Transposition cipher.

Some of the $N!$ enciphering-key combinations will be undesirable, since they leave parts of the message in the same sequence as the plain text, but many acceptable alternatives remain, especially when N is large. The example shows that the use of infrequent uppercase letters exposes a critical part of the message. A large key presents a problem in itself, since it can be difficult to transmit the key required for deciphering to the intended recipient.

Plain text	D	—	1	7	(ETX)		
ASCII* encoding	1000100	0101101	0110001	0110111	0000011		
Regrouping into 5-bit sections	10001	00010	11010	11000	10110	11100	00011
Key	45231	45231	45231	45231	45231	45231	45231
Cipher text sections	01001	00100	10101	00101	10011	00111	11000
Regrouping into ASCII	0100100	1001010	1001011	0011001	1111000		
Cipher text	$	J	K	(EM)	X		

*See ASCII table, Fig. 14-1.

Figure 13-14   Transposition ciphering using a 5-bit transposition key.

In order to obtain a larger effective N and yet operate on shorter messages, individual bits or small bit sequences may be scrambled through transposition. Figure 13-14 gives an example using a short message in the ASCII character encoding. Figure 13-1 provides the bit-pattern table to be used. In the example the transposition key used is very short ($N = 5$) and repeatedly used.

A *substitution cipher* provides replacement of characters of the source message by one or more characters of a cipher alphabet. A *constant substitution cipher* provides an alternate unique character for every character of the source alphabet. The number of alternatives here is again N. The cipher can be described by a substitution table or, alternatively, by the number of positions in the alphabet between the source and cipher character. The substitution must be chosen so that it is reversible; i.e., two different characters from the plain text should not map to the same cipher text character.

A very simple constant substitution cipher is the *Caesar cipher*. The substitution is defined by a displacement of a fixed number of positions, and hence offers only 27 choices for a compact alphabet, of which the "0" displacement is of course unsuitable. The choice of "1" has achieved fame in Arthur Clarke's movie script for "2001" by its use in naming the HAL computer.

A Gronsfeld substitution cipher is not constant. The key specifies the number of steps taken through the alphabet to obtain the cipher character. The number of steps can vary from zero to the number of characters which comprise the plain-text alphabet. The steps can be produced by random permutation generator; the starting value for the generator is the key. Figure 13-15 provides an example of such a Gronsfeld cipher for an alphabet of 27 characters. The number of alternative encodings is now N^2 for an N-character alphabet, with very few choices that are unadvisable. A key containing many zeros would not provide satisfactory enciphering.

P:	A	T		N	O		E	X	P	E	N	S	E		T	O		B	R	A	T	P	U	H	R		A	M	E	R	I	C	A
O:	1	20		0	14	15		0	5	24	16		5	14	19		5	0	20	15		0	2	18		1	20	16	21	8	18	0	
K:	6		2	10	23	27		9	25	18		7	20	24	22	11	14		3	13		5	15	26		4		1	19		8	17	12	21
S:	7	22	10	10	15		9		3	15	23	25	11		14	16	14	23		1		5	17	17		5	21		8		2	25		3
C:	G	vV	J		J	O	I		C	O	W	Y	K		N	P	N	W		A	E	Q	Q	E		U	H	B	Y		C	U	Q

										repeat			
I	C	A						I	L	L			
1	13		5	18	9	3	1		0	23	9	12	12
16	* 6		2	10	23	27	9	25	18		7	20	24
17	19		7	1	5	3	10	25	14	16	5	9
S	G	A	E	C		J	Y	N	P	E	I

P: plain text, *O:* ordinal numbers of plain text, *K:* key, *S:* sum of O and K, mod 27, *C:* cipher text.

Figure 13-15   Gronsfeld cipher.

Instead of using random key numbers, another message can be used. The ordinal values of the characters of the key message provide the amount of displacement in the alphabet value. This technique is called the *Vignere cipher*. The key text, of course, can be of any length, even as long as the message to be enciphered. Blanks in the key may be ignored. For instance, the key string 'AMERICA OF THEE I SING' will generate a sequence $K = 01\ 13\ 05\ 18\ 09\ 01\ 15\ 06\ 20\ 08\ 05\ 05\ 09\ 17\ 09\ 14\ 07$. A Vignere procedure for a larger alphabet is shown in Table 13-16. Ordinal numbers representing the characters are added modulo the size of the alphabet, to determine the ordinal number of the cipher character.

Table 13-16   Vignere ciphering procedure.

```
/* Input is the linein, key, and option = true for enciphering,
   false for deciphering.  The result is in lineout */
cipher: PROCEDURE(linein,key,option,lineout) EXTERNAL;
    DECLARE (linein,lineout,key) CHAR;
    l_line = LENGTH(linein); l_key = LENGTH(key); lineout = '';
                                    /* the typewriter alphabet */
    DECLARE abc CHAR(89) INITIAL('0123456789AaBbCcDdEeFf...
 /* Use one character to define the beginning of the key  */
    k = INDEX(SUBSTR(key,l_key,1),abc); l_key = l_key-1;
    DO i = 1 TO l_line;
         ord = INDEX (SUBSTR(linein,i,1),abc);
         kod = INDEX (SUBSTR(key,k,1),abc);
         IF option THEN kod = -kod;
         cord = MOD(ord+kod,89)+1;
         SUBSTR(lineout,i,1) = SUBSTR(abc,cord,1)
         k = MOD(k,l_key)+1;
    END;
    RETURN; END cipher;
```

An alternative to the addition of ordinal numbers, modulo the size of the alphabet, to determine the ordinal number of the cipher character can be used when the characters use a fixed-bit space. The exclusive-OR operation, used in Chap. 6-1-5 for hashing, provides an operation which is symmetric for both enciphering and deciphering, as shown in Fig. 13-16.

	A	0	0	7
Plain text	A	0	0	7
ASCII encoding	1000001	0110000	0110000	0110111
Key	H	I	H	$\bar{O}$
ASCII encoding	1001000	1001001	1001000	1001111
Exclusive-OR of text and key	0001001	1111001	1111000	1111000
Cipher text	(HT)	Y	X	X

Enciphering   Deciphering

Figure 13-16   Ciphering with the exclusive-OR operation.

More sophisticated methods can be developed based on the two transformations discussed, but we first will describe common procedures of decrypting so that we can evaluate the weaknesses of the basic enciphering techniques.   ╫╫╫╫

⊞⊞⊞ 13-4-2 Decryption

The ease with which a message can be decrypted depends on a number of factors:
- Is the method known?
- Is the source language known?
- How many alternative encipherings did exist?
- How much enciphered text using the same key is available?
- Is any matching plain text available?

A basic tool to aid in the decrypting of a cipher text is the generation of a *tableau*. If the method is known and the number of keys is limited, a tableau can be simply a listing of all possible decipherments. The tableau is scanned by eye and the plain text message will probably stand out.

If many, but yet a reasonably finite number of decipherments are possible, a *heuristic selection* of deciphered text can reduce the volume of the tableau to be listed. Simple heuristic algorithms might be that a vowel should exist in nearly all words, and that capitals and punctuation appear with certain regularity. Tableaux which do not show a reasonable pattern are not presented.

If the source language is known, substitution ciphers can be attacked using known *statistics* of letter frequencies. A simple substitution will generally yield the source text directly if the most frequent letter is replaced by E, the second most frequent letter by T, and so on, according to Table 13-13. Similar tables have been prepared for digrams (combinations of two letters), trigrams, initial and ending letters, and many other features of a language.

Even if such tables do not exist, as is the case when we have enciphered programs in a computer language, it may be possible to generate frequency tables from available source language samples. Programming language text also will be relatively easy to decrypt for a knowledgeable cryptologist, since the syntax is limited. Sequences of data digits will not provide much frequency information for decryption.

In the examples shown for transposition ciphers and Gronsfeld ciphers, *random-digit sequences* have been used that were obtained from a random number generator. Computer-software random-number generators, as well as hardware generators built from shift registers, have perfectly predictable sequences based on a few parameters. The parameters are the initial condition, the multiplicand and shift amount, and the length of the register. The assumption that a random-number generator provides protection equivalent to its cycle length, which for a 21-bit generator can be up to 2^{21}, is not true for someone who has insight into its mechanism. Since random-number generators use parameters which have been carefully selected to give a maximal-length cycle without repeats, the number of alternatives is considerably less. For the 21-bit generator, the number of full cycle sequences is only 84 672 out of the $2^{21} \approx 2\,000\,000$ sequences.

Long encryption keys provide more protection than shorter keys but are awkward for randomly accessed files. For every data block the key is reset to its begin point to enable key synchronization. The key is then always limited to the length of the data unit.

When the *key changes*, decryption has to start over. Changing keys frequently implies more transmission of keys between the enciphering point and the deciphering station, and this increases the susceptibility to having the keys intercepted or stolen.

Determination of the *key length* is important to the cryptographer who needs to reduce the search space. If enough cipher text is available relative to the key length, statistical tests on various groupings of the cipher text can provide clues. It has been stated that a ratio of twenty is adequate. The key length is estimated by generating descriptive parameters of various groupings of the cipher text. The greater cohesiveness of statistical results on the groups which match the original key length versus the groups which are unrelated provides key-length information to a computer-equipped cryptographer. Large amounts of cipher text in a database help to reveal the key patterns.

Still, a considerable effort is required for decryption of nontrivial enciphered text. There is hence a great inducement to obtain some helpful extra information. If the cryptoanalyst obtains a *matching segment* of cipher and plain text, the task is simplified. If the segment is longer than the key, the key used can be determined in most cases where the enciphering method is known. A method to obtain matching text can be the use of index and goal records of sorted data, which allow the conjecture of data values by linkage or position.

If intruders is capable of using the enciphering process, then they can submit data and keys themselves, and in that way obtain matching plain- and cipher-text to help them guess the method. An intruder who masquerades as a legitimate user of entry facilities, may be able to obtain matching plain- and cipher-text based on the legitimate key, and guess both method and key.   ▦▦

▦▦   13-4-3 Countermeasures

Having looked at the tools of the well-equipped cryptoanalyst we can survey counter-measures against attacks to these vulnerable spots. The countermeasures are listed in the same sequence by which the decrypting devices were presented.

To minimize the effectiveness of the use of *tableaus*, we ensure that the number of encipherings is very high. The parameters for the basic methods have been given; combinations of the basic methods may produce the product or the sum of the individual alternatives. For instance, two successive Vignere ciphers — a so-called *two-loop system* — provides only the sum of the two ciphering options, although the key length will be increased if the loops are not of equal length. We always assume that the method is known to the intruder; after all, we all may be using the same computer.

Reducing the redundancy of the source text will aid in disguising the message. In general, blanks and other punctuation will be omitted, and only uppercase characters may be used, transforming an 89-character typewriter alphabet to a 36- or 26-character set. By restricting enciphering to material which truly requires protection, the volume of available cipher text will be less and the analysis will be more difficult.

A number of approaches can be used to hide statistical features of cryptographic text. The use of *homophonic enciphering* can be very effective and relatively easy in a computer-based database. This method makes use of the fact that frequently there are more bit positions available in a computer code than are actually used. If eight bit positions are available so that there are 256 possible characters for our cipher text, and our source alphabet consists of only 26 characters, we can map the frequent characters into multiple cipher characters. Given the relative frequencies of Table 13-12, we can assign to the letter "E" $133 \cdot 256/1032 \approx 33$ different substitution characters in any kind of order and hide the frequency of this particular character. The character "Z", on the other hand, would require $\lceil 1 \cdot 256/1032 \rceil$, or one character position. Some adjusting is needed to assign an integer number of code positions to each character within the total of 256. The letter "U" would receive seven positions. We might assign then to "U" the code values: (17, 30, 143, 145, 173, 225, 249). A random choice of these seven values would be transmitted when enciphering. The receiver would substitute "U" for any of these values. The other characters translate similarly into nonintersecting subsets of the code.

The decrypter is robbed of all single-character frequency information. A more complex homophonic cipher attempts to avoid frequency information not only for all the single characters in the source alphabet but also for other linguistic features which might be useful to a cryptoanalysis. Digrams and trigrams are effectively hidden by providing a transposition in addition to the other techniques. Data which has been encoded prior to enciphering also provides artificial and misleading frequency information.

Random-number sequences used for key generation can become much harder to detect if only a portion of the random number is used in the actual enciphering method. The generators can be restarted from a key value associated with the user to obtain many alternate sequences.

In a database environment, keys can be well protected if the generator of the enciphered record is the same person as the receiver, since then the key itself resides in the system for only a short time. The remainder of the time the key is stored in the user's mind, purse, or wallet. A change of key to foil a suspected intrusion is, however, very costly, since all the data stored under a previous key has to be deciphered and reciphered. Such a process in itself opens opportunities to the intruder.

In order to make the determination of the key from data text more difficult, more than one key might be used. Selection from a number of keys, possibly based on a record number, can weaken statistical analysis operating on large amounts of cipher text.

Varying the key length can cause great difficulty to algorithms which an intruder may use in initial attempts to crack cipher text. The expansion of short messages with data designed to provide noise in the decrypting process also can disturb cryptoanalysis. The additional characters should follow neither random nor natural patterns but should have purposely obfuscating frequencies.

To avoid release of matching plain text and cipher text, the need for enciphering should always be carefully considered. For instance, if in address records the city, but not the zipcode, is enciphered, a large volume of matching text can become available. The problems of system access by intruders in order to obtain matching text are best handled by the existing identification and access logging methods. Since decryption takes time, there is a good chance to catch an intruder when an unusual access pattern has been detected during a periodic review of the access log. ▦▦▦

13-4-4 Summary

The previous two subsections have illustrated a cops-and-robbers game which can be continued ad infinitum. At some point, the effort required to decrypt data will be greater than the cost of other subversion tactics. Literature on cryptology rarely discusses alternative methods of gaining access, so that an overall security trade-off will have to be made by the system designer. Cryptography has been widely applied to data transmission, so that some factors which distinguish data storage from communications should be listed.

In data transmission, there is a continuous stream of characters over a line. The effective message length can be very long and can use a continuous enciphering sequence, subject only to resynchronization in order to cope with transmission errors. In data storage, we want to access records in random order, and frequently encipher only small, critical items of the data record. This places a limit on the key length. An intruder may be willing to gather many such fields from a file to obtain decrypting information equivalent to a long continuous tap of a phone line.

Cryptographic methods also provide tools for joint access control to critical data. Either two successive keys can be applied by two individuals or parts of a key can be allotted, which have to be joined to become useful. Individual and project security can also be accomplished by use of multiple encipherment.

Where data is not generated or analyzed in the processor but simply entered, stored, and retrieved, the ciphering mechanism can be in the remote data terminal. Such devices have been developed and are becoming increasingly feasible because of the increased sophistication of terminals. With such an approach, ciphering methods have to be used that are both transmission- and storage-oriented.

Cryptographic techniques provide only one aspect of the required access protection. Protection from destruction, intentional or accidental, is not obtained by enciphering; in fact, data will be lost if either the cipher text is destroyed or the key is lost.

Enciphering provides the capability to destroy selected data from backup files by destroying the key. This is often the only tool users have to be sure that their data does not become available to someone who happens to reuse a tape which was used for system backup. The implementation of a combination of protection methods, of which cryptography is an important component, can yield a high level of security.

BACKGROUND AND REFERENCES

The representation of information by symbols is a basic human characteristic. Many of the ideas expressed in the initial section are from an excellent exposition by Feinstein[70]. Discussions on the topic are found in Brodie[81]. Pierce[61] provides background information and Reiter in Gallaire[78] considers the limits of encoding. Computer science issues are addressed in papers edited by Kahn[84].

Coding conventions for computers commonly can be found in manufacturers' manuals. Loomis in Stone[75] summarizes codes used by computers to represent data. The IEEE Computer magazine reports regularly on standards, Coonen[80] describes the floating-point standard. A state-of-the-art report of codes used in commerce was provided by McEwen[74].

The patterns of names and words have been studied for a long time; results appear in SSA[57], Schwartz[63], and Lowe[68]. SOUNDEX coding was introduced by Odell and Russel in 1918; it is described by Gilligan in McEwen[74]. OReagan[72] encodes verbal responses. Florentin[76] presents coding conventions for associative relations. Existing code conventions can also be found by looking at usage in available databases, a directory is Williams[85].

An extensive study and implementation of compression algorithms is presented by DeMaine[71] and abstracted in Codd[71]. The file system described in Wiederhold[75] includes compression. Bayer[77] places front-abbreviations into the B-tree. Numeric data files are considered by Alsberg in Hoagland[75]. Young[80] places extracted descriptors at higher levels and Eggers[81] places them into B-trees.

Hahn[74] and Martin[77] discuss character replacement. Huffman coding (Huffman[52]) is also presented in Martin[77], analyzed by Knuth[73S], and applied by Lynch[81]. Compression techniques are surveyed by Gotlieb in King[75]. Welch[84] provides a algorithm to assign frequent strings to 12-bit codes and gives measurements of their effectiveness. Knuth[73S] points out the relation between Zipf's law (Zipf[49]), Heising's 80-20 rule (Heising[63]), and the data by Schwartz[63].

The basic book for cryptographers is Kahn[67]. Meyer[73] describes hardware. Mellen[73] surveys available methods; Stahl[73] presents homophonic enciphering. Friedman[74] evaluates the cost of ciphering. Feistel[73] and Diffie[76] present cryptology for computers. Gudes[80] develops the use for file systems. Bayer[76] applies enciphering to index trees and considers decryption and Davida[81] encrypts fields within records. Needham[78] applies encryption to users in distributed systems.

An implementation of DES for files is described by Konheim[80]. Bright[76] evaluated keys obtained from random-number generators. Gifford[82] considers both communication and databases. Programs for DES algorithms are presented in Press[86].

EXERCISES

1   Determine the field sizes and constants for the floating-point representation on your computer. What is its largest value, what is its smallest? What is its precision?

2   Locate the character-coding table for the computer you are using. How many data and control characters are available? Are there characters which are

usable for compression algorithms? Are all characters usable in files, in terminal output, or on the printer? Can they all be generated from data input without special processing?

3   Locate a standard coding table and describe size, format, density, susceptibility to errors, limitations, suitability for computing, and human-interface effectiveness.

4   Convert your name to Soundex. Do this also for misspellings of your name you have encountered.

5   Devise a check-digit method suitable for

a   Dates encoded as month/day/year

b   Sequentially assigned identification numbers

c   Dollar amounts

6   Design a method to provide TMR for some vital part of a database system. Use flowcharts or a procedural-language description to document the design.

7   Simulate the TMR design of Exercise 6 using randomly occurring errors at several rates.

8   Compress floating-point numbers for the case that only three-digits precision is required. Watch the normalization!

9   Test three algorithms for string compression on a body of text. This exercise can also be assigned as a competition. Discuss the result and the range of its applicability.

10 a   Design a compact code for dates within this century.

b   Design a compact code for the time of day adequate for computer time accounting.

c   Design a compact code for time adequate for the resolution of synchronization problems in your computer.

11   Discuss when the abbreviation scheme used by VSAM (Chap. 8-5-3) is effective, and when it is not.

12   Locate another standard code, similar to those shown in Table 13-2, and describe its domain and utility for data processing.

13   Determine the key used and decrypt the source plain-text message for the following cryptogram. You know that the encoding is a 3-character Vignere cipher.
KMIRLLFXXRXL⊔WXRXSUNIKCDDJIKXD⊔SD⊔QMLQD

14   Write a program to do homophonic enciphering and deciphering. Then make a ranked frequency graph or table on the observed character frequency of text you have enciphered with it.

15^p Define now the domain and the precise representation for all data attributes in your application, as defined in Exercise 1-3.

16^p Suggest a compression scheme for each domain you are using and estimate its effect.

Chapter 14

File-System Evaluation

The purpose of computing is insight, not numbers.

Richard Hamming

The number of computations without purpose is out of sight.

Author's corollary

14-0   INTRODUCTION

We have, up to this point, analyzed the technical performance of individual files and transactions using files. The parameters developed in the previous chapters have yet to be translated into financial costs and economic benefits before we can provide management with information allowing it to judge the appropriateness of a system which uses computer-based files.

We now have to assume that the decision to install a data-processing system is made on rational grounds. Other considerations that have led to the use of computer systems have been based on the expectation that rapid access to information would eliminate existing operational problems. This is unlikely to happen. Decisions have also been made in imitation of *leaders of industry*. Often, substantial pressures are exerted by vendors of computing equipment. These factors are beyond our scope.

In the scope of this book we cannot evaluate all intangible elements which are part and parcel of decisions to install computers, but will rather present a model of a functional evaluation. A number of decisions of a nontechnical nature remain, specifically in the area of attributing financial or social benefits to system performance.

THE PROCESS OF EVALUATION   Evaluation consists of estimating the costs and benefits of a variety of design choices, and selecting the best alternative. The number of choices possible at the various stages of design is already large, and their combination leads to an immense number of alternatives. We can, however, decompose the problem so that many choices can be settled independently. Furthermore, there are practical limits on the number of alternatives we need to consider:

1 The system must produce at least a minimum of adequate services, otherwise it will not be worth any costs.
2 The system must not cost more than what is affordable.
3 The operational benefits of the system must, over time, exceed the cost, in order to pay back the initial investment.

Many candidate alternatives will fail on one of these counts. Figure 14-1 provides an overview of the steps undertaken during design analysis of a file system.

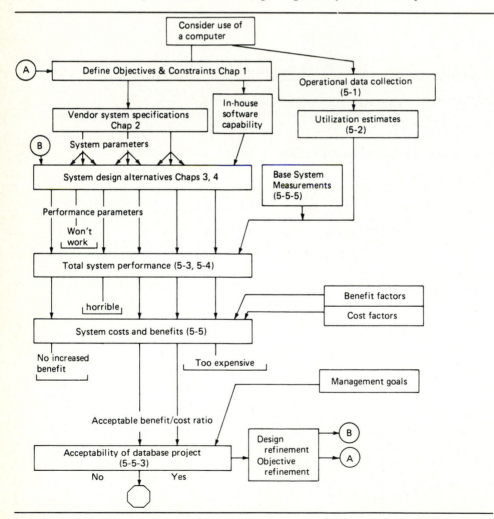

Figure 14-1   The system-analysis process.

CHAPTER OVERVIEW In Sec. 14-1 we assess the benefits of file services and examine how they are affected by system performance, although the issue of benefits due to usage is implied throughout. Section 14-2 deals with the estimation of frequency of system use while Sec. 14-3 considers the aggregate demands and capabilities of a file system. Here we have to deal with parallel operation of multiple devices. Effective use of multiple devices requires of course an operating system which can handle multiple processes and multiprogramming. Section 14-4 considers the evaluation of effects of sharing the computer with multiple users. Section 14-5 presents the comparison of costs and benefits. It includes an assessment of the robustness of the final results. The final review section summarizes the process and discusses its complexity.

Important factors in the analysis of a file system are the seven performance parameters defined in Chap. 4-1 and used throughout. These parameters describe the following:

1   The required data storage: $n_{total}R$
2   The expected search times: T_F, T_N, T_X
3   The expected update times: T_I, T_U
4   The time required for reorganizations: T_Y

The first performance measure (nR), which specifies the quantity of data to be stored, is not directly associated with any system benefits. Except for some historians, the mere collection of data is not an end in itself.

We discussed storage device selection in Chap. 10-2. Having selected storage devices, in Chap. 10-3 we considered transactions composed of several operations described by the timing measures shown above: search and update. This permitted us to estimate the time, T_T, required for individual transactions. We can identify the components of T_T file-by-file. Even though file activities interact in databases, a result of database design theory (*separability*) shows that near-optimal designs can be produced by designing one file at a time, once all its transaction loads are known (Whang[84]).

The special case of transactions which access distributed files was considered in Chap. 11. We now consider only local system costs, so that distributed sites are to be considered separately, one-by-one. This separation of design steps can lead to less than optimal systems, but following the concepts of separability, the results should be reasonable.

The major factor to be combined with the local transaction times is the usage load, i.e., the frequency with which transactions are performed. We will concentrate in this chapter on the elements which relate the load to the performance factors that were developed in Chaps. 4 to 6, and their integration in Chap. 10.

In order to simplify the evaluation procedure we will use methods which can provide rough initial estimates of load on a given system. These values can be refined later when the system being designed has taken a more definite form.

The operation of a computer requires people as well as hardware. Especially to estimate benefits we have to take personnel issues into account. The important issues of data maintenance, which involve personnel issues as well, are summarized in Chap. 16-1-4.

14-1   BENEFITS OF FILE SERVICES

Benefits are obtained due to use of information provided from the files. The form of benefits depends on the application, we distinguish two broad categories:

1 **Operational Services** include all applications which keep an enterprise functioning. This category comprises what is commonly understood as data processing. Products include:

   a Reports for reference by personnel, for instance, an inventory list.

   b Orders for regular activities, for instance, purchase orders for depleted inventory.

   c Inquiry services, for example, to determine the quantity on hand of items for sale.

   d Order entry, to rapidly record and share changes of status, sold items shipped out to customers, for example.

These services are utilized mainly by trained data-processing personnel, often dedicated to that task.

2 **Information Services** for planning purposes. This category is used to aid decision makers in providing management and new directions for an enterprise. Services include:

   a Summaries and comparisons of activities, for instance, sales productivities by category of item.

   b Exception reports, e.g., warnings that an item is not selling as well as last year.

   c Support for *what if* scenarios, to help analyze what would happen if one product line were dropped and another added.

   d Support to deal with external emergencies, such as locating resources when a factory is disabled and analyzing the effect of reallocation of these resources.

We visualize that these information services are needed by management on an irregular basis. Management is often aided by staff in carrying out such work, although, as systems become more capable and *user-friendly*, more of such interactions will be carried out directly by the decision makers.

It is such services that provide the benefits of a computer system, and a cost-benefit analysis has to include these factors.

14-1-1 Benefit Factors

We can compute the benefit from a system by determining the benefit for each transaction type, and multiplying its benefit by how often it will be used. The usage load is considered in Sec. 14-2. The sum over all transactions will yield the total benefit. On systems having a few, long applications the computation is simple; on systems running many arbitrary transactions, it will be more tedious. The 80-20 rule, cited in Chap. 12-1-6, can help again: We need only measure the most important 20% of the transactions in order to obtain a measure of 80% of the benefits.

Most benefit factors can only be estimated, but the fact that the factors are *estimates* does not diminish the importance of assigning quantitative values to all important parameters in a system design. The use of specific, documented, and consistent values for these quantities allows analysis of the decision and the comparison of system and nonsystem alternatives. When design decisions are made without recording the assumptions, the probability of design errors is high, and correction of assumptions to improve the design is impossible. If we have to make very many assumptions, then our conclusions will be mainly of a relative rather than absolute nature. This situation becomes obvious during the design process.

14-1-2 Effectiveness versus Benefit Measures

Systems are not always placed into operation with clear or measurable expectations of benefit. When, for instance, a certain service is mandated by law, only the effectiveness of the implementation can be determined; the benefits of the law have presumably been established already.

If no reasonable measure of benefit can be found, the base benefit is set to zero. It is still possible to proceed through the arguments which follow. Many considerations will reduce the expected benefits. Those reductions will have to be estimated in absolute terms, and by the end of this section only negative benefits will be left. This still will allow the integrated system comparisons in Sec. 14-5 to be made, but the conclusions will have to be presented to management in a relative sense. This approach, termed cost-effectiveness analysis rather than cost-benefit analysis, is common in government operations.

> *Cost-benefit analysis* attempts to obtain quantitative data so that *go/no-go* decisions can be made.
> *Cost-effectiveness analysis* is adequate to select one of several system alternatives which will achieve a goal already recognized to be desirable.

Any system has to achieve a certain level of quality of performance to become effective. The benefits of the transactions can be fully realized only if the entire system performs ideally. The topics following will discuss these effectiveness factors in terms of the performance parameters to be obtained.

14-1-3 Benefit Quantification

The value of a completed transaction is in the actions that it enables. To combine the variety of effects from an action, and compare them with the transaction costs, the benefits are best quantified in financial terms. For instance, in the case that the use of the system is associated with sales, this value can simply be a fraction of the profit expected from sales.

In other cases, the benefit may be established by questioning the potential users to determine what they would be willing to pay for the service. If the situation is one where money does not provide a basis of measurement, a comparison of the desirability between this service and other services whose cost is known can be used to provide measures of service value.

> An example is from the physician's office, where the benefits of perusing the medical record may be compared in terms of diagnostic assistance with some laboratory tests. If the benefits are equal, the value of the record access assigned is taken to be the same as the test cost.

Figure 14-2   Relative benefit estimation.

We can get into trouble with benefit estimation if we accept a statement that the service is essential. Then its value seems infinite.

⊞⊞⊞ **Realization of Benefits**   Frequently benefits are expected from lower personnel costs. Here we have to assure ourselves that these benefits are realizable, and even if they are, that they are socially desirable. Any replacement of untrained personnel by fewer but more expensive trained people must be weighed.

Realization of personnel economies is difficult to achieve if fractions of the effort of a number of individuals are being saved. If new jobs have to be created out of portions of partially eliminated positions, a *benefit realization* effort has to ensure that the new position is viable.

> If a computer in a banking office allows two people to handle the customers previously served by four people, but does not help the reconciliation of cash funds now done after closing at 4 P.M., the daily procedures must change.
>
>   Closing the bank an hour earlier to make more reconciliation time available from 3 to 5 P.M. is not a desirable solution, and has costs in terms of customer satisfaction. To realize the benefits some work done previously after closing should be reallocated to the next morning, when the bank is not as busy,

Figure 14-3   Benefit realization.

Problems can occur if the computer handles routine services but not some task which is to be done infrequently, but requires personnel, as illustrated in Fig. 14-3. It is difficult to schedule people for short time intervals, especially if the time schedule is not flexible. The cost of readjustment of operations also has to be included before summing up the benefits.

Expectations of future benefits are often based on *cost containment*. This term implies a hope that while there is no net saving now, the new system will allow growth at a smaller increase in cost than can be foreseen otherwise. It is obvious that such reasoning requires an even more careful benefit analysis, since the rate of expected growth is always uncertain and affects, when achieved, many aspects of an organization beyond the area of computing systems.   ⊞⊞⊞

14-1-4 Response Time

In our earlier analyses we were often concerned with the speed of the file systems, leading to a good response time for the transactions, T_T. The response time translates into costs and benefits, but the quantification is difficult. We first consider cases where the response time has a gradual effect, and then cases where there are absolute, *real-time limits*, for the response time. A subsequent section relates these effects to personnel costs.

The total response time includes

1 The entry of the request.
2 Computations to analyze the query and start a file transaction.
3 The actual transaction response time (T_T).
4 Computations to analyze and reduce the result of the file transaction.
5 The presentation of the response.

The values for items 1, 2, 4, and 5 must be estimated as well. The first item is highly dependent on the man-machine interface and how well it matches the user. Industrial engineers have measured user interaction times at terminals.

BENEFIT LOSS   Frequently the benefit of file operations diminishes with increased response time. Transaction systems which are in continuous use by trained personnel are designed to require little effort for query entry. A transaction is invoked typing one or two characters and a few parameters. Defaults are used for the common cases.

Figure 14-4 shows the estimated loss of benefit at a city airline counter where the customer has a choice of airlines and much of the business is on a walk-up basis. A logarithmic scale on the abscissa is used in these sketches because we are dealing with a wide range of time values.

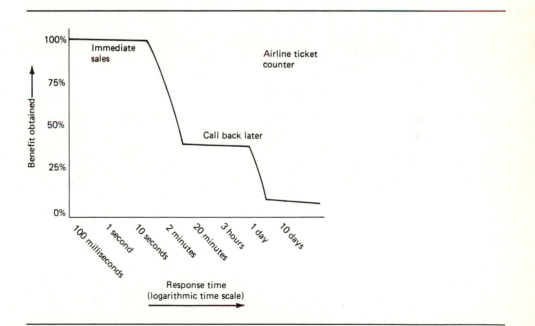

Figure 14-4   Response time and system benefits.

The value of the benefit keeps diminshing, so that if the response time of the system is poor, the data may arrive too late to have any effect effect. This boundary presents us with the *real-time constraint*.

⊞⊞⊞   **Response Time and Use Patterns**   It has been found that different work habits will evolve, depending on the interface that the system provides. The most common distinction is *on-line operation*, as stressed throughout in the transactions we present, and working with printed *data-processing reports*. Even when on-line access is provided patterns of use will be influenced by the response time.

As an example, we will use the financial collection office of a hospital where unpaid accounts are reviewed for follow-up. The computer system is used to provide an up-to-date status report so that all payments, credits, adjustments, and so forth, will be known before a collection effort is made.

A system which responds instantaneously relative to the reaction time of the clerk will allow a continuous performance of the collection task as shown on the left-hand side of Fig. 14-6.

If the system does not respond quickly, some waste of the operator's time will occur. The delay incurred by the operator is generally greater than the system delay which caused it, because the operator's flow of consciousness is disturbed. If the delays become significant, they provide reasons for trips to the coffee machine, checkbook balancing, and such.

At some point, operators will adopt a different mode of operation; they will make a number of requests simultaneously, and during the time the system needs to produce the records, the clerk will process the previous batch.

Now the wasted time is much less, since it consists only of an initial starting time and the overhead of switching attention.

If the delays exceed 8 hours, yet other work procedures will be used. If the delays exceed a week, it is probably not worthwhile to use the system at all.

Figure 14-5   Loss of real-time benefits.

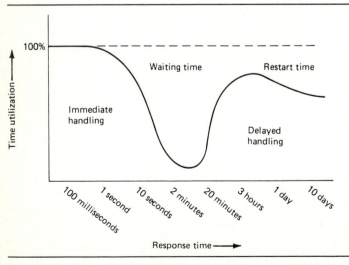

Figure 14-6   Personnel-time utilization.   ⊞⊞⊞

REAL-TIME CONSTRAINTS   The time limit, beyond which the results from a file are no longer useful, constrains the design of the system. The value of this constraint depends on the application and can vary from milliseconds to months.

Table 14-1 lists some estimates of real-time constraints in various areas where computer systems depend on files. The validity of some of the limits may be debatable, but for each of these categories there are instances where systems had a worse response time and were not well accepted. Note that only a fraction of the times shown in Table 14-1 is available for file operations. We also have listed the typical quantity of data expected for one request in these applications.

Table 14-1   Real-time constraints and data volume per transaction.

Application area	Value of constraint	Reason for size of constraint	Search volume/ request (bytes)
Annual accounting	Month	Annual report cycle	10^6
Full auditing report	Week	Audits are preannounced	10^5
Inventory report	2 days	Ordering cycle is a week	10^4
Payroll	2 or 3 days	Accepted by employees	10^3
Stock trade	1 day	SEC requirements	$> 10^3$
Bank account updates	Overnight	Expectation by customers, early detection of problems	10^7
Audit inquiry	Few hours	Request has to be handled via employees of firm	10^2
Fashion model casting agency	10 min	Multiple contacts have to be made in an hour	10^2
Airline-ticket sales	1 to 2 min	Patience of passengers	10
Real-estate sales index	$\frac{1}{2}$ to 2 min	Salesperson does not want to lose continuity	1 to 20
Grocery counter credit check	3 to 20 s	Goodwill	1
Item from medical file	2 to 10 s	Operational cycle of MD	25
Zip+4 code for address	83 ms	Speed ol letter-sorting machine	5
Positioning of a mass spectrometer	100 μs	Vaporization of sample	2

The need to keep within real-time constraints may mean that we will not be able to obtain all the possible information for some decisions, since the time to retrieve all data would be excessive. Decisions taken under operational real-time constraints hence may be less than optimal, but yet better than decisions taken without any data. It helps to avoid data elements which, although they are conceptually useful, do not actually contribute to the decision-making process of the user.

14-1-5 Personnel Costs in Using Systems

Determination of personnel costs is an important part of proper system design. In many systems the cost of terminal operators and other people preparing and receiving data greatly exceeds the cost of the hardware used by a system.

The operator effort required to use a system is often a substantial part of the system expense. If there is a full-time operator the basic costs are easy to determine. How effective the operator is with the system will then determine the overall system cost. A slow or awkward system will increase the basic cost per transaction. If more operators are needed than a fast system would require much benefit can be gained by system improvements.

If the system is operated by people who have additional and perhaps more important tasks, the ease of use of the system will be an essential component of its usage cost. The effort required to use the system is particularly significant where there is direct use of computers by *professional users* such as managers, lawyers, physicians, scientists, and researchers. Cost are measued as a loss of time available for work of primary interest. Delays which distract the users can be costly in terms of productivity, and even reduce resource availability in a transaction-oriented system.

In a number of instances data-processing systems intended for direct use by professionals were found inadequate for the intended users. After installation clerical personnel was hired to operate the terminals. The costs and delays related to the use of such intermediaries seriously affect system economics.

System performance measures other than response time are not easy to quantify. Counting of keystrokes, as has been done when comparing computer editors, seems futile, unless the differences are extreme. Modern systems tend to rely on menus, either presented or recalled by the user. The effort required from the user is easy to underestimate, and predictions by system designers have to be substantiated during pilot operation with the intended users.

Direct time measures of the personnel effort to use the system include:

1 The time required to formulate queries
2 The time spent to describe the format of desired outputs
3 The time needed to enter the search parameters into the system Then the system delay is incurred. When the result appears the user continues:
4 The time needed to locate the significant result on the screen or on a report.
5 The time needed to interpret the result and initiate an action.

Comparison of these times with existing manual systems can provide some idea of the relative demands made on the users.

If queries are complex or long, some of the entry time can be overlapped with processing time. Providing *overlap of entry and processing* makes the transaction management more complex. Overlap of computation and presentation is always desirable. It also permits the user to abort a transaction which produces unintended results.

Another component of personnel effort is the amount of *training* required to use the system. The cost of training will be relatively low for frequent users, but if we expect occasional users to benefit from the system, the amount of requisite training should be minimized. The additional effort of designing data-processing systems so that the user needs little indoctrination can be well justified in terms of overall system cost.

14-2   ESTIMATION OF TRANSACTION USAGE

In order to extract benefits out of stored data, the data has to be used. The benefits which may be obtained, the effectiveness with which they are obtained, and the cost of the data-processing operation are all related to the transaction load placed on the system. The transactions require data storage and operations.

14-2-1 Data, Hardware, and Transaction Performance

We estimated the volume of data expected for a file in Chap. 10-2-1 and we used that estimate to select suitable hardware. Subsequently we computed the cost, T_T, for any single transactions using the files residing on that hardware.

These estimates were made without considering demands made by users on the system. The performance of a transaction which is only used once a day is only of concern if it is used in some critical application. But if users invoke that transaction thousands of times a day its performance becomes critical due to the aggregate demand. We now make an estimation of the frequency of usage so that we can later estimate the total demand made on the files.

The retrieval of data elements is the central objective of a file system. Since a transaction may require data from more than one file, the usage estimates we will make will often address more than one file. On the other hand, several transactions will access the same file. Eventually we will take our results so that we can predict the demands placed by the transactions on each file, one by one.

We measure the utilization of a file in terms of an access frequency or load. Loads can be generated by programs or users operating on a relatively predictable, operational schedule or can be created by ad hoc demands for information. We consider first the load on systems by data processing for services for operational purposes.

14-2-2 Operational Data-Retrieval Load

The operational load L is provided by an estimate of the number of service requests to a file made by the transactions in a given period. Figure 14-7 provides an example for our airline. The number of salable items for the airline is determined by the number of flights between two adjacent points and the number of available seats. A study of its operation generates quantitative estimates. The estimates used in the example may be rough, but it is important that they have been made and have been written down. A change in projected system usage can be accommodated only if the original assumptions are known.

The distribution of these requests over a daily or monthly cycle should also be estimated to determine periods of high demand. The load and time of busy intervals are used to verify that the proposed system is adequate at those times. It is desirable to redo the complete evaluation for both high and low usage estimates in order to be assured that the effects of misestimation are neither fatal in terms of cost nor disastrous in terms of performance.

We wish to design a reservation system for a small airline. The design parameters are based on its operation: With three aircraft of 70 seats each, which complete 20 flight segments per day, there are nearly 30 000 units are for sale each week. The average ticket sale represents 2.7 units because people fly more than one segment and use return flights. The average number of people flying and booking together is 1.61. A survey shows that 20% of all reservations are subsequently changed. During the process of selling a ticket, typically three possible flight schedules are explored.

In this example we consider here two types of transactions:
    CS Check schedule
    ST Sell ticket (as described in Fig. 10-3)
Given the information above the transaction loads, L, on the system are

$$L(\text{CS}) = 30\,000 \cdot 1.20 \cdot 3 = 108\,000$$

$$L(\text{ST}) = \frac{30\,000}{2.7 \cdot 1.60} \, 1.20 = 25\,000$$

Each of these transaction involves multiple `fetch` and `get-next` searches. The ST transaction also generates `inserts` into the `Passenger_list` and updates of the `Seats_counts` file.

Such a computation is carried out for all important transactions. For instance, the refund transaction (RT in Fig. 10-3), being infrequent, may be omitted, but the transaction CP which cleans up the `Passenger_list` should not be omitted, although it is also infrequent, because it is likely to be quite costly.

Figure 14-7   Load for an airline reservation system.

14-2-3 Load for Information Retrieval

For a data-processing system which is to produce primarily *information*, rather than produce data to control sales of services or equipment, the estimation of the load is considerably more difficult. The extent of its use is mainly dependent on user satisfaction. Satisfaction in turn depends on human factors, such as *user friendliness*, utility, and performance. Figure 14-8 illustrates a load estimation for an information system.

A retrospective health-status report on a patient loses its value quickly if the effort to obtain it is greater than the desire of the physician to have the past record available during the encounter with the patient. Such a health report only occasionally contains information which is not obvious to the physician at the time of the visit. The average benefit may be quite low.

    To enable quantification of the design of the system we will assume that the usage factor $\gamma = 25\%$. If each of 100 physicians sees 20 patients per day then the daily load of the transaction, HR, is estimated as

$$L(\text{HR}) = 100\,\gamma\,20 = 500$$

This transaction requires `fetch` plus `get_next` operations for long health records.

Figure 14-8   Information load estimation.

For information systems the estimation of expected load may require investigating similar systems. If no similar situations exist, the operation of a *pilot model* can provide data for load projections. In a pilot model different technology can be employed, since it is allowable to operate at much higher unit cost per query in order to minimize the initial investment, while obtaining performance parameters which match the intended final form of the proposed system.

A prediction based on a pilot model requires reflection and insight when the pilot model was operated with limited files. The designer can only conjecture how system benefits, and hence usage patterns, are related to file size. A careful analysis of the information-producing potential and the power this information provides for users may be required. Usage patterns also change over time. A flexible design is needed to allow the system to grow and adapt.

14-2-4 Load for File Maintenance

We have already considered in the loads above the need to maintain the content of the file by performing updates. But file maintenance also involves periodic reorganization. The frequency of reorganization is largely a function of system design and file dynamics, but affected by practical scheduling concerns. Reorganization may be combined with periodic exhaustive processing so that $L_Y = L_X$. In other cases, reorganization can be specified as a function of the past update activity. Chapter 12-4-3 presented an analytic procedure to determine reorganization frequency.

The small airline of our example may clean up its passenger list, P, once a week as part of a market summary, but reorganize its inventory file, I, more frequently to keep access rapid. Since we expect that after 20% update activity, access to the weekly inventory file is measurably slowed down, we use that limit as the criterion.

$$L_Y(\text{P}) = L_X = 1$$
$$L_Y(\text{I}) = (L_I + L_U + L_Z + L_D)/(0.20 \cdot 30\,000)$$

Figure 14-9   Estimation of reorganization load.

14-2-5 Aggregating the Transaction Load

The outcome of the above considerations should be the frequency of all types of transactions. We cannot directly add the frequencies together; some transaction types are costly and some are simple. Since we have summarized the cost of each transaction type when computing its response time, T_T, we can make an initial guess and estimate the total aggregate system demand, q_{total}, over some period as

$$q_{total} = \sum_i^T L_i\, T_{T,i} \qquad \text{14-1}$$

for all relevant transactions, T. This load has to be applied to the file software and hardware to determine if it is satisfied by the capabilities obtained.

14-3   MATCHING LOAD AND CAPABILITY OF A FILE SYSTEM

Based on the known load and file performance parameters we wish to select a system of adequate capability at a reasonable cost. We can estimate the file performance for any design, but the number of design choices is overwhelming.

DESIGN OPTIMIZATION   One approach is to build a model of all possible file designs, and select an optimum. There is ongoing research based on this approach and methods are available which, for a constrained set of choices, will compute the optimum solution.

For instance, if indexed files are to be used, we can determine which attributes should be indexed. We can also optimize space-time trade-offs for direct files. Given a number of assumptions, we can show that in a database a global optimum can be achieved while optimizing the individual files separately, one by one. In distributed systems the optimal assignment of files or parts of files can also be determined. References to a number of such models can be found at the end of this chapter.

Unfortunately, all these methods have to make many assumptions about the available alternatives, so that their model tends to be simpler than the real world. Many of them are also mathematically complex. Their use will provide an excellent starting point for further determinations and will provide insight into complex design choices.

DESIGN BY ITERATION   The second approach to selecting files follows conventional engineering practice. We assume here either that the choices are practically limited or that a prior modeling analysis has narrowed down the set of alternatives. The process begins with the selection of candidate hardware systems which can deal with the storage requirements estimated earlier. These are then compared and scaled up or down according to the degree of over- or underutilization which we perceive during the analysis.

It is not unusual in data processing that the smallest computer adequate to store the data quantity and support the file programs is adequate to perform the remaining tasks. On the other hand, it does happen that there is no single computer capable of dealing with the data processing between core storage and disk which might be required in an active data-processing environment. Then the tasks will have to be distributed over multiple processors.

After an approximate system is selected, a file design is chosen which matches the expected utilization pattern and can be supported using vendor and in-house resources. The procedure to establish the adequacy of the selected computer system is iterative, and is shown in Table 14-2. In order to simplify the exposition, we will begin with the assumption that the application using the file system will be the only use of the computer. Consideration of the effect of multiprogramming will appear in Sec. 14-3-5.

The measurement used to appraise the demand and the capability of the system is *time*. We will not worry in the presentation about the unit to be employed; in practice, it seems reasonable to scale all values for on-line systems to seconds.

Table 14-2   Evaluation of a storage system for adequate performance.

1 The demand on the system is estimated.

2 The available resources of the system are similarly estimated.

3 The two are compared to see if a *satisfactory match* is obtained. A match is
   satisfactory when the demand is less than the capability of the resources by a
   safety ratio which is a function of the precision used to make the estimates. At
   this point a ratio of demand to capability from $\frac{1}{20}:1$ to $5:1$ is satisfactory, and
   permits skipping the remaining steps.

4 If there is much flexibility in the design it is easiest to skip to step 8 and redesign
   the file organization or change hardware.

5 If the demand is not comfortably within the capability, then both the demand
   and the resources are reestimated more precisely, and a new comparison similar
   to step 3 is made. Now a ratio of demand to capability less than $\frac{1}{4}:1$ is
   satisfactory, and permits skipping steps 6 to 8.

6 If the demand is so close to the capability of the resources, then both the demand and the resources are decomposed into their constituents, as described
   in Sec. 14-3-3, and those constituents are compared individually. This step
   accounts for simultaneous operation of disks, controllers, channels, and processors.

7 If any constituent is unsatisfactorily close, then parallel operation of the devices
   is taken into account. Parallelism leads to factors which modify the capability of the constituents, although not as much as simplistic analyses promise.
   Section 14-3-4 deals with this issue.

8 If there is a major mismatch, the equipment selected, the design of the files,
   or the tasks to be performed are changed and the design process is restarted
   at step 2 or 1.

14-3-1 Aggregate System Demand

The performance parameters, which were derived from the file design, provide estimates of the time required to complete the various transactions, as shown in
Chap. 10-3-2. These can be multiplied by the estimates of the transaction loads to
obtain the gross aggregate demand as shown in Eq. 14-1. In this equation the total
demand, q_{total}, over some period was estimated as the sum of transaction times.

This sum provides a gross initial estimate, but does not tell us anything about
the loads placed on the individual files. Since the performance of a data-processing
system means improving the performance of the files, for a substantial system we
must consider separarly the load for each file, $\mathcal{F}$, generated by all transactions, $\mathcal{T}$.

$$q_{\mathcal{F}} = \sum_i^{\mathcal{T}} L_i(T_{f,i,\mathcal{F}} + T_{n,i,\mathcal{F}} + T_{x,i,\mathcal{F}} + T_{i,i,\mathcal{F}} + T_{u,i,\mathcal{F}} + T_{y,i,\mathcal{F}}) \qquad 14\text{-}2$$

We still assign to the file the CPU constituent, c, required for some file operations,
but omit other computational costs which may be included in Eq. 14-1.

There is an important omission in these estimates: Not all the hardware will be
used during the entire time it takes for a transaction to respond. For instance, the
disk units will be idle, or perhaps used by other transactions, while a transaction, $\mathcal{T}$,

is computing and stressing the CPU. A consideration of these effects will be made now. They require a more precise assignment of loads to the hardware. Since we assign files to specific devices we first look at the file loads.

An alternate way of computing the total load is to consider the set of all files, $\mathcal{F}$:

$$q_{total} = \sum_{j}^{\mathcal{F}} q_j \qquad \langle\text{total file load}\rangle\ 14\text{-}3$$

The sum should be equal to Eq. 14-2.

We will perform the initial demand calculation for a period of high demand. If the daytime activities consist of searches and updates, and insertion of new data and exhaustive searches are delegated to evening operation, then the desired production during the daytime hours is computable as the sum of the file activity times for all transactions, T, carried out in that period. We omit reorganization transactions. The daytime demand is then

$$q_{day} = \sum_{j}^{\mathcal{F}} \sum_{i}^{T'} L_i(T_{f,i,j} + T_{n,i,j} + T_{x,i,j} + T_{i,i,j} + T_{u,i,j}) \qquad 14\text{-}4$$

The total available resource, Q, is, at this level of analysis, simply the available time during this period, perhaps 8 hours.

Demand versus Resource   To compare the values of demand and resources, we will define a utilization ratio,

$$u_{overall} = \frac{q_{period}}{Q} \qquad 14\text{-}5$$

If this value is very low ($u < 0.05$), representing perhaps only a fraction of an hour during the day on a dedicated computer system, then we can expect few problems, and the analyses provided in Secs. 14-3-2, 14-3-3, and 14-3-4 can be omitted. With a very low value, a reevaluation of the amount or type of disks may be in order, to see if costs can be lowered.

Peakloads   Other, highly intensive periods and the effect of other tasks should still be investigated. The careful designer will spend some time with users to determine when loads are high and why.

In a bank the lunch hour and the time before closing may give problems. In a hospital a busy time occurs in the morning when physicians make their rounds prior to opening their offices. Airline ticket sales are highest in the late afternoon.

Figure 14-10   Peak hours.

If the value of the overall u is low, but not negligible during some periods (maybe as high as 0.2), scheduling of the load can be considered to reduce the peak utilization.

Routine processing of bank transactions received by mail can be halted during the lunch hour. The hospital may avoid inventory analysis during peak hours.

Figure 14-11   Scheduling to reduce peak load.

If scheduling does not reduce the utilization significantly, the analysis of Sec. 14-3-3 should be carried out for the busy periods.

14-3-2 Hardware Architecture, Simultaneity, and Parallelism

In Chap. 10 we found that, on large systems, different hardware components such as disks, controllers, channels, and processors carry out distinct constituents of the transaction load. Since they operate at the same time some simultaneity of the constituent operations composing a transaction is possible. These constituents can also be performed in parallel on systems having multiple disks, controllers, and channels.

This means that a computer system having multiple units can support in a given period a number of transactions whose weighted sum, q_{total}, is greater than the available time. The reason is that some operations can be performed in parallel in all but the simplest computer system. Figure 14-12 sketches a simple, but busy system to demonstrate this.

Two types of overlap are possible and will be discussed. We find that at the same time different component types will be *simultaneously* active, for instance, a disk and its channels during data transfer; and some identical component types will be active in *parallel*, for instance, two disks.

In Chap. 10-4-3 we analyzed the simultaneous operation of different component types. To analyze *simultaneity*, we have to consider overlap between dissimilar constituents of the transaction demand: seeks, rotational latencies, and block-transfer times, since the various component types participate in only some of these constituents. Overlap of computing cycles with disk operations was found to be essential for exploitation of buffering in Chap. 3-2-5.

In Sec. 14-3-4 we will analyze the effect of *parallelism* in the operation of multiple hardware components of the same type. Having multiple components permits multiple seeks, latencies, block transfers, and computations to be carried out in parallel, and this permits increased system performance.

In order to overlap operation of either type, it is necessary that the system can handle multiple processes, since individual processes are made up of sections specified to occur in sequential order. In the typical transaction systems there will be one computation associated with every active terminal, so that even if the computations are so simple that they cannot be decomposed into multiple processes, one can expect a considerable amount of parallel aggregate demand.

When a complex information application is being performed on a system, then its internal interaction may prevent or reduce parallel activities. Now retrieval computations may have to be decomposed within the application into parallel processes, so that the capabilities of multiple devices can be exploited.

In Fig. 14-12 data transfers are active between core memory and two disk units, f and i, using both channels and two controllers. At the same time, seeks are taking place on disk units c and g and disk m is reporting the completion of a seek. Which combinations of operations are possible in parallel depends on the *architecture* of the storage system. Data transfer and control lines are bidirectional, so that it does not matter if the transfer activity is read or write, or if the control activity is demand or response.

Table 14-3 defines a number of architectural classes to help analyze the activity of various types of storage-system components during the execution of constituents of disk operations.

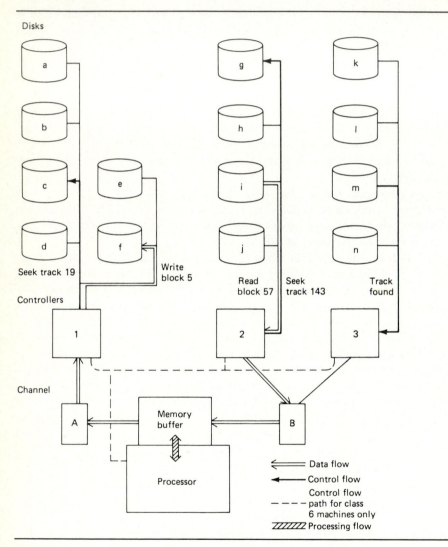

Figure 14-12   Opportunities for parallelism.

We consider for simultaneous operation:

1. The processor and its primary memory, characterized by the value of c.
2. The channel connecting the disks or their controllers and the processor. A channel is busy during the period of data transfer, btt, as well as during initiation of the seeks (s).

3 The controller, which transfers data and control signals to the disks. A controller can often signal to multiple disks as it receives control requests from the processor via the channel. We also find dedicated controllers, where one controller operates exactly one disk.

4 The actual disk drive, which is busy during all of s, r, and btt.

A system is apt to have multiple disk units, so that this type of device, which is used most intensely, also is the device which can most often provide parallel operation. The capability to use multiple disks in parallel is limited, however, by the type and number of controllers and channels available and the demands placed on them for simultaneous operation. For instance, in Fig. 14-12 no additional data transfer can occur, since a channel (such as A, B) is tied up while any one of its attached disks (such as f, i) transfers data.

To determine the amount of simultaneity and hence parallelism possible in a storage system, we recognize six possible architectures of such systems, assigning increasing performance characteristics from class 1 to class 6. Other intermediate combinations are possible and can be analyzed similarly. Table 14-3 lists these architectural options. The architecture class determines the hardware components active during the several constituents (seek, block search, data transfer, and computation) of an operational sequence.

Table 14-3   System components active during storage operations.

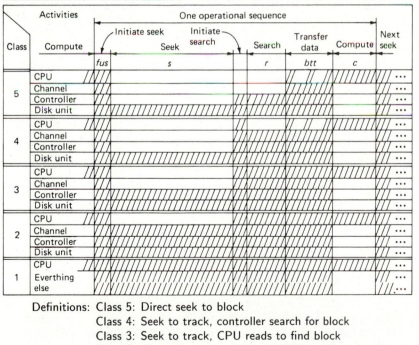

Definitions: Class 5: Direct seek to block
Class 4: Seek to track, controller search for block
Class 3: Seek to track, CPU reads to find block
Class 2: Channel searches for track, CPU reads to find block
Class 1: Processor searches for track and block

▦▦▦ **CLASS DISTINCTIONS**   In the least powerful systems (*class 1*) the processor itself, the channel (if any), the controller (if any), and the disk are fully occupied during any disk operation from the beginning of the seek until the last byte has been transmitted. The processor may be less than fully involved in slightly more sophisticated machines, but its functions may be restricted by frequent control or data-transfer demands. Most microprocessors fall into this class, although microprocessor systems may employ multiple processors and dedicate some to the tasks identified with controllers and channels. Such a system may then be assigned to one of the higher classes.

If the processor only initiates the seek, and the channel, with the controller, executes the seek, then opportunities for simultaneous operation of more than one channel become possible. In such a *class 2* system, however, the processor is required to locate the appropriate block, and hence is tied up during the rotational latency time. If the file system designed for some application often reads blocks sequentially, without seeks, the computer time available will be small, which in turn limits the benefits of multiple channels.

If the channel is not required during the seek (*class 3*), control messages can be transmitted between the CPU and the controller, so that multiple controllers can be started and seek simultaneously.

In a *class 4* system, the channel, after being instructed by the CPU, can search for the proper block and then transmit data to memory. During data transfer the CPU is slowed only somewhat by memory-access interference. In this type of system, the channel, however, is fully tied up during the rotational latency and transfer time.

If the controller accepts combined track and block addresses (*class 5*), then the use of the channel takes place only at the initiation of the combined seek and block search sequence and during transmission of data. We assume that systems of this complexity use *cache memories* for active computations so that memory access interference is negligible.

We reserve *class 6* for systems having direct communication between controllers and CPU, which will allow seek operations to be initiated even when the channel is busy. The importance of this alternative will be discussed later.

In multiprocessor systems each of the machines may fall into one of these classes. Only one active processor will carry out the CPU tasks for one request. Memory interference may occur if memory is shared among processors. Other aspects of computer system architecture also affect performance but are not captured by this classification.   ▦▦▦

14-3-3 Estimating Demand by Constituent

In order to analyze the effect of simultaneity and parallelism we have to consider what the demands are on the constituent capabilities provided by the hardware components. We will decompose the total transaction load into its constituents. Then we are able to make an evaluation separately for each constituent.

Decomposition means recovering the constituents, seek, s; latency, r; block transfer time, btt; and computation effort, c, from each of the terms, T_F, T_N, etc.

The breakdown will provide a measure of the demand for each component type. In the previous derivations of performance measures we have actually been careful to express the parameters T correctly in terms of their constituents, so that we now can safely dissect the earlier results. We will use here the symbols s, r, btt, and c also as subscripts to distinguish the various aspects of the demand parameter, q.

For the seek load

$$q_s = \mathcal{L}_F s(T_F) + \mathcal{L}_N s(T_N) + \mathcal{L}_U s(T_U) + \cdots \qquad \text{14-6}$$

where $\mathcal{L}_F$ represent the fetch frequency to a device for all transactions T and files $\mathcal{F}_d$ residing on the device being analyzed. The measures $\mathcal{L}_N, \ldots$ are similarily defined. In in a more general notation

$$q_s = \sum_{h1} \mathcal{L}_{h1} s(T_{h1}) \qquad \text{for} \qquad h1 = F, N, U, Z, \text{ etc.} \qquad \text{14-7}$$

where $s(T_{h1})$ denotes the seek component of the performance parameter.

Similarly, we can evaluate the total time spent for the rotational delay constituent, for the data transfer constituent, and for the processing constituent, so that for any constituent

$$q_{h2} = \sum_{h1} \mathcal{L}_{h1} h2(T_{h1}) \qquad \text{for} \qquad h1 = F, N, U, Z, \text{etc.}$$
$$\text{14-8}$$
$$\text{and} \qquad h2 = s, r, btt, c$$

Here $h2(T_{h1})$ denotes the constituent $h2$ of the operation T_{h1}. The values q_{h2} give the demand on the system for the constituent due to the load imposed in a given period.

We have not evaluated the processor component, c, throughout, but it is useful to carry it here in symbolic form to verify the assumptions made in Sec. 2-3-2 relative to buffering and the bulk transfer rate, t'. If the final system requires multiple components to satisfy the load, the demand on c grows proportionally, so that faster or multiple processors will be needed.

In Sec. 14-3-4 we will investigate opportunities of parallel operations of various system components, to determine the quantity of basic operations that a computer system can deliver.

UTILIZATION OF SYSTEM COMPONENTS   The constituents of production demand, q, will have to be distributed onto the components of the system in order to obtain estimates of the utilization u for the various types of components. We refer to Table 14-3 to obtain the conditions for the assignment of q, appropriate for the storage-system architecture. We will assume now that we have a class 5 or 6 machine. These machines provide the greatest capability for overlap of constituents. The average utilization for a disk includes all but the computation time so that

$$u_{disks} = \frac{(1 + fus)q_s + q_r + q_{btt}}{Q} \qquad \text{14-9}$$

where fus denotes the fraction of time in terms of s, $\ll 1$ (shown in Table 14-3), needed to get the seek mechanism started. We will discuss this term in the next paragraph. The controller and channel can be evaluated similarly: The controller is free while the disk unit is seeking; the channel is active only during command and data transfer

$$u_{controllers} = \frac{fus\, q_s + q_r + q_{btt}}{Q}$$

$$\hspace{8cm} 14\text{-}10$$

$$u_{channels} = \frac{fus'\, q_s + q_{btt}}{Q}$$

If $s \gg r$, the controller can control multiple disks simultaneously without creating a bottleneck. If $s + r \gg btt$, the channel can control multiple controllers with active disks simultaneously without creating a bottleneck. The term fus' will take into account the control traffic when $s + r \ggg btt$. For the processors

$$u_{processors} = \frac{q_c + fus\, q_s}{Q} \hspace{3cm} \langle\text{computational load}\rangle\ 14\text{-}11$$

If we do not have accurate data on processor usage, we go back to our assumptions about buffering, where we stated that we expect that $c\,Bfr < btt$ (Eq. 2-22), so that we can state initially

$$u_{processors} < \frac{q_{btt}}{Q} \hspace{3cm} \langle\text{buffering constraint}\rangle\ 14\text{-}12$$

EFFECT OF INTERFERENCE BY CONTROL-INFORMATION   There is an unexpected interference when control-information is needed by the channel or controller, while data transfer takes place. The factor fus above accounts for the time it takes to transfer the control information from the processor via the channel to the disk unit. Control information is required to initiate a seek, notify the processor, or perform address or key verification on cylinders and blocks.

In a class 6 machine, there is a data-independent path for such control information via each channel to the controllers. The dotted line in Fig. 14-12 indicates this control flow path. All that is required here is the transfer of a few, (pc), pointers of size P, and if the same transfer rate applies to such control information as applies to data, then for each seek

$$fus' = fus = \frac{pc\, P}{t} = btt\, \frac{pc\, P}{B} \ll btt \approx 0 \hspace{2cm} \langle\text{class 6}\rangle\ 14\text{-}13$$

In the other architectural classes, control information has to share the path used to transfer data, and hence the seek requests will be blocked when the channel is busy with data transfers. We consider that

1 The seek frequency is q_s/s.
2 The channels are busy with data transfer q_{btt}/Q of the available time.
3 The average delay when encountering a data transfer activity is $\frac{1}{2}btt$.

Then, in a period Q, the sum of the delays encountered when attempting to move seek commands to a controller or disk is the product of these three factors. To obtain *fus'* in terms of the seek load, q_s, as *fus* is used in Eqs. 14-9 to 14-12, the delays and the base load from Eq. 14-13 give a factor

$$fus' = \frac{q_s}{s} \frac{q_{btt}}{Q} \tfrac{1}{2} btt \frac{1}{q_s} + fus = \frac{btt}{2s} \frac{q_{btt}}{Q} + pc \frac{P}{t} \qquad 14\text{-}14$$

With large values of *btt*, i.e., large blocks, fast seeks, and active channels, this factor becomes quite large, perhaps adding 25% or more to the seek delays. We find that large block sizes can have significant detrimental effects on the total channel capacity in class 3, 4, or 5 machines. This secondary demand on channel capacity is frequently unjustifiably neglected, and has surprised people who expected better file performance from their systems.

An extreme case is the IBM implementation of ISAM on a 360-type computer. The entire process of following the overflow chain is carried out by a loop in the channel-control program. This reduces the load on the CPU but makes any shared access to other devices on the same channel during this period impossible. Multiplexing capability has been introduced into the channel on the 370 series machines to mitigate this effect.

Figure 14-13   Channel access interference.

EFFECT OF SIMULTANEOUS OPERATION   The decomposition has permitted an analysis of load per constituent. If the demand on a particular constituent was great then the simultaneous operation may have shown relief. However, a significant increase in capability requires that similar components operate in parallel. This analysis follows, and requires also that the demand is phrased in terms of its constituents.

14-3-4 Effect of Parallel Operation of Multiple Devices

In the previous section we have distributed the constituents of the demand over the appropriate hardware-component categories: disks, controllers, channels, and processors. We still can expect to find that the disk component is as heavily loaded as the estimate on the entire system originally indicated, since the disk units are required for all constituents of file activity. We have not yet determined the extent of the beneficial effect of multiple disks, channels, or processors.

Having *parallel components*, that is, multiple units of the same type, permits sharing of the load assigned to the type of device. For instance, if there are two channels, each channel can be used to transmit data up to its own capacity, and it appears that the system's data-transmission capability could be doubled. If there are four disk units, some of them can be seeking and others transmitting data, again greatly increasing the aggregate capability of the system.

Two factors have to be considered when an evaluation of the increase of system performance due to parallel components is to be made:

1 The design of the applications has to distribute the service demands equally over the parallel components.

2 The interference between simultaneous requests has to be assessed.

We will deal with both issues. The problem of interference is one which can be formally addressed. The initial application load distribution requires much judgment.

APPLICATION LOAD DISTRIBUTION   The distribution of the load over parallel storage components has to balance the data quantity and the access rates to the data. Load balancing takes place at several levels.

> **Parallel User Activity**   Users who work during the same time period can have their private files assigned to distinct devices.
>
> **Parallel File Activity**   Files used simultaneously by one application can be assigned to distinct devices. This technique is common in sort programs.
>
> **Distribution of File Fragments**   Fragments of a file, for instance, multiple indexes or pointer lists, can be placed on distinct devices, and the computation which accesses these subfiles can initiate multiple processes to permit parallel utilization.

The discussion which follows will treat the assignment problem in the aggregate sense, and the result can be applied to any level above.

If there is no access load problem, the data files may simply be distributed so that the storage space is well utilized. If we have dev parallel devices, the objective will be to

$$ud_i \approx ud_j \qquad \text{and} \qquad D = \sum_i ud_i \qquad \text{for} \qquad i, j = 1, \ldots, dev \qquad \text{14-15}$$

where ud_k is the data storage volume assigned to component number k of the component type being considered. The total storage requirement, D, is estimated as shown in Eq. 14-1.

If the utilization, u_{comp}, encountered by a system component of some type $comp = \{disks, controllers, channels, processors\}$ is high, the designer will have to consider first of all the distribution of the access load. If the dev parallel devices, $comp_i$, $i = 1, \ldots, dev$ are of equal performance, the distribution will attempt to make uc_i equal.

$$uc_i \approx uc_j \qquad \text{and} \qquad u_{comp} = \sum_i uc_i \qquad \text{for} \qquad i, j = 1, \ldots, dev \qquad \text{14-16}$$

To achieve this objective in practice, the files which receive a higher access load are placed on distinct components, and files which are less critical are distributed subsequently according to the storage capability left on the devices. Optimal placement of files within a disk unit is considered in Sec. 6-3-2.

In systems having parallel components of dissimilar performance (perhaps there are some fast disks and some are larger but slower), the rule of Eq. 14-16 is modified to consider a differential performance factor pf, now

$$uc_i/pf_i \approx uc_j/pf_j \qquad \text{14-17}$$

since the faster device, $(pf_i > pf_{average})$, can handle a larger fraction of the load. This rule could be further refined to consider the actual constituent $h2$ (see Eq. 14-8), leading to the difference in performance among parallel components.

In practice, application loads are not known precisely in advance. The optimal distribution during one period will be different from the optimum a few hours or a few minutes later, and uncertainty about the time patterns can further upset the design of a system. Assignment of loads for optimal usage may hence be deferred to a time when the operation of the file system has achieved a level of demand and stability so that measurements can be made to relate the load, demand, and utilization factors ($\mathcal{L}_{h1}$, q_{h2}, and u_{comp}). Increased loads may also lead to the acquisition of additional disks, channels, and processors. It might even be desirable to get more disk units than are needed for data storage in order to spread the load among more devices.

The most dramatic solution to inadequate performance is an increase of the number of processors in the system. The change from one to multiple processors may involve major changes in the operating system, and its evaluation requires a separate assessment. Once several processors are being used in parallel, further increments of processors should have no deep repercussions and can be considered as any increase in component count.

When more devices are added to a system a redistribution of the utilization is always in order. It is important that file systems provide the flexibility to carry out the reassignments required to keep operations at a near optimal level.

If no satisfactory balance of utilization can be found, *replication* of files or file fragments may be called for. This will of course increase the storage demand and the update requirements, since now multiple copies have to be kept up to date. With the increase of storage devices typically come additional controllers, channels, and possibly processors. As indicated earlier, there is a strong interaction between replication and having multiple processors. Replication becomes easier but is also often needed to keep the demand on communication among processors within bounds.

The extent of benefits from load distribution is not easy to predict. There may also be many other constraints on channel assignments, storage assignments of file-organization components, separation of indexes, and so forth, which work against optimal distribution.

INTERFERENCE OF PARALLEL LOADS   Even after the utilization over similar components has been explicitly balanced, we find that at any instant of time the distribution of demand is such that on some components, $comp_i$, multiple requests are queued, while other components remain idle.

The extent of parallel utilization is limited by the number of simultaneous processes, pr, which request services from the components. In the worst case with a load being present, $pr = 1$ and only one of the parallel components will actually be productive. No parallel operations are enabled, even though parallel components are available.

When a large number of processes generates requests, the probability of simultaneous productivity by parallel components increases. Still, the devices will not be able to be fully productive, since requests from multiple processes for the same device will still interfere with each other. The expected effects of such interference are presented in Table 14-4.

Effects of Interference   The actual operational sequences of parallel processes, and their interactions, are difficult to analyze. However, very simple models give results which match the observed performance when simultaneously accessing parallel components quite well.

We use here a case-analysis approach to estimate the *productivity* of devices, after interference. We assume that the processes request services from one of the *dev* components at random and that all components have an identical performance ($pf_i = 1$). Furthermore, the request intervals are regular. Figure 14-14 develops the case for two devices and two processes.

Let us consider here $pr = 2$ processes (P,Q) and $dev = 2$ devices (A,B). Four (dev^{pr}) combinations are possible and each of the 4 cases is equally likely:

a: (P→A,Q→A),   **b:** (P→A,Q→B),   **c:** (P→B,Q→A),   **d:** (P→B,Q→B).
We do not have to consider here which device receives the most requests. We are concerned with the delays occurring because a request cannot be satisfied while a parallel request needs the same device, and with a complementary issue: A device remains idle whenever none of the requests addresses it.

We find in the example above that in 2 out of the 4 cases (**b,c**) the distribution is good (both devices are being used) and in 2 cases (**a,d**) there is interference. During interference no parallelism occurs, and 1 of the 2 devices will be idle. The fraction of idle devices in these 4 cases is $fr_{idle} = (2 \cdot 1)/(4 \cdot 2) = 25\%$.

This interference reduces the productivity of the two disks by $fr_{idle} = 25\%$ to $Pc = 1$ to 75%. Note that the productivity of a single disk, A, would have been 100% since it would have been in continuous use, but then the using transactions will be delayed. The parallel operation of the second disk, B, only increased the system capacity from $1 \cdot 100\%$ to $2 \cdot 75\% = 150\%$, i.e., by 50%.

Figure 14-14   Productivity of two devices used by two processes.

If the number of processes, P, Q, S,..., is increased the utilization of the devices will increase. However, each process which cannot receive service will be delayed. In the example above two processes were delayed in the four cases. The average number of delayed processes is $pr_{del} = pr - Pc \cdot dev$. These delayed processes have to enter a queue. The relationship of queuing and delay is given in Eq. 12-28.

If the number of devices is large relative to the number of processes, interference will be reduced, but the devices will remain idle more often.

Productivity of Parallel Devices   To estimate the productivity, Pc, of a system with parallel components, a number of assumptions have to be made. Different models of process behavior affect the result. We assume here that a process, after it has had its turn, will immediately make another request and that new request is independent from the previous request. These conditions lead to a stable request pattern. More complex patterns have been explored for similar problems (Baskett[76]) or may be approached by simulation.

The values for the productivity, Pc, in Table 14-4 were derived by case analysis, as shown above, for the small parameters and by binomial were computed as above.

Table 14-4   Productivity of systems having *dev* parallel components.

Num.of devices	Number of active processes *pr*												
	1		2		3		4		6		8		∞	
dev	P_c	pr_{del}	P_c	pr_{del}	P_c	pr_{del}	P_c	pr_{del}	P_c	pr_{del}	P_c	pr_{del}	P_c	pr_{del}
1	1.00	0	1.00	1.00	1.00	2.00	1.00	3.00	1.00	5.00	1.00	7.00	1.00	∞
2	0.50	0	0.75	0.50	0.87	1.26	0.94	2.12	0.98	4.04	0.99	6.02	1.00	∞
3	0.33	0	0.56	0.32	0.70	0.90	0.80	1.60	0.91	3.27	0.96	5.12	1.00	∞
4	0.25	0	0.44	0.24	0.58	0.68	0.71	1.16	0.85	2.60	0.91	4.36	1.00	∞
8	0.12	0	0.22	0.22	0.29	0.66	0.37	1.04	0.55	1.60	0.63	2.96	1.00	∞
∞	0	0	0	0	0	0	0	0	0	0	0	0	0.5	∞

We see in Table 14-4 that the number of active processes, *pr*, should exceed the number of devices, *dev*, if systems with parallel components are to be more than 75% productive, but also that the number of delayed processes becomes significant. A high productivity becomes feasible only if the delays are tolerable, and for most on-line operations they will not be at such a high load.

To increase the productivity when $pr \approx dev$, queuing and buffers can be used to distribute poor short-term request patterns over a longer time. However, when reading records from files randomly, only one buffer can be effectively used by one read process. When writing blocks, multiple buffers can be employed and a good load distribution can be achieved. If some transactions can tolerate larger delays, a priority scheme may help.   ▦

EXPECTED DISTRIBUTION OF LOAD   We have given above estimates for the productivity of similar components when they are used in parallel. The model used here assumed a uniform demand pattern of the processes to the devices.

If the load per device, LpD, has not been explicitly balanced, the components will not receive an equal load from the processes. It is possible to analyze the expected load distribution based on a random behavior. Of interest here is the short-term load distribution; the long-term distribution, given uniform random behavior, will be equal for all devices.

Some values for $LpD(i/dev)$ for two and three devices are presented in Fig. 14-15, with $i = 1$ denoting the active device at any instant. The values appear to stabilize around (0.58, 0.42) and (0.50, 0.33, 0.16). The ideal values would of course have been $1/dev$ or (0.5, 0.5) and (0.33, 0.33, 0.33). These values can in turn be used to estimate a maximum utilization factor, $umax(dev)$, which will limit the eventual productivity. Since the progress of transactions computation is limited by the busiest device, we find, for the limiting cases in Fig. 14-15 (*dev* =2 and 3 parallel devices), that

$$umax(2) = \frac{1/dev}{\lim_{pr \to \infty} LpD(1/2)} = \frac{0.50}{0.58} = 0.86$$

and $$umax(3) = \frac{1/dev}{\lim_{pr \to \infty} LpD(1/3)} = \frac{0.33}{0.50} = 0.66$$

14-18

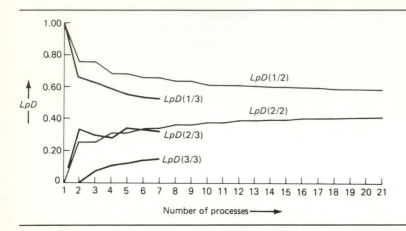

Figure 14-15   Random load distribution.

It is better to measure the imbalance of a system to find *umax* rather than use Eq. 14-18, since the statistical assumptions necessary for this or other analytical results can be quite unrealistic. File-access counts may be obtained by installing utilization-monitoring devices on the computer hardware. Other measurements can be obtained as part of operational statistics of the computer accounting system.

For a new system measurements cannot be taken and the estimates given above may be used as an initial design point. When hardware or its usage is unusual, simulation of the system may be required. If a reasonable facsimile of the system exists, some simple measurement programs can be used to obtain values of the maximum activity. These techniques are particularly important in a multiprogrammed environment.

Load distributions seen in practice match approximately the pattern of *LpD* shown above if known and obvious imbalances are accounted for. It may, for instance, be wise to exclude logging or archival devices, and their assigned load. Figure 14-16 shows a long-term measurement of a file system which had actually been balanced. The test was designed so that $c \ll r, s$, so that the condition that the processes have high request rates was true. The imperfect long-term distribution may not affect the short-time distribution greatly since it is likely that at busy periods the files were used in a randomly balanced pattern. The fact that a component does not carry its "fair" share all the time cannot be helped unless the system can be scheduled in a rigorous lockstep fashion.

Knowledge of disk, channel, and processor utilization based on machines using similar hardware and software architecture can provide further guidelines for prediction of realizable exploitation levels. If load imbalance, interference, or generally low productivity of a system is an issue of concern, operational data should be obtained for analysis.

It is obvious that adding more devices to a system does not increase the system capability in a linear fashion. it is, however, desirable to be able to have many processes available to utilize the available devices effectively.

We indicated earlier that queuing does increase the response time to requests.

Techniques to evaluate the effect of queuing and also the effect of more complex service request distributions on file systems are presented in Chap. 12.

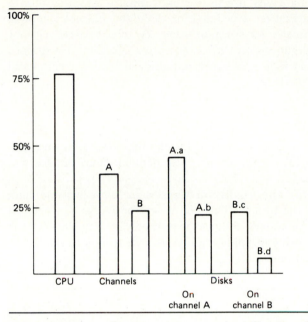

Figure 14-16   System measurement: utilization of components (data from an IBM VS evaluation).

APPLICATION OF INTERFERENCE EFFECTS   The productivity factors obtaine by considering interference can be used to correct the utilization of the multiple disks, controller, channel, and processor components, *comp*, initially estimated in Eq. 14-16. We first apply the productivity factor to all component types having multiple $(dev(comp))$ units.

$$up_{comp(i)} = \frac{uc_i}{Pc(pr, dev(comp))} \qquad \text{for} \qquad i = 1, \ldots, dev(comp) \qquad 14\text{-}19$$

Given the prediction of the imbalance of the load as distributed to the components, it is now possible to state conditions for each device type which are requisite for the system to operate satisfactorily,

$$up_{disk} < umax(dev_{disk})$$
$$up_{channel} < umax(dev_{channel}) \qquad 14\text{-}20$$
$$up_{processor} < umax(dev_{processor})$$

Here, much smaller margins apply than were needed in Eq. 14-3, since now inequalities of load distribution and the observed productivity is taken into account. If these conditions are not adequately met, a change to the hardware or to the file-system design has to be made and another iteration of the analysis is required.

The critical periods evaluated above occurred during daytime processing of transactions. It is still necessary to verify that other operations can be carried out when scheduled. It would be a pity if a user cannot inquire into a system in the morning because the reorganization, scheduled for the night, did not complete in time. The performance parameter for reorganization, T_Y, can be used without further modification. If the reorganization time is excessive, alternate file designs will have to be considered. In very large systems techniques which allow incremental reorganization may have to be used.

14-3-5 Cost versus Capacity

At some point an adequate system configuration for the expected load and performance has been found. The file organization is also defined. This process will typically take several iterations.

It is now necessary to verify the validity of the design for a low and high level of load to be expected in the future. This can reveal problems as shown in Fig. 14-17. For application S, the system design A is optimal; for application T, B is appropriate. At the average value of application U, design A is optimal, but it becomes prohibitive at the high point of the load range.

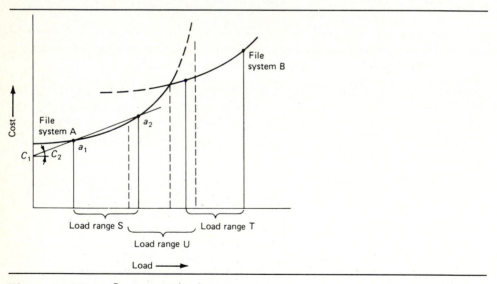

Figure 14-17   Cost versus load curves.

If we choose system A for application U, we will do well if the estimates of load are accurate or high. If the load grows, or the initial estimates were low, the conversion to another design has to be made. If this possibility is not foreseen, its occurrence will be embarrassing. If system B is chosen, the system operates at excessive cost until the load reaches the crossover point. The best alternative is to redesign the system so that effects of miscalculation or poor forecasting of the load will be neither fatal nor costly. The desired relationship had been achieved for applications S and T. The combinations of basic file methods and the selection of alternative hardware should make it possible to design a file system C equally appropriate for application U. The curves shown for file systems A and B are smooth representations of more realistic cost curves as presented in Fig. 10-2, which described storage system costs alone. This allows the cost of the system to be expressed in terms of the load placed on the system without getting bogged down in detailed discussion of hardware or implementation choices. Many of those choices are in fact best deferred until operational experience has been gathered. The presentation of a cost-versus-load curve will make observers aware of incremental costs and limits, and hence is more satisfactory than a statement such as, "Another million dollars will solve our problems".

It is desirable to express incremental cost within the range of the load. Figure 14-17 shows this being done for application S by drawing a line through points a_1 and a_2. The angle at C_2 provides the rate as cost per unit load. Now the costs can be presented as

$$cost = C_1 + C_2 \cdot load \qquad \text{between } \min(L_S) \text{ and } \max(L_S) \qquad 14\text{-}21$$

While this final performance summary is not directly relevant to system design, it is essential to provide management with the cost-to-load ratio which allows managers to make computer-acquisition decisions as effectively as they make decisions in other business areas.

We have employed some greatly simplifying transformations and assumptions. Some experience is required to judge their effects in specific cases. Simplifications, however, are in common use in any situation where the need exists to provide understandable models of complex *real-world* relationships.

14-4　SHARING OF FACILITIES

We have assumed in the analyses to this point that in the data-processing service being analyzed operation was the only user of the hardware facilities. This is rarely the case, although there are many instances where data-processing operations dominate. In a system where the major use is the service being analyzed, and especially in systems where file transactions have priority, the effect of the other tasks will be minor. It can be quite profitable to share the processing capability of a system with other users, who have lower priority, but who still will receive many computational cycles, since the typical on-line data-processing service has to have an excess of computational capability in order to be responsive. If the data storage units are shared, some interference may result.

If the data-processing service is not the major part of system operation, several assumptions made previously are not valid. We will now consider issues where sharing effects are significant.

PROCESSOR COMPETITION　In a heavily shared environment, the condition that $c < btt$ for the file operations will not guarantee that the file system will process sequential data without losing rotational latency because of other computational demands on the processor. Processor usage by tasks which are active at the same time will reduce the share of the processor available to the data-processing computation, so that conditions for continuous data transfer may not be met. This will double or triple the response time when using files as shown in Eqs. 3-22 to 3-24.

DISK COMPETITION   If there is active use of the same disk units by different computations, the probability of having to precede every READ sequence with a seek, s, will be high. In this case, a conservative estimate would associate every block fetch with a seek operation, greatly decreasing the expected performance due to decreased locality. In particular, Get-next operations and exhaustive searches may be affected. The advantages of certain file designs cannot be obtained under these conditions. Where separate disk units and channels are reserved for the data-processing function, the interference may be small. It may be profitable to reduce the degree of multiprogramming to achieve better utilization on specific tasks. This might actually increase the overall throughput.

MEASUREMENT   A pilot system which models the various file transactions within the existing computing environment can provide at a modest effort useful performance estimates. The performance data obtained will be compared with those expected in an isolated operation, which are derived theoretically. The ratio provides us with multiprogramming factors, M_h,

$$M_h = \frac{\text{Measured performance of } h}{\text{Computed performance of } h} \qquad\qquad 14\text{-}22$$

for each of the basic processes, h, which are part of the data-processing computations. These factors may range in practice from 1 to 0.1.

Such tests do not require the existence of the actual files. The pilot study consists of the execution of a proper sequence of random or sequential read or write operations, together with a comparable amount of CPU usage. A program to mimic the proposed operation can often be written and executed on the actual system to be used, at the cost of a few days of effort. The availability of the system is, of course, crucial, and the test has to be made during typical and high-usage periods of the system functions with which the data-processing service will be sharing the resources.

Such a test is not equivalent to a full simulation study, where all computations, as well as the hardware, have to be parameterized and simulated.

MULTIPROGRAMMING ALTERNATIVES   The data-processing application may itself require multiprogramming in order to serve multiple concurrent transactions. This is, for instance, the case if a number of terminals are used for update or retrieval. The operation of one terminal can affect all the others.

Transaction-oriented systems, as presented in Chap. 2, are organized to minimize multiprogramming losses. The strategy is to attempt to finish current transactions before initiating new, possibly conflicting, ones. A transaction in progress may have the privilege of reserving a disk device until the task is completed or until the task frees the disk voluntarily. A transaction computation performing an extensive search has to be programmed by a responsible rather than by a competitive programmer so the device will be yielded at regular intervals.

In multiprogramming and timesharing systems designed to support only scientific or engineering computations, no facilities may have been provided to hold disks to task completion, since their system objective is a fair distribution of capabilities rather than an overall system optimization. Here, measurement or a worst case evaluation is needed to establish the multiprogramming factor.

The initial system-design choices made in Sec. 14-3 have to be adjusted to bring the utilization parameters into acceptable ranges, so that:

$$up_h < M_h umax(dev_h) \qquad\qquad \text{14-23}$$

holds for all system components, h.

14-5   COST-BENEFIT COMPARISON

In the preceding section, we have given a general approach to the estimation of benefits, evaluated the storage costs, and verified that the computer system, or at least its file components, were adequate in terms of capability to handle the expected load. The latter analysis may have to be carried out repeatedly in order to achieve an acceptable solution. We now combine the results of these sections and present them in a fashion related to basic business-economic terms.

14-5-1 Revenue versus Cost

A business which sells consumer goods places a price on its goods and expects to receive an income directly proportional to the amount of sales. Such a revenue curve is shown in Fig. 14-18a. Only a business in a monopolistic position will not be able to increase revenues by increasing sales and will have to resort to other tactics to boost income.

At the same time, costs increase as production increases from a fixed basis at a zero production level. Some of this cost increase may be linear, that is, directly associated with quantity, as would be the cost incurred for supplies consumed in manufacturing. Other costs will increase less in proportion to quantity owing to efficiencies of mass production. The cost associated with sales will tend to increase somewhat faster with quantity since, after an initial demand is satisfied, more effort is required to obtain additional customers. A sample of cost curves is shown in Fig. 14-18b, and their total is presented in Fig. 14-18c.

From the revenue and cost curves, a profit and loss can be derived which shows the break-even quantity, and the volume where the maximum profit as obtained (Fig. 14-18d).

In the information-selling business, the projection of costs and revenues is based on system capability and utilization. While the cost estimation will be similar, the benefit evaluation of an information system is more complex. An understanding of relevant factors is necessary when we wish to appraise the viability of an information system.

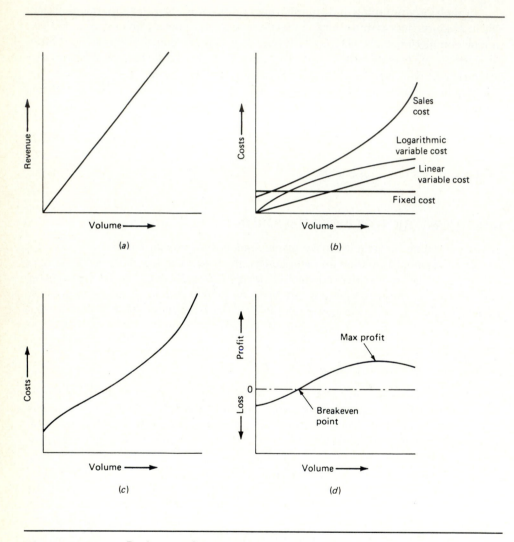

Figure 14-18   Basic manufacturing revenue and costs.

BENEFITS OF INFORMATION   We discussed in Sec. 14-1-2 the factors which control the realization of benefits. In order to relate benefits to costs, we can consider as factors the quantity of data available and the intensity of the use of the information. Figure 14-19 sketches some of these general considerations.

Information theory states that the information content of a nonredundant set of data increases exponentially with its quantity as shown in Fig. 14-19a. In practice, redundancy of information increases rapidly with volume. Once we have, for

instance, the production figures of a factory for a week we can judge annual output reasonably well. Frequently, statistics of relatively small samples can provide
adequate answers with high reliability.

We also have to take into account that users have prior knowledge, so that
much data has a negligible information value. Furthermore, we find that even as
our information increases, our ability to make improved decisions does not keep
pace. Most of the decisions made in enterprises are based on incomplete knowledge
and yet are appropriate to the general situation. This decrease in practical utility
has an effect, as shown in Fig. 14-19b.

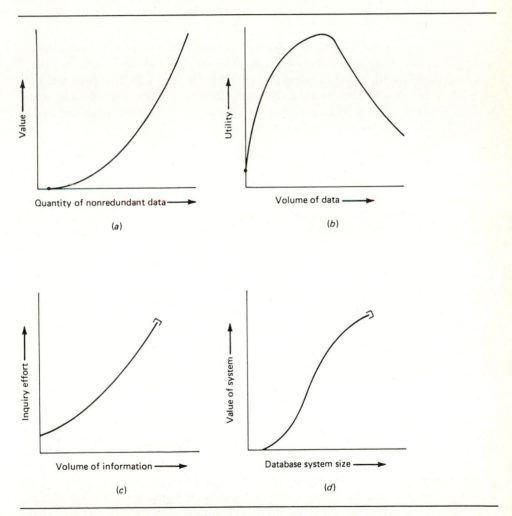

Figure 14-19   Benefits of information.

To extract any information out of the files, they have to be queried and processed. Extracting more information from the files requires more frequent or more
complex processing. The effort to retrieve information will increase more steeply

than the amount of applicable information obtained, as shown in Fig. 14-19c. The cost to process data is often proportional to $n \log n$, where n indicates the data volume being processed. When the value which is returned to users diminishes to the point where it is no longer an effective application of their effort and funds, they cease to inquire further.

When all these factors are combined and displayed relative to file size, the *revenue* curve may be of the form shown in Fig. 14-19d. The actual shape and the values will differ from application to application, but we notice the disparity between benefits from the sale of information and the sale of goods shown as Fig. 14-18a.

14-5-2 Costs

The cost of storage facilities is a major component of file-system cost. There are many instances where the potential value of data is less than the minimal cost of storage. Consequently, one will want to verify that we can afford to store the data we wish to process. In data storage there are often some economies of scale as was seen in Fig. 10-2. The marginal costs of additional storage can be obtained as Cm in Fig. 14-20, which presents the same data in smoothed form.

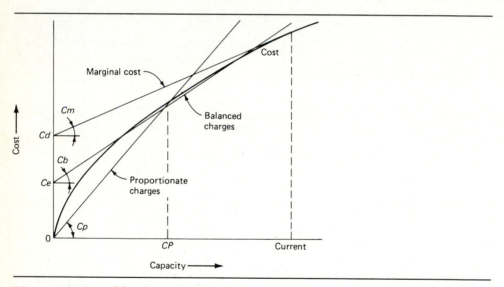

Figure 14-20   Marginal storage costs.

CHARGING FOR STORAGE   When marginal costs are used to justify expansion or new projects, the fact that a low charge based on marginal cost hides a large basic storage expense, Cd, must not be forgotten. If earlier projects are charged at a higher marginal cost for data storage, unhappiness is sure to arise. If the unhappiness causes earlier projects to stop or atrophy, then the marginal cost of the later projects increases so that charges have to be increased. Now everybody is unhappy. A charging rate, Cp, based on strictly proportionate rates does not reflect marginal costs well and leads to losses until the load exceeds capacity, CP, and to excessive profits thereafter. A desirable compromise can be a charging rate, Cb, which matches costs over a large fraction of the operating range. This will leave an amount, Ce, uncovered by storage charges, which will have to be obtained as a surcharge on data processing or data entry.

Companies which provide database services tend to use a balanced charging approach, since this encourages users to store data on their systems, which in turn will encourage data analysis. Companies which sell computer services tend to use the proportionate charging method, since they view file storage as an auxiliary service to the user which must pay its own way. Large files are rarely found on such systems.

COST OF PROCESSING   Processing costs for a given computer system have to be viewed in terms of performance. The addition of devices, such as channels and disks, increases the processing capability of a system, but the increase in capability is less than proportional. Increased interference, inability to distribute the load evenly, and dependence on specific critical components all combine to decrease performance beyond a certain usage volume.

Different systems may have different performance curves, but their shape will remain similar, as shown in Fig. 14-21. Systems B and C may have equal costs but differ in processing and storage access, so that B is better at a relatively low load, but C outperforms B at a high load. System A would be attractive only if the cost is so much less so that the performance difference does not matter.

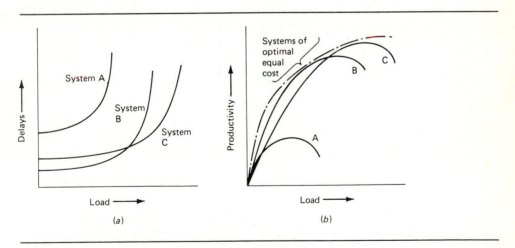

Figure 14-21   System performance versus load.

The difference in these systems leads to different productivity. Productivity is a measure of benefits obtained taking into account that the performance must be realizable (Sec. 14-2). The result is shown in Fig. 14-21b, which combines the effect of increased productivity in terms of requests processed, and the negative effects of poor system performance.

Since there are just about infinitely many systems of equal cost, such as B and C in the figures, then for every load a system could be chosen which would optimize productivity. The dashed line indicates the envelope describing the set of these *optimal systems*.

This information can also be presented on the basis of system cost for a given load. Cost-performance curves have been presented by measuring existing, rather than optimum, systems. It has been shown that the raw hardware (mainly CPU) performance increases steeply with cost. A rule of thumb, referred to as Grosch's law, has been that,

$$\text{Computer performance} = C_G \, \text{cost}^2 \qquad \text{where } C_G \text{ is some constant} \qquad \text{14-24}$$

and this rule has been verified on IBM equipment of the early 360 type using a variety of scientific problems (Solomon[66] and Knight[68]). There is, of course, the possibility that IBM used Grosch's law to determine its equipment prices, since it must be nearly impossible to relate prices to costs for a large integrated company. For data-processing operations, however, the same machines showed

$$\text{Data-processing performance} = C_G \, \text{cost}^{1.5} \qquad \text{14-25}$$

which still indicates advantages of scale, but to a lesser extent than is seen in scientific computation.

The rule is less applicable to file-oriented and interactive systems, since it does not account for interference or loss of productivity due to poor performance at the user terminal. In data-processing systems, raw CPU processing power only indirectly increases throughput. Since file capability is governed more by design decisions than by computer equipment performance alone, software and its implementation become increasingly important. Interference among multiple computations is another area not solved by more powerful hardware.

14-5-3 Summary

If we now combine the three elements, benefits, storage costs, and processing costs, and plot them only over the limited range of interest, we may generate cost-benefit lines as shown in Fig. 14-22.

When benefit and cost curves are similar in shape, the lines are relatively parallel. Parallel lines indicate that small errors in cost or benefit estimation will have a great effect on the range within which the system is profitable or effective. This example presents an undesirable but not unusual operation. Good documentation of the design effort and its parameters is essential, to effectively manipulate the outcomes represented by these curves.

In practice, the cost picture gets even more complex because of discounts, special deals, and peculiar amortization methods. From a technical point of view, these anomalies are best disregarded and left to the financial staff to be dealt with independently of the system design. It is rare that the benefit of *good deals* exceeds the long-range cost of suboptimal system design. To make such issues clear, the processing staff has to produce sensible and understandable numbers when they present their views.

Traditionally, many justifications seen for computer systems were not based on even approximate economic justifications. Today, when most decision-makers will have some familiarity with computer systems, it is no longer a valid assumption that the issues are too difficult to be presented in an understandable form. Proposals containing excessive technical mumbo-jumbo should be rejected.

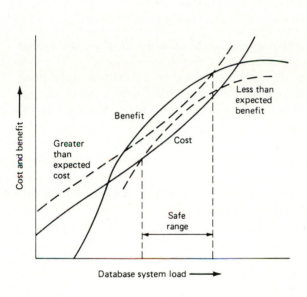

Figure 14-22   Total costs and benefits.

14-6   REVIEW OF FILE DESIGN

It should be obvious by now that the design of a file system which will perform to specifications is a task requiring some effort. Designers and users have to cooperate, because most of the assumptions about load and benefits have to come from the users, while cost figures come from the designers. Yet, the effort is worthwhile, because often years of implementation and data collection work have been lost because nobody analyzed a system prior to implementation, and when the system was completed, it worked so poorly that it was discontinued.

Let us summarize the global rules.

Cost ⇐ (load, design)
Benefits ⇐ (load, performance)
Performance ⇐ (load, design)

There is some circularity, but the load factor is central. If it is possible, it is best to determine the load based on operational parameters; otherwise one must consider the users' information benefit and access cost.

Heavily loaded systems can benefit from parallel operation
    of disks, controllers, channels, and processors;   but
the productivity of each device added is less than its predecessors.

Many parallel processes must be active to exploit the capabilities of parallel system components.

Design implies making reasonable choices that lead to a good balance of benefits, cost, and performance. In system design the people that collect, enter, and use the data must not be forgotten. Conserving the time of professional users requires special consideration.

Personnel costs are part of systems costs.

These costs are often much greater than the computer systems costs we deal with. Poor systems can drive these costs up greatly. Unfortunatly, there are limits in how much data-processing can reduce personnel costs.

There are two major phases in system design itself, here mainly exemplified by Chaps. 10 and 14, although the systems cost and benefits of transaction response time are covered in this chapter.

First, satisfy individual transactions.
Then optimize the aggregate system.

This distinction exists also in distributed design itself, so that, if needed, distribution is considered between the two central phases.

An important observation is that we do not, in general, attempt to *optimize file systems*. Optimization implies having one parameter, as *cost*, which when minimized, defines the absolutely best alternative. No such single parameter can be defined in large systems.

Design objective: a stable, easily maintained, easy to use, reliable system,
    which satisfies performance requirements at a competitive cost.

In all cases one must consider the risk of having poor estimates, and investigate the boundary conditions. Lowered risk can be a good trade-off for optimum system performance. Finally, always make sure that choices made are relevant to the users' objectives.

BACKGROUND AND REFERENCES

The process of system design, evaluation, and acquisition brings together people with technical, financial, and managerial orientation. In such a mixed environment, clarity of expression and measures which seem objective are important communication tools. Graphical presentation can often help to present expectations, but can also be used to hide simplified assumptions. Brooks[75] presents much insight and data regarding the design process. A basic reference on the economics of computers is Sharpe[69], Gotlieb[85] presents recent data. Davis[74], DeMarco[79], and Powers[84] present management-oriented approaches. Davis[82] introduces a number of papers oriented toward requirement analysis of enterprises.

Most implementation descriptions consider benefits and costs, but the data is often difficult to compare. Some references are cited in Chaps. 1, 9, and 10. Batteke[74] has details of a benefit evaluation in water management. Boyd[63] analyzes benefits in a manufacturing system, and Loo[71] describes the real-time needs for airlines. King[78] provides a survey of development trade-offs.

Wiking[71] and Lucas[73] prescribe the evaluation of information systems and Lucas[75] considers the feedback between user benefit, usage, and performance. Alford[77] considers real-time constraints. Sevcik[81] presents a layered technique of load modeling. Robey[82] defines the stages of system development. A language for expressing requirements is presented by Ross[77].

Human factors are cataloged by Martin[73]; an important study is Reisner[77]. The subject has its own journal (*Human Factors*), published by the Human Factors Society in Santa Monica, CA. Important background in this area is provided by Sterling[74,75]. A conference on the subject was sponsored by the National Bureau of Standards (Schneider[82]). The cost of errors is discussed by Stover[73]. Morey[82] considers those errors that are due to delays. Arden[75] contains a number of papers on operating-system aspects of interaction and provides a useful bibliography.

Cost estimates used for projections change rapidly with time. At times projections are incomplete, for instance, reductions in mass-storage costs are projected (Copeland[82]) but the studies do not consider what is happening to processing and software costs. The spread of small computers presents opportunities and problems (Dutta[82] and Hogan[87]).

The structure of file-system hardware is presented by Hellerman[73] and analyzed by Madnick[69]. A new architecture is proposed by Kitsuregawa[87]. The term *database performance* is commonly used in technical papers which actually only deal with the file issues of databases. Salem[86] and Kim[86] deal with parallel disk access. Teorey[78] analyzes parallelism of dissimilar components.

Formal procedures to select file structures have been developed by Schneider in King[75], Hammer[76], Yao[77], Katz[80], and Whang[84]. Waters[74] describes the decision points. Cardenas[84] surveys file design, access structures and analyzes multi-attribute use and selection for partial-match queries. Gambino[77] presents a model for multiring file design. Lowe[68] and Long[71] analyze text files.

Ramamoorthy[70], Arora[71], Parkin[74], Lum[75], and Trivedi[81] evaluate distribution over a hierarchy of components of differing performance, and Major[81] derives the complexity measure. Chu[69], Hoffer in Kerr[75], and Du[82] evaluate the optimal allocation of files to multiple components. Lin[82] considers disk allocation in a local network. Chen[73] and Piepmeier[75] provide optimization policies to balance the load distribution over multiple devices. Dearnley[74], Stocker[77], and Kollias[77], as well as Hammer[77], have done work on automatic optimization of file allocation. Marron[67] trades processing cost versus storage cost.

Interference problems are presented by Atwood[72] and analyzed by Omahen in Kerr[75].

Berelian in Merten[77] considers the effects of paging in a multifile database. Siler[76] and Baskett[76] provide results of straightforward evaluation models which show the limitations of benefits obtained by distributing files over multiple devices. Simulation results by Salza[83] verify the result. Sources of measurements are cited in Chapter 12.

Miller[70] has developed decision procedures for the acquisition of large computer systems. Applications of decision-analysis techniques are presented by Easton[73]; Keith in Cuadra[70] and Miyamoto in Kerr[75] evaluate systems in terms of information. King[81] addresses general evaluation issues. Grosch's law has been tested by Solomon[66] and Knight[68]. McFadden[78] summarizes cost and benefit issues.

EXERCISES

1   Using the manufacturer's description of a hardware file system, determine which class (Table 14-3) of file architecture it belongs to. Then evaluate the software system provided and see whether all the potential of the architecture is available.

2   Describe some of the costs and benefits of the *least* useful file system, including manual data collections, that you have encountered.

3   An inquiry system has 3000 daily requests into a direct file of 50 000 records, each of 250 bytes. When a record is brought into core storage it has to be available for an average of 5 seconds. The system is used 8 hours per day, 300 days per year. A 3330-type disk is used for the file. Determine the minimum-cost file design. Included are the hardware cost ($200/day), the disk storage, and the buffer memory.

4^p Determine the load for the three important transactions of your application. State all assumptions so that management can understand them.

5^p Using the results from Exercise 10-10 determine the total transaction time for each of your files. Also give the total demand for the computer system you have chosen. Assess if this demand requires a refinement of your analysis.

6^p Consider if the three chosen transactions represent tye majority of the load or if other transactions must be brought into the evaluation.

7 a^p Write an introduction for your project giving some conclusions about your application, arguing why the company should invest in it. Do a good *selling* job.

b   Write a critique of such a proposal from the point of view of someone who will be negatively affected in some sense by the system.

c   Now prepare an evaluation for management that lists the arguments for and against as fairly as possible, and then summarizes in management terms the decisions which have to be made by management to evaluate the proposal. Assume that you are a private consultant to management.

Chapter 15

File Security

"I have been misinformed".

Rick (when asked why he came to *take the waters* in Casablanca);
Played by Humphrey Bogart in *Casablanca*, Warner Bros. pictures, 1943

15-0 COMPONENTS OF SECURITY

This chapter reviews the components of security for file systems. The term *security* is used here to describe the protection of systems and their contents from destruction. The term is often used with a scope that varies from discussion to discussion. We will not cover the aspects of security which concern themselves with building and personnel security, although it is obvious that without physical security most computer-system oriented efforts can be brought to naught.

If we wish to secure a database, we will need to

1 Achieve a reliable and predictable mode of operation
2 Provide a protection mechanism to achieve the desired control of access to data
3 Ensure that there will be no destructive interference as users share access to files

The objectives of a file system are to provide quality information to its users. The concerns are well summarized by the statement

The truth, the whole truth and nothing but the truth

and the three topics address overlapping parts of this expectation.

The three issues of security are presented in Secs. 15-1, 15-2, and 15-3:

> *Reliability:* Improving the probability that the system does what it is instructed to do.
>
> *Protection:* Understanding, organizing, and controlling access to data in accordance with specified rights.
>
> *Integrity:* Maintaining of security in a system where multiple users are permitted to access the system and share the database.

There is clearly a strong interdependency among these areas: It is impossible to protect an unrelaible system. Integrity cannot be maintained if we cannot protect access. A system with poor integrity will contain unreliable data. We present the three topics in turn and close in Sec. 15-4 with the mechanisms an operating system may use to protect files.

15-1 RELIABILITY

Reliability is achieved when a computer system, both hardware and software, always produces correct results. One obvious problem is the determination of correctness. We use the term *fault* to denote the cause, and the word *error* for the manifestation of a fault. Lack of correctness is demonstrated by the occurrence of an error.

We start this section with a review of the issues, and in Sec. 15-1-1 define some concepts used to measure reliability. Hardware, programs, and data input mechanisms all contain faults. In Sec. 15-1-2 we discuss how hardware affects file reliability and in the remaining sections we present some techniques for achieving reliability in the presence of faults. These techniques complement the issues of redundant encodings, presented in Chap. 13-2. Finally, in Sec. 15-1-6 we discuss programming faults.

15-1-1 Concepts of Reliability

In order to produce correct results, we need correct data and correct algorithms, and the system has to carry out the algorithms correctly. In each of these areas the problem reduces to two subproblems:

1 The existence of a fault has to be detected, or the absence of faults has to be proven.

2 When an error is detected, a means of correcting and recovering from the error has to be available.

Frequently, a single technique may provide both detection and also some restoration capability.

FAILURE PROBABILIES   Computer systems are composed of many parts that are prone to failure. Success in avoiding errors for a given time period is achieved if no critical part fails. For q parts having each a failure probability of p_f, the probability of successful operation is

$$p_{success} = (1 - p_f)^q \qquad\qquad 15\text{-}1$$

We will look at the effects of failures using some simple numbers in Fig. 15-1.

MTBF Computer-system components have very high reliability. The failure rate of modern electronics is not greatly affected by the number of operations carried out, and hence is specified in terms of operational time. A typical *mean time between failures* (MTBF) for a highly loaded digital switching transistor is 100 000 hours. This time is equivalent to an error probability of only 0.000 010 per hour. A moderately large system containing and using 10 000 such components would, however, have a probability of only $0.999\,990^{10\,000} = 0.905$ of avoiding an error in an hour's span, which is equal to a MTBF of 10.5 hours. The error rate of components may be significantly reduced by conservative usage and a controlled environment. In practice, not all component errors will have a detectable effect in terms of the computer's results, since not all components are contributing to the operation of the computer at any one time, and hence are not actually in use. On highly loaded systems failure rates do increase.

If 10 parts, each with a probability of failure of 1% for a given operation, are used in a logically dependent arrangement, the probability of achieving the correct result is

$$p_{success} = 0.99^{10} = 0.904$$

which amounts to a failure probability of nearly 10%.
For 100 such parts, the probability of system operation decreases to

$$p_{success} = 0.99^{100} = 37\%$$

It should be noted that parallel electric circuits still have dependent failure characteristics. If one bit out of a 16-bit word is not transmitted correctly between storage and a device controller, the entire result is wrong.

Figure 15-1 Failure probabilities.

MTTR The time required to get a system going again is referred to as the *mean time to repair* (MTTR). In this context, repair can range from complete fault identification and correction to merely logging of the error occurrence and restarting of the system. The MTTR can be reduced by having a duplicated computer system. This means that more than twice the number of components have to be maintained, since additional components will be needed to connect the two systems. The trade-off between decreased MTBF due to system complexity and increased MTTR has to be carefully evaluated in any system where a high availability of data is desired.

AVAILABILITY The effect of dealing with faults as seen by the user is often measured as the *availability*, namely the fraction of time that the system is capable of production.

$$\text{Availability} = 1 - \frac{\text{Time for scheduled maintenance}}{\text{Scheduled maintenance interval}} - \frac{\text{MTTR}}{\text{MTBF}} \qquad 15\text{-}2$$

The availability measure does not include the aftereffects of failures to the user. Whenever a failure occurs, the effort expended on the current transactions is lost.

In an environment with long-running programs the cost of recovery increases substantially with a poor MTBF. In a transaction-oriented system, where transactions are short, the impact of a higher MTBF will be less. If users depend greatly on the system for running their businesses, a poor MTTR will be unacceptable.

15-1-2 Storage-System Failures

Mechanical parts of computer systems have higher error rates than electronics. Magnetic storage devices, communication lines, and data entry and output devices are quite prone to errors. Note, however, that human beings are essential elements of computer systems and show even higher error rates.

We can make one important observation about modern disk drives:

> A block will be written either completely or not be written at all.

The electrical and mechanical inertia in storage devices is sufficient to allow a write operation, once started, to finish completely and correctly. This means that, if blocks are properly managed, a high level of system reliability can be achieved.

FAILURE CONTROL   It is important to realize the continued existence of faults and to provide resources to cope with errors as well as to prevent errors. Early detection is needed to stop propagation of errors. For types of errors which occur frequently, automatic correction or recovery is required. Since the same error can be due to more than one fault, the proper recovery procedure may not be obvious.

Halting the entire file system whenever errors occur can have a very high cost, not only in terms of system unavailability but also in terms of confusion generated if the cause for a halt is not clear to everyone affected. In a chaotic environment, fixes and temporary patches are apt to endanger the database more than a reasonable and consistent error recovery algorithm. The formalization of error recovery also allows the application of lessons learned during failure situations, so that the fraction of cases for which the error recovery procedure is correct increases over time.

USE OF REPLICATED SYSTEMS   A duplicate computer facility can be used fully in parallel, or it can be used to provide backup only, and process less critical work up to the time a failure occurs. In the first case, the MTTR can be as small as the time that it takes to detect the error condition and disconnect the faulty computer.

In the second case, programs running in the backup computer will have to be discontinued, and the processing programs from the failing machine will have to be initiated at a proper point. Here, a larger MTTR can be expected; the MTTR in fact may be greater than the time it takes to reinitiate processing on the primary machine if the failures detected were transient. A failure-type analysis will be required to decide which of these two alternatives will be best. Making the decision itself may add to the MTTR.

With two machines which operate in parallel, recognition of a discrepancy of results detects the error but does not allow the system to determine automatically which of the duplicated units caused the error. Replication of systems or subsystems in triplicate, *triple modular redundancy* (TMR), has been used in unusually critical applications. This approach allows two computers to annul the output of the failing computer.

Since the cost of processors is dropping rapidly, replication of processing units is becoming more common, and some "*nonstop*" transaction systems are now being delivered with a minimum of 2 and up to 16 processors.

The space shuttle system uses four computers, so that TMR can be maintained even after a computer has failed. A fifth one is available as a spare. However, a shuttle mission underwent major delay when the fifth computer did not start in synchrony with the four primary computers, so that here the fault was in the additional software to make TMR possible.

Figure 15-2   Using triple modular redundancy.

In practice, many computer circuit failures are transient and will not repeat for a long time. Such errors may be due to a rare combination of the state of the system, power fluctuations, electrical noise, or accumulation of static electricity. Hence, a *retry* capability, replication of a process along the time axis, can provide many of the same benefits.

Complete system replication involves the architecture of the entire computer hardware and operating systems. Selective replication, however, can be employed in various ways by file and database systems. Typical hardware replication is the provision of extra disk units, tape drives, or controllers.

RECOVERY COMPONENTS   To realize the benefit of replicated components, possible failures and their effects must be considered. Those components which are used only to provide recovery capability should be isolated, so that their failures do not affect the productive operation of the entire system. Isolation will inprove the net MTBF.

Errors in recovery components should, however, generate a warning signal, so that repair action can be undertaken. A danger of automatic error correction is that errors signaling faults will be ignored until the fault is so serious that the automated procedure can no longer cope. Many major systems provide hardware logging mechanisms, and software for error recovery should also log its actions.

The repair response should be carefully and formally specified, taking into account the possible effects due to insufficient backup during the repair period. Where file integrity is more important than system availability, an immediate controlled shutdown may be in order. There is a tendency by computer operations staff to continue the provision of services, which they view as their major task, rather than initiate repair procedures to eliminate faults that seem not to affect current system operations.

15-1-3 Redundancy of Data

Instead of duplicating entire storage systems, we can write our data redundantly. Now complete duplication is not needed. Data elements are expanded to provide more information than is strictly necessary, and then be checked for internal consistency.

Adding a little information is adequate for detecting errors; with some more information we can repair correct errors. Several specific schemes were presented in Chap. 13-2. These techniques control errors more effectively than TMR schemes.

DUPLICATION   In Sec. 15-1-2 we considered replicating the hardware. We now consider some data-oriented schemes using duplication and redundancy to improve reliability.

Duplication of data is a simple form of achieving redundancy. It is used during input, in some tape systems, and in the storage of critical data. If the data is processed through different channels and then matched, the error-detection probability will be quite high.   To decide which copy to use for correction requires another indicator, for instance, a parity error. This approach is hence mainly effective for hardware faults; program faults will create the same error in both paths. The cost of duplicate entry and maintenance of data is, of course, quite high.

Duplication of data is used during one small interval of the information-processing cycle when entered data is verified. Data keyed in once is reentered and compared during reentry to verify absence of errors. To avoid errors due to mis-reading the second pass is performed by another person. The original document must remain available to arbitrate when an error is found.

Figure 15-3   Duplication during data entry.

When information is copied or transmitted, a duplicate will exist for some length of time. It can be useful to design the system so that this duplicate remains available until correctness of the copy has been verified. The detection of an error can be used to initiate recopying of the data. This technique is prevalent in the transmission of data over transmission lines. Not only is the vulnerability of data during transmission high, but the size of the damaged areas is frequently large. A reason for errors to occur in bursts is that data is transmitted serially, using separate clocks, one on each end, which are used to define the individual bit positions. A relatively long time will be required to resynchronize these clocks after a timing error.   Burst errors are also caused by transients induced when lines are being switched in the dial-telephone network.

Maintenance of complete duplicate files on disks is now becoming feasible on general-purpose computers. The cost of completely duplicated storage and of extra channel capacity may be excessive if one considers the current high reliability of computer storage devices.   Complete data redundancy also increases the time required for file update. Computer systems designed for *nonstop* operation have fully duplicated channels and controllers to avoid delays in writing to duplicated or mirrored disk units.

To achieve much of the reliability that a fully duplicated system can provide, a small amount of selected critical information may be replicated. In a file system, this may be the index information or the linkage between records. The damage due to loss of a data element can be expected to be minor compared with the effect of the loss of a pointer, which causes all data beyond a certain point to become unavailable. Selective replication will be combined with other error-detection mechanisms, perhaps parity, so that it can be determined which copy is the correct one. Then the erroneous file may be restored. In case of doubt the data file contents, rather than pointer information, will be used for correction.

In order to avoid some of the overhead that would be caused by writing indexes or pointer values into duplicate blocks, a copy of the information required to build the linkages may be written as a preface to the data records themselves. This practice avoids additional seek and rotational overhead times and only adds to the record transmission time and storage cost. Restoration of damaged indexes is now more expensive, since it involves analysis of the bulk of the data files. The larger MTTR is tolerable since such a recovery action should be an infrequent occurrence.

15-1-4 Error Compensation

Careful system design can reduce the effect of some errors. As an example we will show a case where data is acquired periodically.

The electric meter on a house is read every month. If a transcription error occurs, there may be an overbilling in one month, but next month, if the reading is entered correctly, there will be a compensating underbilling. There is, in fact, a duplicate memory here; one is the meter and the other is the computer file. If the meter were reset after each reading, a transcription error would not be compensated.

Figure 15-4   Error compensation.

Wherever errors are not compensated the data values can diverge from the real world. If an inventory is maintained using counts of items sold and items purchased, periodic verification is essential.

When errors are found, they should be corrected via *correcting transactions*; such transaction must be provided when a system is designed. If it is difficult to make corrections they will often not be made, or made after a great delay. Keeping errors too long in the files can lead to other errors, as users make decisions based on the erroneous information, and write their results to the files. If corrections must be made via non-routine procedures the danger of causing disasters is great.

15-1-5 Buffer Protection

File data is most vulnerable while it is in primary memory, especially where computer systems are used for many tasks or undergo frequent change.

Checksums taken of a buffer contents may be used to verify that data has not been changed by other than approved procedures. The maintenance and frequent recalculation of checksums can be quite costly.

Another alternative to protect buffers is the use of *barriers*. These consist of a pair of codes which are apt to occur infrequently. The buffer contents itself is not verified, but the barriers are matched at critical times. Such checks will prevent the use of buffers which have been damaged by overruns or overflows from other areas due to loop or limit code failures. Since a great fraction of programming errors are due to limit failures, and since these errors are not easily detected by their perpetrators, the use of check barriers can provide a fair amount of protection at low cost. No correction capability is provided.

A barrier value which is a very large negative integer, not a defined character code, not a normalized floating-point number, and not a computer instruction is depicted in Fig. 15-5.

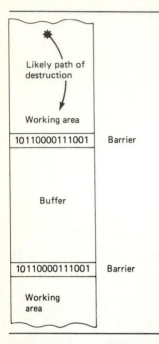

Figure 15-5   Buffer barriers.

15-1-6 Software Reliability

Errors created by program faults or *bugs* are familiar to us all.

Current methods of program debugging by testing are clearly inadequate, since they are limited to the verification of a few sample computations. Analysis of the program structure can create a test plan which ensures that each program section is executed once, but testing of every possible execution sequence is rarely feasible, since the number of combinations is nearly always too large. Extreme values of input data can often induce errors and are useful in testing.

The application of structured programming techniques can lead to a reduction and better identification of *bugs* but will still not eliminate them. Formal verification of programs attempts to eliminate faults. These techniques depend on a detailed specification of the data transforms, and here a comprehensive model of the intended computation is essential.

The modularity provided by *transactions* makes it more convenient to apply formal test and verification techniques. Since the programs are small, the complexity of analysis is reduced. The range of data that the transactions have to process is largely determined by the content of the files, and one can test the files separately to ensure that data is in the expected range or domain.

We will not discuss the important specific issue of program faults further but will concentrate on methods to deal with all kinds of faults found in processing data. Procedures of integrity monitoring (Sec. 15-3-3) can also help in the maintenance of data reliability.

15-2 PROTECTION OF PRIVACY

An important aspect of a secure system is that information, stored with the expectation that it will be kept confidential, will not be divulged. A correllary concern is that, when a request is made, the system will provide all the information, and that it will not be possible for intruders in the system to withhold information.

15-2-1 Components of the Protection Problem

Three types of elements combine to form the system which we use to discuss methods of protection:
1 The accessors
2 The type of access desired
3 The objects to be accessed

Each of these elements has to be properly identified in order to achieve control of access to data. It is also necessary to consider the *envelope*, or the boundary of the area within which the protection system is valid. Sections 15-2-2 to 15-2-5 will define these aspects one by one. This section will discuss various general topics in more detail.

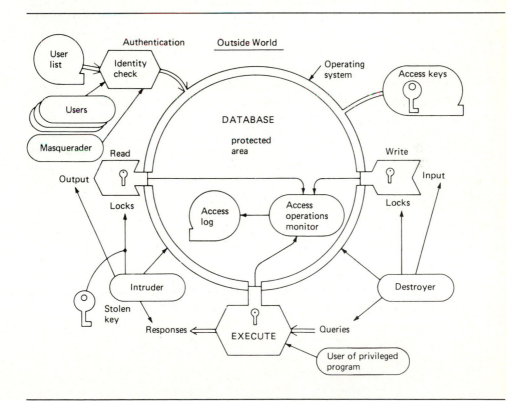

Figure 15-6   Elements of the protection problem.

DEFINITIONS   We define a number of terms to clarify subsequent discussion of the mechanisms for achieving protection:

1 **Envelope** There is an area with a well-defined perimeter which encloses the files to be protected.

2 **Users and Intruders** Within this area there may be active properly identified, *authenticated* or *valid users* , individuals masquerading as valid users, and intruders.

3 **Privileges** Related to an individual's identification are various privileges of data access. The description of privileges is maintained as part of the operating system.

4 **Scope** All data objects are protected to a specified extent while inside the envelope, and lose all system-provided protection when moved out of the area.

Protection, Privacy, and Secrecy   Protection of data provides control over the reading, writing, and use of the data, within the envelope according to the privileges assigned to the users. With adequate controls and specifications we can achieve privacy or secrecy. Many of the methods which we will discuss do not distinguish between the protection of data, the maintenance of privacy, and the assurance of secrecy. Secrecy is achieved when there is no unauthorized access at all to data. Adequate privacy may be achieved when data that is obtainable cannot be linked to specific individuals or cannot be used to impute facts about them. The final section of this chapter will discuss approaches to privacy protection that are supplemental to other protection methods.

VALUE OF PROTECTION   In the area of protection, there are cost considerations similar to those we encountered in our discussion of reliability. Protection of data is always limited. The more protection is implemented to reduce accidental and deliberate access violations, the higher the cost of the system will be. When the cost of protection exceeds the value of the data elements protected, we have reached a limit.

Table 15-1   Protection value of data elements.

	Deliberate	Accidental
Data revealed	Value of effect of information gain to intruder	Value of benefit of privacy of information to owner
Data withheld	Value of effect of information loss to withholder	Value of benefit of use of information to owner

The protection value of a data element can be determined by the benefit gained by a deliberate intruder or by the loss suffered by the owner in the case of an accidental disclosure. In the case of an inability to gain access to data, this value is again dependent on the gain obtained by the withholder or on the loss suffered by the accessor due to willful or erroneous omission of data.

The rules summarized in Table 15-1 are based on the assumptions that any deliberate attempts on privacy are limited by the potential payoff, but that accidental release of information is not so limited. If the manager of the database has the responsibility to maintain the data, costs will be incurred when damaged or lost data has to be replaced. We can assume that the cost the manager will have to bear is limited by the value of the data to the owner.

The substitution of dollars into these value categories may be awkward. Roblems of value measurement occur whenever decisions have to be made involving trade-offs between humanistic values, or utilities, and mechanical values, or costs. Interrogation techniques have been used to obtain quantitative measures of the value of a data item to its owner or to an intruder. By comparing the loss of items which have an assessable value with the loss felt due to a violation of privacy, an approximate value for data can be established. These techniques have been applied in a major study by the state of Illinois (IBM G320-1373[74]) during a project which demonstrated the use of a secure operating system, IBM RSS.

To establish the value of privacy of health information one could ask the question:

"Would you reveal for $5 000 to the public your record of alcoholism?"

For many people, this choice would be simple and affirmative; to some people, however, it would be negative unless the financial loss becomes too great.

Rather than using cash amounts that may be fictional one can impute cash values indirectly:

"Would you request credit to buy this automobile if it revealed
to the public your record of alcoholism?"

To give a value to privacy protection for the category of alcoholism information, the maximum value determined will have to be used.

Figure 15-7   Determining the value of privacy.

The relationship between the quantity of data items lost in a violation of privacy and the information loss may be highly nonlinear. In one instance, the loss of a single fact might be highly incriminating in one instance, and loss of additional data may not matter much afterward. In other cases, the more traditional assumptions that the information value increases with the number of data items released will be valid. The calculation of expected loss aggregates all types of risks and their probable costs for a given system approach. This then provides a basis to assess the cost-to-benefit ratio. In the study a loss reduction by a factor of 50 was feasible, but the optimum was at a factor of 30.

RESPONSIBILITY   It is not clear who, in a legal sense, is responsible for losses suffered because of violation of rules of protection of privacy. In many operations the reponsibility rests on top management, although specific areas may be delegated to data-processing management.

If programming is to be regarded as a professional activity, some responsibility will have to be borne by the members of the profession. The extent of responsibility eventually assigned to data processing and its management will depend on the public perception of the behavior of this group in the operation of database systems. The development of ethical standards for data-processing personnel is an ongoing concern for the professional societies.

COST OF PROTECTION   To achieve protection there will be costs to create physical security (building, personnel supervision), costs to develop adequate software, and increased operational cost. We will consider here mainly the operational cost.

The cost of providing operational protection is high in traditional computers because computer hardware design has stressed capability and efficiency rather than protection. This preoccupation has had the result that costly software mechanisms are required to implement even marginal levels of security.

An example of lack of protection is the degree of accessing freedom accorded to operating systems. Processes executed by the operating system kernel often have unlimited accessing privileges so that they can control other processes efficiently.

Since resource control is a responsibility of the operating system, many services for users' computations are performed by the operating system. In systems where kernel and service routines are not separated, a very wide path of information flow exists between protected and unprotected areas. Such a path may be misused through interspersion of inappropriate information into the stream of data. To protect this path, many validation procedures are required, measurably reducing computer performance. The complexity of the protection mechanism causes unreliability without assuring *confinement* of a malicious and knowledgeable intruder.

The value of adequate protection in commercial systems has been estimated at 10 to 20% of basic data-processing cost. One experiment within RSS caused an increase of 4.2% in file access cost but also limited flexibility and sharing. The total cost of implementation of a truly secure database is today larger by an order of magnitude than its benefit, since it requires development of substitute system programs and the training of personnel to monitor operations. Additional equipment may be needed for redundancy and logging.

Protection of privacy and system security have now been recognized as important concerns, so that we can expect that new systems will be designed with better support for protection. The cost to the user should then become less so that the benefits of a reasonable protection level outweigh the costs.

15-2-2 The Accessor

The external identification of accessors is primarily the name, as entered by them into the system. An accessor may also be identified by a *password*, which has to be typed in on request, or perhaps by a machine-readable key or badge. Methods have been proposed and tested which depend on the biological uniqueness of human beings. Manifestations of this unique coding of individuals are voice prints, fingerprints, and signatures. The database system, as defined here, will not be responsible for the primary decoding and validation or *authentication* of the presented information. Since access to operating-system services is a prerequisite for use of the database, the authentication task is left to modules of the operating system. The method used for authentication of an individual's identification depends very much on the technology available in a specific instance. The authentication subsystem will present to the database system a string of bits which we will consider the access key. This module has to prevent a *masquerader* from obtaining a key. All authorization and privileges given to accessors will depend on the access key.

KEYS To assure that access keys are not available to unauthorized accessors, the *individual's identification* has to be very difficult to mimic or copy. While an individual's name may be unique, this name is easy to mimic by anyone who can observe those who have access to the system, and is hence not suitable for a key. Once a system provided key is obtained, this access key is used to enter the database system from the operating system. The responsibility for manipulating the key rests with both the accessor and the operating system.

Additional parameters may be added to authenticate the accessor more completely: location, time-of-day, etc. The database system proper may remain relatively innocent of these further specifications, since these will be translated into separate access keys; the number of valid access keys may become much greater.

Passwords To protect the process of obtaining a key the system, when the user logs in, requests a password with the user's name. The password is entered without displaying it to protect it from observers. The password will generally consist of a few letters, chosen by the user. A trial-and-error method of entering possible passwords could be used by an intruder to gain access. The time required to carry out a systematic trial is the principal discouragement to potential intruders. The expected time to open a specific lock without any prior knowledge is

$$T(\text{getin}) = \tfrac{1}{2}c^d\, t(\text{try}) \qquad\qquad 15\text{-}3$$

where c^d is the number of possible combinations and $t(\text{try})$ the time required to try a combination. For a three-letter password, let $d = 3$ and $c = 26$ and the time for the interaction with the system be $t(\text{try}) = 3\text{s}$, then $T(\text{getin}) \approx 7$ h. If the authentication process is required only infrequently, an artificial delay in the opening process can increase the safety of the lock. An equivalent method is to allow only two or three attempts to enter a password. An intruder then has to go again through a full access procedure, maybe requiring about 20 seconds. The procedure can be more strict for access to critical data. When the security-control officer using RSS fails twice to provide the password to the security system itself correctly, the entire computer system is shut down. Extending the length of the password and hence number of combinations is the other alternative to increase safety.

A practical problem is that long passwords are harder to remember and will be frequently written down; another problem is that passwords are frequently chosen to be initials, middle names, friends' names, or other *aides-mémoire* and hence are easily guessed. Some systems require nonalphabetic characters in one's password to discourage obvious words. In order to establish legal responsibility, the accessors who have received a password giving them valuable privileges may be required to sign an agreement to keep the password confidential, and to promptly report any suspected loss of confidentiality. A frequent change of passwords can help limit the improper use of leaked passwords. Changing passwords puts an additional burden on users unless they are equipped with some automatic password generator which is matched by the receiving system. If we invent such a device, we also will have to protect its use.

▦▦ **Active Authentication**   Methods beyond passwords are available if increased protection is desired. An *active authentication* procedure is provided by NCSS. A user can place an interrogation routine in the system which requests parameters during the authentication process. The major benefit is that tapping the communication line will not reveal the password.

When the accessor logs into the system it presents a number. The accessor is expected to multiply the number by 3 and add 12 and enter it. This procedure is the "password" the user has to remember.

Figure 15-8   Active authentication.   ▦▦

▦▦ **Keycards**   Authentication methods based on keycards, badges, and so on can positively identify the card and hence the accessor, unless the card is copied, lost, or stolen. A card in combination with a password can be very effective and is used for banking transactions.   ▦▦

▦▦ **MOLES**   An individual who has valid access to the system may, after initial entry, use the identification key to gain access to inappropriate privileges. An accessor may also be defined as a member of two projects. Combining the access rights of two projects may give unexpected capabilities to such a user. These problems require careful management of access privileges.

The existence of masquerading intruders may be determined a posteriori by reporting all access attempts in a given period to the owner of a file. To achieve faster detection, the file user can be informed on every access of the date, time, and a sequence number of the previous access.   ▦▦

CLASS ACCESS   Up to this point, we have characterized the accessor as an individual. Sometimes access authority is given to classes of individuals. Clerical personnel, for instance, may not be individually identified. Authentication by class is not very secure, since there is no individual responsibility.

PROGRAMS AS ACCESSORS   Among the additional accessor attributes to be considered is the *program or process* that is used to access the data. There may be protected programs that are maintained and controlled by one set of accessors, and used by others. Use of such a program may confer unto the user some of the privileges accorded to the controller of such programs. The transfer of privilege is appropriate if the program acts as a filter of the information. Typical of such filters are programs which perform statistical analysis on data. A program which reads data from a set or subset of records and produces only an average of the data performs such a filtering function. The average value may well be appropriate for a general audience, whereas the details of the data are confidential. This program should refuse to produce a result if the number of records selected to provide data for the resulting average is so small that the result can be associated with an individual data record.

A query by a clerk of the United Tamale Company to obtain 'the average salary of all employees with a Beverly Hills zipcode in their address' gives, in effect, the salary of the president of the company.

Figure 15-9   Statistical protection violation.

The concerns of *statistical access* to individual records arise mainly in the maintenance of larger demographic databases, such as health records or census data. It remains possible that, through multiple intersecting queries, some confidential information can be inferred. The result obtained directly by the query of Fig. 15-9 can also be obtained from the average salary of all employees and the average of all employees who do not live in Beverly Hills. Having a file on which all transactions are logged provides at least an ex post facto audit trail for such access attempts. We will discuss in Sec. 15-2-4 other aspects associated with programs as accessors.

ACCESS PARAMETERS   The *location* of the accessor or, more precisely, the destination where the results are to be returned, can be another parameter of the access description. Confidential data is not to be shipped into areas that are not secure. The location also may define the type of device. Access to a check- or ticket-writing device may be made especially secure.

Sometimes it may not be desirable that a permanent paper record be created which should cause later confusion. An example might be an unverified clinical test result that is made available on a display to aid in quick diagnosis but should not become part of the permanent medical record. It may be more advisable to identify such preliminary information specifically rather than to devise separate access keys for hard and soft devices.

The *time and day* of access may be a necessary adjunct to the destination parameter in the accessor description. A location may be considered secure only during normal office hours. There also may be a time component to the value of data, so that data of a certain age may be more liberally accessible than very current information.

The *frequency* with which an element is accessed may be of concern. A sales total may be requested quarterly for the public stockholders' report; the same value produced every hour could be correlated with specific sales activity which a company might wish to keep confidential. An unusually high access frequency would generally indicate an unusual situation and possibly reveal foul play.

ACCESS KEY MANAGEMENT   To lessen the possibility of theft within the system of accessor keys, a transformation which is not uniquely reversible can be applied to the keys. Within the system only the transformed keys are stored and used for access privilege verification, so that the original key is visible within the system only for a short time. The hashing techniques discussed in Chap. 6-1 provide this type of transformation.

The full number of access keys could be as large as:

$$\#(\text{accesskeys}) = \#(\text{individuals}) \times \#(\text{access procedures})$$
$$\times \#(\text{distinct devices or locations}) \times \#(\text{time categories}) \qquad 15\text{-}4$$
$$\times \#(\text{frequency categories})$$

We will discuss in Sec. 15-4-1 methods which can be used to map this set of access keys into a more manageable set of accessor categories or *cliques*.

15-2-3 Types of Data Access

Accesses to data can be categorized by type. Distinctions are commonly made between authorization to read and authorization to write data. Magnetic-tape reels, cartridges, and some disks have inserts which, when removed, make writing physically impossible. Some disk drives have write-protect switches. Many shared operating systems have added an execute-only privilege. Here one can allow an accessor to use a program without allowing reading or copying the program. Such a facility provides a protection for the products of programmers. The execute-only privilege may in turn protect the data used by a protected program, since its access mechanism and identification key are hidden.

Computer systems limited to these three types of authorization still provide fairly unsatisfactory protection. The procedures which are part of the operating system are in general authorized to read or write anything, anywhere, and could not function if this privilege were removed. The read privilege is frequently available to any user and only a knowledge of the structure of another user's data is required to gain access. Various systems have implemented additional protection privileges. We will not survey these in detail but rather will summarize implemented and suggested types of access categories below.

SEVEN ACCESS TYPES   We now present seven distinct access privilege types which in combination allow many choices of control of protection.

1 **READ** access grants the privilege of copying data into the accessor's environment. Once the data is copied, the copy can be manipulated by the accessors as they please.

2 **EXECUTE** access grants the privilege of use of a program or a procedure. The text of the procedure and data read by the procedure are not made available, nor can the program be modified without additional privileges. The **EXECUTE** privilege can protect programs which in turn control statistical access to data.

3 **CHANGE** access provides the accessor with the conventional write access. This access privilege provides capability to destroy stored data.

4 **DELETE** privileges allow destruction of the contents of a data object and also destroys the access path. With the loss of an access path you can no longer determine that the data object existed. This privilege is closely related to write access.

5 **EXTEND** access allows appending data to a file without having the capability to destroy other data in the file and without the privilege to read previous stored

data unless those privileges also were conferred. A file protected in that way will only grow.

6 MOVE access provides the capability to move data fields without the privilege of reading or changing their contents.

7 EXISTENCE VERIFICATION completes the set of privilege types to be considered. Without this privilege an accessor cannot determine if an object, for example, a specific record or an attribute value, exists.

Interaction among Privileges   The use of the EXECUTE privilege gives the users controlled READ access to data otherwise not accessable.

CHANGE access allows destruction of data. It is not clear whether the fine distinction between the CHANGE and DELETE access types is worth it, but a DELETE access causes a change of file size; for this reason it may be desirable to distinguish these privileges. In view of the EXTEND privilege, the CHANGE privilege may be restricted to the updating or changing of existing data items. Files where EXTEND access is appropriate are the files containing system accounting data or audit trails. Many data-entry operations are also EXTEND-only. In many systems WRITE privileges combine CHANGE and EXTEND.

The MOVE privilege describes a concept which is not commonly available. Its desirability is motivated by observing many operations within computing and data-processing systems involve movement of passive data elements associated with key data elements. In order to make decisions, the key has to be read, and READ access to the key has to be granted. But the need to read the key does not imply that all associated data should be available to the moving process.

Specific examples where the MOVE privilege is appropriate and adequate for the tasks can be found in many operating system functions. The movement of users' data to output buffers for blocking as well as the movement of data pages in virtual memory systems requires only move access. The transposition program in Chap. 9-1 has no need to ever READ the data. In user application such as banking, public utility, and medical data processing, records are often sorted and moved based on identification keys. The fact that the programmer who writes the programs that move the data also obtains read and write privileges has aided both intentional fraud and unintentional alteration of other data fields. Not all such errors can be prevented by MOVE constraints but the additional detection capability obtained will help minimize problems.

The MOVE privilege can also be used to reallocate data within a *hierarchy* of high- or low-performance devices to optimize overall system performance. System *tuning* is frequently aided by outside specialists who should not need READ access to data to carry out their business.

EXISTENCE VERIFICATION access may similarily be granted without READ access. It frequently is necessary to determine whether a specific data element exists, leading to decisions to EXECUTE further programs. A program to which this privilege has not been granted cannot even determine the existence of the record. For instance, a program constructing an index of records has a valid need to determine existence and location of a record, and other programs will MOVE and READ the data.

There is a need for two distinct alternate responses for lack of EXISTENCE

VERIFICATION or READ privileges, as shown in Fig. 15-10. In many implementations, the EXISTENCE VERIFICATION gives the privilege of using access paths or indexes to the data, as discussed in Sec 15-2-4.

An intruder who attempts to read a psychiatric record of an individual might receive the message 'No such record' if the person does not have a psychiatric record. If there exists such a record, the intruder who does not possess read privileges would be denied access to the information and might receive a message from the computer stating 'Improper access request'. These innocuous responses actually provide valuable information. Lack of existence verification privilege would result in a message 'Thou shalt not attempt to look for such data'.

Figure 15-10   Inferring existence of a psychiatric health record.

IMPLEMENTATION   The privileges given can be conveniently coded by single bit indicators; for example, '0' disallowing and '1' granting access. The seven distinct access types recognized above provide $2^7 = 128$ combinations as shown in Table 15-2.

Table 15-2   Bit assignment for a protection key byte.

Bit 0	Key byte itself is valid
Bit 1	READ access is granted
Bit 2	EXECUTE access is granted
Bit 3	CHANGE access is granted
Bit 4	DELETE access is granted
Bit 5	EXTEND access is granted
Bit 6	MOVE access is granted
Bit 7	EXISTENCE VERIFICATION access is granted

It is probable that the no-access code ('10000000') and the all-access code ('11111111') combinations will occur most frequently. System programs will refer to users' data with '10000011'. Access keys themselves can be manipulated with this protection level. The validity bit provides safety during manipulation. An understanding of the combinations that these access types provide is necessary in order to be able to specify the access level of a data object for an accessor.

15-2-4 The Objects to Be Locked

The data space, addressed by an accessor for a specific type of access, contains the objects to be provided or defended. Various types of such objects can be distinguished: *data objects*, *access paths*, and *transaction programs*. Each of these objects can have multiple versions over time. We will discuss all of these in turn.

DATA   First of all, there are the recorded facts themselves. A fact becomes interesting to the accessor only when it is bound to a set of attributes which will identify it so that the fact can be related to a real-world person or object. These attributes may have been used as the access path to the element, and hence may be known. On the other hand, there is little probability that a random exposure of a single data field will do much harm. If it could, we should not allow visitors to our computer installation to take a photograph of the console of the shiny machine with its lights displaying some current value of some object.

The size of an object is of greater concern. It is very conceivable that each element of a record has a distinct usage, so that accessor and access type should be specified for one element alone. More practical is that identical access constraints are assigned to all attribute values of the same attribute.

Gathering attribute types which have common access constraints, for example, `street address` and `city`, creates protection segments. In many systems segments defined for protection and record segments defined for manipulation have to be identical. Other systems limit protection boundaries to records, so that the entire file is the data object to be protected.

ACCESS PATHS   In addition to the data elements which represent data values, there are elements in the files organization which indicate relationships and which appear as pointers in the files. Other pointers exist in indexes to the data. These pointers present a separate class of objects to be locked. In many instances there is the need for distinct protection privileges for pointers to objects and for the value of objects.

Let us consider some instances:

1 A data entry has to be updated: The pointer is read, but the data is read and rewritten.
2 A survey wants to know the number of alcoholics on the staff but should not be able to determine who they are. The pointer is read and counted if valid; the data is not accessible.
3 A file-maintenance program reorganizes the file; new pointers are created and written, but the data is only to be moved and is supposedly of no interest to the writer or executor of this task.

In each of the three examples of access to data via a path using pointers, it seems desirable to protect the pointers to a different degree than the data itself.

There is some conceptual overlap between pointers as protection objects and the availability of existence verification as an access type. Complete omission of either may, however, leave some gaps in a protection system.

PROGRAMS   Programs are also objects which already have generated a need for a specific protection type. Since programs can be active elements in a data-processing system, their protection is of equal concern. Where protection for data is reasonably complete, programs, if put under the same rules, also will be protected. The classification of data objects as records with attributes, however, does not apply. The existence of program text has to be specifically recognized. The other aspect of a program, that of an active accessor, was discussed in Sec. 15-2-1. Programs will have to be treated as distinct names units if use of a specific program can convey extended access privileges.

Age   The age of a data object may be of concern in the assignment of access privileges. Data looses information value over time and can be made more generally available outside the system. There are some opposite circumstances where information should no longer be available after a legal statutory time limit, in order to protect individuals from continuing embarrassment or damage.

SUMMARY   The number of data objects that are candidates for protection is the sum of the counts of the object categories (data, access paths, programs) multiplied by a number of time-division categories. Section 15-4-1 discusses how to deal with this large number.

15-2-5 Envelope of Protection

Since file services are an integral part of computer-system facilities, we cannot limit protection consideration to the file system alone, and yet there will be an area beyond which the responsibility for protection is no longer in the hand of the file system. The definition of the *envelope* where protection is maintained is frequently neglected. The omission of a statement defining the envelope, coupled with specifications of the security designed into the internal operation of the system, can easily be misleading. Users of computing systems may be only too willing to believe that adequate protection exists.

PROTECTION-SYSTEM COMPONENTS   Assessment of protection includes the operating system, the input and output subsystems, and the authentication subsystem, as well as the staff involved in the operation. In the ideal case, we can protect the database as a separate unit. If the operating system is included, there is likely to be a lower reliability because of the large part counts and greater number of accessors. The state of security provisions in existing computer systems is such that genuinely secret work is carried out on unshared computers, and in protected buildings, by checked and bonded personnel.

We assume throughout that the database is accessed only through the database or through a file system which recognizes the protection boundaries. In systems where no transaction-log is part of the system, backup files will be created by using *utility* programs which often ignore protection conventions. The backup tapes as well as output from unauthorized execution of utility programs provide convenient opportunities for the breach of protection boundaries.

An example of privacy leakage is the movement of medical record data to insurance carriers and beyond, where the data is used to determine eligibility for insurance coverage and to evaluate claims for health care services provided. An extensive study (Carrol[72]) has shown that this is one of the largest leaks of private information. This transfer proceeds directly from provider to insurance company and then to centralized reference files so that potential loss of privacy is hard to perceive by outsiders.

Another case of leakage is caused by law-enforcement support systems which service more than one state while these states operate under different legislative rules concerning privacy.

The multinational companies, frequently with centralized computing facilities, are difficult to control legally by courts of the countries where they do business and on whose citizens they may keep records.

Figure 15-11   Leakage of private information.

LOSS OF CONTROL OVER DATA   Another problem in the definition of the protection envelope is due to routine exchange of information. Figure 15-11 cites examples.

Rigorous definition of files, control of input and output, and identification of personnel entering the protected envelope are the most important tools currently available to prevent unauthorized access. Logging of all attempts, successful or not, to gain access helps in ex post facto analysis of violations. Genuine concern by management is needed to make the staff aware of the importance of protection.

RESPONSE TO VIOLATIONS   The action to be taken when a violation of the protection mechanism is detected has to be carefully considered.

Not everybody who attempts to access the wrong record has to be thrown instantly into jail. A large number of access violations are due to programmer debugging or inquiry clerk typing errors. A system that exhibits an excessively paranoid behavior is likely to frustrate legitimate use as well. On the other hand, there should be adequate logging of deviant access behavior to allow detection of illicit action and eventual entrapment of perpetrators.

It has been recommended that, with the current level of protection provided by data-processing systems, commercial firms employ one data-processing oriented auditor for every 10 to 20 programmers on the staff (Browne[79]). The high cost of such an approach, as well as the historic failures of auditors to detect glaring instances of computer abuse, should provide an impetus to make improvements in protection systems.

15-3   MAINTENANCE OF INTEGRITY

To get correct results, we need not only reliability and privacy protection, we need also correct data in our files. Low error rates and reasonable cost are essential to data processing. Error management is a wide-ranging subject and we will only indicate a few topics of concern.

1 Entering data as correctly as possible
2 Reducing errors due to programming
3 Monitoring to see that precautions have not failed

Monitoring can also help detect failures due to failures of reliability and destruction of data by intruders.

15-3-1 Data Entry and Feedback

The transfer of source data into computer files for data processing still requires much human effort. Most conversion is performed during data entry. Human error detection can be greatly aided by interaction, selection of a limited number of choices, and playback of entered data.. It cannot be emphasized too much that the best quality control consists of frequent generation of useful output to the various levels of personnel involved in data collection, preparation, and entry. Neither mechanical means nor constant exhortations will keep the contents of a database at an acceptable level when the data is not used regularly.

It is especially important to assure correctness of data which will be stored for long periods of time. A failure in a file of historic data is frequently not correctable, since the source material will have turned to some functional equivalent of dust.

CODING DURING DATA ENTRY   Of particular importance for error reduction are the use of multiple-choice forms or display screens which allow nominal data to be selected as seen in Fig. 15-12. The code for the box checked is entered into the computer system.

The table to translate from code to the intended term has to match the presented form precisely. Since forms and displays change over time, it is desirable that the code does not represent the position of the entry on the form, but is translated into a code which can be maintained over time.

Self-coding forms or multiple-choice questionnaires are seen in most data-processing applications. Digits or arbitrary characters are entered into designated spaces, which correspond in size to available space in the file records. It is possible to generate prototype forms by using data from the data dictionary. This assures that data entered match the file specifications.

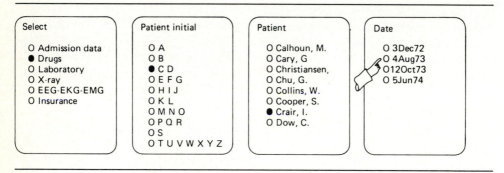

Figure 15-12   Screen selection for input.

15-3-2 Programming Integrity

Most systems allow the programmers to make decisions regarding the use of locks. Problems may be caused by having one individual make decisions which affect programs written by others. A system organization to prevent update interference can be achieved if:

1 The *access protection system* allows only one user, the owner of the data, to modify a protected object or to set a lock for the object.
2 The *access security system* allows only one instance of the user to exist.
3 The *file management system* locks objects which are synonymous with the objects identified for ownership by the access protection system.

The last condition is rarely true. Ownership is allocated to logical entities such as fields, records, files, and databases, whereas physical control is exercised over physical object such as blocks, tracks, files, and devices. If interference problems can be resolved only on the common file level, shared access to data is severely restricted. The rules outlined above do not solve read interference if query regions involve files of more than one user.

If the programmer is not restricted by the access system from potential interference with the activities of others, a higher level of control may be required. Update operations may be permitted only if a claim for exclusive access has preceded the operation. This removes the decision *to lock or not to lock* from the purview of the programmer, although it does not guarantee the locks will cover the correct region. Some systems automatically precede update operations with a claim which will lock the object being updated, but an additional claim facility is required to let the programmer claim regions containing multiple objects. For the sake of programming consistency explicit claims are desirable.

The programmer may decide not to lock on READ operations if the answer does not have to be guaranteed and must be rapid. The decision whether a read operation is of the *audit read* or *free read* type is local to a transaction and program. It is neccessary to let the end user know which choice was made when the results are being transmitted.

Not locking, a *free read*, will be adequate to obtain an estimate of say the total inventory at one location.
To make a sales commitment of a given item an *audit read* should be used.

Figure 15-13   Use of "free read" versus "audit read".

The general problem of assuring the integrity of databases has not been solved. An initial step is the definition of the application requirements by collecting semantic constraints.

15-3-3 Integrity Monitoring

Since a single error in the data can be gradually copied throughout a database, a strategy of regular monitoring of data on files is essential wherever long term data is kept. If results based on data stored for many years are in error, the user's confidence in all the work of past years is suddenly lost.

Monitoring is possible on two levels: structural and content-oriented.
1 *Structural monitoring* can be carried out by the file system without user participation.
2 *Content-oriented monitoring* requires the user to provide assertions regarding data relationships.

In either case monitoring is possible only if there is some redundancy in a database.

STRUCTURAL MONITORING   Structural monitoring is often conveniently combined with periodic dumping operations. One of the areas to be verified is storage allocation: All blocks in the domain of the system should be owned by only one user or belong to the free space list. Some systems may also have a pseudoowner for bad blocks — either physically damaged storage or blocks containing data which may be in error or are backup for data which may be in error.

Where pointers exist, their logic can be verified: Rings should form cycles, trees should not form cycles. Indexes should point only to their primary file. Where data is ordered the sequences can be verified. An entry in a key sequence which is out of order can make successor records unavailable or can make a binary search fail.

CONTENT MONITORING   Some data-checking processes can be driven using additional information about the data. The use of high and low limits and code validity is common. Data content summaries, presented graphically, can be helpful to users who have a certain expectation regarding data. Assertion statements, originally introduced for program verification, can also be used to verify the data values. Possible assertions are:

```
Department.salaries = SUM(Department.employee_salaries)
Apprentice.age < 30
COUNT(Children)  ≤ 12
Manager.salary > Employee.salary | Employee.manager=Manager.name
Employee.social_security_number  ≠ UNDEFINED
```

Figure 15-14   Integrity constraint assertions.

Assertions which are too restrictive will cause excessive inconsistency reports, so that some tuning may be required.

Since data conditions are apt to change frequently, it is desirable that a content monitoring process be table-driven by these statements. If continuous reprogramming is required, frustration will soon lead to disuse of integrity monitoring.

SUMMARY   The maintenance of data integrity is a major problem in any data-processing operation. Unless correct data is reliably available users will not depend on the data systems. If manual backup files are kept in operation by users because of distrust of the computer operation, few economic benefits can be obtained.

15-4   OPERATING SYSTEMS SUPPORT

The file systems must depend a great deal on the Operating Systems of the computers being used. Many good ideas to protect files and databases are actually futile, since most operating systems have minimal protection. Even when users' access is restricted, we find that on large systems there is internal staff and vendor personnel with nearly unconstrained access privileges. On personal workstations, only accessed remotely via formal message protocols, the security issues are more controllable.

15-4-1 Access Key Organization

In order to implement the protection requirements defined in Sec. 15-3, the protection requirements have to be categorized and organized. A three-dimensional access matrix which is the product of the number of accessors, the number of access types, and the number of data elements and links will be excessively large. The dimensions of the matrix can be reduced by grouping accessors into cliques and data elements into protection objects. The entries can be merged by merging the access privileges into a single protection key as shown in Table 15-2.

CLIQUES The effect of a large number of users can be reduced by establishing user categories or cliques. For example, all data entry personnel may be identified as a member of the same clique. Thus there will be a table which maps the individual user identification into a clique identification. A further reduction of number of cliques required is possible if an individual can be a member of more than one clique, since fewer special categories may be needed. On the other hand, unexpected privileges may be the result of multiple, concurrent clique memberships. To avoid this problem, an accessor may have to state the database area to which access is desired, so that only one clique membership is active at a time.

A clique-identification number is assigned internally. Once a clique member is authenticated, this number is hard to forge and will provide a better protection than user-identification keys. It may be desirable to periodically reauthenticate the submitters of clique-identification numbers. A monitoring process can check if the user's identification is appropriate for a legitimate member of the clique or would suggest that a stolen clique number exists. Clique numbers which have been compromised can be withdrawn and new numbers assigned.

DATA OBJECTS The organization of the protection objects depends greatly on the type of database control which is provided in the system. For an object to be protected, it has to be accessed through a *naming* mechanism. Objects on levels where actual addresses are used cannot be identified for protection.

FILES Virtual-memory systems (see Chap. 9-4) can provide a hardware definition of files through the use of named storage segments, so that protection is easier to enforce. In other cases files are defined by software and control information, obtained by the operating system when a file is opened. In either case, files are the smallest units which have symbolic names known to the operating system. The method used for file protection is always determined by the operating system. To identify files uniquely within a system, their names will be prefixed automatically by a qualification term, constructed from the user name.

Login:	NAME? Gio Wiederhold
	PROJECT? DataBase
	. . .
Execution:	. . .
	OPEN FILE(mine) UPDATE;
will define a file named	G_Wieder.DataBase.mine

Figure 15-15 User authentication and file names.

This method is augmented to enable users to access common system files and to enable sharing of files to the extent desired. To access files other than one's own is made possible by specifying the fully qualified names of files such as

SYSTEM.Library.Regression or JCOther.DataBase.Observations

The operating system can check whether Joe Carlos Other has given anybody, or specifically someone with the system name G_Wieder, the privilege to access his data. A list of authorized users can be kept with the file directory and will indicate the type of privilege accorded. Once READ access privilege has been given, the original user has lost control over the data, since the reader can again permit another reader to access the files.

A project name, such as DataBase used above, can be used to imply sharing of data files for all members of a project. A project becomes an external manifestation of a clique organization. A higher level of authorization can be required for access by users outside the project.

File systems can rarely provide much protection beyond the facilities of the operating system and the underlying hardware.

HARDWARE MECHANISMS   The services provided by computer systems can be considerably enhanced by hardware mechanisms which can limit access at the point of data-element fetch or store. Hardware mechanisms are based on matching a protected access key provided by a user with a key field associated with data storage. Two types of methods are in use.

RINGS   A hierarchical assignment of access privileges has been used in some systems. Figure 15-16 illustrates the concept of protection rings where the degree and type of access available depends on a level number assigned to the accessor. The concept models the basic military secrecy hierarchy shown at right.

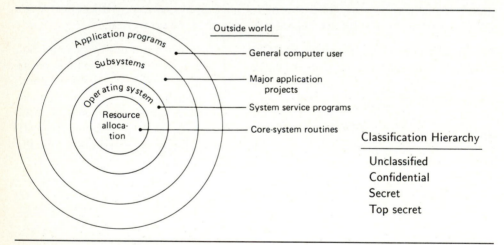

Figure 15-16   Protection rings.

In practice, only few levels are usable, since a single privacy hierarchy of data has to be established appropriate to all accessors. The MULTICS system (Graham[68]) associates ring privileges specifically with processes and storage segments. Systems with rings are effective in protecting operating systems and subsystems, and can contribute much to reliability. For data processing the hierarchical constraints of rings have to be combined with control over files, records, and access paths.

CAPABILITIES   An access privilege allocation not based on a predetermined hierarchy has been provided in so-called *capability-based computer systems*. Here the access control is provided through access keys which are shown and verified when data objects are accessed. Capabilities for access are initially given to a user when new objects are created. To prevent access keysfrom being copied or assembled by intruders, they are kept in a separate mechanism. To share data, the owner of the data can give an access key with selected capabilities to another user. To implement capability management in hardware, a machine architecture with virtual storage segments will be chosen.

SOFTWARE MECHANISMS   No hardware system provides protection adequate for all circumstances, so that operating systems carry much of the responsibility for file protection. We find the two approaches used for hardware mirrored in operating systems.

Common to all software mechanisms is the use of catalogs which relate accessors to file names. Granting any type of access to a combination of user and file will in operating systems provide access to all data in the file.

> Much implicit protection existed when access to computers was difficult. Now most people know how to use computers and many computers are available on nationwide networks. Today all protection must be explit.

USER-BASED ACCESS PRIVILEGE TABLES   Information concerning which files the user is permitted to access may be stored with the user's directory. The names of files which may be accessed by more than one user will appear in multiple directories; the entries will contain the access codes authorized by the user. The system has to protect these codes, so that users cannot change entries in their own directory.

Excessive duplication of file entries may be avoided by having a hierarchical file directory. An entry in the directory such as `Database` → `Database.Directory` can provide a link to a sharable subdirectory in which all the files associated with some project are entered. Multiple users with the same access privilege to the project files may have such a link and share the data. Locking mechanisms have to prevent interference. An extension of this concept was encountered in global file directories in distributed systems.

FILE-BASED ACCESS PRIVILEGE TABLES   Information concerning which files the user is permitted to access is stored with the files. The file directory of every file contains the names of all the users who are authorized to access the file. If many users are authorized to use a file, the list might become excessive.

By now organizing users with similar access privileges into a *clique*, those users can be authorized by having a single clique name in the file directory.

SUMMARY   We have reviewed in this section in a general sense the protection mechanisms available in operating systems. Operating systems are increasingly cognizant of the existence and needs of files and their protection.

15-5   REVIEW

We notice in the examples shown the interrelationship between protection methods and file system design. Such a feedback is difficult to avoid, and makes the design of secure systems an iterative undertaking.

INTEGRATION OF SECURITY PROCEDURES   Protection of privacy depends on reliable hardware and software performance. To avoid gaps in security protection system design and programming techniques must integrate procedures to protect users and gain system reliability.

A large multiuser on-line file system (Frey[71]) developed under management by the author operated for more than 6 years without loss of data stored on files. Control over reliability, security, and data integrity was achieved by integrating access, access protection, and backup. The granule for all operations was the block; fields could be protected only by encryption (Chap. 13-4). Periodic monitoring was performed to locate errors. Backup procedures provided manually initiated rollback.

Figure 15-17   Unit for integrating security management.

Continued integrity of external storage is essential for successful operation. In practical systems today, correctness of integrity protection mechanisms is impossible to prove. Many layers of hardware and software have to work without any faults to permit security protection mechanisms to guarantee their work. Many faults remain undetected for a long time; a histogram giving the rates of errors and fault detection can reveal the approximate fault state.

It remains important for a data-processing manager to review the available facilities and understand their weaknesses. Saltzer[75] has collected 10 principles to be considered in the analysis of protection systems.

1 **Economy of mechanism**: An excessively complex protection system does not allow verification of correctness and completeness.
2 **Fail-safe defaults**: If something goes wrong, access should be denied. Even conscientious users will not report unexpected access privileges.
3 **Complete mediation**: Every access path to the database has to go via the protection mechanism.
4 **Open design**: Protection is not enhanced by keeping the mechanism used for protection secret. A secret mechanism can also install an unwarranted level of faith in the users.
5 **Separation of privilege**: Critical data should be protected so that no single authorized user can subvert the mechanism.
6 **Least privilege**: A program should be granted only the essential access privilege.
7 **Least common mechanism**: Avoid all unnecessary sharing. This means do not mix sharable and private data in one file, and do not share computers with others only for the sake of economy.
9 **Work factor**: The effort to subvert the mechanism must be greater than the benefit which could be gained. The intruder will probably also have access to a computer so that he or she can exert much effort at little cost.
10 **Compromise recording**: Logging of accesses can create the audit trail necessary to correct problems and trap the perpetrators. Intruders into the innards of a system may, of course, be able to avoid creating a trail or can erase the evidence.

Where systems are found inadequate, the application designer may augment the facilities but should also provide to the users a realistic assessment of the available level of protection. If storage of critical data can be avoided, privacy protection is simplified. If the atmosphere of a data-processing operation is open, vandalism will be less of a problem. Since the objective of a database is to enable sharing of information, removal of barriers to sharing is important.

BACKGROUND AND REFERENCES

Basic issues of reliability and redundancy are presented in hardware textbooks, as cited with Chapter 3. After the programming systems stabilized, users began to trust them with large quantities of data, and demands of reliability became more stringent. Protection and integrity became a major concern with the development of multiuser systems, where one failure can impact dozens of users simultaneously, early contributions to understanding of the issues are by Ware[67] and Wilkes[72]. The occasional failures continue to have a major impact on users of files. The relationship of load and failure rates is convincingly demonstrated by Iyer[82].

Physical security is stressed in guidelines for federal installations (NBS[74]) and is an important aspect of an AFIPS sponsored report and checklist (Browne[79]). A major study was sponsored by IBM(G320-1370 TO 1376)[74] and contains many suggestions and experiences, as well as a very detailed bibliography, but does not provide a consistent model. Fernandez[81] provides a text.

TMR was already proposed by Von Neuman, today it is used in the space shuttle (Sklaroff[76]). Some of the other redundancy techniques mentioned were found in actual implementations of file systems, IBM's System R is surveyed by Gray[81]. The field of error-correcting codes is very well developed; the low cost of specialized processing chips makes this solution practical. A basic textbook is Peterson[72]; for recent references a collection of papers on coding theory, Berlekamp[74], may be consulted. Brown[70] presents the method used for tape-error control and Tang[69] covers decimal input checking schemes. Reliability measures for data input are stressed by Stover[73].

Westin[71] and Miller[71] survey historical and legal issues of privacy protection while Petersen[67] describes threats to computer security. Papers on abuse of privacy have been collected and analyzed (Parker[81]) at SRI International. VanTassel[72] also provides samples and guidelines. Carrol[72] shows how private data is used and misused. Many of the cases involve collusion and fraud; technical improvements to protect database access would not have prevented many of the abuses. An environment where reliability and protection is considered important might have discouraged many of the attempts. A professional code of ethics for computer professionals appears as part of a self-assessment procedure of the ACM in Weiss[82].

Two conferences sponsored by NBS (Renniger[74]) provide an overview of security and privacy concerns. Communication with a protected area is considered by Lampson[73]. Evans[74] and Purdy[74] decribe mechanisms to keep passwords secure.

The **MOVE** instruction is proposed by Lewin[69]. Hoffman[77] surveys access protection oriented toward privacy problems. Saltzer[75] provides a comprehensive summary of protection techniques in operating systems and includes a bibliography. Systems with protection features of interest are described by Weissman[69], Molho[70], Needham[72], Feustel[73], and Fabry[74].

Graham[68] presents an extensive model of accessors versus data objects and applies it to several systems. A simple model is formally analyzed by Harrison[76]. That the union of access privileges can be excessive is shown by Minsky[81]. The access model shown here was developed by a SHARE committee (Wiederhold[72]) as part of a requirements study.

MULTICS presents a major effort in the area of protection. Its development can be followed in Daley[65], Graham[68], Schroeder[72], and Saltzer[74]. Capabilities were introduced by Dennis[66], and used by Fabry[74] in 1967. Access privileges are also granted to other users in a method developed by Griffiths[76] and improved by Fagin[78].

Hoffman[71] protects data by procedures controlled by users. The accessor-object matrix is described by Conway[72]. How objects are managed is considered by Lindsay[79]. Friedman[70] defines cliques. How timing problems lead to constraint violations is discussed by Morey[82]. Frey[71] describes several structural verification techniques for a file system.

The TOD system by Wiederhold[75] includes schema directives for audit. Buneman[79] defines *alerters* to monitor the database. Eswaran in Kerr[75], Gray in Neuhold[76], and Chamberlin[76] specify integrity subsystems. In Andler[82], multiple processors are employed. Hammer in Kerr[75] and Stonebraker in King[75] apply integrity assertions at data entry time, but the concept is, of course, extendable to integrity monitoring. Lafue[82] considers the trade-off. Hammer[78] and Bernstein[80] improve the efficiency of integrity-monitoring schemes.

EXERCISES

1   A sign-on procedure consists of the entering of a name and the entering of a character password. Three trials at a password are allowed, and if no correct password is given, the accessor is logged off. Which provides more security: increasing the password from three to four characters or adding 1 minute to the logoff procedure? The following operational times are to be assumed:

$T(\text{name}) = 2$ s

$T(\text{password}) = 0.1$ s/character

$T(\text{response: "bad password"}) = 1$ s

$T(\text{basic logoff}) = 1$ s

Ninety-six different characters are allowed in the password.

2   Given the computer system you are currently using, investigate the types of access control available for user's data stored:

  a In primary memory

  b In secondary storage

3   How would you implement some of the access types listed in Sec. 15-2-3 that are not now available on the equipment you are currently using?

4   Rewrite the file-transposition program of Fig. 9-3 with a MOVE operation so that the privacy remains protected.

5^p For your application, define the cliques of users which will be using your files, and estimate the size of each clique. Then augment your data dictionary with by assigning for each data object or attribute one or more of the seven access types for each clique. If you have many attributes which have similar sets of access types it may be best to assign a protection category to each attribute and present the protection assignment as a clique-protection category matrix.

Chapter 16

Future Directions

The list could surely go on, and there is nothing more wonderful than a list, ...

Umberto Eco;
The Name of the Rose, After Nones.

16-0 OVERVIEW

In this final chapter we will summarize what has been covered, point out topics we have missed, and then provide a bridge for further study, specifically of database design, database management systems, and knowledge-based data management. In the final section we indicate where we expect file systems to undergo change, as the applications and settings of computers change in the future.

REVIEW   After defining the data-processing environment in Chap. 1, the operating system environment in Chap. 2, and the hardware in Chap. 3, we covered fundamental files, their combinations, and specialized files in Chaps. 4 to 9. This material was integrated into general storage system concerns in Chap. 10.

More specialized topics of file access were addressed in Chaps. 11, 12, and 13. In Chap. 14 the costs and benefits of entire file systems are evaluated. The security provided by file systems was addressed in Chap. 15.

PERFORMANCE ANALYSIS PRIOR TO IMPLEMENTATION   We have gone in this book beyond simply describing file systems. We have developed a characterization of hardware which permits us to deal consistently with a wide variety of devices. We have developed consistent measures of file performance which enable the evaluation of arbitrary file systems. Applying quantitative methods permits the evaluation of design alternatives for files and the suitability of the best designs for the tasks specified. Learning how to simplify the apparently complex systems is also an important result. Throughout we have developed an ability to weigh alternatives in system design.

Translating the descriptions to simple performance formulas provides the ability to predict performance. The predictions apply equally well to new file applications and new file structures. File design is a typical engineering activity:

1 Sketch out alternatives.
2 Evaluate the alternatives to the precision required for selection.
3 Refine the selected alternative.
4 Partition the problem if possible.
5 Iterate through steps 2, 3, and 4 until the design can be built with the confidence that it will perform as desired

Quantitative modeling of performance, before one actually builds the programs, is essential to engineering, but often omitted in programming. It is indeed possible to write simple programs without analysis, just as it is possible to whittle toys without planning. But, as applications require more investment before they are completed, planning and analysis become essential.

The analytic concept is important beyond file systems as well, and the quantitative techniques presented here will be applicable to software development in general. We see these engineering activities as an extension of the scientific process. The results of engineering activities, whether constructed from hard materials or composed of less tangible software, are added to our world. They can be observed and studied as natural phenomena are.

The Scientific Process
Collect observation relevant to the problem at hand.
Build a model which explains the observations.
When not all observations are explained, refine and start over.

The Engineering Process
Specify the desired behavior of an object.
Select reasonable building blocks and tools.
Use the model to evaluate which combinations produce the desired result.
Select the most effective combination of building blocks and tools.
Build it as well as possible.
Observe and monitor its behavior.

We have not stressed in this book the specification of complex application tasks. These require the interaction of multiple files, and such modeling belongs in the realm of database design itself.

The costs incurred in developing data-processing systems and supporting software systems are such that a thorough analysis is always warranted before implementation. It is rare that the costs of an analysis exceed 5% of systems; it is also rare that the cost of problems avoided is less than 25% of the system cost. Analysis prior to implementation is clearly very beneficial.

The results of such a performance analysis are not precise. We have made simplifying assumptions, and ignored interaction effects within the programs and due to other, parallel activities. This lack of precision does not make the analysis effort invalid. Frequently the predictions are within 20% of any measurements of results made after implementation; they are nearly always within a factor 2 of the outcome. That is much better than the alternative: guessing and hoping that the project will turn out successfully. If a series of quantitative estimates for a range of assumptions have been prepared trends will become clear as well. If the cost changes modestly with higher loads, then system growth can be well accomodated. The relative results produced by varying parameters tend to be quite accurate.

Defining systems, and the expectations of their performance prior to implementation also has intangible benefits. Clarification of the objectives and their trade-offs made in the design process helps people work together. In Sec. 16-1 we introduce some tools to help in design communication.

16-1   TOOLS FOR SYSTEM DESIGN

It is surprising that design of computer systems is often carried out without assistance by the computer. Even computer-aided design (CAD) systems are often designed and built today without systematic design tools. We are advocating here using tools whose use should precede the bulk of the programming effort. The programmer uses of course compilers, operating systems services, and subroutine libraries. Table 16-1 lists some design tools and their functions.

Table 16-1   Tools for developing data-processing systems.

1 Data dictionaries collect all information on data elements to be stored in the system files.
2 Database design tools help with the allocation of attributes to files, and the definition of linkages among related files.
3 Project management (PERT) charts permit not only scheduling of implementation tasks, but can also define the dependencies of transactions on each other. Systems using primary copies and derived data are especially dependent on correct execution sequences.
4 Spreadsheets can be used to predict the performance of proposed design and permit rapid assessment of the effect of proposed changes.
5 Simulations to predict system performance can elucidate complex relationships. This topic was addressed in Chap. 12-2.
6 Software design methodologies, with tools provided by consulting firms, help in the development of large programs.

In transaction-oriented systems the programs are typically small. Here the data dictionary and database design tools play an important role to help assure that all transactions treat the data consistently. The data dictionary is used by programmers as the prime documentation for writing the transaction and application programs.

16-1-1 Data Dictionaries

A data dictionary is a table listing for each data element the information needed to assure its correct use. We encountered some of the needed information already in Table 1-1 of Chap. 1-1-1, when we were defining data fields, and in Chap. 4-1-1, where file directories were described. Table 16-2 expands further on that list.

Table 16-2   Content of a data dictionary.

Data Attribute	Definition and Usage
Identifier	Short name used in programs and displays
Full name	A complete name to avoid ambiguity
Domain	Abstract data type
Range	Limits or list of permissible values
Representation	Format of data values, i.e., REAL, CHAR, etc.
Owner	Individual responsible for data values
Source file	Primary file for new data values
Secondary files*	Other files containing this data
Source program*	Program used to update these values
Use programs*	Programs using this data
Accessors, access type*	Users having access privilege
. . .	. . .
Comments	For anything not categorized above

these attributes have multiple entries

Data dictionaries have become critical to many large data-processing applications. A number of software packages are available to serve the need, and organizations have often standardized their content. Federal efforts at standardization are also in progress.

In practice data dictionaries are often not well maintained. Pressures to get programs finished, and then to go on to handle errors in old programs, often leave too little time to update the data dictionairies with the results of program additions and changes. An obsolete data dictionairy can of course cause further problems.

Advanced Roles for Data Dictionaries   A data dictionary lends itself to further expansion. More information can be brought into the dictionary, so that most of the documentation for the programs operating on the files is contained within the dictionary.

Some *business rules* may be incorporated into these data dictionairies. For instance, including in the **Range** specification for a `salary` attribute that its value may not be greater than the managers salary does not affect the file structure, but does control decisions made in the operation of the personnel department.

Data dictionaries for database design also contain constraints on the *relationships between files*. Important constraints are not permitting entries in the `Billing` file for customers that are not listed in a `Customer` file, or that have a poor `credit_rating`.

16-1-2 File Schemas

We can also let the dictionary be processed automatically. This requires, of course, quite rigid formatting and consistent encoding of all descriptions. Such a dictionary is called a *schema*. The use of a schema distinguishes database management systems from file systems. A system which manages multiple files, and has a schema is a database management system. We do find some file systems which already use schemas, or at least structures closely related to schemas.

An example of a file schema is provided by the record management system, RMS, for the DEC VAX VMS operating system. With the operations for (1) creating a file, (2) opening a file, and (3) closing a file, it specifies *parameter areas* which can be accessed to determine the structure of the file, as shown in Fig. 16-1.

---

1 The structure of the file
2 Naming of the file, including path names for distributed access
3 Record access specification
4 Disk allocation for the file
5 Dates to log creation, backup, revision, and expiration
6 Versions of the file
7 Key fields
8 Compression
9 Protection

Figure 16-1   Code blocks defined in RMS for file control.

Systems now in development extend such specifications to permit automation of linkages between programs and files. After all, it should not be necessary for a user to specify the format of the file to be read, this information can perfectly well be obtained by the program during compilation or linking, prior to execution. If the cost of schema processing is not critical, then the information can be interpreted during execution.

16-1-3 Data Engineering

Design methodologies which depend on data analysis are now circumscribed by the term *data engineering*. Data engineering provides in an important sense an alternative to traditional *software engineering* approaches. Rather than defining software by decomposing a procedural objective into its components, as is the dominant approach in software engineering, in data engineering we find an initial focus on the meaning and structure of the data. This focus is appropriate when data *persist* longer than programs.

Data engineering analysis proceeds also *top down*, first considering the meaning of data objects, their relationships to other data elements, and then their proper structure and representation. For each data element defined in the dictionary we analyze its dependencies on other values. Such dependencies may imply that the value must change when another value changes, so that we can define an *invariant expression*. These dependencies, and constraints we derive from them, represent knowledge about the data.

The steps by which data may become information is the next concern. These steps are initiated by defining the desired goal result attributes and checking backwards to resolve their dependencies. We must verify that all source data elements are available and timely.

If the system is to be event-driven rather than goal-driven, then a forward analysis is applicable. A mixed system may permit cost minimization: some file contents are derived based on changes in source values, and these are used for the computation of goal results. Notions employing derived data were already introduced with distributed files in Chap. 11-4-4.

Data engineering approaches to system design are motivated by several observations:

1 The data structure is more permanent than the program structure. New programs may be developed to use the data, and earlier programs may fall into disuse, but the organization of the data remains.
2 The use of small transactions modularizes and simplifies the programming effort, but the data becomes the medium which links all activities together.
3 The spread of distributed approaches emphasizes data issues, since data is shipped across the communication links, whereas programs remain bound to their sites.

In data-processing situations, where these observations are common, the use of data engineering methods is fundamentally better than a process-oriented design methodology. Furthermore, with data-oriented approaches, it becomes easier to move from file management to database management.

16-1-4 Long-term File Maintenance

The long lifetime of data means that data maintenance is an important, and often costly aspect of data-processing systems.

PERSISTENCE   We noted in the introduction to this book that an important aspect of data stored on files is their persistence. From the programming point-of-view we noted that files live longer than programs, and hence require documentation that permits successor programs to share their content.

Files can also outlive the computers they were developed on. When they are moved to new equipment, the data representation may have to change. The concept of a domain remains unaffected by changes in representation, so that an understanding of the domain provides the guidance when representations must be changed. Each unique domain value must correspond to a unique value in the new representation.

In Chap. 2-1-4 we presented documentation requirements to assure usability of files. Data dictionaries play an important role. We now also consider some economic aspects.

LIFETIME It can take a long time before the investment in a data-processing system and the collection of data necessary for its operation begin to pay off. Once such a system is working, however, there is a great reluctance to worry about investing in its long-term viability.

Since files are long-lived, some ongoing maintenance costs are inevitable. Good maintenance lets a system perform longer, but the time will also come when the software supporting the files has to be redesigned. That point may be when the file has grown in size or in terms of load that it can no longer deliver the required performance. such a spoint should be predictable, so that a redesign can be completed well before the system is overstressed.

If the files are used within an accounting framework, then their development cost can be depreciated. A depreciation period should be estimated to be less than a reasonable system *lifetime*. At the end of the depreciation period, funds should have been accumulated that will pay for the redesign. The cost of redesign and reestablishment of the files include changing of software and documentation, and then the conversion costs of the files themselves.

The cost of redoing the software depends mainly on the quality of the documentation. It is rare that any programmers who participated in the original design will still be available. We can expect that improved systems support will permit simplification of application software in the future. As database management systems become more versatile, more file-processing functions will be taken over by them. When a redesign is completed, the contents of the obsoleted files has to be placed into the new system. Typically, new fields and subfiles will be added. If the files will be distributed, then fragmentation and replication requireds further effort.

Since a redesign is a major effort, it is wise to plan ahead. A system which has only a few years of life remaining can receive reduced maintenance, but the users have to be assured that schedules and resources for its replacement are in place.

MAINTENANCE OF DATA INTEGRITY In files the major long-term maintenance cost is due to the need to maintain integrity. As files are updated, errors will be entered into the files. Techniques to keep error rates low were presented in Chap. 15-3-3. Error rates can be measured by auditing file contents versus source data or actual inventories.

The error rates found have been typically in the range of 0.5% to 5.0% on well maintained systems. It should be noted that the error rate tends to be less on important data elements, for example, employees' salaries, and worse on less important data items, such as their addresses. Lower-end rates occur on files containing counts and financial data; error rates are higher when data being entered is subjective and complex.

Figure 16-2 illustrates the *feedback loops* that can be used to maintain integrity in large file systems. The cost of establishing the loops initially is always less than the effort needed to correct excessive erroneous results.

At the time it must remain clear that any realistic approach to data processing must consider that errors will be present. Long logical derivations are especially susceptible to errors, whereas statistical analyses are much less so.

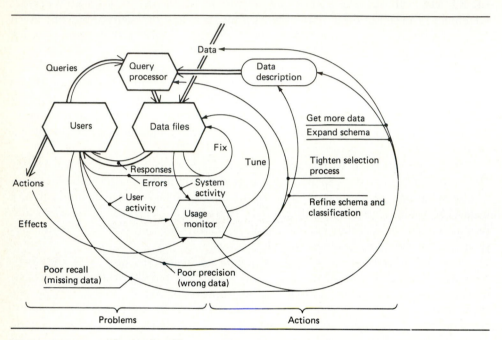

Figure 16-2   Monitoring files.

BACKUP AND VERSIONS   Since serious errors can render entire files unusable, it is important to provide backup for important files. If only protection for disasters is needed, then periodic backing up of entire files may be adequate. If possible the *backup file* is created as a *snapshot* at a quiescent period so that no updates intervene.

█████ **Backup of Very Large Files**   If the file is *very large*, so that the time to copy it is greater than the maximum feasible interval between updates, the file will never be quiescent. In that case we write the backup file while the source file is being changed. The updates entered in this period should be logged and appended to the backup file when the copying is done. If rapid restoration is important, it can be wise to incorporate the intervening updates into the backup files before putting it away.

Copies of backups may be duplicated as well, and one kept locally for rapid recovery and one remotely. The remote copy protects us from site disasters, which could destroy both active storage and local backup storage. All backups must be carefully *time-stamped*, so that they are easy to identify and retrieve when they are needed.   █████

VERSIONS   If access to past data is routinely required, then we speak of having *versions*. Versions may be required when a historical data analysis is needed, for instance, a summary of business changes at quarter year intervals.

In *computer-aided design* applications, it is often necessary to go back to past versions. For instance, a promising design turns out to be infeasible, and *alternative version*, rejected earlier, must be retrieved.

The methods to maintain versions are much like making backups, but a number of points differ.

- Versions are created at points in time determined by external factors, and version creation cannot always be deferred to times of low usage.
- Alternative versions are not simply identified by a linear point in time but also by their content and conditions. Work on alternative files can continue in parallel. We can now speak of a tree of versions and alternatives.

Without adequate file system support for alternative versions, all alternatives must be given distinct names. Version management is mainly addressed today in engineering settings. Design files in such systems are maintained by specialized software.

Alternative versions can also be created, intentionally or unintentionally, in replicated files of distributed systems. Communication difficulties can hamper concurrent updates of active files. In all cases, versions are used for *read-only access*. This constraint simplifies version management and may permit alternative indexing strategies. Indexes can be dense, rather than sparse B-trees, and structures such as *tries*, as described in Chap. 8-3-5, provide effective choices.

16-2   MOVING TO DATABASE MANAGEMENT

We can now define the bridge which leads from file management to database management. A database contains a diversity of related data so that typically several files are used to hold the data. Other files may be needed to hold descriptive information about the data and its relationships.

The analysis of files is characterized by an emphasis on performance issues. The analysis of databases concentrates on logical structures. The result of this analysis is a precise specification of the contents and the required manipulations of the database. Files and support programs chosen for implementation of a database have to satisfy the database specification and provide adequate performance for the users of the database.

The combination of software and the files to support a variety of applications becomes a database system.

An integrated collection of support programs and file structures to support databases, their logical requirements, and provide generalized interfaces to users and user programs is called a database management system or DBMS.

Table 16-3 lists some of the features we may find in a DBMS, but which are uncommon in file management. Yet both share many of the same concerns of performance, correct and reliable operations, and a need for data-engineered design.

Table 16-3   Features of a DBMS.

DBMS features	Availability
Access to multiple files at the same time	Essential
A schema to place and locate the data	Essential
A query language for convenient access	Common
Provisions for multiple simultaneous users	Common
Support for a choice of file organizations	Frequent
Facilities to define the beginning and end of transactions	Frequent
Logging and recovery services	Frequent
Formal privacy privilege specification of fields	Frequent
Programs to generate reports, using schema information	Frequent
Utility programs to help with data administration	Frequent
Support for variable length records	Often
Support for complex data elements	Sometimes
Support for constraints between files	Sometimes
Automated triggering of transactions on file changes	Sometimes
Support for structured data objects	Rare
Support for arbitrary constraint expressions	Rare

While much remains to be presented about database management, the reader of this book should have acquired an understanding of the essential foundation for database management: accessing data on external storage.

16-3   THE FUTURE OF FILE SYSTEMS

With the emphasis in the literature on database systems one may wonder if files and file systems will remain relevant. The answer is: of course! A database system cannot deliver performance which files cannot provide. As users of databases become more demanding, a larger variety of file organizations will have to be supported. File systems will also continue to develop further. Some of the reasons for further development are:

1 New hardware devices and device organizations
2 Increased distribution of processing
3 New programming methods
4 Technologies which avoid programming

We will indicate these directions in turn.

16-3-1 New Hardware Devices

File development is partially driven by improvements in technology. Whenever new devices appear, new file structures must be considered. Sometimes hardware innovations have not taken hold because the required investment in software was not made.

Optical Storage   Optical discs have characteristics which require new file organizations. Our techniques for multiattribute access, indexes using B-trees and ring organizations require rewriting of file contents for updating, but WORMs (as defined in Chap. 3-1-4) only permit the appending of information. Keeping B-trees on distinct magnetic devices seems to be one solution, but is not economically viable when many indexes are being maintained, since index storage costs then become much greater than the data storage cost.

Semiconductor Storage   The reduction in cost of semiconductor components also permits new device configurations. It should now be possible to keep all data required by a transaction in memory. The benefit is immediate for applications which now make repeated accesses to file storage, and retrieving sometimes the data over and over. Research into massive-memory databases is also in progress. Now external storage becomes mainly the logging device, necessary to assure persistence.

Some specialized systems now use associative memory. If software can routinely benefit from having associative memory within data systems then such memory should become common.

Mixed Storage Devices   Optimization of cost-benefit ratios can mean that file components will be stored on a *hierarchy of devices*. Use of multiple devices to store a single file introduces new complexity. Device failures can cause inconsistencies. A good allocation of functions to the devices can make great differences in performance.

16-3-2 Distribution of Files

As files become more frequently fragmented and replicated over multiple nodes, new techniques must be developed to assure their currency and consistency. A failure in one node can be restored by using data from partner nodes, but such a restoration requires careful management of file directories and references.

The data may be kept on nodes which use different hardware and operating systems. To permit joint management, the information kept about files must be kept at a higher level of abstraction. To assure recoverability, that information itself must be replicated at multiple nodes.

Transparency   An open question is whether the distribution of files should be *transparent*, i.e., not visible to the user. It is generally agreed that a human end-user should not have to modify programs and procedures when data is relocated or rearranged. The end-user will of course be able to observe differences in performance if data is removed from local nodes.

16-3-3 New Programming Methods

As new data structures become better understood, they enter as basic objects into programming languages. Arrays and matrices were the only structures supported by the languages of the 1960s, but now records, lists, and queues are becoming routinely available. Object-oriented programming languages permit the definition by composition of arbitrarily complex object structures, and such objects may in turn be composed into super objects.

The storage of these objects presents new challenges, since they are more difficult to describe than records composed of a simple list of attributes. The length of their elements and the number of elements within an attribute becomes variable, so that simple file structures are no longer adequate.

Complex objects will also be more difficult to share. What is a suitable object configuration for one program may not be best for another. Traditionally, data structures have not been shared among programs, so that new problems must be resolved if files can contain complex and variable objects. To delineate the elements of such objects, marking strategies have to be devised and shared.

16-3-4 Using Files without Programming

Files are also becoming important to new technologies which avoid the notion of programming. Examples of such technologies are spreadsheets and artificial intelligence systems. As their capabilities increase they begin to rely on files or databases for external storage. Many of the services offered by a DBMS are actually irrelevant to these approaches, since they manage data according to their needs, and do not need the complexity of a DBMS. A file schema, as presented in Sec. 16-2-2, may be useful so that the file and processing modules are not bound together too tightly.

Files for Spreadsheets A spreadsheet consists of a matrix with two representations for each cell:

1 A value — as seen on the output screen. Source data and results are indistinguishable here.
2 A formula — used to compute this value from other elements in this, or from a referenced, spreadsheet. Base data is provided by formulas which only contain a constant.

The values always present the results for a given case, a case typically presents a plan, the base constants represent resource inputs, and the other formulas presented expected transformations of these resources into expected outcomes, for example, business profits. A user can try out alternative plans and actions on a spreadsheet by modifying the formulas, frequently those containing base constants. With a change in only one or a few formulas, for example, an estimate of future sales, the derived values may change drastically.

Storage of spreadsheets involves some special concerns. The formulas are variable in length and complexity, and awkward to store on simple files. Often the spreadsheets are irregular in form, so that a rectangular representation will contain many null values as well.

If a user wishes to retain alternative versions of the spreadsheet for later reference, typically the entire set of formulas is saved, though only a few constant formulas may differ. However, a 100×100 spreadsheet of formulas can occupy 100K bytes. Storing spreadsheets for several contemplated alternatives can be a significant load for the disks on personal computers.

If the data from a spreadsheet is to be used for other applications, then the values rather than the formulas are required. So now the first representation, values, has to be stored. Simple updates in the spreadsheet formulas involve updates of many values in the resulting presentation of the spreadsheet.

If the spreadsheet must be reevaluated when source data change, then the spreadsheet should accommodate linkages to the operational files for the business. Such linkages are becoming available, but are rarely smooth or troublefree.

Knowledge-based Systems   Systems based on artificial intelligence technology store knowledge about tasks and procedures in largely declarative form. An interpreter obtains the knowledge for a given task. This knowledge can refer to facts stored on files. The combination of the task specification, the general knowledge, and specific facts can then automatically generate the desired results.

A knowledge-based system can also easily obtain its data directly from files. Having a file schema is again beneficial to provide a well-defined interface to the knowledge base. The knowledge base will link to the schema and provide access functions for selected data. For instance, a task to plan a new product will obtain information about product development plans in general and data about specific similar products, their users, and their sales patterns. The data may come from files which are maintained in the company for other purposes. Data from these operational files may be selected and copied to the files used for the knowledge-based analysis. When time is a critical fcator in planning, for example, to respond to an emergency situation, then a knowledge-based advice system will need to access the base files directly.

16-4   EPILOGUE

We have covered the topic of files quite extensively although many specific topics can be considered in yet much greater depth. The readings in the Background sections provide access to further material. The presentation should permit this book to serve as a reference as well as a text on files.

The topic of files also included many issues in system design — the need for description of objectives, the evaluation of alternatives, and the use of effective technology. These issues will be further refined in a successor volume, *Database Design and Implementation*.

BACKGROUND AND REFERENCES

Issues of software design are addressed at a variety of levels. Popular magazines, such as *Datamation*, regularly carry articles which present new methods and tools. The concept of the Chief Programmer was first applied by Baker[72] during the development of a large information system. More formal approaches are found in journals such as the IEEE *Transactions on Software Engineering*, as, for instance, Cameron[86] and Wasserman[86]. Modeling tools for design are presented in Brägger[85] and Farmer[85], and their development is projected by Carlson[85]. It is difficult to prove that any approach is better than another. Small scale analyses tend to be unrealistic, and it is too costly to replicate major design and implementation efforts. An IEEE CS conference series on data engineering is intended to stress the data-oriented approach (Berra[84], Wiederhold[86DE], Wah[87]), some papers have been published with Shuey[86]. Any reasonable method will probably improve the process of developing software, and occasional changes of methods and tools will keep the use of methodological processes exciting through the *Hawthorne effect*. The term *data engineering* was used first by Gilb[76].

Maintenance of long term data was one of the objectives of work by Teichrow[77]; Smith[81] considers their migration. Severance[76] sees economies in storing differential files. Restructuring of data is addressed by Fry[74], Navathe[76], and Shu[87]. A standard for sharing files, including a machine readable description is ANSI[85].

File growth and lifetimes are studied by Satyanarayanan[81]. Fuchs[87] addresses the problem of keeping replicated files consistent and Sarin[87] deals with discarding obsolete information. Laudon[86] reports distressing error rates. Tichy[82] and Katz[84] introduce the problems of versions and alternatives. Papadimitriou[84] uses versions to assure consistent access and Weihl[87] develops the read-only case.

Entire books (Ross[81], LeongHong[82]) and conferences (Fong[86]) have been devoted to data dictionaries, and standardization is being considered; Dolk[87] provides a prototype implementation. An early review is by Uhrowczik[79]. The first use is documented by McGee[59], later examples are presented by Sakamoto[82] and Symons[82]. Sharability of data will be enhanced if standards are adopted. In specific fields data standards can go to greater depths and use codes as described in Chap. 13-1-3.

References to developments in hardware and distribution of processing were already provided in Chaps. 3 and 11. An object-oriented language with file access, C++ is implemented by Stroustrup[86], objects in database are suggested by by Baroody[81] and a workshop proceedings considered the database interface for such programming techniques (Dittrich[86]). Problems in combining object approaches and databases are presented in Wiederhold[87].

Interest in artificial intelligence approaches is explosive. Formal logic-based methods are motivated in Gallaire[84] and covered in depth by Jacobs[85]. Some applications of these techniques to databases are described by Wiederhold[84]. An edited collection of papers on knowledge-based approaches is Brodie[86] and useful material from a workshop on *Expert Databases* is in Kerschberg[86]. This field is advancing rapidly.

The knowledge required by these approaches is in part obtained from the contents of data dictionaries and schemas. Keeping, updating, and maintaining the knowledge about the data being manipulated closes the left-hand side of the information loops introduced in Fig. 1-4.

FILE PRODUCTS

The systems in this list were chosen either because of their ubiquity, their historical interest, their potential for experimentation, or their significance for study. The list is obviously not complete. Current information is best obtained from the manufacturers. Further references to file systems, data dictionaries, transaction processing systems, as well as related software can be obtained from commercial software catalogs (DATAPRO, Auerbach, ICP Quarterly) or from surveys in computer magazines. A similar list of database systems is included in Wiederhold[83,88].

*Most of the product names cited are protected by trademarks

File Systems

Name	Year	Developer location	Computer* OPER.SYS*	Type and features [reference]
ALPINE	1983	Xerox Research Lab Palo Alto CA	Xerox 1108 CEDAR	Inst DFMS ixf vlr obj pri dbs(CYPRESS) Brown[85]
AMIGOS	1970	Comress Inc Rockville MD	IBM370	FMS slc hli isf
ASI/ST	1969	Applications Softw. Torrance CA	IBM370 Univac70	QUS slc rpg tbq sch *for* sqf isf IMS TOTAL
ASM2		Cambridge Syst.Grp Santa Clara CA	IBM370	FMS rpg pri *for* DL/1 files
APL (Associative Prog.Lang.)	1965	General Motors Res. Warren MI	IBM360-67	Inst FMS rnf hli(PL/1) gra [Dodd[66]]
Btrieve	1983	SoftCraft Inc Austin TX	IBM-PC	FMS hli(BASIC PASCAL COBOL C) ixf
CDMS	1974	Digital Eq Corp Maynard MA	DEC-11	FMS slc hie trf *see* MUMPS

Name	Year	Developer location	Computer OPER.SYS	Type and features [reference]
Dataease	1984	Software Solutions Milford CT	IBM-PC MS-DOS	FMS slc rel rpg ixf
CFS	1980	Carnegie-Mellon U. Pittsburg PA	DEC-LSI-11s	Exp DFMS
DATAMAN	1975	Dataman Ltd Calgary Alberta	IBM370	FMS slc rpg sch sqf
DATAMASTER	1980	Microsoft Seattle WA	Apple 8080	FMS rpg sch sqf
dBASEII/III	1981	Ashton-Tate Torrance CA	Z-80, IBM PC CP/M, DOS	FMS *with* Join, stq rpg ixf(1 *updated*)
DBMS990	1980	Texas Instruments Austin TX	Ti990	FMS hli(PASCAL COBOL FORTRAN) hie tbq isf
DISAM	1975	Four Phase Systems Cupertino CA	4phase70	FMS *for* DFMS hli(COBOL) isf ixf
DL/1	1968	IBM White Plains NY	IBM370 MVT MFT, DOS-VS	FMS dbs(IMS) hli sch hie sqf isf hsf stq(CICS)
DMS/1700	1975	Dedicated Systems Chicago IL	Burr.1700	FMS ixf
DYL250	1971	Dylakor Comp Syst Encino CA	IBM370	FMS slc rpg stq sqf isf
EDEN	1982	Univ of Washington Seattle WA	DEC-VAX	Exp DFMS obj [Jessop82]
FLASH	1979	Stanford Univ. Stanford CA	DEC-20,VAX; IBM370	Exp FMS ixf vlr sch dbs hli(PASCAL) [Allchin80]
FOCUS	1978	Information Builders New York 10001 NY	IBM 370 CMS,TSO	QUS irq rpg isf,DL/1,IDMS pri
FORTE	1959	Burroughs Corp Paoli PA	B2500/3500 B1700-7700	FMS hli(COBOL) sqf isf hsf ixf rnf [Chapin69]
GIS	1966	IBM White Plains NY	IBM370	QUS hli(COBOL PL/1) hie stq sch sqf isf
INFOS	1975	Data General Southboro MA	DG-Nova, -Eclipse	FMS hli hie isf ixf stq
Infostar+	1983	Micropro San Raphael CA	IBM-PC MS-DOS	FMS txt

Name	Year	Developer location	Computer OPER.SYS	Type and features [reference]
ISAM	1964	IBM White Plains NY	IBM 370	FMS isf flr hli(COBOL PL/1) [Grosshans[86]]
ISAM70	1974	Software70 Anaheim CA	Any FORTRAN system	FMS hli(FORTRAN) isf
LAN:DataCore	1983	Software Connections Sunnyvale CA	IBM PC, TI prof. MS-DOS	DFMS ixf sec pri cip dbs
LEADER	1967	Lehigh Univ Bethlehem PA	CDC6400	Inst IRS irq bib ixf [Hillman[69]]
LEAP	1968	Stanford Univ.AI lab Stanford CA	DEC 10	Inst FMS rnf mem [Feldman[69]]
MARKIV	1967	Answer Systems Canoga Park CA	IBM370 Univac900	FMS slc rpg tbq hie isf(ISAM,VSAM)
MUMPS	1966	Mass Gen Hospital Boston MA	DEC-PDP15,11 DG 8080 ao.	FMS slc hie trf [Greenes[69]]
Omnifile	1983	SSR corp. Rochester NY	IBM-PC MS-DOS	FMS slc rpg ixf
Pfs:File, Report	1983	Software Pub.Corp. Mountain View CA	IBM-PC MS-DOS	FMS slc rpg isf
PICKLE-CSA	1982	Lawrence Berk. Lab. Berkeley CA	DEC VAX VMS	FMS tnf *for statistics on census*, [McCarthy[1982]]
PLUS/4	1979	Century Analysis Pacheco CA	NCR 101 etc.	FMS hli
Power-base	1983	Powerbase Systems New York 18 NY	IBM-PC MS-DOS	FMS slc rel(1 file) rpg sch
QID/1 RMS/RTP	1978	Reiter Software Sys. Haifa Isr., SanFrancisco	IBM-series-1 RPS	DFMS hie(1-level):ixf-hsf rec
RMS	1979	DEC Colorado Springs Co	DEC VAX VMS	FMS isf sch sec dbs cpr hli(FORTRAN PL/1)
SAM, XRM RSS	1968	IBM Scientific Center Cambridge MA	IBM360*modified later on* 370	Exp FMS rel vrf [Date[85]] dbs(SYSTEM R)
SAS/FSP	1972	Univ.N.Carolina & SAS Inst., Cary NC	IBM370,XT; VAX DG Eclipse; Prime	FMS(*statistics*) slc stq rpg sqf
SCORE	1969	Programming Meth-ods, New York NY	*Any* COBOL system	FMS hli(COBOL) hie tbq sqf isf

Name	Year	Developer location	Computer OPER.SYS	Type and features [reference]
SESAM	1973	Siemens München FRG	S4004	FMS stq rpg sqf isf
SIS	1963	CDC Minneapolis MN	CDC 6600, Cyber SCOPE	FMS isf hli(FORTRAN COBOL) [Claybrook[83]]
SHOEBOX	1970	MITRE Corp Bedford MA	IBM360	Exp FMS slc txt plf stq [Glantz[70]]
SWALLOW	1980	Mas Inst Tech Cambridge MA		Exp DFMS plf *optical dics* obj [Svobodova[84]]
TDMS	1966	System Dev Corp Santa Monica CA	IBM360-50 (ADEPT)	Inst FMS slc hie ixf sch irq [Bleier[68]]
TIM IV	1983	Innovative Software Overland Park KS	IBM-PC MS-DOS	FMS slc rel rpg ixf
TURBO-Access	1984	Borland Int. Scotts Valley CA	IBM PC	FMS ixf sec hli(PASCAL)
VISIFILE	1982	Visicorp San Jose CA	IBM-PC Apple	FMS slc ixf stq flr
VSAM	1968	IBM White Plains NY	IBM 370	FMS isf sec vlr hli(COBOL PL/1) [Atkinson[83]]
WSS	1983	Univ.of Wisconsin Madison WI		Exp FMS ixf [DeWitt[85]]

Data Dictionairies

Name	Year	Developer location	Computer OPER.SYS	Type and features [reference]
DATACATALOG	1974	Synergetics Bedford MA	IBM370 OS,DOS UNIVAC	DIC slc isf scg(DMS1100 IDMS IMS S2K) rpg
DATAMANAGER	1976	MSP Inc. Lexington MA	IBM 370	DIC slc scg(ADABAS DL/1 IDMS MARKIV S2K TOTAL UDS) rpg
DB/DC	1975	IBM White Plains NY	IBM370 IMS	DIC rpg scg(DL/1) hie (CMIS *for manufacturing*)
FACETS *was* PRISM	1981	Synergistics/TSI Int. Bedford MA	IBM 370	DIC slc rpg
LEXICON	1976	Arthur Anderson Chicago IL	IBM370, System 3	DIC slc scg(IDMS IMS TOTAL)
LINC II	1984	Burroughs Corp Paoli PA	B1000	DIC rpg

Name	Year	Developer location	Computer OPER.SYS	Type and features [reference]
MANTIS	1971	Cincom Inc Cincinnati OH	IBM370	DIC apg
TSI		Technology Inf.Prods. Burlington MA		DIC
UCC TEN	1976	DSIMS Corp. Dallas TX	IBM370	DIC slc rpg sch scg(IMS)

Transaction Processing Systems

Name	Year	Developer location	Computer OPER.SYS	Type and features [reference]
CICS		IBM Armonck NY	IBM 370 DOS, MVS	TPS dbs(DL/1) [Eade[77]]
COM-PLETE		software ag Darmstadt FRG	IBM370 Siemens	TPS dbs(ADABAS)
ENVIRON TIS	1971	Cincom Inc Cincinnati OH	IBM370 DOS, MVS	TPS dbs(TOTAL, SUPRA)
TMF	1978	Tandem Computers Tandem Non-Stop	Cupertino CA ENCOMPASS	TPS [Borr[81],Svobodova[84]]
TPF ACP	1959	IBM White Plains NY	IBM370	TPS slc *used for airlines* (PARS) [Siewic[77]]

Legend for type and features of systems

apg application generator
bib bibliographic application
cip ciphering
cpr compression
dbs database support
DFMS Distributed FMS
DIC Data Dictionary System
Exp experimental
FMS file-Management System
flr fixed length records
hie hierarchical file organization
hli host language interface
hsf hashed file organization
Inst Institutional
int integrated package
IRS Information-Retrieval System
irq interrogative query processor
isf indexed-sequential file
ixf indexed files
mem in-memory system

plf pile file organization
pri privacy protection
QUS query and update system
rel support for relational operations
rec recovery support
rnf ring file organization
rpg report generator
sch schema
scg schema generation
sec secondary indexes
slc self-contained system
sqf sequential file organization
stq statement driven query processor
tbq table driven query processor
tnf transposed files
TPS Transaction Processing System
trf tree-structured files
txt textual data
vlr variable length records
vrf virtual file support

Symbols Used

MATHEMATICAL SYMBOLS USED

$+, -$	addition, subtraction
$\times, \cdot$	multiplication
$a/b, \frac{a}{b}$	division of a by b
$\leftarrow$	assign right-hand side to left-hand side
$=$	equality
$\approx$	approximately equal
$\gg$	much greater than
$\lceil\ \rceil$	CEIL, next higher integer
$\lfloor\ \rfloor$	FLOOR, next lower integer
$!$	factorial
#	number of
$\log_y x$	logarithm base y of x
$\log x$	natural logarithm of x, base $e = 2.71828182846$
$\sum_k f(k)$	sum of all $f(k)$ for the integer k's specified
$\max_k f(k)$	greatest value of all $f(k)$ for the integer k's specified
$\binom{n}{k}$	binomial coefficient; the #of combinations of n objects taken k at a time for integers $= (n!)/(k!(n-k)!)$
$\wedge$	and, true if both sides are true
$\vee$	or, true if either side is true

PROGRAMMING AND SYNTAX SYMBOLS AS USED

`a + b`	addition
`a - b`	subtraction
`a * b`	multiplication
`a / b`	division
`MOD(a,b)`	modulo, remainder of division
`CEIL(a)`	ceiling, smallest integer greater than or equal to **a**
`FLOOR(a)`	ceiling, largest integer less than or equal to **a**
`a ** b`	exponentiation, **a** to the power **b**
`a = b`	depending on context in PL/1, assignment or equality comparison
`a > b`	greater than comparison, true if **a** greater than **b**
`a ≥ b`	greater or equal comparison, true if **a** greater or equal to **b**
`a ∧ b`	and, true if both **a**, **b** true (& in PL/1)
`a ∨ b`	or, true if either **a**, **b** true (| in PL/1)
`¬ c`	not, true if **c** false and vice versa
`s ‖ w`	catenation, string **s** connected to string **w** to form a single new string
`;`	statement separator
`.`	termination of computational section
`/* Note */`	explanatory comments
`variable`	program variable, to be declared
`a.b`	qualification of variable **b** by a higher-level variable **a**, i.e., `Employee.name`
`File_name`	File names, node names, and transaction commands are Capitalized
`DECLARE`	program keywords are in UPPERCASE
`1023`	numeric constant
`'Word'`	character string constant
`10DEC86`	date constant
`_`	(underline) pseudo-alphabetic character without syntactic meaning used for legibility within variable names. (In COBOL – is used for this function.)

VARIABLES USED IN PERFORMANCE FORMULAS

A	average space required for attribute name	Chap. 4-3-1
a	number of different attributes in a file	Chap. 4-2-1
a'	average number of attributes in a record	Chap. 4-2-1, 6-3-2
B	blocksize	Chap. 3-2
b	blockcount	Chap. 3-2-2
btt	block transfer time $= B/t$	Chap. 3-2-5, Eq. 3-13
Bfr	blocking factor $\approx B/R$	Chap. 3-2-4, Eqs. 3-5 to -7, -20
C	Cost factors	Chap. 14-3-5, Eq. 14-21
c	computational overhead per record, when not negligible	Chap. 3-3-4
D	space for data storage Chap. 10-1-1, Eq. 10-1, Chap. 10-2-1 Eqs. 10-2 to -4	
d	number of records that have been invalidated	Chap. 4-3-7
F	subscript denoting a fetch for a specific record	Chap. 4-1-3
G	space required for an interblock gap	Chap. 3-2-3
G	Giga or a thousand million (1 073 741 824) times	
h	classification variable	Chap. 10-3-1
I	subscript denoting insertion of a record	Chap. 4-1-3
j	number of cylinders	Chap. 3-2-1, Table 3-1
K	Kilo or thousand (1024) times	
k	number of tracks per cylinder	Chap. 3-2-5, Table 3-1
L	load frequency factors	Chap. 14-2-2
M	multiprogramming factor	Chap. 14-3-5, Eq. 14-22
M	Mega or million (1 048 576) times	
m	number of available slots for records	Chap. 6-1
N	subscript denoting getting the next serial record	Chap. 4-1-3
n	number of records in a file	Chap. 4-2-1
$\mathcal{O}$	order of magnitude	Chap. 1-3-1
o	number of records that overflow Chaps. 4-3-7, -5-1, 5-2-7, 6-2-1, 12-1-5	
P	space required for a pointer	Chap. 3-2-4
p	collision cost, also probability Chap. 6-2-2 Eqs. 6-6 to -9, -11 to -12, Fig. 6-10	
q	production demand by a file application Chap. 14-2-4, -3-1 Eq. 14-1 to -3, -6	
R	space required for a complete record	Chap. 4-1-3
RW	subscript indicating rewriting	Chap. 3-3-5
r	rotational latency time	Chap. 3-2-2, Eq. 3-3
SI	storage space for index	Chap. 5, Eqs. 5-7, -28 to -29
s	average seek time	Chap. 3-2-1, Eq. 3-2
T	the time required for various operations	Chap. 4-1-3
T_{sort}	the time required to sort a file	Chap. 4-3-8, Eq. 4-12
t	transfer rate from a storage unit to processing memory	Chap. 3-2-5
T	subscript denoting total transaction time	Chap. 10-3-1, Eq. 01-5
t'	bulk transfer rate	Chap. 3-2-5, Eqs. 3-17, -18, -19
U	subscript denoting an update of a record	Chap. 4-1-3
u	utilization	Chap. 14-3-1, Eqs. 14-5, -9 to -20, -23
uf	utilization factor	Chap. 12-3-2, Eqs. 12-25, -29
V	average space for value part of an attribute	Chap. 4-3-1
w	wait time in queues	Chap. 12-3-2, Eq. 12-26
W	wasted space due to gaps per record	Chap. 3-2-4, Eqs. 3-9 to -11, -21
X	subscript denoting an exhaustive search	Chap. 4-1-3
x	number of levels in an index, master level	Eqs. 4-27, -49, -97, Chap. 6-3-4
Y	subscript denoting a reorganization of a file	Chap. 4-1-3
y	fanout ratio	Chap. 5, Eq. 5-26, -48

Bibliography

A FILE BIBLIOGRAPHY

This bibliography is extracted from a much larger bibliography on files, databases, and knowledge-based systems maintained by the author. Except where material was directly extracted from a publication only references that are commonly available are cited here. To get some information about the contents of the listed publications one can go via the indexed name of the first author to the background sections of the various chapters.

ABBREVIATIONS USED IN THE BIBLIOGRAPHY:

ACM	Association for Computing Machinery (ACM), New York NY.
AFIPS	American Federation of Information Processing Societies, Arlington VA.
ASIS	American Society for Information Science, Washington DC.
BIT	*Nordisk Behandlings Informations Tidskrift*, Copenhagen Denmark.
CACM	*Communications of the ACM*, ACM, New York NY.
CIPS	Canadian Information Processing Society, Toronto Canada.
Comp. J.	*Computer Journal* of the British Computer Society, London UK.
DE	*IEEE CS Data Engineering Conference*, Los Angeles CA.
FJCC	*Fall Joint Computer Conference* (sponsored by AFIPS).
IBM JRD	*IBM Journal of Research and Development*, Armonk NY.
IBM Sys. J	*IBM System Journal*, Armonk NY.
IEEE	Institute of Electrical and Electronics Engineers, New York NY.
IEEE CS	IEEE Computer Society, Washington DC.
IFIP	International Federation for Information Processing, Geneva Switzerland.
IPSJ	Information Processing Society of Japan, Tokyo Japan.
JACM	*Journal of the ACM*, ACM, New York NY.
NCC	*National Computer Conference* (sponsored by AFIPS).
PODS	*ACM Conference on Principles of Database Systems*.
SIGMOD	ACM Special Interest Group on Management of Data.
SJCC	*Spring Joint Computer Conference* (sponsored by AFIPS).
TC	*IEEE Transactions on Computers*.
TOCS	*ACM Transactions on Computer Systems*.
TODS	*ACM Transactions on Database Systems*.
TOPLAS	*ACM Transactions on Programming Languages and Systems*.
TSE	*IEEE Transactions on Software Engineering*.
VLDB	*Very Large Data Base* conferences, pub. Morgan Kaufman, Los Altos CA.

Some information on these and other periodicals covering file topics is provided in the background section of Chap. 1.

Acton,Forman S.[70]: *Numerical Methods That* Usually *Work*; Harper and Row, 1970.

Abiteboul,S.[85]: "Disaggregation in Databases"; *JACM*, vol.32 no.1, Jan.1985, pp.79–101.

Acker,R.D. and Seaman,P.H.[82]: "Modeling Distributed Processing across Multiple CICS/VS Sites"; *IBM Sys.J.*, vol.24 no.4, 1982.

Addis,T.R.[82]: "A Relation-Based Language Interpreter for a Content Addressable File Store"; *ACM TODS*, vol.7 no.2, Jun.1982, pp.125–163.

Adiba,M.[81]: "Derived Relations: A Unified Mechanism for Views, Snapshots and Distributed Data"; *VLDB 7*, Zaniolo and Delobel(eds.), Cannes, .1981, pp.293–305.

Agarwala,A.K.[70]: "Learning with a Probabilistic Teacher"; *IEEE Trans. Information Theory*, vol.IT-16 no.4, May 1970.

Aho,A.V. and Ullman,J.D.[79U]: "Optimal Partial-Match Retrieval When Fields Are Independently Specified"; *ACM TODS*, vol.4 no.2, Jun.1979, pp.168–179.

Alford, M. W.[77]: "A Requirements Engineering Methodology for Real-Time Processing Requirements"; *IEEE TSE*, vol.SE-3 no.1, 1977, pp.60–69.

Allen,A.O.[75]: "Elements of Queuing Theory for System Design"; *IBM Sys.J.*, vol.14 no.2, 1975, pp.161–187.

Allen,Roy P.[68]: "OMNIBUS, A Large Data Base Management System"; *Proc.1968 FJCC*, AFIPS vol.33, Thompson Books, pp.157–164.

Allen,S.I., Barnett,G.O., and Castleman,P.A.[66]: "Use of a Time-shared General Purpose File Handling System in Hospital Research"; *Proc.IEEE*, vol.54, 1966, pp.1641–1648.

Allchin,J., Keller,A.M., and Wiederhold,.G[80]: "FLASH: A Language-Independent Portable File Access System"; *ACM-SIGMOD 1980*, May 1980, pp.151–156.

Allgeyer,K. and Kratzer,K.[87]: "Expert System Based Configuration of VSAM Files"; *IEEE CS DE 3*, LA, Feb.1987.

Amble,O. and Knuth,D.E.[74]: "Ordered Hash Tables"; *Comp. J.*, vol.17 no.2, Feb.1974, pp.135–142.

Ammon,G.J., Calabria,J.A., Thomas,D.T.[85]: "A High-Speed, Large Capacity, 'Jukebox' Optical Disk System"; *IEEE Computer*, vol.18 no.7, Jul.1985, pp.36–45.

Anderson,H.D. and Berra,P.B.[77]: "Minimum Cost Selection of Secondary Indexes for Formatted Files"; *ACM TODS*, vol.2 no.1, Mar.1977, pp.68–90.

Andler,S., et al.[82]: "System-D Distributed System for Availability" ; *VLDB 8*, McLeod and Villasenor(eds.), Mexico City, 1982, pp.33–44.

ANSI (American National Standards Institute)[86]: Medium and System-independent File and Data Record Formats for Information Interchange; ANSI-ISO Standard 8211-1985, American National Standards Inst., New York.

Anzelmo,Frank D.[71]: "A Data Format for Information System Files"; *IEEE TC*, Jan.1971, vol.C-20, pp.39–43.

Apers,P.M.G.[81]: "Centralized or Decentralized Data Allocation"; *Proc.Internat. Seminar on Distributed Data Sharing Systems 1*, vandeRiet and Litwin (eds.), Amsterdam, Jun.1981, pp.101–116.

Apers,P.M.G. and Wiederhold,G.[85]: "Transaction Handling in a Loosely Coupled Environment"; *Proc.ACM-ICS conf.1985*,Florence,Italy: 'Computing 85,A Broad Perspective of Current Developments' Bucci and Valle(eds.), pp.25–36, North-Holland 1985.

Arden, Bruce W.(ed.).[75]: "Interactive Computer Systems"; *IEEE Proc.* , vol.63 no.6, Jun.1975, pp.883–979.

Armisen,J.P. and Caleca,J.Y.[81]: "A Commercial Back-End Data Base System"; *VLDB 7*, Zaniolo and Delobel(eds.), Cannes, 1981.

Aron,J.D.[69]: "Information Systems in Perspective"; *ACM C.Surveys*, vol.1 no.4, Dec.1969, pp.213–235.

Arora,S.R. and Dent,W.T.[69]: "Randomized Binary Search Techniques"; *CACM*, vol.12 no.2, Feb.1969, pp.77–80.

Arora,S.R. and Gallo,A.[71]: "Optimal Sizing, Loading and Re-loading in a Multi-Memory Hierarchy System"; *Proc. 1971 SJCC*, AFIPS vol.38, pp.337–344.

Astrahan,M.M., Schkolnick,M., and Whang,K-Y.[87]: "Approximating the Number of Unique Values without Sorting"; *Information Systems*, vol.12 no.1, 1987.

Atkinson,M.P. and Morrison,M.[85]: "Procedures as Persistent Objects"; ACM TOPLAS, vol.7 no.4, Oct.1985, pp.539–559.

Atkinson,W. and DeSanctis,P.[83]: *Introduction to* VSAM; Hayden Book Co., 1983.

Atwood,J.W., MacLeod,A., and Yu,K-C.[82]: "An Empirical Study of a CDC 844-41 Disk Subsystem"; *Perform.Eval.*, vol.2 no.1, May 1982, pp.29–56.

Atwood,R.C.[72]: "Effects of Secondary Storage I/O Contention on the Performance of an Interactive Information Management System"; *ACM National Conf. 27*, Aug.1972, pp.670–679.

Baber,R.L.[63]: "Tape Searching Techniques"; *JACM*, vol.10 no.4, Oct.1963, pp.478–486.

Bachman,C.W. and Williams,S.B.[64]: "A General Purpose Programming System for Random Access Memories"; *Proc. 1964 FJCC*, AFIPS vol.26, pp.411–422.

Bachman,Charles W.[66]: "On a Generalized Language for File Organization and Manipulation"; *CACM*, vol.9 no.3, Mar.1966, pp.225–226.

Bachman,Charles W.[72]: "The Evolution of Storage Structures"; *CACM*, vol.15 no.7, Jul.1972, pp.628–634.

Bachman,Charles W.[73]: "The Programmer as a Navigator"; *CACM*, vol.16 no.11, Nov.1973, pp.653–658.

Baer,Jean-Loup[75]: "Weight-Balanced Trees"; *Proc. 1975 NCC*, AFIPS vol.44, pp.467–472.

Baker,F.T.[72]: "Chief Programmer Team Management of Production Programming"; *IBM Sys.J.*, vol.11 No. 1, 1972, pp.56–72.

Barbara,D. and GarciaMolina,H.[82]: "How Expensive is Data Replication, An Example"; *IEEE Internat. Conf. on Distr. Comp. Sys. 3*, 1982, pp.263–268.

Baroody,A.J.,jr. and DeWitt,D.J.[81]: "An Object-Oriented Approach to Database System Implementation"; *ACM TODS*, vol.6 no.4, Dec.1981, pp.576–601.

Baskett,F. and Smith,A.J.[76]: "Interference in Multiprocessor Computer Systems with Interleaved Memory"; *CACM*, vol.19 no.6, Jun.1976, pp.327–334.

Batory,D.S.[79]: "On Searching Transposed Files"; *ACM TODS*, vol.4 no.4, Dec.1979, pp.531–544.

Batory,D.S. and Gotlieb,C.C.[82]: "A Unifying Model of Physical Databases"; *ACM TODS*, vol.7 no.4, Dec.1982, pp.509–539.

Batteke,J.P.H., Heaps,D.M., and Mercier,M.A.[74]: "Canadian Water Resources Information A Network Approach"; *Inf. Stor. and Retr.*, vol.10 nos.3,4, Mar.1974, pp.85-99.

Bayer,R. and McCreight,E.M.[72O,S]: "Organization and Maintenance of Large Ordered Indexes " and "Symetric Binary B-trees: Data Structure and Maintenance Algorithms"; *Acta Inf.*, vol.1 no.3, Feb.1972, pp.173–189 and no.4, Nov.1972, pp.290–306.

Bayer,R. and Metzger,J.K.[76]: "On the Encipherment of Search Trees and Random Access Files"; *ACM TODS*, vol.1 no.1, Mar.1976, pp.37–52.

Bayer,R. and Unterauer,K.[77]: "Prefix B-trees"; *ACM TODS*, vol.2 no.1, Mar.1977, pp.11–26.

Bays,Carter[73]: "The Reallocation of Hash-Coded Tables"; *CACM*, vol.16 no.1, Jan.1973, pp.11–14.

Bell,A.E.[83]: "Critical Issues in High Density Magnetic and Optical Storage" ; *Optical Data Storage*, Chen(ed.), Proc. Soc. for Photo-optical Instr. Eng., vol.382, 1983, pp.2-15.

Bell,A.E.[84]: "Optical Data Storage — A Status Report" ; *Proc. IEEE Symp. on Mass Storage Sys. 6*, 1984, pp.93–98.

Benner,F.H.[67]: "On Designing Generalized File Records for Management Information Systems"; *Proc. 1967 FJCC*, AFIPS vol.31, pp.291–304.

Bentley,J.L.[75]: "Multidimensional Binary Search Trees Used for Associative Searching"; *CACM*, vol.18 no.9, Sep.1975, pp.509–517.

Berlekamp,E.R.(ed.)[74]: *Key Papers in The Development of Coding Theory*; IEEE Press, 1974, 296pp.

Bernstein,P.A.(ed.)[79]: *Proc. of the ACM SIGMOD Int. Conference*; ACM, NY, 1979.

Bernstein,P.A.,Blaustein,B.T., and Clarke,E.M.[80]: "Fast Maintenance of Semantic Integrity Assertions Using Redundant Aggregate Data"; *VLDB 6*, Lochovsky and Taylor(eds.), Oct.1980, pp.126–136.

Bernstein,P.A.. and Goodman,N.[81]: "Concurrency Control in Distributed Database Systems"; *ACM C. Surveys*, vol.13 no.2, Jun.1981, pp.185–221.

Berra,Bruce(ed.)[84]: *Proceedings First Internat. Conference on Data Engineering*; Los Angeles CA, IEEE CS, Apr.1984.

Bhargava,B.(ed.)[81]: *Symp. on Reliability in Distributed Software and Database Systems*; IEEE Pub. 81-CH1632–9, 1981.

Bhattacharya,C.C.[67]: "A Simple Method of Resolution of a Distribution into Gaussian Components"; *Biometrics*, Mar.1967.

Bihan,J.L., Esculier,C., LeLann,G., Litwin,W., Gardarin,G., Sedillot,S., and Treille,L.[80]: "SIRIUS: A French Nationwide Project on Distributed Data Bases"; *VLDB 6*, Lochovsky and Taylor(eds.), Montreal, Oct.1980, pp.75–85.

Billings. John Shaw[1892]: "Mechanical Methods Used in Compiling Data of the 11th U. S. Census, with Exhibition of a Machine"; *Proc. Am. Ass. Adv. of Science*, 1892.

Bleier,R.E. and Vorhaus,A.H.[68]: "File Organization in the SDC TDMS"; *Information Processing-68*, Proc. 1968 IFIP Congress, North-Holland, pp.F92–F97.

Bobeck,A.H. and DellaTorre,E.[75]: *Magnetic Bubbles*; North-Holland — Elseviers, 1975.

Borr,A.J.[81]: "Transaction Monitoring in ENCOMPASS: Reliable Distributed Transaction Processing"; *VLDB 7*, Zaniolo and Delobel(eds.), Sep.1981, pp.155–165.

Bose,R.C. and Koch,Gary G.[69]: "The Design of Combinatorial Information Retrieval Systems for Files with Multiple Valued Attributes"; *SIAM J. Appl. Math.*, vol.17 no. 6, Nov.1969, pp.1203–1214.

Bouros,Michael P.[85]: *Getting into VSAM; An Introduction and Technical Reference*; John Wiley, 1985, 435pp.

Boyd,D.F. and Krasnow,H.S.[63]: "Economic Evaluation of Management Information Systems"; *IBM Sys.J.*, Mar.1963, pp.2–23.

Bradley,James[85]: "Use of Mean Distance between Overflow Records to Compute Average Search Lengths in Hash files with Open Addressing"; *Comp. J.*, Aug.1985.

Brägger,R.P., Dudler,A.M., Rebsamen,J., and Zehnder,C.A.[85]: "GAMBIT: An Interactive Database Design Tool for Data Structures, Integrity Constraints, and Transactions"; *IEEE TSE*, vol.SE-11 no.7, Jul.1985, pp.574–583.

Brainerd,W.(ed.)[78]: "FORTRAN 77"; *CACM*, vol.21 no.10, Oct.1978, pp.806–820.

Bright, H. S. and Enisa,. L.[76]: "Cryptography using Modular Software Elements"; *Proc. 1976 NCC*, AFIPS vol.45, pp.113–123.

BrinchHansen,Per[73]: *Operating System Principles*; Prentice Hall, 1973, 366 pp.

Brodie,M.L. and Zilles,S.N.[81]: *Data Abstraction, Databases and Conceptual Modelling*; *ACM SIGMOD Record*, vol. 11 no. 2. Feb.1981; republished as *Perspectives in Conceptual Modelling*; Springer Verlag, 1984.

Brodie,M.L. and Mylopoulos,J.[86]: *On Knowledge Base Management Systems, Integrating Artificial Intelligence and Database Technologies*; Springer Verläg, Jun.1986.

Brooks,F.D.,jr.[75]: *The Mythical Man-Month: Essays on Software Engineering*; Addison-Wesley, 1975, 195 pp.

Brown,D.T. and Sellers,F.F.,jr.[70]: "Error Correction for IBM 800-bit-per-inch Magnetic Tape"; *IBM JRD*, vol.14 no.4, Jul.1970, pp.384–389.

Brown,D.T., Eibsen,R.L., and Thorn,C.A.[72]: "Channel and Direct Access Device Architecture"; *IBM Sys.J.*, vol.11 no.3, 1972. pp.186–199.

Brown,M., Kolling,K., and Taft,E.[85]: "The ALPINE File System"; *ACM TCS*, vol.3 no.4, Nov.1985, pp.261-293

Browne,P.S.(ed.)[79]: *Security, Checklist for Computer Center Self-Audits*; Best Practices Series, AFIPS, Arlington VA, 1979.

Buchholz,Walter[63]: "File Organization and Addressing"; *IBM Sys.J.*, vol.2 no.2, Jun.1963, pp.86–111.

Buchholz,Walter[69]: "A Synthetic Job for Measuring System Performance"; *IBM Sys.J.*, vol.8 no.4, 1969, pp.309–318.

Buneman,O.P. and Clemons,E.K.[79]: "Efficiently Monitoring Relational Databases"; *ACM TODS*, vol.4 no.3, Sep.1979, pp.368–382.

Burge,W.H. and Konheim,A.G.[71]: "An Accessing Model"; *JACM*, vol.18 no.3, Jul.1971, pp.400–404.

Burkhard,Walter A.[76,79]: "Hashing and Trie Algorithms for Partial-Match Retrieval" and "Partial-Match Hash Coding: Benefits of Redundancy"; *ACM TODS*, vol.1 no.2, 1976, pp.175–187 and vol.4 no.2, Jun.1979, pp.228–239.

Burkhard,Walter A.[83]: "Interpolation-based Index Maintenance"; *BIT*, vol.23 no.3, 1983, pp.274–294.

Burkhard,W.A., Martin,B.E., and Paris,J-F.[87]: "The GEMINI Replicated File System Test-bed"; *IEEE CS DE 3*, LA, Feb.1987.

Bush, Vannevar[45]: "As We May Think"; *The Atlantic Monthly*, vol.176 no.1, Jan.1945, pp.110-108, reprinted in Kochen[67].

Cameron,J.R.[86]: "An Overview of JSD"; *IEEE TSE*, vol.SE-12 no.2, 1986, pp.222–240.

Canaday,R.H., Harrison,R.D., Ivie,E.L., Ryder,J.L., and Wehr,L.A.[74]: "A Back-end Computer for Data Base Management"; *CACM*, vol.17 no.10, Oct.1974, pp.575–582.

Cardenas, Alfonso F.[73]: "Evaluation and Selection of File Organization - A Model and a System"; *CACM*, vol.16 no.9, Sep.1973, pp.540–548.

Cardenas, A. F. and Sagamang, J. P.[77]: "Doubly-Chained Tree Data Base Organization - Analysis and Design Strategies"; *Comput.J.*, vol.10 no.1, 1977, pp.15–26.

Cardenas,A.F.[84]: *Data Base Management Systems*, 2nd ed.; Allyn and Bacon, 1984.

Carlson,C.R. and Arora,A.K.[85]: "Towards the Next Generation of Data Modeling Tools"; *IEEE TSE*, vol.SE-11 no.9, Sep.1985, pp.966-970.

Carrol,John M.[72]: "Snapshot 1971 - How Canada Organizes Information about People"; *Proc.1972 FJCC*, AFIPS vol.41, pp.445–452.

Casey,R.G.[73]: "Design of Tree Networks for Distributed Data"; *Proc.NCC 1973*, AFIPS vol.42, pp.251–257.

Ceri, S. Pelagatti, G. , and Bracchi, G.[81]: "Structured Methodology for Designing Static and Dynamic Aspects of Database Applications"; *Information Systems*, vol.6 no.1, Jan.1981.

Ceri,S., Negri,M., and Pelagatti,G.[82]: "Horizontal Data Partitioning in Database Design"; *ACM-SIGMOD 82*, Schkolnick(ed.), Orlando FL, Jun.1982.

Ceri,S., Navathe,S., and Wiederhold,G.[83]: "Distribution Design of Logical Database Schemas"; *IEEE TSE*, vol.SE-9 no.4, Jul.1983, pp.487–563.

Ceri,S. and Pelagatti,G.[84]: *Distributed Database Design: Principles and Systems*; McGraw-Hill, 1984.

Chamberlin,D.D.[76]: "Relational Data-Base Management Systems"; *ACM C.Surveys*, vol.8 no.1, Mar.1976, pp.43–66.

Chan,A., Dayal,U., Fox,S., Goodman,N., Ries,D.R., and Skeen,D.,[83]: "Overview of an ADA Compatible Distributed Database Manager"; *ACM-SIGMOD 83*, San Jose, May 1983, pp.228–237.

Chang,J.M. and Fu,K.S.[81]: "Extended K-d Tree Database Organization: A Dynamic Multiattribute Clustering Method"; *IEEE TSE*, vol.SE-7 no.3, May 1981, pp.284–290.

Chang,S.K. and Cheng,W.H.[80]: "A Methodology for Structured Database Decomposition"; *IEEE TSE*, vol.SE-6 no.2, Mar.1980.

Chang,S.K. and Liu,A.[82]: "File Allocation in a Distributed Database"; *Internat. Journal of Computer and System Sciences*, vol.11 no.5, 1982, pp.325–340.

Chapin, Ned[68]: *360 Programming in Assembly Language*; McGraw-Hill, 1968, 532 pp.

Chapin,Ned[69]: "Common File Organization Techniques Compared"; *Proc. 1969 FJCC*, AFIPS vol.35, pp.418–422.

Charles,William R.[73]: "Some Systems Should Not Use Paired File Techniques"; *Data Management*, Sep.1973, pp.33–37.

Chen, Peter P.S.[73]: "Optimal File Allocation in Multi-Level Storage Systems"; *Proc.1973 NCC*, AFIPS vol.42, pp.227–282.

Chen,P.P.S. and Akoka,J.[80]: "Optimal Design of Distributed Information Systems"; *IEEE TC*, vol.C-29 no.12, Dec.1980, pp.1068-1081.

Cheng,P.S.[69]: "Trace Driven System Modelling"; *IBM Sys.J.*, vol.8 no.4, 1969, pp.280–289.

Cheng,W.K. and Belford,G.G.[80]: "Update Synchronization in Distributed Databases"; *VLDB 6*, Lochovsky and Taylor(eds.), Montreal, Oct.1980, pp.301–308.

Cheriton, D.G. and Zwaenepoel,W.[83]: "The Distributed V Kernel and Its Performance for Diskless Workstations"; *ACM Symp. on Operating Systems Principles 9*, Bretton Woods NH, Oct.1983.

Cheung,T-Y.[82]: "Estimating Block Accesses and Number of Records in File Management"; *CACM*, vol.25 no.7, Jul.1982, pp.484–487.

Chi,C.S.[82]: "Advances in Computer Mass Storage Technology"; *IEEE Computer*, May 1982, pp.60–74.

Christodoulakis,Stavros[83]: "Estimating Record Selectivities"; *Information Systems*, vol.8 no.2, Jun.1983.

Christodoulakis,Stavros[84]: "Implications of Certain Assumptions in Data Base Performance Evaluation"; *ACM TODS*, vol.9 no.2, Jun.1984, pp.163–186.

Chu,W.W.[69]: "Optimal File Allocation in a Multiple Computer System"; *IEEE TC*, vol. C-18 no.10, Oct.1969, pp.885–888.

Chu,W.W.and Hurley,P.[82]: "Optimal Query Processing for Distributed Database Systems"; *IEEE TC. vol.C-31 no.9*, Sep.1982, pp.835–850.

Chu,W.W.. and Hellerstein,J.[85]: "The Exclusive-Writer Approach to Updating Replicated Files in Distributed Processing Systems"; *IEEE TC. vol.C-34 no.6*, Jun.1985.

Clark,W.A.[66]: "The Functional Structure of OS/360: Part III Data Management"; *IBM Sys.J.*, vol.5 no.1, 1966, pp.30–51.

Claybrook, Billy G.[83]: *File Management Techniques*; John Wiley, 1983.

Codd,E.F.[70]: "A Relational Model of Data for Large Shared Data Banks"; *CACM*, vol.13 no.6, Jun.1970, pp.377–387.

Codd,E.F. and Dean,A.L.(eds.)[71]: *Data Description Access and Control*; ACM, 1971.

Coffman,E.G.,jr.[69]: "Analysis of a Drum Input-Output Queue under Scheduled Operation in a Paged Computer System"; *JACM*, vol.16 no.1, Jan.1969, pp.73–90.

Coffman,E.G., jr., Klimko,L.A., and Ryan,B.[72]: "An Analysis of Seek Times in Disk Systems"; *SIAM J. on Comp.*, vol.1 no.3, 1972, pp.269–279.

Coffman,E.G.,jr., Gelenbe, E., and Plateau, B.[81]: "Optimization of the Number of Copies in a Distributed Data Base"; *IEEE TSE*, vol.SE-7 no.1, Jan.1981, pp.78–84.

Collmeyer,A.J., and Shemer,J.E.[70]: "Analysis of Retrieval Performance for Selected File Organization Techniques"; *Proc. 1970 FJCC*, AFIPS vol.37, pp.201–210.

Comer,D.[78]: "The Difficulty of Optimum Index Selection"; *ACM TODS*, vol.3 no.4, Dec.1978, pp.440–445.

Comer,D.[79]: "The Ubiquitous B-tree"; *ACM C.Surveys*, vol.11 no.2, Jun.1979, pp.121–137.

Comer,D.[81]: "Analysis of a Heuristic for Full Trie Minimization"; *ACM TODS*, vol.6 no.3, Sep.1981, pp.513–537.

Comer,Douglas[84]: *Operating System Design,the XINU approach*; Prentice Hall, 1984.

Connors,T.C.[66]: "ADAM — A Generalized Data Management System"; *Proc. 1966 SJCC*, AFIPS vol.28, pp.193–203.

Conway,R.W., Maxwell, W.L., and Morgan,H.L.[72]: "On the Implementation of Security Measures in Information Systems"; *CACM*, vol.15 no.4, Apr.1972, pp.211–220.

Coonen,Jerome T.[80]: "An Implementation Guide to a Proposed Standard for Floating Point Arithmetic"; *IEEE Computer*, vol.13 no.1, Jan.1980, pp.68–79.

Copeland,G.[82]: "What If Mass Storage Were Free"; *IEEE Computer*, vol.15 no.7, Jul.1982, pp.27–35.

Copeland,G., Khoshafian,S., Smith,M., and Valduriez,P.[86]: "Buffering Schemes for Permanent Data"; *IEEE CS DE 2*, Los Angeles, Feb.1986.

Cornell,D.W. and Yu,P.S.[87]: "A Vertical Partitioning Algorithm for Relational Databases"; *IEEE CS DE 3*, LA, Feb.1987.

Cuadra,C.R. and Lake,R.(eds.)[66−77]: *ARIST: Annual Review of Information Science and Technology*; Wiley 1966–1970, vol.1–4, Encyclopedia Brittanica, 1971–1973, vol.5–7. ; later vols. published by ASIS.

Czejdo,B.,Rusinkiewicz,M., and Embley,D.W.[87]: "An Approach to Schema Integration and Query Formulation in Federated Database Systems"; *IEEE CS DE 3*, LA, Feb.1987.

Daley,R.C., and Neuman,P.G.[65]: "A General Purpose File System for Secondary Storage"; *Proc. 1965 FJCC*, AFIPS vol.27, pp.213–229.

Daniell,T.P., Harding,R.C..jr., and Nauckhoff,S.H.[83]: "Dynamic Replication, an Overview"; *Proc. 1983 NCC*, AFIPS vol.52.

Date,C.J.[85]: *An Introduction to Database Systems*; Addison-Wesley, 2 vols., vol.1 4th ed. 1985.

Davida,G.I., Wells,D.L., and Kam,J.B.[81]: "A Database Encryption System with Subkeys"; *ACM TODS*, vol.6 no.2, Jun.1981, pp.312–328.

Davies,A.C.[80]: "The Analogy between Electrical Networks and Flowcharts"; *IEEE TSE*, vol.SE-6 no.4, Jul.1980.

Davis,Gordon B.[74]: *Management Information Systems,Conceptual Foundations, Structure, and Development*; McGraw Hill, 1974, 481 pp.

Davis,Gordon B.[82]: "Strategies for Information Requirements Determination"; *IBM Syst.J.*, vol.21 no.1, 1982.

Davis,Lou[70]: "Prototype for Future Computer Medical Records"; *Comp. and Biomed. Res.*, vol.3 no.5, Oct.1970, pp.539–554.

Dayal,U. and Hwang,H.Y.[84]: "View Definition and Generalization for Database Integration in a Multibase System"; *IEEE TSE*, vol.SE-10 no.6, Nov.1984, pp.628–645.

De,P., Haseman,W.D., and Kriebel,C.H.[78]: "Toward an Optimal Design of a Network Database from Relational Descriptions"; *Operations Research*, vol.26 no.5, Sep.-Oct.1978, pp.805–823.

Dearnley,P.A.[74]: "The Operation of a Self Organising Data Management System"; *Computer J.*, vol.17 no.3, Aug.1974, pp.205–210.

DeGreene,Kengon B.[73]: *Socio-technical Systems: Factors in Analysis, Design and Management*; Prentice Hall, 1973, 416 pp.

DeMaine,P.A.D.[71]: "The Integral Family of Reversible Compressors"; *IAG Journal*, vol.4 no.3, 1971, pp.207–219.

DeMarco,Tom[79]: *Structured Analysis and System Specification*; Prentice Hall, 1979.

Demolombe,Robert[80]: "Estimation of the Number of Tuples Satisfying a Query Expressed in Predicate Calculus Language"; *VLDB 6*, Oct.1980, Montreal, pp.55–63.

Demurjian,S.A. and Hsiao,D.K.[87]: "The Multi-Lingual Database System"; *IEEE CS DE 3*, LA, Feb.1987.

Denning,Peter J.[67]: "Effects of Scheduling on File Memory Operations"; *Proc.1967 SJCC*, AFIPS vol.30, pp.9–21.

Denning,Peter J.[71]: "Third Generation Computer Systems"; *ACM C.Surveys*, 1971, vol.3 no.4, pp.145–216.

Denning,Peter J.[72]: "A Note on Paging Drum Efficiency"; *ACM C.Surveys*, vol.4 no.1, Mar.1972, pp.1–3.

Denning,P.J. and Buzen,J.P.[78]: "The Operational Analysis of Queueing Network Models"; *ACM C.Surveys*, vol.10 no.3, Sep.1978, pp.225–261.

Dennis,J.B. and vanHorn,E.C.[66]: "Programming Semantics for Multiprogrammed Computations"; *CACM*, vol.9 no.3, Mar.1966, pp.143–155.

Desmonde,W.H.[64]: *Real Time Data Processing Systems*; Prentice Hall, 1964.

Deutscher,R.F.,Tremblay,R.P,and Sorenson,P.G.[75]: "A Comparative Study of Distribution-Dependent and Distribution-Independent Hashing Functions"; *ACM Pacific-75 Conf.*, SF, Apr.1975, pp.56–61.

Devor,C., ElMasri,R., and Rahimi,S.[82]: "The Design of DDTS: A Testbed for Reliable Distributed Database Management"; *IEEE Symp.on Reliability in Distributed Software and Database Systems 2*, Wiederhold(ed.), Pittsburgh PA, Jul.1982, pp.150–162.

DeWitt,D.,Chou,H-T.,Katz,R.,and Klug,T.[85]: Design and Implementation of the Wisconsin Storage System; *Software Practice and Experience*, vol.15 no.10, Oct.1985, pp.943–962.

Diffie,W.,and Hellman,M.E.[76]: "New Directions in Cryptography"; *IEEE Trans.Information Theory*, vol.IT-22 no.6, Nov.1976, pp.644–654.

Dimsdale,J.J. and Heaps,R.S.[73]: "File Structure for an On-Line Catalog of One Million Titles"; *Journal of Library Automation*, vol.6 no.1 Mar.1973, pp.37–55.

Dittrich,K.R. and Dayal,U.(eds.)[86]: *Proc. 1986 Internat. Workshop on Object-Oriented Database Systems*; IEEE CS Order no.734, Sep.1986.

Dittrich,K.R.[87]: "Controlled Cooperation in Engineering Database Systems"; *IEEE CS DE 3*, LA, Feb.1987.

Dixon,W.J.and Massey,F.J.jr.[69]: *Introduction to Statistical Analysis*,3rd ed.; McGraw-Hill, 1969, 638 pp.

Dodd,George G.[66]: "APL - a Language for Associative Data - Handling in PL/1"; *Proc. 1966 FJCC*, AFIPS vol.29, pp.677–684.

Dodd.George G.[69]: "Elements of Data Management Systems"; *ACM C.Surveys*, vol.1 no. 2, Jun.1969, pp.117–133.

Dolk,D.R. and Kirsch,R.A.II[87]: "A Relational Information Resource Dictionary System"; *CACM*, vol.30 no.1. Jan.1987. pp.48–60.

Doty,K.L., Greenblatt,J.D., and Su,S.T.W.[80]: "Magnetic Bubble Memory Architectures for Supporting Associative Searching of Relational Databases"; *IEEE TC. vol.C-29 no. 11*, Nov.1980, pp.957–970.

Dowdy,L.W. and Foster,D.V.[82]: "Comparative Models of the File Assignment Problem"; *ACM C.Surveys*, vol.14 no.2, Jun.1982, pp.287–313.

Du,D.H.C., Ghanta,S., and Maly,K,.J.[87]: "An Efficient File Structure for Document Retrieval in the Automated Office Environment"; *IEEE CS DE 3*, LA, Feb.1987.

Du,H.C. and Sobolewski,J.S.[82]: "Disk Allocation for Cartesian Product Files on Multiple-Disk Systems"; *ACM TODS*, vol.7 no.1, Mar.1982, pp.82–101.

Dunnigan,Mike[84]: "5.25-In. Fixed/Removable Disk Products Resolve Data Integrity Problems"; *Computer Technology Review*, Spring 1984, pp.19–22.

Dutta,A., Koehler,G., and Whinston,A.[82]: "An Optimal Allocation in a Distributed Processing Environment"; *TIMS*, vol.28 no.8, Aug.1982, pp.83.

Eade,D.J., Homan,P., and Jones,J.E.[77]: "CICS/VS and its Role in System Network Architecture"; *IBM Sys.J.*, vol.16 no.3, 1977, pp.258–286.

Easton,A.[73]: *Complex Managerial Decisions Involving Multiple Objectives*; Wiley, 1973.

Easton,M.C.[69]: "A Streamlined Statistical System for a Medical Computer Center"; *ACM National Conf. 24*, 1969, pp.494–475.

Effelsberg,W. and Härder,T.[84]: "Principles of Database Buffer Management"; *ACM TODS*, vol.9 no.4, Dec.1984, pp.560–595.

Eggers,S.J., Olken,F., and Shoshani,A.[81]: "A Compression Technique for Large Statistical Databases"; *VLDB 7*, Zaniolo and Delobel(eds.), Sep.1981, pp.424–433.

Eisner,M.J. and Severance,D.G.[76]: "Mathematical Techniques for Efficient Record Segmentation in Large Shared Databases"; *JACM*, vol.24 no.4, Oct.1976.

Ellis,Carla Schlatter[85]: "Concurrency and Linear Hashing"; *ACM-PODS 4*, Mar.1985.

Ellis,M.E. Katke,W., Olson,J., and Yang,S.C.[72]: "SIMS - An Integrated, User-Oriented Information System"; *Proc. 1972 FJCC*, AFIPS vol.41, pp.1117–1132.

Epstein,R. and Hawthorne,P.[80]: "Design Decisions for the Intelligent Database Machine"; *Proc. 1980 NCC*, AFIPS vol.49, pp.237–241.

Eswaran,Kapali P.[74]: "Placement of Records in a File and File Allocation in a Computer Network"; *Information Processing 74*, Proc. IFIP Congress, North-Holland, 1974, pp.304–307.

Evans, A., jr., Kantowitz, W., and Weiss, E.[74]: "A User Authentication Scheme Not Requiring Secrecy in the Computer"; *CACM*, vol.17 no.8, Aug.1974, pp.437–442.

Everest,Gordon C.[86]: *Database Management: Objectives, System Functions, and Administration*; McGraw-Hill, 1986, 816 pp.

Fabry,R.S.[74]: "Capability Based Addressing"; *CACM*, vol.17 no.7, Jul.1974, pp.403–412.

Fagin,Ronald[78]: "On an Authorization Mechanism"; *ACM TODS*, vol.3 no.3, Sep.1978, pp.310–319.

Farmer,D.B., King,R., and Meyers,D.A.[85]: "The Semantic Database Constructor"; *IEEE TSE*, vol.SE-11 no.7, Jul.1985, pp.583–591.

Feinstein,A.R.[70]: "Taxonorics"; *Archives of Internal Medicine*, vol.126, Oct.1970, pp.679–693; Dec.1970, pp.1053–1067.

Feistel,H.[73]: "Cryptography and Computer Privacy"; *Scientific American*, vol.228 no.5, May 1973, pp.15–23.

Feldman,J.A. and Rovner,P.D.[69]: "An Algol-Based Associative Language"; *CACM*, vol.12 no.8, Aug.1969, pp.439–449.

Feller,William[71]: *An Introduction to Probability Theory and Applications*; John Wiley: vol.1, 3rd ed., 1968; vol.2, 2nd ed., 1971.

Fernandez,E.B, Summers,R., and Wood,C.[81]: *Data Base Security and Integrity*; Addison-Wesley, 1981, 320 pages.

Ferrari,Domenico[86]: "Considerations on the Insularity of Performance Evaluation"; *IEEE TSE*, vol.SE-12 no.6, Jun.1986, pp.678-683.

Ferrari,D., Serazzi,G., and Zeigner,A.[83]: *Measurement and Tuning of Computer Systems*; Prentice-Hall, 1983.

Feustel,E.A.[73]: "On the Advantages of Tagged Architecture"; *IEEE TC*, vol.C-22 no.7, Jul.1973, pp.644–656.

Files,J.R. and Huskey,H.D.[69]: "An Information Retrieval System Based on Superimposed Coding"; *Proc.1969 FJCC*, AFIPS vol.35, pp.423–432.

Fischer,M.J., Griffeth,N.D., and Lynch,N.A.[81]: "Algorithms for Placing Identical Resources in a Distributed System"; *Proc. Int. Symp. on Distributed Data Bases 2*, Litwin(ed.), Paris, Apr.1981.

Fishman,George S.[67]: "Problems in the Statistical Analysis of Simulation Experiments"; *CACM*, vol.10 no.2,Feb.1967, pp.94–99.

Flajolet,P. and Martin,G.N.[85]: "Probabilistic Counting Algorithms for Data Base Applications"; *J. of Computer and System Sciences*, vol.31 no.2, Sept.1985, pp.182-209.

Flajolet,P., Regnier,M., and Sotteau,D.[86]: "Algebraic Methods for Trie Statistics"; *JACM*, vol.33 no.2, Apr.1986, pp-371–407.

Florentin,J.J.[76]: "Information Reference Coding"; *CACM*, vol.19 no.1, Jan.1976, pp.29–33.

Flores,Ivan[70]: *Data Structure and Management*; Prentice Hall, 1970.

Floyd,R.W.[74]: "Permuting Information in Idealized Two-Level Storage"; *Complexity of Computer Computations*, Miller et al(eds.), Plenum NY 1974.

Fong,E.N., Goldfine,A.H., and Navathe,S. (eds.)[86]: Data Base Directions: Information Resource Management – Making It Work; IEEE CS Database Eng.Bull., Jun.1986.

Franaszek,P.and Robinson,J.T.[85]: "Limitations of Concurrency in Transaction Processing"; *ACM TODS*, vol.10 no.1, Mar.1985, pp.1–28.

Frank,H.[69]: "Analysis and Optimization of Disk Storage Devices for Time-Sharing Systems"; *JACM*, vol.16 no.4, Oct.1969, pp.602–620.

Fredkin,E.[60]: "Trie Memory"; *CACM*, vol.39, 1960, pp.490–499.

Freiberger,W.(ed.)[72]: *Statistical Computer Performance Evaluation*; Academic Press, 1972.

Freund,J.E.[62]: *Mathematical Statistics*; Prentice Hall, 1962.

Frey,R., Girardi,S., and Wiederhold,G.[71]: "A Filing System for Medical Research"; *Bio-Medical Computing*, vol.2 no.1, Elseviers, Jan.1971, pp.1–26.

Friedman, Theodore D.[70]: "The Authorization Problem in Shared Files"; *IBM Sys.J.*, vol.9 no.4, pp.258–280, 1970.

Friedman, T.D. and Hoffman, L.J.[74]: "Execution Time Requirements for Encipherment Programs"; *CACM*, vol.17 no.8, Aug.1974, pp.445–449.

Fry,J.P.and Jeris,D.W.[74]: "Towards a Formulation and Definition of Data Reorganization"; *ACM-SIGMOD 74*, Rustin(ed.), 1974, pp.83–100.

Fuchs,W.K.,Wu,K-L.,and Abraham,J.A.[87]: "Comparison and Diagnosis of Large Replicated Files"; *IEEE TSE*, vol.SE-13 no.1, Jan.1987.

Fujitani,Larry[84]: "Laser Optical Disk: The Coming Revolution in On-Line Storage"; *CACM*, vol.27 no.6, Jun.1984, pp.546-554.

Fuller,S.H.[75]: *Analysis of Drum and Disk Storage Units*; Lecture Notes in CS, vol.31, Goos and Hartmanis(eds.), Springer Verlag, 1975, 283 pp.

Gallaire,H. and Minker,J.(eds.)[78]: *Logic and Data Bases*; Plenum Press, 1978.

Gallaire,H., Minker,J., and Nicolas,J-M.[84]: "Logic and Databases: A Deductive Approach"; *ACM C.Surveys*, vol.16 no.2, Jun.1984, pp.153–185.

Gambino,T.J., and Gerritsen,R.[77]: "A Database Design Decision Support System"; *VLDB 3*, Merten(ed.), Tokyo, Japan, Oct.1977, pp.534–544.

GAO (U.S. Government Accounting Office)[80]: Continued Use of Costly, Outmoded Computers in Federal Agencies Can Be Avoided; Report to the Congress of the United States, AFMD-81-9, Dec.1980.

GarciaMolina,Hector[81]: *Performance of Update Algorithms for Replicated Data*; UMI Research Press, Ann Arbor MI, 1981.

GarciaMolina,H. and Wiederhold,G.[82]: "Read-Only Transactions in a Distributed Database"; *ACM TODS*, vol.7 no.2, Jun.1982, pp.209–234.

GarciaMolina,H., Germano,F..jr., and Kohler,W.H.[84]: "Debugging a Distributed Computing System"; *IEEE TSE*, vol.SE-10 no.2, Mar.1984, pp.210–219.

Garg,A.K. and Gotlieb,C.C.[86]: "Order Preserving Key Transformations"; *ACM TODS*, vol.11 no.2, Jun.1986, pp.213–234.

Gaynor,Jerry[74]: "Determining Access Time for Moving Head Disks"; *Digital Design*, Sep.1974.

Gentile,R.B. and Lucas,J.R.[71]: "The TABLON Mass Storage System"; *Proc. 1971 SJCC*, AFIPS vol.38, pp.345–356.

Ghosh,S.P. and Senko,M.E.[69]: "File Organization: On the Selection of Random Access Index Points for Sequential Files"; *JACM*, vol.16 no.4, Oct.1969, pp.569–579.

Ghosh,Sakti P.[76]: *Data Base Organization for Data Management*; Academic Press, 1976.

Gifford,D.K.[82]: "Cryptographic Sealing for Information Secrecy and Authentication"; *CACM*, vol.25 no.4, Apr.1982, pp.274–286.

Gifford,D.K. and Spector,A.[84]: "The TWA Reservation System"; *CACM*, vol.27 no.7, Jul.1984, pp.649–665.

Gilb,Tom[77]: *Data Engineering*; Studentlitteratur, Lund, Sweden, 1977.

Gilb,Tom[87]: *Principles of Software Engineering Management*; Addison-Wesley, 1987.

Gildersleeve,T.R.[71]: *Design of Sequential File System*; Wiley 1971.

Glantz,R.S.[70]: "SHOEBOX, A Personal File Handling System for Textual Data"; *Proc.1970 FJCC*, AFIPS vol.37, pp.535–545.

Glinka,L.R., Brugh,R.M., and Ungur,H.J.[67]: "Design through Simulation of a Multiple Access Information System"; *Proc.1967 FJCC*, AFIPS, vol.31, pp.437–447.

Goldberg,R.P., and Hassinger,R.[79]: "The Double Paging Anomaly"; *Proc. 1979 NCC*, AFIPS vol.48, 1979, pp.195–199.

Gopalakrishna,V. and Veni Madhavan,C.E.[80]: "Performance Evaluation of Attribute-Based Tree Organization"; *ACM TODS*, vol.6 no.1, Mar.1980, pp.69–87.

Gordon,G.[69]: *System Simulation*; Prentice-Hall, 1969.

Gotlieb,C.C. and Borodin,A.[73]: *Social Issues in Computing*; Academic Press, 1973.

Gotlieb,C.C.[85]: *The Economics of Computers: Costs, Benefits, Policies, and Strategies*; Prentice-Hall, 1985, 339pp.

Gould,I.H.[71]: *IFIP Guide to Concepts and Terms in Data Processing*; North-Holland, 1971.

Graham,G.S.(ed.)[78]: "Queuing Network Models of Computer System Performance"; *ACM C.Surveys*, vol.10 no.3, 1978, pp.219–224.

Graham,R.M.[68]: "Protection in an Information Processing Utility"; *CACM*, vol.11 no.5, May 1968, pp.365–369.

Grant,J.[84]: "Constraint Preserving and Lossless Database Transformations"; *Information Systems*, vol.9 no.2, North-Holland, 1984.

Gray, James N.[78]: "Notes on Data Base Operating Systems"; *Operating Systems*, Bayer, Graham, Seegmüller (eds.), Springer 1978, pp.393–481.

Gray,James N.[81]: "The Transaction Concept: Virtues and Limitations"; *VLDB 7*, Cannes, France, Sep.1981, pp.144–154.

Gray,James,N[86]: "An Approach to Decentralized Computer Systems"; *IEEE TSE*, vol. SE-12 no.6, Jun.1986, pp.684–692.

Gray,P.M.D., Moffat,D.S., and duBoulay,J.B.H.[85]: "Persistent PROLOG: A Secondary Storage Manager for PROLOG"; *Proc. Appia Workshop on 'Data Types and Persistence'*, Atkinson(ed.), 1985; *Proc.ACM SIGMOD 1985*, Navathe(ed.), 1985, pp.437–443.

Greenes, R.A., Pappalardo,A.N., Marble,C.M., and Barnett,G.O.[69]: "A System for Clinical Data Management"; *Proc. 1969 FJCC*, AFIPS vol.35, pp.297–305.

Griffiths,P.P. and Wade,B.W.[76]: "An Authorization Mechanism for a Relational Database System"; *ACM TODS*, vol.1 no.3, Sep.1976, pp.242–255.

Groner,L.H. and Goel,A.L.[74]: "Concurrency in Hashed File Access"; *Proc. 1974 IFIP Congress*, North-Holland.

Grosshans, Daniel[86]: *File Systems Design and Implementation*; Prentice Hall, 1986.

GSA (US General Services Administration)[57,···]: Authorized Federal Supply Schedule Price List; FSC Class 7440, Electronic Data Processing Machines, annually.

Gudes,E. and Taur,S.[80]: "Experiments with B-tree Reorganization"; *ACM-SIGMOD 1980*, pp.200–206.

Guibas,L. and Sedgewick,R.[78]: "A Dichromatic Framework for Balanced Trees"; *Proc. IEEE Symposium On Foundations of Computer Science*, 1978.

Gurski,Aaron[73]: "A Note on the Analysis of Keys for Use in Hashing"; *BIT vol.13 no.1*, 1973, pp.120–122.

Guttman,A.[84]: "R-Trees: A Dynamic Index Structure for Spatial Searching"; *ACM-SIGMOD*, Jun.1984.

Hac,A.[87]: "A Performance Model of Concurrency Cona Distributed File System"; IEEE CS DE 3, LA, Feb.1987.

Hagmann,R.B.[86]: "An Observation on Database Buffering Performance Metrics"; *VLDB 12*, Aug.1986.

Hahn,Bruce[74]: "A New Technique for Compression and Storage of Data"; *CACM*, vol.17 no.8, Aug.1974, pp.434–436.

Hakola,J. and Heiskanen,A.[80]: "On the Distribution of Wasted Space at the End of File Blocks"; *BIT*, vol.20 no.2, 1980, pp.145–156.

Hammer,M. and Chan,A.[76]: "Index Selection in a Self-Adaptive Data Base Management System"; *ACM-SIGMOD 76*, Rothnie(ed.), 1976, pp.1–8.

Hammer,Michael[77]: "Self-Adaptive Data Base Design"; *Proc. 1977 NCC*, AFIPS vol.46, pp.123–129.

Hammer,M. and Sarin,S.K.[78]: "Efficient Monitoring of Database Assertions"; *ACM-SIGMOD 78*, 1978, pp.159–168.

Hammer,M. and Niamir,B.[79]: "A Heuristic Approach to Attribute Partitioning"; *ACM-SIGMOD 79*, Bernstein(ed.), pp.93–100.

Hanan,M. and Palermo,F.P.[63]: "An Application of Coding Theory to a File Address Problem"; *IBM JRD*, vol.7 no.2, Apr.1963, pp.127–129.

Härder,Theodor[78]: "Implementing a Generalized Access Path Structure for a Relational Database System"; *ACM TODS*, vol.3 no.3, Sep.1978, pp.285–298.

Harrison,M.S.,Ruzzo,W.L.,and Ullman,J.D.[76]: "Protection in Operating Systems"; *CACM*, vol.19 no.8, Aug.1976, pp.461–471.

Hawthorn,P.B.and DeWitt,D.J.[82]: "Performance Analysis of Alternative Database Machine Architectures"; *IEEE TSE*, vol.SE-8 no.1, Jan.1982, pp.61–75.

Heising,W.P.[63]: "Note on Random Addressing Techniques"; *IBM Sys.J.*, vol.2 no.2, Jun.1963, pp.112–116.

Held,G. and Stonebraker,M.[78]: "B-Trees Re-examined"; *CACM*, Feb.1978, pp.139–143.

Helland,P.[86]: "The Transaction Monitoring Facility (TMF)"; *Database Engineering*, vol.3, IEEE CS press 1986.

Hellerman,H.[73]: *Digital Computer System Principles*; McGraw-Hill, 1973.

Hellerman,H. and Conroy,T.F.[75]: *Computer Systems Performance*; McGraw-Hill, 1975, 380 pp.

Hertz, D. B.[69]: *New Power for Management-Computer Systems and Management Science*; McGraw-Hill, 1969.

Hevner,A.R.[82]: "A Survey of Data Allocation and Retrieval Methods for Distributed Systems"; *IEEE Symp. on Reliability in Distributed Software and Database Systems 2*, Wiederhold(ed.), Pittsburgh PA, Jul.1982, pp.1–10.

Hibbard,Thomas N.[62]: "Some Combinatorial Properties of Certain Trees with Applications to Sorting and Searching"; *JACM*, vol.9 no.1, 1962, pp.13–28.

Hill,F.J. and Peterson,G.R.[73]: *Digital Systems: Hardware Organization and Design*; Wiley, 1973.

Hill,T.R. and Srinivasan,A.[87]: "A Regression Approach to Performance Analysis for the Differential File Architecture"; *IEEE CS DE 3*, LA, Feb.1987.

Hillier,F.S. and Lieberman,G.J.[67]: *Introduction to Operations Research*; Holden Day, 1967.

Hillman, D.J. and Kasarda, A.J.[69]: "The LEADER Retrieval System"; *Proc. 1969 SJCC*, AFIPS vol.34, pp.70–74

Hoagland, A.S., and Rice, R.(eds.)[75]: "Large Capacity Digital Storage Systems"; *IEEE Proceedings*, vol.63 no.8, Aug.1975, pp.1092–1240.

Hoagland,Albert S.(ed.)[84]: *Mass Storage Systems*; IEEE Computer Society, 1984.

Hoagland,Albert S.[85]: "Information Storage Technology: A Look at the Future"; *IEEE Computer*, vol.18 no.7, Jul.1985, pp.60–67.

Hoffman,L.J.[71]: "The Formulary Model for Access Control"; *Proc. 1971 FJCC*, AFIPS vol. 39, pp.587–601.

Hoffman,L.J.[77]: *Modern Methods for Computer Security and Privacy*; Prentice Hall, 1977.

Hogan,P.D. and Kotlarek,T. L.[87]: "Satellite Data Management for Effective Data Access"; *IEEE CS DE 3*, LA, Feb.1987.

Holt,G.A. and Stern,H.C.[75]: "Cost-Benefit Evaluation of Interactive Transaction Processing Systems"; *Proc. 1975 NCC*, AFIPS, vol.44, pp.687–694.

Horowitz,E. and Sahni,S.[78]: *Fundamentals of Computer Algorithms*; Computer Science Press, 1978.

Hsiao,D.K. and Harary,F.D.[70]: "A Formal System for Information Retrieval from Files"; *CACM*, vol.13 no.2, Feb.1970, pp.67–73; corrigenda in no.3, Mar.1970, pp.266.

Hu,T.C. and Tucker,A.C.[71]: "Optimal Computer Search Trees and Variable-Length Alphabetic Codes"; *SIAM Jour. Appl. Math.*, vol.21 no.4, Dec.1971, pp.514–532.

Huang,S-C. and Goel,A.L.[74]: "An Analytical Model for Information Processing Systems"; *Proc. 1974 NCC*, AFIPS vol.43, pp.41–44.

Huang,S-H.S.[85]: "Height-Balanced trees of Order (β, γ, δ)"; *ACM TODS*, vol.10 no.2, Jun.1985, pp.261–284.

Huff, Darrel[54]: *How to Lie with Statistics*; Norton, 1954.

Huffman,D.A.[52]: "A Method for the Construction of Minimim Redundancy Codes"; *Proc. of the IRE*, vol.40, Sep.1952, pp.1098–1101.

IBM F20-0007[71]: *Analysis of Some Queuing Models in Real Time Systems*, 2nd ed.; IBM Data Processing Division, White Plains NY, 1971.

IBM GC20-1649[69]: *Student Text: Introduction to IBM-360, Direct Access Storage Devices and Organization Methods*; IBM Data Processing Division, White Plains NY, 1969.

IBM G320[74]: *Data Security and Data Processing*, 6 Vols., G320-1370 to 1376; IBM Data Processing Division, White Plains NY, 1974.

Inglis,J. and Dee,E.G.[73]: "Flexibility of Block-length for Magnetic Files"; *Comp. J.*, vol.16 no.4, Nov.1973, pp.303–307.

Inglis,J.[74]: "Inverted Indexes in Multi-list Structures"; *Comp. J.*, vol.17 no.1, Feb.1974, pp.54–63.

Inmon,W.H. and Bird,T.J.,jr.[86]: *The Dynamics of Data Base*; Prentice-Hall, 1986, 394pp.

Inmon,William H.[86]: "Stalking the Elusive Maximum Transaction Rate"; *Data Management*, Jan.1986.

Iyer,R.K., Butner,S.E., and McCluskey,E.J.[82]: "A Statistical Failure/Load Relationship: Results of a Multicomputer Study"; *IEEE Computer*, vol. C-31 no. 7, Jul.1982, pp.697–706.

Jacobs,Barry[85]: *Applied Database Logic,vol.1: Fundamental Database Issues*; Prentice-Hall 1985.

Jajodia,Sushil[87]: "Managing Replicated Files in Partitioned Distributed Database Systems"; *IEEE CS DE 3*, LA, Feb.1987.

Jajodia, S. and Meadows, C.A.[87M]: "Mutual Consistency in Decentralized Distributed Systems"; *IEEE CS DE 3*, LA, Feb.1987.

Javitt,Jonathan[86]: *Computers in Medicine, Applications and Possibilities*; Saunders, 1986.

Jenq,B-C., Kohler,W.H., and Towsley,D.[87]: "A Queueing Network Model for a Distributed Database Testbed System"; *IEEE CS DE 3*, LA, Feb.1987.

Jessop,W.H., Noe,J.D., Jacobson,D.M., Baer,J-L, and Pu,C.[82]: "The EDEN Transaction-Based File System"; *IEEE Symp.on Reliability in Distributed Software and Database Systems 2*, Wiederhold(ed.), Pittsburgh PA, Jul.1982, pp.163–170.

Jewell,W.S.[67]: "A Simple Proof of $L = \lambda \times w$"; *Operations Research*, vol. 15, 1967, pp.1109–1116.

Johnson,Clayton T.[75]: "IBM 3850/Mass Storage System"; *Proc. IEEE*, vol. 63 no. 8, Hoagland(ed.), Aug.1975, pp.1166–1170.

Johnson,L.R.[61]: "An Indirect Chaining Method for Addressing on Secondary Keys"; *CACM*, May 1961, pp.218–222.

Judd,D.R.[73]: *Use of Files*; American Elseviers, 1973, 164 pp.

Kahn, David[67]: *The Codebreakers*; Macmillan, 1967.

Kahn,G., MacQueen,D.B., and Plotkin.,G.(eds.)[84]: *Semantics of Data Types*; Springer Verlag, 391pp, Internat.Symp.Proc., 1984.

Kaiman,Richard A.[73]: *Structured Information Files*; Wiley-Becker-Hayes, 1973, 161 pp.

Karlton,P.C., Fuller,S.H., Scroggs,R.E., and Kaehler,E.B.[76]: "Performance of Height-Balanced Trees"; *CACM*, vol.19 no.1, Jan.1976, pp.23–28.

Katter,R.V. and Pearson,R.M.[75]: "MEDLARS II: A Third Generation Bibliographic Production System"; *Journal of Library Automation*, vol.8 no.2, Jun.1975, pp.87–97.

Katz,R.H. and Wong,E.[80]: "An Access Path Model for Physical Database Design"; *ACM-SIGMOD*, Chen(ed.), May 1980, pp.22–28.

Katz,R.H. and Lehman,T.J.[84]: "Database Support for Versions and Alternatives for Large Files"; *IEEE TSE*, vol.SE-10 no.2, Mar.1984, pp.191–200.

Kearns,J.P. and DeFazio,S.[83]: "Locality of Reference in Hierarchical Database Systems"; *IEEE TSE*, vol.SE-9 no.2, Mar.1983, pp.128–124.

Keehn,D. and Lacy,J.[74]: "VSAM Data Set Design Parameters"; *IBM Sys. J.*, vol.3, 1974, pp.186–202.

Kelton,W.David[85]: "Transient Exponential-Erlang Queues and Steady-State Simulation"; *CACM*, vol.28 no.7, Jul.1985, pp.741–749.

Kent,William[78]: *Data and Reality, Basic Assumptions in Data Processing Reconsidered*; North-Holland, 1978.

Kerr, Douglas S.(ed.)[75]: *Proc.of the Internat. Conf. on Large Databases*; ACM, 1975.

Kerschberg,Larry(ed.)[86]: *Expert Database Systems*; Benjamin-Cummings, Jan.1986.

Kim,Michelle Y.[86]: "Synchronized Disk Interleaving"; *IEEE TC*, Vol. C-35 no.11, Nov.1986.

King,J.L. and Schrems,E.L.[78]: "Cost-Benefit Analysis in Information Systems Development and Operation"; *ACM C.Surveys*, vol.10 no.1, Mar.1978, pp.19–24.

King,J.M.[81]: *Evaluating Data Base Management Systems*; VanNostrand-Reinhold, NY, 1981, 275 pp.

King,W.F.III(ed.)[75]: *Internat. Conf. on Management of Data*; ACM-SIGMOD 75, ACM 1975.

King,W.F.III[80]: "Relational Database Systems, Where Do We Stand Today?"; *Information Processing 80*, Proc. 1980 IFIP Congress, North-Holland. 1980.

Kitsuregawa,M. and Mikio,T.[87]: "Functional Disk System for Relational Database"; *IEEE CS DE 3*, Feb.1987.

Kiviat,P.J.,Villanueva,R.,and Markowitz,H.M.[69]: *The Simscript II Programming Language*; Prentice Hall, 1969.

Kleinrock, Leonard[75]: *Queuing Systems, vol.1: Theory*; Wiley 1975, 417 pp.

Knight,K.E.[68]: "Evolving Computer Performance"; *Datamation*, Jan.1968, pp.31–35.

Knott, Gary D.[75]: "Hashing Functions and Hash Table Storage and Retrieval"; *Comp. J.*, vol.18 no.3, 1975, pp.265–278.

Knuth,Donald E.[69]: *The Art of Computer Programming, vol.2: Seminumerical Algorithms*; Addison-Wesley, 1969, 634 pp.

Knuth,Donald E.[73F]: *The Art of Computer Programming, vol.1 - Fundamental Algorithms*; Addison-Wesley, 2nd ed., 1973, 634 pp.

Knuth,Donald E.[73S]: *The Art of Computer Programming, vol.3 - Sorting and Searching*; Addison Wesley, 1973, 722 pp.

Knuth,D.E.[79]: T_EX and METAFONT, *New Directions in Typesetting*; Digital Press, 1979.

Kobayashi,H.[78]: *Modeling and Analysis: An Introduction to Performance Evaluation Methodology*; Addison-Wesley, 1978, 446 pp.

Kochen,Manfred (ed.)[67]: *The Growth of Knowledge*; Wiley, 1967.

Kollias,J.G., Stocker,P.M., and Dearnley,P.A.[77]: "Improving the Performance of an Intelligent Data Management System"; *Comp. J.*, vol.20, 1977, pp.302–307.

Kollias,J.G. and Hatzopoulos,M.[83]: "Some Additional Models and Studies of the File Assignment Problem"; *ACM C.Surveys*, vol.15 no.1, Mar.1983, pp.81–82.

Konheim,A.G., Mack,M.H., McNeill,R.K., Tuckerman,B., and Waldbaum,G.[80]: "The IPS Cryptographic Programs"; *IBM Sys.J.*, vol.19 no.2, 1980, pp.253–283.

Korth,H. and Silberschatz,A.[86]: *Database System Concepts*; McGrawHill, 1986.

Kral,J.[71]: "Some Properties of the Scatter Storage Technique with Linear Probing"; *Comp. J.*, vol.14 no.2, May 1971, pp.145–149.

Kriegel,H-P. and Seeger,B.[87]: "Multidimensional Dynamic Quantile Hashing is Very Efficient for Non-Uniform Record Distributions"; *IEEE CS DE 3*, LA, Feb.1987.

Krinos,J.D.[73]: "Interaction Statistics from a Data Base Management System"; *Proc. 1973 NCC*, AFIPS vol.42, 1973, pp.283–290.

Kroenke,David M.[78]: *DATABASE: A Professional's Primer*; Science Res. Associates, 1978, 323 pp.

Kroenkhe,David M.[83]: *Business Computer Systems: An Introduction*, 2nd ed.; Mitchell Pub., Santa Cruz CA, 1983, 576pp.

Kronwal,R.A. and Tarter,M.E.[65]: "Cumulative Polygon Address Calculation Sorting"; *ACM National Conf. 20*, 1965, pp.376–34.

Kuehler,J.D. and Kerby,H.R.[66]: "A Photo-Digital Mass Storage System"; *Proc. 1966 FJCC*, AFIPS, vol.28, pp.753–742.

LaFue,Gilles M.E.[82]: "Semantic Integrity Dependencies and Delayed Integrity Checking"; *VLDB 8*, McLeod and Villasenor(eds.) 1982, pp.292–299.

Lampson, Butler W.[73]: "A Note on the Confinement Problem"; *CACM*, vol.16 no.10, Oct.1973, pp.613–615.

Lampson,B.W., Paul,M., and Siegert,H.J.[81]: *Distributed Systems – Architecture and Implementation*; Lecture Notes in CS, vol.105, Springer-Verlag, 1981, 510 pp.

Lancaster,F.W.[79]: *Information Retrieval Systems*, 2nd ed.; Wiley-Becker-Hayes, 1979.

Landauer,W.I.[63]: "The Balanced Tree and its Utilization in Information Retrieval"; *IEEE Trans. in Electronic Computers*, vol.EC-12 no.6, Dec.1963, pp.863–871.

Landers,T. and Rosenberg,R.L.[82]: "An Overview of MULTIBASE"; *ISDD 2*, Schneider(ed.), North-Holland 1982, pp.153-184.

Lang,C.A. and Gray,J.C.[68]: ASP - *A Ring Implemented Associative Structure Package*; *CACM*, vol.2 no.8, Aug.1968, pp.550–555.

Langdon,G.G.,jr.(ed.)[79]: "Data Base Machine, An Introduction"; *IEEE TC*, vol.C-28 no.6, Jun.1979.

Langworthy,George[86]: "Mass Storage"; *Digital Review*, vol.3 no.9, Jun.1986, pp.84–91.

Larson,J.A. and Rahimi,S.[85]: *Tutorial: Distributed Database Management*; IEEE CS, Jan.1985.

Larson,Per-Åke[81]: "Analysis of Index-Sequential Files with Overflow Chaining"; *ACM TODS*, vol.6 no.4, Dec.1981, pp.671–680.

Larson,Per-Åke[83]: "Analysis of Uniform Hashing"; *JACM*, Oct.1983.

Larson,P-Å.and Kajla,A.[84]: "File Organization: Implementation of a Method Guaranteeing Retrieval in one Access"; *CACM*, vol.27 no.7, Jul.1984, pp.670–677.

Larson,Per-Åke[85]: "Linear Hashing with Overflow-Handling by Linear Probing"; *ACM TODS*, vol.10 no.1, Mar.1985, pp.75–89.

Laudon,Kenneth[86]: "Data Quality and Due Process in large Interorganizational Record Systems"; *CACM*, vol.29 no.1, Jan.1986 pp.4–11.

Lee,D.L.[86]: "A Word Parallel, Bit Serial Signature Processor for Superimposed Coding"; *IEEE CS DE 2*, Los Angeles, Feb.1986.

Lee,D.T. and Wong,C.K.[80]: "Quintary Trees: A File Structure for Multidimensional Database Systems"; *ACM TODS*, vol.5 no.3, Sep.1980, pp.339–353.

Lefkovitz,David [74]: *Data Management for On-line Systems*; Hayden Book Co., 1974.

LeongHong, B.W. and Plagman, B.K.[82]: *Data Dictionary/Directory Systems: Administration, Implementation and Usage*; Wiley-Interscience, 1982

Leung,C.H.C. and Choo,Q.H.[82]: "The Effect of Fixed-Length Record Implementation on File System Response"; *Acta Informatica*, vol.17, 1982, pp.399-409.

Leung,C.H.C.[86]: "Dynamic Storage Fragmentation and File Deterioration"; *IEEE TSE*, vol.SE-12 no.3, 1986, pp.436–441.

Levin,K.D. and Morgan,H.L.[78]: "A Dynamic Optimization Model for Distributed Databases"; *Operations Research*, vol.26 no.5, Sep.-Oct.1978, pp.824–835.

Levy,M.R.[82]: "Modularity and the Sequential File Update Problem"; *CACM*, vol.25 no.6, Jun.1982, pp.362–369.

Lewin,M.H.[69]: "A Proposed 'Background Move' Instruction"; *Computer Group News of the IEEE*, vol.2 no.12, Nov.1969, pp.20–21.

Li,Z.J. and Wong,H.K.T.[87]: "Batched Interpolation Searching on Databases"; *IEEE CS DE 3*, LA, Feb.1987.

Lide,D.R., jr.[81]: "Critical Data for Critical Needs"; *Science*, vol.212 no.4501, Jun.1981, pp.1343–1349.

Lim, Pacifico Amarga[86]: CICS/VS *Command Level with* ANS *Cobol Examples*, 2nd ed.; VanNostrand Reinhold, 1986.

Lin,C.S., Smith,D.C.P., and Smith,J.M.[76]: "The Design of a Rotating Associative Array Memory for a Relational Database Management Application"; *ACM TODS*, vol.1 no.1, Mar.1976, pp.53–65.

Lin,J.J. and Liu,M.T.[82]: "System Design and Performance Evaluation of a Local Data Network for Very Large Distributed Databases"; *IEEE Symp. on Reliability in Distr. Software and Database Sys. 2*, Wiederhold(ed.), Pittsburgh PA, Jul.1982, pp.134–143.

Lindsay,B. and Gligor,V.[79]: "Migration and Authentication of Protected Objects"; *IEEE TSE*, vol.SE-5, Nov.1979, pp.607–611.

Lindsay,B. et al[84]: "Computation and Communication in R-*, A Distributed Database Manager"; *ACM TCS*, vol.2 no.1, Feb.1984, pp.24-38.

Litwin,W.[80]: "Linear Hashing: A New Tool for File and Table Addressing"; *VLDB 6*, Lochovsky and Taylor(eds.), Montreal, Oct.1980, pp.212–223.

Litwin,W.[81]: "Trie Hashing"; *ACM-SIGMOD 1981*, pp.19–29.

Litwin,W.[84]: "MALPHA: A Multi-Database Manipulation Language"; *IEEE DE 1*, Los Angeles, Apr.1984.

Lochovsky,F.H. and Taylor R.D.(eds.)[80]: *Proc. of the 6th VLDB*; IEEE publication 80 CH-1534-7C, 1980, 435 pp.

Lohman,G.M. and Muckstadt,J.A.[77]: "Optimal Policy for Batch Operations: Backup, Checkpointing, Reorganization, and Updating"; *ACM TODS*, vol.2 no.3, Sep.1977, pp.209–222.

Lomet,D.B.[75]: "Scheme for Invalidating Free References"; *IBM JRD*, vol.19 no.1, Jan.1975, pp.26–35.

Long, P.L. et al[71]: "Large On-Line Files of Bibliographic Data. An Efficient and a Mathematical Prediction of Retrieval Behavior"; *Information Processing-71*, North-Holland, pp.473.

Loo,J., O'Donald,B.T., and Whiteman,I.R.[71]: "Real Time Considerations for an Airline"; *Proc. 1971 SJCC*, AFIPS vol.38, pp.83–92.

Lorie,Raymond(ed.)[83]: *Engineering Design Applications*; ACM-SIGMOD 83, vol.2, Proc., Database Week, San Jose, May 1983.

Lowe,Thomas C.[68]: "The Influence of Data Base Characteristics and Usage on Direct Access File Organization"; *JACM*, vol.15 no.4, Oct.1968, pp.535–548.

Lucas,Henry C., jr.[73]: *Computer Based Information Systems in Organizations*; Science Research Associates, 1973.

Lucas,Henry C.,jr.[75]: "Performance and the Use of an Information System"; *Management Science*, vol.21, Apr.1975, pp.908–919.

Lucas,Henry C.,jr.[81]: *The Analysis, Design, and Implementation of Information Systems*; McGraw-Hill 1981, 419 pp.

Luk,W.S.[83]: "On Estimating Block Accesses in Database Organizations"; *CACM*, vol.26 no.11, Nov.1983, pp.945–947.

Lum,Vincent Y.[70]: "Multi-Attribute Retrieval with Combined Indexes"; *CACM*, vol.1 no.11, Nov.1970, pp.660–665.

Lum,V.Y. and Ling,H.[71L]: "An Optimization Problem on the Selection of Secondary Keys"; *ACM National Conf. 26*, 1971, pp.349–456.

Lum,V.Y., Yuen,P.S.T., and Dodd,M.[71]: "Key-to-Address Transformation Techniques: A Fundamental Performance Study on Large Existing Formatted Files"; *CACM*, vol.14 no.4, Apr.1971, pp.238–239.

Lum, V.Y.[73]: "General Performance Analysis of Key-to-Address Transformation Methods Using an Abstract File Concept"; *CACM*, vol.16 no.10, Oct.1973, pp.603–612.

Lum,V.Y., Senko M.E., Wang,C.P., and Ling,H.[75]: "A Cost Oriented Algorithm for Data Set Allocation in Storage Hierarchies"; *CACM*, vol.18 no.6, Jun.1975, pp.318–322.

Lynch,C. and Brownrigg,E.B.[81]: "Application of Data Compression Techniques to a Large Bibliographic Database"; *VLDB 7*, Zaniolo and Delobel(eds.), Sep.1981, pp.435–447.

MacDougall,M.H.[82]: "Computer System Simulation: An Introduction"; *VLDB 8*, McLeod and Villansenor(eds.), Mexico City, Sept.1982.

Madnick,Stuart E.[75]: "INFOPLEX: Hierarchical Decomposition of a Large Information Management System Using a Microprocessor Complex"; *Proc.1975 NCC*, AFIPS vol. 44, pp.581–586.

Maier,D. and Ullman,J.D.[81]: "Fragments of Relations"; ACM XP2 Workshop on Relational Database Theory, Jun.1981.

Maier,David[83]: *The Theory of Relational Databases*; CS Press, 1983, 637 pp.

Maio,D., Scalas,M.R., and Tiberio,P.[84]: "Dynamic Non-dense Indexes in Relational Databases"; *Information Processing Letters*, Sep.1984.

Major,J.B.[81]: "Processor, I/O Path, and DASD Configuration Capacity"; *IBM Sys.J.*, vol. 20 no.1, 1981, pp.63–85.

Maloney,J. and Black,A.[87]: "File Sessions: A Technique and Analysis of Dynamic File Usage Patterns in UNIX"; *IEEE CS DE 3*, LA, Feb.1987.

Mano,Morris M.[82]: *Computer System Architecture*, 2nd ed.; Prentice-Hall, 1982.

March,S.T. and Severance,D.[77]: "The Determination of Efficient Record Segmentations and Blocking Factors for Shared Files"; *ACM TODS*, vol.2 no.3, 1977, pp.279–296.

March,S.T.[83]: "Techniques for Structuring Database Records"; *ACM C. Surveys*, vol.15 no.1, Mar.1983, pp.45–79.

March,S.T. and Scudder,G.D.[84]: "On the Selection of Efficient Record Segmentations and Backup Strategies for Large Shared Databases"; *ACM TODS*, vol.9 no.3, Sep.1984, pp.409–438.

Marill,T. and Stern,D.[75]: "The DATA-COMPUTER - A Network Data Utility"; *Proc.1975 NCC*, AFIPS vol.44, AFIPS Press, pp.389–395.

Marron,B.A. and deMaine, P.A.D.[67]: "Automatic Data Compression"; *CACM*, vol.10 no. 11, Mar.1967, pp.711–715.

Martin,James[67]: *Design of Real-Time Computer Systems*; Prentice Hall, 1967, 640 pp.

Martin,James[72]: *Systems Analysis for Data Transmission*; Prentice Hall, 1972, 896 pp.

Martin,James[73]: *Design of Man-Computer Dialogues*; Prentice Hall, 1973, 496 pp.

Martin,James[76]: *Principles of Data-Base Management*; Prentice Hall, 1976, 352 pp.

Martin,James[77]: *Computer Data-Base Organization*, 2nd ed.; Prentice Hall, 1977, 576 pp.

Martin,James[83]: *Managing the Database Environment*; Prentice-Hall, 1983, 766 pp.

Martin,T.H. and Parker,E.B.[75]: "Comparative Analysis of Interactive Retrieval Systems"; *ACM-SIGPLAN-SIGIR*, Nance (ed.), 1975 (Proc.of 1973 meeting), pp.75–85.

Maruyama,K. and Smith,S.E.[76]: "Optimal Reorganization of Distributed Space Disk Files"; *CACM*, vol.19 no.11, Nov.1976, pp.634–642.

Maryanski,Fred J.[80]: "Backend Database Systems"; *ACM C.Surveys*, vol.12 no.1, Mar.1980, pp.3–25.

Maryanski,Fred.J.[83]: *Digital Computer Simulation*; Hayden Book Co., 1983.

Maurer, W.D. and Lewis, T.G.[75]: "Hash Table Methods"; *ACM C. Surveys*, vol.7 no.1, Mar.1975, pp.5–20.

McCarthy,John L.[82]: "Metadata Management for Large Statistical Databases"; *VLDB 8*, Mexico City, Sep.1982, pp.234–243.

McCormick,W.T.,jr.., Schweitzer,P.J., and White,T.W.[72]: "Problem Decomposition and Data Reorganization by a Clustering Technique"; *Oper. Res.*, vol.20 no.5, Sep.1972, pp.993–1009.

McCreight,E.M.[77]: "Pagination of B*-trees with Variable-Length Records"; *CACM*, Sep.1977, pp.670–674.

McEwen,H.E.(ed.)[74]: *Management of Data Elements in Information Processing*; US Dept. of Commerce, COM 74-10700, NTIS, Springfield VA, Apr.1974.

McFadden,F.R. and Suver,J.D.[78]: "Costs and Benefits of Database Systems"; *Harvard Business Review*, vol.56 no.1, Jan.1978, pp.131-138.

McFadden,F.R. and Hoffer, J.A.[85]: *Data Base Management*; Benjamin-Cummings, 1985.

McGee, W.C.[59]: "Generalization - Key to Successful Electronic Data Processing"; *JACM*, vol.6 no.1. Jan.1959. pp.1-23.

Mealy,George H.[67]: "Another Look at Data"; *Proc.1967 FJCC*, AFIPS vol.31, pp.525-534.

Mellen,G.E.[73]: "Cryptology, Computers, and Common Sense"; *Proc. 1973 NCC*, AFIPS vol.42, pp.569-579.

Merten,A.G.(ed.)[77]: *Proc.of the 3rd VLDB Conf.*; IEEE, 1977, 570 pp.

Meyer,C.H.[73]: "Design Considerations for Cryptography"; *Proc.1973 NCC*, AFIPS vol.43, pp.603-606.

Meyers,Glenford J.[81]: *Advances in Computer Architecture*; Wiley, 1981.

Michael,G.A.[80]: "An Archival Memory System Specification"; *Fourth IEEE Symp. Mass Storage Systems*, Apr.1980, pp.62-66.

Michaels, P.C. and Richards, W.J.[75]: "Magnetic Bubble Mass Memory"; *IEEE Trans. Magnetics*, vol.11, Jan.1975, pp.21-25.

Miller, Arthur R.[71]: *The Assault on Privacy*; The Univ.Michigan Press, Ann Arbor, 1971.

Miller,J.R.[70]: *Professional Decision Making*; Praeger Publisher, NY, 1970.

Miller,S.W. and Collins,W.W.[85]: "Towards a Reference Model of Mass Storage Systems"; *IEEE Computer*, vol.18 no.7, Jul.1985, pp.9-22.

Minoura,T. and Wiederhold,G.[82]: "Resilient Extended True-Copy Token Scheme for a Distributed Database"; *IEEE TSE*, vol.SE-8 no.3, May 1982, pp.173-189.

Minsky,N.[81]: "Synergistic Authorization in Database Systems"; *VLDB 7*, Zaniolo and Delobel(eds.), Sep.1981, pp.543-552.

Mohan,C.[84]: *Tutorial: Recent Advances in Distributed Data Base Management*; IEEE CS Press EHO218-8, Dec.1984.

Molho,L.[70]: "Hardware Aspects of Secure Computing"; *Proc. 1970 SJCC*, AFIPS vol.36, pp.135-141.

Morey,R.C.[82]: "Estimating and Improving the Quality of Information in a MIS"; *CACM*, vol.15 no.5, May 1982, pp.337-342.

Morgan,Howard Lee[74]: "Optimal Space Allocation on Disk Storage"; *CACM*, vol.11 no.3, Mar.1974, pp.139-142.

Morgan,H.L. and Levin,K.D.[77]: "Optimal Program and Data Locations in Computer Networks"; *CACM*, vol.20 no.5, May 1977, pp.315-322.

Moroney,M.J.[56]: *Facts from Figures*, 3rd ed.; Pelican Books, 1956, 472 pp.

Morris,R.[68]: *Scatter Storage Techniques*; *CACM*, vol.1 no.1, Jan.1968, pp.38-44.

Mullin,James K.[71]: "Retrieval-Update Speed Trade-offs Using Combined Indexes"; *CACM*, vol.14 no.12, Dec.1971, pp.775-776.

Mullin,James K.[72]: "An Improved Indexed-Sequential Access Method Using Hashed Overflow"; *CACM*, vol.15 no.5, May 1972, pp.301-307.

Mulvany,R.B.[74]: "Engineering Design of a Disk Storage Facility with Data Modules"; *IBM JRD*, vol.18 no.6, Nov.1974, pp.489-505.

Navathe,S.B. and Fry, J.P.[76]: "Restructuring for Large Data Bases: Three Levels of Abstraction"; *ACM TODS*, vol.1 no.1, Mar.1976, pp.138-158.

Navathe,S., Ceri,S., Wiederhold,G., and Dou,J-L.[84]: "Vertical Partitioning for Physical and Distribution Design of Databases"; *ACM TODS*, vol.9 no.4, Dec.1984, pp.680-710.

NBS (US National Bureau of Standards)[74]: *Guidelines for Automatic Data Processing Physical Security and Risk Management*; NBS-FIPS pub.31, Jun.1974, 92 pp.

Needham,Roger M.[72]: "Protection Systems and Protection Implementation"; *Proc. 1972 FJCC*, AFIPS vol.41, pp.571-578.

Needham,R.M. and Schroeder,M.D.[78]: "Using Encryption for Authentication in Large Networks of Computers"; *CACM*, vol.21 no.12, Dec.1978, pp.993–999.

Neuhold,E.J.(ed.)[76]: *Modelling in Data Base Management Systems*; North-Holland 1976.

Neuhold,E.J. and Walter,B.[82]: "An Overview of the Architecture of the Distributed Database System POREL"; *Proc. Int. Symp. on Distributed Data Bases 2*, Schneider(ed.), North-Holland 1982., pp.247-289.

Nevaleinen,O. and Vesterinen,M.[77]: "Determining Blocking Factors for Sequential Files by Heuristic Methods"; *Computer J.*, vol.20, 1977, pp.245–247.

Newell,G.F.[71]: *Applications of Queuing Theory*; Chapman and Hall, 1971.

Nielsen,Norman R.[67]: "The Simulation of Time Sharing Systems"; *CACM*, vol.10 no.7, Jul.1967, pp.397–412.

Nievergelt,Jürg[74]: "Binary Search Trees and File Organization"; *ACM C. Surveys*, vol.6 no.3, Sep.1974, pp.195–207.

Nievergelt,J.,Hinterberger,H.,and Sevcik,K.C.[84]: "The Grid File: An Adaptable Symmetric Multikey File Structure"; *ACM TODS*, vol.9 no.1, Mar.1984, pp.38–71.

O'Connell,M. L.[71]: "A File Organization Method Using Multiple Keys"; *Proc.1971 SJCC*, AFIPS vol.38, pp.539–544.

O'Lear,B.T. and Choy,J.H.[82]: "Software Considerations in Mass Storage Systems"; *IEEE Computer*, vol.15 no.7, Jul.1982, pp.36–44.

O'Neill,J.T.(ed.)[76]: *MUMPS Language Standard*; NBS Handbook 118,Government Printing Office, Washington DC, 1976.

O'Reagan, Robert T.[72]: "Computer Assigned Codes from Verbal Responses"; *CACM*, vol. 15 no.6, Jun.1972, pp.455–459.

Orr,Ken[81]: *Structured Requirements Definition*; QED Information Sciences, 1981, 235pp.

Ousterhout,J.K. et al[85]: "A Trace-driven Analysis of the UNIX 4.2 BSD File System"; *ACM Symp. on Operating Systems Principles 12*, Dec.1985, pp.15–24.

Overholt,K.J.[73]: "Optimal Binary Search Methods"; *BIT*, vol.13 no.1, 1973, pp.84–91.

Ozkarahan,E.A., Schuster,S.A. and Sevcik,K.C.[77]: "Performance Evaluation of a Relational Associative Processor"; *ACM TODS*, vol.2 no.2, Jun.1977, pp.175–195.

Özsu,M.Tamer[85]: "Modeling and Analysis of Distributed Database Concurrency Control Algorithms using an Extended Petri Net Formalism"; *IEEE TSE*, vol.SE-11 no.10, Oct.1985, pp.1225–1240.

Palvia,P.[85]: "Expressions for Batched Searching of Sequential and Hierachical Files"; *ACM TODS*, vol.10 no.1, Mar.1985, pp.97-106.

Papadimitriou,C.H.and Kanallakis,P.C.[84]: "On Concurrency Control by Multiple Versions"; *ACM TODS*, vol.9 no.1, Mar.1984, pp.89–99.

Parker,D.B.[81]: *Ethical Conflicts in Computer Science and Technology*; AFIPS, 1981.

Parkin,A.[74]: "Bringing Cost into File Design Decisions"; *Comp. J.*, vol.18 no.3, 1974, pp.198–199.

Pechura,M.A. and Schoeffler,J.D.[83]: "Estimating File Access Time of Floppy Disks"; *CACM*, vol.26 no.10, Oct.1983, pp.754–763.

Petersen,H.E. and Turn,R.[67]: "System Implications of Information Privacy"; *Proc. 1967 SJCC*, AFIPS vol.30, 1967, pp.291–300.

Peterson,J. and Silberschatz,A.[85]: *Operating System Concepts*, 2nd ed.; Addison-Wesley, 1985.

Peterson,W.W.[57]: "Addressing for Random Access Storage"; *IBM JRD*, vol.1 no.2, Apr.1957, pp.130–146.

Peterson,W.W. and Weldon,E.J.[72]: *Error Correcting Codes*; MIT Press 1972, 285 pp.

Piatetsky-Shapiro,G. and Cornell,C.[84]: "Accurate Estimation of the Number of Tuples Satisfying a Condition"; *SIGMOD 1984*, Yormark(ed.), pp.256–276.

Piepmeyer, William F.[75]: "Optimal Balancing of I/O Requests to Disk"; *CACM*, vol.18 no.9, Sept.1975, pp.524–527.

Pierce,J.[61]: *Symbols, Signals, and Noise*; Harper and Row, 1961.

Popek,G., et al.[82]: "The LOCUS Distributed File System"; *ACM Symp. on Operating Systems Principles 9*, Bretton Woods NH, Oct.1982.

Powers,M.J., Adams,D.R., and Mills,H.D.[84]: *Computer Information Systems Development: Analysis and Design*; South-Western Pub.Co, Cincinnati OH, 1984, 686 pp.

Press,W.H., Flannery,B.P., Teukolsky,S.A., and Vetterling,W.T.[86]: *Numerical Recipes, The Art of Scientific Computing*; Cambridge Univ.Press, 1986, 818 pp.

Prywes,N.S.and Gray,H.J.[59]: "The Organization of a Multi-List Type Associative Memory"; *ACM National Conf. 14*, 1959; *IEEE Trans. Comp. and Elec.*, Sep.1963, pp.488–492.

Pugh,E.W.[71]: "Storage Hierarchies: Gaps, Cliffs, and Trends"; *IEEE Trans. Magnetics*, vol.Mag-7, Dec.1971, pp.810–814.

Purdy, George B.[74]: "A High Security Log-in Procedure"; *CACM*, vol.17 no.8, Aug.1974, pp.442–445.

Quarterman,J.S. and Hoskins,J.C.[86]: "Notable Computer Networks"; *CACM*, vol.29 no.10, Oct.1986, pp.932–970.

Ramamoorthy,C.V. and Chandy,C.V.[70]: "Optimization of Memory Hierarchies in Multi-programmed Systems"; *JACM*, vol.17 no.3, Jul.1970, pp.426–445.

Ramamoorthy,C.V. and Wah,B.W.[79]: "The Placement of Relations on a Distributed Relational Database"; *IEEE Internat.Conf.on Distr.Comp.Sys. 1*, Huntsville AL, Oct.1979, pp.642–650.

Rathmann,Peter[84]: "Dynamic Data Structures on Optical Disks"; *IEEE DE 1*, Los Angeles, Apr.1984, pp.175-180.

Ray-Chaudhuri,D.K.[68]: "Combinatorial Information Retrieval Systems for Files"; *SIAM J. Appl. Math. vol.16 no.5*, 1968, pp.973–992.

Reisner,P.[77]: "The Use of Psychological Experimentation as an Aid to Development of a Query Language"; *IEEE TSE*, vol.SE-3 no.3, May 1977.

Reitman,W.R. et al[69]: "AUTONOTE, a Personal Information and Storage System"; *ACM National Conf. 24*, 1969, pp.67–76.

Renniger, Clark R.(ed.)[74]: *Approaches to Privacy and Security*; National Bureau of Standards, Wash.DC, Spec. Pub. 404, Sep.1974.

Riley,M.J.(ed.)[81]: *Management Information Systems*, 2nd ed; Holden-Day, 1981.

Rivest,R.L.[76]: "Partial Match Retrieval Algorithms"; *SIAM J. on Computing*, vol.5 no.1, 1976, pp.19–50.

Robey,D. and Farrow,D.[82]: "User Involvement in Information Systems Development: A Conflict Model and Empirical Test"; *Management Science*, vol.28 no.1, Jan.1982, pp.73–85.

Robinson,T.J.[86]: "Order Preserving Linear Hashing Using Dynamic Key Statistics"; *ACM-PODS*, Cambridge MA, Mar.1986.

Rochkind,M.J.[82]: "Structure of a Database File System for the UNIX Operating System"; *Bell System Technical Journal*, vol.16 no.9, Nov.1982, pp.2387–2405.

Rodriguez-Rosell,J.[76]: "Empirical Data Reference Behavior in Data Base Systems"; *IEEE Computer*, vol.9 no.11, Nov.1976, pp.9–13.

Rosenberg,A.L. and Snyder,L.[81]: "Time- and Space-Optimality in B-Trees"; *ACM TODS*, vol.6 no.1, Mar.1981, pp.174–183.

Ross,D.T.[77]: "Structured Analysis (SA): A Language for Communicating Ideas"; *IEEE TSE*, vol.SE-3 no.1, 1977, pp.16–34.

Ross,Ronald G.[81]: *Data Dictionaries and Data Administration*; AMACOM, New York NY, 1981, 454 pp.

Rothnie,J.B.,jr. and Lozano,T.[74]: "Attribute Based File Organization in a Paged Memory Environment"; *CACM*, vol.17 no.2, Feb.1974, pp.63–79.

Rothnie,J.B.,jr. et al[80]: "Introduction to a System for Distributed Databases (SDD-1)"; *ACM TODS*, vol.5 no.1, Mar.1980.

Ruchte,W.D. and Tharp,Alan L.[87]: "Linear Hashing with Priority Splitting"; *IEEE CS DE 3*, LA, Feb.1987.

Rudolph,J.A.[72]: "A Production Implementation of an Associative Array Processor — STARAN"; *Proc. 1972 FJCC*, AFIPS vol.41, pp.229–242.

Rustin, Randall,(ed.)[72]: *Data Base Systems*; Prentice Hall, 1972.

Saccà,Domenico and Wiederhold,G.[85]: "Database Partitioning in a Cluster of Processors"; *ACM TODS*, vol.10 no.1, Mar.1985, pp.29–56.

Sacco,Giovanni Maria[82]: "A Mechanism for Managing the Buffer Pool in a Relational Database System Using the Hot Set Model"; *VLDB 8*, Mexico City, Sep.1982, pp.257–262.

SacksDavis,R. and Ramamohanarao,K.[83]: "A Two Level Superimposed Coding Scheme for Partial Match Retrieval"; *Information Systems*, vol.8 no.4, 1983.

Safran,C., Sobel,E., Lightfoot,J., and Porter,D.[86]: "A Computer Program for Interactive Searches of a Medical Data Base"; *Medinfo 86*, North-Holland 1986, pp.545-549.

Sakamoto,G.J.[82]: "Use of DB/DC Data Dictionary to Support Business Systems Planning Studies: An Approach"; *The Economics of Information Processing*: vol.1, Management Perspectives, Goldberg and Lorin(eds.), John Wiley, 1982, pp.127–136.

Salasin,John[73]: "Hierarchial Storage in Information Retrieval"; *CACM*, vol.16 no.5, May 1973, pp.291–295.

Salem,K. and GarciaMolina,H.[86]: "Disk Striping"; *IEEE CS DE 2*, Los Angeles, Feb.1986.

Saltzer, Jerome H.[74]: "Protection and the Control of Information Sharing in Multics"; *CACM*, vol.17 no.7, Jul.1974, pp.388-402.

Saltzer,J.H. and Schroeder,M.D.[75]: "The Protection of Information in Computer Systems"; *Proc. of the IEEE*, vol.63 no.9, Sep.1975, pp.1278–1308.

Salza,S., Terranova,M. and Velardi,P.[83]: "Performance Modeling of the DBMAC Architecture"; *Intern. Workshop on Database Machines 3*, Sep.1983, Munich, Missikoff(ed.), Springer Verlag, 1983.

Salza,S. and Terranova,M.[85]: "Workload Modeling for Relational Database Systems"; *Intern. Workshop on Database Machines 4*, Mar.1985, Bahamas, DeWitt and Boral(eds.), Springer Verlag, 1985.

Salzberg,Betty Joan[86]: *An Introduction to Data Base Design*; Academic Press, 1986.

Sarin,S.K., Kaufman,C.W., and Somers,J.E.[86]: "Using History Information to Process Delayed Database Updates"; *VLDB 12*, Aug.1986.

Satyanarayanan,M.[81]: "A Study of File Sizes and Functional Lifetimes"; *ACM Symp. on Operating Systems Principles 8*, ACM Order no.534810, Dec.1981, pp.96–108.

Savage,P.[85]: "Proposed Guidelines for an Automated Cartridge Repository"; *IEEE Computer*, vol.18 no.7, Jul.1985, pp.49–58.

Saxton,L.V., Ip,M.Y., and Raghavan,V.V.[83]: "On the Selection of an Optimal Set of Indexes"; *IEEE TSE*, vol.SE-9 no.2, Mar.1983, pp.135–143.

Schay,G.jr. and Spruth, W.G.[62]: "Analysis of a File Addressing Method"; *CACM*, vol.5 no.8, Aug.1962, pp.459–462.

Schay,G.,jr. and Raver,N.[63]: "A Method for Key-to-Address Transformations"; *IBM JRD*, vol.7 no.2, Apr.1963, pp.121-126.

Schkolnick,Mario[75]: "The Optimal Selection of Secondary Indices for Files"; *Information Systems*, vol.1, 1975, pp.141–146.

Schkolnick,M.[77]: "A Clustering Algorithm for Hierarchical Structures"; *ACM TODS*, vol.2 no.1, May 1977, pp.27–44.

Schkolnick,M. et al[83]: "A Multiprocessor System for High Availability"; *Proc. IEEE COMPuter Systems and Applications Conference*, San Francisco, 1983.

Schneider,M.(ed.)[82]: *Proceedings Human Factors in Computer Systems*; Inst. for Science and Technology, NBS, Mar.1982, Gaithersburg MD.

Scholl,M.[81]: "New File Organizations Based on Dynamic Hashing"; *ACM TODS*, vol.6 no.1, Mar.1981, pp.194–211.

Schroeder,M.D. and Saltzer,J.[72]: "A Hardware Architecture for Implementing Protection Rings"; *CACM*, vol.15 no.3, Mar.1972, pp.157–170.

Schroeder,M.D., Birrell,A.D., and Needham,R.M.[84]: "Experience With GRAPEVINE: The Growth of a Distributed System"; *ACM TCS*, vol.2 no.1, Feb.1984, pp.3–23.

Schwartz,Eugene S.[63]: "A Dictionary for Minimum Redundancy Encoding"; *JACM*, vol.10 no.4, Oct.1963, pp.413–439.

Seaman,P.H., Lind,R.A., and Wilson,T.L.[66]: "An Analysis of Auxiliary Storage Activity"; *IBM Sys.J.*, vol.5 no.3, 1966, pp.158–170.

Seaman,P.H. and Soucy,R.C.[69]: "Simulating Operating Systems"; *IBM Sys.J.*, vol.8 no.4, 1969, pp.264–279.

Selbman,H.K.[74]: "Bitstring Processing for Statistical Evaluation of Large Volumes of Medical Data"; *Methods of Information in Medicine*, vol.13 no.2, Apr.1974, pp.61–64.

Senko,M.E., Altman,E.B. Astrahan,M.M., and Fehder,P.L.[73]: "Data Structures and Accessing in Data Base Systems"; *IBM Sys.J.*, vol.12 no.1, 1973, pp.30–93.

Senko,M.E.[77]: "Data Structures and Data Accessing in Data Base Systems Past, Present, Future"; *IBM Sys.J.*, vol.16 no.3, 1977, pp.208–257.

Sevcik,K.C.[81]: "Data Base System Performance Prediction Using an Analytical Model"; *VLDB 7*, Zaniolo and Delobel(eds.), Sep.1981, pp.182–198.

Severance,D.G.and Merten,A.G.[72]: "Performance Evaluation of File Organizations through Modelling"; *ACM National Conf. 27*, 1972, pp.1061–1072.

Severance,D.G. and Lohman,G.M[76]: "Differential Files: Their Applications to the Maintenance of Large Databases"; *ACM TODS*, vol.1 no.3, Sep.1976, pp.256–367.

Shannon,C.E. and Weaver,W.[62]: *The Mathematical Theory of Computation*; Bell System Technical Journal, 1948; reprinted by The Univ. of Illinois Press, 1962, 80 pp.

Sharpe,William F.[69]: *The Economics of Computers*; Columbia Univ.Press, NY, 1969.

Shaw,David[80]: "A Relational Database Machine Architecture"; *ACM-SIGIR*, vol.XV, Apr.1980, pp.84–95.

Shneiderman,Ben[73]: "Optimum Data Base Reorganization Points"; *CACM*, vol.16 no.6, Jun.1973, pp.362–365.

Shneiderman,Ben[74]: "A Model for Optimizing Indexed File Structures"; *Internat. Journal of Computer and Inf. Sciences*, vol.3 no.1, 1974, pp.93-103.

Shneiderman,B. and Goodman,V.[76]: "Batched Searching of Sequential and Tree Structured Files"; *ACM TODS*, vol.1 no.3, Sep.1976, pp.268–275; comments in vol.10 no.2, Jun.1985, pp.285–287.

Shneiderman,B.[77]: "Reduced Combined Indexes for Efficient Multiple Attribute Retrieval"; *Information Systems*, vol.1 no.4, 1977, pp.149–154.

Shneiderman,B.(ed.)[78]: *Databases: Improving Usability and Responsiveness*; Academic Press, NY, 1978.

Shu,N.C.[87]: "Automatic Data Transformation and Restructuring"; *IEEE CS DE 3*, LA, Feb.1987.

Shuey,R. and Wiederhold,G.[86]: "Data Engineering and Information Systems"; *IEEE Computer*, Jan.1986, pp.18–30.

Siler,K.F.[76]: "A Stochastic Evaluation Model for Database Organizations in Data Retrieval Systems"; *CACM*, vol.19 no.2, Feb.1976, pp.84–95.

Siwiec,J.E.[77]: "A High-Performance DB/DC System"; *IBM Sys.J.*, vol.16 no.2, 1977, pp.169–174.

Skeen,D., Cristian,F., and ElAbbadi,A.[85]: "An Efficient Fault-Tolerant Algorithm for Replicated Data Management"; *ACM-PODS 4*, Mar.1985.

Skinner,C.E.[69]: "Effects of Storage Contention on System Performance"; *IBM Sys.J.*, vol.8 no.4, 1969, pp.319–333.

Sklaroff,J.R.[76]: "Redundancy Management Technique for Space Shuttle Computers"; *IBM JRD*, vol.20 no.1, Jan.1976, pp.20–30.

Slonim,J. et al[82]: "A Throughput Model, Sequential versus Concurrent Accessing in Very Large Data Bases"; *Information Systems*, vol.7 no.1, Mar.1982, pp.65–83.

Smith,A.J.[81]: "Analysis of Long-Term File Migration Patterns"; *IEEE TSE*, vol.SE-7 no.4, Jul.1981, pp.403–417.

Smith,A.J.[85]: "Disk Cache – Miss Ratio Analysis and Design Considerations"; *ACM TCS*, vol.3 no.3, Aug.1985, pp.161–203.

Snedecor,G.W. and Cochran,W.G.[67]: *Statistical Methods*; Iowa State Univ.Press, Ames IO, 1967, 593 pp.

Sockut,G.H.[78]: "A Performance Model for Computer Data-Base Reorganization Performed Concurrently with Usage"; *Operations Res.*, vol.26 no.5, Sep.-Oct.1978, pp.789–804.

Sockut,G.H. and Goldberg,R.P.[79]: "Data Base Reorganization - Principles and Practice"; *ACM C.Surveys*, vol.11 no.4, Dec.1979.

Solomon,Martin B.[66]: "Economics of Scale and the IBM System/360"; *CACM*, vol.9 no.6, Jun.1966, pp.435–440.

Solomon,M.K. and Bickel,R.W.[86]: "A Self-Assessment Procedure Dealing with File Processing"; *CACM*, vol.29 no.8, Aug.1986, pp.745–750.

Sprague, R. H.. jr. and Carlson, E. D. [82]: *Building Effective Decision Support Systems*; Prentice-Hall, Feb.1982, 329 pp.

Sreenivasan,K. and Kleinman,A.J.[74]: "On the Construction of a Representative Synthetic Workload"; *CACM*, vol.17 no.3, Mar.1974, pp.127–133.

SSA (US Social Security Administration)[57]: Report of Distribution of Surnames in the SS Account Number File; HEW, SSA, Bureau of Old Age and Survivors Insurance 1957.

Stahl,Fred A.[73]: "A Homophonic Cipher for Computational Cryptography"; *Proc. 1973 NCC*, AFIPS vol.42, pp.565–568.

Stanfel,Larry E.[70]: "Tree Structures for Optimal Searching"; *JACM*, vol.17 no.3, Jul.1970, pp.508–517.

Steel,Tom B.,jr.[64]: "Beginnings of a Theory of Information Handling"; *CACM*, Feb.1964, pp.97–103.

Sterling,T.D.[74,75]: "Guidelines for Humanizing Computerized Information Systems, A Report from Stanley House"; *CACM*, vol.17 no.11, Nov.1974, pp.609–613; *Science*, vol.190 no.4220, 19 Dec.1975, pp.1168–1172.

Stocker,P.M.[77]: "Storage Utilization in a Self-Organizing Data Base"; *Proc. 1977 NCC*, AFIPS vol.46, pp.119–122.

Stone,Harold S.[72]: *Introduction to Data Structures and Computer Organization*; McGraw-Hill, 1972, 1974.

Stone,H.S. and Fuller,S.F.[73]: "On the Near-Optimality of the Shortest-Access-Time-First Drum Scheduling Discipline"; *CACM*, vol.16 no.6, Jun.1973, pp.352–353.

Stone, Harold S.(ed.)[75]: *Introduction to Computer Architecture*; SRA, Palo Alto 1975.

Stonebraker,Michael[74]: "The Choice of Partial Inversions and Combined Indices"; *Journal of Computer and Information Science*, Jun.1974, pp.167–188.

Stonebraker,M.,et al.[79]: "Concurrency Control and Consistency of Multiple Copies of Data in Distributed INGRES"; *IEEE TSE*, vol.SE-5 no.3, May 1979, pp.188–194.

Stonebraker,Michael[80]: "Retrospection on a Data Base System"; *ACM TODS*, vol.5 no.2, Jun.1980, pp.225–240.

Stonebraker,Michael[81]: "Operating System Support for Database Management"; *CACM*, vol.14 no.7, Jul.1981.

Stonebraker, Michael(ed.)[85]: *The INGRES Papers: Anatomy of a Relational Database System*; Addison-Wesley, 1985.

Stover,R.F. and Krishnaswamy,S.[73]: "Ensuring Input Data Integrity in a High-Volume Environment"; *Proc. 1973 NCC*, AFIPS vol.42, pp.M54–M59.

Streeter,D.N.[73]: "Centralization or Dispersion of Computing Facilities"; *IBM Sys.J.*, vol. 12 no.3, 1973, pp.283–301.

Stroustrup,B.[86]: *The C++ Programming Language*; Addison-Wesley, 1986.

Studer,Rudi[80]: "A Dialogue Interface for Data Base Applications"; *VLDB 6*, Lochovsky and Taylor(eds.), Oct.1980, pp.167–182.

Su,S.Y.W. et al[80]: "Database Machines and Some Issues on DBMS Standards"; *Proc.1980 NCC*, AFIPS vol.49, pp.191–208.

Sussenguth,E.H.[63]: "Use of Tree Structures for Processing Files"; *CACM*, vol.6 no.5, May 1963, pp.272–279.

Svobodova,Liba[84]: "File Servers for Network-Based Distributed Systems"; *ACM C.Surveys*, vol.16 no.4, Dec.1984, pp.353–398.

Symons,C.R. and Tijsma,P[82]: "A Systematic and Practical Approach to the Definition of Data"; *Computer J.*, vol.25 no.4, Nov.1982, pp.410–422.

Tanenbaum,A.S.[81]: *Computer Networks*; Prentice Hall, 1981, 517 pp.

Tang, Donald T. and Chien, Robert T.[69]: "Coding for Error Control"; *IBM Sys.J.*, vol.8 no.1, Mar.1969, pp.48–80.

Teichrow,Daniel(ed.)[71]: "Education Related to the Use of Computers in Organizations"; *CACM*, Sep.1971, vol.14 no.9, pp.573–588.

Teichrow,D. and Hershey,E.A.[77]: "PSL/PSA: A Computer Aided Technique for Structured Documentation and Analysis of Information Processing Systems"; *IEEE TSE*, vol. SE-3 no.1, 1977, pp.41–48.

Teng,J.Z. and Gumaer,R.A.[84]: "Managing IBM Database 2 Buffers to Maximize Performance"; *IBM Sys.J*, vol.23 no.2, Jul.1984, pp.211-218.

Teorey, T.J. and Pinkerton, T.B.[72]: "A Comparative Analysis of Disk Scheduling Policies"; *CACM*, vol.15 no.3, 1972, pp.177–184.

Teorey,Toby J.[78]: "General Equations for Idealized CPU-I/O Overlap Configurations"; *CACM*, vol.21 no.6, Jun.1978, pp.500–507.

Teorey,T.J. and Fry,J.P.[82]: *Design of Database Structures*; Prentice-Hall, 1982.

Terdiman,J.B.[70]: "Mass Random Storage Devices and Their Application to a Medical Information System (MIS)"; *CBR*, vol.3 no.5, Oct.1970, pp.518.

Thiele,A.A.[69]: "The Theory of Cylindrical Magnetic Domains"; *Bell System Journal*, vol. 48, 1969, pp.3287–3335.

Thomas,D.A., Pagurek,B., and Buhr,R.J.[77]: "Validation Algorithms for Pointer Values in DBTG Databases"; *ACM TODS*, vol.2 no.4, Dec.1977, pp.352–369.

Tichy,Walter F[82]: "Design Implementation and Evaluation of a Revision Control System"; *Proc. 6th Int. Conf. Software Eng.*, Tokyo, Sept.1982.

Trivedi,K.S. and Sigmon,T.M.[81]: "Optimal Design of Linear Storage Hierarchies"; *JACM*, vol.28 no.2, Apr.1981, pp.270–288.

Tsichritzis,D.C. and Bernstein,P.A.[74]: *Operating Systems*; Academic Press, 1974.

Tsichritzis,D.C. and Lochovsky,F.H.[82]: *Data Models*; Prentice Hall, 1982, 381 pp.

Tuel,W.G., jr.[78]: "Optimum Reorganization Points for Linearly Growing Files"; *ACM TODS*, vol.3 no.1, Mar.1978, pp.32–40.

Uhrowczik,P.P.[73]: "Data Dictionary/Directories"; *IBM Sys.J.*, vol.12 no.4, Dec.1973, pp.332–350.

Ullman,J.D.[83]: *Principles of Database Systems*, 2nd ed.; Computer Science Press, 1983.

vanderPool,J.A.[73]: "Optimum Storage Allocation for a File in Steady State" and "Optimum Storage Allocation for a File with Open Addressing"; *IBM JRD*, vol.17 no.1, Jan.1973, pp.27–38 and no.2, Mar.1973, pp.106–116.

vanTassel,D.[72]: *Computer Security Management*; Prentice Hall, 1972.

Veklerov,E.[85]: "Analysis of Dynamic Hashing with Deferred Splitting"; *ACM TODS*, vol. 10 no.1, Mar.1985, pp.90–96.

Vitter,J.F.[85]: "An Efficient I/O Interface for Optical Disks"; *ACM TODS*, vol.10 no.2, Jun.1985, pp.129–162.

Vold, Havard and Sjogren, Bjorn H.[73]: "Optimal Backup of Data Bases: A Statistical Investigation"; *BIT vol.13 no.2 1973*, pp.233–241.

Vonnegut,Kurt, jr.[52]: *Player Piano, America in the Coming Age of Electronics*; Charles Scribner's Sons, 1952, 295 pp.

Wagner,H.M.[75]: *Principles of Management Science*; Prentice Hall, 2nd ed., 1975, 562 pp.

Wagner,Robert E.[73]: "Indexing Design Considerations"; *IBM Sys. J.*,vol.12 no.4, Dec.1973, pp.351–367.

Wah,Benjamin W.[81]: *Data Management on Distributed Databases*; UMI Research Press, Ann Arbor MI, 1981.

Wah,Benjamin W.[84]: "File Placement on Distributed Computer Systems"; *IEEE Computer*, vol.17 no.1, Jan.1984, pp.23–33.

Wah,Benjamin W.(ed.)[87]: *Proceedings Third Internat. Conference on Data Engineering*; Los Angeles CA, IEEE CS, Feb.1987.

Ware,Willis[67]: "Security and Privacy"; *Proc. 1967 SJCC*, AFIPS vol.30, pp.279–282, 287–290.

Warnier,Jean-Dominique[79]: *Logical Construction of Systems*; vanNostrand-Reinhold, 1979.

Wasserman,A.I., Pircher,P.A., and Shewmake,D.T.[86]: "Building Reliable Interactive Information Systems"; *IEEE TSE*, vol.SE-12 no.1, Jan.1986, pp.147–156.

Waters,S.J.[72]: "File Design Fallacies"; *Comp. J.*, vol.15, Feb.1972, pp.1–4.

Waters,S.J.[74]: "Methodology of Computer System Design"; *Comp. J.*, vol.17 no.1, 1974, pp.17–24.

Waters,S.J.[75]: "Estimating Magnetic Disk Seeks"; *Comp. J.*, vol.18 no.1, Feb.1975, pp.12–17.

Weihl,William E.[87]: "Distributed Version Management for Read-Only Actions"; *IEEE TSE*, vol.SE-13 no.1, Jan.1987.

Weingarten,Allen[66]: "The Eschenbach Drum Scheme"; *CACM*, vol.9 no.7, Jul.1966, pp.509–512.

Weingarten, Allen[68]: "The Analytical Design of Real-Time Disk Systems"; *Proc.1968 IFIP Congress*, North-Holland, pp.D131–D137.

Weiss,E.A.(ed.)[82]: "Self-Assessment Procedure IX: Ethics"; *CACM*, vol.25 no.3, Mar.1982, pp.181–195.

Weissman,Clark[69]: "Security Controls in the ADEPT-50 Time-Sharing System"; *Proc.1969 FJCC*, AFIPS, vol.35, pp.119–133.

Welch,Howard[84]: "Data Protection in a Shared Memory Multiprocessor"; *IEEE CS DE 1*, Los Angeles, Apr.1984.

Westin,A.F.(ed.)[71]: *Information Technology in a Democracy*; Harvard Univ.Press, 1971.

Weyl,S., Fries,J., Wiederhold,G., and Germano,F.[75]: "A Modular, Self-Describing Clinical Databank System"; *CBR*, vol.8, 1975, pp.279–293.

Whang,K-Y., Wiederhold,G., and Sagalowicz,D.[82]: "Physical Design of Network Model Databases Using the Property of Separability"; *VLDB 8*, McLeod and Villasenor(eds.), Mexico City, Sep.1982, pp.98–107.

Whang,K-Y., Wiederhold,G., and Sagalowicz,D.[83]: "Estimating Block Accesses in Database Organizations - A Closed Noniterative Formula"; *CACM*, vol.26 no.11, Nov.1983, pp.940–944.

Whang,K-Y., Wiederhold,G., and Sagalowicz,D.[84]: "Separability: An Approach to Physical Database Design"; *IEEE TC*, vol.33 no.3, Mar.1984, pp.209–222.

Whang,Kyu-Young[85]: "Index Selection in Relational Databases"; *Int.Conf.on Foundations of Data Organization*, IPSJ, Kyoto, 1985.

White,L.J. and Cohen,E.I.[80]: "A Domain Strategy for Computer Program Testing"; *IEEE TSE*, vol.SE-6, May 1980, pp.247–257.

Wiederhold,G.et al[72]: Report on the San Diego SHARE Data Base Committee on Technical Objectives meeting, Dec.1972; SHARE Inc. Proceedings, 1972.

Wiederhold, G., Fries, J.F., and Weyl,S.[75]: "Structured Organization of Clinical Data Bases"; *Proc.1975 NCC*, AFIPS vol.44, pp.479–486.

Wiederhold,Gio[81]: *Databases for Health Care*; Lecture Notes in Medical Informatics no. 12, Lindberge and Reichertz(eds.), Springer-Verlag, Heidelberg, 1981, 75pp.

Wiederhold, Gio[83]: *Database Design*; McGraw-Hill, Computer Science Series, 1977, 2nd ed. 1983.

Wiederhold,Gio[84]: "Knowledge and Database Management"; *IEEE Software*, vol.1 no.1, Jan.1984, pp.63–73.

Wiederhold,Gio[84a]: "Databases"; *IEEE Computer*, Centennial issue, vol.17 no.10, Oct.1984, pp.211-223.

Wiederhold,Gio(ed.)[86DE]: *Proceedings Second Internat. Conference on Data Engineering*; Los Angeles CA, IEEE CS, Feb.1986.

Wiederhold,Gio[86]: "Views, Objects, and Databases"; *IEEE Computer*, Dec.1986, pp.37–44.

Wiederhold,Gio and Qian,XiaoLei[87]: *Modeling Asynchrony: The Identity Connection*; *IEEE CS DE 3*, LA, Feb.1987.

Wiederhold, Gio[88]: *Database Design and Implementation*; McGraw-Hill, to appear 1988.

Wiking,Donald[71]: *The Evaluation of Information Services and Products*; Information Research Press, Washington DC, 1971.

Wilhelm,Neil C.[76]: "An Anomaly in Disk Scheduling: A Comparison of FCFS and SSTF Seek Scheduling Using an Empirical Model for Disk Accesses"; *CACM*, vol.19 no.1, Jan.1976, pp.13–17.

Wilkes, Maurice V.[72]: "On Preserving the Integrity of Data Bases"; *Comp. J.*, vol.15 no.3, 1972, pp.191–194.

Willard,D.E. and Lueker,G.S.[85]: "Adding Range Restriction Capability to Dynamic Data Structures"; *JACM*, vol.32 no.3, Jul.1985, pp.597–617.

Willard,D.E.[86]: "Good Worst-Case Algorithms for Inserting and Deleting Records in Dense Sequential Files"; *ACM-SIGMOD Proceedings*, 1986, pp.251–260.

Williams,Martha(ed.)[85]: *Computer Readable Databases; A directory and data sourcebooks*; ASIS, 1985.

Williams,R. et al[82]: "R-*: an Overview of the Architecture"; *Databases*, Shneiderman(ed.), Academic Press, Jun.1982.

Wilms,Paul F., Lindsay,B.G., and Selinger,P.G.[83]: "'I wish I were over there': Distributed Execution Protocols for Data Definition in R*"; *ACM-SIGMOD 83*, San Jose, May 1983, pp.238–242.

Winick,Robert M.[69]: "QTAM: Control and Processing in a Telecommunications Environment"; *ACM National Conf. 24*, ACM 1969.

Withington,F.G.[80]: "Coping with Computer Proliferation"; *Harvard Business Review*,
May-Jun.1980, pp.152.

Wong,C.K.[80]: "Minimizing Expected Head Movement in One-Dimensional and Two-
Dimensional Mass Storage Systems"; *ACM C. Surveys*, vol. 12 no. 2, Jun.1980,
pp.167–211.

Wong,E. and Chiang, T-C.[71]: "Canonical Structure in Attribute Based File Organization";
CACM, vol.14 no.9, Sep.1971, pp.593–597.

Wong,H.K.T. and Jianzhong,L.[86]: "Transposition Algorithms for Very Large Compressed
Databases"; *VLDB 12*, Kyoto Japan, Aug.1986.

Yamamoto,S., Tazawa,S., Ushio,K., and Ikeda,H.[79]: "Design of a Balanced Multiple-Valued
File-Organization Scheme with the Least Redundancy"; *ACM TODS*, vol.4 no.4,
Dec.1979, pp.518–530.

Yao,Andrew[78]: "Random 3-2 Trees"; *Acta Inf.*, vol.2 no.9, 1978, pp.159–170.

Yao,Andrew C.[85]: "Uniform Hashing is Optimal"; *JACM*, vol.32 no.3, Jul.1985, pp.687–693.

Yao,S.B., Das,K.S., and Teorey,T.J.[76]: "A Dynamic Database Reorganization Algorithm";
ACM TODS, vol.1 no.2, Jun.1976, pp.159–174.

Yao,S.B.[77]: "An Attribute Based Model for Database Access Cost Analysis"; *ACM TODS*,
vol.2 no.1, 1977, pp.45–67.

Yoshida,M., Matsushita,Y., et al[85]: "Time and Cost Evaluation Schemes of Multiple Copies
of Data in Distributed Database Systems"; *IEEE TSE*, vol.SE-11 no.9, Sep.1985,
pp.954-959.

Young,J.W.[74]: "A First Order Approximation to the Optimum Checkpoint Interval";
CACM, vol.17 no.9, Sep.1974, pp.550–531.

Young,T.Y. and Liu,P.S.[80]: "Overhead Storage Considerations and a Multilinear Method
for Data File Compression"; *IEEE TSE*, vol.SE-6 no.4, Jul.1980, pp.340–347.

Yourdon,Edward[72]: *Design of On-line Computer Systems*; Prentice Hall 1972, 608 pp.

Yu,C.T.,Siu,M.K.,Lam,K.,and Chen,C.H.[85]: "File Allocation in Star Computer Network";
IEEE TSE, vol.SE-11 no.9, Sep.1985, pp.959-965.

Yue,P.C. and Wong,C.K.[78]: *On a Partitioning Problem*; *ACM TODS*, vol.3 no.3, Sep.1978,
pp.299–309.

Zipf, George K.[49]: *Human Behavior and the Principle of Least Effort*; Addison-Wesley,
1949.

Index

COVERAGE   This index contains entries for all terms defined in the text, the first authors of cited papers, and cross references for some file terms often used by manufacturers or in other publications, but not specifically defined in this book. The first instance of a pagenumber refers to the primary discussion of the topic, so that the pagenumbers are sometimes out of order. Since Appendix A provides access to products and companies, they are not cited here.

Abbreviation of index entries, 455.
   use of, 269.
  of names, *see* compression of character
    strings.
  of TIDs, 269.
  other opportunities for, 269.
  used in the bibliography, 571.
Abiteboul, S., 52, 572.
Abort, 35, 380.
Abuse, *see* protection (violation of).
Access, 105.
  by attribute, *see* indexed file.
  control, *see* protection of privacy.
  frequency, *see* load.
  group, 99.
  key management, 533.
  key organization, 542.
  methods, 27.
    see file organization.
    summary, 124.
  parameters, 533.
  paths, 536–537.
  protection system, 540.
  security system, 540.
  types, 534.

Accessing data blocks, 276.
  federated nodes, 383.
  remote nodes, 377.
  the directory, 100.
Accessor, 530.
Acker, R.D., 387, 572.
Active authentication, 532.
Acton, F.S., 436, 572.
Addis, T.R., 360, 572.
Additions file, *see* transaction log file.
Addresses, 32.
Addressing, 283.
  versus naming, 32.
Adiba, M., 387, 572.
Advanced roles for data dictionaries, 552.
Affinity matrix for fragmentation design,
  372.
Agarwala, A.K., 436, 572.
Age, 537.
Aggregate computation, 351.
Aggregate system demand, 491.
  transaction load, 489.
Aho, A.V., 171, 572.
Alerters, 548.
Alford, M.W., 517, 572.

Allchin, J., 564, 572.
Allen, A.O., 438, 572.
Allen, R.P., 20, 170, 572.
Allen, S.I., 324, 572.
Allgeyer, K., 292, 572.
Allocation and record management, 280.
   for distribution, 364–370, 374, 376.
   for sequential processing, 347.
   in clustered distributed systems, 373–375.
   in remotely distributed systems, 378.
   of free storage, 344.
Alphabetic identifiers, 179.
Alternate file organizations, 293.
Alternative version, 557.
Amble, O., 221, 572.
Ammon, G.J., 95, 572.
Analysis method, 98.
Analysis of variance, 411.
Analysis techniques, 389.
Ancestors, 307.
Anchorpoint, 137.
Anderson, H.D., 171, 572.
Andler, S., 360, 548, 572.
ANSI, 562, 572.
Anzelmo, F.D., 95, 572.
Apers, P.M.G., xii, 387, 388, 572.
APPEND statement, 104.
   -only, 36.
Applications, 15, 21–23.
   load distribution, 500.
   of interference effects, 505.
Architecture, 493–496, 365.
   multifile, 328.
Archive, 7, 60, 95.
   files, see large capacity storage.
Archive data staging systems, 353.
Arden, B.W., 517, 572.
Armisen, J.P., 360, 572.
Aron, J.D., 18, 572.
Arora, S.R., 324, 438, 517, 573.
Artificial intelligence, 255, 10.
Artificial keys, 118.
Assigning portions, 340.
Assisted sequential, see sequential and blocking.
Association, 252.
Associative addressing, 356.
   memory, 61, 356.
   processing, 356.

Associative retrieval, 103.
   storage, 356.
Astrahan, M.M., 171, 573.
Atkinson, M.P., 29, 51, 292, 573.
Attribute name, 107.
   name-value pair, 107.
   selection, 351.
   sizes in indexes, 160.
   value, 107.
Atwood, J.W., 437, 573.
Atwood, R.C., 517, 573.
Audit read, 541.
Audit trail, see transaction log file.
Authentication, 528, 531.
Automated-tape libraries, 57.
Autonomy, 365.
AV pair, see attribute name-value pair.
Availability, 521, 200, 365.
AVL tree, see balanced tree (binary).
Aztec coding, 458.

B-tree, 155, 231.
   index, 133.
B+ tree, 275.
Baber, R.L., 95, 573.
Bachman, C.W., 18, 204, 206, 221, 255, 256, 573.
Back-end, 364.
   processor, 352.
Backspace, 90.
Backup, 25, 95.
   and versions, 556.
   copies, 438.
   file, 556.
   of very large files, 556.
Badal, D., 387.
Baer, J-L., 324, 573.
Baker, F.T., 562, 573.
Balanced trees, 299.
Band, see track, may be a set of adjoining tracks.
Barbara, D., 388, 573.
Baroody, A.J., jr., 562, 573.
Barriers, 525.
Basic files, 97.
Baskett, F., 502, 518, 573.
Batch checking, 451.
   insertion, 201.
   of requests, 110.
   operating system, 24.

Batch processing, 41.
  storage allocation, 343.
  totals, 451.
  transactions, 45.
  update, 119.
    see reorganization.
Batory, D.S., 323, 438, 573.
Batteke, J.P.H., 517, 573.
Bayer, R., 170, 255, 292, 324, 475, 573.
Bays, C., 221, 573.
BCH code, see Bose-Chaudhuri code.
Begin-point, 99.
Bell, A.E., 94, 95, 573, 574.
Benefit and cost of sharing, 39.
  factors, 480-483.
  loss, 483.
  of information, 510.
  quantification, 481.
  realization, 482.
Benner, F.H., 324, 438, 574.
Bentley, J.L., 324, 574.
Berelian, E., 518.
Bernstein, P.A., 387, 388, 438, 548, 574.
Berra, B., 562, 574.
Best fit, 344.
Bhargava, B., 387, 574.
Bhattacharya, C.C., 436, 574.
Big-$\mathcal{O}$ notation, 14.
Bihan, J.L., 387, 574.
Bill-of-materials, 15, 307.
Billings, J.S., 94, 574.
Bimodal distribution, 410, 396.
Bin, see bucket or slot in hashed access.
Binary arranged index tree, 271.
  search, 122.
    in index blocks, 270.
  trees, 299.
Binding, 254.
Bit table, 345.
Bit vector, 456.
Bits-per-inch — BPI, 55.
Bitstrings, 441.
Bleier, R.E., 171, 566, 574.
Block, 81-84, 65.
  anchors, 137.
  identifier, 85.
  marking, 76.
  overflow due to record variability, 401.
  pointer, 73, 84.
  size, 66.

Block size and track capacity, 73.
  transfer time, 78.
Blocking, 74, 280.
  factor, 74, 76.
  of the index, 285.
  when sorting, 114.
Blum, R., xii.
Bobeck, A.H., 94, 574.
Bogart, H., 519.
BOM or B/M, see bill of materials.
Borges, J.L., 327.
Borr, A.J., 51, 360, 387, 567, 574.
Bose, R.C., 170, 171, 574.
  -Chaudhuri code, 454.
Bouros, M.P., 292, 574.
Boyd, D.F., 517, 574.
BPI, 55.
Bradley, J., 221, 574.
Brägger, R.P., 561, 574.
Brainerd, W., 255, 574.
Bright, H.S., 475, 574.
BrinchHansen, P., 51, 359, 425, 438, 574.
Brodie, M.L., 475, 562, 574, 575.
Brooks, F.D., jr., 517, 575.
Brother, see sibling.
Brown, D.T., 547, 95, 170, 575.
Brown, M., 360, 563, 575.
Browne, P.S., 539, 547, 575.
Bubble memories, 62.
Buchholz, W., 221, 436, 437, 575.
Bucket, 176, 180–182, 229, 407.
  accessing, 233.
  addresses, 182.
  search, 182.
Buffer, 81–87.
  management, 87.
  protection, 525.
  requirements, 87.
Buffering overhead, 89.
Bugs, 526.
Building a database, 23.
Bulk allocation, 279.
  storage, see external storage.
  transfer rate, 69, 78–80.
  update, see batch update.
Bunching, see clustering.
Buneman, O.P., 548, 575.
Burge, W.H., 437, 575.
Burke, E., 223.
Burkhard, W.A., 221, 256, 291, 292, 387, 575.

Bus, 331, 6.
Bush, Vannevar, 1, 18, 575.
Business rules, 552.
Byte, 55, 64.

c.d.f., *see* cumulative distribution function.
Cache memory, 6, 7, 95, 331, 496.
    directory, 367.
Caesar cipher, 469.
Cameron, J.R., 561, 575.
Campbell, T., 363.
Canaday, R.H., 360, 575.
Candidate key, *means* any unique key.
Capabilities, 544.
Card, *see* Hollerith card.
Cardenas, A.F., 19, 255, 517, 575.
Carlson, C.R., 562, 575.
Carrol, J.M., 538, 547, 575.
Cartridge tape, 55.
Casablanca, 519.
Cascading index, *see* index $(x > 1)$.
Casey, R.G., 387, 575.
Cassette, 55.
CD-ROM, 60.
Cellular file organization, *see* parallel
    devices.
Central limit theorem, 401.
    tendency, 395.
Ceri, S., xii, 386, 387, 388, 438, 575, 576.
Chain, 139, 314.
Chained, *see* linked list of records.
    files, *see* ring files.
    overflow records, 139, 183.
    portions, 345.
Chamberlin, D.D., 548, 576.
Chan, A., 387, 576.
Chang, J.M., 171, 302, 324, 576.
Chang, S.K., 256, 292, 387, 576.
CHANGE statement, 534.
Channel, 328-330, 493-499.
Chanson de Roland, 134.
Chapin, N., 95, 170, 255, 564, 576.
Character string data, 444.
Charging for storage, 512.
Charles, W.R., 128, 576.
Chebyshev's inequality theorem, 410, 429.
CHECK statement, 289.
Check bit, 54.
    digits, 451.
Checksums, 451.

Chen, P.P.S., 517, 438, 576.
Cheng, P.S., 437, 576.
Cheng, W.K., 388, 576.
Cheriton, D.G., 52, 576.
Cheung, T-Y., 291, 576.
Chi, C.S., 95, 576.
Chi-square, 404, 397.
Child, 307.
Chin, Y.H., 292.
Christodoulakis, S., 171, 436, 576.
Chu, W.W., 171, 387, 388, 438, 517, 576.
Cipher, 467-468.
Claiming the CPU, 39.
Clark, W.A., 51, 576.
Class access, 532.
Class distinctions, 496.
Classification of operating systems, 41.
Claybrook, B.G., 51, 566, 576.
Clear text (cryptography), *see* plain text.
Clique, 534, 543-545.
CLOSE a file, 100, 288.
Closely coupled, 331.
Cluster, 183, 103, 211.
Clustered index, *is an* index as seen in
        indexed-sequential files.
    processor system, 49, 331, 370-376.
Clustering, 446, 84.
    of hashed records, 183-184.
    of rings, 211.
Coalesced hashing, *uses* open addressing
        and chains.
Codd, E.F., 387, 475, 576.
Code block(DEC-RMS), *see* parameter area.
Code book, *see* data dictionary.
Coding during data entry, 540.
    for precision, 457.
    for small domains, 457.
    of names of individuals, 446.
Coffman, E.G., jr., 388, 419, 437, 576, 577.
Collision, 174, 177-180.
    probability, 406-408.
    resolution, 181.
    set, 184.
    in the TID space, 240.
Collmeyer, A.J., 255, 577.
Combined abbreviation, 268.
    indexes for partial-match, 167-169.
Combining file methods, 223, 225-252.
    associative memory and storage, 357.
    results from multiple files, 352.

Comer, D., 51, 170, 171, 291, 577.
Command, 329-330.
Commit, 35, 380.
Communication networks, 366.
Compaction, *see* abbreviation, compression.
Complex attributes, 107.
Compression of data, 455–466.
  of an index, *see* abbreviation of index entries.
  of character strings, 458.
  of numeric data elements, 455.
  of sparse data, 455.
  processing point, 465.
Computation, 37.
  scheduling, 38–39.
  on files, 22.
Computer network, 331.
Computer-aided design, 557.
Concepts of reliability, 520.
Concordance, 134.
Concurrent update of replicated data, 380.
Confinement, 530.
Conflict, *see* collision.
Connors, T.C., 324, 577.
Consecutive files, *see* sequential files.
Consistency of data and knowledge, 11.
  of retrieval, 381.
  units, 36.
Constant substitution cipher, 469.
Constraint expression, 554.
Content addressability, *see* associative addressing *or* retrieval.
Content monitoring, 541–542.
Control area (IBM-VSAM), *see* portion.
  block (IBM-VSAM), *see* parameter area.
  characters, 444.
  data, 27–28.
  flow, 27.
  interval (IBM-VSAM), *see* train.
  language, 46.
  of processing, 28.
Controller, 328–329, 493-498.
Conversion, 449.
Conway, R.W., 548, 577.
Coonen, J.T., 475, 577.
Coordinate index, *is an* index used for partial-match.
Coordination, 382.
Copeland, G., 95, 517, 577.

Copy of the file, 379.
Copy-on-write (TENEX), *means* updating a file by linking in new blocks, instead of rewriting them.
Coral rings, 248.
Core storage, *see* memory.
Cornell, D.W., 387, 577.
Correcting transactions, 525.
Correlation variable, *see* TID.
Cosequential, 120.
Cost, 512–514, 335478, 516.
  benefit comparison, 509.
  containment, 482.
  estimates, 63, 64.
  increment, *see* 335.
  of personnel, 486, 516.
  of processing, 513, 332.
  of protection, 530.
  of storage, 332–335, 63, 64.
  versus capacity, 506.
  versus revenue, 509.
Count area, *see* block identifier.
Countermeasures, 472.
Counting the attributes, 108.
Counting the devices needed, 334.
Create-date, 99.
Criteria, *is the* value of the search key.
  for hierarchical data files, 308.
Critical section, 40.
Cross indexes, *see* indexed files.
CRT, *see* display terminals.
Cryptography, 466.
CSCAN scheduling, 421.
Cuadra, C.R., 577.
Cumulative distribution function), 396.
Currency of derived data, 384.
Cursors, *see* pointers.
Cylinder, 59, 64, 78.
  indexes, 260, 137.
  overflow areas, 183.
  scheduling policies, 418.
Czejdo, B., 387, 577.

Daley, R.C., 324, 548, 577.
Daniell, T.P., 388, 577.
DASD, *see* disk drive, etc..
Data, 9, 2, 107, 536.
  access types, 534.
  aggregate, *see* group of records.
  and the world, 441.

Data dictionary, 26, 552, 566.
  engineering, 553.
  entry and feedback, 539.
  flow, 27.
  independence, 13.
  objects, 536, 543.
  reduction, 24.
  representation, 441.
  set (IBM), see file.
  staging systems, 353.
  versus knowledge, 10.
  volume, hardware, and performance, 487.
Data-processing reports, 484.
  card, see Hollerith card.
Database, 4.
  descriptions, see schema.
  machines, 350–352, 358.
  management system, 3, 557.
  system, 2.
Datalogical, see file organization.
Date, 6.
Date, C.J., 18, 565, 577.
Davida, G.I., 475, 577.
Davies, A.C., 51, 577.
Davis, G.B., 20, 51, 517, 577.
Davis, L., 324, 577.
Day and time, 533.
Dayal, U., 387, 577.
De, P., 438, 577.
Dearnley, P.A., 517, 578.
Decipher, 467.
Decision rule, 178.
Declarative description of files, 26.
Decomposing a transaction, 336.
Decrypting, 467, 471.
Deferred update, see batch update.
  of indexes, 263.
DeGreene, K.B., 21, 578.
DELETE statement, 534.
Deleting blanks, 460.
  records, 104.
  from hashed files, 184.
  in a B-tree, 156, 264.
Delta coding, 458.
DeMaine, P.A.D., 464, 475, 578.
Demand distributions, 391.
Demand versus resource, 492.
DeMarco, T., 517, 578.

Demolombe, R., 359, 578.
Demurjian, S.A., 387, 578.
Denning, P.J., 324, 420, 437, 438, 578.
Dennis, J.B., 548, 578.
Dense index, see exhaustive index.
Density, 176.
Density and locality, 83.
Derived data, 384.
Derived fragmentation, 372.
Descendants, 307.
Design, 25, 490.
  evaluation, 478.
Desmonde, W.H., 18, 578.
Detail file, see transaction file.
Detail records, 120.
Determinant, see key.
Deterministic procedure, 188.
Deutscher, R.F., 195, 437, 578.
Device-name, 99.
Device-type, 99.
Devor, C., 387, 578.
Dewitt, D., 566, 578.
Differences among storage devices, 93.
Diffie, W., 475, 578.
Digit analysis, 189.
Dimsdale, J.J., 20, 171, 256, 578.
Direct access, 174, 175.
  access (IBM), see hashed files.
  access storage device, is a disk drive, magnetic drum, etc..
  access to sequential files, 226.
  storage drives, 57.
Direct address, see KAT.
Directory, 153, 47, 280.
  contents, 99.
  for distributed files, 367.
Dirty pages, 319.
Disadvantages of sequential files, 119.
Disk drive, 57.
  file, see disk drive.
  competition, 508.
  pack, 58.
  scheduling policies, 420.
  versus drum, tape, 93.
Distributed systems, 331, 377.
Distribution (of data), 364–367, 436, 391.
  of file fragments, 500.
  of files, 559, 48, 239, 363.
  steps, 269.

Distributions (statistical), 391, 436.
  other, 408.
  non-uniform update, 163.
  dependent hashing methods, 188.
Dittrich, K.R., 387, 562, 578.
Dixon, W.J., 436, 578.
Documentation, 25.
Dodd, G.G., 256, 255, 563, 578.
Dolk, D.R., 562, 578.
Domain, 441–446, 5–6, 55.
  of accessors, *see* cliques.
Doty, K.L., 94, 360, 578.
Double buffering, 88.
Dowdy, L.W., 387, 579.
Du, D.H., 255, 579.
Du, H.C., 517, 579.
Dunnigan, M., 95, 579.
Duplication of data, 524.
Duration of file assignment, 47.
Dutta, A., 387, 517, 579.
Dynamic, 23.
  allocation policy, 342.
  replacement, 464.

ERASE statement, 289.
Eade, D.J., 567, 579.
Early binding, 254.
Easton, A., 517, 579.
Easton, M.C., 323, 579.
Eco, U., 549.
Effectiveness versus benefit measures, 481.
Effelsberg, W., 95, 437, 579.
Eggers, S.J., 475, 579.
Eisner, M.J., 387, 579.
Ellis, C.S., 221, 579.
Ellis, M.E., 20, 579.
ElMasri, R., xii.
Enciphering, 467.
Encoding groups of characters, 459.
Encryption keys, 471.
End-of-file pointer, 99.
ENDREQ statement, 289.
Engineering accuracy, 98.
Engineering information system, 25.
Entry, 131.
  see record.
  point, 204.
  variable, *see* TID.
  sequenced data set (VSAM), *see* pile file.
Envelope of protection, 538, 527.

Epstein, J., 519.
Epstein, R., 360, 387, 579.
Equilibrium density, 83.
Erasmus, D., 389.
Erlang, A.K., 437.
  distributions, 426–429, 166, 409, 425.
Error, 520.
  compensation, 525.
  correcting codes, 452, 547.
Escape procedures, 289.
Eschenbach scan scheduling, 423.
Estimates, 481.
  of demand by constituent, 496.
  of index height, 138.
  of overflow costs, 146.
  of transaction usage, 487.
Eswaran, K.P., 387, 579, 548.
Ethernet, 370.
Evans, A., jr., 547, 579.
Everest, G.C., 20, 579.
Exclusive-OR, 189.
EXECUTE statement, 534.
Executive, *see* operating system.
Exhaustive indexes, 154.
EXISTENCE VERIFICATION, 535.
Expected distribution of load, 503.
Exponential distributions, 394.
  transformation, 189.
EXTEND statement, 534.
Extensible, 186.
Extent (IBM), *see* portion.
External key abbreviation, 265.
External sorting, 114–117, 113.
  storage, 2, 5-7.
Extrapolation, 409.

F-test, 405.
Fabry, R.S., 548, 579.
Fagin, R., 221, 548, 579.
Failure, 521.
  control, 522.
  probabilities, 520.
False drops, 245.
Fanout ratio, 132–133, 137.
Farmer, D.B., 561, 579.
Fascicle, *is a set of pages or blocks.*
Fault, 520.
FCFS polling, *see* FIFO.
Federated systems, 382, 331.
Feedback loops, 555.

Feinstein, A.R., 475, 579.
Feistel, H., 475, 579.
Feldman, J.A., , 579.
Feller, W., 436, 437, 579.
Fernandez, E.B., 547, 579.
Ferrari, D., x, 96, 436, 579, 580.
Fetch a record, 103.
    not in the file, 196.
    hashed file, 193.
    indexed file, 160.
    indexed-sequential file, 144.
    multiring file, 214.
    pile, 109.
    sequential file, 122.
    performance, 262.
    procedure, 178.
Feustel, E.A., 548, 580.
Fields, 5.
FIFO, 417, 420.
File, 2, 5, 543.
    access interpreter, 367, 373, 386.
    access program, 5.
        privilege tables, 545.
    address, see pointer.
    allocation table, 376.
    and record structure, 106.
    creation, 47.
    contents, 312.
    definition, see data dictionary.
    description and use, 100.
    design, review, 515.
    dictionary, 26.
    directories, 99.
    distribution, 363–369, 385.
    hardware for, 92.
    hierarchical structure, 92.
    indexes, 131.
    organization, 99, 7, 25, 27.
    performance parameters, 102.
    scanning, 351.
    schemas, 553.
    security, 519.
    servers, 353.
    system evaluation, 477.
        products, 563.
    transactions, 31.
    using virtual memory, 319.
    without programming, 560.
File management system, 3, 540.
        and database management, 3.

Files for spreadsheets, 560.
    text, 230.
Files, J.R., 256, 292, 580.
Final fragmentation, 373.
Finkelstein, S., xii.
First fit, 344.
First in first out (FIFO), 417, 420.
Fischer, M.J., 388, 580.
Fishman, G.S., 437, 580.
Fixed blocking, 74.
Fixed head disks, 59.
Flajolet, P., 171, 324, 580.
Flat distribution, see uniform distribution.
Floppy disks, 57, 64.
Florentin, J.J., 475, 580.
Flores, I., 51, 580.
Flowcharts, 27.
Floyd, R.W., 295, 580.
Folding and adding, 191, 189.
Fong, E.N., 562, 580.
Fragmentation, 370–373, 69, 383.
    is waste due to portion management.
Franaszek, P., 52, 580.
Frank, H., 437, 580.
Fredkin, E., 291, 580.
Free characters for encoding, 462.
    read, 541.
    storage space management, 340.
Freiberger, W., 324, 436, 580.
Frequency of access, see load.
    (protection), 533.
Freund, J.E., 436, 580.
Frey, R., 255, 359, 546, 548, 580.
Friedman, T.D., 475, 548, 580.
Front-end processor, 364, 352.
Fry, J.P., 562, 580.
FSCAN scheduling, 420, 423.
Fuchs, W.K., 562, 580.
Fujitani, L., 95, 580.
Fuller, S.H., 437, 580.
Fully inverted file, see phantom file.
Fundamental files, 97–98, 224.
Future directions, 549.
Future of file systems, 558.

Gallaire, H., 475, 562, 580.
Gambino, T.J., 517, 580.
GAO (General Accounting Office), 95, 580.
Gap, 72–73, 64.
    effect on the transfer rate, 78.

Garbage collection, *see* reorganization.
GarciaMolina, H., 52, 387, 388, 581.
Gardarin, G., 387.
Garg, A.K., 221, 581.
Gather writing, 349.
Gaussian distribution, *see* normal distribution.
Gaynor, J., 95, 581.
Generalization of multiattribute ring access, 251.
Gentile, R.B., 95, 581.
Geometric objects, indexing for, 303.
Get, *see* fetch a record.
GET statement, 288.
Get the next record, 103.
   hashed file, 197.
   indexed file, 160.
   indexed-sequential file, 147.
   multiring file, 215.
   pile, 110.
   sequential file, 124.
GFF (Greedy—first-fit) algorithm, 375.
Ghosh, S.P., 52, 95, 129, 170, 171, 475, 581.
Gifford, D.K., 51, 475, 581.
Giga, 55.
Gilb, T., 51, 562, 581.
Gildersleeve, T.R., 128, 581.
Gilligan, M.J., 441.
Glantz, R.S., 128, 566, 581.
Glinka, L.R., 437, 581.
Global allocation problem, 374.
   directory, 367.
   variables, 309.
Goal data, 107.
Goldberg, R.P., 437, 581.
Goodness of fit testing, 404.
Gopalakrishna, V., 324, 581.
Gordon, G., 437, 581.
Gotlieb, C.C., 20, 517, 581.
Gotlieb, L.R., 475, 581.
Gould, I.H., 18, 581.
Graham, G.S., 438, 581.
Graham, R.M., 544, 548, 581.
Grant, J., 387, 581.
Gray, J.N., 51, 386, 547, 581.
Gray, P.M.D., 128, 581.
Greedy—first-fit algorithm (GFF), 375.
Greenes, R.A., 324, 565, 582.
Grid-file, 256.

Griffiths, P.P., 548, 582.
Groner, L.H., 129, 221, 582.
Grosshans, D., 51, 128, 565, 582.
Group, *is a* segment of a record.
Growth, 365.
GSA (General Services Admin.), 95, 582.
Guaranteeing service, 421.
Gudes, E., 475, 582.
Guibas, L., 291, 582.
Gurski, A., 221, 582.
Guttman, A., 171, 303, 324, 582.

Hac, A., 388, 582.
Hagman, R.B., 95, 582.
Hahn, B., 475, 582.
Hakola, J., 95, 582.
Hammer, M.M., 171, 387, 517, 548, 582.
Hamming, R.W., 477.
   distance, 451.
   weight, 450.
Hanan, M., 221, 582.
Hard disks, 348.
Hard sectoring, 65.
Härder, T., 256, 582.
Hardware, 53.
   architecture, 493.
   choices, 54.
   mechanisms, 544.
   new devices, 558.
   parameters, 65, 92.
Harrison, M.S., 548, 582.
Hashed files, 173–202, 220.
   accommodating growth of, 185.
   and rings, 249.
   multiattribute, 235.
   use of, 192.
   with a TID-list and rings, 251.
Hashing, 220, 85.
   methods, 189.
   structures for partial-match, 242.
   techniques, 188.
Hawthorn, P.B., 360, 582.
Hawthorne effect, 562.
Heacox, H.C., 437.
Head-per-track devices, 59.
Header records, 208.
Heap file, *see* pile file.
Height of indexes, 138, 156, 269, 304–305.
Heising, W.P., 221, 475, 582.
   's rule, 409.

Held, G., 171, 582.
Helical scanning, 57.
Helland, P., 51, 582.
Hellerman, H., 438, 517, 582.
Hertz, D.B., 437, 583.
Heuristics, 14.
    selection, 471.
Hevner, A.R., 387, 583.
Hibbard, T.N., 324, 583.
Hierarchical storage organization, 353.
    storage system, 364.
    structured data, 307, 315.
        versus arrays, 310.
Hierarchy of devices, 7, 559.
    of protection, 535.
High-order key abbreviation, 266.
High-speed memory, *see* memory.
Hill, F.J., 95, 583.
Hill, T.R., 436, 583.
Hillier, F.S., 437, 583.
Hillman, D.J., 565, 583.
History maintenance, 25.
Hoagland, A.S., 95, 475, 583.
Hoffer, J.A., 387, 517.
Hoffman, L.J., 547, 548, 583.
Hogan, P.D., 517, 583.
HOL policy, *see* PRIority disk scheduling.
Hollerith card, 54, 94.
Holt, G.A., 51, 583.
Home address, 70.
Homophonic enciphering, 472.
Horizontal fragmentation, 371.
Horowitz, E., 170, 583.
Hsiao, D.K., 255, 583.
Hu, T.C., 291, 583.
Huang, S-C., 437, 583.
Huang, S-H.S., 291, 583.
Huff, D., 436, 583.
Huffman, D.A., 475, 583.
    coding, 461.

IBM, ubiquitous.
    card, *see* Hollerith card.
    tape, *see* industry compatible magnetic
        tape.
    VSAM, 82.
Identifier, 444.
    block, 85.
    track, 70.
    tuple, 132.

Immediate-access storage, *see* memory.
Implementation, 536.
    of a fundamental data structure, 252.
    of a tree-structured file, 306.
    of an indexed-sequential file, 278.
    of compression, 465.
Independence of attributes, 165.
Index, 131–172, 259–292.
    B-trees, 155.
    block sizes, 277.
    for an indexed-sequential file, 136–138.
    for geometric objects, 303.
    for partial-match queries, 165–167.
    manipulation, 283.
        processing, 270.
    search, 286.
    selection, 166.
    shape of, 132.
    trees, 270.
Indexed file, 131, 152-169.
    use of, 157.
Index point, *is the* beginpoint of a track.
Indexed-sequential file, 131, 135–142.
    use of, 142.
    with secondary indexes, 231.
Indirect accessing, 233.
Individual's identification, 531.
Industry-compatible magnetic tape, 55.
Information, 9, 24, 488.
    hiding, 13.
    services, 480.
Infrequent events, 401.
Inglis, J., 95, 256, 583.
Initial state, 340.
Initialization, 179.
Inmon, W.H., 51, 52, 583, 584.
Input-output, 7.
    devices, 38.
Insert a record, 104.
    hashed file, 197.
    indexed file, 160.
    indexed-sequential file, 150.
    multiring file, 215.
    pile, 111.
    sequential file, 125.
    using a separate overflow area, 198.
Insertion, 155.
    procedure, 177.
    successive, 201.
    two-pass, 201.

Integers, 443.
Integration of security procedures, 546.
Integrity, 520.
    monitoring, 541.
Interaction among privileges, 535.
Interaction of block size and index pro-
        cessing, 276.
Interblock gaps, 72.
Interference, 502.
    by control-information, 498.
    of parallel loads, 501.
Interleaving of blocks, 348.
Interlinked rings, 204.
Internal key abbreviation, 266.
Interpolation, 409.
Interval, *see* critical section.
    (IBM-VSAM), *see* train.
Invariant constraint expression, 554.
Inventory theory, 433.
Inverted file, 133.
Inverted list, 133.
    see indexed file.
Iyer, R.K., 547, 584.

Jacobs, B., 562, 584.
Jajodia, S., 387, 388, 584.
Jamison, B., 168.
Javitt, J., 20, 584.
Jenq, B-C., 437, 584.
Jessop, W.H., 52, 564, 584.
Jewell, W.S., 419, 584.
Job, *see* application *or* transaction.
Johnson, C.T., 95, 584.
Johnson, L.R., 256, 407, 436, 584.
Journal file, *see* transaction log file.
Judd, D.R., 18, 129, 255, 584.
Jump index search, 271.
Jumps, 271.

K-d tree, 302.
Kahn, D., 475, 584.
Kahn, G., 475, 584.
Kaiman, R.A., 221, 256, 584.
Karlton, P.C., 300, 584.
KAT (Key-to-address transformation),
        175–176, 188–192.
Katter, R.V., 18, 584.
Katz, R.H., 20, 25, 562, 517, 584.
Kearns, J.P., 96, 584.
Keehn, D., 292, 584.
Keith, N.R., 518.

Keller, R.M., xii.
Kelton, W.D., 437, 584.
Kendall's notation, 425.
Kent, W., 18, 584.
Kerr, D.S., 584.
Kerschberg, L, 562, 584.
Key, 24, 107, 356, 531.
    see search argument.
    abbreviation, 264–270, 285–286.
    size and file address space, 179.
    changes, 472.
    compression, *see* key abbreviation.
    field on a disk, *see* block identifier.
    length, 472.
    sequenced dataset (IBM-VSAM), *see*
        indexed-sequential file.
    to-address transformation, 175–176,
        188–192.
    tree, *see* index.
    type, *see* attribute name.
    variable-length, 265.
    work tree, *see* temporary index.
Keycards, 532.
Keyed record access, *see* indexed files.
Kilo, 55.
Kim, M.Y., 517, 584.
King, J.L., 517, 584.
King, J.M., 518, 585.
King, W.F.III, 360, 585.
Kitsuregawa, M., 517, 585.
Kiviat, P.J., 437, 585.
Kleinrock, L., 437, 585.
Knight, K.E., 514, 518, 585.
Knott, G.D., 221, 585.
Knowledge, 9–10, 2.
Knowledge-based systems, 10-11, 561.
Knuth, D.E., xii, 51, 95, 113, 115, 123, 128,
        170, 194, 199, 221, 291, 299, 300, 324,
        336, 360, 408, 436, 585.
Kobayashi, H., 438, 585.
Kochen, M., 575, 585.
Kollias, J.G., 517, 387, 585, 585.
Konheim, A.G., 475, 585.
Korth, H., 19, 388, 585.
Kral, J., 221, 585.
Kriegel, H-P., 221, 585.
Krinos, J.D., 437, 517, 585.
Kroenke, D.M., 19, 20, 585.
Kronwal, R.A., 221, 585.
Kuehler, J.D., 95, 585.

Labeling TIDs, 237.

LaFue, G.M., 548, 585.

Lampson, B.W., 52, 386, 547, 585, 586.

Lancaster, F.W., 292, 586.

Landauer, W.I., 170, 324, 586.

Landers, T., 387, 586.

Lang, C.A., 221, 586.

Langdon, G.G., jr., 360, 586.

Langworthy, G., 95, 586.

Large-capacity storage devices, 60.

Larson, J.A., 386, 586.

Larson, P-Å., 170, 221, 256, 586.

Last-in-first-out (LIFO), 420.
    -used date, 99.

Late binding, 254.

Latency, 70–71, 65.

Laudon, K., 562, 586.

Layering and files, 13.

LCFS (last-come-first served) policy, *see*
        LIFO.

Lee, D.L., 256, 586.

Lee, D.T., 324, 586.

Lefkovitz, D., 291, 586.

Length indicator, 76.

LeongHong, B.W., 562, 586.

Leung, C.H., 95, 128, 586.

Levels, 283.

Levin, K.D., 438, 586.

Levy, M.R., 129, 586.

Lewin, M.H., 547, 586.

Li, Z.J., 129, 586.

Lide, D.R., jr., 18, 586.

Lifetime, 555.

LIFO (last-in-first-out), 420.

Lim, P.A., 52, 586.

Limits in VSAM, 283.
    of abbreviation, 265.
    of storage devices, 60.

Lin, C.S., 360, 586.

Lin, J.J., 517, 587.

Lindsay, B., 387, 548, 587.

Line (text files), *is* a record.

Line (communication), *is* a network link.

Linear hashing, 187.
        see Sequence maintaining KATs.
    processing if index blocks, 270.
    Programming, 438.
    search in a hashed file, 181, 183.

Link, *see* pointer.

Linkage to colliding records, 183.
    to overflow records, 139.

Linked list of records, 139.

Linked lists, *see* rings.

List, *see* chain.

Little's formula, 419.

Litwin, W., 187, 221, 291, 387, 587.

Load, 487-489, 333, 352, 516.
    for file maintenance, 489.
    for information retrieval, 488.

Loading a hashed file, 201.
    density, 83, 281.

Local networks, 331.

Locality, 83, 103.
    control, 287.

Locate, *see* fetch.
    the successor block, 196.

Location, 533.

Lochovsky, F.H., 387, 587.

Lock, 35, 38.

Log file, 119.

Logging, 44.

Logical record, *see* record.

Lohman, G.M., 438, 587.

Lomet, D.B., 128, 587.

Long, P.L., 517, 587.

Long-term file maintenance, 554.

Loo, J., 517, 587.

LOOK scheduling, 421.

Lorie, R., 20, 587.

Loss of control over data, 539.

Low-order key abbreviation, 268.

Lowe, T.C., 475, 517, 587.

Lucas, H.C., jr., 18, 517, 587.

Luk, W.S., 291, 587.

Lum, V.Y., 170, 171, 190, 195, 255, 437, 517,
        587.

Lynch, C., 475, 587.

M-way trees, 133.

MacDougall, M.H., 437, 588.

Machine representation, 443.

Machines with rapid storage access, 354.

Madnick, S.E., 387, 588.
    disk, 57.
    drums, 59.
    tape storage, 55.

Maier, D., 18, 387, 588.

Maintenance of data integrity, 539,555.
  files, *see* reorganization.
  indexes, 154.
  long-term, 554.
  trees, 300.
Maio, D., 170,588.
Major, J.B., 517,588.
Maloney, J., 437,588.
Management of allocated portions, 342.
Management science, 425.
Manipulation of rings, 209.
Mano, M.M., 95,588.
March, S.T., 95,170,291,387,588.
Marill, T., 360,588.
Mark, 109.
Marron, B.A., 517,588.
Martin, J., 18,20,51,438,475,517,588.
Martin, T.H., 129,255,588.
Maruyama, K., 292,588.
Maryanski, F.J., 360,438,588.
Masquerader, 531.
Master file, 120.
Master index, *see* root block.
Master records with indexes, 249.
Matching load and capability of a file system, 490.
Matching segment, 472.
Mathematical symbols used, 568.
Maurer, W.D., 221,588.
Maximum size, 99.
McCarthy, J.L., 565,588.
McCormick, W.T., jr., 373,588.
McCreight, E.M., 291,588.
McEwen, H.E., 441,475,588.
McFadden, F.R., 19,518,589.
McGee, W.C., 562,589.
Mealy, G.H., 18,589.
Mean, 397.
  time between failures, 521.
    to repair, 521.
Measurement, 437,508.
Mechanical storage, 54.
Mega, 55.
Mellen, G.E., 475,589.
Memory, 38,62.
Memory-based files, 62,278,559.
Merge-sort, 113–117.
Merten, A.G., 518,589.
Method of analysis, 98.
Meyer, C.H., 475,589.

Meyers, G.J., 95,589.
Michael, G.A., 95,589.
Michaels, P.C., 94,589.
Miller, A.R., 547,589.
Miller, J.R., 518,589.
Miller, S.W., 95,589.
Minimization of combined indexes, 168.
Minoura, T., xii,388,589.
Minsky, N., 548,589.
Mix of distributions, 429.
Mixed blocking techniques, 82.
Miyamoto, I., 518.
Model of a system, 390.
Modes of file operation, 24.
Modularity and transactions, 36.
Module, 36.
Modulo-two addition, *see* exclusive-OR.
Mohan, C., 386,589.
Moles, 532.
Molho, L., 548,589.
Monitor, 425.
Morey, R.C., 517,548,589.
Morgan, H.L., 387,438,589.
Moroney, M.J., 436,589.
Morris, R., 221,589.
Motivation and architecture, 365.
Motivation and organization, 364.
MOVE, 535.
Moving to database management, 557.
MTBF (mean time between failures), 521.
MTTR (mean time to repair), 521.
Mullin, J.K., 171,256,589.
Multi-attribute access, *see* partial match.
  hashed access, 235.
  index trees, 302.
  indexes for partial-match queries, 167.
  improving the schemes, 244.
Multidatabases, 382.
Multidimensional trees, 302.
Multifile architecture, 328.
Multilists, 202,165.
Multiple files with common hashed access, 238.
  regression, 411.
  units, 329.
Multiprocessor computer systems, 331.
  use of, 330.
Multiprogramming, 41,508.
Multiring file, 202-220.
  use of, 212.

Multiway access, *see* partial-match.
Mulvany, R.B., 95, 589.
MUMPS, 309–314.

N-step scan scheduling, 420, 423.
Naked variables, 316.
Name spelling variations, 447.
Naming versus addressing, 32.
Natural redundancy, 449.
Navathe, S.B., xii, 372, 387, 562, 589.
Navigation, 206.
NBS (National Bureau of Standards), 547,
    589.
Needham, R.M., 475, 548, 589, 590.
Network file servers, 353.
Neuhold, E.J., 548, 387, 590.
Nevaleinen, O., 128, 291, 590.
Newell, G.F., 438, 590.
Next record, path choices, 147.
Nielsen, N.R., 437, 590.
Nievergelt, J., 292, 324, 256, 590.
Nijssen, G.M., 221, 364.
Node, 364.
Non-audit results, 381.
Non-return-to-zero recording, 55.
Nondense index, *see* index with block
    anchor points.
Nonremovable disks, 59.
Nonstop, 524.
Nonunique record keys, 178.
Normal distribution, 400, 166, 393.
Not-ready queue, 41.
Notation, *see* code representation.
Numbers, 335.
Numeric data, 443.

$\mathcal{O}$ notation, 14.
Objects to be locked, 536.
O'Connell, M., 171, 590.
Off-line, 63.
O'Lear, B.T., 95, 590.
Omahen, K., 517.
On-line, 63.
    operation, 25, 484.
    transaction scheduling, 43.
O'Neill, J.T., 309, 324, 590.
OPEN a file, 100, 288.
Open addressing, 178, 181, 194.
    with chaining, 183–184.

Operating system, 8, 37, 51.
    control, 46.
    support, 542.
Operational data-retrieval load, 487.
    services, 480.
Operations Research, 425–437.
Optical discs, 60, 559.
    storage devices, 61.
    technology, 60.
Optimization by change of the hierarchy,
        317.
    database machine performance, 352.
    of allocation for variable-length records,
        403.
    of overall file systems, 516, 487, 509,
        513–514.
Order-preserving, *see* sequence-maintaining.
O'Reagan, R.T., 475, 590.
Organization of data for processing, 13.
Organization, 364.
Orr, K., 51, 590.
Ousterhout, J.K., 437, 590.
Out-of-place-insertion, *see* overflow file.
Overflow, 138.
    area, 135, 182–183.
    chains, 141.
    file, *see* transaction log file.
Overhead caused by buffering, 89.
Overholt, K.J., 324, 590.
Overlap of entry and processing, 486.
Owner, 382, 99.
Ozkarahan, E.A., 360, 590.
Özsu, M.T., 437, 590.

Pages, 42.
    see block.
Paged memory, *see* virtual memory.
Paging, 42.
Palvia, P., 128, 590.
Papadimitriou, C.H., 562, 590.
Paper tape, 54.
Parallel components, 493, 499.
    operation of multiple devices, 499.
        productivity of, 502.
    file activity, 500.
    processing of storage functions, 355.
    storage access, 355.
    user activity, 500.
Parameter area, *see* 288, 553.
    of models, 390.

Parent, 307.
Parity, 450–451.
Parker, D.B., 547, 590.
Parkin, A., 517, 590.
Partial index, 154.
Partial-match, 164-169, 274.
  by address catenation, 242.
  by precomputing hash entries, 243.
  with hashed access, 241.
Partially inverted file, 133.
Partitioned file, *is* a file with a single level
      index to large record groups.
Partitioning, 108, 210, 270, 302.
  effectiveness, *see* selectivity.
Password, 288, 530-531.
Path choices for next record, 147.
Peakloads, 492.
Pechura, M.A., 95, 590.
Peirce, C.S., 97.
Pelegatti, G., 438.
Percentiles to define performance, 428.
Performance, 2, 14, 364.
  analysis prior to implementation, 550.
  gains, 350.
  of hashed files, 192.
  of indexed files, 158.
  of indexed-sequential files, 143.
  of multiring files, 212.
  of piles, 109.
  of sequential files, 121.
  percentiles, 428.
Periodicals, 20.
Permutation index, *see* concordance.
Perpendicular recording, 57.
Persistence, 2, 28, 554.
Personnel costs, 486-487, 516.
Petersen, H.E., 547, 590.
Peterson, J., 51, 590.
Peterson, W.W., 191, 221, 436, 547, 590.
Phantom files, 290.
Phase-encoding, 55.
Physical clustering, 103.
Physical disk address, 84.
Physical record, *see* block.
Piatetsky-Shapiro, G., 166, 171, 590.
Piecewise-linear-transformation, 189.
Piepmeier, W.F., 517, 591.
Pierce, J., 475, 591.
Pile file, 106–108, 254.
  use of, 108.

Piling, *see* clustering.
Pilot model, 489.
Pipelining, 354.
Pipes, 9.
Plain text, 467.
Planning, 25.
POINT statement, 289.
Pointer, 85.
  array, *see* TID-list.
  to the master record, 247.
  use of, 85.
Poisson distribution, 403, 395.
Pope, A., 131.
Popek, G., 387, 591.
Portion, 279, 340.
  size versus number, 341.
Position table, 76, 270, 306.
Positive integers, 443.
Power of an index, *see* fanout ratio.
Powers, M.J., 19, 517, 591.
Predecessor pointers, *see* prior.
Prefix B-tree, 266.
Prefix, *see* attribute-name.
Presplitting, 161, 260-262.
Press, W.H., 436, 475, 591.
Primary copy update, 381.
Primary index, 137, 231.
Prior pointers, 246.
PRIority disk scheduling, 420–421.
Probing, 124.
Procedural descriptions, 26.
Process, 39.
Processor, 38.
  competition, 507.
Productivity, 502.
Productivity of parallel devices, 502.
Professional users, 486.
Prognosis, 386.
Program files, 29.
Programming file transactions, 22–31.
  integrity, 540.
  methods, 559.
  files without, 560.
  symbols, 569.
  VSAM, 287.
Programs, 537.
  as accessors, 532.
  as persistent objects, 29.
  for transactions, 25, 536.
Progressive overflow, *see* open addressing.

Property, *see* attribute value.
Protection of access, 520, 540.
  of privacy, 527.
Protection-system components, 538.
Prywes, N.S., 221, 591.
Pugh, E.W., 94, 591.
Purdy, G.B., 547, 591.
Push-through, 139–140, 232.
Put, *is* inserting a record.
PUT statement, 289.

Qualifier, *see* attribute value.
Quantifying the shape of an index, 137.
Quarterman, J.S., 386, 591.
Queue, 414.
  access, *see* buffer management.
  length and delays, 419, 428.
  management, 416.
    program, 417.
  scheduling, 437, 417.
    techniques, 414.
  and processes, 415.
Queuing analysis, 438.
  distributions, 425.
Quib, *see* buffer.

R-trees, 303.
Ramamoorthy, C.V., 438, 517, 591.
Random access to records or blocks, 81.
    see hashing or indexes.
  drive, *see* disk drive.
  memory, *used for* memory *and* disk.
  time, 65.
Randomizing, *see* key-to-address transfor-
    mation.
Randomizing hashing functions, 176–188.
Range queries, 274–275, 231, 241.
Rathmann, P., 95, 291, 591.
RayChaudhuri, D.K., 171, 591.
READ statement, 534.
Read entire hashed file, 200.
  indexed file, 163.
  indexed-sequential file, 151.
  multiring file, 218.
  pile, 112.
  sequential file, 126.
  entire file, 105.
Read-only, 60.
  access, 557.
  transaction, 36, 52.
Ready queue, 42–43.

Real-time constraint, 482–485.
  systems, 163.
Real-valued numbers, 443.
  categorizing, 212.
Realization of benefits, 482.
Recoding, 459.
Record, 66, 5, 74.
  (MUMPS), *see* entry.
  anchors, 232.
  and blocking, 74.
  formats, 208.
  identity number, *see* TID.
  insertion, 280.
  marks, 75.
  segments, 310–311, 315.
  selection, 351.
  size, 102.
  size in a hashed file, 193.
    indexed file, 158.
    indexed-sequential file, 143.
    multiring file, 213.
    pile, 109.
    sequential file, 121.
  variable-length, 74, 106, 229, 232, 466.
Recovery, 365, 523.
Reducing the access costs of indexes, 260.
Redundancy, 100, 449.
  and error correction, 449.
  of data, 523.
  versus correction and detection, 453.
Regional 1 file (IBM), *see* hashed file.
  2 file (IBM), *is a* file using hashing and
    buckets.
  3 file (IBM), *is a* file using hashing and
    buckets holding variable-length
    records.
Reisner, P., 517, 591.
Reiter, A., 437.
Reitman, W.R., 255, 591.
Relationships between files, 553.
Relative access (IBM), *see* hashed file.
  address, 84, 86, 176–179.
Reliability, 520.
  in allocation, 346.
Remainder-of-division, 189, 177.
Remotely distributed systems, 377.
Renniger, C.R., 547, 591.
Reorganization, 141, 105.
  analyses, 438.
  hashed file, 200.

Reorganization of an indexed file, 164.
  indexed-sequential file, 151.
  multiring file, 219.
  pile, 113.
  sequential file, 126.
Repeating keys, 269.
Replacement, 462.
Replication, 239, 377–381, 383–384, 501.
  systems, use of, 522.
Report generators, 27.
Representation of data, 441, 6.
Request stringing, *see* queue management.
Requirements for KATs, 176.
Rerandomization, 183, 181.
Resolution of indexes, *see* anchorpoint.
Resource, 35, 38, 47.
Response time, 337–339, 482.
  and use patterns, 484.
Response to violations, 539.
Responsibility, 529.
Restriction, *see* selectivity.
Retrieval, 24, 105.
Retrieval field, *see* key.
Retry, 523.
Revenue versus cost, 509.
Rewriting records in one revolution, 90.
Riley, M.J., 18, 591.
Ring files, 173, 202–220.
  and hashed access, 249.
  in combinations, 245-252.
  with a TID-list and hashed access, 251.
Rings for protection, 544.
Rivest, R.L., 256, 292, 591.
Robey, D., 517, 591.
Robinson, T.J., 221, 591.
Rochkind, M.J., 51, 591.
RodriguezRosell, J., 95, 128, 591.
Role of files in data processing, 9.
Root block, 138, 307.
  in memory, 260.
Rosenberg, A.L., 171, 591.
Ross, D.T., 517, 591.
Ross, R.G., 562, 591.
Rotating magnetic storage, 57.
Rotational latency, 70–71, 64.
  delay, *see* latency.
  position sensing, *see* architecture (class
    5).

Rothnie, J.B., jr., 324, 387, 592.
RSS (random service scheduling), 420.
Ruchte, W.D., 221, 592.
Rudolph, J.A., 360, 592.
Ruskin, R., 259.
Rustin, R., 171.

Saccà, D., xii, 376, 388, 592.
Sacco, G.M., 95, 592.
SacksDavis, R., 256, 592.
Safran, C., 324, 592.
Sakamoto, G.J., 562, 592.
Salasin, J., 95, 592.
Salem, K., 517, 592.
Saltzer, J.H., 546, 547, 548, 592.
Salza, S., 437, 518, 592.
Salzberg, B.J., 19, 592.
Sarin, S.K., 291, 562, 592.
SATF (Shortest Access Time First) pol-
  icy, *see* SSTF.
Satyanarayanan, M., 562, 592.
Savage, P., 95, 592.
Saxton, L.V., 171, 592.
SCAN scheduling, 420–423.
Scatter block reading, 348.
Scatter reading, 348.
Scatter storage, *see* hashing.
Schay, G., jr., 221, 592.
Scheduler, 38.
Scheduling, 417–419.
  for multiple computations, 38.
  on-line transactions, 42–43.
  policies for a cylinder, 418.
    for disks, 420.
  use of, 424.
Schema, 553, 26, 153.
Schkolnick, M., 171, 292, 360, 592, 593.
Schneider, L.S., 517.
Schneider, M., 517, 593.
Scholl, M., 221, 256, 593.
Schroeder, J.R., 324.
Schroeder, M.D., 387, 548, 593.
Schwartz, E.S., 448, 464, 475, 593.
Seaman, P.H., 170, 437, 593.
Search, 105.
  see fetch.
  argument, 107, 24, 170.
  in the bucket, 182.
  key, 24.

Secondary access paths, *see* partial match.
   indexes, 231.
   storage, *see* external storage.
Sections of a process, 39.
Sector, 65.
   addressing, 71.
Secrecy versus protection of privacy, 528.
Security, 519.
Seek time, 65, 66-70.
   and latency combined, 71.
   effect on the transfer rate, 78.
Segment (hardware), *see* block *or* band.
   of records, 310–311, 315.
Selbman, H.K., 323, 593.
Selecting the key, 137.
Selectivity, 108, 166, 209, 236, 302.
Self-describing fields, 107.
Self-indexing file, *see* deterministic proce-
     dure (hashing).
Semaphores, *see* locks.
Semiconductor storage, 61, 559.
Senko, M.E., 255, 324, 593.
Separate overflow area, 198.
Separator marker, 76.
Sequence numbers, 452.
Sequence-maintaining KATS, 188-189, 399.
Sequential access, 287.
   of blocks, 81.
   of records, 81.
Sequential file, 118–120.
   use of, 120.
   combinations with, 225.
Sequential search, 104, 122.
Serial reading, 104.
     see read entire file.
   and indexes, 274–275.
   for hashed files, 240.
   for pile files, 112.
Servers for large files, 352.
Service demand transients, 430.
Sevcik, K.C., 517, 593.
Severance, D.G., 128, 438, 593.
Shadow pages, 44.
Shakespeare, W., 21.
Shannon, C.E., 10, 18, 593.
Sharability, 28, 2.
Shared KAT for multiple attributes, 238.
Shared TID-list, 236.
   to distributed data, 239.
Sharing of facilities, 507.

Sharpe, W.F., 95, 517, 593.
Shaw, D., xii, 360, 593.
Shneiderman, B., 128, 129, 171, 438, 593.
Shortest service time first (SSTF), 418–
     421, 418.
Shu, N.C., 562, 593.
Shuey, R., 562, 593.
Sibling record, 307, 311.
Sigma, 397.
Signed integers, 443.
Siler, K.F., 518, 594.
Simplification of get-next estimate, 150.
Simulation, 411–414, 437.
Simultaneity, 493, 499, 558.
SIRO policy, *see* RSS.
Sites, 48.
Siwiec, J.E., 51, 567, 594.
Size of files, 28.
   allocated, 99.
   of overflow areas, 141.
   used, 99.
Skeen, D., 388, 594.
Skewed distribution, 409, 395.
Skinner, C.E., 437, 594.
Skip sequential, *see* index sequential.
Sklaroff, J.R., 547, 594.
Slonim, J, 128, 594.
Slot, 176.
SLTF (Shortest Latency Time First) pol-
     icy, *see* SSTF.
Small value changes, 162.
Smith, A.J., 95, 594.
Snapshot, 384, 556.
Snedecor, G.W., 436, 594.
Sockut, G.H., 438, 594.
Soft sectoring, 65.
Software engineering, 553.
   mechanisms, 545.
   reliability, 526.
Solomon, M.B., 514, 518, 594.
Solomon, M.K., 360, 594.
Sorensen, P., 221.
Sort block, 115.
Sorting, external, 114–117, 113.
   and block writing, 201.
Soundex coding, 447.
Source programs, 29.
Space allocation, 279.
   key-to-address transformation, 227.
Spanned blocking, 74.

Spawning, *means* collection and submission for execution of a transaction.

Specialization, 47.

Spelling-checking programs, 449.

Split, 155.

Spooling, 41.

Sprague, R.H., jr., 18, 20, 594.

Sreenivasan, K., 437, 517, 594.

SSA (Social Security Administration), 446, 447, 464, 475, 594.

SSTF scheduling, 418–421.

Stable sorting, 115.

Staging storage systems, 353.

Stahl, F.A., 475, 594.

Standard codes, 446.

Stanfel, L.E., 438, 594.

Static database, 23.
   versus dynamic trees, 133.

Statistical access, 533.
   methods, 390.

Statistics, other, 411.

Steady state density, 158.

Steel, T.B., jr., 18.53, 594.

Sterling, T.D., 517, 594.

Stocker, P.M., 517, 594.

Stone, H.S., 51, 437, 438, 475, 594.

Stonebraker, M., 171, 52, 255, 387, 548, 594, 595.

Storage, 6, 38.
   access processors, 355-356.
   allocation, 317.
   and input-output, 6.
   for archiving, *see* archive.
   capacity, 333, 64, 355.
   device types, 335, 559.
   hardware selection, 332.
   organization, 327.
   processors, 355.
   requirement, 333.
   structure, 310.
   system components, 328.
   utilization, 333.
   control tables, 344.
   system failures, 522.

Stover, R.F., 517, 547, 595.

Stratum, *see* cylinder.

Stream files, 9.

Streeter, D.N., 387, 595.

String handling, variable-length, 462.

Stroustrup, B., 562, 595.

Structural dependency, 103.
   monitoring, 541.

Structured file, *see* ring file.

Studer, R., 387, 595.

Su, S.Y., 360, 595.

Substitution cipher, 496.

Sums of normally distributed values, 402.

Superimposed coding, 245.

Support for DBMS, 558.

Sussenguth, E.H., 324, 595.

Svobodova, L., 360, 567, 566, 595.

Symbionts, *see* input-output *and* processes *of an* operating system.

Symbol encoding, variable-length, 461.

Symbolic address, 85.

Symons, C.R., 562, 595.

Synchronization, 25.

System, 2.
   cost, 369.
   analysis, 26.

T-access, *see* get the next record.

t-test, 405.

Table of contents, 344.

Tableau, 471–472.

Tag (associative search), *see* key.

Tanenbaum, A.S., 52, 386, 595.

Tang, D.T., 547, 595.

Task, *see* computation.

Taxonorics, *see* data representation.

Teichrow, D., 562, 595.

Teng, J.Z., 95, 595.

Teorey, T.J., 18, 255, 437, 517, 595.

Terdiman, J.B., 95, 595.

Termination, 178.

Textbooks, 18.

Thiele, A.A., 94, 595.

Thomas, D.A., 221, 595.

Threaded lists, 202.

Tichy, W.F., 562, 595.

TID, 132, 287.

TID-list, 234.
   for a sequential file, 227.
   for hashed access to rings, 251.

Time and day, 533.

Time-out, 380, 417.

Time-stamped, 556.

Timesharing, 42.

TMR (triple modular redundancy), 522.

Token-passing, 370.

Tolkien, J.R., 173.
Tombstone, 105, 112, 184.
Tools for system design, 551.
Top down, 554.
TPS (Transaction Processing System),
    43–46.
Track, 54.
  identifiers, 70.
  length, 72, 65.
  stagger, 349.
Trailing-portion abbreviation, *see* low-order
    key abbreviation.
Train, 82.
Training, 486.
Transaction, 21–28, 36, 526.
  allocation table, 376.
  command, 31–34, 338.
  cost, 337–339.
    in a distributed system, 368–369.
  log file, 119.
  numbering, 452.
  origin node, 370.
  read-only, 36, 52.
  performance, 336.
  processing, 43, 370.
    system, 37, 43–46, 567.
  program, 25–29, 536.
  protection, 44.
  response time, 337.
  replicated update, 379.
  scheduling, 42.
  sequence numbers, 452.
  types, 35.
Transfer rate, 77–81.
Transients in service demands, 430–433.
Transparency, 365, 373, 383, 559.
Transposed files, 294–297.
Transposition cipher, 468.
  of digits, 451.
Transverse recording, 56.
Travel time, *see* seek time.
Tree-structured file, 298–302.
    see indexes.
  used as a single index, 305.
  multidimensional, 302.
Tries, 270-272, 557.
Triggering transactions, 558.
Triple modular redundancy, 522.
Trivedi, K.S., 517, 595.
Tsichritzis, D.C., 18, 51, 595.

Tuel, W.G., jr., 438, 596.
Tuning, 535.
Tuple, *see* record.
  identifier, 132.
Two's complement, 443.
Two-loop system, 472.
Two-pass insertion, 201.
Two-phase concurrency control protocols,
    380.
Type, 443–444, 5, 552.
  token ratio, 464.

U-access, *see* fetch.
Uhrowczik, P.P., 563, 596.
Ullman, J.D., 18, 596.
Uncertainty, 10.
Unexplained, 390.
Uniform distribution, 397, 166, 391.
Uninitialized number, 444.
Unique, 178, 269.
Unordered attributes, 216.
  sequential, *see* pile file.
Unrecognizable distributions, 410.
Unspanned blocking, variable-length, 74.
Update a record, 105.
  by distributed transaction, 379.
  distribution, non-uniform, 163.
  hashed file, 199.
  indexed file, 161.
  indexed-sequential file, 150.
  multiring file, 216.
  pile, 112.
  sequential file, 125.
Updating a file, 23.
  see insert a record.
  blocks, 90.
  federated files, 383.
  indexes, 263.
  replicated files, 379.
Use patterns, 484.
User friendly, 480, 488.
User-based access privilege tables, 545.
User-provided variable-length blocking,
    229.
Utilization factor, 418.
  of system components, 497.

Valid users, 528.
Validation, 195.
Value of protection, 528.
vanderPool, J.A., 221, 596.

VanTassel, D., 547, 596.
Variability, effect of, 427.
Variable-length keys, 265.
    records, 229, 182, 232.
        see bucket.
    spanned blocking, 74.
    string handling, 462.
    symbol encoding, 461.
    unspanned blocking, 74.
Variables used in performance formulas,
    570.
Vector, see bucket.
Veklerov, E., 221, 596.
Verify, 73.
Version, 557, 29, 48-49, 381, 384.
Vertical fragmentation, 372.
Very large files, 556.
Vignere cipher, 469.
Virtual addressing, 319.
    memory, 63, 42.
    storage, 278.
Vitter, J.F., 95, 596.
Volatile database, 23.
Vold, H., 438, 596.
Volume (CII, IBM), see disk pack.
    of data, means data quantity.
    table of contents (IBM), is a directory
        for a device.
Vonnegut, K., jr., 293, 596.

Wagner, H.M., 437, 596.
Wagner, R.E., 291, 292, 596.
Wah, B.W., 386, 387, 562, 596.
Waiting line, see queue.
Ware, W., 547, 596.
Warnier, J-D., 51, 596.
Wasserman, A.I., 561, 596.
Waste, 76, 81, 333.
Waters, S.J., 95, 221, 517, 596.
Weihl, W.E., 562, 596.
Weingarten, A., 437, 596.
Weiss, E.A., 547, 596.
Weissman, C., 548, 596.
Welch, H., 475, 596.
Welch, J.W., 170.
Westin, A.F., 20, 547, 596.
Weyl, S., 323, 597.
Whang, K-Y., xii, 171, 221, 276, 291, 437, 479,
    517, 597.
White, L.J., 94, 597.

Width of memory acess path, 330.
Wiederhold, G., 12, 18, 20, 28, 438, 388, 475,
    548, 562, 597.
Wiking, D., 517, 597.
Wilhelm, N.C., 437, 597.
Wilkes, M.V., 547, 597.
Willard, D.E., 128, 291, 597.
Williams, M., 475, 597.
Williams, R., 387, 597.
Wilms, P.F., 387, 597.
Winchester drives, 57.
Winick, R.M., 424, 598.
Withington, F.G., 388, 598.
Wong, C.K., 95, 598.
Wong, E., 256, 292, 598.
Wong, H.K.T., 323, 598.
Words, 443, 62.
Working set, is a group of pages used
    together.
WORM, 60.
Write verification, 72.
Write-multiple-times, 60.
Write-once, 60.
Writing a simulation, 414.

X-Or, 190.

Yamamoto, S.B., 171, 598.
Yao, A.C., 156, 171, 221, 438, 598.
Yao, S.B., 171, 276, 291, 517, 598.
Yoshida, M., 388, 598.
Young, J.W., 438, 598.
Young, T.Y., 475, 598.
Yourdon, E., 51, 598.
Yu, C.T., 291, 598.
Yue, P.C., 128, 598.

Zato coding, see superimposed coding.
Zipf, G.K., 475, 598.
    's Law, 408–409, 463.
Zipfian distributions, 463, 166, 408.